To Grandpa
From Kimberly

world .
mountaineering

a bulfinch press book
little, brown and company
boston • new york • london

general editor
audrey salkeld

foreword by
chris bonington

world
mountaineering

First published in 1998 by Mitchell Beazley,
an imprint of Octopus Publishing Group Ltd,
Michelin House, 81 Fulham Road, London SW3 6RB

First United States Edition
Second printing, 1999

ISBN 0-8212-2502-2

Library of Congress Catalog Card Number 98-71505

Executive Editor: **Samantha Ward-Dutton**
Executive Art Editor: **Emma Boys**
Project Editor: **Claire Musters**
Senior Art Editor: **Kathryn Gammon**
Editor: **Jo Weeks**
Designers: **Glen Wilkins and Alison Verity**
Production: **Rachel Lynch**
Picture Researcher: **Jenny Faithfull**
Map Illustrator: **Raymond Turvey**

The publishers wish to thank all those who contributed
in collating reference material for the mountain routes.

Page 1: **On summit of Mount Kinabuk with Asgard in the background**
Pages 2–3: **The Hillary Step close to the top of Mount Everest**
Pages 4–5: **Top of the East Face of Aconcagua on the 'Polish Glacier Route'**

Front endpaper: **View of Mount Logan**
Back endpaper: **Among the crevasses in the Khumbu Icefall on Mount Everest**

Bulfinch Press is an imprint and trademark of Little, Brown and Company (Inc.)

Printed in Hong Kong

contents

foreword

chris bonington

During the 200 years or so that mountaineering has evolved as a sport, there has been a steady development from an activity that was essentially exploratory adventure to a much more technical, no less demanding or risky, pastime in which what were once unknown mountain ranges are now charted, fairly accessible, and extensively climbed. *World Mountaineering* is a superb compilation of this change, assembling within the covers of a single book the wealth of climbing that has taken place around the world, particularly in the last 20 years or so. As well as inspiring all those interested in mountaineering, it will inform pioneering climbers of possible gaps – even complete valley systems – just awaiting first ascents, and will show those wanting to repeat routes where some of the best climbing is to be found.

Today climbing throughout the world has become similar to that in the Alps, with Everest superficially resembling a giant Mont Blanc with a network of routes up its flanks and ridges. Just the same as in an early morning start from the Goûter Hut on Mont Blanc or the Hörnli Hut on the Matterhorn, when guides and clients race for their respective summits, on Mount Everest, in the tight windows of opportunity when the weather is right for a summit bid, up to 60 guides, Sherpas, and clients might set out from the South Col. On Everest the pace is slow and the penalties, because of altitude and the ferocity of the weather, are more serious, but the principles are similar.

In every mountain area there has been a gradual taming of natural wilderness – an imposition of man's needs on the environment. Roads reach up valleys and, in the case of the Alps, cable cars and climbing huts claw their way into the heart of the mountains. The latest and most controversial invasion is at the foot of the Zmutt Ridge of the Matterhorn, first climbed by A F Mummery with the guides Burgener, Petrus, and Gentinetta in 1879. There is a new climbing hut on the spot where they had a chilly bivouac, fortified with red wine, beer, and cognac. This has been followed by the fixing of stanchions and ropes on the ridge above the hut to make the route safer and easier. It represents a sanitization of both the wilderness and the quality of the experience. The same can be seen in the

Left Climbers trudge up the Western Cwm between Everest, Lhotse, and Nuptse. Swiss mountaineers, who were the first to enter this basin, called it, aptly, the Valley of Silence.

further ranges, with a proposal for a hotel at the site of the base camp on the North Side of Everest; a road up to, and a hotel on, the beautiful Fairy Meadow below Nanga Parbat; and hotels and prepared paths in the Paine Region of Patagonia. There is a creeping erosion of the spirit of adventure for a more synthetic, tamed experience.

It is easy to regret these changes, to yearn for the unexplored and the unknown. I first visited the Himalaya in 1960 when, although all but one of the 8000m (26,000ft) peaks had been climbed, few mountains had been climbed by more than one route and few of the 7000m (23,000ft) and 6000m (19,700ft) peaks had even been attempted. In Nepal there was just one road between Kathmandu and the Nepalese/Indian border, only one Western-style hotel in the city and you started your approach march from the suburbs of Kathmandu. We made the first Annapurna circuit, approaching the mountain from the east, establishing a base camp just short of Manang, making the first ascent of Annapurna II and then returning by crossing the Tilicho Pass in the Kali Gandaki and dropping down to Pokhara. In a period of eight weeks the only foreigners we saw were two Swiss climbers, members of Max Eiselin's Dhauligiri Expedition. Today you would see several hundred.

I don't believe you should begrudge people the opportunity of wandering through this wonderful terrain, or the local people who are exploiting a growing tourist industry with their tea houses and lodges. It is a question of balance – one that is not always easy to achieve and one that, all too often, is at the cost, not just of the environment, but of the spirit of adventure and wonder that attracts us to these high places.

There still are, and I believe always will be, obscure valleys and mountain ranges off the beaten track where climbers can find untouched faces and ridges, even unclimbed peaks, but the numbers desiring to pioneer are dwindling and becoming comparatively small. The vast majority have always preferred the reassurance of following where others have been before, be it in the Alps or in the Himalaya and other greater ranges. In Nepal the majority of expeditions are going for the 8000m (26,000ft) peaks, usually via their trade routes, or for classic routes on particularly well known mountains like Ama Dablam or the popular trekking peaks.

Guided climbing has arrived in the Himalaya, but prices are extremely high and guides here have enormous responsibility. The high costs are due to a combination of the peak fee imposed by the Nepalese government and the expense of organizing an expedition. At Himalayan altitudes guides cannot possibly look after their clients in the way that they can in the Alps or on other mountains of similar height. This was tragically demonstrated in 1996 when both guides and clients lost their lives as they were caught in a violent storm high on Everest. Most of the guides did their best to save their clients. Rob Hall, a New Zealander, arguably the most successful of the Everest guides, stayed with his client not far from the summit even though he probably could have got back down himself, knowing full well that this would almost certainly cost him his life. It was ironic that the expedition had every high-tech device – from super-lightweight Russian oxygen bottles to a satellite phone that could be patched into their VHF radio net on the mountain. Rob was able to talk to his wife back in New Zealand from his bitterly cold bivouac just below Everest's summit but his team was helpless in its efforts to rescue him because of the altitude and furious storm.

An increasing number of local people in the Himalaya are becoming guides, employed both by commercial expeditions taking clients up Everest or other peaks and by inexperienced climbing expeditions. All too often, however, local guides are paid only a fraction of what visiting guides would receive, though they are taking on the same kind of responsibility.

Many expeditions are allowed onto the mountain at the same time, undoubtedly compounding the problem by causing traffic jams high on the mountain. This can be exacerbated when some climbers do not feel responsible for the plight of others in trouble. There have been cases where climbers have ignored other people's problems because of their hunger to reach the summit.

Surely the climbing community, alongside the Nepalese and Chinese governments, should be able to find a solution to the problem. Everest is such a special place. It was certainly very important to me to stand on that highest point.

We must remember that there are alternatives to Everest and the other 8000m (26,000ft) peaks. There is a wealth of superb climbing to be had around the world, as described in this book, in places where there are few, if any, other people and still no tell-tale signs of man. This is where the leading innovative climbers are beginning to turn their attention. In 1997 Mick Fowler, Stephen Sustad, Andy Cave, and Brendan Murphy put up a superb new route on the North Face of Changabang in India. Hosts of challenging lines have been climbed in Patagonia, Baffin Island, Greenland, Antarctica, around the Baltoro and Biafo

Glaciers in the Karakoram, and the Gangotri in northern India. It is significant that Paul Pritchard, a brilliant young climber, was given the

Right **Luke Laeser jumaring during the first ascent of 'Friggin in the Riggin' on Shiprock, an isolated monolith in the New Mexican desert.**

Boardman Tasker Award for Mountain Literature in 1997 for his book, *Deep Play*. It is not just the quality and originality of his writing but also the boldness of his climbs and his climbing philosophy that make this book so important. I can remember the inspiration I received from W H Murray's *Mountaineering in Scotland* when I started climbing in the early 1950s. For me this was followed by Hermann Buhl's *Nanga Parbat Pilgrimage*, encouraging me to head for the Eastern Alps to try climbs like the Comici Route on the North Face of Cima Grande and the Cassin on the Cima Ouest. I hope young climbers will be inspired by writers like Paul Pritchard. There is certainly a mass of information in *World Mountaineering* to help them stretch their own limits.

In 1996 and 1997 I visited a range of mountains in north-east Tibet as extensive as the whole of Switzerland with over 20 magnificent jagged peaks in the 6000m (19,700ft) range. None of these had been climbed or even attempted. There are other places like this but in our fast-shrinking world they are not an infinite resource.

It is important that we try to preserve the unspoilt beauty of these mountains, not only in our own behaviour by taking away with us everything that we carry in, but also in trying to influence governments to protect such ranges. An approach that aims to make the minimum impact on nature and is attuned to the environment is one that is going to help preserve the natural beauty of the world's highest places for those who venture among them, those who gaze upon them, and for those who find inspiration in reading about them.

introduction

audrey salkeld

This book is a celebration of mountaineering and the world's mountains. In it, we have selected 52 peaks around the world to give a taste of the variety and choice that are available. Each is described by a leading climber with specialist knowledge of the peak and its surroundings.

There are thousands of mountains, and few without charm or attraction, so what appears here can be only a token. However, we have had the unique opportunity of featuring some of the great favourites alongside lesser known, but no less exciting, peaks, some of which have rarely been described in any detail in the literature of mountaineering. As well as comprehensive mountain profiles, first-hand accounts of memorable adventures have been included for some peaks to illustrate a little of their history, drama and continuing appeal.

the roots of climbing

People have been climbing mountains for as long as humans and mountains have coexisted, yet perhaps their reasons for doing so have varied over time. Early on, simple practicalities like hunting or trading were probably the prime motivations, but there is plenty of evidence from early cultures testifying to the spiritual pull of mountains. Whatever changes a more materialistic world has brought, it is hard to imagine that human emotions have changed significantly. Our ancestors surely experienced moments of exultation and sheer joy, as they would have done of fear and timidity. While seeking out the easiest passage through mountain barriers, there will have been the adventurous few tempted to clamber higher for no more reason than the thrill of the morning, or for elevation and prospect and the satisfaction of going where none had been before.

Mountaineering, formally defined – though whether as a sport, a pastime, or a calling depends very much on your view-point – is a little over 200 years old. That's if we count the first ascent of Mont Blanc in 1786 as the beginning. Certainly that inspired other adventurous individuals to repeat the feat – not that this was universally welcomed. Baedeker's guide, with peremptory authority, pronounced that 'a large proportion of those who have made this ascent have been persons of unsound mind'.

The lunacy took hold, however, slowly at first but

Left **Packed with deadly power, an avalanche thunders down from the Mazeno Peak on Nanga Parbat in the Himalaya.**

Above **Gustav Doré's graphic representation of the Matterhorn disaster in 1865. Four men died when their thin rope broke; they were coming down after the first successful ascent of the peak.**

Above **Climbers investigating a crevasse on the Pers Glacier below Piz Palu and the Diavolezza Pass in the Bernina Alps. The photograph dates from _c._1910, when Alpine glaciers were more extensive than they are now.**

gathering momentum. In the early days there were many who wanted to be the first to scramble up this or that peak so that their names might be written forever in the climbing annals. Throughout what is called the Golden Age of Mountaineering, occupying the years between 1854 and 1865, no fewer than 180 great Alpine peaks were climbed for the first time. As accessible virgin peaks grew scarcer, dedicated climbers attempted ever-harder lines on known peaks, while the peak-baggers searched further afield for fresh areas of conquest.

The reason that most early climbing took place in the Alps was largely attributable to the question of accessibility. New railways in Europe pushing as far as Basle and Geneva resulted in the construction of a rash of mountain inns and brought visitors flocking to the main Alpine centres. Other mountain areas took longer to reach this level of development so that, for a while, there was a curious anomaly; North American climbers, for instance, kept making the long journey to the Alps, seemingly unaware of the vast tracts of unexplored alpine country on their own continent. It wasn't until the construction

of the Canadian Pacific railroad several decades later that the Selkirks and Rocky Mountains were opened up to mountaineers.

British gentleman-climbers and their guides dominated the Golden Age by claiming no less than 30 of the 39 greatest peaks of the Alps, culminating in Edward Whymper's ascent of the Matterhorn in 1865. But that climb cost the lives of four men and severely dented the mountain brotherhood's confidence. An outspoken leader in _The Times_ demanded by what right illustrious Alpine Club members dared to throw away the precious gift of life? Even Queen Victoria wondered what might be done to prevent such catastrophes happening again. And it is true that, with the growing feeling that the Alps were almost played out from a climbing point of view and were fast becoming vulgarized by the trappings of tourism, many disenchanted members resigned from the Alpine Club. Others looked east, to the Caucasus – again following the latest railway

continent and country in the world. In between travelling to the great ranges, climbers looked to lower local crags for training. Rock climbing as a distinct activity in its own right was discernible in Britain and the Alps by the 1880s. First ascents were no longer the only spur: climbers did not give up as soon as their goal was achieved or claimed by someone else. Peak after peak, route upon route were achieved, not once but many times; climbs were attempted and repeated with enthusiasm. Sea cliffs, crags, quarries, boulder problems, buildings sometimes, artificial walls – all were called into play to supply raw material for dedicated practice and enjoyment.

the unwritten codes

Climbing is a restless urge needing regular satisfaction. It has often been described as 'constructive anarchy'. It assumes rules and conventions, venerating its own traditions at the same time as flouting accepted orthodoxies and continually pressing for change. It is a world within a world, at odds with wider society, while representing what many feel to be the purest essence of that society. Its adherents can be spread through every walk of life and every 'age of man'. One dedicated climber will instinctively recognize another, will accept the world on climbers' terms. That is not to say that climbers share an affinity of ideas or aspirations, though it seems that the concurrence of peers is important. Climbing involves action, expression, and a demonstration of the possible. It incorporates an element of competition, though this is not always acknowledged. Above all else, it involves the recognition and acceptance of risk – and it is at this level that it most deviates from society's conventions.

Since the beginning, then, climbing has been an activity of continual evolution, balanced by tradition. The spearhead, or growing tip, is not always one-directional. At any time there may be several vigorous sideshoots, which may or may not thrive. There is constant positing and questioning, and no new step is

Above **In deference to the beliefs of their Sherpas, few expeditions in Tibet or Nepal start without a puja, or ritual ceremony, at which offerings are made to placate the mountain gods.**

development. Here the peaks were higher and wilder than the Alps; there was no comforting network of huts and hotels, nor was the area accurately mapped. Caucasian climbing was pure pioneering, yet in the decade between 1886 and 1896 the majority of major summits were climbed – once again, mostly by British Alpine Club parties and their Swiss guides.

Then it was to New Zealand and Canada that climbers turned, and on to South America and the Indian Himalaya. And the pattern has followed, at different stages, thoughout almost every

ever taken without an outcry from traditionalists. Crampons have been deplored, as have dynamic rope techniques, the use of bottled oxygen at high altitude, pegging and bolting, Sherpa support... The articulated ethos of mountaineering favours practice as near to the purest possible essentials: the peak, the person, and the very minimum of additional aids. Different disciplines within the sport, however, have drawn up their own codes of acceptable aid and practice, and by and large over the years there has been tolerance between them.

Of course, climbing is influenced by trends in society at large. There have been unedifying displays of nationalism and politics on mountains, and there has been a fashion for climbing seen as an educational or, dubiously, as a character-developing ploy. The arguments we hear now against the tide of commercial climbing are reminiscent of those that accompanied the advent of competition climbing: here, it is said, are outsiders waltzing in with no concern for the sport's traditions, seeking short-term gratification, and displaying no wish to pay the price of long years of apprenticeship. The fear is that by their very numbers they could topple the delicate edifice of tolerance and ethics that characterizes climbing as we know it. And the biggest threat these incomers are seen to pose lies in their reluctance to confront the inherent risk.

Primitive people were geared to facing danger in almost everything they did. We have evolved a society that seeks to eliminate risk almost entirely – even to hold someone else accountable when anything does go wrong. In providing this expectation of safety, we fail to encourage the acquisition of skills, experience, and above all the common sense which would help us, if not to manage it, at least to react to risk constructively. We lose the empowering sense of our own judgement. This is what climbing is most about – taking back the responsibility for one's own existence – and climbers react dramatically when they perceive this essence is being threatened or compromised.

modern-day controversies

Every so often in mountaineering an extreme event takes place that focuses attention on the developments and controversies of the day. One such event was the sudden storm on Everest in 1996, mentioned by Chris Bonington in his Foreword. I was there as an expedition reporter at Everest Base Camp during the emergency: as winds lashed the upper slopes of the world's highest mountain and darkness fell, more than 20 people were

caught in a chaos of sleet and snow on their way back from the summit. Anatoli Boukreev, the great Russian guide (who died on Annapurna in 1997 on Christmas Day), ventured into the storm several times to lead people into the top camp on the South Col at 8000m (26,000ft). We huddled helplessly around the radio at base camp as survivors trickled in throughout the next day and desperate attempts were made to reach those who were too frostbitten and too exhausted to make it back unaided. Ultimately, it became clear that five climbers had perished on the southern, Nepalese, side of the mountain, and a further three on the northern, Tibetan, side. This became an enormous international news story, which would go on to generate many books and films; and the complicated issues it has thrown up continue to stir passions.

Putting aside questions over whether or not you ought to be able to buy your way onto big expeditions, rather than be selected on suitability, it is easy to see that, with forces like these, scaling Everest at least is put almost out of the frame for

Above **Climbing the 'Hillary Step' on summit day on Everest. Ten metres (40ft) in height, it bars the way to the top for all those on the upper South East Ridge. Sometimes in the post-monsoon season the rock is entirely hidden under snow.**

serious young climbers whose means and sponsorship opportunities are modest. Additionally, with no limitations on numbers, and a natural bottleneck high on the most popular route, overcrowding becomes a critical issue. Any accident or weather change affecting climbers high on the mountain also affects all the others on that flank of the mountain at the time. Initiating a rescue effort puts further lives at risk, particularly among the Sherpa contingent. Pulling out these necessary extra resources, and the attendant delays, may well spell the end of any chance of summit success for expeditions that are inadvertently caught up in the incident.

There has been a lot of talk that climbers are becoming more cynical and selfish, steeling themselves against the needs of those in trouble, clambering over others in their rush for the summit. And there appear to be documented instances of this. However, from what I saw on Everest, quite the reverse can happen. Not only was Boukreev selflessly braving the storm to save fellow climbers during the night of 10 May and throughout the next day, but from the moment it was clear a serious situation was developing, there were no longer a dozen expeditions on the South Side of Everest. All climbing stopped and everyone's main concern was focused on helping down the victims, two of whom were very seriously frostbitten indeed.

Inevitably, a tragedy such as this, involving high-profile guides and clients, provokes great soul-searching and conflict. There is nothing intrinsically wrong with the concept of guiding. The tradition is as old as 'sporting mountaineering' but, whereas a local guide can confidently lead a client up a known peak and be responsible for that client's safety, many additional factors come into play at heights above 8000m (26,000ft). Then, the client is still paying for the guide's experience and judgement, and to be shepherded in the right direction, but he or she cannot expect to be 'led' in the same intimate manner as on Alpine or

similar peaks. The margin of safety diminishes the higher you go on the basis of scale as much as anything else. But over and above that are problems of altitude compatability, which can affect client and guide alike. Three of the five who died on the Nepalese side of Everest in 1996 were guides. Not all accredited guides feel happy taking on the responsibility for others' lives at altitudes requiring them to pay additional attention to their own wellbeing. Individual guides will impose their own height ceiling and choose the mountains they are prepared to work on.

Another controversial issue that has surfaced recently is the extent of the communications gadgetry some of these large-scale

Above **Digging in on Cerro Torre. Ice caves make better homes than tents in the fierce Patagonian winds.**

expeditions take along. Satellite telephones, faxes and access to the Internet allow up-to-the-minute news to be relayed to the outside world.

media pressure

What became obvious on Everest in 1996 (and on K2 the year before) was the huge appetite the public has for high-level drama. I suppose it should be no surprise that tragedy on a mountain can be as compulsive a subject as any other form of disaster reporting. We may deplore voyeurism of this nature, wherever it occurs, but it is difficult to argue that news stories involving mountaineers should be considered of less human interest than those at football grounds or motor-racing circuits. You can plead for good taste to be shown by the media, but not for immunity from it. By introducing high-tech toys on climbing expeditions, we have invited the media in. As Anatoli Boukreev said, after the Everest débâcle, 'The world now has an appetite for what we do. The big question is, will it eat us?'

Improved communication brings safety advantages to an expedition. Conceivably it could also increase sponsorship

Above **Catherine Destivelle climbing the red granite wall of 'El Matador' (5.11) on Devil's Tower in Wyoming, USA.**

opportunities. But against this must be the strong argument that one of the main reasons for going into a mountain wilderness is to get away from the trappings of everyday life.

The big philosophical question facing today's climbers is how might a team's concentration, judgement, or performance be affected, knowing the world is watching its every move? There has been debate lasting many years over whether corporate sponsorship could influence decision-making, and could exert pressure on a team to continue out of reasons of obligation when rational mountaineering judgement demands retreat. Climbing in the media spotlight can be seen as an augmentation of this effect. Yet, for all the talk, and the occasional, regrettable incident where publicity or commercial concerns are deemed to have played a part in an unfortunate accident, the overwhelming evidence is that most climbers on most mountains make their decisions based on matters of moment, disregarding all outside influences. And, whereas Everest in some ways might

Above **A helicopter lands at K2 base camp to evacuate a frostbitten Polish climber during the first winter attempt on the mountain.**

be an indicator of the way things are going in mountaineering, in others it is absolutely unique, with scarcely any bearing on what happens elsewhere in the Himalaya, let alone on all the other mountains and crags worldwide. In fact, at probably no other time has there been more opportunity open to climbers to do their own thing, away from all distractions. Travel is easy and it is perfectly possible for a small group of friends to find affordable adventure almost anywhere. As Joe Simpson pointed out recently, for the price of booking on a commercial Everest trip, you could have 15 brilliant trips of your own.

future opportunities

Technology changes, and changes perceptions. There are aids available to the modern climber that our ancestors never dreamed of. Protection is safer than ever before. The Global Positioning System (GPS), based on satellite signals, has revolutionized navigation. With a GPS receiver, you need never

be lost. Anywhere in the world, in any kind of weather, night or day, you can determine your position to within 100m (330ft); that is, using civilian models – the military can do this with even greater accuracy. In emergencies, helicopters can be called out for search or rescue at altitudes below 5000–6000m (16,400–19,700ft). Heroic pilots have plucked casualties from the steep walls of the Eiger; and in 1996 the Himalaya Lt Col Madan Khatri Chhetri took his B2 Squirrel above the dangerous Khumbu Icefall, twice, to lift two seriously frostbitten climbers from Everest, knowing how risky the operation was. One year later, he wrote off a similar aircraft, coming in to land at base camp. Climbers admit an ambivalence towards such support. To the victim the throb of an approaching chopper is the most welcome sound in the world; to the climber poised on a delicate

move high on the Eiger it can seem a violent intrusion. The big change such developments and new technology make is in that delicate balance of risk acceptance and personal responsibility, and in your conception of wilderness. With the continual extension of what is being considered possible in the mountains, it may be that the risk margins will remain similar.

As always, climbers can choose what to use and what to lose. There is nothing compelling them to take the latest technical wizardry away with them, no need to go where services are most developed. Yet what tends to happen is a readjustment of traditional mores to accommodate the situation of the day. The erosion of wilderness is a greater problem – physically more so than philosophically. Deep commitment is required of all visitors, but of mountaineers especially, who press into places even the adventurous traveller cannot reach. Where there is no one to clear up, nothing should be left behind.

It is encouraging to note – from the practical, boxed information sections throughout this book – what initiatives are being taken in many wilderness areas and national parks to combat environmental degradation. In some places, you will see that even faecal waste has to be removed. With a little care and concern, and a healthy regard for those who live locally,

Above **The well earned reward. Two climbers on the summit of the Matterhorn, the best-known mountain in the Alps, and the most recognizable peak in the world.**

climbers can continue to enjoy the high places on this planet, at the same time preserving them for future generations.

Assembling all the information on the following pages has been a great and rewarding task, and only possible thanks to our many contributors and to a vast amount of help from many other individuals (a list appears on page 301). We offer you the result of this labour in the hope and expectation that all of you, whether new to the activity or old hands, will find plenty here to enjoy and illuminate. *Bon aventure!*

Audrey Salkeld

how to use this book

World Mountaineering explores 52 mountains and reveals the climbing opportunities to be found on them. The experienced mountaineer authors present an insider's look at the peak(s) they know best, commenting on the climbing difficulties involved and suggesting many exciting future challenges. Whether you are an 'armchair enthusiast' wishing to discover more about the exhilarating world of mountaineering or an active mountaineer intending to use this book to plan expeditions, you will be inspired by the wealth of information that it contains. If planning a trip, however, please ensure that you refer to the local guidebooks and contact specialist organizations and guides for detailed advice.

These two pages explain exactly what information you can expect to find within the main profiles of each mountain.

marmolada

lindsay griffin

The Marmolada, at 3342m (10,965ft), is the highest of all the Dolomite summits. Situated more or less centrally in this region of Italian limestone spires, which lies entirely in the South Tyrol, the mountain is bordered to the north by the Avisio River Valley and by the road connecting Canazei to Malga Ciapela. To the south-west lies the Contrin Valley, and to the south the Ombretta. Seen from the north, the gentle icy slopes of one of the region's few permanent glaciers would hardly merit a second glance by today's climber – a cable car rises to the summit ridge and various lifts allow glacier slopes to be used for both winter and summer skiing – however, a peek over the top of the rim reveals one of the most impressive of all Dolomite walls. Although not quite as extensive as the North West Face of the Civetta, clearly visible across the valley to the east, the South Face of the Marmolada, at around 850m (2800ft) high and 3km (2 miles) long, is the modern crucible of Dolomite climbing.

ridges, faces, and peaks

The mountain's summit ridge has three main tops: the Penia, the highest at 3342m (10,965ft); the Rocca at 3309m (10,850ft); and the Ombretta at 3259m (10,700ft). The western top of the Ombretta has the top station of the cable car built on it.

The extensive South Face is at its highest and most impressive below the Ombretta. Running west, it turns a corner at the conspicuous South Pillar of the Penia and continues as a slightly shorter South West Face above the Contrin Valley. Much of the central section of the South Face has a huge but discontinuous terrace, splitting the wall at half-height.

A large proportion of the limestone in the Dolomites is poor, even on many of the so-called popular classics. However, on the Marmolada's South Face most of the rock on the open walls is more or less perfect, and ideal for the continued development of high-standard free climbing. Many of the finest names in Dolomite pioneering appear in the roll of first ascensionists. Descent from the big routes is either along the summit ridge to the top station of the cable car or straight down the Marmolada Glacier. Although 'pisted' in places, and benign in appearance, it is worth noting that one of the great Dolomite activists, Graziano Maffei, was killed when he fell into a crevasse on this glacier.

The North Side of the Marmolada is gentle and largely glaciated, with a number of small subsidiary summits such as the 2792m (9200ft) Cima Undici.

future climbing

Commendably, the current activists have, in the main, preserved traditional ethics when opening their hard new routes and this has resulted in some very bold climbing. It would be scandalous to see these efforts derogated by the creation of adjacent, fully-bolted alpine sport routes, as has happened in other regions. The scope for pioneering magnificent high-standard free ascents is still large and some of the best climbs of the future will result from talented performers eliminating the aid on established mixed, free, and artificial routes.

A free ascent of Maffei's 'Via della Cattedrale' (VI+/A4) is considered one of the biggest challenges. For those with the vision to see a line up those crackless but pocketed walls, the story of the Marmolada is far from over.

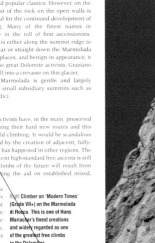

Right Climber on 'Modern Times' (Grade VII+) on the Marmolada di Rocca. This is one of Hans Mariacher's finest creations and widely regarded as one of the greatest free climbs in the Dolomites.

Title The mountain described in each piece may be a single peak, a huge massif with many summits (ie Tirich Mir *see pages 212–15*), a whole area such as Kamchatka (*see pages 208–11*), part of a mountain, or even a single monolithic wall (ie El Capitan *see pages 114–19*). This reveals the full range of snowy and rocky places that climbers are now visiting.

Locator map Specially illustrated aerial locator maps clearly show the mountain and the surrounding area, highlighting country borders, nearest towns, summits, ridges, faces, and glaciers (*see key below*).

Introduction Along with the locator map, this section sets the scene, describing where the mountain is situated. It also explains exactly what attracts climbers to the area, and what this mountain offers them.

Future climbing The authors speculate on what they think the future holds, discussing possible new lines and revealing where there are still unexplored faces.

Key to locator maps

All aerial maps are orientated north/south unless otherwise indicated. The following symbols are used throughout the book on these maps:

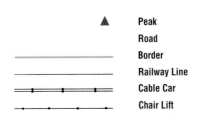

▲ **Peak**

Road

Border

Railway Line

Cable Car

Chair Lift

Key to route photographs

The route photographs include coloured lines (actual colours not significant) that show the approximate lines of major routes. The line variations are as follows:

(11) the line of route shown as accurately as possible

(14) an arrow shows the general direction of the route or indicates when it is subject to change, depending on conditions

a dashed line is used where the line is obscured on the photograph

Timeline The mountain's climbing highlights are charted in this easy-to-follow timeline. First ascents, major new lines, and remarkable achievements are included to give you an instant guide to the history of climbing on each peak.

Main route sections These cover each of the specific sides or faces on the mountain. They also enable you to cross-refer quickly to the photographs illustrating the routes.

A general comment on the climbing to be found on the side/face is given. If there is more than one peak or face within a side, each one is given its own subsection (*see marmolada di penia, marmolada di rocca etc*).

Route photographs Magnificent black-and-white photographs of the different sides of the mountain are overlaid with coloured lines that plot the major routes (*see key below left*).

Route numbers Each route line is numbered to cross-refer to the relevant text entry.

Face annotation Major features of the mountain face, mentioned in the route descriptions, are pointed out.

and the route widely considered the most demanding of the major lines on the South Face.
1994 R Lacher (Italian) placed (well-spaced) bolts on the lead up a 4-pitch route left of 'Specchio di Sara' to create 'Coitus Interruptus', the first X- on the South Face.
1995 M Giordani and M Girardi (Italian) spent three days on the South Face

creating 'Fantasia', a 33-pitch route left of 'The Fish' with a crux of X-. Austrians L Reiser and I Knapp completed 'Steps across the Border' (an 11-pitch route they had first tried 11 years before). Giordani and the Austrians are noted for their very bold climbing and traditional ethics, and none of them appear to have placed a single protection bolt.

SOUTH FACE: MARMOLADA DI PENIA
SOUTH FACE: MARMOLADA DI ROCCA AND OMBRETTA

south face
The South Face has well over 100 established routes. This selection is just a fraction of the worthwhile climbing. Light and fast, 1-day ascents are the norm but can have serious repercussions for climbers caught out in the sudden electrical storms that are notoriously common.

marmolada di penia
1 West Ridge
Dittman, L Rizzi, and Seyffert 1898
Now one of the most popular of the 12 well-equipped Via Ferrata, this route is ungraded. It is 450m (1480ft) and should take two hours.

2 South West Face: Original Route VI
U Conforto and G Soldà 1936
A classic, although not so popular these days. The crux is reaching the exit chimneys and is best tackled after a good dry spell. This route is 550m (1800ft) and takes 8–10 hours.

3 South Pillar VI
D Christomannos, L Micheluzzi, and R Perathoner 1929
Loose rock with a normally very wet section adds to the seriousness of this old classic. It follows the line of weakness on the right flank of the pillar, but the crest itself is taken by the 1979 Brandsatter-Jovane-Kroll-Mariacher Route, a modern free climb at VI+. The route is 550m (1800ft), about 9–10 hours.

4 South Face: Original Route IV+
M Bettega, B Zagonel, and B Tomasson 1901
An old but still popular route that was impressive in its day. The alternative start, right of Gorby's Wall, avoids the notorious stonefall in the initial chimneys. It is 650m (2100ft) long and takes five hours.

5 Viva Gorby VIII
I Koller and D Kuran 1991
The first of four routes (up to IX in standard) added to the 150m (500ft) vertical wall of perfect limestone to the right of the 'Original Route' (4). Good protection and bolted rappel descents give it an ambience between big-wall and sport climbing. There are very few ascents of this route; it is very hard and times vary.

6 Sud Tiroler Weg VI and AO/A1
R Messner and K Renzler 1969
Another well-known problem that fell to the talented Messner. Generally easy climbing on good rock to reach, and then follow, the left-facing diedre between the Penia

and the Rocca. This diedre can often remain wet and is best climbed after a long period of dry weather. It is 700m (2300ft) and takes 7–8 hours.

marmolada di rocca
7 Via del Cinquantenario Fisi VII-
B Allemand, A Dovigani, A Giambisi, and A Gogna 1970
Superb and well protected climbing that has no summit chimneys to remain wet or icy after bad weather. Originally climbed at VI and A1 but all free in 1982. The route is 800m (2600ft) and takes 12–15 hours.

8 Modern Times VII+
L Iovane and H Mariacher 1982
Mariacher's finest creation is regarded as one of the best free climbs in the Dolomites with only 5m (16ft) of less-than-perfect rock. Steep slabs with relatively little in-situ gear and no exit chimneys. The 800m (2600ft) takes 12–14 hours.

9 Vinatzer Route VII
E Castiglioni and G Vinatzer 1936
Direct Finish (VI+): R Messner 1969
One of the great Dolomite classics. Loads of in-situ gear allows an ascent of the original at V+, VI- and AO, but the section below the great terrace is equipped for a rappel descent. The Direct Finish is rarely attempted as most parties require more than one day to complete it and modern climbers prefer to ascend unencumbered by bivouac gear. The route is 800m (2600ft), allow 10 hours for the original.

marmolada di ombretta
10 Via dell'Ideale VII-
A Aste and F Solina 1964
Still a very serious line with obligatory hard moves due to missing bolts. There is also a VI-VI+ waterfall pitch high on the wall so the route should only be tried in settled periods of fine weather. The upper gully taken on the original ascent used to be a depository for refuse from the cable car station; a more popular variant today follows the left rib. The 850m (2800ft) route will probably take two days, but the first winter ascent took a week.

11 The Fish IX-
I Koller and J Sustr 1981
This route was originally a bold climb up an unobvious line. It remains a long, relatively serious, and highly coveted undertaking, and is one of the most popular hard routes on the South Face. With skilful use of skyhooks it is possible

at VII-VII+ and A3, and there have been several winter ascents. The 850m (2800ft) will take two days.

12 Andromeda IX+
M Giordani and R Manfrini 1989
Despite the compact nature of the superb rock, Giordani refused to resort to bolts. He climbed the route at about VIII with a number of bold skyhook sections but it was freed the next year by R Mittersteiner. Allow two days, 850m (2800ft).

13 Don Quixote VI
H Mariacher and R Schiestl 1979
This route and the next one form popular modern classics of around 23 pitches. The 750m (2500ft) normally takes eight hours. This one dries fast; the rock is mostly perfect.

14 Swallow Tail VI
L Reiser and R Schiestl 1978
Not as popular as route (13), despite some wonderful climbing on the slabs above the mid-height terrace.

15 Hatschi Bratschi VI-
H Mariacher, L Reiser, and R Schiestl 1978
Another accessible free climb of medium difficulty. However, it still features a bold crux pitch near the top of the face.

16 Specchio di Sara IX
M Giordani and R Manfrini 1988
A tour de force by Giordani, who had to resort to bolts on the first ascent (VIII with skyhook moves) but still took a 30m (100ft) fall. Climbed free by Mittersteiner the following year. Very bold climbing, up vertical compact limestone, and a must for the talented adventure climber. It is 500m (1640ft) and takes a long day.

17 Filo di Ariana VIII+
M Guerrini and R Vettori 1993
A much-attempted line that was eventually climbed in two days with many rests on skyhooks. Not a single bolt was placed. Awaits a free ascent. It is 450m (1500ft) and is now done in one long day.

18 Savana VII-
S Svetic 1992
Sveticic achieved this excellent free solo first ascent of a much-eyed line on the Elephant Pillar. Protection appears to be rather scant and the climb possibly still unrepeated. It is 750m (2500ft) and takes a day.

19 Progetto Teseo VIII+
M Marisa and R Vettori 1992
Perhaps the most overhanging piece

of rock to be free climbed, and in excellent style with no bolts, on the Marmolada. Unrepeated.

penia north side
This is one of the very few great snow and ice walls of the Dolomites, but is rarely climbed by anyone other than the regular German or Italian visitors. The North Face is 500m (1640ft), the North West Face 400m (1300ft).

20 North Face Direct AD+
G Lori and G Micheluzzi 1935
Although not direct, this line gives excellent mixed climbing in cold, snowy conditions. It is generally impracticable in the summer months. Takes 3–4 hours.

21 Via Paladin D-
L Paladin and S Zappi 1985
A direct route, with steep climbing in the upper section. Difficulty

depends on the state of the summital sérac barrier. Takes four hours.

22 North West Face Direct AD-
G Corenselli, M Ghezzi, and G Todeschini c 1940
A straightforward, highly recommended outing, reached in two hours from the cable car station. There is a short passage of 50 and the route has minimal atonefall in good conditions. The route is approximately three hours long.

how to get to the marmolada
You could fly to Munich, Venice, or Milan and either hire a car (very expensive in Italy) or get the local bus to the villages of Canaze in the west and, convenient for the South Face, Malga Ciapela in the east. Canaze is the larger centre. From these, walk via the Contrin Hut up the Contrin Valley, or up the Ombretta Valley past the Faller Hut, to get to the South Face. The nearest railway station is at Bolzano.

facilities
Major centres (ie Canaze) offer best facilities: accommodation (campsites tend to be booked up in summer), shops selling climbing gear, and supermarkets.

when to climb
June–September; many routes are best late in the season or in autumn. In dry conditions, winter climbing on open walls may be no more arduous than in summer.

gear
Comprehensive rack, including two good skyhooks. Some rely on TriCams in pockets.

maps and guidebooks
Maps 'Tobacco', 1:25,000 (Val di Fassa – Marmolada) or the 'Geografica Carta Escursionistica No 30' (Dolomiti Ladini). Best guides: *Marmolada Parete Sud*, *La parete*, or *Selected Climbs in the Dolomites*, Ron James (Alpine Club).

language
Italian is the main language but German is understood. English not widely spoken.

rescue and insurance
Sophisticated helicopter rescues are possible via the local police. Full alpine insurance is highly recommended.

red tape
None.

Route headings Route names may reflect a particular feature that the line climbs, may be the name bestowed by the original climbers, or may take the name of those climbers.

Where possible, the official grading for each route is given, following the relevant system of the country that the mountain is in. A comparison grading table (*see page 298*) gives equivalent grades for all systems in the book.

The next line gives the first ascensionists and the date the route was put up by them.

Route description The specific difficulties on the route are highlighted, together with personal comments from the writer.

Practical boxed information This covers how to get to the area, the facilities nearest to the mountain, the best time to climb, the gear you will need, maps and guidebooks, the language spoken, rescue service, and any red tape, such as compulsory permits.

This symbol indicates when a route or side of the mountain is not illustrated. This may be because the mountain is extremely complex and it would take several pages to cover all its sides, or because there are no photographs available that show the route/side.

ROMSDAL

● Åndalsnes
Store Trolltind

N O R W A Y

● Oslo

Western Highlands
Fort William ●
Ben Nevis
S C O T L A N D
● Glasgow

North Sea

Wasdale ●
Scafell
Irish Sea

E N G L A N D

● London

Atlantic
Ocean

P O L A N D

A U S T R I A

Tatras ● Zakopane
Mieguszowiecki Group

● Paris

F R A N C E

S W I T Z E R L A N D

S L O V E N I A

S L O V A K I A

Bay of
Biscay

Alps   Eiger   ● Bolzano
Matterhorn   Marmolada
Mont Blanc   Triglav
● Ljubljana

● Lourdes   ● Lyon
Vignemale
Pyrenees

● Milan

Julian Alps

S P A I N

● Barcelona

I T A L Y

Black
Sea

Sierra
Nevada
Mulhacen ⊿   ● Almeria

Mediterranean
Sea

europe

Mountaineering, as a recreation, was born in the European Alps and for many years most climbers were European. At first this meant that, except for those lucky enough to live in one of the Alpine regions, all activity was restricted to a few weeks of annual holiday. But soon alpinists began looking around for other climbable hills and mountains, both for enjoyment and to keep themselves in training for the big mountains. Once rock climbing had developed as an activity in its own right, almost any cliff or crag came under scrutiny, so that now there is probably no sizeable boulder or outcrop anywhere in Europe that has not been investigated by local climbers.

The Alps remain the focus, however, because of their extent, beauty, and accessibility. Rising from the shores of the Mediterranean Riviera, they form a crescent of some 1000km (330 miles), through Monaco, France, Switzerland, Italy, Germany, Liechtenstein, Austria, and into Slovenia, before tangling with the outliers of the Carpathians. Within this great sweep are to be found more than 50 separate peaks above 4000m (13,125ft) – we have described Mont Blanc, the Matterhorn, Marmolada, Triglav, and the Eiger.

The Caucasus is wilder and less developed than the Alps, and has at least a dozen summits higher than anything the Alps have to offer. They are less well known – during the years of the Cold War it was extremely difficult for anyone outside the Soviet bloc to visit them – but, as the pieces on Shkhara will show you, provide excellent climbing opportunities.

Below left **North Face of Ben Nevis on left** Below right **The Eiger (on the left) with neighbouring peak the Mönch**

Nationalities: Norwegian unless stated.
1880 Trollryggen was climbed by J Venge and H Fieve, from Stigfoss over the southern flank.
1882 Store Trolltind was first ascended by C Hall (Danish) with an escort, also from Stigfoss.
1931 The steeper rocks on Store Trolltind were first broached by the celebrated tailor/climber A Randers Heen. With his cousin E Heen, he climbed 'Fivaruta' on the East Face.
1958 A Randers Heen and R Høibakk climbed the long sweeping buttress of Trollryggen's East Pillar (the Troll Pillar) on Heen's seventh attempt. This 40-pitch route was a breakthrough, marking the start of the modern free climbing era in Norwegian alpinism. Today, the climb is known simply as 'Trollryggen'.
1965 Trollveggen became the focus of attention. In parallel siege climbs, a Norwegian team put up a route (see route 3) and a British team put up the 'Rimmon Route'. After five days of continuous climbing the teams reached the summit simultaneously.
1967 C Deck, Y Boussard, P Cordier, J Brunet, and J Fehel (French), practising orthodox siege tactics, forced a magnificent direttissima up Trollveggen over three busy weeks.
1968 Wanda Rutkiewicz and Halina Krüger-Syrokomska (Poland) made the first all-female ascent of Trollryggen.
1972 E and H Drummond (British) created the epic 'Arch Wall' climb over 20 days. This route involved desperate A4+ hooking as well as some fragile nailing.

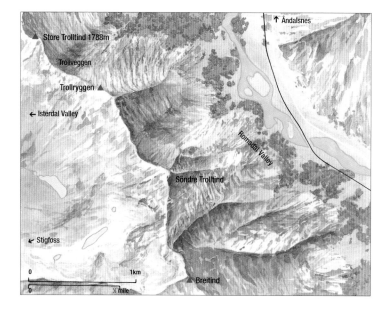

store trolltind and trollveggen

anders lundahl

Store Trolltind, 1788m (5900ft), is the main summit in the long and rugged Trolltindegg chain, which forms an impressive ridge of interconnected peaks, dominating the western flank of the Romsdal Valley in Norway. The chain runs roughly 8km (5 miles) south to north, culminating in Store Trolltind. Trollveggen, the famous 'Troll Wall', is a sheer 1000m (3300ft) drop down into the Romsdal Valley, not from the main peak of Store Trolltind, but from the lesser Trollryggen, 1742m (5700ft), to its south. The rock is made up of quartz, feldspar, and mica, presented sometimes as gneiss, sometimes as granite – solid rock existing side by side with more brittle material.

Early ascents were not made from the abrupt Trollveggen side, which gives access onto the Romsdal, but from Stigfoss in the gentler Isterdal Valley, climbing up over the southern flank of the mountain. This is easy walking, in part over snow and ice, and with a little scrambling in the upper sections. The nearest town, Åndalsnes, is by the fjord 10km (6 miles) north of the massif.

ridges, faces, and peaks

The main summits in the Trolltindegg chain, from south to north, are: Breitind, 1707m (5600ft); Söndre Trolltind, 1536m (5050ft); Trollryggen (the three east-facing Pillars of Romsdal); and Store Trolltind. Trollveggen, often dubbed (without too much exaggeration) Europe's only vertical mile, is a largely north-facing wall in the amphitheatre between Trollryggen and Store Trolltind. It is bounded to the left by the famous East Buttress (Troll Pillar) of Trollryggen, and to the right by the pioneer 'Fivaruta' on Store Trolltind's furrowed East Face.

There are very few outstanding or obvious features on the Trollveggen itself. The left part of the face has a girdle of clearly visible overhangs two-thirds of the way up; it looks somewhat like a crumpled curtain as it is almost entirely covered with interconnected systems of cracks and grooves.

climbing on store trolltind and trollveggen

Arne Randers Heen was the first person to unlock the steeper rock shields of the Trolltindegg, establishing a route of alpine character on the East Face in 1931. In 1958 he and Ralph Høibakk climbed the East Buttress of Trollryggen, conquering the chimney that had defeated many previous attempts.

Trollveggen became the main focus of activity in the 1960s, culminating in the simultaneous arrival at the summit of two teams after epic climbs in 1965. Bolts have never been inserted on the 'Rimmon Route' or the 'Swedish Route' – only pegs. Free climbing emerged in the mid-1970s, but nearly half of the first ascent of the 'Swedish Route' (1978) was done by artificial means.

Today, Norway's multi-day big-wall routes are internationally famous. Here, solitude still rules. Importantly, too, perhaps as much as 1 sq km ($\frac{1}{2}$ sq mile) of virgin rock still awaits climbers.

future climbing

A couple of magnificent direttissimas have been established, as has an entirely artificial climb at the back of the amphitheatre, but the pattern is to free what can be freed. In future, a free ascent of the 1967 French direttissima is a possibility. Or, the ultimate, a ropeless excursion into the corners and cracks of the 'Swedish Route'.

Right **High up on Trollryggen's steep 'Troll Wall', overlooking the Romsdal Valley.**

1976 The 'Rimmon Route' saw its first winter ascent by a Czech team. In the summer J Liliemark (Swedish) and A Lundahl climbed it 95 per cent free.

1978 L Göran Johansson and T Nilsson (Swedish) created the excellent 'Swedish Route' ('Svenskeruta'), a sustained climb in the modern idiom.

1979 H-C Doseth made the first free ascent of the 'Rimmon Route'.

1980 F Perlotti (Italian) soloed 'Trollryggen' (1958) with a new variation.

1981 The 'Swedish Route' received its first winter ascent by H-C Doseth, H and S Nesheim, and K Svanemyr (13 days). In the summer it was free climbed by H-C Doseth, S Bancroft, and C Brooks.

1982 The 'Rimmon Route' was soloed (roped) by B Östigaard in a fast 30 hours. H-C Doseth forced a new line, 'Trollkjerringruta', to the right of the 'Swedish Route'.

1985 Ö Vadla and L Magnussen climbed 'Trolldom' with some aid, but mainly free, in two days.

1986 Ö Vadla and partners put up an entirely artificial climb in winter, 'Död åt Alla'. It took 10 days of continuous A3+ nailing and hooking to complete.

1992 The first all-female ascent of the 'Rimmon Route' was made by Berit Skjevling and Anne Grete Nebel.

1997 The Russians A Ruchkin and J Koshelenko put up a new route on Trollveggen, forcing a mainly artificial line between 'Arch Wall' and the 'French Route'. The first roped solo ascent of the 'Swedish Route' was made by Christian Eek (Norway).

East Buttress — Trollryggen — Trollveggen — Store Trolltind

Please note that American grading is used throughout this section.

east face

The angle of the rock is much less here than on the Trollveggen proper, but you can encounter some delicate slab climbing, with sparse protection in a few places.

1 The East Pillar: Trollryggen 5.9
R Høibakk, A R Heen 1958
Solo (roped with variations): F Perlotti 1980
A great classic on solid rock, this is a 40-pitch rock climb with a few exposed sections bordering on 5.10. Ascent 1300m (4300ft); the route takes 11–16 hours.

2 Fivaruta 5.3
A Randers Heen and E Heen 1931
A long route with more scrambling than real climbing. Seldom done nowadays. Ascent 1800m (6000ft); takes 5–8 hours.

trollveggen

In contrast to the type of climbing in Yosemite, USA (*see pages 114–17*), pure crack climbing is not at the forefront on the Troll Wall. Also, in contrast to the limestone towers of the Dolomites in Italy, there are few repugnant chimneys to be found on the face. Steep and rather continuous face climbing on positive holds prevails, often following indefinite but interconnected seams or rifts. Corners involving bridging and stemming have to be reckoned with. In places fissures become orthodox – solid cracks take good protection and you can move with confidence on clean rock.

3 Norwegian Route 5.9
L N Patterson, J Teigland, O D Enerson, and O Eliassen 1965
A line close to the East Buttress, finishing on the actual summit of Trollryggen. Repeated a few times. The quality of the rock deteriorates in the upper part. 1300m (4300ft); normally takes 16–20 hours.

4 Arch Wall 5.10, A4+
E and H Drummond 1972
An epic climb of some 20 days, involving desperate A4+ hooking as well as fragile nailing. Nonetheless, it has been repeated once. Pitches 13–16 overlap the 'French Route' (5). Ascent 1200m (3900ft); can be done in 8–10 days.

5 French Route 5.9, A4
C Deck, Y Boussard, P Cordier, J Brunet, and J Frehel 1967; Winter: Polish team 1974
This is a long and serious direct route that was climbed by its first ascensionists in siege style over three busy weeks. Repeated a handful of times. Ascent 1200m (3900ft); Takes 5–6 days.

6 Rimmon Route 5.10
J Amatt, T Howard, and B Tweedale 1965
Winter: Czech team 1976
Free: H-C Doseth 1979
Solo (roped): B Östigaard 1982
Takes the well defined line sweeping across the face from right to left. The first ascent took just over five days of continuous climbing, much of it 5.9 with long sections of artificial climbing. Nowadays, one bivouac is normal, although it has been done in just eight hours. The level of difficulties never exceeds hard 5.10, but the easier nature of the top grooves detracts from the overall impression. The quality of the rock leaves something to be desired – the 'Nick' bivvy-ledge let go with a big bang a few years ago. The ascent is 900m (3000ft) and it takes around 1–2 days.

7 Trolldom 5.11, A3
Ö Vadla and L Magnussen 1985
An inspiring route, with some aid but mainly prolonged free climbing, originally completed in good style in two days. Ascent 1050m (3400ft); allow 2–3 days.

how to get to store trolltind
Fly to Oslo, take another plane to Aalesund, and then a bus to Åndalsnes. You can then hire a taxi from Åndalsnes – this is an easy and cheap way to get to the campsites, which are a few kilometres up the Romsdal Valley.

facilities
There are all sorts of hostels and campsites in Romsdal. The official climbing centre at Aak (a few kilometres up the valley) offers year-round courses and outdoor activities. You can also stay there for a moderate cost.

The staff at Aak should be consulted if qualified climbing assistance is required (Aak A/S, Box 238, 6301 Åndalsnes). All supplies, except for specialized climbing gear, can be obtained in Åndalsnes.

when to climb
There is no real darkness from the end of May to August, so it is possible to dispense with alpine starts.

At higher levels, new snow is possible, even at the height of summer, so be prepared. March tends to be the best month for winter climbing, as conditions have stabilized and the days are beginning to lengthen.

gear
For the free routes, a standard rack including at least 25 karabiners and up to 13 friends, plus the same amount of steelwires, will do the job perfectly. The big artificial climbs call for more specialized hardware (you can ask the staff at Aak for advice).

You should take a double rope of 45m (150ft) as a safeguard for quick abseils in an emergency. You will also need to take a crash helmet.

Portaledges are a must on the artificial climbs, but unnecessary on all free routes. In late summer you will have to carry all water from below. Take standard bivouac gear, including a primus, for the longer routes.

maps and guidebooks
A splendid map is 'Romsdalen', 1:50,000, the M-711 series. It is available in many bookshops and equipment stores.

Walks and Climbs in Romsdal, Norway, Tony Howard (revised ed n.o.m.a.d.s., 1998) is excellent. In 1994 a selected guide of popular routes was published in Norwegian and is on sale in mountaineering shops.

language
Norwegian, although many people speak excellent English.

rescue and insurance
An organized rescue service – Fjellreddningen – exists in Norway, but climbers should be individually insured.

red tape
There are no restrictions for climbers, but BASE jumping is forbidden.

Trollryggen

Great Wall

8 Svenskeruta (Swedish Route) 5.11

L G Johansson and T Nilsson 1978
Winter: H-C Doseth, H and S Nesheim,
and K Svanemyr 1981
Free: H-C Doseth, S Bancroft, and C Brooks
(televised) 1981

A 'modern' route of continuous
quality, the 'Svenskeruta' begins
under Rimmon's Great Wall and
aims for the big triangular roof
higher up, which is passed to the
right. Climbed free it involves
a steady 5.10 and even 5.11, and
should only be considered by an
experienced party. There are a
couple of good bivvy ledges; as
the cliff faces north, warm clothes
cannot be dispensed with.
The ascent of 1000m (3300ft)
normally takes two days.

9 Raspberry Dream 5.12

Unknown Japanese climbers 1986
Winter: unknown team 1987
Free: Ö Vadla and A Aastorp 1987

This fine route was first ascended
using artificial methods, but was
free climbed a year later by Norse
climbers Vadla and Aastorp. Two
good bivvy ledges make portaledges
unnecessary. The hardest route on
the Troll Wall. Ascent 950m (3100ft);
allow 2–3 days.

10 Spanish Route: Via El Cami Dels Somnis 5.9, A3

Spanish team of three 1986

A variation of 'Raspberry Dream' (9)
and the 'Swedish Route' (8). Ascent
1000m (3300ft); it takes about
seven days.

11 Trollkjerringruta 5.11

H-C Doseth and a Japanese climber 1982
Winter: H-C Doseth, H and S Nesheim,
and an unknown British climber 1982

This route shares its start with
the 'Rimmon Route' (6), then soars
straight as an arrow to the ridge rim.
Seldom below 5.10 or 5.11, all
climbed free. Ascent 900m (3000ft);
takes two days.

12 Död åt Alla (Death to Everyone) A3/A4

Winter: Ö Vadla and partners 1986

This climb took a total of 10 days and
involved continuous A3+ climbing.
No bolts were used. Gently
overhanging, this is the steepest
of all the routes on the Troll Wall.
Ascent 600m (2000ft).

Nationalities: British unless stated.

1771 The first recorded ascent of Ben Nevis by the botanist J Robertson, made during a tour of Scotland collecting specimens.

1818 John Keats climbed the mountain with his friend C Brown and a local guide. ('It was not so cold as I expected,' he wrote, 'yet cold enough for a glass of whiskey now and then.')

1883 An observatory was opened on the summit by the Scottish Meteorological Society and a bridle path built to service it. Climbers were charged a shilling to use it, or five shillings to ride a pony to the top. Most by-passed the toll gate. An ascent of a gully by persons unknown on the North East Face was the first technical climb on the mountain.

1889 The Glasgow mountaineer W Naismith proposed the establishment of the Scottish Mountaineering Club, which led to a surge in climbing.

1892 J, B, and C Hopkinson made the first ascent of the North East Buttress and descended Tower Ridge, two of the best-known climbs in Britain.

1896 Following the opening of the West Highland Railway, the SMC held regular meetings on Ben Nevis. W Naismith made the first winter ascent of the North East Buttress, still graded IV.

1906 H Raeburn climbed 'Green Gully', the hardest ice route yet managed on the Ben and still graded IV.

1929 The SMC opened a climbers' hut below Coire na Ciste as a memorial to Charles Inglis Clark, who was killed in the Great War.

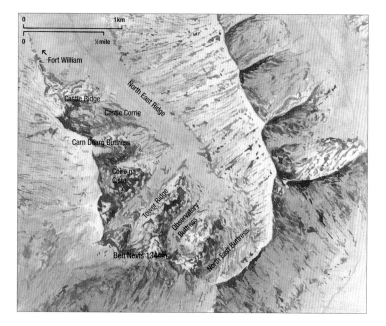

ben nevis

ed douglas

Ben Nevis, at 1344m (4406ft), is Britain's highest mountain and is found in Scotland near the Lochaber town of Fort William. The mountain is best known for its winter routes, which are good enough to draw French climbers away from the Alps. It also has some outstanding summer routes.

The name Nevis is obscure in origin. The Irish word 'neamhaise' means terrible, and in Gaelic the word 'neamh' means 'a raw atmosphere'. Any climber with some experience of struggling down 'the Ben' on a wild winter's night would agree with both.

The mountain boasts the biggest crags in Britain but their exposed position close to the Atlantic creates a great deal of bad weather. The wild variance in temperature at the summit often turns the mountain into an ice factory, producing some of the best winter conditions in the world with superlative snow and ice climbing, and technical face climbs and icefalls. In recent years winters have been leaner but in most seasons the higher climbs will be in good condition for much of the winter. The Ben's ridges give superb mixed climbing. During the short summer season, rock climbers have an excellent range of easy routes on the mountain's long ridges, while on Carn Dearg Buttress they can attempt some of Scotland's best routes between HVS and E3 on compact volcanic rock. Ben Nevis has seen more than a century of mountaineering and remains a forcing ground for winter climbing standards and the pre-eminent mountaineering arena in Britain.

ridges, faces, and peaks

The mountain's North East Side is the most dramatic, its architecture intricate and compelling as though some giant had taken a bite from the rounded summit to leave jagged tooth marks, creating buttresses and gullies for people to follow. The North East Face, the only aspect of the mountain regularly climbed, is usually approached along the Allt a' Mhuilinn track that runs from north-west to south-east and offers a long and tedious approach to the huge cliffs below the bleak summit plateau. The first of these cliffs is the huge Castle Ridge that runs eastwards into the glen.

Between Castle Ridge and the vast Carn Dearg Buttress is Castle Corrie, which holds Castle Buttress. On the other side of Carn Dearg Buttress, the highest point on the north-west corner of Ben Nevis, is Coire na Ciste with its tiny green lochan visible in summer. It is surrounded on three sides by huge cliffs and bounded to the north by Carn Dearg Buttress and to the south-east by Tower Ridge. Running between the two is a series of buttresses and gullies, beginning with Number Five and the Moonlight and Trident Buttresses which extend round to Number Four Gully. To the left is Creag Coire Na Ciste, which is divided from Number Three Gully Buttress and The Comb by Number Three Gully.

Beyond the Creag Coire Na Ciste is Number Two Gully, as well as a series of minor buttresses leading to Tower Ridge and stretching down almost to the CIC Hut. The third of the great buttresses on the mountain, Tower Ridge, is also the most striking, starting at 700m (2300ft) just above the CIC Hut and extending for almost 600m (1970ft), culminating in the Great Tower that is found just below the summit slopes. Next is the broad Observatory Gully, which splits at the top either side of Gardyloo Buttress, with Gardyloo Gully on the left and

Right Climbing 'The Curtain' route on the Carn Dearg Buttress of Ben Nevis. When conditions are right, Scottish winter climbs can be among some of the best in the world.

1954 J Brown and D Whillans put up 'Sassenach' (E1) on the Carn Dearg Buttress and so opened a post-war boom in new routes both in winter and summer.

1959 'Point Five Gully' was climbed after a 6-day siege. The 4-man team used tactics some regarded as unethical.

1978 M Fowler and V Saunders climbed the steep right flank of the

Carn Dearg Buttress to give the 'Shield Direct' route, a major leap in modern standards.

Tower Gully on the right. Overlooking the East Side of Observatory Gully is a huge sweep of impressive buttresses and walls, beginning with Indicator Wall, Observatory Buttress, Point Five and Observatory Buttress, Orion Face, and culminating in the steep North East Buttress, which holds the Minus Face. The route up the North East Buttress, first climbed in 1896, contained the Mantrap, a difficult but avoidable step that still checks many competent parties.

future climbing

With more than 200 routes already done, most of the best lines on the mountain have now been completed. However, Ben Nevis gets more attention than any other mountain in Scotland and climbers will continue to find gaps and difficult new climbs for some time to come. Modern ice tools may have made climbing the famous ice routes technically easier, but the mixed routes continue to have a big reputation for serious climbing.

Orion Face

Observatory Buttress

Minus Face

North East Buttress

Most routes will take a day for competent parties to complete, but it is generally a 4-hour walk in to the start of the routes.

north east buttress

This facet of Ben Nevis arguably contains more world-famous and world-class ice climbs than that of any other mountain in the world. The first-ascensionist list reads like a who's who of British climbing.

1 North East Buttress IV, 4
W Naismith, W Brunskill, A Kennedy, W King, and F Squance 1896
One of the finest mountaineering expeditions in the country, with the difficult step known as the Mantrap high on the ridge slowing even the strongest parties. This route is 300m (1000ft) in length.

2 Minus Two Gully V, 5
J Marshall, J Stenhouse, and D Haston 1959
Often overshadowed by the celebrity of its neighbours, Minus Two has some of the best climbing of its grade with the added bonus of finishing up the top section of the North East Buttress. 275m (900ft).

3 Minus One Gully VI, 6
K Crocket and C Stead 1974
The most technical of the famous Nevis gullies, the crux is a difficult overhang at one-third height but the route requires good conditions and ascents are rare. The route is 275m (900ft) in length.

4 The Long Climb VS
J Bell and J Wilson 1940
With more than 420m (1378ft) of climbing, this alpine rock climb gives one of the best mountaineering routes in the country.

5 Orion Direct V, 5
R Marshall and R Smith 1960
One of the three big Nevis winter routes, this sustained and open face is Scottish winter climbing at its best. It was first climbed before the age of modern ice tools by two of the biggest contributors to Scottish climbing. It is 300m (1000ft).

6 Slav Route VI, 5
D Lang and N Quinn 1974
This long grade VI is not as technically demanding as some more modern desperates but

nevertheless it is continuously interesting. The route is 420m (1378ft) in length.

7 Zero Gully V, 4
H MacInnes, A Nicol, and T Patey 1957
This famous and historic route was the first grade V on Ben Nevis and is still considered very serious, if technically amenable. 300m (1000ft).

8 Observatory Ridge VD
H Raeburn 1901
A highly rated and popular climb both in summer and winter (when it is graded at IV, 4) and can be serious under powder snow conditions. 420m (1378ft).

9 Point Five Gully V, 5
J Alexander, I Clough, D Pipes, and R Shaw 1959
Known simply as 'The Point', this narrow and initially steep gully is one of the most famous ice routes in the world. 325m (1100ft).

10 Albatross VII, 6M
Geddes and C Higgins 1978
A difficult line up a thinly iced corner, this is just one of several excellent and difficult shorter climbs

situated on the Indicator Wall. It is 170m (560ft).

tower ridge
If done in its entirety, Tower Ridge gives the longest technical climb in Britain. Parties should move quickly to avoid being benighted, especially early in the year.

11 Tower Ridge III
J Collie, G Solly, and J MacLean 1894
In scale and length, this is a great climb, building to an impressive climax on the Great Tower and beyond. 820m (2700ft).

12 Vanishing Gully V, 5
R Marshall and G Tiso 1961
Superb route with good protection and belays. The main difficulties are in the first two pitches. Requires good conditions to form. 200m (660ft).

carn dearg buttress
Carn Dearg has some of the best mid-grade rock climbs in the world and some of the most impressive ice and mixed climbs too.

13 The Curtain IV, 5 ⊠

J Knight and D Bathgate 1965

A hugely popular introduction to the hard Nevis ice routes. 110m (360ft).

14 The Bullroar HVS

J Marshall and J Stenhouse 1961

One of the best HVS in Britain through impressively steep terrain. 285m (940ft).

15 Torro E2J

McLean, W Smith, and W Gordon 1962

A superb and sustained 8-pitch E2 that takes an elegant line up slabs to the left of 'Centurion' route. 215m (700ft).

16 Centurion HVS

D Whillans and R Downes 1956

Possibly the best HVS route in Britain, this brilliant line takes in some unlikely positions for its grade, especially through the upper overhangs. 190m (620ft).

17 King Kong E2 ⊠

B Robertson and J Graham 1964

The initially wet and technical start of this route is often by-passed, but the central section offers some of the best climbing on the mountain through overlapping slabs right of 'Centurion'. 275m (900ft).

18 The Bat E2

D Haston and R Smith 1959

Takes a narrow corner to the right of the buttress's central slabs. There are a number of long, swooping falls, giving the route its name. 270m (890ft).

19 Gemini VI, 6 ⊠

A Paul and D Sanderson 1979

One of the best modern ice climbs, with an atmospheric and exposed lead up an ice-smeared detached flake one-third of the way up. 300m (1000ft).

how to get to ben nevis

The main valley base for Ben Nevis is Fort William, 2-hours drive north of Glasgow. You can take an overnight sleeper rail service from London to Fort William or fly to Glasgow or Inverness. The North East Face is often reached from the Allt a' Mhuilinn track that starts north-east of Fort William near the golf course.

facilities

Several hotels and bunkhouses at Fort William, as well as climbing shops.

when to climb

Winter climbing on Ben Nevis normally happens from early January–late April (and even early May) but the best time to go is late February–March when the weather is more settled and the days are longer. The Ben's ridges are often snowed up from late October onwards. Conditions are not predictable so monitor conditions constantly: daily weather and avalanche reports are posted in the major climbing areas. Summer season is short, usually confined from late May–early September.

gear

In Scotland, protection from wind and cold in winter is essential. On steep ice, short, technical ice axes are obligatory. (The easier mixed ridges are alpine in scale and speed is as important as technique.) Ice screws are widely used but are not as reliable as they are on waterfalls. A compass is essential for navigating off the summit plateau.

rescue and insurance

There is a rescue service; dial 999.

maps and guidebooks

The Scottish Mountaineering Council guide *Ben Nevis* is the standard guidebook. The Ordnance Survey 'Outdoor Leisure' series map, 1:25,000, is the best map available.

red tape

None.

Nationalities: British unless stated.

1802 Descent of Broad Stand to Mickledore by poet S T Coleridge.

1882–1892 Most of the main gully lines were climbed: Deep Gill, Slingsby's Chimney, Moss Gill. Leading characters included W G Haskett-Smith, J N Collie, and C Slingsby.

1896 O Glynne Jones emerged as one of the first rock athletes with his bold

departure from the gullies onto the steeper adjacent rock with 'Jones' Route Direct'. Unrepeated for 14 years.

1903 F W Botterill and companions climbed 'Botterill's Slab', an astonishing lead for the time.

1914 Central Buttress was climbed by S Herford, G Sansom, and C F Holland, employing combined tactics to overcome the infamous chockstone

section of the 'Great Flake' pitch. Far harder than anything done since.

1926 'Moss Gill Grooves' was completed by gritstone maestro H Kelly, the culmination of seven years of effort above and right of the Central Buttress.

1931 C Kirkus breached the extremely steep East Buttress with 'Mickledore Grooves' (VS 4c). J M Edwards free climbed the Central Buttress.

1932 M Linnell made a bold solo first ascent of 'Bayonet Shaped Crack', a variation finish to 'Central Buttress'.

1933 'Overhanging Wall' on East Buttress was climbed by M Linnell, using controversial pitons for aid.

1952 P Greenwood and A Dolphin forced the line of 'Hell's Groove' through the overhanging left end of the East Buttress.

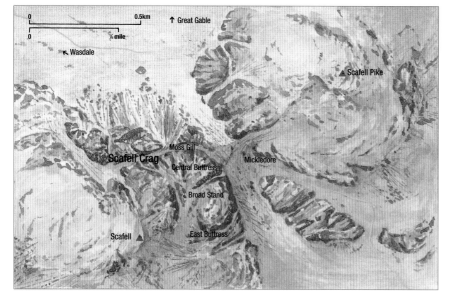

professional classes. It was obvious to dedicated British climbers that training was needed for the Alpine climbs, so attention was focused on the seemingly modest crags and gullies of upland Britain. Wasdale, with its convenient public house and fine crags, quickly became the first British climbing 'resort'.

The rock of Scafell, like that of the rest of the Lake District, comprises ancient lava flows. More recent glaciation and prolonged weathering have carved out crags and provided countless cracks and edges for hands and feet. Thus a perfect environment has been created for climbing styles and techniques to evolve with the minimum of technology. The structure of the rock offered just enough natural protection to encourage a striving for ethical purity.

scafell crag and east buttress

bernard newman

Situated at the head of Wasdale in the heart of the Cumbrian Mountains, the Scafell massif is the hub of the radial pattern of ridges, valleys, and lakes that comprise the English Lake District. Scafell Crag lies near the summit of Scafell, 964m (3162ft), the sister peak to Scafell Pike which, at 978m (3208ft), is England's highest mountain.

The crags of Scafell and Great Gable, 899m (2949ft), across Wasdale to the north, are accepted as the birthplace of British rock climbing and the routes here are steeped in history. Every major phase and advance of British rock climbing is mirrored in the cliffs of Scafell. It was early Wasdale activists who developed rock climbing as a valid pursuit in its own right.

During the second part of the 19th century, alpinism became a well established sport among both the idle rich and the

ridges, faces, and peaks

The main areas of climbable rock on Scafell are confined to two huge buttresses – Scafell Crag on its northern flank and the East Buttress – lying to either side of Broad Stand, an open chimney that drops down to Mickledore, which is a strange green col joining Scafell to Scafell Pike.

As you stand on the col facing west, the huge, steep, black, north-facing wall of Scafell Crag sweeps off to the right. It is cut into three monolithic buttresses, each nearly 120m (400ft) high, separated by deep gullies. Nearest is the clean wall of the Central Buttress, topped out by slanting grooves and slab lines. Further right, across the deep gash of Moss Gill, is the more broken pillar of Pisgah and, beyond that, across Steep Gill, the aptly-named Scafell Pinnacle, a miniature Chamonix aiguille.

To the left of Mickledore Col, an elongated, barrel-shaped cliff drops away southwards. Smaller than the main crag, at around 75m (250ft), the East Buttress drips with cracks, blind grooves, and hanging arêtes, topped by steep walls and slabs.

future climbing

Even though Scafell Crag and the East Buttress could be said to have reached 'maturity' in terms of being climbing venues, there are still many new lines awaiting the bold and fit. The natural lines on the latter demand to be climbed.

Right **Martin Berzins leads the overhanging 'Siege Perilous' on the East Buttress.**

1957 The Rock & Ice Club announced its presence with 'Phoenix', R Moseley's soaring groove-and-wall line to the right of 'Hell's Groove'.

1960 G Oliver put up 'Ichabod'. It is still the definitive East Buttress route.

1966 Attention returned to the Central Buttress. 'The Nazgul', the unrelenting diagonal line left of the 1914 Central Buttress climb, succumbed to L Brown.

1969 'The Lord of the Rings', a girdle traverse of East Buttress, was solved by J Adams and C Read in 19 hours over two days. Unrepeated for six years.

1976 A quantum leap in standards was launched with P Livesey's route 'Lost Horizons' on the East Buttress.

1976 J Eastham and E Cleasby climbed the blank wall and hanging crack to the right of the Central Buttress to produce 'Saxon', one of the most popular extreme rock climbs in the Lake District.

1977 E Cleasby and R Matheson climbed 'Shere Khan', which is the companion route to 'Lost Horizons' on the East Buttress.

1978 'Cullinan' on the East Buttress was the first of a series of desperately hard and very serious climbs from M and B Berzins.

1981 'The Almighty', the short, thin, overhanging crack on the East Buttress, was put up by P Botterill and J Lamb.

1986 C Sowden and M Berzins climbed 'Borderline', a fearsome overhanging groove in the blank wall left of centre on the East Buttress.

1989 M Berzins forged 'The Siege Perilous', a futuristic *tour de force* up the leaning wall right of 'Shere Khan'.

Mickledore · Central Buttress · Moss Gill · Pisgah · Steep Gill · Scafell Pinnacle

All climbs on Scafell are excellent; these are just some of the best. Several routes can be done in one day, depending on conditions and how experienced you are.

scafell crag

This definitely has a 'big' feel to it. In gloomy conditions it can be forbidding but, in the afternoon sun, all the routes seem do-able.

1 Botterill's Slab VS, 4c

F W Botterill, H Williamson, and J E Grant 1903
This tackles the obvious, clean, slanting slab line, picked out by the evening sun, to the left of the Central Buttress. 87m (285ft).

2 White Wizard E3, 5c

C Bonington and N Estcourt 1971 (6 points of aid)
Free: M Berzins and G Higginson 1976
This gives magnificent, sustained groove-and-crack climbing in a superb position above 'Botterill's Slab' (1). 96m (315ft).

3 Ringwraith E5, 6b

M Berzins, R H Berzins, and C Sowden 1977
A typical Berzins route: steep and uncompromising. The leaning wall between 'White Wizard' (2) and the Central Buttress. 94m (310ft).

4 The Nazgul E3, 5c

L Brown and K Jackson (3 points of aid)
Free: P Botterill and S Clegg 1975
This takes the breathless steep crack on the wall left of 'Central Buttress' (5), then finishes more reasonably in superb position. 84m (275ft).

5 Central Buttress E1, 5b

S W Herford, G S Sansom, and C F Holland 1914
Six pitches of classically superb climbing, winding up the smoothest part of the face. The famous flake crack moves are much harder (5c) since the chockstones came away (sadly killing the climber on them) but can be avoided by an excursion onto the left wall at 5b. If you only do one route, do this. 121m (400ft).

6 Saxon E2, 5c

J Eastham and E Cleasby 1976
This steep wall and hanging crack is popular. Here, commitment pays dividends. 120m (400ft).

east buttress

This always presents a fierce aspect. Approaching along the path at its foot, the whole place seems neck-achingly steep and it's always cold!

7 The Almighty E5, 6b

P Botterill and J Lamb 1981
This follows a thin, fierce, overhanging crack. 18m (60ft).

8 Ichabod E2, 5c

G Oliver, G Arkless, and L Willis 1960
The classic of the East Buttress. Soaring line; good rock. 45m (145ft).

9 Borderline E6, 6c

C Sowden and M Berzins 1986
A technical masterpiece up the central overhanging flake-and-groove wall. Protectable – just. 54m (180ft).

10 Shere Khan E5, 6a

E Cleasby and R Matheson 1977
A scary climb whose main feature is a steep diagonal ramp that turns out to be precarious and overhanging. Persistence is rewarded with little protection and a fierce short crack to the stance. 72m (240ft).

11 The Siege Perilous E7, 6b

M Berzins and C Sowden 1989
Free: M Berzins and A Phizacklea 1992
Possibly the hardest and most serious route in the area, this takes the overhanging wall right of 'Shere Khan' (10). 37m (120ft).

12 Mickledore Grooves VS, 4c

C F Kirkus, I M Waller, and M Pallis 1931
This is a sweeping diagonal line across the right-hand side of the East Buttress. The first ascent was way ahead of its time. 67m (220ft).

how to get to scafell

Wasdale, the natural starting point, is reached by car via the A595. The approach from the head of Wastwater is via Brown Tongue, a steep rounded bluff between two streams, which leads to Mickledore (GR211068). It is 4km (2½ miles) with 760m (2500ft) of ascent so allow two hours. Most of the routes can easily be reached from the col along well-worn paths.

facilities

There is camping and a hotel and climbing shop at Wasdale Head. More campsites and accommodation are located further down the valley.

when to go

Scafell is predominantly a summer (May–October) venue and even then it needs four consecutive dry days to bring the routes into condition.

gear

Two 50m (165ft) ropes are essential. Carry a full rack of nuts and friends.

maps and guidebooks

The best map is the 'Outdoor Leisure 6: The English Lakes, South Western area', 1:25,000, (Ordnance Survey).

Scafell, Wasdale & Eskdale, Al Phizacklea (Fell & Rock Climbing Club, 1996) is the definitive rock-climbing guide to the crag and its locality. Look no further than this.

rescue and insurance

Mountain rescue is extremely efficient. The nearest rescue post is at Wasdale Head Hotel. A kit for the rescue team's use is stored in the lee of Mickledore. Dial 999 and ask for the Police.

red tape

None.

Left **Scafell Pike, the sister peak of Scafell (in the distance) is the highest summit in England.**

Nationalities: Polish unless stated.
1575 The first information was written about the area. It grew in popularity after the beginning of the 19th century.
1877 Wielki Mięguszowiecki was climbed to the summit by local guides M Sieczka and W Roj with their client L Chalubiński.
1906 North Face of Wielki Mięguszowiecki was climbed for the first time by guides

J Marusarz-Startszy, J Stopka-Ceberniak, and client S Krygowski.
1910 The North Face of Pośredni Mięguszowiecki (Middle Peak) was first climbed by G Komarnicki, R Komaricki, and J Roguska-Cybulska.
1934 The first route on the Kazalnica Mięguszowiecki on the Czarny (Black) Summit was put up by Z Korosadowicz and J Staszel.

1935 The North East Pillar of Wielki Mięguszowiecki was climbed by Z Korosadowicz and J W Zulawski.
1936 The first winter ascent of the North Face of Wielki Mięguszoweicki was made by Z Korosadowicz and J Staszel.
1942 The classic 'Lapinski-Paszucha Route', or 'La-Pa', was first climbed by C Lapinski and K Paszucha.

1948 The Orlowski Pillar on the North Face of the Pośredni Mięguszowiecki was climbed by T Orlowski and J W Zulawski with D Schiele.
1955 The 'Dlugosz-Momatiuk Route' on the Kazalnica was put up by J Dlugosz and C Momatiuk.
1962 New lines continued to be drawn on the Kazalnica: 'The Pillar' was climbed by the strong team

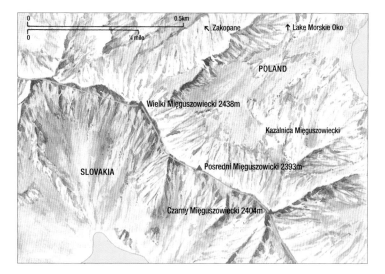

ridges, faces, and peaks

The Mięguszowiecki group consists of three peaks: Wielki 2438m (8000ft), Pośredni 2393m (7851ft), and Czarny, or Black, 2404m (7887ft). Part of the main ridge of the Tatra mountains, all three are approximately 1000m (3300ft) above the valley, from where they present an impressive view for visitors.

The Main Summit, Wielki Mięguszowiecki, has always been an ambitious goal. Its fine granite affords quality climbing, and the grassy and broken North Face, rising over 800m (2600ft) high above the picturesque Morskie Oko Lake ('the eye of the sea'), offers difficult routes and particularly good winter climbing.

The middle peak, which is called Pośredni Mięguszowiecki, has a 350m (1150ft) high North Face. Compared to the other peaks, it is relatively rarely climbed.

Some of the most difficult climbing is found on a lower crag on the Czarny (or Black) Mięguszowiecki. Called Kazalnica Mięguszowiecki, this is the 'El Cap' (*see pages 114–17*) of the Polish Tatra. The crag is 570m (1870ft) high, with about 250m (820ft) vertical or overhanging. It boasts some of the longest and most serious climbs in Poland and provides adventurous climbing to tempt international interest. In foul weather, it is possible to practise ice climbing on the many short icefalls in the area.

mięguszowiecki group

piotr konopka

The Tatra Mountains, which form part of the Carpathian arc, are situated on the border between Poland and Slovakia. A small, compact range, occupying no more than 50 by 15km (30 by 10 miles), and alpine in character, they have been described as big mountains on a small scale. From a climber's point of view, some of the most interesting and impressive peaks in the range are the Mięguszowiecki group (highest point 2438m/8000ft) of the High Tatra. These present some of the biggest walls in the Tatra; the summits are not accessible by footpaths. The national border runs across the Main Summit, Wielki.

Only one-fifth of the Tatra Mountains lies within Poland, yet these rugged peaks and ridges have been the forcing ground for a disproportionate number of top-class Polish mountaineers. In the past 20 years, Polish climbers have out-performed all other nations in the field of exploratory alpinism on the world's highest peaks. Inured by the harsh winter conditions in their native mountains, they introduced winter climbing to the Himalaya.

climbing on the mięguszowiecki group

The development of climbing in the Tatra has, more or less, reflected changes elsewhere. The 1960s was a period of long, big climbs, very stylish and mostly with aid, the 1970s saw the start of free climbing, and the 1980s brought the speed ascents. The latter were best achieved on the Kazalnica Pillar, which was climbed in under two hours (first ascent took two days). This style persisted into the early and mid-1990s, when, unfortunately, a trend for new bolted routes began to appear. This is a controversial move and is by no means accepted by all climbers.

future climbing

More than 100 climbs exist in the massif. However, there are still new things to do. People who have a knowledge of the massif, a lot of imagination, and are bold enough (backed up by the very latest gear and training), put up a sprinkling of new routes every year, or make first winter ascents.

Right **The Mięguszowiecki peaks from the north-east. From the left: Czarny, Pośredni, and Wielki Mięguszowiecki. The crag Kazalnica Mięguszowiecki is in the centre foreground.**

of E Chrobak, A Heinricyh, J Kurczab, and K Zditowiecki; in addition, the 'Momatiukowka' (VI/A3) was climbed over 11 days by C Momatiuk, K Jurkowski, A Nowacki, A Szurek, and A Wojnarowicz.

1968 One of the most serious winter climbs to be undertaken on the Kazalnica, 'Wielki Zaciecie' (The Big Dihedral), was completed by the team of J Kielowski, T Piotrowski, and Z Prusisz.

1973 'Super Ściek' (Super Gully), another major winter route, was established over two days by P Jasinski, V Kurtyka, K Pankievicz, and Z Wach.

1992 The 'Momatiukowka' (IX) was climbed free by W Derda and A Marcisz on 8 August.

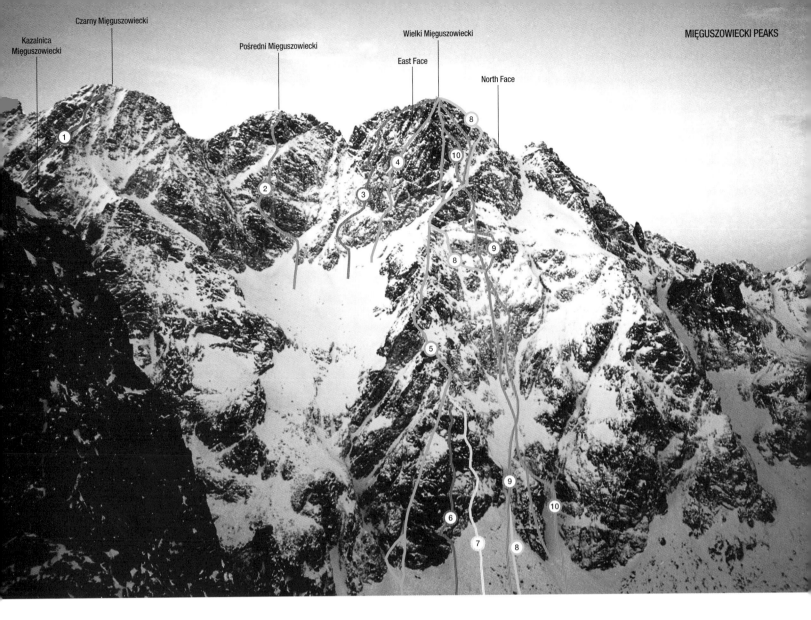

Czarny Mięguszowiecki
Kazalnica Mięguszowiecki
Pośredni Mięguszowiecki
Wielki Mięguszowiecki
East Face
North Face

Grades given here are mostly for summer climbing; in winter the routes below can be serious alpine rock routes.

czarny mięguszowiecki

1 East Face
P Konopka 1994
This 300m (1000ft) face has little to interest climbers, but it is recommended for good skiers, offering an exciting 55° ski descent.

pośredni mięguszowiecki

2 Orlowski Route V
T Orlowski, J W Zulawski, and D Schiele 1946
Highly recommended, as are all Tadeusz Orlowski routes. 4¹/₂ hours.

wielki mięguszowiecki

The route lines on the North Face and the North East Pillar are up to 900m (2950ft) high. The very lowest part of the North Pillar, Czolowka Mięgusza, 180m (600ft), and the East Face, 350m (1150ft), offer good rock-climbing opportunities.

east face

This 400m (1300ft) face has some particularly good rock climbing.

3 The Surdel Route V/V+
J Surdel and B Uchmański 1964
The most popular climb on this face. Four hours.

4 The Świerz Route V-
J Humpola and M Świerz 1921
First climb on this face. Three hours.

north face

This has 800m (2600ft) of excellent winter climbing.

5 Classic North East Pillar V
Z Korosadowicz and J W Żulawski 1935
Winter: J Dlugosz and A Pietsch 1956
One of the longest climbs in the area, particularly interesting in winter. The ascent was reduced to 10 hours by C Lapinski and S Siedlecki in 1946.

6 Czarny Zacięcie (The Black Dihedral) VI+, A1
J Hobrzanski and K Lozinski 1972
A popular rock climb, very often done in winter. Connected to route (5), this offers a very long climb. 120–180m (400–600ft); eight hours.

7 North East Pillar Headwall: Starek-Ushmański Route VI, A3/ freed VI
A Starek and B Uchmański 1964
The first climb on this 160m (500ft) high headwall. A popular route, and very long if climbed in conjunction with the 'Classic North East Pillar' route (5). 250m (800ft); 10 hours.

8 North Face Route III
S Krygowski, J Marusarz, and J Stopka-Ceberniak 1906
Winter: Z Korosadowicz and J Staszel 1936
Vertical climb of 1045m (3400ft). Not recommended in summer. Six hours.

9 North Face Direttissima V
S Biel, J Honowski, and Z Rubinowski 1953
Follows a straighter line than route (8) in the upper part of the face. The original climb took two days; now allow 8–10 hours. The route is approximately 850m (2800ft) long.

10 North Face Superdirettissima V-VI (ice 85°–90°)
W Kurtyka, J K Rusiecki, and D Davis 1974
Recommended only in winter, this route takes 12 hours. 15m (50ft).

kazalnica mięguszowiecki

This legendary climbing crag on Czarny Mięguszowiecki has played an important role for generations of Tatra climbers and is the site of a large part of Polish climbing history. Grades V/V+ up to IX+, with only one easy route (III). The longest routes have up to 12 full pitches.

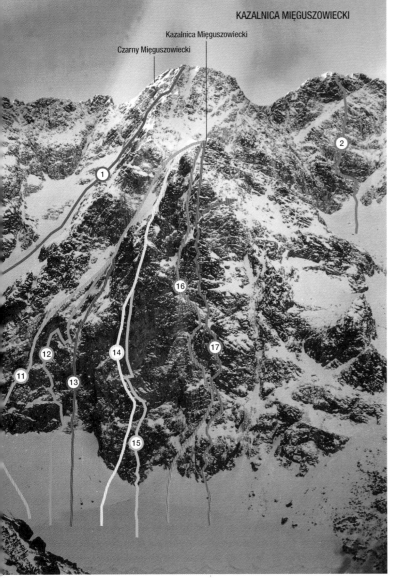

KAZALNICA MIĘGUSZOWIECKI

Kazalnica Mięguszowiecki

Czarny Mięguszowiecki

11 Dlugosz-Popko Route VI, A1

J Dlugosz and M Popko 1958

A typical winter climb, with a lot of steep turf. Not too long. Very popular and recommended. 230m (750ft) of ascent; 4–6 hours.

12 Sprężyna (The Spring) VI, A0

R Berbeka and M Gryczynski 1961

A popular summer and winter climb, taking 4–10 hours.

13 Super Ściek (Super Gully) VI, A2/A3

P Jasinski, V Kurtyka, K Pankiewicz, and Z Wach 1973

A typical winter climb, which has only had one summer ascent. 90° water ice; aid climbing through the roofs; delicate mixed climbing when coming out, with permanent risk of avalanches from the big gully above. Probably one of the most serious routes in the Tatras. Not very often climbed. 210m (700ft). It originally took two days; allow 10–15 hours.

14 Lewa Kazalnica or Dlugosz-Momatiuk Route – originally VI, A1, now VIII

J Dlugosz and C Momatiuk 1955

A good summer and winter climb. Quite popular. Allow 12 hours.

15 The Pillar – originally VI, A2/A3, now IX+

E Chrobak, A Heinrich, J Kurczab, and K Zditowiecki 1962

Climbed free as 'the last big problem of the Kazalnica' in 1995. One of the longest routes with 370m (1200ft) of ascent; a long day (20–25 hours).

16 Lapiński-Paszucha Route – originally V1, A1, now V+/VI-

C Lapiński and K Paszucha 1942

The first climb through the main section of this wall, and still an interesting winter route. 560m (1800ft). Originally took seven hours; now allow five.

17 Schody do Nieba (Steps to Heaven) VI/VI+

Z Czyżewski and M Aderek 1977

Probably the most popular summer route. Good climbing on mostly solid rock. 560m (1800ft); six hours.

how to get to the mięguszowiecki group

You can easily reach the town of Zakopane at the northern foot of the Tatras by train or bus.

Zakopane is the jumping-off place/starting point for climbing in the Tatras. A popular Polish tourist and winter-sports resort, it is linked by road to the Morskie Oko Lake, a beauty spot and the centre for climbing.

From the Slovakian side, you can travel by air to Poprad. It is then 90km (55 miles) by road to Zakopane via the border station of Lysa Polana.

facilities

Zakopane boasts many hotels and *pensions*, and there are comfortable refuges in the mountains. For climbing in the Morskie Oko area you can stay in the Roztoka refuge (halfway up to the lake) or the Morskie Oko refuge.

Prices are higher than most people expect (a little cheaper than the Alps – but not much).

Guides are compulsory for people who are not members of a national climbing organization, but they are also recommended for anyone who is not an independent climber. For information on guides, contact the Polish Mountain Guides Association: PO Box 289, First Floor, 35 Krupówki Street, Zakopane, Poland.

when to climb

Try to avoid the main tourist seasons, which are 10 July–30 August and 26 December–5 January.

Climbing is possible almost all the year round, but the summer is usually short with changeable weather.

Rock climbing can normally be done from May–October; September and October are the best months. The end of October–early December produces the worst and most dangerous conditions so should be avoided. There is good winter climbing from January–March; the best conditions for extreme skiing are in mid-April–mid-June. February–April produce the best snow for ski mountaineering and ski touring.

gear

Besides the usual gear, you will need a selection of pitons, a rock hammer, (summer and winter), and some Warthogs (when climbing in winter).

maps and guidebooks

Good maps are available in Zakopane, the best being the 'Tatrzanski Park Narodowy', 1:30,000.

As yet there are no guidebooks in foreign languages.

language

Polish (on the Polish side of the border). English is understood in most places.

rescue and insurance

The professional mountain-rescue service TOPR can be contacted at Pilsudski Street, Zakopane. In Slovakia, climbing insurance is now compulsory.

red tape

The Tatra Mountains are very overcrowded. Take care to protect this heavily used environment. Restrictions are posted beside each entrance to the national park so please respect them – unfortunately climbers are not the local rangers' favourite people. All climbers need to have documents from their own national climbing association.

1741 The Chamonix valley was 'discovered' by two Englishmen.
1744 The name Mont Blanc first appeared on a map published in London.
1760 H B de Saussure, who was a scientist from Geneva, promised a large sum of money to the first person discovering a route to the summit of Mont Blanc and in doing so unwittingly created a new activity – alpinism.

1786 J Balmat, a chamois hunter and glass cutter, and Dr M G Paccard (French) stood atop the highest point of Mont Blanc and made history by not only climbing the highest peak in the Alps but also making the first ascent of any major summit in the range.
1787 H B de Saussure made the third ascent with Balmat, who had made the second a month earlier.

1859 The 'Grands Mulets Route' was opened up by C Hudson's largely British party.
1861 Goûter Ridge was first climbed in its entirety by L Stephen and F Tuckett (British) and guides.
1865 The first ascent was made from the Italian side. A Moore's largely British party climbed the great snow and ice ridge bounding the right side of the

fearsome Brenva Face. Despite four repeats in the next 30 years, the 'Brenva Spur Route', affectionately known afterwards as the Old Brenva, was way ahead of its time and is still considered a relatively serious undertaking.
1872 The first ascent was made of the main Miage Face by T Kennedy's party.
1876 The first winter ascent was made by Mary Isabella Straton (British) and

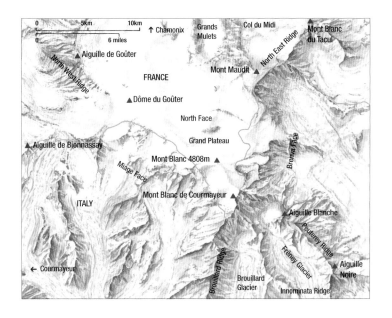

mont blanc

lindsay griffin

Mont Blanc, at 4808m (15,771ft) the highest mountain in Western Europe, straddles the frontier between France and Italy. The actual summit lies entirely in France; Italy must make do with the 4748m (15,577ft) Mont Blanc de Courmayeur, situated just over 0.5km (⅓ mile) to the south-east.

To committed climbers, the importance of Mont Blanc lies not so much in its high altitude but in the fact that it forms the culminating point of a massif that has undoubtedly been the forcing ground of alpinism since the activity began. Mont Blanc's compact range lies towards the western end of the Alps – Europe's finest collection of glaciated mountains. The spectacular rock and ice peaks of Mont Blanc are formed mostly from a granite of excellent quality, and so it is not surprising that the vast majority of the world's greatest alpinists all served part of their apprenticeship here, or that trends in climbing style and ethic, developed in the massif, have been later mirrored throughout the world's ranges.

ridges, faces, and peaks

Mont Blanc is a complex yet beautiful mountain with four long ridges, plus a fifth somewhat lesser crest, that demarcate five main faces. It has a grandeur and sheer bulk that are often compared favourably with many of the great Himalayan peaks. Well over 100 routes have now been created on the various flanks of the mountain. Together, these offer almost the widest variety of climbing possible, and each year many thousands of alpinists reach the summit.

the french side Viewed from Chamonix, France's world-famous resort to the north, Mont Blanc presents its least dramatic aspect. The long North West Ridge above the 3863m (12,700ft) Aiguille de Goûter rises gently over several rounded snowy humps to the Main Summit, which from this angle looks somewhat undistinguished. To the left lies the equally lengthy North East Ridge, which ascends from the Col du Midi over the peaks of Mont Blanc du Tacul, 4248m (13,940ft), and Mont Maudit, 4465m (14,650ft). Between the two ridges lie the vast, rambling, and dazzling white, glaciated slopes of the North Face, with its wide corridor, generally referred to as the Grands Mulets, leading to the Grand Plateau below the final summit rise.

the italian side This side is altogether a different kettle of fish. There are two main ridges, both of which converge on Mont Blanc de Courmayeur. And what ridges! The jagged crest of the South East or Peuterey Ridge is one of the finest sights in the Alps. Beginning with the needle-sharp granite spire of the Aiguille Noire de Peuterey, it continues over the ethereal snowy crest of the 4112m (13,500ft) Aiguille Blanche and, turning west, climbs the flanks of the Grand Pilier d'Angle to reach the upper crest – interminable ice slopes, perched high above the awesome Brenva Face to the north and the chaotic Frêney Glacier to the south. Running south-south-west from the summit is the Brouillard Arête, a long crest of rotten rock that flanks the most remote facet of the mountain: the South West or Miage Face.

The remarkable 1400m (4600ft) Brenva Face is, together with the East Face of Monte Rosa, over 70km (40 miles) away, the largest sweep of snow and ice in the Alps. It is characterized by huge, threatening sérac barriers and the frequent roar of gigantic avalanches as they scour the deep couloirs.

Right **Climbers completing the Cosmiques Arête on the Aiguille du Midi, 3800m (12,500ft). The shoulder of Mont Blanc du Tacul, Mont Maudit, and Mont Blanc are rising up behind.**

three French guides who reached the summit via the 'Grands Mulets Route'.

1878 J Eccles (British) and his two guides climbed the upper section of the Peuterey Ridge.

1909 Innominata Ridge was first traversed by A Aufdenblatten, S Courtalauld, E Oliver, and A and H Rey.

1911 The Brouillard Ridge was first traversed by K Blodig (Austrian), H Jones (British), J Knubel (Swiss), and G Young (British).

1927 Today's classic approach to the Peuterey Ridge via the Aiguille Blanche was first completed by L Obersteiner and K Schreiner.

1933 T G Brown's (British) ascent of the highly dangerous Pear Buttress completed a magnificent triptych of routes on the mighty rock and icewall of the Brenva Face. These routes remained the classic ambitions of serious alpinists until the 1980s, when encroaching desiccation in the Alps increased the objective dangers on the face. Climbing fashions change: nowadays routes like the 'Pear' exert little magnetism and ascents of this particular route have become increasingly scarce.

1940 The great Italian rock climber and pioneer, G Gervasutti, with P Bollini, became the first person to climb one of the Frêney Pillars.

1957 Pioneering work on Mont Blanc, as elsewhere in the Alps, began to be taken over by local guides. The foremost activist, the great Italian guide W Bonatti, teamed up with T Gobbi (Italian) to make the first ascent of the

Grand Pilier d'Angle on the Brenva Face, which was considered the hardest creation in the Western Alps at the time.

1959 W Bonatti (with A Oggioni) was the first to explore the potential of the remote Brouillard Face with his ascent of the Red Pillar, the most beautiful of the four vertical towers that rise towards the lower crest of the Brouillard Ridge.

1961 W Bonatti attempted the other outstanding problem on Mont Blanc, the Central Pillar of Frêney. In the disaster that followed, four of his partners lost their lives in a vicious storm. Soon after, the British trio of C Bonington, I Clough, and D Whillans, together with J Djuglosz (Polish), tried it again in better weather. After an inspired piece of climbing on the upper section, the Chandelle, they reached the summit, creating the hardest climb on the mountain.

1962 W Bonatti returned to the Grand Pilier with C Zappelli (Italian), climbing the North East Face. This was considered the ultimate challenge in hard mixed climbing, with an almost unjustifiable risk of objective danger. It was not repeated until 1975.

1965 The multi-national team of R Baillie, C Bonington, J Harlin, and B Robertson made the first ascent of the Right Hand Pillar of Brouillard, though they did not continue to the summit.

1967 R Desmaison and R Flematti (French) made the first winter ascent of the Central Pillar of Frêney.

1971 Exploiting new techniques in ice climbing, W Cecchinel and G Nomine

In contrast, the Frêney Face, above the Upper Frêney Glacier, is a collection of slender granite pillars, rising steeply for 700m (2300ft) to the summit ridge. Further left, the rocky Innominata Ridge separates these pillars from an equally fine, though shorter, group of pillars on the Brouillard Face.

Finally, the South West or Miage Face is more comparable in structure to the Brenva, though with less objective hazard. However, a complicated and lengthy approach has ensured that this remains the 'Big One's' secret facet.

climbing on mont blanc

By the late 1970s, top French rock climbers were taking their EBs to higher altitudes in an attempt to eliminate the aid from classic routes on big rock features around Mont Blanc. Rappeling from the end of the main technical difficulties or from the top of a particular feature became commonplace, allowing parties to make light, fast ascents, rather than having to carry cumbersome equipment over the mountain. The summit was no longer the natural conclusion to every climb. Increasingly dry summers in the 1980s, coupled with the rapid rise in rock climbing standards and a widespread acceptance of the use (and misuse) of bolts, brought a proliferation of modern rock climbs throughout the massif, spearheaded by the Swiss climber, Michel Piola.

Meanwhile, a revolution in ice equipment and a change in attitude towards ice/mixed climbing brought about a rapid development in this area of the sport. Soon, ice lovers were turning to the massif's more ephemeral lines in order to be creative on steep ice. This required a certain visionary talent, and two great protagonists emerged: the Italian, Gian-Carlo Grassi, and Frenchman Patrick Gabarrou. Both were very active in creating innumerable hard lines on Mont Blanc, its satellite peaks, and many other corners of the range, some of which are currently enjoying immense popularity.

future climbing

Although a number of distinctive unclimbed lines remain and several established routes await first winter ascents, it seems inconceivable that a major future classic has yet to be pioneered on Mont Blanc. However, alpinists are sure to make ever faster

Left **Descent from the Aiguille du Midi to the Vallée Blanche.**

Right **The Mer de Glace and Vallée Blanche, seen from the Dru (another mountain in the range). The Mer de Glace, at 14km (8½ miles), is the longest glacier in the Mt Blanc group.**

(French) climbed their historic new route on the Grand Pilier d'Angle.

1972 R Desmaison soloed the 'Peuterey Ridge Integral'.

1975 The French alpinist, N Jaeger, was responsible for the first major modern *enchainement* in the Western Alps, when, over two days in August, he made the first solo ascent of the 'Original Route' (1957) on the Grand Pilier d'Angle, then descended to the upper Frêney Glacier and made the second solo ascent of the Central Pillar of Frêney, climbing to the summit of Mont Blanc.

1982 P A Steiner (Swiss) and P Gabarrou (French) opened up the ephemeral ice-climbing potential on the Italian Flank of the mountain with their ascent of the difficult 'Hypercouloir'.

1983 G-C Grassi (Italian) with J-N Roche (French) opened up modern climbing on the remote Miage Face with an ascent of the Red Pillar.

1984 Probably the most significant ascent of the 1980s was P Gabarrou's and F Marsigny's 'Divine Providence', up the big red shield to the left of Bonatti's 'Original Route' on the Grand Pilier d'Angle.

1988 Incredibly, the 'Bonatti-Zappelli Route' on the North Face of the Grand Pilier d'Angle was skied, albeit with several rappels, by the French ace, P Tardivel.

1990 'Divine Providence' was climbed with only three points of aid. The first person who manages to free climb this route will have completed the hardest line in the Mont Blanc Range.

speed ascents, perform more daring ski descents, include greater media-sponsored stunts in their climbs, perform more mind boggling *enchainements*, weave distressingly hard new variations to existing lines, and generally swarm all over the mountain in escalating numbers. Although Mont Blanc will definitely continue to attract attention from alpinists of all abilities, those with an inclination for remoteness and exploration, in any season, will increasingly have to look elsewhere.

CHAMONIX SIDE

Mont Blanc du Tacul

Col du Midi

Mont Maudit
Col de la
Brenva

North East Ridge

Mont Blanc

Grands
Mulets

Goûter Ridge

Dôme du
Goûter

Grands Mulets

Bossons
Glacier

Overall grades relate to a complete ascent to the summit of Mont Blanc. Approximate ascent times are from the highest mountain hut normally used, unless otherwise stated.

chamonix side

There are many routes and variations on this side, generally over non-technical but serious and crevassed glacier terrain.

1 North East Ridge from the Col du Midi PD/PD+

R Head, J Grange, A Orset, and J Perrod 1863

A fine ascent via the snow slopes of Mont Blanc du Tacul and Mont Maudit. In the future, it may become the normal route. Takes 6–7 hours.

2 Grands Mulets Route PD-

M Anderegg, F Couttet, and two unnamed guides, plus E Headland, G Hodgkinson, C Hudson, and G Joad 1859

A glacier expedition that now provides the normal route for spring skiers and the most reliable descent in bad weather. One section is exposed to sérac fall and has been the scene of several major fatal

accidents in the last few years. Takes 6½–7 hours.

3 The Goûter Ridge PD-

M Anderegg, J Bennen, P Perren, L Stephen, and F Tuckett 1861

The most frequented ascent route with little technical difficulty in good conditions, but exposed snow crests in the upper section. The approach to the Aiguille du Goûter is subject to stonefall. Takes five hours.

grand pilier d'angle

All 14 routes on the Grand Pilier are serious expeditions because the only logical way off is a lengthy continuation up the Peuterey Ridge and over the summit of Mont Blanc. Ascent times and heights given are to the top of the Grand Pilier. Allow an additional four to eight hours to reach the summit about 600m (2000ft) above.

4 Divine Providence ED3

P Gabarrou and F Marsigny 1984

The four really hard pitches can be negotiated entirely on aid (A3), but, climbed free (ED5 and 7c), there

is no other route of this technical standard set in such a committing situation anywhere in the Alps. Ascent 900m (3000ft); two days.

5 Original Route TD+/ED1

W Bonatti and T Gobbi 1957

Classic stuff, though still infrequently climbed. Difficult and sometimes loose rock in the chimney system leads to icy mixed ground on the upper North East Face. Ascent 900m (3000ft); takes a long day.

6 Cecchinel-Nominé Route TD+/ED I

W Cecchinel and G Nominé 1971

A classic mixed route that heralded the introduction of modern ice techniques on Mont Blanc. It is probably the safest and arguably the best line on the face. Ascent 750m (2500ft); 11–13 hours.

7 Dufour-Fréhel Route with the Boivin-Vallençant Direct Finish TD+/ED1

G Dufour and J Fréhel 1973
J-M Boivin and P Vallençant 1975

This combination of routes has proved to be the easiest, quickest, and most popular means of ascent.

The crux is a 70° goulotte. Ascent 750m (2500ft); 10 hours.

8 Bonatti-Zappelli Route ED I

W Bonatti and C Zappelli 1962

The original route on the North East Face gives bold mixed climbing with considerable objective danger in the lower section. Like other routes on this face, it should only be attempted in cold, snowy conditions. Ascent 750m (2500ft); 12–15 hours.

9 Peuterey Ridge D+; Integral ED1

L Obersteiner and K Schreiner 1927
First complete ascent: R Hechtel and G Kittelmann 1953

The normal approach to the upper Peuterey Ridge is to traverse the Aiguille Blanche, giving the finest ridge route of its class in the Alps. Climbed integral over the Aiguille Noire it presents the longest, and probably most difficult, traverse of its kind in Western Europe.

brenva face

There are around nine routes and their variants on this 1400m (4600ft) face; most exit close to the summit.

10 The Pear Buttress TD/TD+

A Aufdenblatten, A Graven, and T G Brown 1933

This is a magnificent route but it is harder and considerably more dangerous to climb than the 'Route Major' (11). Until quite recently, the route was a leading ambition for all serious alpinists, but fashions change and it is rarely climbed today. Takes 11–14 hours.

11 Route Major TD-

T G Brown and F Smythe 1928

The finest route on the face, with equal difficulties on both rock and ice. The approach is very serious but, once on the route, objective dangers are minimal. Takes 10½–13½ hours.

12 Red Sentinel D+

T Graham Brown and F Smythe 1927

A masterpiece of route finding on mixed terrain. Generally the route is low in technical difficulty but high in potential objective danger. Allow 8½–10½ hours.

13 Brenva Spur AD+/D-

J and M Anderegg, G Mathews, A Moore, and F and H Walker 1865

This is the easiest and the safest line on the Brenva Face, and one of the world's classic snow/ice climbs. Fitness and good acclimatization are as important as technical competence, though crossing the ever-changeable sérac barrier near the top of the route can be difficult. This route takes 9–11 hours.

brouillard face

Remarkably, 20 routes and variations have now been completed on the four pillars and various couloirs of this 600m (2000ft) face. However, parties rarely continue on to climb towards the Brouillard Ridge, which is far above the end of the major difficulties. (*See page 46 for picture.*)

14 Brouillard Ridge D

K Blodig, H Jones, J Knubel, and G Young 1911

This is not a technically difficult route in good conditions but it is a long, serious, and committing ascent at high altitude with its fair share of rotten rock. Nowadays, seldom climbed in its entirety. Ascent 1400m (4600ft) and around 12 hours to the summit from the foot of the approach couloir.

15 Red Pillar: Original Route ED1

W Bonatti and A Oggioni 1959

The most popular route on the pillars, although the climbing is somewhat overrated; it is not too difficult if the chimneys are dry. It takes 10–12 hours to reach the Brouillard Ridge.

16 Red Pillar: Directissima ED2/3

P Gabarrou and A Long 1984

A brilliant route on the most beautiful pillar. It has gained modern classic status and was climbed completely free at F7a+ on the third ascent. Allow 1–1½ days.

17 Cascade de Notre Dame ED2

P Gabarrou and F Marsigny 1984

Gabarrou felt this elegant line was equal in quality to the 'Hypercouloir' (20) and it has been repeated on several occasions. It will take a long day to complete the route.

18 Hypergoulotte ED3/4

B Grison and L Mailly 1984

Rarely in condition, this is the hardest of all the Mont Blanc icefalls. This route must be completed within a day, or not attempted at all.

19 Right Hand Pillar ED1

R Baillie, C Bonington, J Harlin, and B Robertson 1965

The first of four splendid routes on this fine granite feature, which still sees few ascents. Allow 10–14 hours to the Brouillard Ridge.

20 Hypercouloir ED2/3

P Gabarrou and P-A Steiner 1982

This succession of quasi-vertical icefalls is considered one of the finest and most difficult ice routes on Mont Blanc. 16–19 hours.

frêney face

A long approach with the prospect of an arduous retreat in bad weather makes the 15 or so existing routes on this 800m (2600ft) face very serious. It is usual to continue over the summit, although parties have rappelled the Central Pillar. Ascent times given are from the foot of the route only. (*See page 46 for picture.*)

21 Innominata Ridge D+

A Aufdenblatten, S Courtauld, E Oliver, and A and H Rey 1909

This is a splendid, classic, and

Dôme du Goûter · Brouillard Ridge · Brouillard Glacier · Mont Blanc · Mont Blanc de Courmayeur · Innominata Ridge · Mont Maudit · Frêney Glacier

middle-grade expedition at high altitude. The route presents greater difficulties on rock, ice, and mixed terrain than are found on the 'Peuterey Ridge' (9) but it is less committing. In dry conditions the crossing of the huge central basin is seriously exposed to stonefall. Ascent of this route is about 950m (3100ft) from the Eccles Huts; takes 8–11 hours.

22 Fantomastic ED3

P Gabarrou and F Marsigny 1985

This route is one of the hardest of the south-facing goulottes and has been completed only to the end of the difficulties. So far unrepeated. A long day.

23 Hidden Pillar ED2

T Frost and J Harlin 1963

A short, but rarely climbed, rock route that is exposed to objective danger. The two American first ascensionists put their advanced aid techniques and revolutionary equipment to good use for the first time on Mont Blanc but the route has now been climbed free at F6c. Takes a long day.

24 Central Pillar: Jori Bardill Route ED2

J Bardill, M Piola, and P-A Steiner 1982

Although considered inferior to the original line, this route allows parties the dubious pleasure of clipping the highest bolt in Europe. 1–1½ days.

25 Central Pillar: Original Route ED1

C Bonington, I Clough, J Djuglosz, and D Whillans 1961

An outstanding route and one of the classic, high-altitude alpine rock climbs. Although the hard sections on the Chandelle can be negotiated on *in-situ* aid, the route has been climbed free at F7a. A long day.

26 Freneysie Pascale ED2/3

P Gabarrou and F Marsigny 1984

A discontinuous but logical line of icefalls giving climbing very much in the modern idiom. About 20 hours.

27 North (Gervasutti) Pillar TD+/ ED1

P Ballini and G Gervasutti 1940

A fine, but rarely climbed, high-altitude rock route. It was a bold undertaking for the era but is now often overshadowed by its famous neighbour, the Central Pillar. The route takes a long day.

28 Great Frêney Couloir TD+/ ED1

M Bernardi, G-C Grassi, and R Luzi 1980

A direct ascent involves the only vertical icefall above 4500m (14,800ft) in Europe. 10–12 hours.

miage face

The very long and serious approach required to reach Mont Blanc's most remote face has ensured that the many climbs here have been reserved for lovers of solitude.

29 Aiguille Grises Route PD

G Bonin, J Gradin, L Grasselli, A Proment, and A Ratti (later Pope Pius XI) 1890 in descent

The normal route from Italy, coinciding with the route from France above the Dôme de Goûter. A long, varied expedition on snow and ice with seriously crevassed terrain. Ascent 1750m (5700ft); 6–7 hours.

30 Rocher du Mont Blanc or Tournette Spur AD+

J Carrel, J Fischer, and T Kennedy 1872

The original route on this side, and for a while the normal route from Italy until route (29) was discovered. A direct, classic line that has become

more difficult in the upper section. 1100m (3600ft); 6½–8½ hours.

31 Left Hand Spur D

B Domenech, D de Frouville, C Jaccoux, and J Perrodeau 1976

A magnificent route comparable to the 'Red Sentinel' (12) but remaining in the shade until much later in the day. 1100m (3600ft); 8–10 hours.

32 Central Spur D-

E and J Gentinetta, R Kaufmann, T Kesteven, and A Marshall 1893

An elegant mixed route. The spur is fairly sheltered from objective danger. 1100m (3600ft); 8–10 hours.

33 Fantacouloir TD+

G-C Grassi and E Tessera 1984

Beautiful ice climbing but watch out for stonefall even in extremely cold conditions. 600m (2000ft); 10 hours.

34 Red Pillar TD-

G-C Grassi and J-N Roche 1983

The first modern route in this secret corner has excellent climbing on the 350m (1150ft) granite pillar, followed by rotten rock to the crest. Ascent 550m (1800ft); about six hours.

Mont Blanc

Mont Blanc de Courmayeur

how to get to mont blanc

The main valley bases on both sides of the mountain, Chamonix in France and Courmayeur in Italy, are highly frequented resorts, served by a fast and excellent road network, and they are linked by the Mont Blanc Tunnel.

Both places can be reached by public transport (road and rail: frequent services). Chamonix lies less than 90km (56 miles) from Geneva airport.

facilities

Chamonix is a major tourist resort and offers extremely good facilities, although these are at significantly inflated prices. There are plenty of campsites in the valley, plus a variety of accommodation from *dortoirs* and *gîtes* to 5-star hotels.

The Office de la Haute Montagne provides an excellent service, offering information on routes and mountain conditions plus supplying detailed weather forecasts and snow/avalanche reports. The Aiguille du Midi *téléphérique*, the highest cableway in Europe, with a connection to Entreves just above

Courmayeur, allows rapid access to the high glaciers.

Courmayeur is still expensive and cannot match the facilities of Chamonix, though the Office du Val Veni offers all the mountain and weather reports. Most climbers use the Veni Valley campsite.

Mont Blanc is served by a number of guarded and often overcrowded huts. Reserving a place is essential in high season; ring the warden or get in touch with the Office de la Haute Montagne.

when to climb

These days, climbing can take place during every month of the year, although the high season and prime time for rock climbing is obviously July and August. A series of very hot summers and mild winters during the 1980s had disastrous effects on many Mont Blanc snow/ice routes, and some classic ice climbs of yesteryear are now only practicable out of season. Excellent conditions in the goulottes and on the great ice faces have been found recently during April–May and October–November. Full-blooded winter

ascents of all routes are officially recognized from 21 December–20 March but, despite the south-facing aspect of much of the established rock climbing, the serious approach difficulties have ensured that many still await a winter ascent.

gear

An ascent of one of the normal routes may require little more than a rope, a harness, an axe, and crampons, plus the ability to navigate in poor visibility and travel safely over glaciated terrain. However, this is big country (an ascent from the snowline at the Plan de l'Aiguille will involve a vertical rise of some 2400m/7900ft); bear in mind, too, that bad weather, even in summer, can produce surprisingly low temperatures and ferocious winds. Adequate clothing should be carried to cover this possibility. Routes of the highest standard will require the full armoury of modern alpine gear and may demand one or more bivouacs.

maps and guidebooks

The best map available on the Mont Blanc Range is the French IGN 'Series

3531 est: St Gervais-les-Bains Mont Blanc' 1:25,000.

The best definitive guidebook is probably the *Monte Bianco*, Gino Buscaini (Italian Alpine Club). *Selected Climbs in the Mont Blanc Massif Vol I*, Lindsay Griffin (The Alpine Club) is in English. *Le Topo du Massif du Mont Blanc (Vol 2)*, Michel Piola, covers most modern rock climbing in a topo-diagram format.

language

A smattering of the local language (French or Italian) is desirable, but English is generally understood.

rescue and insurance

Rescue facilities on both sides of the range are excellent, but parties should carry adequate insurance to cover the high costs of helicopter evacuation and medical expenses.

red tape

There are no restrictions on climbing on Mont Blanc.

the great ridge: five days ... and a moment of grace

kurt diemberger

If you have stood in the meadows of Val Ferret, looking up towards Mont Blanc, the fascination of the unique skyline of the Peuterey Ridge will not have escaped you. The dark, pointed Aiguille Noire, Aiguille Blanche's elegant white crest, and the immense snowy dome that is Mont Blanc itself – from the bottom of the valley to the distant summit the ridgeline is incredibly harmonious, a threefold sweep, pulling your eyes and mind ever higher.

My heart has belonged to the Peuterey Ridge since I saw it first as a crystal-hunting boy. To me, the silhouette resembled a sequence of rising crystals, and my dream was to follow it, up and down, to its end. The attraction lay not in the 8km of climbing it offered, but in a magic pull, a strong radiation of feeling that has attracted me to the heights and hills from the beginning. Perhaps, too, it was an awareness that the Peuterey Ridge embodies everything a mountain can offer: fantastic granite, steep ice, snow ridges, surrounded by fabulous architecture and unlimited space, a sense of freedom, hours and hours of climbing and abseil descents, and bivouacs – a cavalcade over the sharp edges of peaks, on and on, through nights and days – a condensed life of mountaineering. Even now, 40 years and many visits later, I still admire it. Its beauty never fades.

From the meadows and woods of Val Veni and Val Ferret, the smell of hay and trees always brings back memories of erecting our old tent and setting out to climb the great ridge for the first time, of Wolfi Stefan and me experiencing our chilly apprenticeship bivouacking below the summit of the Aiguille Noire. The years pass by in my mind and again I go up, with other friends and companions, sometimes in vain, forced to turn around; other times right to the top. And once – yes, that was a close-run thing – with Tona (my wife), Walter, Bianca, Terenzio, and others, when we were shaken by the electric forces of eight thunderstorms and Tona was struck by lightning. Even then, we made it back down, if only at the very edge of being alive. I have climbed the South Ridge of the Aiguille Noire three times, but only once succeeded in capturing it on film – a once-in-a-lifetime reward when stubbornness, conviction and luck collided. 'Five days and a moment of grace' are the last words of this film, uttered as Franz Lindner and I reached the top of the 'White Mountain', the great ridge behind us:

It is September 1958. We have prepared everything for a full week and, after a summer of climbing in the Alps, are in top form. The weather is beautiful, even if the days are short. We reach the Noire Hut, cross the wide cwm of the Fauteuil des Allemands, and scramble up easy rock to our ridge.

We are roping up. The pinnacles of the South Ridge are already touched by the fingers of dawn. The rock under our hands is gloriously rough, every hold, solid as steel.

Up it goes, up and up, slab after slab, cliff upon cliff, tower on tower, all of it steep, and always above the sheer abyss on either side. Mists drift up from the séracs of the Frêney Glacier to dance around the pinnacles and about us as we climb on.

All around us lies sunlight and valley and vast distances; the banks of cloud building slowly in the sky, the turquoise eye of the little Chécrouit lake far below, and the warm scent of autumn rising from the foothill meadows.

The rock is beautifully varied. We meet slabs whose rounded surfaces are covered with grey-green lichens; white feldspar crystals protrude here and there, asking to be touched. There are ledges offering a firm foothold to the groping boot, wrinkles in the rock inviting you to entrust your bodyweight to them.

We come to a huge overhang and use one another's shoulders to surmount it. Then we are over the second tower and on our way to the next, the Pointe Welzenbach.

After an abseil descent into the notch behind the Pointe Welzenbach, Franz, and I tackle the difficult Pointe Brendel, the fourth granite tower on the ridge, looming vertically above us. But it is dark as we reach its summit. We find a marvellous granite 'bed' for our bivouac and even a patch of snow to give us water. Soon a thousand stars shine down on us.

Throughout the next day we are busy with the hardest section of the climb – the precipitous sweep up to the Pointe Bich and all those indentations to the summit of the Aiguille Noire. For

... fantastic granite, steep ice, snow ridges surrounded by fabulous architecture ...

us, it also means the most difficult filming of the ridge. But we are happy. 'Don't let's hurry!' Franz begs. 'We want this to last; not to be over and gone!' We bivouac again on top of the Aiguille Noire.

Morning on the third day, and all has changed: grey mist everywhere around us. Is the weather breaking? Shall we go on or give up? We decide to risk it.

It's a hairy business, going down some 500m, along a vertical ridge and inside a giant chimney, all in the fog. We have two ropes of 40m and a good number of slings and pitons, but we

Above **The great Peuterey Ridge of Mont Blanc, seen from Mont Mallet. The peaks from left to right are Aiguille Noire, Aiguille Blanche, and the dome of Mont Blanc.**

Right **Kurt Diemberger climbing the Aiguille Blanche de Peuterey.**

Far right **Following the spectacular cornice of the Aiguille Blanche at 4000m.**

move down very slowly, obsessively checking and rechecking every abseil. It pays off. We discover that, after a short abseiling pitch, instead of continuing vertically down the face, we have to follow a ledge to the right, eastwards, from where we can gain the shoulder of the North Ridge of Aiguille Noire, hidden in the thick cloud. So far, so good ... then one of our ropes gets stuck! No amount of pulling will free it. Finally, Franz climbs 40m in prusik slings to sort out the dilemma.

After descending the monstrous chimney just to the west of the ridge, we have to skirt the slim needles of the 'English Ladies', an altogether endless task. It is pitch dark by the time we reach the bivouac box in the Brèche Nord.

Definitely a serious day, but from now on it looks as if we may win! We have enough food, as we stashed a supply here (film material, too) several days before setting out.

Incredibly, the next morning brings bright sunshine. But it's too late to start out so we enjoy a day of relaxation. Below us, the shadow of the Peuterey Ridge expands slowly and impressively across the séracs of the Brenva Glacier. Tomorrow we will follow the dark edge of this silhouette all the way to the summit of

Mont Blanc. It's a pleasure even to think of it. The great ridge will then be ours! But it will be over, too.

Aiguille Blanche, the fifth day of our traverse. Although we are heavily loaded, we enjoy moving along the aiguille's beautiful white crest, swinging from peak to peak between its three summits. Here, over 4000m high, we are yet well short of the summit of Mont Blanc. In front of us, and below, the giant arena of the Col de Peuterey has opened up. High above, to the left, gleam rust-coloured buttresses, one of them the Frêney Pillar. This is an awe-inspiring place: you truly feel that you are standing before the peak of the continent.

Night approaches again. From the Col de Peuterey to the top of Mont Blanc is 900m. In the last glimmer of light we tackle the cornice at the end of the ridge. The horizon is still tinted with orange. A short while ago the shadow of Mont Blanc was cast eerily across all the peaks to the east, while the night, like an ocean of darkness, was creeping up from below.

We are now sitting on top, looking down to the lights of Courmayeur and Chamonix. The ascent is over. But it lives with us forever. Five days ... and a moment of grace.

1865 M Croz (French), and F Douglas, D Hadow, and C Hudson (British) died on the North Face, having climbed Hörnli Ridge with E Whymper (British) and the two Peters Taugwalder (Swiss), father and son. J-A Carrel climbed Lion Ridge with J-B Bich (Italian).
1867 The Maquignaz brothers (Italian) made the exposed direct ascent of the summit tower on Lion Ridge.

1871 Lucy Walker (British) became the first woman to reach the summit.
1879 A F Mummery (British) and Swiss guides climbed Zmutt Ridge. W Penhall with Swiss guides F Imseng and L Zurbrücken reached the summit in 17 hours from Zermatt, having climbed a direct line up the West Face of the mountain to reach the top section of Zmutt Ridge.

1882 J-A, J-B, and L Carrel and V Sella (Italian) made the first winter ascent of Lion Ridge and, by descending Hörnli Ridge, the first winter traverse.
1930 E Benedetti, M Bich, and L Carrel (Italian) climbed Fürggen Ridge by the route now used as standard.
1931 The first ascent of the North Face of the mountain was made by F and T Schmid (German).

1933 A Crétier (French) and A Gaspard and B Ollietti (Italian) made the first true ascent of the Cresta de Amicis. All died descending the Italian Ridge.
1936 G Gervasutti (Italian) made a brilliant first winter solo ascent of the peak in three days, via Lion Ridge.
1953 W Bonatti and R Bignami (Italian) made first winter ascent of the Fürggen Ridge, creating a superdirect finish.

the matterhorn

lindsay griffin

Situated on the Swiss-Italian border in the heart of the Valais or Pennine Alps, the Matterhorn, at 4477m (14,701ft), entirely dominates the area. More has been written about this eroded, rock pyramid than almost any other mountain in the world. No other peak is more readily recognized by its form or by its name, which has become generic for similarly shaped mountains everywhere. Even California has its own replica – thanks to Walt Disney.

Not surprisingly, this is one of the summits most coveted by alpinists at some stage in their career, and it has been subjected to all sorts of media attention – and many unusual climbs. The normal route can attract a couple of hundred climbers per day and, on occasion, some may have to join a long queue in order to reach the highest point. The rock is notoriously variable and stonefall is an ever-present threat. The Matterhorn gives life to the two famous resorts at its foot: Zermatt, high in the Mattertal to the north; and Cervinia (the modern version of Breuil), at the head of the Valtournénche to the south.

ridges, faces, and peaks

The four ridges and four faces of the Matterhorn converge to a horizontal crest, 85m (280ft) long, with the Swiss summit, 4477m (14,701ft) at the west end, and the Italian summit, 4476.4m (14,686ft) at the east, adorned with a large metal cross.

The 1000m (3300ft) East Face and 1200m (3900ft) West Face are rarely climbed due to poor rock and high objective danger. On the East Face, just below the large summit block, a series of ledges – the Mummery Ledges – connect the Hörnli, or North East, Ridge (the least steep and most frequented of the ridges) with the more or less rocky Fürggen, or South East, Ridge.

Between the East and West Faces lies one of three great North Walls in the Alps (the Grandes Jorasses and Eiger are the other two). The most prominent features on this 1000m (3300ft) face are a left-to-right slanting couloir in the middle third (taken by the classic 1931 'Original Route') and a huge vertical-to-over-hanging rock wall like a giant prow coming down from the Zmutt Nose and forming an inset North-North-West Face.

The stone-swept, 1200m (3900ft) South Face is in Italy, above the Lower Cervino Glacier. It is a huge, concave wall with a marked central recession. The main face is demarcated on the left by the Cresta de Amicis, coming down from a shoulder known as Pic Tyndall on the South West Ridge, and on the right by a splendid pillar descending from the Picco Muzio, the third step on the Fürggen Ridge.

The South West (Italian or Lion) Ridge forms the right edge of the West Face, rising from the Col de Lion, which is the lowest point on the ridge between the Matterhorn and the 3715m (12,200ft) Tête du Lion. Two-thirds of the way up the ridge is the prominent shoulder Pic Tyndall.

future climbing

There are just over 30 routes and major variations to the summit. All are, to a certain degree, serious climbs. The potential for major new lines is pretty much non-existent, although impressive sections of uncharted rock still exist on the South Face.

Despite the intense and unsightly development at its feet and the often chaotic events on its flanks, the peak remains aloof, its reputation assured. The Matterhorn will continue to be an obligatory objective for the vast majority of alpinists. Hopefully, they won't come away disappointed.

Right **The Matterhorn's East Face. The Cresta de Amicis to the left and Zmutt Ridge to the right form the skyline. Part of the South Face can be seen on the left of the picture.**

1962 The first winter ascent of the North Face was achieved by Swiss guides, H von Allmen and P Etter, despite strong competition from two Austrians and a 3-man German team, who reached the summit just one day later.

1965 W Bonatti bid farewell to supreme alpinism with one of the great exploits of the decade – a solo winter ascent of a new direct route on the North Face.

1966 Swiss guides R Arnold and J Graven completed the astonishing feat of two complete traverses (taking in all four ridges) within a day (19½ hours).

1969 L Cerruti and A Gogna (Italian) ascended the vertical rock wall of the North-North-West Face to the Zmutt Nose without fixed ropes or bolts.

1970 Some of the great Italian alpinists of the day (G Calcagno, L Cerruti, G Machetto, and C di Pietro) combined forces on the South-South-East Pillar of Picco Muzio to create one of the best rock climbs on the mountain.

1981 Taking up the challenge of the direttissima on Zmutt Nose, M Piola and P-A Steiner (Swiss) made a superb and almost totally free rock climb.

1984 The first winter and second overall ascent of the Casarotto-Grassi Route on the South Face of Pic Tyndall was made by Italians Barmasse, Cazzanelli, and Tomone.

1995 B Brunod set the record for the fastest ascent of the mountain when he reached the summit in just two hours, 12 minutes, and 29 seconds from the village of Cervinia.

Labels on image: Tête du Lion · Lion Ridge · Cravate · Pic Tyndall · South Face · The Shoulder · Fürggen Ridge · East Face · Hörnli Ridge · Upper Cervino Glacier · Lower Cervino Glacier

north face

Optimum climbing conditions occur on this face when temperatures are low and the friable, often downward-sloping rock is well plastered with ice and good névé. Even in summer this sombre wall receives little sun.

1 Original Route ED1
F and T Schmid 1931

A classic mixed route and highly prestigious test piece for the traditional breed of aspiring alpinist. Its reputation is due more to the overall ambience and historical significance than to quality climbing, and route finding presents one of the biggest difficulties. Average of 13–16 hours for the 1000m (3300ft).

2 Bonatti Direct ED2/3
W Bonatti solo 1965

Because this historic mixed route captures much of the stonefall on the North Face and involves either very compact or totally rotten rock, it is a logical winter objective that has seen few ascents. Protection and belays are always well spaced and often unreliable. About 1000m (3300ft); allow four days.

3 The Zmutt Nose (North-North-West Face) ED2/3
L Cerruti and A Gogna 1969

After 400m (1300ft) of mixed ground, this route gives a hard free and aid climb (originally graded VI+ and A3), sheltered from objective danger but technically comparable to many of the big-walls in the Dolomites being climbed in the same era. 1000m (3300ft); this route takes several days.

4 Zmutt Nose Direttissima ED2
M Piola and P-A Steiner 1981

Largely free climbing with only four partial pitches of aid (VI and A2). Above the initial mixed ground (85° ice), it offers 12 steep pitches on rock that is surprisingly good quality for the Matterhorn. Allow two days for this route, which has about 1000m (3300ft) of ascent.

south face

This entirely rocky wall above the Lower Cervino Glacier is the most complex of all the faces, and more exposed to serious stonefall than any other. There are many established lines but few repeat ascents.

5 The Italian or Lion Ridge AD/AD+
J-B Bich and J-A Carrrel 1865

This historic route remains a superb rock climb, despite the proliferation of fixed ropes. The rock is relatively good. Purists could climb it free at IV+ with one or two harder moves. Allow five hours to climb the 650m (2100ft) from Carrel Hut.

6 Cresta de Amicis AD+/D-
A Crétier, A Gaspard, and B Ollietti 1933

This would be the easiest and most direct route to the Cravate if 'The Italian Ridge' did not have fixed ropes. It is 800m (2600ft) to Pic Tyndall; allow 9–11 hours to reach the summit.

7 South Face of Pic Tyndall TD+/ED1
R Casarotto and G Grassi 1983

This quasi-vertical rock pillar gives sustained climbing at V to VI. The 1000m (3300ft) ascent takes from 12–14 hours.

8 Direttissima ED1
M Barmasse and V de Tuoni 1983

Offers high-standard free-climbing difficulties on generally solid rock. 1200m (3900ft) of ascent; this route takes 1–1½ days.

9 SSE Pillar of Picco Muzio TD+
G Calcagno, L Cerruti, C di Pietro, and G Machetto 1970

Sheltered from stonefall and on mostly sound rock, this is one of the safest routes on the face. It is 800m (2600ft) to Picco Muzio and will take a long day.

10 Zmutt Ridge D
A Burgener, A Gentinetta, A F Mummery, and J Petrus 1879

One of the greatest mixed routes in the Alps and widely considered the best way up the Matterhorn. The difficulty, while nowhere excessive (rock III+ when dry), is sustained, particularly on the long crest between the rocky teeth and the Zmutt Nose. Allow 8–10 hours for this 1200m (3900ft) climb. A new hut (1997) at the foot of the ridge, plus controversial equipping of its difficult sections, will increase the route's popularity in the future.

east face

This rarely climbed, triangular face above the Fürggen Glacier steepens abruptly above the Mummery Ledges. It is bounded on the right by the normal route up the Hörnli Ridge.

South Face

Zmutt Ridge

West Face

South Face

Fürggen Ridge

East Face

SOUTH FACE

NORTH FACE

Hörnli Ridge

Lion Ridge

The Shoulder

11 East Face Direct TD

E Benedetti, M Bich, L and L Carrel, A Gaspard, and G Mazzotti 1932
This route is on a relatively straightforward, uniform slope of rotten rock, best covered with good-quality névé. The summit block gives very steep rock climbing on loose terrain. The route is 1000m (3300ft) long and it takes between 14–15 hours.

12 Hörnli Ridge AD

M Croz, F Douglas, D Hadow, C Hudson, and P Taugwalder and son, and E Whymper 1865
This is still a very long, serious and often severely underestimated route. In perfect conditions the rock-climbing difficulties are not high, but they are sustained. Snow is nearly always present on the Shoulder and close to the summit. On busy days some stonefall is inevitable.

Heavyweight fixed ropes have long been in place above the Shoulder, so you can ascend the ridge direct. 1220m (4000ft) of ascent; 5–6 hours.

13 Fürggen Ridge D-/D

J Carrel, J Gaspard, and M Piacenza 1911
Probably the most technical, least climbed, and possibly most objectively dangerous of all the ridges. Entirely rocky, the route is best left

till later in the season when it should be relatively free of snow. Allow eight hours for the 1150m (3800ft).

14 Fürggen Direct Finish TD

L Carrel, G Chiara, and A Perino 1941
The true and logical finish up the final step above the Fürggen Shoulder gives pitches of V. This 1150m (3800ft) climb takes 9–10 hours and is still infrequently climbed.

how to get to the matterhorn

The popular and expensive resort of Cervinia is easily reached by car or public transport (bus) from the main Aosta Valley. The equally expensive Zermatt in Switzerland is closed to visitors' cars. There is a huge car park 5km (3 miles) down the valley at Täsch, or a small and scenic railway runs all the way to Zermatt from Visp in the Rhône Valley. From these two resorts you can walk up to the closest wardened hut.

facilities

Both resorts have a variety of generally expensive accommodation. Zermatt has

a campsite; on the Italian side it is better to camp lower down the valley than Cervinia. All you need is available at both resorts, including climbing equipment. Each resort also has a guides' office.

when to climb

Peak season is July–August, but many face climbs are subject to stonefall, needing the cold conditions of autumn or winter. Nowadays, winter is the classic period for attempting lines on the North Face; full-blooded winter ascents of routes are officially recognized from 21 December to 20 March. All are long undertakings – a very early start is essential.

gear

An axe and crampons are essential. Many parties have been caught unprepared for sudden and violent weather, and it can quickly become surprisingly cold near the top, even in summer. The hard face routes often require multiple bivouacs, and a selection of friends and blade pegs will prove useful, in addition to the full complement of rock and ice gear.

maps and guidebooks

The best map is the CNS (Cartes Nationales de la Suisse), 1:25,000. The definitive guidebook is the *Guide des Alpes Valaisannes (Vol III: Col Collon to*

Theodul Pass), (Swiss Alpine Club), in French or German. *Selected Climbs in the Valais Alps West*, Lindsay Griffin (The Alpine Club), is in English.

language

German on the Swiss side; Italian on the other. English is usually understood.

rescue and insurance

Rescue services are sophisticated, with expert helicopter evacuation, but very expensive; carry full alpine insurance.

red tape

No permits are needed.

1858 C Barrington (British) with C Almer and P 'Glacier Wolf' Bohren (Swiss), made the first ascent of the Eiger by the South West Flank and West Ridge.
1874 The South West Ridge was climbed by Miss Meeta Brevoort and W A B Coolidge (USA), with guides A Almer, U Almer, and C Bohren (Swiss).
1876 G Foster (British) with guides H Baumann and U Rübi (Swiss),

climbed the Eiger Glacier to the northern Eigerjoch and South Ridge.
1885 A descent was made of the Eiger's Mittellegi Ridge by M von Kuffner with local guides J Beiner, A Burgener, and A Kalbermatten.
1921 The first ascent of the Mittellegi Ridge was made by Yuki Maki (Japanese) with guides F Amatter, S Brawand, and F Steuri (Swiss).

1932 H Lauper, climbing with fellow Swiss A Zürcher, J Knubel, and A Graven, completed the 'Lauper Route'.
1935 M Sedlmayer and K Merhinger (German) attempted a direct line up the Eigerwand only to perish of cold at Death Bivouac.
1937 M Rebitsch and L Vörg (German) were the first to make it safely down from Death Bivouac. A new route was

made on the South East Face by O Eidenschink and E Moeller (German).
1938 First ascent of the Eigerwand made over four days in July by A Heckmair, L Vörg, H Harrer, and F Kasparek (German and Austrian). It is the only reasonable line up the complex face. Every feature on the route has a name.
1950 Austrians E Waschak and L Forstenlechner climbed the wall

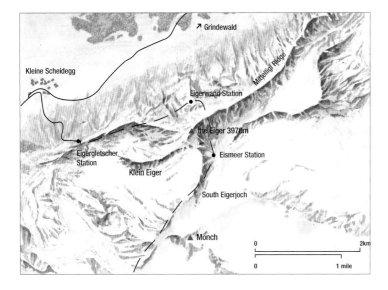

the eiger

victor saunders

The Eiger, 3970m (13,041ft), is the best-known mountain in the history of extreme alpinism. Along with the Mönch and the Jungfrau, it completes the photogenic trio of great peaks that make up the northern bulwark of the Bernese Oberland in Switzerland. Its abrupt North Face, Nordwand, is known variously as the Eigerwand, the Eiger Wall, the North Wall, or the Mördwand, meaning Killer Wall.

The North Face is the only major north wall in the Alps that has no glacier beneath it. It looms over the resort of Grindelwald, and can be approached over the grazing meadows of Alpiglen. Most climbers concentrate on the 1800m (6000ft) high north-west half of the face, the Eigerwand. It is best seen in Kleine Scheidegg, from where activities on the face appear as if on a gargantuan stage. Ever since the 1930s, 'Eigerwatchers' on the hotel balconies of Kleine Scheidegg have witnessed a series of tragedies and spectacular rescues on this notorious wall.

The face seems to have its own microcosmic weather system: storms can rage there while holidaymakers in Kleine Scheidegg sunbathe. The sense of contrast is increased by the Jungfrau

Railway, built in 1912, which bores right through the heart of the mountain and has two openings that overlook the Eigerwand. The train always stops to allow tourists to gaze out from these brilliant vantage points.

ridges, faces, and peaks

The Eiger has three main faces, defined by three principal and two subsidiary ridges. The West Ridge and South West Flank were used in the first ascent of the mountain. The South Ridge runs down to two cols, the Eigerjochs, and onto the Mönch; while the very long Mittellegi Ridge, running north-east from the summit, almost reaches Grindelwald. The Klein Eiger, 3472m (11,400ft), is a bump on the South West Ridge.

The North East Rib divides the North Face, creating, in effect, a North East and a North West Face. The left (eastern) side contains the 'Lauper Route', while the right (western) side is the Eigerwand proper.

The North East Face, silhouetted by the Mittellegi Ridge on the left and the pillars of the North East Rib on the right, is characterized by a broad icefield above and rock barriers below.

The triangular North West Face, the Eigerwand, consists of tiered limestone cliffs in its lower parts and a black slatey gneiss above the Spider icefield. The right side of the face is bounded by cliffs 1000m (3300ft) high and, though the routes here appear to finish well below the summit, they are still bigger than almost any other vertical climbs in the Alps.

The right-hand edge of the North West Face is the West Ridge, which, together with the West Flank, offers the 'traditional' means of descent to Kleine Scheidegg. The very loose ground here has caused some serious accidents, often in descent.

The 800m (2600ft) South East Face has only two routes but they are fine climbs of middling difficulty. This is the only face on the mountain with a glacier beneath it, the Fiescher.

future climbing

There are currently 30 or so major routes on the Eiger, and it is difficult to predict key future additions. The most recent major new route, 'Metanoia' (1991), found difficult climbing in ground that seems little more than a variation on existing routes. There are only two routes on the South Face, but this is less attractive than the North Face, being half the height and subject to stonefall.

Right **On the summit of the Eiger. Too often climbers reach this point in bad weather, for which the mountain is infamous.**

(its fourth ascent) in a single day of only 18 hours (including a wait of five hours at the Spider to assist a Swiss team).

1961 First winter ascent of the 1938 Route by W Almberger, T Hiebeler, A Kinshofer, and A Mannhardt (Austrian).

1963 The Eigerwand was first soloed by M Darbelley (French).

1966 Two teams laid siege to a new and difficult direct line on the Eigerwand

during February and March. J Harlin (American), one of the leaders, was killed in a fall from below the Spider, and the teams combined to finish the route in his memory. D Haston (British), and S Hupfauer, J Lehne, G Strobel, and R Votteler (German) reached the summit – assisted at stages during the climb by C Bonington (British), L Kor (American), D Whillans (British), and

K Golikow, P Haag, R Rosenzopf, and G Schnaidt (German).

1974 On the South East Face a new route was made by K Moser and W Muller (Swiss).

1979–88 M Piola (Swiss) made a series of hard rock climbs (*see routes 10, 12,13*) on the right side of the Eigerwand.

1979 The 'Geneva Pillar' was climbed by G Hopfgartner and M Piola.

1981 C Howald, H Howald, and M Ruedi (Swiss) climbed 'North Corner'.

1983 R Ghilini (French) and M Piola climbed a new ED3 route. The Austrian T Bubendorfer soloed the Eigerwand without using any rope and in a record time.

1988 'The Sanction' was climbed by D Anker and M Piola (Swiss).

1991 J Lowe (USA) soloed 'Metanoia'.

north east face

The North East Face is less steep, less elegant, and not as continuously difficult as the North West Face. It has only one major line up the middle of the face. This face is 1800m (6000ft) in height.

1 Lauper Route TD+

H Lauper, guides A Zürcher, J Knubel, and A Graven 1932
Winter: H Trachsel and G Siedhoff 1964
The last of the classic lines on the Eiger, this is an ice climb, taking the right-slanting diagonal snowfields

on the face. In good conditions, the route is quick, reasonably easy and is often soloed. Allow 8–12 hours.

north east rib

The next two routes take the North East Rib, or Pillar, which separates the North East Face from the North West Face.

2 North East Pillar, Austrian Route TD

T Hiebeler, R and G Messner, and F Maschka 1968
This route is considered to be safer than the Lauper (1) and offers about the same amount of climbing as the '1938 (Heckmair) Route' (4).

3 North East Pillar, Scottish Route ED3

I MacEacheran, A McKeith, and K Spence 1970
Clearly visible from Grindelwald, this route takes the three pillars directly with a considerable amount of artificial climbing (VI and A3).

north west face

The Eigerwand consists of steep, mixed climbing in the centre of the face, with modern rock climbs on the right flank. The routes are characterized by their sheer size. This is the largest North Face in the Alps and retreat can be very

difficult in bad weather, giving the climbs their atmosphere of seriousness. This is an 1800m (6000ft) face. Allow 2–3 days for most of the routes on this face.

4 1938 (Heckmair) Route ED2

A Heckmair, H Harrer, L Vörg, and F Kasparek 1938
This is the classic one. Although very fast ascents, winter ascents, and solos have become almost commonplace, the 1938 Route remains a magnificent outing – logical, committing, and one of the best climbs in the Alps.

south ridge

This is a short ridge linking the Eiger to the Mönch. Allow 6–9 hours for the ascent and a similar amount of time for the descent.

12 South Ridge AD

G Foster, guides H Baumann and U Rübi 1876
Done from the Mönchjoch Hut, this route is a straightforward and popular climb.

south east face

The routes on this face are somewhat overshadowed by the other routes on the mountain. They see little traffic.

13 1974 Route TD+

K Moser and W Muller 1974
This rock climb takes a fairly direct line from the Eismeer Railway Station to the summit of the Eiger.

14 1937 Route TD

O Eidenschink and E Möller 1937
Although the route mainly consists of reasonable rock climbing, there is some stonefall danger.

15 Mittellegi Ridge D

Y Maki, F Amatter, S Brawand, and F Steuri 1921
This route traverses under the South East Face before climbing up to the Mittellegi Hut at 3355m (11,000ft). This fine outing continues spectacularly to the summit.

5 Harlin Route ED3/4

D Haston, S Hupfauer, J Lehne, G Strobel, and R Votteler, with help from J Harlin, C Bonington, L Kor, D Whillans, K Golikow, P Haag, R Rosenzopf, and G Schnaidt 23 February–25 March 1966
This very hard route takes the direct line running through Death Bivouac and more or less follows the fall-line from the Spider. Bear in mind that the route is only considered safe in cold conditions and has therefore seen few summer ascents.

6 Metanoia ED4

J Lowe 1991
Contains the only section of A5 recorded in the Alps.

right side

The big west-facing walls are here, including the Rote Fluh on the right side of the face. This is very steep ground with generally sound rock, which the Swiss climber M Piola seems to have dominated with a trio of fine rock climbs.

7 Ghilini-Piola Route ED3/4

R Ghilini and M Piola 1983
1400m (4600ft) of climbing up the overhanging pillar on the right side of the Rote Fluh, requiring five bivouacs on the first ascent.

8 North Corner ED3

C Howald, A Howald, and M Ruedi 1981
1200m (3900ft) of hard, free climbing, with sections of poor rock and poor protection.

9 The Sanction ED3

D Anker and M Piola 1988
An impressive climb of 1000m

(3300ft), it is exposed and difficult to retreat from after the seventh pitch.

10 Geneva Pillar ED2

G Hopfgartner and M Piola 1979
This route climbs the big pillar that can be seen clearly from the '1938 Route' (4) and contains some very good rock climbing.

west side

This flank presents the only low-angle route to the summit. Allow

how to get to the eiger

The nearest international airports are Bern or Basle. The usual valley base for the Eiger is Grindelwald, though you can use Kleine Scheidegg. Both bases are well served by efficient railway and road systems. Allow about three hours to drive from Chamonix, two hours from Zermatt (via the Lötschberg tunnel), and one hour from Bern.

The South East Face and Mittellegi Ridge routes can be reached by a long hike from Grindelwald up the Unter Grindelwald Glacier and the Fiescher Glacier, but are usually approached from the Eismeer Station (3160m/10,700ft) on the Jungfrau Railway.

facilities

In Grindelwald there is a wide range of accommodation, from hotels to hostels and camping. Food and climbing equipment can also be purchased here. It is common practice to bivouac near Alpiglen (halfway between Grindelwald and Kleine Scheidegg) the evening before setting out for the North Face.

approximately 7–10 hours for the ascent, and around 4–6 hours for your descent.

11 South West Flank and West Ridge AD

C Barrington, guides C Almer and P Bohren 1858
The first ascent route. This is tedious in the summer, often with long stretches of debris-covered ledges. It is difficult to find the route in bad weather, and there is some danger from stonefall generated by other parties. Quite reasonable in winter.

For route (11) either bivouac near Eigergletscher or use the hostels in Kleine Scheidegg. There are two mountain huts serving the South Side of the mountain; the Mönchjoch Hut, 3650m (12,000ft), has 120 beds and the Mittellegi Hut, 3355m (11,000ft), has 30 beds – both are owned by the Grindelwald guides.

when to climb

Ascents of the Eiger by the easier routes are best from June–September, when the hut system is fully functional, but winter and out-of-season ascents of the North Face are fairly common. In the early 1990s a succession of very mild winters made it possible to climb the Eigerwand in near summer conditions. Though the climbing tends to be harder in winter, there is usually less stonefall.

gear

For the easier routes you will need little more than glacier-crossing equipment, such as a couple of prusik loops and an ice screw. For the harder routes on the North Face the equipment will vary, but

it is essential to allow for long retreats in bad weather – a selection of pegs and ice screws will be useful.

maps and guidebooks

The most useful map to the area is the 'LKS 254 Interlaken', Landeskarte der Schweiz series, 1:50,000.

The best guidebook is *Bernese Oberland: Selected Climbs*, Les Swinden (Alpine Club, 1993).

language

German, but most people speak English almost as well as an average English person does.

rescue and insurance

Helicopter rescue insurance should always be carried – in Switzerland this can be bought over the counter at post offices. Only the rich need not carry medical insurance!

red tape

None – climbers do not need permits.

breaking the jinx
anderl heckmair

In 1938 the Eigerwand was the big alpine problem. Several fine climbers had died attempting it, but the safe retreat of Matthias Rebitsch and Ludwig 'Wiggerl' Vörg from Death Bivouac the year before had proved it was not necessarily a killer. That summer I felt the time was right to attempt it. Rebitsch suggested I partner Vörg. When we met I was surprised how stocky and plump 'der Wiggerl' was. Still, I recognized something of the good mountaineer about him; indeed, although he was my complete opposite, I never had another companion with whom I harmonized so well.

Early on our first day on the Eiger we caught up with Heini Harrer and Fritz Kasparek in the Second Icefield. I was all for overtaking them, as our pace was much faster than theirs. We had equipped ourselves with the very latest crampons, and one long and one short ice axe. The others were expecting to climb mostly on rock and had not brought axes. Heini didn't even have crampons. Despite my reservations, Wiggerl persuaded me to team up with them and we soon became great friends.

By 2pm we were brewing up beside the Third Icefield. The sky, which had been clear earlier, began to haze over. Moving on, we crossed a rib of snow onto virgin ground.

The Ramp is an easy gully running 150m (500ft) up towards an amphitheatre of cliff, split by a single vertical chimney. I'd begun to worry that the whole route might prove an anticlimax, but one look at that chimney changed my mind. A waterfall gushed down it, sufficient to soak us to the skin in minutes. Not wanting to bivouac in wet clothes – it was now 7pm – we retreated to the Ramp. At that moment the clouds parted to reveal just how high and exposed we were, with the wall falling away at our feet. We banged in a couple more pitons to anchor ourselves, then put on every stitch of clothing we had. I was amused to see that Wiggerl had some fur bootees; in the event, he was the only one of us not to suffer frostbitten toes. Soon, he had his stove going and was producing endless cups of coffee.

By 4am we were cooking again and, by 7am, were ready to go. The waterfall had now frozen to an icy crust. I couldn't see any ice higher up, and decided, unwisely, to attack the chimney without crampons. Luckily, I put in a couple of pitons, one of them really solid, for, just as I reached around an overhang to place another peg, my handhold gave way and I was left dangling on the good piton. That was my first fall.

After telling myself that these things happen, I strapped on my crampons and tackled the icy wall to the side before regaining the chimney at a point above where I had come off. There I cut a stance, belayed, and brought up my companions.

A canopy of massive icicles beckoned. To get a piton into it, I needed to attack the icicles. Warning the others to take cover, I chopped away, sending icicles hurtling down like thunderbolts. I took another tumble on the rope, trying to scramble onto the icy canopy. In the end, it was really fury that propelled me over it, only to be greeted with a steep, blank slope of hard ice.

This long, difficult section ate up the hours as we tried to gain the extended 'legs' of the Spider. The first rolls of thunder came during the afternoon, but the idea of retreat appealed even less than battling on through a storm. To speed up, we divided into two pairs again. Wiggerl and I gained the Spider, only to realize that the others had all our ice pitons. This was no place to hang about, so we belayed with our axes, a dubious technique up here.

Once above the spidery icefield, we awaited our companions on a pulpit of rock. By now the storm was almost overhead and we sheltered under our bivouac sack. Suddenly Wiggerl shouted, 'There's an avalanche coming!' A stream of ice fragments broke over our heads and poured down the mountain. I stabbed my axe in the ice beside me and grabbed Wiggerl with my other hand, clinging to both for what seemed like ages as my bare hand turned white with cold.

> **... before the others could join us, the next avalanche came down.**

Slowly the air cleared and the pressure eased. I was up to my haunches in ice crystals and still clutching Wiggerl, but what of the others, who must have been halfway up the steep ice of the Spider when the avalanche struck? By some miracle they were still there, although Kasparek had lost all the skin from the back of his hand. I bound the raw wound with sticking plaster, which was soon saturated in blood. He didn't complain.

It was already 6pm but we decided to climb higher in search of a safer spot to bivouac. We found one ledge, but not big enough for us all to sit together, so we hacked out another, a few metres away. Then we rigged a line between the two so that we could pass a billycan between us. Once more, Wiggerl manned the stove, and once more we had no appetite for anything solid. I tossed away the leg of ham I'd brought. Wiggerl snuggled into his fur slippers, but Fritz and I had to keep our crampons on to stop ourselves sliding downhill. We could hear the storm raging above but, in the lea of the West Ridge, I slept well enough, oblivious to the small avalanches pouring over us.

When morning came I surveyed the possibilities. Treacherous new snow had built over all the ice-coated slopes. We could climb either the open wall that, though hard, would be the safer

Above **July 1938, the successful Eiger climbers return to Kleine Scheidegg. From left to right: Heinrich Harrer, Fritz Kasparek, Anderl Heckmair, Ludwig 'Wiggerl' Vörg.**

Far right **Heinrich Harrer sack-hauling.**

Right **Anderl Heckmair and Ludwig Vörg enduring a cold bivouac on the Eigerwand.**

option; or a steep groove, down which all the avalanches were funnelling. Starting up the wall, I soon realized that it would take too much time and energy. So the groove it had to be, though there was a barrier of ice to cross first. Wiggerl belayed me as, with a lurch, I managed to pendulum myself into it. I waited as an avalanche swept the face then front-pointed up the chute, chipping handholds with my ice hammer. When the angle eased, I brought up Wiggerl but, before the others could join us, the next avalanche came down. We barely had time to bang in another piton and raise our rucksacks over our heads for protection.

As Wiggerl belayed our friends, I climbed on. The steepening gully was blocked by a bulge that I had to climb before the next avalanche. It had a light covering of ice and snow, but nothing to hold a piton. Before I knew it, both feet had skidded from under me. 'Watch out!' I shouted, as I sailed towards Wiggerl. He dropped the rope to grab me, catching only my crampons, which ripped his hand. I snatched the rope, flipping a complete somersault, before landing upright some distance below. I'd knocked Wiggerl

off, but was able to catch him before he fell far. Shaken, we scrambled back to the stance and hammered in another peg.

The crampon spike had pierced right through Wiggerl's hand. He looked rather green. I pulled out the first-aid tin to bind the wound, and noticed a phial of heart-stimulant drops. Shaking half the bottle into Wiggerl's gaping mouth, I swallowed the rest.

'I'm going to try the overhang again,' I told him. He fixed me with a wan gaze. 'Just don't fall on me,' he said. This time I swarmed up and ran out the whole rope before belaying to a rock piton. Down poured another avalanche.

Up and up we went. We cleared the gully. A steep ice slope now rose before us, exposed to the full fury of the storm. Our windproofs iced up like armour as we stomped on stiffly, zigzagging up the final metres. Earth and sky were one in fog. Suddenly, Wiggerl yelled, 'Get back! You're on the cornice!'

I looked down. Through a hole at my feet I could see rocks way, way below. 'Close!' I whistled to myself, thinking what a terrible thing it would have been to have made the first ascent of the Eiger's North Face, only to fall straight down the other side.

Nationalities: Slovene unless stated.

1777 B Hacquet (French) climbed Mali Triglav from the south. Later the next year he reached the summit with guides.

1778 Š Rozžic, M Kos, L Korosec, and L Willomitzer made the first climb to the summit from Bohinj.

1882 J Kugy and A Tožbar traversed under the summit along the ledge on the Triglav Glacier, now the 'Kugy Ledge'.

1890 The first ascent via the North Wall is thought to have been made on a poaching expedition by the hunter, I Berginc-Štrukelj, taking a line in the extreme eastern section (the route now known as the 'Slovene Route').

1895 J Alijaz erected a small turret on the summit, now named after him.

1906 First alpine style ascent made via the Wall by F König, H Reinl, and K Domenigg (German). The 'Long German Route' made by G Jahn and F Zimmer.

1924 K Jug was killed on a solo climb of the Wall on the Jug Pillar.

1926 G Kuglstatter and H Unger (German) climbed the 'Bavarian Route'.

1927 J Čop and S Tominšek climbed the 'Jug Ravine', dedicating it to Klement Jug – regarded as the conceptual leader of that generation of alpinists.

1929 P Jesih and M Gostiša climbed the 'Skalaška Route'. A German rope comprising K Prusik and R Szalay successfully climbed the western crest of the Triglav Pillar to create the 'Prusik-Szalay Route'.

1931 J Čop, S Tominšek, M Potočnik, and M Frelih completed 'Zaltorog Ledges' – a traverse of the entire Wall from east to west.

triglav

marko prezelj

Triglav, 2864m (9397ft), stands in north-west Slovenia, close to the borders with Italy and Austria, and is the focal point of Triglav National Park. It is the highest mountain in the Julian Alps and in Slovenia. It is so embedded in the national consciousness that a stylized version of its skyline appears on the Slovenian crest and it has become a place of pilgrimage for almost every Slovene. In the summer months an endless procession of hikers labours up well-trodden paths to the summit, although it cannot be regarded as an easy climb. On the most frequently used route from the Kredarica Lodge, the rocks are worn to a shine in places.

The name Triglav would suggest three peaks, but does not in fact refer to the shape of the mountain – ancient people believed it to be the home of a three-headed god and kept well away. Generations of artists, however, have drawn inspiration from Triglav and it features in many folk tales: some people accord it a veneration akin to Mount Olympus. Though relatively small in scale, its topography is intricate and full of surprises. Every corner reveals sudden visions of cliffs and valleys. The great mountain explorer and lover of the Julian Alps, Tom Longstaff, used to say that compared to Triglav the Dolomites were 'obvious'.

ridges, faces, and peaks

Triglav's spectacular North Wall falls away from the Kugy Ledge, below the summit pyramid. To the east of the Main Summit, there is a shoulder called Mali Triglav (Little Triglav). Below Mali Triglav on the North Side, the Triglav Glacier flows towards the edge of the Wall.

Although Triglav's southern and western faces have some routes on them, people nowadays travel chiefly to the North Wall, which is referred to by Slovenes simply as 'the Wall'. A fine example of a limestone face, its varied expanse offers more than 100 separate routes and variations. Over 3km (2 miles) wide, it rises over 1000m (3300ft) at its highest point. The Wall has had a decisive influence on the development of alpinism both in Slovenia and further afield, comparing proudly with many of the better-known rock faces in the West.

The Wall is distinguished by its extent and by its dynamic topography. The limestone is in layers set in horizontal strata, creating ledges with small breaks that extend in waves across its extremely varied relief. Four pillars (the famous Slovene, German, Central, and Jug) are separated by ravines, the most famous being the Slovene, German, Black, and Jug ravines. Outstanding features on the Wall include the Kugy Ledge, the White Slab, the Slovene Steeple, the Castle, the German Window, the Small Black Wall, the Big Black Wall, the Ship, the Pulpit, the Amphitheatre and, importantly, the Sphinx, at the western end, where so much of the modern climbing development has taken place.

climbing on triglav's north wall

The outside world rather lost touch with the Wall following World War II but, before World War I and between the wars, roped parties of various nationalities vied with each other on the face – Slovene and German ropes enjoying particular success.

German climbers began attempting the Wall in 1906 and were very active at the beginning of its climbing history. In every period of recent history, the Wall has served climbers as a yard-stick of ability, and is always a serious challenge.

Immediately after World War II, Joža Čop, who is legendary in Slovene alpinism, and his climbing partner, Pavla Jesih, attacked the Central Pillar. After three days of climbing, Jesih was completely exhausted and Čop continued to the edge of the Wall without her, soloing a seriously exposed traverse. He then descended to the valley and returned with a rescue team for his partner. Even today, climbers must exercise great caution in approaching this same traverse, which Čop managed alone in 1945 at the age of 52.

The generation of alpinists who climbed on the Wall in the 1960s and 1970s completed most of the direct routes and tackled a number of the plentiful, short monolithic problems. The Wall enjoyed a kind of renaissance through the extraordinarily strong and active generation of climbers in the 1980s, who set about freeing established routes, and focusing on winter repeats and new routes.

Applying a more sports-like approach to climbing, this generation gave the Wall several modern and original routes, particularly on the Sphinx. The leading alpinist of this decade, Franček Knez, gave the Wall a systematic working over, tracing more than 30 new routes, and in the 1990s he crowned this with 'Korenina', climbing the entire route freestyle. This style of climbing has become the guiding principle for the latest generation of alpinists.

The Sphinx, on the western part of the Wall, presented particular problems. This is a perpendicular, monolithic pillar, about 150m (500ft) high and wide, just under the edge of the Wall. Climbers eventually broke through it, free climbing the Face (Obraz) Route for the first time in 1995.

future climbing

If only because of its mighty expanse, the Wall still represents a challenge to climbers. Even though it is now encased in an intricate web of established routes, there remains some capacity for new ideas, and for the innovative linking of existing lines.

Right **Pavle Kozjek reconstructs the great solo traverse on Triglav, originally created by Joža Čop.**

Triglav
Big Black Wall
Kugy Ledge
Mali Triglav
Central Pillar
Small Black Wall
The Amphitheatre
Slovene Pillar
White Slab
German Pillar
Jug Ravine
Sphinx

Selected routes are presented as they are climbed today, and may not be as followed by the first climbers. Some are in fact more attractive now than they were originally.

the wall

Almost all routes end at the edge of the Wall, at around 2200–2400m (7200–7900ft), from where climbers can continue along the northern ridge to the summit, or go down to the Vrata Valley by one of the trails.

1 Zlatorogove Police (Goldenhorn Ledges) IV/I–II
J Čop, M Frelih, M Potočnik, and S Tominšek 1931
Major traverse of the entire Wall. This is an excellent tour of more than 3km (2 miles).

2 Slovenska Smer (Slovene Route) III/II
I Berginc 1890
This easiest and first route on the Wall has also been skied. Numerous combinations and variations are possible. 750m (2400ft).

3 Nemška Smer (German Route) IV/III
K Domenigg, F König, and H Reinl 1906
This long and popular route is a logical exit to the summit. It is 1000m (3300ft).

4 Sanjski Ozebnik (Couloir of Dreams) V–VI
Lower part: F Knez and L Cajzek 1983
Complete: B Mrozek and I Ullsperger 1985
This route is climbed only in winter. Ascent 1000m (3300ft).

5 Na Drugi Strani Časa (On the Other Side of Time) VIII-/VI–VII, A1
M Kajzelj and T Jokofčič 1994
Difficult route with excellent rock, demanding a modern approach. Ascent 300m (1000ft).

6 Bergantova (Borut Bergant Memorial Route) IX-/VI+
F Knez, S Karo, and M Frešer 1985
A route first climbed technically, with full gear, and then repeated in freestyle. The most difficult section requires precision climbing over rock slab. The total ascent is about 350m (1150ft).

7 Helba (Riko Salberger-Helba Memorial Route) VII+/VI-
L Anderle, L Rožič, D Strečnik, F Bence, and S Frantar 1974
A very popular route, joining up with the Skalaška Route (8). Good start for Čop Pillar (9). 350m (1150ft).

8 Skalaška z Ladjo (Skalaška with the Ship) V+/IV
M Gostisa and P Jesih 1928
J Čop, M Potočnik, and S Tominšek 1929
Popular classic over the central section of the Wall, with some direct variations. 1000m (3300ft).

9 Čopov/Osrednji Steber (Čop/Central Pillar) VI+/IV–V
J Čop and P Jesih 1945
This starts in the middle of the Wall. It is a popular continuation of Skalaška route (8) or 'Helba' (7). The route is 350m (1150ft).

10 Korenina (Root Route) VIII+/VI–VII
F Knez and D Tič 1992
Here, the difficulties facing the climber are ranged one after another in a sheer rise from foot to summit.

This climbing *tour de force* of Franček Knez is probably the most difficult route on the Wall. The route is 1000m (3300ft).

11 Prusik-Szalayeva Smer (Prusik-Szalay Route) IV-/III–IV
K Prusik and R Szalay 1929
Popular long route with a natural line. 1000m (3300ft).

12 Jugova Grapa (Jug Ravine) II–III
J Čop and S Tominšek 1927
Direct and fast approach to the right part of the Sphinx. 900m (3000ft).

13 Smer Klementa Juga (Klement Jug Memorial Route) IV
M Gostiša and P Jesih 1926
Klement Jug was killed attempting a solo climb on this route six years before the first ascent. 900m (3000ft).

14 Zahodna Zajeda (Western Notch) IV+
J Hudeček and Juvan 1959
A classic, obvious route with a connection to the 'Klement Jug Memorial Route' (13). 450m (1500ft).

15 Slosarska Smer (Slosar Route) V–VI
P Gross and B Krivic 1968
This is a popular route without a simple line. It winds around overhangs and roofs. 550m (1800ft).

16 Pandorina Skrinjica (Pandora's Box) VII-/V
F Knez and J Zupan 1981
Modern, in good rock. 500m (1600ft).

17 Ljubljanska Smer (Ljubljana Route) V–VI
N Fajdiga, A Mankota, L Juvan, and T Sazonov 1961
A popular route with difficulties in lower part. In the upper part, the rock is poor. 600m (2000ft).

18 Serenada (Serenade) VII-/V–VI
P Kozjek and C Jagodic 1988
Good route in the part where it reaches the edge of the Wall over long, easy terrain. 550m (1800ft).

19 Smer Sandija Wisiaka (Sandi Wisiak Memorial Route) IV-V
I F Ogrin and U Župančič 1933
The classic route in the western part of the Wall. 600m (2000ft).

the amphitheatre
20 Johan-Silvo VI+/A2
S Karo and J Jeglič 1983
Interesting, good rock. 200m (650ft).

21 Smer Jakoba Aljaza (Route of Jakob Aljaz) VI+, AI/VI-
S Karo and J Jeglič 1987
Good route with one solo winter ascent. 200m (650ft).

CLOSE-UP OF THE AMPHITHEATRE

22 Smer Kunaver-Drašler (Kunaver-Drašler Route) VII+/VI
A Kunaver and K Drašler 1961
The first route on the Sphinx. 250m (820ft).

23 Smer Mojstranskih Veveric (Route of the Mojstrana Squirrels) VIII+/VII-
J Ažman and Z Kofler 1969
This route is popular when combined with the 'Prusik-Szalay Route' (11). 250m (820ft).

24 Obraz Sfinge (Face of the Sphinx) IX+/X-
A Majkota and P Ščetinin 1966
Famous route, now climbed free. 150m (500ft).

25 Kljuc Srece (Key to Happiness) VII+/VI–VII
F Knez, J Jeglič, and S Karo 1984
This was the first route on the Sphinx to have been climbed at the first ascent entirely free, and without the use of bolts. It is 150m (500ft).

26 Pajkove Police (Spider Ledges Traverse) VI+, AO
S Karo 1986
This route has only been climbed once, a solo ascent.

how to get to triglav
The Wall is normally approached from the village of Mojstrana, which lies on the main road running west from Ljubljana through Kranj, Jesenice, and Kranjska gora to Tarvisio in Italy. Trains run from Ljubljana or Villach in Austria to Jesenice, which is 10km (6 miles) down the road to the east of Mojstrana. Ljubljana's international airport at Brnik is 50km (30 miles) from Mojstrana.

A road running 11km (7 miles) from Mojstrana (2½-hour walk) takes you to the Aljaž Lodge (Aljazev dom), 1015m (3330ft), in the Vrata Valley below Triglav. From there to the foot of the Wall is another 1½-hour walk.

facilities
During the summer all the mountain lodges in the Triglav range are open for overnight stays. However, the best starting point for ascents of the Wall is the Aljaž Lodge, where you should leave details of your intended climb together with your envisaged time of return. A rather higher level of tourist comfort is offered by the villages in the Upper Sava Valley, and particularly in the town of Kranjska gora.

when to climb
The best time for ascents of the Wall is June–October. In summer there may be sudden weather changes with accompanying low temperatures. However, the Wall offers numerous comfortable places for bivouacking. In winter, besides mixed climbing on the Wall, the Triglav mountain range is excellent ski-touring terrain.

gear
Climbers need the proper gear for rock faces: it is important to take a hammer as well as a range of pitons. There are plenty of fixed pitons on the more popular routes, although these may not always be secure. The routes are not normally crowded, but given the Wall's composition you must wear a helmet.

maps and guidebooks
Maps are: 'Julian Alps – Triglav', 1:25,000; 'Triglav National Park', 1:50,000; and 'Julian Alps – Eastern Section', 1:50,000 (PZS, the Planinska Zveza Slovenije or Mountaineering Association of Slovenia, Ljubljana).

In addition to the many guidebooks written in Slovene, the following are recommended: *How to Climb Triglav/Triglav, ein Kurzer Führer*, Stanko Klinar (PZS, 1991); *Julian Alps, Mountain Walking and Outline Climbing Guide*, Robin Collomb (West Col, Reading, 1978); and the *Lonely Planet Guide to Slovenia*, Steve Fallon (1995).

language
A knowledge of Slovene is desirable but not essential, as English and German are understood almost everywhere visitors come into contact with local people. It is also possible to hire a guide.

rescue and insurance
Rescue services are currently still provided free of charge. The Mountain Rescue Service (GRS) is well organized. It is advisable to discuss any intended ascent with mountain lodge wardens; the Aljaž Lodge has an automatic alarm pager for emergency calls in winter.

red tape
The Triglav National Park is governed by all the normal national park rules. Pay special attention to protection of the rich wildlife and plants. Camping is strictly forbidden.

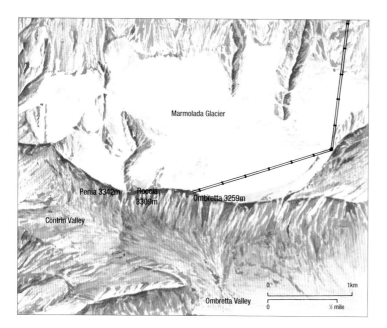

marmolada

lindsay griffin

The Marmolada, at 3342m (10,965ft), is the highest of all the Dolomite summits. Situated more or less centrally in this region of Italian limestone spires, which lies entirely in the South Tyrol, the mountain is bordered to the north by the Avisio River Valley and by the road connecting Canazei to Malga Ciapela. To the south-west lies the Contrin Valley, and to the south the Ombretta. Seen from the north, the gentle icy slopes of one of the region's few permanent glaciers would hardly merit a second glance by today's climber – a cable car rises to the summit ridge and various lifts allow glacier slopes to be used for both winter and summer skiing – however, a peek over the top of the rim reveals one of the most impressive of all Dolomite walls. Although not quite as extensive as the North West Face of the Civetta, clearly visible across the valley to the east, the South Face of the Marmolada, at around 850m (2800ft) high and 3km (2 miles) long, is the modern crucible of Dolomite climbing.

ridges, faces, and peaks

The mountain's summit ridge has three main tops: the Penia, the highest at 3342m (10,965ft); the Rocca at 3309m (10,850ft); and the Ombretta at 3259m (10,700ft). The western top of the Ombretta has the top station of the cable car built on it.

The extensive South Face is at its highest and most impressive below the Ombretta. Running west, it turns a corner at the conspicuous South Pillar of the Penia and continues as a slightly shorter South West Face above the Contrin Valley. Much of the central section of the South Face has a huge but discontinuous terrace, splitting the wall at half-height.

A large proportion of the limestone in the Dolomites is poor, even on many of the so-called popular classics. However, on the Marmolada's South Face most of the rock on the open walls is more or less perfect, and ideal for the continued development of high-standard free climbing. Many of the finest names in Dolomite pioneering appear in the roll of first ascensionists. Descent from the big routes is either along the summit ridge to the top station of the cable car or straight down the Marmolada Glacier. Although 'pisted' in places, and benign in appearance, it is worth noting that one of the great Dolomite activists, Graziano Maffei, was killed when he fell into a crevasse on this glacier.

The North Side of the Marmolada is gentle and largely glaciated, with a number of small subsidiary summits such as the 2792m (9200ft) Cima Undici.

future climbing

Commendably, the current activists have, in the main, preserved traditional ethics when opening their hard new routes and this has resulted in some very bold climbing. It would be scandalous to see these efforts derogated by the creation of adjacent, fully-bolted alpine sport routes, as has happened in other regions. The scope for pioneering magnificent high-standard free ascents is still large and some of the best climbs of the future will result from talented performers eliminating the aid on established mixed, free, and artificial routes.

A free ascent of Maffei's 'Via della Cattedrale' (VI+/A4) is considered one of the biggest challenges. For those with the vision to see a line up those crackless but pocketed walls, the story of the Marmolada is far from over.

Right **Climber on 'Modern Times' (Grade VII+) on the Marmolada di Rocca. This is one of Hans Mariacher's finest creations and widely regarded as one of the greatest free climbs in the Dolomites.**

named 'Modern Times'. This all-free route on the Rocca is still regarded as one of the most wonderful.

1986 H Mariacher created the 8-pitch 'Tempi Modernissimi' (IX+) on the Cima Undici. First winter ascent of 'The Fish' by M Giordani (Italian) and party.

1987 All 39 pitches of 'The Fish' were redpointed by H Mariacher with crux sections of IX-.

1990 M Giordani (Italian) made the first solo of 'The Fish' (with a backrope). R Mittersteiner made first free ascent of Giordani's 'Andromeda'.

1991 I Koller (Slovakian) returned to create a bold new route, 'Fram'. Some aid was used, but this was dispensed with on the second ascent during the same season by R Mittersteiner. The climbing is characteristically 'run out'

and the route widely considered the most demanding of the major lines on the South Face.

1994 R Lacher (Italian) placed (well-spaced) bolts on the lead up a 4-pitch route left of 'Specchio di Sara' to create 'Coitus Interruptus', the first X- on the South Face.

1995 M Giordani and M Girardi (Italian) spent three days on the South Face

creating 'Fantasia', a 33-pitch route left of 'The Fish' with a crux of X-. Austrians L Resier and I Knapp completed 'Steps across the Border' (an 11-pitch route they had first tried 11 years before). Giordani and the Austrians are noted for their very bold climbing and traditional ethics, and none of them appear to have placed a single protection bolt.

south face

The South Face has well over 100 established routes. This selection is just a fraction of the worthwhile climbing. Light and fast, 1-day ascents are the norm but can have serious repercussions for climbers caught out in the sudden electrical storms that are notoriously common.

marmolada di penia

1 West Ridge
Dittman, L Rizzi, and Seyffert 1898
Now one of the most popular of the 12 well-equipped Via Ferrata, this route is ungraded. It is 450m (1480ft) and should take two hours.

2 South West Face: Original Route VI
U Conforto and G Soldà 1936
A classic, although not so popular these days. The crux is reaching the exit chimneys and is best tackled after a good dry spell. This route is 550m (1800ft) and takes 8–10 hours.

3 South Pillar VI
D Christomannos, L Micheluzzi, and R Perathoner 1929
Loose rock with a normally very wet section adds to the seriousness of this old classic. It follows the line of weakness on the right flank of the pillar, but the crest itself is taken by the 1979 Brandsatter-Iovane-Kroll-Mariacher Route, a modern free climb at VI+. The route is 550m (1800ft); about 9–10 hours.

4 South Face: Original Route IV+
M Bettega, B Zagonel, and B Tomasson 1901
An old but still popular route that was impressive in its day. The alternative start, right of Gorby's Wall, avoids the notorious stonefall in the initial chimneys. It is 650m (2100ft) long and takes five hours.

5 Viva Gorby VIII
I Koller and D Kuran 1991
The first of four routes (up to IX in standard) added to the 150m (500ft) vertical wall of perfect limestone to the right of the 'Original Route' (4). Good protection and bolted rappel descents give it an ambience between big-wall and sport climbing. There are very few ascents of this route; it is very hard and times vary.

6 Sud Tiroler Weg VI and A0/A1
R Messner and K Renzler 1969
Another well known problem that fell to the talented Messner. Generally easy climbing on good rock to reach, and then follow, the left-facing diedre between the Penia and the Rocca. This diedre can often remain wet and is best climbed after a long period of dry weather. It is 700m (2300ft) and takes 7–8 hours.

marmolada di rocca

7 Via del Cinquantenario Fisi VII-
B Allemand, A Dorigatti, A Giambisi, and A Gogna 1970
Superb and well protected climbing that has no summit chimneys to remain wet or icy after bad weather. Originally climbed at VI and A1 but all free in 1982. The route is 800m (2600ft) and takes 12–15 hours.

8 Modern Times VII+
L Iovane and H Mariacher 1982
Mariacher's finest creation is regarded as one of the best free climbs in the Dolomites with only 5m (16ft) of less-than-perfect rock. Steep slabs with relatively little *in-situ* gear and no exit chimneys. The 800m (2600ft) takes 12–14 hours.

9 Vinatzer Route VII
E Castiglioni and G Vinatzer 1936
Direct Finish (VI+): R Messner 1969
One of the great Dolomite classics. Loads of *in-situ* gear allows an ascent of the original at V+/VI- and A0, and the section below the great terrace is equipped for a rappel descent. The Direct Finish is rarely attempted as most parties require more than one day to complete it and modern climbers prefer to ascend unencumbered by bivouac gear. The route is 800m (2600ft); allow 10 hours for the original.

marmolada di ombretta

10 Via dell'Ideale VII-
A Aste and F Solina 1964
Still a very serious line with obligatory hard moves due to missing bolts. There is also a VI/VI+ waterfall pitch high on the wall so the route should only be tried in settled periods of fine weather. The upper gully taken on the original ascent used to be a depository for refuse from the cable car station; a more popular variant today follows the left rib. The 850m (2800ft) route will probably take two days, but the first winter ascent took a week.

11 The Fish IX-
I Koller and J Sustr 1981
This route was originally a bold climb up an unobvious line. It remains a long, relatively serious, and highly coveted undertaking, and is one of the most popular hard routes on the South Face. With skilful use of skyhooks it is possible at VII/VII+ and A3, and there have been several winter ascents. The 850m (2800ft) will take two days.

12 Andromeda IX+
M Giordani and R Manfrini 1989
Despite the compact nature of the superb rock, Giordani refused to resort to bolts. He climbed the route at about VIII with a number of bold skyhook sections but it was freed the next year by R Mittersteiner. Allow two days; 850m (2800ft).

13 Don Quixote VI
H Mariacher and R Schiestl 1979
This route and the next one form popular modern classics of around 23 pitches. The 750m (2500ft) normally takes eight hours. This one dries fast; the rock is mostly perfect.

14 Swallow Tail VI
L Reiser and R Schiestl 1978
Not as popular as route (13), despite some wonderful climbing on the slabs above the mid-height terrace.

15 Hatschi Bratschi VI-
H Mariacher, L Reiser, and R Schiestl 1978
Another accessible free climb of medium difficulty. However, it still features a bold crux pitch near the top of the face.

16 Specchio di Sara IX
M Giordani and R Manfrini 1988
A *tour de force* by Giordani, who had to resort to bolts on the first ascent (VIII with skyhook moves) but still took a 30m (100ft) fall. Climbed free by Mittersteiner the following year. Very bold climbing, up vertical compact limestone, and a must for the talented adventure climber. It is 500m (1640ft) and takes a long day.

17 Filo di Ariana VIII+
M Guerrini and R Vettori 1993
A much-attempted line that was eventually climbed in two days with many rests on skyhooks. Not a single bolt was placed. Awaits a free ascent. It is 450m (1500ft) and is now done in one long day.

SOUTH FACE: MARMOLADA DI PENIA

Penia

West Ridge

18 Savana VII-

S Sveticic 1992

Sveticic achieved this excellent free solo first ascent of a much-eyed line on the Elephant Pillar. Protection appears to be rather scant and the climb possibly still unrepeated. It is 750m (2500ft) and takes a day.

19 Progetto Teseo VIII+

M Marisa and R Vettori 1992

Perhaps the most overhanging piece of rock to be free climbed, and in excellent style with no bolts, on the Marmolada. Unrepeated.

penia north side ⊠

This is one of the very few great snow and ice walls of the Dolomites, but is rarely climbed by anyone other than the regular German or Italian visitors. The North Face is 500m (1640ft), the North West Face 400m (1300ft).

20 North Face Direct AD+

G Lori and G Micheluzzi 1935

Although not direct, this line gives excellent mixed climbing in cold, snowy conditions. It is generally impracticable in the summer months. Takes 3–4 hours.

21 Via Paladin D-

L Paladin and S Zeppi 1955

A direct route, with steep climbing in the upper section. Difficulty depends on the state of the summital sérac barrier. Takes four hours.

22 North West Face Direct AD-

G Corenselli, M Ghezzi, and G Todeschini c.1940

A straightforward, highly recommended outing, reached in two hours from the cable car station. There is a short passage of 50° and the route has minimal stonefall in good conditions. The route is approximately three hours long.

how to get to the marmolada

You could fly to Munich, Venice, or Milan and either hire a car (very expensive in Italy) or get the local bus to the villages of Canazei in the west and, convenient for the South Face, Malga Ciapela in the east. Canazei is the larger centre. From these, walk via the Contrin Hut up the Contrin Valley, or up the Ombretta Valley past the Falier Hut, to get to the South Face. The nearest railway station is at Bolzano.

facilities

Major centres (ie Canazei) offer best facilities: accommodation (campsites tend to be booked up in summer), shops selling climbing gear, and supermarkets.

when to climb

June–September; many routes are best late in the season or in autumn. In dry conditions, winter climbing on open walls may be no more arduous than in summer.

gear

Comprehensive rack, including two good skyhooks. Some rely on TriCams in pockets.

maps and guidebooks

Maps: 'Tobacco', 1:25,000 (Val di Fassa – Marmolada) or the 'Geografica Carta Escursionistica No 30' (Dolomiti Ladin). Best guides: *Marmolada Parete Sud, La parete*, or *Selected Climbs in the Dolomites*, Ron James (Alpine Club).

language

Italian is the main language but German is understood. English not widely spoken.

rescue and insurance

Sophisticated helicopter rescues are possible via the local police. Full alpine insurance is highly recommended.

red tape

None.

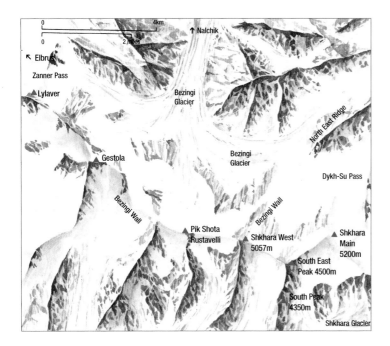

shkhara

josé luis bermúdez

Shkhara, at 5200m (17,060ft) high, is the undisputed king of the Bezingi, part of the Caucasus Mountains, which form a 900km (550 mile) natural frontier between Europe and Asia. It is the highest mountain in the Bezingi region, the second highest in the Caucasus, and is guarded on all sides by faces of near-Himalayan proportions.

At each end of the Caucasus range stands a peak of 5000m (16,400ft), higher than anything in the Alps. Elbrus, the highest mountain in Europe at 5633m (18,480ft), commands the west. Kazbek, at 5047m (16,550ft), dominates the east. However, both are dormant volcanoes, offering little in the way of challenge to the serious mountaineer. They impress through sheer size, but have none of the architectural defences and seeming impregnability that mark the truly great mountains. For that, the mountaineer has to travel from Nalchik, capital of the autonomous region of Kabardina-Balkaria, to the Russian side of the Bezingi region. This is the heart of the Caucasus. Here the other eight of Europe's 5000m (16,400ft) peaks are crammed into the two valleys of the Bezingi Glacier and the Mishirgi Glacier. And here is Shkhara, dominating the chaotic tangle of peaks that forms the innermost citadel of the central Caucasus. It lies at the eastern end of the great 12km (7½ mile) ridge known as the Bezingi Wall, which stretches the length of the horizontal section of the T-shaped Bezingi Glacier.

Summers go by with only a handful of climbers standing on Shkhara's summit. It has a reputation for malevolence that is easy to understand when you stand beneath its 1500m (4900ft) North Face and listen to the constant sound of falling ice. You have to wait for the summit to make an appearance from behind the swirling clouds, which keep it almost constantly hidden – it is a summit not easily won and not easily forgotten.

ridges, faces, and peaks

The Shkhara massif has a complex structure. There are two main summits: Shkhara Main, at 5200m (17,061ft), and Shkhara West, at 5057m (16,587ft), separated by a 2km (1¼ mile) ridge running east to west. This ridge is part of the celebrated Bezingi Wall, which continues west over the gendarmes of the Saw of Shkhara and a further seven summits, six of which are just above or just below the 5000m (16,400ft) mark, before descending to the Zanner Pass.

north side The North Face is a terrifying cascade of steep icefields and tottering séracs with the odd scattered rock buttress. It is bounded on its left (easternmost) side by the beautiful North Rib, a great ridge that plunges down from the summit of Shkhara Main in the Caucasus' answer to the Walker Spur on the Grandes Jorasses. Left of the North Rib the North West Face drops to a high plateau guarded by an icefall. The North West Face is smaller and more rocky than the North Face proper, although even more threatened by avalanches and sérac fall from the summit snowfields. The easternmost part of the Shkhara massif is dominated by the huge aesthetic curve of the North East Ridge, rising from the Dykh-Su Pass.

south side The southern side is less austere and more broken than the great sweep of the northern Bezingi Wall, although each of its great faces bears comparison with the Brenva Face of Mont Blanc.

Shkhara's two main summits each have a subsidiary peak. Its South Peak, 4350m (14,270ft), lies on the South Ridge of

Above **Neil Wilson climbing the Cockin Couloir towards the Main Summit of Shkhara. This fine route was first climbed in 1888.**

Shkhara West, while the South East Peak, 4500m (14,760ft), is on the South East Ridge of Shkhara Main. The ridges delimit the main faces.

The South Ridge of Shkhara West marks the right-hand (easternmost) edge of the mountain's great South West Face, which stretches westwards to the ridge descending from Pik Shota Rustaveli (the next peak along from Shkhara West on the Bezingi Wall). The South West Face itself is rocky in comparison with the vast expanses of ice that lie on the other side of the Bezingi Wall, and has a prominent steep rib in its centre – the focus for the routes on the face.

The South East Face stretches between the South Ridge of Shkhara West and the South East Ridge of Shkhara Main, reaching up the Shkhara Glacier, at the head of the Inguri Valley. This is the largest and most complex face on the southern side

of the mountain – with several distinct buttresses and rock ribs, it provides numerous routes.

On the other side of the South East Ridge lies Shkhara's rocky and imposing East Face. This is the least visited face on the mountain.

future climbing

Hundreds of people from all over the world come each year to plod their way up the uninspiring Elbrus, but barely a handful make the journey to test their mettle on Shkhara. We can only hope that future generations will see the potential of one of the most formidable and impressive of Europe's large mountains. There is little scope for new routes on the northern side, where the unclimbed lines (and several of the climbed ones) are objectively dangerous, but the harder routes have had few repeats. The greatest challenges are on the Georgian side, where the remoter faces await adventurous and competent parties.

Cockin Couloir
North East Ridge
Shkhara Main
North Rib
North Face
South West Ridge
Shkhara West

All the routes described are multi-day, with the precise timescale depending upon snow and ice conditions, weather, and the competence of the party. For routes on the faces, allow 3–5 days. A week would be a good time for the traverse of the Bezingi Wall.

Routes on Shkhara are generally longer and more serious, but technically more straightforward, than those of an equivalent grade in the European Alps.

north side

These routes are all reached from Camp Bezingi in Russia. They can all be started off from the Austrian Bivouac.

1 Traverse of the Bezingi Wall 6a

K Poppinger, K Moldan, and S Schintlmeister 1931
The complete traverse of the Bezingi Wall is surely Europe's longest, most arduous, and most committing expedition. The easiest traverse starts up the North East Ridge and then crosses east–west for 12km (7½ miles) over the seven summits

of the Wall, but the traverse has also been done starting up the harder North Rib. The most logical and most difficult route is from west to east, with Shkhara as the fitting final summit.

shkhara main

2 The North East Ridge 5a

J Cockin, U Almer, and C Roth 1888
This route provides one of the finest, and longest, snow-and-ice ridge climbs in Europe. Although occasionally climbed from the Dykh-Su Pass, it is more usual to join the ridge from the plateau via the Cockin Couloir (400m/1300ft of 50° ice). The ridge itself is heavily swept by winds and is correspondingly corniced.

3 The North East Face 5b

P Baudish, Hysek, Jurse, and Zahoransky 1964
This takes a line up the prominent pillar on the right-hand edge of the face. It was one of many pioneering routes climbed in the Caucasus by Eastern European climbers before the fall of communism.

4 The North Rib 5b

H Tomaschek and W Müller 1930
A long route taking perhaps the most logical line on the mountain. The climbing is nowhere near as hard as on classic alpine routes like the Walker Spur, but its length and seriousness place it firmly in their class.

5 The North Face: Russian Route 5b

Y Bushmanov, B Maleev, A Nekrasov, and V Panasjuk 1985
This route takes a horrifically dangerous line up the iceface on the right of the North Rib.

6 The North Face: Czech Route 5b

Durane, Tschunkol, and Zahoransky 1965
This route, with an average angle of 60°, is even more dangerous than route (5), as it is continually threatened by collapsing séracs and avalanches from the summit snowfields. A slightly less direct version was climbed in 1983 by a party led by Krainov, who is usually credited in Russia as the first ascensionist.

shkhara west

7 The North Face: Razumov Route 6a

Y Razumov, V Alimov, A Kolchin, and B Silin 1981
This takes a steep line up technically challenging, mixed ground. As with the next route, a successful ascent is only half the battle, because the descent involves traversing the most difficult section of the Bezingi Wall and then descending the North East Ridge of Jangi-Tau East.

8 The North Face: Blankovski Route 6a

A Blankovskhy, I Krainov, A Levin, and V Melentejev 1980
A more logical line than the 'Razumov Route' (7), the 'Blankovski Route' actually finishes on the summit of Shkhara West. Perhaps this is the route for an ambitious visitor to the Bezingi Glacier.

south side ⊠

The climbs on the southern side of the Shkhara massif are in the independent state of Georgia and cannot be reached from Camp Bezingi. These routes receive even fewer ascents than those on the Russian side. Being so remote, the South Side is rarely photographed.

shkhara west
south west face

The earliest route on this face was a rather circuitous line on the South West Rib (5B), climbed in 1958 by a Georgian team led by D Oboladze. The 1958 route was straightened out in 1970 by another Georgian team, this time led by S Mirianashvili. The 1970 route has 1500m (4900ft) of climbing and required seven bivouacs on the first ascent.

Visiting Czech climbers put up two routes. The left-most route on the face was climbed by a Czech party in 1977, a complement to the line more or less up the middle climbed by another Czech party the previous year.

It is unclear what the relationship is between the 1976 'Czech Route' and the route climbed in 1978 by O Haradze's Georgian team.

The South Ridge itself is a classic at 5A, climbed in 1903 by the visiting British team of T L Longstaff and L Rolleston. Longstaff described it as the finest climb he had ever made. The route is mainly on rock.

south east face

The three principal routes on this face are: the 1952 'Khergiani Route' (5A), which takes the buttress falling down directly from the summit; the 1969 'Mirianashvili Route' (5B), a variant that follows the Khergiani Route and then breaks off up the

next buttress to the left; and the 1963 'Tikanadze Route', which takes a completely independent line up the buttress just left of the 'Mirianashvili Route'.

shkhara main
east face

The South East Ridge, which forms the southern boundary of the face, was climbed in 1933 by the Georgian climbers A Gavalia and V Cheishvili. At 4B it is technically the easiest route up the mountain. Two other routes take the face direct. The first was climbed in 1963, the second in 1965 by a Georgian party led by

the great Misha Kerghiani who, together with Vitali Abalakov, was responsible for most of the major developments in the Caucasus during the 1950s and 1960s. Unlike most of Khergiani's climbs, this one is mainly on rock.

Above **Looking back along the Bezingi Wall at a small part of the long ridge separating Shkhara West and Jangi-Tau East.**

---

how to get to shkhara

The easiest approach to the mountain is to fly from Moscow to either Mineralnye Vodye (safer planes) or Nalchik (slightly nearer but more of a gamble). There is an alpinists' hotel at Nalchik where a night will have to be spent in transit.

You can hire a jeep to drive direct to Camp Bezingi at the head of the Bezingi Glacier but this is the most expensive option. The hardy can take a public bus to Bezingi village and walk the last 25km (15½ miles). However, I do not recommend this as there is a particular threat to climbers from bandits in the area.

facilities

Camp Bezingi provides food and comfortable accommodation at negotiable prices. It is a 5–6 hour walk up the Bezingi Glacier from Camp Bezingi to the Austrian Bivouac. The bivouac is a comfortable hut ideally located for routes on Shkhara.

when to climb

The main climbing season in the Bezingi region is July–August because it is the only time that Camp Bezingi is open. Winter climbing in the area is a serious challenge for all competent parties, but access would have to be on foot from Bezingi village (c.25km/15½ miles).

gear

A bivouac tent will be essential on the longer routes. Bring rack suitable for mountain/alpine climbing.

rescue and insurance

A mountain-rescue service is run at Camp Bezingi. Local hospital facilities are primitive and a comprehensive rescue and evacuation insurance is recommended.

maps and guidebooks

Maps of the region are readily available in Russia.

Camp Bezingi has an excellent stock of photographs, which Russians use instead of guidebooks. *Classic Climbs in the Caucasus*, Friedrich Bender (Diadem) is out of date although better than nothing. Useful historical background can be found in *At the Edge of Europe: Mountaineering in the Caucasus*, Audrey Salkeld and José Luis Bermúdez (Hodder & Stoughton, 1993).

language

Russian. English is not widely spoken in the Caucasus.

red tape

No permit is required to climb in the Bezingi region.

sideways on shkhara
josé luis
bermúdez

" **'You may bivouac here',** said the saturnine Yuri Saratov, pointing his finger somewhere to the leftmost end of the panoramic photo of the Bezingi Wall. He looked hard at us and walked about four paces to his right: 'Next bivouac', he announced, pointing straight in front of him. Then, in case we hadn't got the message, he swung his arm back to the left and repeated: 'No bivouacs from Shkhara Main to Shkhara West'. By his standards, he was being rather chirpy. Saratov's usual reaction to a proposed route was to pore over his prized collection of photos and point out the noted accident blackspots of the last 30 years.

Neil Wilson and I were in the Bezingi area in 1995 to attempt a traverse of the Bezingi Wall from west to east. The mountain tolerated us for a while and then violently spat us out. Although we retreated before finishing the entire climb, we did manage to traverse the splendid Shkhara massif, up the North East Ridge, over the Main Summit, the West Summit, and then the jagged crenellations of the so-called Saw of Shkhara. It was a sobering experience, and one of the most memorable I have had.

Poor weather and a broken ice axe put an end to our first attempt. We set off for the second time from the Austrian Bivouac at 1am the next day. This time the weather was fine and we made good progress. We bivvied on the North East Ridge. It was a perfect bivvy site, large and flat. It was a while before we saw another one of those.

The next day was a short one. We pressed on up the magnificently corniced ridge to the 5200m summit, where we enjoyed the first of several very chilly and extremely scenic bivvies, looking out to the north across the whole of the Central Caucasus and to the south over a remarkably lush Georgia. The contrast between the two sides of the wall was striking. Georgia has trees, fields, and villages. Russia has glaciers and moraine. But the good thing about the Russian side, apart from the pork fat at Camp Bezingi, is that they don't shoot foreigners there.

A broad whaleback ridge descended westwards from the summit of Shkhara. We thought it was great. Unfortunately we could only gambol down it for 200m before the serious business of climbing sideways started. The ridge narrowed to a corniced crest, falling away steeply on both sides. We front-pointed sideways just below the crest, moving together on very insecure ice. Most of the time we stayed on the Georgian side, but occasionally we crossed the cornice and shifted operations into Russia to avoid some particularly foul stretches of ice. It was a rather peculiar feeling, creeping sideways like a crab for hour

after hour above a 2000m drop. But we were making good time and just managed to beat the evening storm to a plateau where we bivvied, near the West Peak of Shkhara.

But the good times couldn't last for ever. On day four we set out just after dawn. As the cloud had come down, we followed the crest of the ridge westwards. The ice was awful but we had got used to it by then, and breezed along. But after 30 minutes or so the topography of the ridge started to get more complicated, with ridges appearing off to the side. We hadn't bargained for that, and the last thing we wanted to do was charge off down the wrong ridge into Georgia. All we could do was take regular compass bearings, head westward and hope for the best. The next misfortune hit us when we got out my compass to check that Neil's was working properly. My expensive prescription Raybans came out with it and bounced off down the face into Georgia. As neither of us had spares, I was guaranteed snowblindness.

Things got worse. Even with two compasses, we still got lost and headed off down the wrong ridge and had to retrace our steps. The cloud refused to lift, so we side-pointed sideways, hoping that we would at least find somewhere flat enough to bivvy. Nowhere appeared. Eventually the clean crest of the ridge gave way to shattered pinnacles. We had come to the first of the Seven Gendarmes forming the technical crux of the route, the Saw of Shkhara. We didn't immediately work out that this (first) was the seventh gendarme (they are confusingly numbered in reverse). It looked too big and complicated, and we still thought we could be on the wrong ridge. For some bizarre reason we decided to abseil into a couloir between two of the pinnacles to

see if we could work round at a lower level. This was a mistake. Just as the second man was down the wind got up and it started hailing. Stones came flying down, along with little avalanches. Neil's Scottish training came in handy here, as he teetered back up the snow-covered slabs we had just foolishly abseiled down.

On the pinnacles the weather was getting even worse. There wasn't much daylight left, and we clearly needed to bivvy. We poked at heaps of snow that looked as if they might become snow holes, but they all fell apart to reveal drops to the Bezingi Glacier. Then I remembered falling into a crevasse not long before the pinnacles. We found it could be expanded into a snow hole so we had a home for the night. Still things were not looking good. We were stranded in a storm in a crevasse halfway between the summits of Shkhara and Jangi-Tau. Since Shkhara West, we had been going more or less steadily downhill, and we didn't fancy our chances of reversing the route. Ahead of us lay the Seven Gendarmes, which were supposedly the hardest part of the traverse. And I was swiftly going snowblind.

> ... he managed to hold the fall before we both went flying into Georgia.

The next morning things had picked up slightly. The storm had cleared and we could see the way ahead. Or rather, Neil could. I couldn't see a thing. My glasses were covered with sticking plaster, leaving just a slit in the middle, in a vain attempt to recreate the Rayban effect. We set off across the gendarmes. Number seven seemed to be either one very big gendarme about a mile long, or hundreds of little ones. It would have been good fun if I had been able to see anything, but it turned out rather awkward, not least since we had to rope every pitch. Neil went in front to do the route finding and talked me past the obvious (to him) cornices and snow-covered slabs. This was all very well going up, but rather traumatic coming down the other side when it was my turn at the sharp end of the rope.

Progress was excruciatingly slow on day five. We didn't make it through the gendarmes but bivvied at the first flat place we found. I dosed my eyes with amethocaine and by the morning I could see again. The weather held and we were reasonably optimistic about finishing the route. But day six didn't go well. We were moving at a snail's pace. Neil had given me his sunglasses and he was now paying the price by slowly going snowblind. It took the whole day to get to the Sandro Saddle. Just before the final gendarme I slipped on a particularly brittle ice traverse. Neil's ice axe belay pulled out, but he managed to hold the fall before we both went flying into Georgia. In a moment our attitude to the climb changed completely. It was clear that the odds were on another stupid mistake from one or the other of us.

That night we bivouacked on the Sandro Saddle. We had traversed Shkhara. Despite our original intention to continue the length of the Bezingi Wall, the fleshpots of Camp Bezingi were starting to look pretty tempting. We succumbed at dawn the next day, arriving back at the Austrian Bivouac at about 10pm. Sideways climbing had taken its toll, but we had had a glorious adventure on one of Europe's most challenging mountains.

Far left **Neil Wilson descending the North East Ridge of Jangi-Tau after the traverse of the Shkhara massif.**

Left **The long sideways descent from Shkhara.**

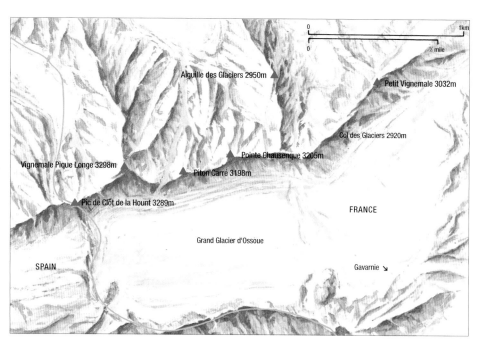

the vignemale

araceli segarra roca

Located in the Central Pyrenees, the massif of the Vignemale, 3298m (10,820ft), has long been a source of inspiration for mountaineers. Among its many charms, it can boast the greatest rock wall, the most developed glacier, and the most celebrated ice climb in the Pyrenees. Although the Main Summit is situated on the border of Spain and France, most of the massif is in France. The majority of climbers approach Vignemale from the two closest French villages of Cauterets and Gavarnie.

The mountain is made of limestone, which forms into tilted slopes with fragile flakes and few cracks. Many of the routes are not climbed regularly because it is difficult to place pitons, and there is usually a shortage of ice in winter. But, in optimum conditions – abundant ice in winter or dry rock in summer – climbers can enjoy the pleasures of alpine climbing in this unique atmosphere of solitude, peace, and immensity.

ridges, faces, and peaks

The Vignemale forms a ridge west to east, along which all the summits are located. The North Faces are the most interesting for climbers. From the Oulettes de Gaube Hut, just below these faces, all the summits can be admired. Following the ridge, from east (left) to west (right), first is the Petit Vignemale, 3032m (9947ft), followed by the Col des Glaciers, 2920m (9581ft); the Aiguille des Glaciers, 2950m (9678ft); the Pointe Chausenque, 3205m (10,516ft); the Piton Carré, 3198m (10,493ft); the Grand Vignemale or Pique Longue (the Main Summit), 3298m (10,821ft); and, finally, the Pic du Clôt de la Hount, 3289m (10,790ft). Vignemale's southern aspect is much more gentle, with a huge glacier that constitutes the usual ascent to all the summits.

The West Face of the Petit Vignemale and the South Face of the Grand Vignemale by the Grand Glacier d'Ossoue are the classics. They both see numerous ascents each summer, and make particularly fine faces for skiers in winter.

future climbing

Most of the logical climbing lines on the North Faces have been put up by French climbers, and some of these routes have been repeated frequently. However, there is still room for new modern routes, such as 'Mixed Emotions' and 'Les Délinquants de l'Inutile', which were created by strong young climbers from Catalonia and France.

The Vignemale still offers great possibilities for the skilled mountaineers of the future.

Right **Looking down the South Face and the Grand Glacier d'Ossoue on the Vignemale massif. This is where the normal route is situated.**

Arlaud-Souriac) was made by French Pyrénéistes P Bellefon and M Haegelin:

1965 The brothers J and P Ravier (French) made the first ascent of the left branch of the central gully named Couloir de l'Y, probably the most difficult gully in the Vignemale. During the same year P Bellefon, R Despiau, P Mirabal, and S and T Sarthou (French) climbed the extremely steep Central Buttress of the Main Summit, Pique Longue.

1994 The young French climber R Thivel climbed the three difficult gullies: the Couloir Arlaud-Souriac, the Couloir de l'Y, and the Couloir de Gaube, in a single day.

1994–95 Two extremely difficult new routes were climbed in winter: 'Les Délinquants de l'Inutile' climbed by B Dandoneau, C Ravier, and R Thivel (French), and 'Mixed Emotions' by F Latorre (Catalán) and P Vilarasau (French).

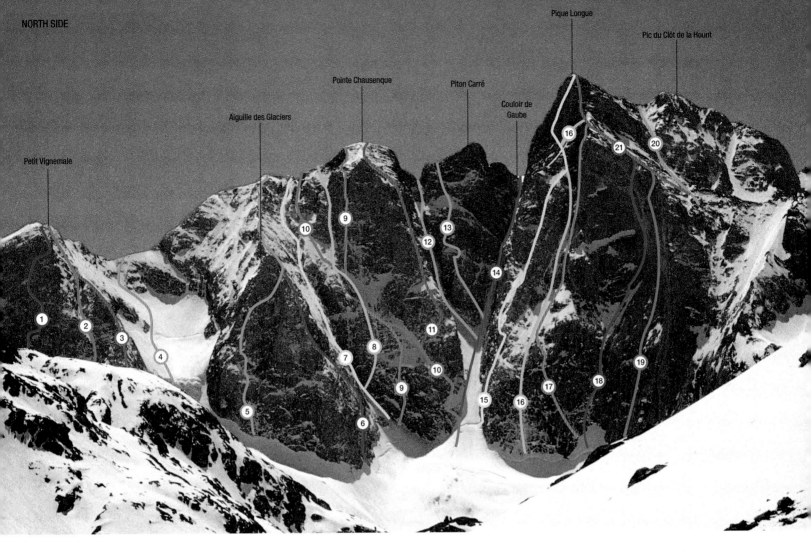

Petit Vignemale · Aiguille des Glaciers · Pointe Chausenque · Piton Carré · Couloir de Gaube · Pique Longue · Pic du Clôt de la Hount

north side

There are 21 routes shown, along with their variants, on the North Side of the Vignemale massif. These are often long routes that follow beautiful and logical lines, and make the North Faces of this mountain unquestionably the most interesting for climbers.

Some of the routes have been repeated frequently; others await the dexterity and skill of mountaineers of the future.

The selection provided here is described from east to west. All the routes can be climbed in a day, except for some winter mixed climbs, which may require a couple of days in bad conditions.

petit vignemale
1 North Face Direct TD+
J Couzy and J Soubis 1958
Not repeated very often as the quality of the rock is poor. 300m (1000ft).

2 Goulotte Lechêne TD- (IV/4+, 70°)
J L Lechêne and C Santoul 1975
Very narrow gully, where it is possible to find mixed passages.

It is not often in condition, but is a wonderful climb when it does have enough ice. The route is 300m (1000ft).

3 North West Buttress AD+
H Brulle, C Passet, and F B Salles 1890
One of the most beautiful routes on the mountain, this is frequently repeated. The route is approximately 350m (1150ft).

col des glaciers
4 Séracs Route PD+ (III/3, 60°)
M Orte, J Arlaud, and C Laffont 1928
Depending on the size of the sérac, this route can be difficult. It is frequently ascended. This route is 300m (1000ft) long.

aiguille des glaciers
5 North Face D-,
R Ollivier and A Pracherstofer 1936
This route is not repeated very often by climbers because the quality of the rock is poor. It is approximately 300m (1000ft) long.

6 North West Buttress D
G Chabanneau and R Ollivier 1946
A nice route but not often repeated. It is 350m (1150ft).

pointe chausenque glaciers
7 Couloir Arlaud-Souriac TD+ (V/5-, 80°)
Summer: P de Bellefon and M Haegelin 1960
Winter: T Bedel, D Gillerau, and B Prat 1978
Interesting and popular winter route with some mixed passages. It is not often in condition, but is a great climb when it has enough ice. It is 600m (2000ft).

8 Mixed Emotions ED (A3+, V, 80°)
F Latorre and P Vilarasau 1995
This new route, with difficult aid climbing in the first pitches, may require a couple of days. At the end, it follows an angle and goes through a huge rock arch. The route is about 600m (2000ft).

9 Direct North Face ED (A3, 6a)
J Bescos, R Montaner, J Vicente, P de Bellefon, P Mirabal, H Paradis, and S Sarthou 1962
This is a long route, and is not often repeated. It is approximately 600m (2000ft).

10 Diagonal Route TD
P Marchand, R Ollivier, and L Thiard 1945
This route is not very interesting as it follows the easy ground from right to left. The length of the route is 600m (2000ft).

11 North West Buttress TD
F Boyrie and J Simpson 1945
A classic route, this is often repeated and does have quite good rock. It is 700m (2300ft).

piton carré glaciers
12 Couloir de l'Y TD+ (V-/5+, 60–90°)
J and P Ravier 1965
A very interesting and difficult gully with mixed passages. The route is not often in good condition, but is a wonderful climb, following a logical line, when it does have enough ice. 600m (2000ft).

13 North Face TD
J Teillard, and J and P Ravier 1954
This classic and frequently ascended route is located between two central gullies, which give it an impressive atmosphere. It is 600m (2000ft).

pique longue
14 Couloir de Gaube TD (IV/ 4+, 70–85°)
H Brulle, J Bazillac, R de Monts, C Passet, and F B Salles 1889
One of the most famous and mythical climbs in the Pyrenees, this is still also considered to be one of the hardest. In winter it has an elegant ice exit to the col. Later in

spring, the last pitches have to be done following the right-hand wall (easy rock climbing, IV+). The route is 600m (2000ft) long.

15 North Face D+
H Barrio and R Bellocq 1933
One of the most beautiful climbs with several variants. The first ascensionists climbed this route in four hours without using pitons. In summer, teams are to be found on this line nearly every day. This route is approximately 900m (3000ft).

16 Les Délinquants de l'Inutile ED (VI/6-, A3)
B Dandoneau, C Ravier, and R Thivel 1994
A new, very difficult technical route, which is very rarely in condition as it needs a lot of ice on the face. The length of the route is approximately 900m (3000ft).

17 North Buttress ED+
P de Bellefon, R Despiau, P Mirabal, and S and T Sarthou 1965
Today, this route is a revered classic and often repeated. It can be climbed free (to 6b+) or with some easy aid (5+) and it is 750m (2500ft) in length.

18 Yellow Angle ED (A2, 6b)
J and P Ravier 1964
This route has had very few ascents. It is approximately 550m (1800ft).

19 Despiau-Lucquet ED+ (A3, 6b+)
R Despiau and J C Lucquet 1969
This route has only been repeated twice. The quality of the rock is quite awful. It is 500m (1650ft) in length.

20 Clôt de la Hount Gully D- (IV/3+, 50°)
J Bazillac, Bordenave, H Brulle, and Sarettes 1879
This route can provide some mixed climbing and is often repeated in good conditions. It is approximately 350m (1150ft).

21 Gaube Ridge AD
Date and first ascensionists are unknown
This route is around 400m (1300ft) in length.

how to get to the vignemale
Cauterets can be reached by car or bus from Pau via Lourdes (south of France). From Cauterets, take the route to Pont d'Espagne for 8km (5 miles). When you reach the National Park sign, take the obvious, signposted path heading left. This will bring you to the Oulettes de Gaube Hut, 2158m (7080ft), in 2½ hours – the base camp of all North Face climbs. From December–March you can take a chairlift from Pont d'Espagne, which will cut your journey time by half an hour.

To climb all the summits by the normal route (south), you have to go via the Baysellance Hut, at 2651m (8700ft). It can be reached from Oulettes de Gaube in an hour or directly from the village of Gavarnie in three hours.

facilities
Cauterets and Gavarnie are the nearest villages. They have hotels, huts, and shops to buy equipment and food. The Oulettes de Gaube Hut has 82 beds. The Baysellance Hut has 70 beds; book both through the Club Alpin Français.

when to climb
Normal routes are feasible all year round. The rock-climbing routes are best tackled in summer. The gullies are in condition from December–May, but this varies.

gear
A set of nuts, friends, pitons, helmet, and rope for the rock routes. Crampons are often necessary to reach the bases of the climbs. Ice axes, crampons, and ice screws are needed for the gullies and winter ascents. In winter, skis can be useful for approaches and descents.

maps and guidebooks
The best maps are: French IGN 'Série Bleue', 1:25,000 (Institut Geographique National) and 'Ordesa-Vignemale', 1:25,000 (Spanish Editorial Alpina).

Books include *Les 100 Plus Belles Courses des Pyrénées,* Patrice de Bellefon (Ed Denoël) and *Vignemale-Monte Perdido*, R Ollivier (Ed Ollivier). *Rock Climbs in the Pyrenees*, Derek Walker (Cicerone, 1990), is in English. All the above can be purchased in Cauterets and Gavarnie.

language
French, although people do speak some Spanish and English.

rescue and insurance
Rescue services are available and it is always best to carry insurance.

red tape
None.

Above **Grand Glacier d'Ossoue, Grand Vignemale. The longest glacier in the Pyrenees, it lies on the French side of the border.**

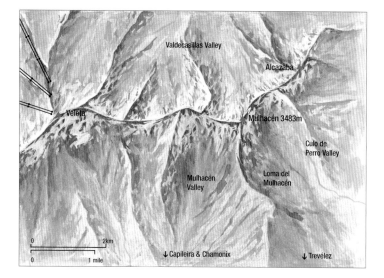

mulhacén

lindsay griffin

Situated more or less in the middle of the 110km (70 mile) Sierra Nevada range and less than 30km (18 miles) south-east of the famous old Moorish capital Granada, Mulhacén, at 3483m (11,428ft), is the highest summit on mainland Spain. The mountain's name was derived from Mulay Hassan, the penultimate Moorish King of Granada, whose body is reported to be buried beneath the summit.

In summer the Sierra Nevada is dry and barren, with little mountaineering interest. It is in winter, when the temperatures drop to -20°C (-4°F) and the generally stony terrain becomes well snow-covered, that the range takes on a splendid new appearance. The weather is often settled for long periods, so snow can quickly consolidate into excellent névé, and ice can form on the sheltered northern faces. Mulhacén then offers considerable rewards to the middle-grade mountaineer with axe and crampon, and it is also popular with the adventurous ski tourer. A recent praiseworthy proposal to create a National Park around the upper reaches of the Sierra's high mountains may be offset somewhat by the suggestion that the Ministry of Defence wants to install a radar site on the summit.

ridges, faces, and peaks

Mulhacén, in common with all the big peaks in the Sierra, has very gentle, south-facing slopes, ambling down to the small communities of white-washed houses in the upper Alpujarras. The nearest villages include Capileira, which lies at the end of a partially unmade road running from the ski resort of Sol y Nieve, south across the range to the west of Mulhacén, and the sleepy Trevélez, the closest settlement to the summit and, at 1476m (4800ft), the highest inhabited village in Spain.

The west slopes are also gentle and fall into the Mulhacén Valley, which drains south to Capileira. The so-called West Ridge is hardly a ridge at all but simply the point where these slopes end abruptly above the much steeper North Face. The Ridge falls gradually from the summit in about 1km (½ mile) to the high pass of the Collado del Clervo, then continues for another 4km (2½ miles) over several minor summits to Veleta, at 3398m (11,100ft) the second highest peak in the Sierra Nevada.

The east slopes are somewhat steeper, especially towards the summit, although they are still far from difficult. They are bounded to the north by the North East Ridge, which is not steep on its south side, and, after dropping from the summit to its lowest point at the Collado de Siete Lagunas, continues for a total of about 2km (1¼ miles) to the summit of Alcazaba, 3363m (11,000ft). The east slopes drain into the upper Culo de Perro Valley, descending to the Rio Trevélez. Running south from the summit, and dividing the west from the east slopes, is the very broad, rounded ridge of the Loma del Mulhacén.

The northern slopes are abrupt, with moderately steep rocky walls comprised of a kind of friable schist. These walls provide nothing in the way of decent rock but offer classic mixed climbing during the winter, most often at a relatively accessible standard. Two features are prominent: a central couloir rising the full height of the face towards the summit, and a continuous rock buttress immediately to the left that is split in its lower section by a narrow gully. Running north from the foot of this face is the Valdecasillas Valley, which leads into the Rio Real.

future climbing

All obvious lines have long since been climbed on Mulhacén. In an attempt to restore some tranquillity to the area, the Félix Méndez Hut, near the foot of the West Ridge, has been removed and replaced by the Poqueira Hut, at 2500m (8200ft), in the Mulhacén Valley. Prospective summiteers now have three hours and almost 1000m (3300ft) of ascent to reach the summit.

Collado de Siete Lagunas

North Face

West Flank

Collado del Clervo

None of the winter routes to the summit demands high levels of technique on snow or ice. All the routes were probably climbed many years ago. Apart from the North Face, the flanks of the mountain can be ascended by winter hill walkers used to handling an axe and crampons. Grades are only given where appropriate.

1 South Flank ⊠

A long, gently angled, snow walk with no technical difficulty up the Loma del Mulhacén above the Capileira jeep road. The broad South Flank of the mountain can be ascended anywhere. About 1000m (3300ft) and 3–4 hours from the Poqueira Hut or a point at the same altitude on the road.

2 West Flank

By far the most frequented route of ascent due to the proximity of the jeep road in summer and the cable car from Sol y Nieve to Veleta in winter. Gentle snow slopes with no technical difficulty. Around 1000m (3300ft) and 3–4 hours from the Poqueira Hut, or 650m (2100ft) of ascent and 3½ hours from the top of the cable car.

3 East Flank via Culo de Perro Valley ⊠

A long but easy snow plod with steeper ground to finish. This route gets the first sun, and the snow deteriorates quickly; the best conditions are found shortly after dawn. Not nearly as popular as routes

(1) and (2). About 2000m (6500ft) of ascent, this route should take eight hours in good snow conditions.

4 North East Ridge F

Easy snow slopes, passing the prominent rocky buttress at half-height on the left to reach a broad snow gully on the South East Flank. As with (3), this gets the first sun and snow conditions deteriorate quickly, so it is best climbed shortly after dawn. Around 250m (820ft), taking an hour or less from the Collado de Siete Lagunas.

5 Via the Siete Lagunas Couloir and North East Ridge PD-

Really only a couloir in the initial section, where it slants left through the lower rock barrier. Due to its north-westerly orientation, the couloir can often be found in good condition late in the day. It is 280m (900ft) to the Collado de Siete Lagunas from the foot of the North Face and takes one hour or so for a party moving together; 2–3 hours to get to the summit.

north face

The only interesting facet of the mountain for alpinists. It forms a moderately steep, mixed face rising about 500m (1600ft) above the upper Valdecasillas Valley. At one time or another parties have climbed all over this face, but the two main lines are as follows.

6 El Paria AD

A classic winter buttress climb. The lower section gives moderately steep snow climbing in a narrow gully; the upper section is more mixed. 520m (1700ft); allow five hours.

7 Central Couloir AD-

The classic of the face with the

steepest section and crux (55°) in the narrows at around half-height. The easiest exit slants up left to the North East Ridge but it is possible to finish direct on steeper mixed ground. About 500m (1600ft), this route normally takes 4–5 hours.

how to get to mulhacén

Get a cheap charter flight to Málaga, then a train or bus to Granada. Local buses go to Sol y Nieve and various villages. Car hire is relatively inexpensive.

There are various approaches: via the road between Granada to Capileira (summer); via the Poqueira Hut (a 6-hour walk from Capileira); and via the cable car to near the top of Veleta to the west. Approach the North Face by descending snow slopes below the Colloda Del Clervo or via the Valdecasillas Valley.

facilities

Granada has everything you might need. Sol y Nieve has typical ski-resort facilities; many of the South Side villages are basic. There is a bivouac hut near the Collado del Clervo; Poqueira Hut has 75 beds.

when to climb

November–May, with ice being best in January and February. Avalanches are less common than in other European ranges, but beware of windslab formation on north-facing slopes.

gear

Summer alpine or Scottish winter gear, although temperatures can reach -25°C (-13°F) and it is often windy. A small selection of rock gear, including blade pegs, will be sufficent for the North Face.

maps and guidebooks

Try the IGN map to the Sierra, 1:50,000.

Sierra Nevada, Guia Montanera, Bueno Porcel (University of Granada, 1987) is a useful guide, and *En Esquis Sierra Nevada*, Lorenzo Arribas, although about skiing, has route maps and some excellent photographs.

language

Spanish, English spoken in tourist resorts.

rescue and insurance

Mountain rescue in the Sierra Nevada is carried out by the Guardia Civil and helicopter evacuation is a possibility. Full alpine insurance is recommended.

red tape

Permits are not needed.

Arctic
Ocean

GREENLAND

ALASKA

BAFFIN
ISLAND

● Mt McKinley
Alaska Range
● Anchorage

Nalumasortoq ▲

St Elias Mtns
YUKON
TERRITORY

▲ Mt Logan

Mt Asgard ▲
● Pangnirtung

Narsarsuaq ●

● Whitehorse

R
O
C
K
Y

BRITISH
COLUMBIA

CANADA

Hudson
Bay

Pacific
Ocean

▲ Mt Robson
● Jasper

Mt Waddington ▲ *Canadian Rockies*
● Calgary

*Coast
Range*

M
O
U
N
T
A
I
N
S

● Vancouver

▲ Devil's Tower
● Sundance

▲ Grand Teton
● Jackson

CALIFORNIA

Teton Range

UNITED
STATES OF
AMERICA

WYOMING

Sierra Nevada
● San Francisco
▲ El Capitan

● Shiprock
▲ Shiprock

NEW MEXICO

Atlantic
Ocean

Gulf of Mexico

M E X I C O

*Cordillera
Anahuac*
● Mexico City
▲ Orizaba

arctic & north america

Exploration of the highest of North America's mountains is relatively recent. There was no permanent route across the Canadian Rockies until the Canadian Pacific Railroad was built towards the end of the 19th century. Mount McKinley received its first confirmed ascent in 1913, and Mount Logan was not climbed until 1925. Other peaks in the far north saw no one until as recently as the 1930s and 1940s. The first rock climbs began to be traced on the sheer faces in California's Yosemite Valley during the 1930s, but 'big-wall' climbing only took off with the revolution of climbing hardware in the 1960s. The weirdly eroded sandstone towers and canyon walls of the American South West have a special appeal; then there are freaks of geography, like the extraordinary Devil's Tower. As you would expect in such a big continent, practically every style of climbing is represented.

Mount Asgard in Baffin Island lies within the Arctic Circle, as does most of Greenland, which is why they have been included here.

Clockwise from left: **Mount Asgard from the south; East Side of the Tetons; Summit Ridge of Mount McKinley**

1975 First ascent of Nalumasortoq by five members of a French party, via the South Face. Five other members of the same team ascended the East Ridge.
1994 Having completed a long and demanding climb on Ulamertorsuaq, S Glowacz (Austrian), D Langen (German), and B Masterson (British) attempted a line on the fissured face between the Central and Left Pillars.

The attempt concluded seven pitches up when the climbers ran out of time.
1995 A British team visited the area with the intent to climb the Central Pillar, but arrived to discover a Swiss team, led by veteran big-wall climber C Dalphin, firmly ensconced on the route. They turned their attention to the unfinished line of 1994 and successfully completed the ascent in a relatively short time,

reaching the crest of the ridge in one continuous push with only one bivouac.
1996 C Dalphin returned with P Berthet (French), J Flugi (Swiss), and S Brambati and P Vitali (Italian) to complete a prominent line on the Central Pillar, 'Cheese Finger at 3 o'clock'. It took six days in June for all the team to climb the route. Later that summer, J Gore and T Penning (British) with S Karo (Slovenia)

claimed 'Mussel Power', on the West Face of Left Pillar, to the left of the Dring route. M Turner and L Thomas (British) put up 'Umwelten', to the right of the Dring line. In the same year I Wilson and N Shepherd (British) established the first seven pitches of a hard new route, 'Candle in the Wind', on the Right Pillar. The climb had to be abandoned due to an accident on pitch eight.

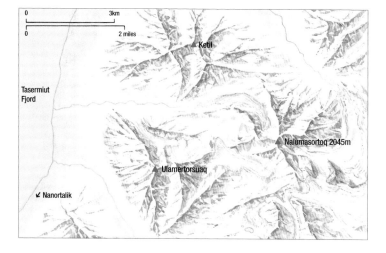

nalumasortoq

nigel shepherd

In recent years, considerable climbing attention has focused on the southern parts of Greenland, where towering granite spires thrust skyward, presenting challenging opportunities for big-wall climbing – often on perfect granite. The region offers an abundance of very varied mountaineering opportunities at almost any difficulty, but much of the exploration has centred on peaks along the eastern shore of Tasermiut Fjord.

Nalumasortoq is the highest mountain in the immediate vicinity of Tasermiut Fjord. It stands at 2045m (6710ft) above sea level, between Ulamertorsuaq and Ketil, and represents massive potential, attainable and achievable by many climbers. Most people access the area through the small fishing town, Nanortalik, at the entrance to the Fjord.

ridges, faces, and peaks

Nalumasortoq is an important peak whose walls and towers were not fully explored until the mid-1990s. Huge, moderately angled slabs and ridges lead to its summit but, like much of the low-angle rock in the region, it exfoliates readily and is lichenous. The Nalumasortoq Pillars are significantly more appealing to climbers than other faces in the immediate area. They are a satellite of the main mountain, running along a ridge in a generally north-west direction from the summit. Collectively known as the South Face, the three Pillars (Left, Central, and Right) are composed of solid, golden-coloured granite. They usually catch most of the sun from late morning through to mid-evening, which gives them a stunning appearance.

The Central Pillar is the most strikingly impressive, its profile presenting an alluringly clean and steep outline. The Left Pillar is a large, compact mass, seamed only by a few possible climbing lines, many of which end abruptly in blank walls. In the background on the approach from the fjord, the Right Pillar appears less significant but is, in fact, equally dramatic, and is topped by an elegant tower, shaped like a candle flame.

A small buttress separates the Left and Central Pillars from the Right Pillar, and a 100m (330ft) rock barrier must be overcome before any of the climbs to its left can be reached. This leads to a snowy ledge system, below the Central and Left Pillar climbs, which can be reduced to steep, loose scree and large boulders when there has not been much snow. The ledge below the Right Pillar is reached by solid, clean granite slabs and is much more accommodating, with ample bivouac sites.

The East Arête is a long and narrow crenellated ridge, the start of which is gained via the col at the head of the glacier in front of the Pillars.

future climbing

There are many climbing possibilities on these walls. A huge corner between the Central and Right Pillars is a striking and obvious line, and the cracks that sear their way through the wall between the Central and Left Pillars are numerous. The very prow of the Left Pillar has yet to be climbed, and there are no routes on the North West Face of Nalumasortoq, which is situated behind the Pillars. A glacier has carved a cirque of steep slabs and walls which, though on the shady side of the mountain, have clean sweeps of rock and innumerable crack lines.

Across the glacier in front of the Pillars are some impressive walls – one curves outwards for its entire length to finish in a huge prow and roof resembling a diving board. For generations to come, these walls and gigantic slabs will offer climbs of great quality in a remote and wonderful setting.

Right **Jumaring fixed ropes on the lower section of the Right Pillar of Nalumasortoq. There is still plenty of fine virgin rock in this part of southern Greenland.**

Left Pillar

Central Pillar

Right Pillar

the nalumasortoq pillars

1 Left Pillar: Mussel Power ED with pitches of A4

J Gore, S Karo, and T Penning 1996

An 800m (2600ft) climb, mainly on very difficult aid, but with hard free climbing towards the top. Completed over five days although thought to be possible in four days. Descent is down the line of the Dring route (2).

2 Left Pillar ED with pitches of 6c/A2

I and C Dring, P Tattersall, and D Anderson 1995

This 800m (2600ft) climb follows a continuous crack line between the Central and Left Pillars. The first ascensionists report that it might be possible to free climb the route in 2–3 days. Descent is by rappel.

3 Left Pillar: Umwelten ED with pitches of 7a

M Turner and L Thomas 1996

An excellent, mainly free climb of 800m (2600ft), following a line of obvious cracks to the right of the Dring route. Was done in four days, but could be done in two. Descent is by the same line as the ascent.

4 Central Pillar: Cheese Finger at 3 o'clock ED with pitches of 6b and A4

P Berthet, C Dalphin, J Flugi, S Brambati, and P Vitali 1995/6

A fine line of 900m (3000ft) – including lower tier – up the obvious prow, giving steep, sustained, high-standard climbing on excellent rock. Repeat ascents possible in 3–4 days. Hard aid with some free. The descent is down the line of ascent.

5 Right Pillar: Candle in the Wind

Attempted by I Wilson and N Shepherd 1996

The climbing up to the high point is mainly free with two pitches of 6c+. Seven pitches were done in total; there were another possible 12 or so.

6 South Face Route TD with pitches of V

B Domenech, F Guillot, P Chapoutot, M Perrotet, and B Gorgeon 1975

A steep slab climb of 1000m (3300ft) up solid rock. The climbing is exquisite, although there is barely enough protection.

7 East Arête D

M Agier, B and Mme Amy, B Domenech, F Guillot, and C Laurendeau 1975

This is a ridge climb of 1000m (3300ft) with some moderately difficult sections. Loose rock covered in thick, black lichen makes the route a little more tricky.

Right **The North East Face of Nalumasortoq is 760m (2500ft) of sheer granite.**

how to get to nalumasortoq

Flights to southern Greenland are few and very expensive. The closest international airport is at Narsarsuaq, an ex-US Airforce base in the south-west. From there, you can catch a ferry that plies its way between all the villages in the south. The journey to Nanortalik takes two days, but you can save time by taking a helicopter. This takes about 1½ hours and gives you an opportunity to view the spectacular scenery from the air.

From Nanortalik there are three ways to get to the base camp area at the head of Tasermiut fjord: charter a helicopter, hire your own inflatable Zodiac, or pre-arrange for a boat to take you. The latter two options depend on the state of the pack ice – the entrance to the fjord and the harbour around Nanortalik can rapidly become ice bound, prohibiting any movement in or out.

facilities

Accommodation is available in two hotels (expensive) or through the tourist office which can arrange bunkhouse or self-catering accommodation. It is possible to buy leaded petrol and Camping Gaz in Nanortalik, as well as essential food supplies, but there is nowhere that sells specialist rations for use on the mountain.

Two main campsites are used, one on the shores of the fjord and the other about three hours walk up the valley, just below the glacier leading to the Pillars. It is worth collecting some of the large, fresh, and tasty mussels on the nearby shore. You can also pick an edible plant called angelica below the glacier that leads to the Pillars.

when to climb

May–early September is the best time. Most expeditions opt for the period from mid-June to mid-July. Expect bad weather to interfere with climbing plans whatever time of year you go.

Daylight hours are long – in midsummer there is only about one hour of twilight and no complete darkness. It can be very cold during the 'night time' but scorchingly hot in full sun.

gear

The climbing is all of big-wall nature, so take a good selection of nuts, camming devices, pegs, and other hardware. Any ascent that takes more than a day will require the use of a portaledge as roomy ledges on the faces are few. A haul bag, water containers, and fixed rope are also necessary for a multi-day ascent. Crampons and ice axes are advisable.

Take insect repellent and special hats as the fjord and low swampy areas are often swarming with mosquitoes.

maps and guidebooks

An excellent series of maps, produced in 1995 by the Greenland Tourist Board, includes details such as suggested walking routes. There are no guidebooks in existence but information can be obtained by reading through copies of the *American Alpine Journal* and the *Alpine Club Journal (UK)*.

language

The native people speak Inuit, but almost everyone also speaks Danish and there are some people who speak English in Nanortalik.

rescue and insurance

Insurance is absolutely essential. There is no formal rescue facility and any emergency will be dealt with by Greenlandair helicopters. Be warned that there is a hefty charge for this service. Climbing teams should be prepared to take care of themselves as complex cliff rescues are impossible to arrange quickly.

red tape

To avoid expensive air freighting, it is advisable to send out all expedition equipment by sea freight in advance. Make sure that at least six weeks elapse between the despatch date and your expected arrival in Greenland, to allow for the cargo ship being unable to get through pack ice.

There are, at present, no restrictions on climbing in the area and it is not necessary to have a permit. If you wish to take a radio, you must obtain a permit from Danish Telecom.

1585 J Davis (British) was the first to visit the region and his names for many of the coastal features and mountains are still on modern maps.

Early 1920s The Hudson Bay Company and the Royal Canadian Mounted Police established a settlement at Pangnirtung and went on patrols up Weasel Valley, over Pangnirtung Pass, and down Owl Valley.

1953 The higher of the twin summits of Asgard, the North Peak, was first climbed by H Webber, J Marmet, and Rothlisberger, Swiss scientists attached to the Arctic Institute Baffin Island Expedition, which was organized by P Baird (Canadian). Altogether, eight mountains were climbed for the first time, including the highest mountain in the area, Tête Blanche.

1971 The first ascent of the South Peak of Asgard was made by G Lee, R Wood, and P Koch on perfect rock and in brilliant weather. They bivouacked on the summit, awoke to a full-blown blizzard and had to descend in white-out conditions. The first attempt was made on the West Side of the North Peak by D Scott (British) and D Hennek (American).

Two weeks of storm at the end of August put paid to this effort.

1972 The East Pillar of North Peak was climbed by P Braithwaite, D Hennek, and D Scott. This has proved to be one of the world's great free climbs and has been repeated six times to date. It was the first high mountain route climbed on Baffin Island unsupported by mechanical means from the fjord-head.

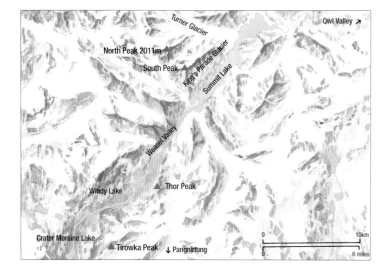

mount asgard

doug scott

Asgard is the most remarkable – and now most famous – of the mountains of the Cumberland Peninsula of Canada's Baffin Island. This peninsula is about the size of Switzerland with a coastline indented by numerous fjords. Pangnirtung Fjords, North and South, provide routes into the main climbing area, which is concentrated along Weasel and Owl Valleys and around Summit Lake. Before any climbers came to the area, pilots flying between Eskimo settlements and on geological surveys had reported the spectacular shape of Asgard, 2011m (6598ft). From most angles it resembles giant twin sawn-off chimney stacks; a great granite barrel of a mountain rising out of the ice 900m (3000ft) on most sides with few easy lines of weakness – and none that do not require mountaineering and rock-climbing skills.

There is no easy approach to Asgard, especially now that it and the surrounding mountains are included in the huge Auyuittuq National Park. The area is still very much pristine wilderness and the use of helicopters is discouraged within the park so climbers have to come in overland. Yet, far from being a deterrent, this remote setting has acted like a magnet to those climbers who seek a total mountain experience.

Most expeditions to the Cumberland Peninsula aim to establish base camp at Summit Lake and from there hump loads to the foot of individual peaks, establishing smaller camps with enough supplies to survive storms and long periods of bad weather. One characteristic of climbing in Baffin Island is the huge loads that have to be carried, especially if the full range of big-wall climbing equipment is taken along.

It is a remarkable 40km (25 mile) journey from the fjord-head along the glaciated, flattish but steep-sided Weasel Valley to Summit Lake, with all the truncated spurs, and glaciers in-between that come down from icecaps and snowfields on either side. It is obvious that the ice has retreated in relatively recent times, for nature is still re-establishing itself. Streams wander through boulder and tundra, dotted with willow herb and arctic poppy, sometimes in flood, especially during the summer afternoons when the 24-hour sun is strong and the snows are melting fast. Negotiating these streams with 45kg (100lb) loads is exhausting and dangerous work. This is not easy country, even for the young in heart and limb.

A visit to Baffin Island is much enhanced by making contact with the Inuit. Although making use of modern conveniences, they are still firmly rooted in their traditions, and are a gentle and helpful people, providing most of the services for climbers.

ridges, faces, and peaks

From all angles Asgard is a huge monolith of granite. The higher North Summit, 2011m (6598ft), is capped with the bigger snow dome. The South Summit is only a few metres lower, and the saddle is 120m (390ft) below both summits. The longest continuous rock for climbing is presented by the East Pillar of the North Peak, 1200m (4000ft); the steepest faces are the North and West, both practically vertical for 800m (2600ft). On the South Side the line of weakness is via the South East Basin to the saddle. This basin sometimes collects snow that can be extremely difficult to surmount. The South Buttress offers a classic free climb on excellent rock with stupendous views down the West Face, but, as with many of the climbs on Asgard, it remains steep all the way to the summit.

future climbing

There is room for much more climbing on both peaks.

Right **Looking south from Asgard: the Weasel River is on the right and the Highway Glacier is on the left.**

1975 The first ascent of the West Side of the North Peak of Asgard by C Porter (American), solo. Not only was this ascent and epic retreat a remarkable achievement, it was also the first Baffin modern, multi-day, technical, big-wall climb. Porter's solo climb up 40 pitches of Asgard granite at Grade VI, his descent in a storm down the Swiss route, and his 10-day walk-out to the fjord-head, without food and with frost-damaged feet, took him into realms no other climber had gone before. In the same year, the one and only parachute jump off the summit took place for a James Bond movie and a subsequent whisky advertising campaign. The stunt man who skied off Asgard into space was R Sylvester (American).

1994 Big-wall climbing of the modern multi-day extreme kind arrived with the ascent by N Craine, P Pritchard, S Quinlan (British), and J Tosas (Spanish) of the West Face of the North Tower. This was closely followed by an ascent of the North Face of the North Tower in alpine style by Americans C Breemer and B Jarrett.

South Face
South Buttress
South Peak
North Peak

North Peak
North Face
East Pillar

King's Parade Glacier

East Pillar

Turner Glacier

Only some of the free climbs on Asgard have been repeated and none of the technical big-wall climbs has had a second ascent. There is no local climbing scene and the first ascensionists have come from many countries, so there is no guaranteed standard of grading.

east side

1 Original South Peak Route TD V, 5.8
G Lee, P Koch, and R Wood 1971
The route ascends the couloir from King's Parade Glacier to the shoulder beneath the South Buttress of the South Peak. The first ascent took one long day from glacier to summit.

2 South Face of the South Peak: Arctic Dreams
R Tanner and J Eysell 1991
This is a new route almost to the summit but bad weather persuaded the climbers to finish by the 'Italian Route' (13). They retreated by abseil the same way. Takes one long day.

3 Original Route VI, 5.8/5.9 A.I.
H Weber, J Marmet, and Rothlisberger 1953
The route ascends the snow basin and rocky ribs to the saddle between the North and South Peaks. From there it is 150m (500ft) over sometimes loose rock to the summit. On the first ascent a peg was used for direct aid because of water pouring down from the summit snowfields. Conditions on this route vary from year to year and from month to month on account of the snow, which can be horrendously soft. It is the most-travelled route and is the usual way off both peaks.

4 East Pillar Route VI, 5.10
P Braithwaite, D Hennek, P Nunn, and D Scott 1972
The climbing here is superb and logical. It goes up over slabs with the difficulties at each overlapping until the final 305m (1000ft) headwall. The penultimate squeeze-chimney pitch is particularly hard. On the first ascent the 1200m (4000ft) route was climbed in a continuous 38 hours.

5 East Pillar: German Variant VI
F Perchtold, A Fuchs, W Wahl, and C Krah 1991
This route takes the first eight pitches of the 'East Pillar Route' (4) before deviating to the left and then climbing up chimneys and crack systems that lead to the summit.

6 East Pillar: American Variant 5.7/5.8/5.9
M Hesse and H Kent 1977
After climbing some 20 pitches from the south-east this route eventually joins the original 'East Pillar Route' (4) to the summit. The climbing was found to be on good rock and was nearly all free.

north peak
north face
7 American Route: Valkyrie VI, A4+ 14 pitches
C Breemer and B Jarrett 1994
So far this is the only route on the North Side of the North Peak. It is an extremely difficult aid climb. The route took 14 days with bivouacs on portaledges. This was the first modern aid route not to use fixed routes and yet the climbers only had two days of good weather. They were also plagued by falling ice and stone. They abseiled back down the route of ascent, leaving the last pitch of fourth-class rock to the snow dome as it was so wet and miserable. The team had the advantage of being brought to Asgard by helicopter.

west side
8 Swiss Route: Inukshuk VI, 5.10, A3+
J-M Zweiacker, D Burdet, C Choffat, and P Robert 1995
The Swiss first attempted the route in 1994 but had been stormed off. They returned to fix rope to the lower pitches before completing the route, which was found to be 800m (2600ft) and not absolutely desperate. A possible popular route for the future.

9 Spanish Route VI, 5.8 (6A, A4)
T Lizarraga, R Melero, M Berazaluze, and N Barriuso 1995
The route takes a difficult line up hard, compact rock and took the first ascensionists 17 days to complete to the summit. 800m (2600ft) of ascent.

10 British Route A4+, E4 6A
N Craine, P Pritchard, S Quinlan, and J Tosas 1994
This was the first of the very hard modern aid routes involving the full array of artificial climbing equipment – rivets, hooking, and portaledges. Altogether, 19 pitches were forged and 11 days spent on the wall. Fixed lines were utilized up to approximately half-height, from where the climbers continued

capsule style from a portaledge camp. 1000m (3300ft) of ascent.

north west face
11 Charlie Porter route VI, 5.10
Solo: C Porter 1975

Using just one bolt and his ice axe, Porter gained the prominent dihedral to make a direct route to the summit. He made 40 pitches – the most remarkable achievement on Asgard, Baffin Island, and probably anywhere!

south peak
12 West Face Direct VI 5.10 A4
J Bagley, J Barbella, W McCartney, and E Redfern 1988

This route had been attempted three times before – once by Earl Redfern. This team used *in-situ* fixed rope up to Redfern's previous high point and continued to the summit. 800m (2600ft) of ascent.

13 Southern Edge: Italian Route
F Leoni, L Luca, F De Francesco, and M Manica 1988

The summit was reached after 27½ hours of climbing – from the Turner Glacier, up the ribs leading round to the 'Original Route' (3).

how to get to mount asgard
Fly from Montreal to Pangnirtung. First Air do the round trip – they may charge for freight on top of the basic price.

From Pangnirtung take a boat to the fjord-head and walk the 40km (25 miles) along Weasel Valley to Summit Lake. The cost of the boat varies upon the size of your group, and several relays may be needed to carry all your equipment to base camp. In spring, when the fjord is frozen, the boat is put on a sledge and pulled by skidoo. If the ice is breaking up, you may have to wait up to a week or more before the boat can be used. If you are in a hurry, the tedious walk along the fjord is the only option. In all, the 100km (60 mile) journey from Pangnirtung to Asgard takes at least five days with heavy loads.

Helicopters are not a permanent feature at Pangnirtung and the policy of the Auyuittuq National Park authorities is ambivalent on their use – occasionally helicopters have taken climbing parties in. For information on the policy, as well as costs of boat and skidoo transport, write to: Auyuittuq National Park, Baffin Island, North West Territories, XOA OHO, Canada.

facilities
Fuel and all types of food, except freeze-dried, are available at Pangnirtung.

Most climbers use the campsite 3km (2 miles) north-east of Pangnirtung as the night hotel is expensive. Alcohol is not allowed at Pangnirtung.

Three bivouac shelters are provided by the park authorities: one at the fjord-head, one at Windy Lake, and the last at Summit Lake. They have radios for emergency use and for arranging to meet a boat or skidoo at the fjord-head.

when to climb
The best time to climb is early July to mid-August. Earlier in the season the weather tends to be clearer, but with snow and ice on the rock. By September the weather is colder and bleaker, but the glaciers are dry of snow and the rock is free of snow and ice.

gear
Besides big-wall climbing gear, food, fuel, tents, and bivouac equipment, for most of the summer (except towards the end of August) it is wise to have snowshoes or touring skis as the snow can be very soft on the upper glaciers.

maps and guidebooks
The best map is 'Pangnirtung District of Franklin North West Territories' (1964).

There is no guidebook to the climbing on Baffin Island, and no complete coverage in any magazines. Try: 'Baffin Island Expedition 1953', Pat Baird, *Mountain World* (1954); *Big Wall Climbing*, Doug Scott; 'Baffin Commentary', Eugene Fisher, *High* Magazine (February 1995); and 'Baffin Island Dream Wall', Chris Breemer, *Canadian Alpine Journal* (1996). Also comb American and Candian Alpine Journals. *Desnivel* is useful for all climbing activity done by Spaniards.

language
English and Inuit.

rescue and insurance
There is no resident rescue team at Pangnirtung so you must be self-sufficient.

red tape
None.

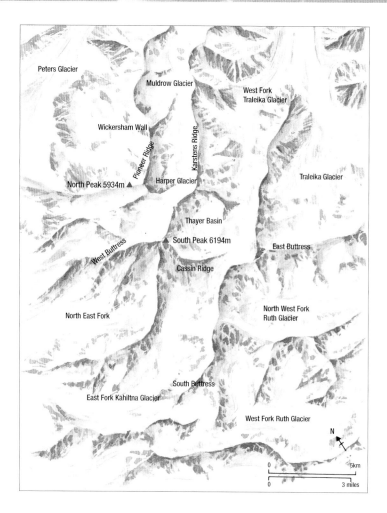

it with the Himalayan giants. In addition, its position at latitude 63°N makes it arguably the coldest mountain outside Antarctica and, because of the lower barometric pressure near the poles, the problems of acclimatization are similar to those experienced at 7000m (23,000ft) in the Himalaya. The nearest town is Talkeetna and the mountain is situated within Denali National Park and Preserve.

Each year more than a thousand people from many nations come to climb Denali. On the normal route, guided parties predominate, campsites are sociable and, during periods of good weather, the trail is apparent. Yet even this onslaught does not subjugate the mountain. Nearly half fail in their attempts to reach the summit, turned aside by snowfall, cold, wind, or altitude. Whether they succeed or fail, visitors return from Denali knowing that they have met with a formidable mountain whose popularity belies its seriousness. On all routes, crevasses, avalanches, and icefall are significant threats. High on the mountain, even on the popular western slopes, there is a real sense of isolation and commitment.

ridges, faces, and peaks

Denali is a majestic mountain of high glacial basins divided by a complex system of ridges and spurs. The mountain has two summits, the North Peak, at 5934m (19,470ft), and the higher South Summit, at 6194m (20,320ft). But it is the ridges, often knife-edged and dramatically corniced, that most epitomize Alaskan climbing. Three large glaciers entangle the massif: to the north-east the Muldrow; to the south-east the Ruth and its tributaries; and to the south-west the Kahiltna, from which the airstrip on the South East Fork gives access to most of the popular routes.

The 17.5km (11 mile) Pioneer Ridge stretches from Gunsight Pass to North Peak, 5934m (19,470ft), forming the western bank of the Muldrow and Harper Glaciers. It affords superb views across the Wickersham Wall and the tundra to the north. Awkward 'sawteeth' pinnacles lower down on the Pioneer Ridge proved a barrier to the first comers but, higher up, towards North Peak, though it is still steep, the difficulties moderate. Most ascents are made from the Muldrow Glacier, gaining the ridge at 4000m (13,100ft). The ridge was not climbed in its entirety until 1988.

mount mckinley

roger mear

Mt McKinley or, to give it its native name, Denali, is the highest peak in North America. The Alaskan Range, with Denali at its hub, rises dramatically from the surrounding plains, giving a vertical interval between tundra and summit of almost 6000m (19,700ft) in less than 50km (30 miles). Such a rise is surpassed only in the Himalaya, by the plunge from the summit of Nanga Parbat into the Indus Valley. Denali's stature, if not its altitude, ranks

Right **Air taxi is the only practical way to approach Denali and the other high Alaskan peaks.**

1932 The first use of aircraft by climbers on McKinley, when Allen Carpé and Theodore Koven were landed on the Muldrow Glacier by Pilot Joe Crosson. Aeroplane assistance is now an integral part of Denali climbing.

1951 B Washburn's American expedition climbed the West Buttress, which soon replaced the Muldrow Glacier as the normal route.

1954 First ascent of the enormous South Buttress of Denali and the first traverse of the mountain by E Thayer, L Viereck, M Wood, and G Argus (Thayer was killed during the descent).

1961 R Cassin's Italian team climbed the elegant and difficult spur on the South Face – the Cassin Ridge.

1963 P Lev, R Newcomb, and A Read reached the summit via the East Buttress in a team including W Bleser, J Williamson, and F Wright. A Canadian team made the first ascent of the West Side of the Wickersham Wall. The North Peak was reached by G Prinz, H Schwarz and H Gmoser. In the same month a dangerous new route up the East Side of the Wickersham Wall was climbed by members of the Harvard Mountaineering Club: H Abrons, P Carman, C Goetze, J Graham, D Jensen, R Milikan, and D Roberts.

1967 First winter ascent of the mountain by an 8-man team; the summit was reached by A Davidson and R Genet. A Japanese team made the second ascent of the Cassin Ridge, climbing the 60° couloir that has become the standard route.

1967 The difficult South Face ('American Direct Route') was climbed by Eberl, Laba, Thompson, and Seidman. They fixed over 2000m (6500ft) of rope.
1970 N Uemura (Japanese) was the first to make a successful solo ascent of the mountain.
1976 D Scott and D Haston (British) climbed the South Face in alpine style in 14 days by a variation of the 'American Direct'. This was the first time a major new route had been climbed without recourse to fixed ropes. C Porter soloed the Cassin Ridge in two days.
1980 J Roberts and S McCartney climbed a new route on the South West Face. McCartney was rescued from 6000m (19,700ft) on the Cassin Ridge.
1982 M Young, R Mear (British), and J Waterman made the first winter ascent of the Cassin Ridge in eight days (only the second time Denali had been climbed in winter). The remote Isis Face was climbed by J Tackle on his third attempt. M Hesse soloed the Haston/Scott route.
1983 B Becker led R Graage up the Denali Diamond on the South West Face, probably the most technically difficult route on the mountain.
1984 N Uemura (Japanese) disappeared while descending the West Buttress. He had reached the summit on his birthday, becoming the first to climb Denali alone and in winter.
1985 R Casarotto (Italian) climbed the 'Ridge of No Return'. This was the first significant new route climbed solo.
1988 The complete Pioneer Ridge of North Peak was climbed by R Laver

northern side The Wickersham Wall makes up the vast northern face of Denali, a gigantic 7km (4½ mile) sweep of hanging glaciers and séracs that slide from North Peak to the Peters Glacier, 4000m (13,100ft) below.

The massive North West Buttress rises steeply from the Peters Glacier, eventually linking with the North Peak. Its base is reached in 17km (11 miles) from the South East Fork of the Kahiltna Glacier.

western side The West Buttress forms the watershed between Peters and Kahiltna Glaciers, with the Kahiltna Pass at 3140m (10,300ft) offering passage between the two. Because of its accessibility from the air-taxi base on the South East Fork of Kahiltna Glacier, the West Buttress remains the most popular route on the mountain and it has spawned a host of direct starts, variations, and eliminates for added spice. It is 27km (17 miles) from the Kahiltna Base. The West Rim is a subsidiary ridge joining the West Buttress at Windy Corner. The West Rib, too, rises from this side, from the North East Fork of the Kahiltna Glacier. It provides a shorter, more direct route to the summit, but its closeness to the Cassin Ridge means that it tends to get overlooked in favour of its neighbour.

southern side The majestic southern aspect of McKinley rears above the heads of the North East and East Forks of the Kahiltna Glacier, divided by the shadowed edge of the Cassin Ridge. This is the definitive image of Denali, and the Cassin is internationally recognized as one of the world's great

Below **Descending the upper Karstens Ridge, with the upper Muldrow Glacier on the left.**

climbs. Although there are direct routes that are harder and more demanding on the overpowering 3000m (10,000ft) granite walls found to the right of the ridge, none has the classic elegance of this giant spur running straight to the summit.

McKinley's South Buttress, extending a massive 20km (12 miles) to the Kahiltna South East Fork airstrip, has only recently been climbed in its entirety.

south-eastern side Cradled between the giant arms of the South Buttress, the South East Spur, and the East Buttress lies Mt McKinley's remote and magical land, the Ruth. Here, from beginnings in the West or North West Forks of the Ruth Glacier, there are climbs without summits, fantastically sculpted crests with romantic names and formidable reputations, that deposit the climber a long way from home, high on one of McKinley's main ridges. Some climbs, like the 'Ridge of No Return', 'Reality Ridge', or the 'Isis Face', are among the most difficult on McKinley.

The Isis Face in particular is an elegant and difficult ice arête, and the double-corniced Ridge of No Return, culminating on the South Ridge, is surely the supreme Alaskan experience. It was first climbed, solo and alpine style, by the Italian mountaineer Renato Casarotto in 1985. However, even the climbs of earlier generations, such as the aptly named, crevassed Catacomb Ridge, and the South East Spur itself, are long excursions into a remote corner of the mountain.

eastern side The North East or Traleika Spur rises between the West and Main Forks of the Traleika Glacier and joins the East Buttress, east of the Thayer Basin. It affords a high-level expedition, crossing two 3500m (11,500ft) peaks and two avalanche-threatened icefalls, finished via the North East Ridge.

The Thayer Basin, tucked under the North East Ridge and the Main Summit, gives access to the hidden, icefall-threatened, unclimbed East Face – the last virgin face of Denali.

The long north–south Karstens Ridge provides the eastern bank of the Muldrow Glacier and, avoiding the icefall at its head, gives access to the higher Harper Glacier.

future climbing

Beyond the obvious challenge that the East Face presents, there are significant variations to existing routes possible, though all will be harder and more dangerous than those that were done previously.

Right **Jon Waterman during the first winter ascent of the Cassin Ridge.**

East Buttress

South Peak

North Peak

Denali Pass

Pioneer Ridge

Wickersham Wall

Gunsight Pass

1

Harper Glacier

23

23

2

5

4

23

3

1

Traleika Glacier

Muldrow Glacier

1

north side

Long and remote glacier climbs, these routes are popular with those looking to get away from the crowds on the West Buttress.

1 The Muldrow and Harper Glaciers Alaskan Grade 2

W Harper, H Karstens, 'Tatumand', and H Stuck 1913; North Peak: P Anderson and W Taylor 1910
This route was the normal route to the summit until 1951. Today, the relative solitude and the 30km (18 mile) approach from Wonder Lake add the element of wilderness missing on the south-east fork of the Kahiltna. The route has 30–40° ice and snow and takes 14–28 days. Overall distance is 30km (18 miles).

2 The Pioneer Ridge Alaskan Grade 4

A Baur, D Lyon, L Fowler, D Haumann, and S Heiberg 1961
Ascent is up the Muldrow Glacier, gaining the ridge at 4000m (13,000ft), avoiding the pinnacles of route (3).

3 Integral route

R Laver, C Maffei, T Cancroft, and R Waitman 1988
This route has up to 70° snow and

ice, and class 5 rock pinnacles. It is 17km (11 miles) long and takes 14–29 days.

the wickersham wall

Because of the high threat of icefall, the technicality of the routes, and the avalanche risk on account of its general low angle, the Wickersham Wall has never been and is unlikely to become popular.

4 Wickersham Wall Harvard Route Alaskan Grade 4+

H Abrons, P Carman, C Goetze, J Graham, D Jensen, R Millikan, and D Roberts 1963
So far unrepeated, this generally low-angle route is highly threatened by icefall and avalanches. It takes 13–25 days and is 11km (7 miles).

5 Wickersham Wall Canadian Route Alaskan Grade 3

G Prinz, H Schwarz, and H Gmoser 1963
Alpine style: Nobel, McLean, Lees, and Wyatt 1910
This route has 10–45° snow and ice climbing with little technical terrain. The first part of the route is exposed to hanging glaciers and the latter part is particularly dangerous after

snowstorms. It is about 16km (10 miles); allow 12–24 days.

west side

These are the most popular routes on the mountain due to their accessibility. They offer the most straightforward as well as the most difficult lines on Denali.

6 North West Buttress Alaskan Grade 4

Beckey, Hackett, McClean, Maybohm, and Wilson 1954
A remote and seldom climbed route to the North Peak, with ice up to 65°, offering mixed rock and ice climbing. The 14km (9 mile) route takes 12–25 days.

7 West Buttress Alaskan Grade 2

Ambler, Bishop, Buchtel, Gale, Griffiths, Hackett, More, and B Washburn 1951
The most popular route on the mountain and, with a 40–50° snow and ice headwall from 4600–4900m (15,000–16,000ft), always a serious proposition. There is significant crevasse risk on the Kahiltna and commitment above 5200m

(17,000ft). Despite the infilling, the parent route remains supreme. Allow 10–24 days for the 27km (17 miles).

8 West Rim Alaskan Grade 4

Ehman and Morrow 1977
This is the 1200m (4000ft) buttress rising out of the north east fork of the Kahiltna Glacier, ending at 4300m (14,000ft), on the edge of the basin on the West Buttress. It provides airy and spectacular climbing on a knife-edge ridge, and ice up to 70°. It should take approximately 3–5 days and is around 1.5km (1 mile) long.

9 West Rib Alaskan Grade 3

Breitenbach, Buckingham, Corbet, and Sinclair 1959
A superb, moderately difficult, snow and ice climb, 40–50° up the initial couloir. The possibility of a 'bale out' at half-height (4300m/14,000ft), into the basin on the West Buttress, means it is not such a committing proposition as it sometimes first appears. Allow 14–24 days for this 5km (3 mile) route.

North West Buttress
North Peak
South Peak
West Rib
West Rim
Denali Pass
West Buttress
Kahiltna
Glacier North East
Fork
Kahiltna
Glacier

how to get to mount mckinley

Fly to Anchorage International airport where Denali, Mount Foraker, and Mount Hunter are visible 220km (140 miles) to the north. Getting around Anchorage, like most American cities, is difficult without a car. There are several operations offering transportation by road between Anchorage and Talkeetna, and most of the Talkeetna air services will shuttle climbers back and forth from Anchorage. The Alaska Railroad runs a once-weekly train in spring, and begins its daily service in May. The train has a licensed buffet car.

The small, thriving town of Talkeetna is the jumping-off point for those routes on the west, south, and east of the mountain. Denali Park, the next stop up the line, is for those heading to Muldrow Glacier and the northern routes. There is a 40-minute flight from Talkeetna over One Shot Pass onto the South East Fork of the Kahiltna Glacier. West Buttress climbers must continue up the arduous Ski Hill until just below Kahiltna Pass, where the Glacier turns east to squeeze under the base of the West Buttress at

Windy corner and into the snow basin at 4200m (13,800ft).

There are four air-taxi operators who fly onto the southern glaciers from Talkeetna, and one in the town of Denali Park who will fly into Kantishna before the road to Wonder Lake opens at the end of May each year.

facilities

Anchorage is the last dependable place for provisioning an expedition, but be aware that the availability of specialist mountain food and equipment is limited.

In Talkeetna, camping is free; there are restaurants, bars, a couple of small hotels, and a post office, but no bank. There is a general store with limited supplies, and some of the guide services sell or hire sledges and equipment.

when to climb

The winter climbing season runs from 21 December–21 March, when the hills are silent and empty but there is little light and it is intensely cold. The normal climbing season starts in late April.

The weather is thought to be more stable then, but high winds still sweep the mountain and even in May temperatures can drop well below -40°C (-40°F). Be wary of route descriptions measured in days, for endless daylight enables an Alaskan day to be as long as it takes. June and July are warmer, but the moist maritime air blowing in from the south brings summer storms that can last several days and dump feet of snow. By August the warm temperatures make the glaciers and lower slopes hazardous.

gear

Plastic double boots should be the warmest available and loose-fitting; an extra layer of 5mm (¼in) close cell foam under your foot between the inner boot and the shell adds insulation where you most need it. Overboots are advisable for high on the mountain. A good wind shell is essential: many climbers wear 1-piece suits, and you'll need a large hood. Ski goggles and face protection are a must. A duvet jacket is recommended and insulated pants should be considered.

Camp bootees are nice! Hand protection should be well integrated, so that layers, including spares, are compatible with each other. The cold affects the performance of every mundane task as materials stiffen, so pay particular attention to fitting crampons. Gloves, stuffsacks, and rucksacks all need to be twice as big as you imagine. Fit wrist-loops to mitts and long tags to all zips, on clothing, tent, and pack. It is a good idea to preserve the loft in down sleeping bags: a Gore-Tex shell and a vapour-barrier liner will help.

Though the normal route presents no particular technical difficulty, crevasses on the Kahiltna are a serious hazard. All members of the party should be practised in roped travel and improvised rescue. Carry wands to mark snow caves and caches and to add to those marking the route. Skis or snowshoes are used by many parties and, while they are not essential, skis in particular make the glacier safer. Multi-fuel stoves are the norm; white gas the standard fuel.

(continued on page 97)

Cassin Ridge

South East Ridge

Kahiltna Glacier East Fork

south face

The stupendous face of Denali, offering steep technical routes of great quality.

10 South West Face Alaskan Grade 6

J Roberts and S McCartney 1980
Difficult, mixed climbing and rock difficulties up to 5.9. 20–24 days.

11 Denali Diamond Alaskan Grade 6+

B Becker 1983
Extremely difficult, mixed climbing including an 8m (25ft) roof (5.9, A3), combined with sections of vertical ice, makes this arguably the most difficult route. Allow 20–24 days.

12 Cassin Ridge Alaskan Grade 5

Airoldi, Alippi, Canali, R Cassin, Perego, and Zucchi 1961
A superb, justifiably renowned classic with ice up to 70° in the

Japanese Couloir, a fine corniced arête and short sections of 5.7 climbing on sound, red granite through the rock bands below 5000m (16,500ft). The route takes 7–14 days.

13 Czech Direct Alaskan Grade 6+

Adam, Krizo, and Korl 1984
This is objectively safer but technically harder than the other South Face routes, with sustained difficulties, 60–100° ice and 5.6 rock, and poor bivouac sites on the first 1500m (5000ft). About 12–21 days.

14 American Direct Alaskan Grade 6

Eberl, Laba, Thompson, and Seidman 1967
An indirect route that climbs the buttress on the right side of the South Face and gains the South East Ridge at 5800m (19,000ft). The sustained snow and ice climbing

(50–65°) in the lower part is swept by powder slides during snow storms, and is followed by difficult mixed climbing on the upper buttresses (5.7, A2). The route takes 7–14 days.

15 Scott/Haston route

D Scott and D Haston 1976
This was the first time a major route had been done in alpine style on Mt McKinley. It took 14 days.

the ruth and the east

Remote ridges, which see few people but offer the epitome of Alaskan climbing.

16 South Buttress Alaskan Grade 3

P Lev, R Newcomb, and A Read 1963
A 20km (12 mile) level journey with the Ramp and Ruth Glacier

approaches exposed to avalanche. This route can take anything between 14 and 28 days.

17 Ridge of No Return Alaskan Grade 6

R Casarotto 1985
A spectrally double-corniced ridge giving sustained climbing on snow and ice at 50–70° with some overhanging sections followed by 1200m (3900ft) of mixed climbing, finishing at 4500m (14,800ft) on the South Buttress. About 12–21 days; the first climb made five bivouac sites; 11km (7 miles).

18 Isis Face Alaskan Grade 5+

Stutzman and J Tackle 1982
Elegant and exposed climbing on a knife-edged ridge. 60° ice with overhanging sections; rock 5.8 and A1. This route takes 10–21 days and is 10km (6 miles) long.

Ridge of No Return

South Buttress

Reality Ridge

South East Spur

Catacomb Ridge

Traleika Spur

Ruth Glacier North West Fork

19 Reality Ridge Alaskan Grade 4+

Thuermer 1975

A spectacular fluted, knife-edged ridge with rock gendarmes (5.5, A2) and considerable cornicing, leading to a remote position on the South East Spur. The route will take approximately 12–24 days and is 11km (7 miles).

20 South East Spur Alaskan Grade 4

Cochrane and Everett 1962

A difficult and unfrequented climb. Ice up to 65° and lots of cornicing. The route is about 13km (8 miles); allow 12–24 days.

21 East Buttress Alaskan Grade 4

P Lev, R Newcomb, and A Read 1963

This long (15km/9 mile) route is remote with some exposure to avalanche. It takes approximately 12–26 days.

22 Catacomb Ridge Alaskan Grade 4

Anderson, Brenner, Davidson, Fries, Given, Jones, and Reagan 1969

A spectacular knife-edged and corniced ridge with ice up to 70°. About 14–28 days and 15km (9 miles).

23 Traleika Spur Alaskan Grade 3

Jacober, Johnson, Pettigrew, Stewart, Schmidt, and Ruth 1973

A 17km (11 mile), unrepeated, high-level expedition crossing two 3600m (12,000ft) peaks and two avalanche-threatened icefalls *en route* to the summit. It takes about 16–30 days.

Your tent will need to be dug out (perhaps daily) and you'll need to erect snow walls to give it shelter – a large aluminium snow shovel is necessary.

maps and guidebooks

The best map is 'Mount McKinley', Dr Bradford Washburn, 1:50,000 (Boston Museum of Science). A useful book is *High Alaska, a historical guide to Denali, Mount Foraker and Mount Hunter*, Jonathan Waterman (American Alpine Club, 1988).

language

English.

rescue and insurance

It is the policy of Denali National Park to assist those in need, but rescue is not automatic and it is best to be self-sufficient. Rescue bills are often high but, if your expedition has complied with all the regulations, the park often waives them. It is wise to be insured.

red tape

You must register with the Talkeetna Ranger Station at least 60 days before you arrive. The address is: Denali National Park and Preserve, PO Box 588, Talkeetna, Alaska 99676. You must also check in and out at the Station. Backcountry permits are required for any overnight stay on the North Side of Denali; obtainable at the Backcountry Desk in the Denali Visitor Centre.

Leave nothing behind. You can be fined for improper disposal of garbage and human waste.

six hard days
on the cassin
barry
blanchard

Climbers' feet have compressed a track into the broken surface of the North East Fork of the Kahiltna Glacier. My black crampons bite into the firm snow and lead me through a giant's jumble of castle-sized blocks, moated and delineated by the deep, sagging troughs of bottomless crevasses. Kevin and I keep the rope tight, ice climbing through sways and over walls towards Mt McKinley. Overhead, tiers of blue séracs reach into a sky one shade darker. We do not dawdle. Ahead the Cassin Ridge slices cleanly into the sky.

'Oh man, there's something wrong with the stove!' Kevin hisses out the words. A plume of blue flame escapes from a fractured brazing just below the burner. Snow pressed into the pot minutes ago is an opaque damp grey. It should have melted and boiled by now. Instantly I have the feeling our attempt is threatened, a sinking sensation, as if my heart is being dragged under black water. We are camped inside the bergschrund at the base of the Japanese Couloir and without the stove we'll be screwed. 'OK, we might be able to fix it. Give me a chocolate bar.' Kevin-the-carpenter takes charge. I roll tinfoil from the bar wrapper into tight match-size pieces and Kev tamps them into the broken braze with the micro-driver from his Swiss Army knife. An hour later the stove is burning hotter than when new, but a seed of doubt has been planted: will it keep working? More seeds will sprout during the climb. Given enough doubt and fear we will retreat, but it is the last week of May 1982 and we are both 23 years old so it takes quite a field of doubt to turn us around – far more than it will in later years.

It took us 10 hours to climb the Japanese Couloir; the storm caught us five hours into it. Looking back, there are things I would do differently. Less weight. Accept that I am going to lose bodyweight – 9kg of it. Pare things down until I can lead with a pack and the second can follow on jumars ... or climb.

The top of the couloir is a spider's web of rotting fixed lines, worse than we'd ever seen. Really ugly. We get our tent three-quarters pitched on the only ledge, where the storm batters us all night.

I lead over shattered granite, which is like a decaying Celtic ruin, yet solid to the grip because of ice setting the pieces in place. At the anchor I rappel to jumar with my pack, the ground

being too serrated to haul over. Two carries again. The storm is getting mean. Wind-raking waves of ice shards across my face push the sick work of advancing the packs into an annoying labour. And anger rises in us: 'We can suffer more. We are good at suffering.'

On our second trip across, the storm begins to break up and we catch brief glimpses of the sun, momentary rushes of its heat. The powdery storm snow over steel-grey ice demands attention. A tightrope of ice traverses the edge of the storm as it quits the sky one mile up. We camp at 4260m on a large shelf just below the hanging glacier. Doubts quieten, anger is long gone. Bundled up, we stay outside for as long as we can, gorging ourselves on food and drinks and Denali.

Morning. Kevin explodes up the hanging glacier and it is all I can do to keep up. We climb with our full packs. Heavy work. All the pores in my skin dilate at once and I am glazed in sweat by the time I catch him. I feel as if I've been dipped in cooking oil. In front of us is a rock band, its golden walls already awash in mist. We climb up clean dihedrals cleaved into bronze-coloured granite. The rock is as angular as quarry-cut blocks but rising in clean sweeps of hundreds of metres. Occasional fixed pitons provide protection and I place one large friend, the only rock runner we put in on the route. The mist matures to a storm through the day and again we are slapped by the wind and abraded by snow. Spindrift forces our jaws onto our chests. Hoods drawn, heads bowed, penitent – suffering again.

The light is feeble and fading, the storm strong. We lash the tent to ice screws on a sloping ledge right on the edge of the

Left **Barry Blanchard at the 4260m (14,000ft) camp on Cassin Ridge.**

Below **Barry Blanchard climbing on the Tent Arête.**

Cassin. Inside we pile our packs and food and ropes in an effort to get horizontal. We're too exhausted to cook. We've climbed 38 out of the last 44 hours. I pry my feet from frozen supergaiters and boots. Diaphragm-cramped, breath-compressed, I wrestle into my two sleeping bags. The small final arrangements are made during brief fits of being wakened by hands going numb outside the bag, by my skull burning from the bite of the helmet.

The first 160kph blast of wind flattens the tent and pulls ripstop nylon over my face like a clingfilm seal. The fly shears instantly, spinning and flapping from its sole remaining anchor. It goes. Light floods into my eyes as if someone has switched on a searchlight. My reaction is reflexive. I swear and bolt upright, clawing my hands free of the bag and thrusting at the suffocating nylon. The wind backs off, then smacks us again, driving my face into my knees. I choke on the fear of having the wind reach under the tent and pry us off the mountain!

Then he oversteps the edge ... tumbles into the white-out ...

'Blanch! We have to hold the shape of the tent! It'll blow apart if we don't hold the shape!' Kevin screams from close by. I see nothing but a trembling tunnel of white nylon and shattered plates of frost vibrating away from it.

For the next three hours we fight the wind. I wrap the draw cord from the snow portal around my hand like a leather rein. Kevin does the same with the cord to the door. We lean our backs hard into the wind, haul on the cords, and try to keep the dome of the tent established. The wind pummels us. It is like large men running at the tent and hurling their shoulders and weight and speed into our backs. I feel their punches in my ribs in the surges of breath beaten from my lungs.

In time our hands go numb from the choke of the draw cords and we plan when to regain our grips so that one of us is always holding the shape. Our breath stands as mist and the ambient tension is visible in it: the mist jerks and quivers to the slapping of the tent walls. After two hours the violence and frequency of the hits diminish and we prepare to leave the tent. Outside, the sky has blown clear. We hear and see the wind screaming over the South Shoulder: it has taken the mountain down to ice there. At 4740m we feel exposed, unprotected ... lucky. All the tent poles have deformed, one has been snapped. A seam in the body of the tent has split for 15cm and the fly has lost all its anchoring toggles save one. We carry out our makeshift repairs and climb away.

Three pitches of mixed ground lead us into the large glacial couloirs that form the top half of the route. We drag the ropes behind us, cramponing up slowly and beside each other. At 5190m we find a good platform, pitch our crippled tent, and set about catching up on fluids and food.

The evening has become one of the precious gems that I have sifted from 20 years of mountaineering. Kevin and I: truly happy, exactly where we want to be, have wanted to be, have strived to the limit of our entire abilities to be. We stand content and firm on our balcony hacked from the edge of Denali.

The tops of clouds tumble by at 48kph. We catch stroboscopic flashes of sunlight far off on the shadowed lowland, the glowing shoulders of Denali. These framed images give the illusion of motion, as if we're sailing through the sky. 'Pretty damn cool, eh Blanch?' 'Beautiful, man, too beautiful.'

Two hours into the next day, at 5640m, I reach my limit. Flashes of pain ring in my skull every time I force 20 steps; scary moments of dizziness. My stoic friend informs me that he's been pushing past this point for two days. We stop and camp.

Morning. Our sixth day on the route. Visibility pulsates from a white-out to a misty 100m. Kevin cannot be persuaded to stop. We solo together through the clouds. It is cold and each breath a labour but the climbing is fun. Our packs are finally light enough to climb with.

Cresting the Summit Ridge, visibility contracts to 6m at best. Kevin leads with our one set of goggles (his) and only ski poles (also his). He uses the ski poles like white canes, halting abruptly, and often, when he can no longer sense the ridge. I follow close on his heels, practically blind in my glacier glasses. Then he oversteps the edge and is hauled away, as if some claw has surfaced from the underworld and yanked him down. He tumbles into the white-out, limbs splaying, torso churning, carving a swathe into the white. I scream, 'KEVIN!' He stops 10m down, spread-eagled in the snow. Lowering him an axe and a rope end, I step back onto the South Face to belay him up.

No higher ground, a cluster of wands and pickets and rope, 6194m – the summit. Can't see three metres...it's just like the inside of a Ping-Pong ball. We snap two photographs, shoulder our packs, and stagger off – and down – Mt McKinley.

1925 A joint Canadian/American expedition succeeded in climbing the mountain. The achievement was an exceptional *tour de force* involving a reconnaissance during the summer of 1924, a provision expedition during the bitterly cold winter of 1925, and, finally, the first ascent during May and June 1925. Led by A H MacCarthy, the summit team included F Lambart,

N Read, A Taylor, A Carpe, and W W 'Billy' Foster.
1957 An American party, led by D Monks, ushered in a new era of climbing on the mountain. Rather than repeating the 'King Trench' route, they climbed the East Ridge, the first of the dozen major ridge routes.
1965 A group of California mountaineers completed the ascent of the South

Ridge (The Hummingbird Ridge). This set a new standard for boldness, and it was several decades before the ridge received a second ascent (it is unlikely to have been repeated in its entirety).
1977 A group of Canadian climbers from Vancouver ascended the Warbler Ridge on Logan.
1979 A group of Calgary climbers, led by J Lauchlan, climbed the technically

demanding South West Buttress in a 15-day, alpine style push.
1984 In March, a group from Vancouver climbed to the West Summit.
1986 The mountain received its first winter ascent on 16 March, when a group of Alaskan climbers reached the Central Summit.
1987 Prominent climbers D Cheesmond (Canadian) and Catherine Freer

mount logan

chic scott

Mount Logan is the highest mountain in Canada, standing at 5959m (19,550ft) above sea level. It forms the centre of the St Elias Range and, located at about 60° north latitude, in Canada's Yukon Territory, is only 50km (30 miles) from the Pacific Ocean. The combination of its high altitude, the extreme arctic temperatures, and the storms from the Gulf of Alaska make it one of the most heavily glaciated regions on the planet.

Mount Logan remains one of the undiscovered treasures of the mountaineering world. Although popular with Canadian climbers, it has largely been ignored by the rest of the international climbing community, being somewhat overshadowed by Alaska's Mount McKinley or Denali (*see pages 90–97*). Only about 12 parties reach the summit of Mount Logan each year, and they usually follow the classic 'King Trench' route or go via the East Ridge. This small number of visitors is surprising considering that the mountain offers some of the greatest climbing challenges outside the Himalaya, but it does mean that there is plenty of scope for those who make the trip.

ridges, faces, and peaks

Logan is a complex mountain, about 30km (18½ miles) long and 20km (12½ miles) wide. At the core is a glacial plateau, from which arise numerous peaks, the main summits being the West 5925m (19,440ft), Central 5959m (19,550ft), and East 5900m (19,360ft). Radiating like spokes from the central plateau is a multitude of long ridges and flying buttresses, extending up to 10km (6 miles) out into the surrounding glaciers. There are two major faces, the South Face and the North Face.

Above the huge, icy expanse of the Seward Glacier, the South Face rises some 4000m (13,000ft) and is 30km (18½ miles) wide. It has long ridges and its steep walls are hung with séracs.

The North Face, also about 4000m (13,000ft), is very similar to the South Face, only more heavily glaciated. The routes on the North Face are not as long as those on the South because the summit plateau dips lower on that side of the mountain.

There are several faces on the South East Side, between the Hummingbird Ridge and the Hubsew Ridge. The Hummingbird Ridge has it own special place in North American climbing mythology, and is the ultimate in long, narrow, corniced ridges. The adjacent Warbler Ridge is also extremely difficult, offering some of the finest climbing on Mount Logan.

climbing on mount logan

Mount Logan is a wilderness mountain, and, unlike European peaks, where decades of ascents and epic struggles have given definition to routes, there is little in the way of man-made character to its climbs. Each one is long, icy, often heavily corniced, dangerous, and exposed to extreme weather and avalanche hazard. The rock, which is simply frost-shattered granite-diorite, shows through on some of the faces, but the climbing is generally on snow on top of ice. The exception is the South West Buttress, on which there is a significant amount of rock climbing.

future climbing

The rocky faces of the mountain have not yet been touched by climbers, as they are very dangerous propositions. The unclimbed walls of the South East Face are the great future alpine challenges. Over 3000m (10,000ft) high, technically difficult, and subject to violent weather in this arctic environment, they offer exciting climbs for the next millennium.

Right **Among the séracs on Mount Logan, one of the great wilderness mountains of the world.**

(American) disappeared from the Hummingbird Ridge. A tent was found hanging from the side of the corniced ridge. It is likely that they had plunged to their deaths when a cornice broke. **1992** Following confusion over Logan's height, a Geological Survey of Canada expedition took a satellite dish to the summit, and ascertained it to be 5959m (19,550ft).

Hubsew Ridge

East Ridge

Catenary Ridge

West Peak

South
West
Buttress

All of the climbs described here are serious, wilderness, Himalayan-style undertakings. Only one piece of rock on the entire mountain has ever been given a grading – the Renshaw Chimney at 5.8.

Each route will take 7–21 days depending on acclimatization and whether the climbing is done alpine or expedition style. The routes are all 15–20km (9½–12½ miles) long.

east flank

The routes here rise steeply, making it a popular destination.

1 Hubsew Ridge

V Hoeman, A Bittenbinder, D Shaw, W Harrison, and E Ward 1967

A high-altitude snow and ice ridge, rarely climbed today.

2 East Ridge

D Collins, D Monk, C Ouellette, G Roberts, and K Ross 1957

One of the finest routes on the mountain – a true classic. The first 2000m (6500ft) follow a narrow crest offering exciting, but not difficult, climbing. The upper part of the mountain is simply a cold snow slog.

3 Catenary Ridge

C Plummer, S Connary, D Schmechel, J Given, W Bleser, and D Ingalls 1967

This ridge proved quite difficult on the first ascent and has probably not been repeated.

south face

One of the great mountain walls in the world, towering 4000m (13,000ft) above the glacier. Its flying buttress and intervening faces offer some of the best climbs in North America.

4 South West Buttress

J Lauchlan, J Elzinga, R Jotterand, and A Burgess 1979

A very difficult route, offering technical ice and rock climbing in a Himalayan setting. Climbed only once in a 15-day, alpine style push.

5 Hummingbird (South) Ridge

A Steck, J Wilson, J Evans, D Long, F Coale, and P Bacon 1965

A long and exciting ridge climb that is exceptionally difficult. This knife-edged corniced ridge offers few level places to erect a tent. The route weaves in and out of unstable masses of snow – not for the fainthearted.

6 Warbler (South East) Ridge

D Jones, F Baumann, F Thiessen, J Page, and R Bucher 1977

One of the finest difficult routes on the mountain, but rarely repeated.

7 Schoening Ridge

P Schoening, D McGowan, G Reynolds, and B Niendorff 1952

This is a short route rising about 2000m (6500ft) to join route (13) at King Col. Be wary of the complex, heavily crevassed approach.

north face

The North Face is swathed with innumerable hanging glaciers, but little has been written about it or about the routes accomplished. All the ridges are similar so there are no individual route descriptions here. Each one is long, icy, corniced, and ripe with avalanche hazard.

8 Independence Ridge

R Springgate, R Baker, D Stelling, T Stewart, G Blomberg, E Amstutz, W Bassett, E Coleman, and F Magary 1964

9 Centennial Ridge

D Jones, G Holdsworth, and J Wyss 1976

10 North Ridge

B Balderston, A Mathews, D Sweet, and K Schuttenberg 1974

11 Amenity (North West) Ridge

R Carter, M Down, J Howe, P Kindree, and J Whitmayer 1979

west flank

The mountain was first climbed from this side and 'King Trench' remains its most popular route.

12 West Ridge

S Davis, R Hirt, G Sievewright, and J Waterman 1978

The longest and most indirect route to the summit. Technical climbing on corniced ridges.

13 King Trench

A H MacCarthy, W W Foster, F Lambart, A Carpe, N Read, and A Taylor 1925

This route is over 20km (12½ miles) in length and technically easy. Skis can be used almost to the summit.

how to get to mount logan

You can reach Mount Logan by flying to Vancouver, BC, then on to Whitehorse in the Yukon Territory (serviced by commercial jet). From here, rent a car and drive to Haines Junction where a check-in with the Kluane National Park Wardens is required. Drive on to the Arctic Institute of North America on the shores of Kluane Lake, where you can camp. A 100km (62 mile) flight, over glaciers and icefields, will take you to the base of Mount Logan. Contact Icefield Ranges Expeditions, 59 13th Ave, Whitehorse, Yukon Territory, Y1A 4K6, Canada for flight information.

You can also reach Mount Logan from Alaska. Gulf Air Taxi operates from Yakutat, and Ultima Thule Expeditions operates from the Chitina Valley.

facilities

The nearest town is Haines Junction, where the Park Wardens are situated. The nearest city is Whitehorse, with a population of 20,000. Here you can find all modern amenities, including supermarkets, banks, hospitals, hotels, and car-rental agencies. Limited dehydrated food and climbing equipment is available in Whitehorse sports shops.

when to climb

Most parties climb Mount Logan in June or July. The weather is stable earlier in the season, but temperatures are colder.

gear

Expedition gear of Himalayan quality is required. Storms of up to a week in duration are common, with winds of 100kph (62mph) and temperatures as low as -40°C (-40°F). Very strong tents, warm clothing, high-altitude boots, and overboots are essential. You should take food for at least three weeks, as air pick-up is always subject to weather. Note: all unwanted material should be packed out after your expedition. It cannot be assumed that rubbish will be buried by snow and gone forever.

maps and guidebooks

There are no guidebooks to Mount Logan, but there are some good maps to the area that you can purchase via: Canada Map Office, 130 Bentley Ave, Napean, Ontario, K1A OE9, Canada. TOPO Maps 'Mount Saint Elias 115 B' and 'Mount Saint Elias 115 C' are very helpful, as is 'Mt Logan, Yukon', 1:100,000 (Arctic Institute of North America). The *Mount Logan Map, Research, and Reference Folio* provides a map of Mt Logan, information on all the routes described, and some history and climbing-journal references.

language

English.

rescue and insurance

Rescue is provided by Kluane National Park. However, it is expected that groups will be self-sufficient. It is advisable to get insurance cover.

red tape

Mount Logan is in Kluane National Park and permission is required to climb the mountain. Normally the authorities prefer groups of four or more people capable of self-rescue in the event of an emergency. For more information contact: Kluane National Park, Box 5495, Haines Junction, Yukon Territory, Y0B 1L0, Canada.

1907 First attempt to climb Mount Robson by Dr A P Coleman, his brother L Q Coleman, and the Rev G B Kinney (Canadian). They reached the base of the mountain after 39 days, but only advanced a short distance up the South Face before retreating.

1908 Second attempt by the Coleman brothers and Rev Kinney. They reached the base of the North East Face

(later to be known as the Kain Face). Kinney, climbing alone, discovered a potential route to the summit on the North West Flank.

1909 Rev Kinney with D 'Curly' Phillips (Canadian) reached the summit via the North West Flank. Although Phillips later revealed that they had not climbed the final 20m (65½ft) summit snow mushroom, Kinney

continued to maintain that they did reach the ultimate point.

1913 Austrian guide C Kain led A H MacCarthy (American) and W W Foster (Canadian) to the summit of Robson via the North East (Kain) Face. Kinney's ascent was discredited.

1913 Mount Robson Provincial Park was created by the British Columbian government. The construction of

a railway past the mountain enabled climbers to reach Robson without the 400km (250 mile) approach walk.

1924 C Kain led a party, including M D Geddes, T B Moffat, and M Pollard (Canadian), to the summit of Robson via the South-South-West Ridge.

1924 Phyllis Munday (Canadian) and Annette Buck (American) became the first women to climb Mount Robson.

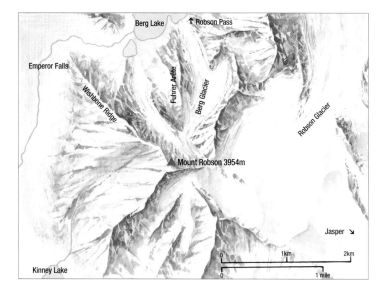

mount robson

chic scott

Mount Robson, 3954m (12,972ft), is the highest and most striking mountain in the Canadian Rockies. Located towards the northern end of the range, the peak is surrounded by the Mount Robson Provincial Park and, viewed from the Yellowhead Highway, at a distance of 10km (6 miles), it towers more than 3000m (10,000ft) above the surrounding valleys. This ice-encrusted fortress is truly 'King of the Rockies'.

Mount Robson is composed of banded, sedimentary limestone of dubious quality. Most of the climbing, however, takes place on ice and snow, and is very difficult. Moist Pacific winds blast the mountain continually, depositing snow and thick rime at higher elevations. During the winter time, the snow is deep, resulting in extensive glaciation.

Although the region is wilderness by most people's definition, the nearby town of Jasper, about 110km (70 miles) away, is a world tourist destination. Here it is possible to have the best of both worlds – solitude in a wild and virgin landscape with modern conveniences only a few hours away.

Despite the fact that Canada has many mountains, the country has attracted little international attention and Mount Robson does not see many climbers from around the globe. The Americans, however, love the Canadian Rockies, and many of them make a pilgrimage north of the border each year. In recent years, it has mainly been Americans who have pioneered climbing development on Mount Robson.

ridges, faces, and peaks

Mount Robson has two distinctly different characters. The South and West Sides get the sun and are therefore largely bare rock; the sedimentary banding can clearly be seen from the valley floor. The North Side is ice-clad and is characterized by two glaciers that stream from the mountain – the Berg Glacier, which cascades steeply down from beneath the North Face into Berg Lake; and the Robson Glacier, which makes its way from beneath the North East Face to the gravel flats near Robson Pass. The Helmet is a subsidiary upthrust from the case of the Fuhrer (North) Ridge, and is linked to it by the Helmet Col.

When hiking into Mount Robson, the complete panorama unfolds. Starting up the trail, the South Face and the South-South-West Ridge are directly in front. Past Kinney Lake and the Emperor Falls, the rocky West Flank and the Wishbone Ridge appear, with their steep cliffs interspersed with ledges covered in rubble. Heading out onto the shingle flats towards Berg Lake, the North Face gradually comes into view – first the Emperor Face, then the true North Face. This is a classic and elegant ice face, about 50°–55° and about 800m (2600ft) high. Further along towards the Robson Pass, the Fuhrer Arête comes into view, then the North East or Kain Face, a 45°, 500m (1600ft) sheet of ice.

It appears that during some years the winds form a mound of snow and ice, a 'snow mushroom', at the top of the mountain.

future climbing

The Emperor Face is *the* big climb to do on Mount Robson; there is still plenty of room for new routes on it, and it should be noted that neither of the existing routes has been repeated. A winter ascent of one of those routes would be impressive.

Right **Mount Robson from the south. At 3954m (12,972ft) this is the highest peak in the Canadian Rockies.**

1939 Swiss guide H Fuhrer, led J W Carlson and W R Hainsworth (American) up the elegant shoulder, which is now known as the Fuhrer Arête, dividing the North East Face from the North Face.

1958 The West Ridge (Wishbone Arête) was successfully climbed by the Americans D Claunch, H Firestone, and M Sherrick.

1961 R Perla and T M Spencer (American) climbed the North West (Emperor) Ridge.

1963 The North Face was climbed by Americans P Callis and D Davis.

1965 Americans A Bertulis, F Beckey, L Patterson, and T Stewart ascended the Kain Face; the first winter ascent.

1978 North Face climbed by American T Sorenson and Canadian A Henault.

1978 Americans T 'Mugs' Stump and J Logan climbed the Emperor Face.

1997 B Blanchard and J Josephson (Canadian), and S House (American) attemped the Emperor Face. They began a new route in winter, but were forced to descend when their stove malfunctioned and they were without water.

Please note that all the times given for the routes include the long walks in and out.

north face

Big and icy, the northern faces of Mount Robson offer the highest-quality routes as well as the most difficult climbing.

1 North East (Kain) Face IV ⊠

W W Foster, A H MacCarthy, and C Kain 1913

The classic route on the mountain and an outstanding achievement for its day. Not to be underrated, this is a complex, big mountain route, requiring experience, judgement, and ice-climbing skills. It is 2290m (7500ft) from the foot of the Robson Glacier and takes about four days.

2 North East (Fuhrer) Arête IV, 5.4

J W Carlson, W R Hainsworth, and H Fuhrer 1939

This route is rarely climbed, but is a high-quality, mixed rock and ice climb that takes four days. Its height is around 670m (2200ft) from the Helmet Col.

3 North Face IV

P Callis and D Davis 1963

A popular climb, this classic alpine ice route of 760m (2500ft) takes about 3–4 days.

4 Emperor Face: Cheesmond/Dick Route VI, 5.9, A2

D Cheesmond and T Dick 1981

A modern, technically difficult route of 2200m (7200ft). The first ascent required three bivouacs.

5 Emperor Face: Stump/Logan Route VI, 5.9, A2

T Stump and J Logan 1978

A modern, technically difficult route. Takes the prominent rib in the middle of the 2200m (7200ft) Emperor Face. The first ascent required four bivouacs. Rockfall is a serious hazard.

6 North West (Emperor) Ridge V, 5.6

R Perla and T M Spencer 1961

One of the biggest alpine routes in the Canadian Rockies. The lower rock ridge is not technically difficult, but is loose. The gargoyle-like snow formations at the top, stretching for hundreds of metres, are very time-consuming and insecure. This 2290m (7500ft) route normally takes about three days.

west face

Exposed to the heat of the sun, the West Face soon loses much of its snow cover. The rock is poor and the routes are rarely climbed.

7 Kinney Route IV

G B Kinney and D Phillips 1909

This is the route of the controversial first ascensionists. There is no record of it ever being repeated but it would offer a very direct line to the summit. Its length is about 2290m (7500ft) from the base of the West Face.

8 Wishbone Arête IV, 5.6

D Claunch, H Firestone, and M Sherrick 1958

This route, which is characterized by loose rock, is rarely climbed. The snow gargoyles at the top are usually the crux. The arête is about 2950m (9700ft) from the valley floor to the summit, and it normally takes three days to complete the route.

south face

This is the side of the mountain that can be seen from the Yellowhead Highway. It has the shortest approach march.

9 South-South-West Ridge IV

M D Geddes, T B Moffat, M Pollard, and C Kain 1924

This is often considered the 'normal' route and is a popular ascent, offering the fastest approach and a very direct line to the top of the mountain. The climb is not particularly technical but is long, committing, and subject to some objective hazard. It is necessary to traverse under the séracs of the South Glacier on the ascent. A small hut, Ralph Forester Hut (sleeps eight), is situated at 2500m (8200ft). Should take three days, or two if your team is particularly fast. The ridge is about 2950m (9700ft) from the Kinney Lake to the summit.

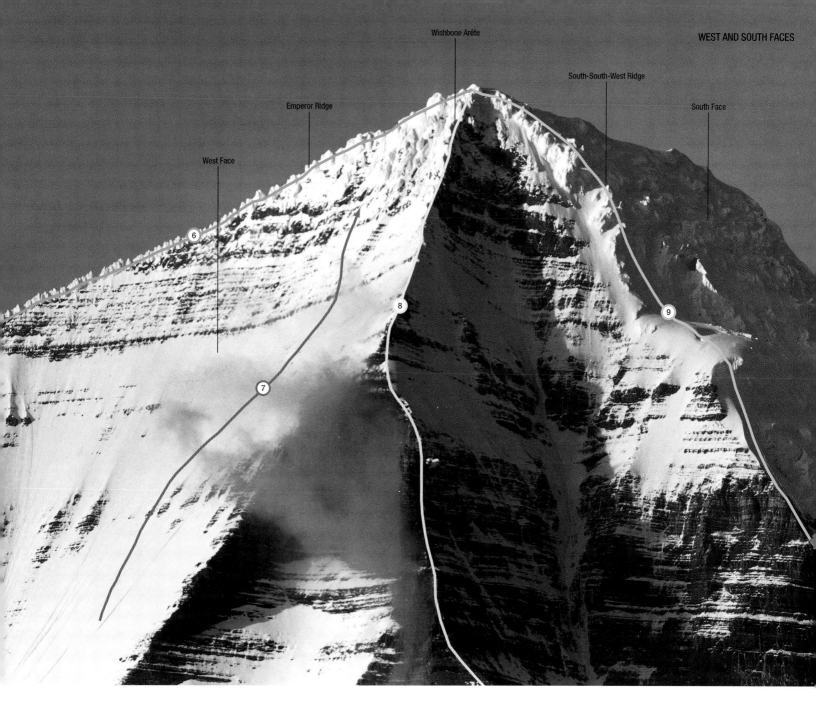

Wishbone Aréte

South-South-West Ridge

Emperor Ridge

South Face

West Face

6

7

8

9

how to get to mount robson

Mount Robson is easily accessible via the airports in Calgary or Edmonton. From there it is best to rent a car and drive to the trailhead, 90km (56 miles) west of the nearest town of Jasper.

Park your car in the large parking lot at the entrance to the valley, a short distance beyond the Mount Robson Park Headquarters, where signs will clearly indicate the trail to Mount Robson. The hike along the well-maintained trail will take you to the base of the mountain in only a few hours.

facilities

Jasper has a permanent population of about 4500, but this swells to 10,000 during the summer tourist season. Every modern convenience – medical resources, financial services, food, fuel, and auto repairs – is readily available there.

when to climb

July– September are the best months. Expect snow early in the season; later on expect ice.

gear

You will need standard alpine equipment. Few complete an ascent in a day, so it is recommended that you take bivouac gear.

maps and guidebooks

Topographical Maps for all of Canada can be purchased through the Canada Map Office at the following address: 130 Bentley Ave, Napean, Ontario, K1A OE9, Canada.

The following topographical maps are recommended: 'Mount Robson 83E', 1:250,000 and 'Mount Robson 83E/3' 1:50,000. Both are available from the Canada Map Office.

Good books are *The Rocky Mountains of Canada, North*, Robert Kruszyma and William L Putnam (the American and Canadian Alpine Clubs) and *Selected Alpine Climbs in the Canadian Rockies*, Sean Dougherty (Rocky Mountain Books).

language

English.

rescue and insurance

The mountain is located in Mount Robson Provincial Park, which is patrolled and managed by highly trained park rangers. Mountain rescue is available, but there is likely to be a charge. It is best to carry insurance.

red tape

No permits are required.

blue skies on
mount robson
ed webster

"Mount Robson, 'King of the Rockies', is daunting both in size and myth. My climbing partner, Bryan Becker, had already failed on it once; I'd only heard the legends of scouring avalanches, van-sized cornices, and rain of biblical proportions. On average, only a dozen teams attain Robson's summit annually. Defeats far outnumber the successes. For Bryan Becker and myself, this high uncertainty was one of the mountain's great attractions.

september 16, 1982 Not a single cloud! Bryan warned me it was a bear of a hike to Berg Lake. He was right – 12 miles uphill, carrying monstrous packs. The last time Bryan tried Robson, he bivvied in the rain for three days; this time we carried a tent. At milky-green Kinney Lake, we ate a trailside lunch, then ascended steep switchbacks into the Valley of a Thousand Falls.

The day was picture-perfect – the sky glowing velvet blue, the leaves turned gold by autumn's first frost, the distant glaciers dazzling. An invigorating dip in a glacial stream restored our tired legs, then more switchbacks led to beautiful Emperor Falls.

Later, from beside Berg Lake, we enjoyed our first view of Robson's North Face. No more a mythical, mist-enshrouded peak, its 7000ft of storm-raked snow and icefields exceeded my wildest expectations. The Mist Glacier rose diagonally right to left, beneath the Emperor Face and towards the North Face, our goal. Bryan casually pointed at a possible new line starting up the Mist Glacier and trending left onto the North Face's upper icefield. It was direct, feasible-looking, and objectively safe. On the spur of the moment we agreed to give it a try.

Hobbling across the frigid, thigh-deep torrent gushing from Berg Lake, I leaned on my driftwood staff like a vulnerable old man. The sun was setting; we needed a comfortable home. Above a mountainous moraine, in a tiny glen, we found one. After dinner, we discussed climbing strategy. We recognized the importance of reaching the summit in one day: bivvy sites midway were nil. To achieve such vertical mileage, we'd have to climb most of the way, if not the entire route, unroped.

Undoubtedly our plan was foolhardy. But we bet on it because we knew we made a good team. Our strength was our mutual trust, a bond forged over eight years' mastering long, hard, free routes in Colorado's Black Canyon, sandstone spires in Arizona, and New Hampshire icefalls. Tandem-soloing, a new variation up Robson's North Face, did seem impulsively dangerous, but we'd survived other harebrained climbs, so why not this, too?

Left **'And they say you can't climb overhanging ice!' Bryan Becker bouldering on the North Face of Mount Robson.**

Below left **Ed Webster on the Emperor Ridge, above the North Ridge.**

september 17 Bone-tired from the approach, we didn't leave camp till 9am. Mt Whitehorn flamed in sunshine, while icy shadows clung to Robson's North Face. Hoisting my pack, I felt a thousand nervous butterflies take flight. Yet there was no room for self-doubt. After a deep draught of crisp air, I followed Bryan up grassy slopes onto the Mist Glacier.

Fresh avalanche debris lay strewn across the run out. Donning crampons and harnesses and holstering ice tools, we scrambled over the mountain's sweepings, dodged small crevasses, then headed right into a 45° snow gully. Zigzagging up, we settled into self-controlled rhythms, Bryan in the lead.

The angle steepened near the gully's top. We switched to front-pointing, reached simultaneously for ice hammers, but our ⅜in rope stayed in Bryan's pack. Then, without warning, I needed the rope – both my crampons came off. The neoprene straps had slipped over the toes of my plastic boots. I frantically chopped a step as my boots skittered. 'Hold on, Bryan,' I yelled,

... we'd survived other harebrained climbs, so why not this, too?

feigning only slight alarm. 'I'm having a bit of trouble.' Down-climbing to investigate, Bryan had a hearty laugh at my expense.

An hour later we lunched beneath a huge sérac. Bryan appeared typically fresh; he bouldered up the sérac's 110° wall, quipping, 'And they say you can't climb overhanging ice!'

His antics made for excellent photography, which in turn gave me a good excuse not to emulate him (not that I could have done), and dispelled my nervous tension – we'd accomplished less than half the face and done none of the 'real' climbing. The 'schrund was, as expected, awkward. Sugary snow forced us to highwire-walk the sharp spine of an enormous detached ice boulder. After surmounting a fragile snow tongue, we stood at the base of the final ice slope. Only 3000ft to go.

The summit icefield, a featureless frozen blanket, humbled us. We continued soloing – Bryan remained in front, eventually by 300ft. We were united only by an occasional yell. Locked into patterned movements, which I varied every few minutes to avoid fatigue and cramping, I concentrated solely on the next 50ft. The voice of self-preservation whispered, then shouted, into my brain, and told me not to stop.

Except for the expansive views of nearby mountains and the now unnerving exposure dropping fathoms below, the climbing was tiringly monotonous. Ankles, calves, knees, and forearms burned with unstoppable fatigue. My helmeted head dropped to the slope with increasing frequency as I battled exhaustion, trying to maintain a semblance of self-control. Never before had I felt my safety so jeopardized; one slip and I'd be dead. Moment to moment, only three vital movements mattered – the firm thrust of my axe and the secure kick of each crampon.

I was grateful for Bryan's steps and axe placements, which I now used. Looking up, I noticed he'd stopped. Gossiping like two birds on a limb, we shared encouragement, food, and water. We were surprised how well everything had gone. Afterwards, I photographed Bryan climbing at close range. Always an admirer of his technique, I was speechless as he sure-footed up the 65° slope, completely at ease French technique-ing with only one ice axe above hundreds of metres of exposure.

Just below the top of the face, we encountered the route's crux – a 6ft limestone band topped by loose, granular snow. Balancing up gingerly, I sought a secure axe placement above the rock band, but the axe pick bounced off the limestone lurking beneath. Anger welled up. Bryan had paused 200ft higher, the rope still nestled in his pack. He wasn't about to downclimb and lower me an end. 'It's only one move, Ed, then it gets easier!' he encouraged. I swallowed hard; if I slipped, my next stop might be splashing into Berg Lake, a full 7000ft below. Insanity! Slowly my anger at Bryan for not offering me a belay subsided as adrenalin surged through my veins. I kicked the front-points of my left crampon into the soft limestone, gently at first, then with increasing ferocity until I'd carved two small nicks. Gritting my teeth, I muscled up – and when I felt my crampon hold, scrambled over the rock impasse. Five minutes later, I'd calmed down enough to continue.

Overhead, a figure stood erect and backlit by brilliant sunshine. Snow crystals, a stream of white sparks, blew around him, creating an unearthly apparition. Bryan had topped out onto the Emperor Ridge. I waded up the final slope of unstable windslab, asked Bryan for a belay, then thought better of it. I couldn't take the rope now, not after getting past the rock band. Bryan chuckled while I gasped up the last few steps. 'I didn't think you wanted the rope,' he grinned, 'but we might want it now. Look!'

An unforgettable sight, the infamous gargoyles, 60ft towering cream puff cornices, graced the ridge. We roped up and plunge-stepped carefully up the ridge. The snow, softened by the blazing sun, was mushy, making each belay stance a bad joke. And threading our skinny rope between the cornices gave only a hint of protection. But neither of us slipped, and after five rope-lengths of spine-tingling climbing, we scrambled onto the highest point in the Canadian Rockies.

For the first time in seven hours, we let down our guard and relaxed in the warm rays. Victory was sweet, and I savoured it even more fully with Bryan, my constant ropemate and friend. Blue skies tugged at the horizon – a rarity, we well knew – the weather was still perfect, and joyful emotions flooded to the surface as we hugged and took each other's picture. Earlier in the day I'd resolved never to do anything so impulsively dangerous again, but I now cherished this tangible summit, our memorable reward for all the perils we'd vanquished.

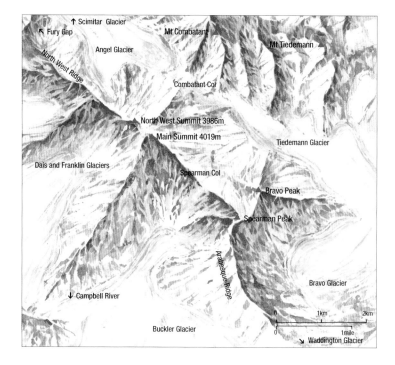

mount waddington

rob wood

At 4019m (13,186ft) Mount Waddington is the highest mountain in the British Columbia Coast Range, Canada. It lies 290km (180 miles) north-west of Vancouver and is right in the middle of one of the biggest blank sections on the road map, a heavily glaciated mountain wilderness, which even by Canadian standards is extremely rugged. The nearest town is Campbell River, 160km (100 miles) due south on Vancouver Island. Tatla Lake is a small village 80km (50 miles) to the north-east on Highway 20, which crosses the Chilcotin Plateau from Williams Lake 200km (125 miles) to the north-east, to the coast at Bella Coola, about 160 miles (100 miles) to the north-west.

The mountain is the high point on a continuous ridge forming the Crest of the Coast Range and stretching 60km (35 miles) south-east to north-west between two mighty rivers, the Homathko and the Klinaklini. Both originate in the Interior Chilcotin Plateau and slice through the range with precipitous, forested canyons, dispensing their loads of glacial silt into two majestic fjords: Bute Inlet and Knight Inlet.

The combination of big mountains and big ocean presents a tough landscape with a haunting beauty as well as an array of severe weather conditions – the dramatic and extremely harsh winters occur when the intensely cold arctic outflow meets the very wet air pumping in off the Pacific. In the past, these elements provided a formidable shield against conventional transport systems and, together with the remoteness, fostered a rich tradition of self-reliance and self-sufficiency in the pioneers.

In recent times, technology has reduced the natural defence of the wilderness and, like most valleys in the Coast Range, the Homathko and Klinaklini have been heavily logged. However, the wide, open landscape is appealing to adventurers, and the complete absence of any regulations is a rare and refreshing commodity that reinforces the pioneering opportunities offered by the expansive environment. In spite of increasing popularity, it is possible to find here, in the heart of this magnificent wilderness, a unique blend of the essence of mountaineering.

ridges, faces, and peaks

Waddington's form is a masterpiece of natural architecture. The clean-cut ramparts of gneiss are unusually steep for such a high and large massif, especially near the top, where they culminate in a fin-like tower, honed to a sharp-pointed summit so small that only one person can stand on it. Most of the estimated *c.*60m (*c.*200ft) of annual snowfall slides away to the convoluted icefalls and heavily crevassed glaciers that guard the lower slopes. However, it is not uncommon to find, even in summer, that the rock – especially high on the mountain – is deeply encrusted in ice. Although it can be dangerous, this can also make for superb, mixed rock and ice climbing.

The mountain is shaped like a huge wafer, long and thin, with two main ridges, running south-east and north-west, forming the crest of the high ridge system that is the divide between the Homathko tributary glaciers, Scimitar, Tiedemann, and Waddington, to the north and east, and the various arms of the Franklin Glacier, to the south and west. There are few feasible ways of crossing the divide in the vicinity of the mountain so expeditions tend to be committed to one side or the other.

From neighbouring Mount Munday to the east, the crest connects directly along the dramatic and unclimbed Arabesque

Above **High on the South East Ridge of Mount Waddington. This remote peak was known as 'Mystery Mountain' until the mid-1930s.**

Ridge past Spearman Peak, connected to Waddington by the Spearman Col, and onto the South East Ridge of Waddington. It then rises to the spectacular rock spire called the Tooth and the final 300m (1000ft) Main Summit Tower. A deep cleft separates this from the slightly lower North West Summit, 3986m (13,078ft), as the crest descends the North West Ridge to a low spot at Fury Gap, the West Col.

The North East Side of the mountain is a continuous 1000–2000m (3300–6500ft) escarpment. It runs around the East Face, above the Tiedemann Glacier, with its subsidiary Bravo Glacier, past the upper and lower tiers of the North East and Northern Faces, and up to the North West Face, consisting mainly of the steep Angel Glacier, a subsidiary of the Scimitar Glacier. A steep and impressive North Buttress descends the lower tier of the North Face to the North Col separating Tiedemann and Scimitar Glaciers and connecting Waddington to its northern neighbours Mount Combatant and Mount Tiedemann.

The South West Side of the mountain has more exposed rock and less ice than the north, draining down into the Buckler, Dais, and Regal Glaciers, all tributaries of the Upper Franklin Glacier.

Separating the Buckler and Dais Glaciers is a rather indistinct South Ridge that connects the mountain through a South Col to its southerly neighbours, Mount Jester and Mount Cavalier.

climbing on mount waddington

In the late 1920s–early 1930s the heroes of Canadian climbing, Don and Phyllis Munday, spent 10 years exploring and mapping Waddington. Although the summit eluded them they showed the way for subsequent ascents, mainly up the Franklin Glacier from Knight Inlet. This traditional route is now inhibited because the snout of the glacier has receded into a deep and dangerous gorge. During the 1950s, floatplanes began providing access to the regular route on the North East Side, flying to Ephemeron Lake near the snout of the Tellot Glacier, 16km (10 miles) east of the mountain. The popularity of this approach was consolidated by the building of the Plummer Hut beside the Upper Tellot Glacier in 1969.

future climbing

Future possibilities include a grand traverse of the crest of the Waddington massif from Mystery Pass to Fury Gap as well as a few remaining rock buttresses and ice gullies. There also remain winter ascents of the harder routes.

NORTH EAST SIDE

Main Summit
Tooth
North West Summit
Spearman Col
Bravo Glacier

SOUTH WEST SIDE: SOUTH FACE

Main Summit
Mt Spearman

north east side

Climbing on this side of the mountain is made serious by the remoteness which, when combined with bad weather, can make emergency access very difficult.

east face and upper north face

These routes are on the east and upper tier of the northern faces from Tiedemann Glacier. Routes 1–4 normally take two bivouacs.

1 Bravo Glacier Route IV, 5.6

W Long, O Cook, R de Saussure, and R Houston 1950

The regular and most popular route involves a long and tricky snow climb, with superb mixed rock and ice climbing in the South East Chimney of the Main Summit Tower. 2300m (7500ft).

2 The Tooth III (some direct aid)

W Long, A Steck, R de Saussure, and P Bettler 1950

This rarely climbed route follows the South East Ridge. 150m (500ft).

3 North East Face: Summit Tower III, 5.7

P Bettler and A Steck 1950

Mixed rock and ice climbing

rightwards from below the Tooth notch to the North West Ridge of the Main Summit. 200m (650ft).

4 North West Peak from North East Side

British Columbia Mountaineering Club and Alpine Club of Canada 1962

Easy snow ledge contours the North Side of the Main Summit Tower to the North West Ridge, providing a link to the South West Side (*see route 15*).

lower north face ⊠

These routes are on the lower tier of the North Face from Waddington/Combatant Col, at 3000m (10,000ft), which is normally accessed by helicopter. Routes 5–8 normally take one bivouac.

5 North Ridge (Kiwi Route) IV

A Richards and S Ross 1979

Fine low-grade ice climbing to 50° following left-hand ice rib out of the Col to join regular route (1) on the Main Summit Tower. This route is 1000m (3300ft).

6 North East Pillar V, 5.10

P and N McNerthney 1986

Sound rock, tricky route finding. 1000m (3300ft).

7 North East Couloir IV 5.8 A14

S Flavelle and D Lane 1982

Weaving ice gully to 55° (steeper at bergschrund) left of pillar. Short rock finish. 1000m (3300ft).

north west face

The route on this face ascends from the Upper Scimitar Glacier.

8 Firey Route ⊠

P Renz, D Knudson, K and J Beebee, and J and J Firey 1972

No technical challenge so the route is ungraded. Hazard of crossing under ice cliffs to gain Angel Glacier and route (15) to the North West Peak. Ascent 2150m (7000ft).

south west side

Although the mountain itself is steep with serious objective danger created by the sun melting and loosening ice-bound rock, the surrounding terrain is mellower, warmer, and more easily accessible than the northern side.

south face

These routes are on the South Face above the Buckler Glacier and normally take one bivouac.

9 Cowboy Way IV, 5.9

J Harlin and M Jeakins 1995

Steep rock and ice gullies (water-ice W13) on the right side of the face link to the upper South East Ridge and the regular route (1) near base of Summit Tower. 1150m (3770ft).

10 Towers Couloir WI4

J Elzinga and D Serl 1995

Right centre of face to Spearman Col, with ice to 90°. Links to route (1) as above. 700m (2300ft).

south west face

These routes are above the Dais Glacier. Route 11 can be done in one long day; routes 12–14 will require one bivouac.

11 Risse Route IV, 5.8 A13

S Risse and A Tuthill 1987

This climbs the South Face of the North West Summit by a series of prominent but sometimes thin couloirs and ramps left of the Central Couloir and leads to a rib on the upper face. 700m (2300ft).

12 Central Couloir III, A13

B Ash and J Farrel 1980

Ice gully (alpine ice to 50°) leading directly to the notch between Main

North West Summit

Central Couloir

Main Summit

Tooth

13

12

11

9

Dais Glacier

Buckler Glacier

Summit and North West Summit.
Very loose rock at top. The route is
600m (2000ft).

13 Original South West Face Route
IV, 5.7

F Wiessner and W House 1936
Original and classic route. Its
popularity has been marred by
a reputation for falling rock and
ice in the heat of the day. Several
variations have now been done.
750m (2500ft).

14 Dais Couloir II

H Fuhrer, H Hall, and D and P Munday 1934
North West Ridge direct from Dais
Glacier. Short cut joins the Main
Ridge halfway (*see route 15*).
300m (1000ft).

15 North West Ridge from Fury Gap IV

D, P, and B Munday 1928
Superb, low difficulty but long and
strenuous expedition. Lower part
follows the ridge, upper part follows
the Angel Glacier north of the ridge.
(*See route 4 for crossing the divide and
linking with regular route on Main
Summit.*) 1500m (5000ft). The first
ascensionists did this route in one
long day. Now, most people require
one bivouac.

how to get to mount waddington

The mountain is usually reached by
helicopter from the White Saddle Ranch
near the Tatla Lake in the Chilcotin
Plateau, which is one full day's drive north-
west of Vancouver; or from Campbell
River on Vancouver Island. Alternatively,
you can take a floatplane from Vancouver
or Campbell River to Ephemeron Lake,
near the snout of the Tellot Glacier,
or a wheeled plane to the Scar Creek
logging camp. In the spring and early
summer ski planes run from Squamish.

You can also travel by boat from the
Campbell River area to the head of Bute,
then arrange a ride with loggers to Scar
Creek. Or, you can bushwhack down
either branch of Homathko River from
Interior, or up through Canyon from Scar
Creek. Dirt roads run from the Inlets
to the canyons with a logging camp
and airstrip at 37km (20 miles) up the west
side of the Homathko at Scar Creek.

Ocean to Alpine Wilderness Adventures
offers an access service and guided
tours into the Waddington area. They are
based in the Campbell River area (Box 23,
Surge Narrows, BC, Canada VOP 1W0).
Helicopters are now the most popular

mode of access, especially for climbers
in the summer, facilitating a wave of fine
new routes of high technical standard.

facilities

The Plummer Hut (run by the BC
Mountaineering Club) is situated at
51 22 N, 125 9 W. It is mainly used as
a base for the Tiedemann peaks.

Basics can be found in Campbell River
or Williams Lake. There are campsites
at Campbell River, Tatla Lake, and White
Saddle helicopter base. Campbell River
also has a variety of hotels.

when to go

July and August give best alpine climbing
conditions, but unpredictable weather and
difficult glacier travel. May and September
often have better weather. It is best to use
skis in May, as this gives safer glacier travel.

gear

A normal selection of alpine gear should
include harnesses with prusik loops for
crevasse rescues, along with helmets
for falling rock and ice. Helicopters
cannot be relied on to function well
in bad weather and radios require strong

batteries, good weather, and adequate
line of sight. Several days' emergency
rations are recommended.

maps and guidebooks

1:50 000 topographical maps are
available from Geological Survey
of Canada, Worldwide Books and Maps
in Vancouver. Guidebooks include:
Climber's Guide – Coastal Ranges of BC,
Dick Culbert (1969); *Exploring the Coast
Mountains on Skis*, John Baldwin (1994);
and *Climber's Guide to Waddington*,
Don Serl (1998).

language

English.

rescue and insurance

In case of emergency, phone the
nearest Royal Canadian Mountain Police
station. Foreign visitors may have
to pay for any rescue services, so
private insurance is recommended.
A phone service is available
at Scar Creek logging camp.

red tape

Permits are not necessary.

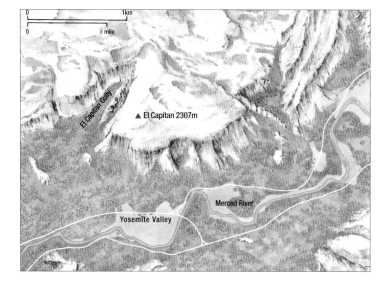

el capitan

steve roper

Tourists and climbers alike are immediately struck by the enormous granite monolith, El Capitan, that guards the portal of Yosemite Valley, a great gorge in the Sierra Nevada Range of eastern California. The huge cliff is about 900m (3000ft) high and 1.6km (1 mile) wide, and is said to be the largest chunk of exposed granite on earth. Since the rock is incredibly solid and Yosemite's weather so often superb, climbers from all over the world flock to test their mettle on this splendid formation.

The mountain was named the Rock Chief by Indians, but the first white men to visit the valley gave the monolith another equally apt name, El Capitan, which is Spanish for The Captain. To climbers it is now simply El Cap or The Captain.

In comparison with many other areas, climbing in Yosemite is amazingly safe. Weather and rockfall cause minimal problems, and the rock is most often solid. Despite this, many climbers have died on El Cap, usually because of misuse of equipment. It goes without saying that before setting hand to El Cap, all would-be climbers should be highly experienced in all phases of difficult aid climbing, hauling techniques, and living on vertical rock for days at a time.

El Cap was avoided by climbers until the 20th century. In 1933, the first Yosemite rock climbers hardly looked at El Capitan, they found it so overpowering. In the early 1950s, however, climbers with superior equipment (nylon ropes and pitons of varying sizes) began to make tentative approaches to the wall – but, even then, only at its edges. In 1957 they began looking at the main cliff in a new light. Using sophisticated aid techniques and new, wide-angle pitons, they decided it might be possible to put up a route: but where?

ridges, faces, and peaks

El Cap is not one single plane of granite, though from certain viewpoints it appears to be. Rather, two faces, the South West and the South East, intersect at a great prow of stone called the Nose.

The enormous wall left of the Nose, the South West Face, is characterized by solid granite, many small ledges perfect for bivouacs, and an abundance of less-than-vertical rock. The shorter wall to the right, the South East Wall, is dead vertical, lacks big ledges, and is composed of darker, looser rock. This wall has a huge dark intrusion of diorite, shaped like the North American continent. The Nose itself is a classic prow, and is characterized on its upper 300m (1000ft) by long and bold dihedrals. Climbing up through these gleaming white facets of rock is like being inside a cut diamond.

Royal Robbins, a superb climber and a visionary, dominated El Cap during the 1960s, putting up many routes in fine style. Using very few bolts and eschewing fixed ropes, Robbins set the standard for those who would follow.

future climbing

What lies ahead? Ground-to-top routes that don't follow existing routes partway will be hard to come by; most of the recent 'new' routes start up an established route, branch off for a while, and then follow another existing route to the top. Each new climb will be given a name by its first ascensionists, so the total number of routes, which now stands at around 80, is likely to double. Although most of these will be 'mere' 200m (650ft) variations of existing routes, and the day of long, separate routes is gone forever, climbers will still find enough challenge to keep them occupied for years.

Right **Xavier Bongard during an ascent of 'The Shield' on El Capitan. This route was first climbed in 1972 and is still highly prized.**

first woman to solo an El Cap route. J Bridwell, D Bard, and D Diegelman established 'Sea of Dreams', a route with 16 A4 and A5 pitches.

1984 'Wyoming Sheep Ranch', the first route with super-extreme aid climbing (A5+), was put up by R Slater and J Barbella.

1988 T Skinner and P Piana climbed 'The Salathé Wall' route free at 5.13b.

1989 M Wellman climbed 'The Nose', forever putting to rest the idea that 'handicapped' people cannot aspire to their dreams – he is a paraplegic.

1993 First free climb of 'The Nose' was accomplished by L Hill and B Sandahl.

1994 S Schneider and H Florine completed three El Cap routes in 23 hours: 'The Nose', 'Lurking Fear', and 'The West Face'.

West Buttress

The Nose

This is just a representative sample of 14 routes. Most are recommended for experienced big-wall climbers; a few are of historical interest or possess cutting-edge difficulty.

south west face

With its obvious crack systems and many bivouac ledges, this wall was the scene of most of the early routes.

1 Lurking Fear VI, 5.10, A3

D Bircheff and J Pettigrew 1976

A direct route up the 600m (2000ft) West Buttress and one of the easier big-wall routes on El Cap, with long stretches of relatively simple climbing. Proficient parties do it in a long day; the record is nine hours.

2 The Salathé Wall VI, 5.13b (or 5.11, A3)

R Robbins, C Pratt, and T Frost 1961

Dozens of bolts and scores of fixed pitons have been added to this 800m (2600ft) route since the epic first ascent, tarnishing a climb done in

impeccable style by masters of the craft. Nevertheless, with its slabs, pendulums, jam cracks, roofs, and famous headwall, the climb remains one of the most varied and desired on El Cap. Most parties will bivouac twice; speedsters can try to break the record of nine hours.

3 The Shield VI, 5.9, A3+

C Porter and G Bocarde 1972

One of the first 'half routes'. The first ascensionists climbed 275m (900ft) up 'The Salathé Wall' route, then headed into virgin territory. They encountered a dead-vertical wall, apparently devoid of cracks, where Porter placed 35 successive thin pitons into a hairline crack. This was one of the gutsiest leads ever done in Yosemite, and is still sought out. Allow about four days for this 800m (2600ft) route.

4 The Nose VI, 5.13b (or 5.11, A2)

W Harding, W Merry, and G Whitmore 1958

As the most historic Valley climb, the 900m (3000ft) Nose still attracts

an enormous number of climbers. Regardless of overcrowding, the upper part of the route, with its clean, soaring dihedrals, is one of the most aesthetic places imaginable. The route has now been done in an incredible 4½ hours – but most will take two or more days.

south east face

While this wall is generally only two-thirds as high as the South West Face, its steepness makes it equally forbidding. The dead-vertical (and sometimes overhanging) cliff contains numerous sections of black diorite, often fractured and loose. One gigantic patch of diorite is shaped remarkably like the North American continent, and several routes have names associated with this feature.

5 Mescalito VI, 5.9, A4

C Porter, S Sutton, H Burton, and C Nelson 1973

This popular 900m (3000ft) route, one of the longest on the face, takes a line just right of The Nose. It is noted for its many fixed copperheads and its 'tied-off' placements. Plan 4–5 days for this route.

6 Pacific Ocean Wall VI, 5.9, A4

J Bridwell, B Westbay, J Fiske, and F East 1975

The most intimidating El Cap route of the 1970s, the 850m (2800ft) P O Wall involves intricate nailing, copperheading, and hooking. With nine pitches of A4 and 15 sling belays, this is hardly a route for the novice big-wall climber. Many fixed placements have badly frayed cables, creating the potential danger of long leader falls. Allow five days for this hair-raiser.

7 Sea of Dreams VI, 5.9, A5

J Bridwell, D Bard, and D Diegelman 1978

This 600m (2000ft) route, Bridwell's masterpiece, involves seven pendulums, four A5 pitches, and much desperate hooking. The recommended equipment list is revealing: 75 pitons, 35 friends, hooks of all sizes and shapes, and 100 copperheads. Most parties take about four days.

8 North America Wall VI, 5.8, A3

R Robbins, C Pratt, Y Chouinard, and T Frost 1964

Characterized by awkward nailing, loose rock, and complex pendulums, this 600m (2000ft) route is included here more for its history than its superb climbing. The four first ascensionists, the best big-wall climbers of the 1960s, believed the

route to be the world's most difficult technical climb. Allow 3–4 days.

9 Wyoming Sheep Ranch VI, A5+

R Slater and J Barbella 1984

This 520m (1700ft) line, which slices upward through the centre of the 'North American continent', is presently the only El Cap route rated A5+. As such, it ranks among the hardest artificial climbs yet. When it is done, which is rarely, it usually takes 4–5 days.

10 Gulf Stream VI, 5.9, A4

S Gerberding, J Harpole, and J Smith 1993

This recent 490m (1600ft) route is one of the hardest, involving 200 hook placements. Only suitable for bold, confident climbers, it will take about a week.

11 Tangerine Trip VI, 5.9, A3+

C Porter and J de St Croix 1973

One of Porter's early routes attacks the overhanging wall to the right of the 'North America Wall' (8). Few ledges mar this featureless climb, which requires 15 sling belays in a row. Although the difficulty is hardly extreme, the fact that two climbers have died low on the route lends it a sombre aura. Allow 2–3 days for this 500m (1640ft) route.

12 Lost in America VI, 5.9, A5

G Child and R Leavitt 1985

This difficult 500m (1640ft) route took the first ascensionists 10 days.

13 Zodiac VI, 5.11, A3+

C Porter 1972

Charlie Porter's El Cap career was relatively short – four seasons in the early 1970s. But what a record! His eight new routes are testaments to skill and commitment – and four are included in this list of noteworthy climbs. 'Zodiac' is perhaps the most repeated, as the artificial climbing is straightforward. Honed climbers can do it in a long day with headlamps – the record is 15 hours – but most parties will bivouac at least once on this 430m (1400ft) route.

14 East Buttress IV, 5.10b

A Steck, W Siri, W Long, and W Unsoeld 1953

This 300m (1000ft) route is the easiest way up El Cap's escarpment. Although not a big-wall route, the line is a classic, and a popular 1-day outing. The cliff abounds with 'chickenheads' (erosional knobs) that allow easy free climbing on steep sections. A seasonal waterfall just to the west means this climb is not usually feasible until July.

how to get to el capitan

From the international airports at San Francisco or Los Angeles, you can hire a car and follow the excellent highways to Yosemite Valley; allow a day for the trip from each city. Public transport from the big cities is hardly adequate so it is best to have a car. The walk to El Cap is 15–45 minutes depending on the route to be climbed.

facilities

Yosemite Valley is becoming excessively crowded, so climbers must plan ahead. Several lodges offer rental cabins, but most climbers camp. Most campsites must be reserved and are booked weeks ahead of time: book through Destinet Services at 9450 Carroll Park Drive,

San Diego, CA 92121, USA. However, Sunnyside is the traditional climbers' site, and no reservations are needed here. The site is always jammed, but people are normally willing to share a spot. Supplies and equipment are available at stores in the valley, and restaurants and a market can be found near the campsites.

when to climb

Spring is the best time to climb El Cap as the days are long and the weather is often perfect for weeks at a time, although multi-day storms can occur. By early June the temperatures rise, and during a heatwave the wall can become an inferno. In late September the temperatures are fine again, but the days are short and the nights can often be chilly.

gear

Many El Cap routes require long stretches of artificial climbing, so take a huge selection of nuts and camming devices. Pitons are still used extensively on most routes, and hooks, rivet hangers, and copperheads are needed on many pitches. Other big-wall equipment, such as portaledges or hammocks, sturdy haul bags, and ascending devices are necessary.

maps and guidebooks

The free map given out to all visitors at the entrance gates is adequate for finding your way along the roads of Yosemite Valley.

A necessary guidebook is *Yosemite Climbs: Big Walls*, Don Reid (Chockstone Press, 1993).

language

English.

rescue and insurance

Be prepared for storms and self-rescue; carry a bolt kit for emergencies. Although a highly competent rescue squad is on hand on the valley floor, weather conditions in the off-season can hinder it. Insurance is not compulsory.

red tape

Peregrines make their nests on the South East Face so many routes can actually be closed by park rangers until 1 August.

nine days on the wall
greg child

"I've been accused by my friends of having a love affair with El Capitan these past few years, and since all love affairs are of an indulgent and obsessive nature I, of course, wanted a part of her for myself. The routes I had repeated on El Cap had produced excitement and challenge, but I'd always felt a little envious of those who'd been there first, who had felt out the way and pushed their minds and bodies to the limit.

The plotting of a new route on El Cap traditionally takes place on your back in the meadows. If you look at the wall long enough you may find something to climb, and if you look at that long enough you might climb it. A route or 'line' occurs when enough flakes, cracks, and ledges connect to form a natural path to the top. While blank sections can be crossed by drilling for bolts or rivets, this alone does not constitute a route; if it did an 'unnatural' 2000m line of bolts could appear every three metres on any wall or mountain, a pointless exercise that would be ugly and horrific in terms of time and effort.

It was with a lot of imaginative staring, and not a little wishful thinking, that Peter Mayfield and I visualized a line on the overhanging East Face. We planned to follow an existing route, the Tangerine Trip, for three pitches to a point where it traverses right under a huge arch, a point where we would climb left for 60m to an untouched line of weakness.

In the autumn of 1981, we humped enough food, water, and equipment for 10 days to the base and then set off.

Climbing walls is by nature a slow business; and climbing new ones even slower. The type of climbing, aid climbing, is a process by which you hang off a piton or similar gadget, supported in an étrier or little sling ladder. Stretch as high as you can, place the next piece, clip it, hang, and then repeat. Each placement is different and may be no more than a wafer of steel gently tapped into a crack a few millimetres wide. Concentration and patience are of the essence. So it was no surprise that we found ourselves ascending a mere one or two pitches a day.

The first day involved hauling our 100kg of gear to the top of our ropes where the virgin ground began. Although we hauled this in two equal loads through a pulley to give a mechanical advantage, it remained a backbreaking task that never grew easier. We followed the arch left, slamming pins up into it, until it opened up into a huge bomb-bay chimney. To all appearances

... in a couple of days we would have our own piece of real estate on El Cap.

from below, we had disappeared, swallowed by the rock. A cave-like alcove at its end capped by a large roof became our hanging home where we spent the night in portaledges.

Over the next two days our route began to fall into place even better than we had hoped. Sections that appeared blank turned out to be subtly featured. Peter led out of the cave, through bulging overlaps, past a crack inhabited by shrieking bats which, along with the swallows, frogs, toads, moths, and mice that live in the deep cracks and ledges of the walls, reminded us that we were never quite alone. El Cap may appear to be a granite desert, but soaks of water squeezing out onto the surface sustain tiny oases of moss and plants, forming ecosystems even on the vertical.

The next lead involved a series of scallops that were too shallow to drive a piton into but would accept copperheads. Being so soft, copperheads only just take body weight – a fall would rip them straight out. I moved cautiously from one to the next until, several hours later, I reached a welcome ledge, mentally and physically drained.

The following morning Peter free climbed for 20m to a red-coloured tower, then began hooking across diorite flakes to a

stance barely big enough for our feet. Above us was the most barren-looking section of the climb. Should the rock turn blank we would have no choice but to break out the hand-drill and hammer and twist until we punched out a 0.5cm hole. But not a single hole was needed as delicate features appeared, revealing themselves only when we came face to face with them. This was the stuff we were there for. My mind was rapt; for the moment we were just two flies on a wall hunting out a path. Some people may think that climbing is a sort of forced entry, a violation, a pounding of spikes and a smashing of the rock into submission. But here I felt that I wasn't doing anything that El Cap didn't let me do. Every move and placement flowed as naturally as the stone that accepted it.

Peter jumared up, cleaning the pitch, and we returned to our ledge, leaving the ropes fixed above us. The evening star flickered into life and the air turned crimson with dusk. Suddenly a wild scream and a whoosh cut through the twilight. We gazed in amazement as, one after another, eight dots hurtled down for 600m then jerked upwards as their parachutes flew open to float them down like feathers to the meadow below. So now they take running jumps off El Cap.

Left **Greg Child on the first ascent of Aurora. He is in A5 territory heading towards the bivouac spot, the American zone.**

Below **Climbing high on Aurora, near the end of the route. With swollen hands and waists pinched from hunger and their harnesses, both climbers were looking forward to standing on flat ground, on top of El Cap.**

On day six Peter carefully negotiated a flake that expanded as he pounded pitons into it; it expanded so much that his placements wobbled limply behind him as he gently tapped on a higher piton. I stared boggle-eyed at the flapping guillotine poised above my head and nearly jumped out of my skin when a whoosh and a blur swooped by to my left. Not jumpers this time, but haul bags, barrelling to the scree below, thrown off, as used to be the custom, by climbers who had just topped out.

Setting up our portaledges on the seventh afternoon we talked about how smoothly the climb had gone. With about four pitches left, we knew that it was in the bag and that in a couple of days we would have our own piece of real estate on El Cap. Both of us had tasted that feeling of isolation and acute awareness on our leads, and for a week now we had been a self-sufficient microcosm, drifting up the wall, scarcely aware of the rest of the world. From our bivouac on the headwall, which leaned out at an angle of 120°, we had a panoramic view of the acres of granite around us, with the symmetrical baseline curving beneath us and the High Sierras rising above the valley rim. But the longer we looked, the more our feeling of isolation receded. To either side were teams on other routes, acres away, yet their voices amplified in the afternoon calm. And the longer we looked the more the activity increased. A rope the length of El Cap snaked slowly down the wall, lowered from a steel tripod and winch for some daredevil to abseil in space, a stunt never to eventuate, as the rope fell whip-cracking to the ground, narrowly missing a crowd below. Then there was more shouting and soon the air was filled with blasting megaphones and the eerie sound of helicopter blades whipping up the dusk. Someone had taken a fall on Dawn Wall and was injured. As the helicopter hovered close by to ascertain the situation, the curious peregrine falcons, roused from their eyrie on the wall, flew in rings around the intruding machine.

Removing the stricken climbers posed an interesting challenge – 300m from the top and every bit overhanging, they would be no easy job for the rescuers. Various hypothetical solutions had been dreamed up but the solution came next morning. A nearby team on Mescalito would traverse the void between the two routes and assist them to the top, a manoeuvre accompanied by two days of yelling and shouting. During this time Peter led across a blank traverse, interspersing rivets with hook moves until we rejoined the last of the Tangerine Trip, which led us quickly to the top of what we came to call Aurora.

Before we began the walk down to the valley floor on legs still wobbly after nine days on an overhanging world, I looked back down the shiny beast one last time. We had blazed a trail through a wilderness and, even though our only marks are a few rivets and bolts, it will never be the same again. We, like other climbers and explorers, were guilty of a small and incurable imperialism. The urge to be the one to leave those first footprints, to go where no others have been, is precisely what will eventually kill the wilderness, because that is what opens up the path for others. Although we all have an inalienable right to these rare places, whether a new route on a wall or a journey into the tundra, as the popularization of the wilderness experience catches on, it diminishes the aura of the once impenetrable and uncharted.

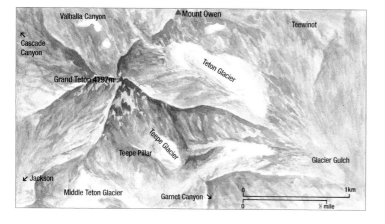

grand teton

al read

The Teton Range is in the northern Rocky Mountains in the north-west state of Wyoming, North America. Along with Jackson Hole, a huge valley between the Teton and Gros Ventre Ranges, the massif constitutes Grand Teton National Park. The scenery in this area is stunning. Jagged peaks are set within pine forests and sagebrush plains, and wildlife abounds: there are moose, elk, bison, bears, and eagles – even an occasional wolf and grizzly bear.

Sweeping abruptly 2000m (7000ft) above Jackson Hole, the Grand Teton is 4197m (13,770ft) high. One of the most dramatic and spectacular mountains in North America, it dominates the entire Teton Range and dwarfs the clusters of satellite peaks, such as Middle Teton, Mt Owen, and Teewinot, and numerous needles and spires. At the south end of the valley, 32km (20 miles) from the mountain, is the town of Jackson.

Probably no area in the United States can match the Tetons for their variety of mountaineering, and the Grand Teton is the principal climbing objective. It is composed primarily of crystalline rock interwoven with a profusion of granite dikes, providing modern routes and challenging climbs of all difficulties. The Grand Teton's long alpine climbs have been used as a training ground, enabling Teton climbers to go on to pioneer groundbreaking routes throughout the world.

ridges, faces, and peaks

The Grand Teton's striking presence is caused by an immense westward-tilted, wedge-shaped fault block of metamorphic and igneous rocks thrusting out of Jackson Hole. Once covered by sedimentary rock, the mountain was carved by valley glaciers. The ice sheets from the Yellowstone Plateau to the north created the level plain of Jackson Hole, which contrasts so dramatically with the mountains.

the north side The North Face sweeps across from the East Ridge to the North Ridge. Because of its awesome appearance from Jackson Hole, this wall is the most famous in the United States. Racked by rockfall, it plummets 1200m (3900ft) from the summit of the Grand Teton onto the Teton Glacier. The western edge of the face, called the North Ridge, is a nearly vertical corner that runs from the summit down to a buttress called the Grandstand. Across the Grandstand's horizontal backbone is Gunsight Notch, a deep cleft that separates the Grand Teton from Mount Owen.

the east side Facing Jackson Hole and falling 1200m (3900ft) into Glacier Gulch, near the terminus of the Teton Glacier, the long East Ridge has two huge towers: the Molar Tooth and the Second Tower. The upper part of the ridge is a long snowfield, the East Ridge Snowfield, which looms above the North Face and may be corniced in early season. On the south-east side of the East Ridge is the 'Otterbody', a large, otter-shaped snowfield. Below it, separated by a steep face, chimneys, and runnels, is Teepe Glacier, named after Theodore Teepe, who was killed while descending the Grand Teton (the mountain's first death), and Teepe Pillar, a huge pillar at the west edge of the glacier.

the south side The Grand Teton is flanked on the south by the Lower Saddle, a windy col separating the Grand and Middle Tetons. The Lower Saddle is the key to the many popular South Side routes. Gigantic buttresses sweep out of the deep Garnet Canyon approaches to the Lower Saddle, but they end as pinnacles, severed from the Grand Teton itself by the Black Dike, a dark diabase intrusion slicing through the South Side buttresses east to west at about 3660m (12,000ft). Beyond the dike the buttresses become the three main southern ridges, the Exum, Petzoldt, and Underhill (all names commemorating pioneer climbers). Teepe Pillar, technically the lower section of the Underhill Ridge, is severed from it by the Black Dike. These ridges have some of the most frequented routes. The Exum Ridge is the most popular,

1960 The North West Chimney on the West Face was ascended by D Dornan, and L and Irene Ortenberger.
1961 H Swedlund and R Jacquot climbed the Black Ice Couloir.
1962 A Read, P Lev, and J Greig climbed the Enclosure Ice Couloir, and combined it with the upper North West Ridge – now one of the most popular alpine climbs on the Grand Teton.

1981 M Stern and S Quinlan climbed the last of the major ice problems, Visionquest Couloir.
1985 R Jackson and S Rickert put up a difficult North Face route, which they called 'Emotional Rescue'.

accessed from the west by a near-horizontal ledge, Wall Street. The Beckey, Ford, and Stettner Couloirs separate the ridges, providing climbs that vary from steep snow to ice and rotten rock.

the enclosure Above the Lower Saddle and west of the Exum Ridge, two couloirs and a labyrinth of lesser gullies, buttresses, and towers lead to the Upper Saddle at 4012m (13,160ft). This col separates the summit block from the Enclosure, 4048m (13,300ft), which is the great western massif of the Grand Teton, as well as its West Summit. The Enclosure is the culmination of the South West Ridge, which drops steeply into Dartmouth Basin 900m (3000ft) below and west of the Lower Saddle, and the long North West Ridge, which plummets 1700m (5500ft) into Cascade Canyon, to the north of the Grand Teton, Mt Owen, and Teewinot. The name, the Enclosure, was originally used to describe the man-made rock structure found on the summit of this peak by explorers.

Between the Enclosure and the West Face is the Black Ice Couloir, a narrow cleft that leads from an almost hidden icefield above Valhalla Canyon to the Upper Saddle. To the west of the Black Ice Couloir, separated by a buttress, is the Enclosure Couloir, the other famous ice route on the mountain. Between the Black Ice Couloir and the Enclosure Ice Couloir is a massive buttress, and slanting across its upper section is the steep Visionquest Couloir, which leads from the Black Ice Couloir almost to the summit. The standard approach to the west side of the Grand Teton, the North Ridge, upper North Face, and most of the Enclosure, is the Valhalla Traverse, a ledge system traversing from the Lower Saddle around the west side of the Enclosure.

the west side Between the Black Ice Couloir and the North Ridge is the huge West Face, which drops 900m (3000ft) into Valhalla Canyon. Cold and dark, hidden from the sun most of the day by the mass of the Enclosure, the West Face is cleft by two huge fissures, the Great West Chimney and the North West Chimney. It also has a huge, almost vertical, smooth and featureless buttress, Loki's Tower, and an array of icefields and slanting ramps.

future climbing

Almost all obvious aesthetic lines, and their many variations, have now been climbed. Minor (mostly obscure or very difficult) variations are still possible.

There are, however, many winter, solo, and speed climbs awaiting first ascents.

Right **The West Face of the Grand Teton seen from Lake Solitude, the upper part of Cascade Canyon.**

There are approximately 108 routes on the Grand Teton (including the Enclosure). Degrees of difficulty range from scrambling to serious alpine routes on enormous features, snow climbs, ice couloirs, and glacier approaches. Below is a selection of the most important routes.

Most ascents are done in two days from the Valley but all times listed below are from base camp to the summit.

south side

Most climbs are done from this side, even those on the West Face and the Enclosure are best begun here, using the Valhalla Traverse. The Lower Saddle provides an accessible high camp, 1550m (5085ft) above Jackson Hole. Routes are sunny and mainly less of a serious undertaking than on other sides of the mountain.

1 Owen-Spalding Route II 5.4 (UIAA III)

W Owen, F Spalding, F Peterson, and J Shive 1898
The easiest route to the summit unless iced. Approach is from the Lower Saddle to the Upper Saddle, then out across the West Face and up chimneys and slabs. Takes 4–5 hours from the Lower Saddle or 6–8 hours from Garnet Canyon; 640m (2100ft).

2 Upper Exum Ridge II 5.5 (UIAA IV)

G Exum 1931
A beautiful climb and the most popular route. Not usually difficult. Takes 5–6 hours from the Lower Saddle. Ascent 640m (2100ft).

3 Lower Exum Ridge III 5.7 (UIAA V)

J Durrance and K Henderson 1936
Steep and exposed with excellent rock. It is eight hours from the Lower Saddle to the summit including 'Upper Exum Ridge' (2). Ascent 640m (2100ft).

4 Petzoldt Ridge III 5.6 (UIAA V-)

P Petzoldt and E Cowles 1941
Steep, with great sweeps of quality rock. Eight hours from the Lower Saddle. Ascent 640m (2100ft).

5 Underhill Ridge II 5.6 (UIAA V-)

R Underhill, P Smith, and F Truslow 1931
The shortest of the three south ridges. Often cold. Five hours from Lower Saddle. Ascent 640m (2100ft).

east side

The East Ridge is approached from Amphitheater Lake by descending ledges to the terminal moraine of Teton Glacier. Or bushwack up

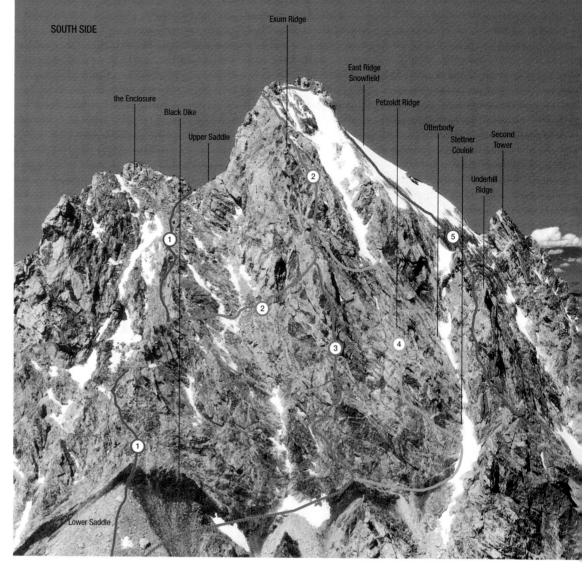

Glacier Gulch past Delta Lake. East Face routes are usually approached via Garnet Canyon or by crossing the Black Dike from the Lower Saddle.

6 East Ridge III 5.7 (UIAA V)

R Underhill and K Henderson 1929
The Molar Tooth defied early attempts. Not difficult in condition. 10½–13 hours; 1200m (3900ft).

7 Petzoldt-Loomis Route III 5.1 (UIAA III) ⊠

P Petzoldt and W Loomis 1935
In perfect conditions, this is one of the easiest routes on the mountain. Rockfall danger. It takes 5½ hours; 1048m (3770ft).

8 Smith-Otterbody II 5.6 (UIAA V-) ⊠

P Petzoldt, P Smith, and W House 1937
Often running with water from the 'Otterbody', making it cold and unpleasant. 8½ hours; 1048m (3770ft).

9 Beyer East Face III 5.9 (UIAA VI) ⊠

J Beyer 1979
Steep, clean, and excellent rock. A difficult route. 8½ hours; ascent is 1048m (3770ft).

north side

The huge North Face is approached via the Teton Glacier, and all routes except those from the Grandstand (accessed via the Valhalla Traverse) begin here. In bad weather, retreat is possible by traversing the top of the West Face to route (1). Times given are from Ampitheater Lake.

10 Route Canal IV WI5 5.9 (UIAA VI)

J Lowe and C Fowe 1979
A narrow, nearly vertical chute. Serious, mixed climbing. Seldom in condition. 8–12 hours. 1048m (3770ft).

11 North East Couloir IV 5.6 (UIAA V-)

J Hossack and G MacGowan 1939
Long, mixed route. 8–12 hours. 1048m (3770ft).

12 North Face IV 5.6 and IV 5.8 (direct finish – UIAA V- and UIAA V-)

P Petzoldt, J Durrance, and E Petzoldt 1936
Direct finish: R Pownall, R Garner, and A Gilkey 1949
High rockfall danger below the First Ledge. The direct finish is hard, but can be avoided by rappelling from

the Third Ledge and traversing the West Face to route (1). 12–15 hours; 1048m (3770ft).

13 North Ridge IV 5.8 (UIAA VI-)

R Underhill and F Fryxell 1931
Actually a corner. Difficult pitches and wonderful positions; 12–15 hours. 1048m (3770ft).

west face & the enclosure ⊠

An exciting side, but not often visited. Unless otherwise stated, ascent times are from the Lower Saddle. The routes are remote, long, and often verglased.

14 North West Chimney IV 5.9 (UIAA VI)

D Dornan, and L and I Ortenberger 1960
One of the best alpine routes when combined with the Black Ice and West Face variations. 12–15 hours; 640m (2100ft).

15 Loki's Tower IV 5.9+ (UIAA VI+)

M Whiton and M Stern 1981
The massive, featureless buttress between the North Ridge and North

West Chimney. Spectacular.
10–13 hours; 640m (2100ft).

16 West Face IV 5.8 (UIAA VI-)

J Durrance and H Coulter 1940
Mixed ice and rock. An outstanding
alpine route. 12–15 hours from
Valhalla Canyon. 1040m (3700ft).

17 North West Ridge V 5.7 (UIAA V)

J Durrance and M Davis 1938
In its entirety, the longest climb
on the mountain. Two days from
Cascade Canyon. 1433m (4700ft).

18 Black Ice Couloir IV AI3+ 5.7 (UIAA V)

H Swedlund and R Jacquot 1961
Steep, long, and subject to rockfall.
7–10 hours; 640m (2100ft).

19 Enclosure Ice Couloir IV AI3 5.7 (UIAA V-)

A Read, P Lev, and J Greig 1962
A classic alpine ascent. 7–9 hours;
ascent 640m (2100ft).

20 North Face of the Enclosure: Lowe Route IV 5.9 (UIAA VI)

G and M Lowe 1969
A mixed climb; seldom in condition.
9–13 hours. Ascent 640m (2100ft).

21 Visionquest Couloir IV AI3+ 5.8 (UIAA VI-)

M Stern and S Quinlan 1981
This is more difficult than the 'Black
Ice Couloir' (18), with mixed ice
and rock runnels. Rockfall danger.
8–12 hours. Ascent 640m (2100ft).

22 Emotional Rescue IV 5.11 (UIAA VII+)

R Jackson and S Rickert 1985
Follows the left prow of the huge
buttress separating the Black Ice and
Enclosure Ice Couloirs. 8–11 hours;
640m (2100ft).

EAST AND NORTH SIDES

North Face · East Ridge · North East Couloir · North Ridge · Grandstand · Gunsight Notch · Molar Tooth · Teton Glacier

how to get to grand teton

You can reach Jackson by car, from Salt
Lake City, Denver, Boise, and Yellowstone
National Park, or you can fly then hire a
car – public transport is poor. Approaches
are by trails, usually about 8km (5 miles)
with up to 1500m (5000ft) of ascent.
Trailheads can be reached by good roads
in Grand Teton National Park.

facilities

Accommodation is widely available in the
area – there are campsites in the National
Park and National Forest. There is also the
modestly priced American Alpine Club's
Climbers' Ranch, at the foot of the range,
which provides bunks and cooking
facilities. Alpine Club membership is not
required to stay there. There are no
refuges, cable cars, or lifts in Grand Teton
National Park.

when to climb

The climbing season is short, from
mid- to late June–September. The
prime months are July and August. May
and June sometimes offer early season
ice and snow climbs. Winter is snowy
and bitterly cold, and temperatures can
plummet to -51°C (-60°F) with winds
on the peaks in excess of 195kph
(120mph). Winter ascents are problematic;
only a few major routes have been
done in winter.

gear

Ascents of the great faces and ridges of
the Grand Teton require serious climbing
gear, usually including crampons and ice
tools. Weather changes rapidly so bring
protective clothing. Many unprepared
climbers have died from exposure.

maps and guidebooks

There are many good maps and
guidebooks that are available locally. The
best map is 'Grand Teton', 1:24,000,
produced by the US Geological Survey.

The best books include *A Climber's
Guide to the Teton Range*, Ortenberger and
Jackson (1996), and *Teton Skiing, a History
and Guide*, Tom Turiano (1995).

language

English.

rescue and insurance

The Park rescue team prides itself on
being the best in the United States.
Rescue insurance is not readily available
to climbers.

red tape

There are very few restrictions to climbing
in the area but, as it is a National Park,
camping registration is required and
environmental restrictions are strongly
enforced. Clean climbing is the ethic here,
and there are very few fixed pins on
the mountain.

getting to know the grand

christian
beckwith

Familiarity is a journey beneath the surface towards an object's essence, a slipping through the portals of time to the dreamscape where all moments exist at once. I know its unhurried rhythms best on the coast of Maine, where I grew up. Each year, as I return for the holidays to rejoin family and friends, I am struck by the depth of my connections to the land. Simple drives through the back roads become extended journeys with my youth; the landscape is intimately entwined with the memories of my childhood. In a 20-mile radius around our old farmhouse I can hardly set foot on ground without being flooded by a sense of the familiar. Slowly, though, I am watching familiarity unfold in the home I have chosen as an adult. And more than that: I am watching it unfold in the mountains I have chosen to climb.

The first time I went to climb the Grand Teton in Wyoming, I was frightened the entire day. Beyond its physical dimensions loomed the mystique of a full-blown mountain, laced in ice and snow, and adrenalin washed into me from when I woke in the morning until we baled out at Wall Street and stumbled back to camp. I didn't try again that whole year.

Late the next spring I went with some friends to climb the South Teton. Snow still blanketed the ground from the Meadows on up, and we kicked our way through a billowing storm, up the North West Couloir and across the summit ridge until we could go no higher. By the time we got back to Jackson I was exhausted. At Mark's house I flopped onto the couch and fell deeply asleep.

Sean woke me with a rough shake of the shoulder. 'Hey,' he said, his face a few inches from mine. 'Do you want to climb the Grand tomorrow?' His disembodied head hovered above me, haloed by the ceiling lights.

'Wha? Huh?'

'The Grand. Do you want to climb the Grand?'

'Yuh.'

'Great. See you at four.'

The next morning I found myself in Sean's car with a coffee mug in my hand and a vague idea that we were headed back into the Park snapping at my synapses. By the Headwall I had woken up with enthusiasm. Sweat mixed with the early morning light, prickling my body with a tingling joy. The cold air stung my throat and lungs. On the Lower Saddle I looked over into Idaho, which was tentatively budding into the year's first green.

Sean guided us up the Owen Spalding Couloir to the Upper Saddle. I followed his tracks closely, careful not to look at the drop below. As we roped up he calmly handed me the rack. 'Your lead,' he said. I shimmied around a bulge, scrambled onto a ledge, and nudged out until I could see the Crawl. Valhalla Canyon fell away beneath it. My head spun. I quickly pulled back to the safety of the ledge and practised breathing.

There wasn't really any turning around. What would I say to Sean? I lowered myself to the hand ledge as best I could, but it was covered in snow too hard to brush away. I jabbed at it with my fingers, groping for purchase. Slowly my fingers went numb. Legs shook; chest palpated. I wedged as much of my body onto the hand ledge as possible, got on my belly, and wiggled my way, inch by inch, across.

An eternity later, shaking and white, I pulled myself up the second chimney and atop a triangular block, hauling with all my strength against the rope drag. I put Sean on belay. Within moments I saw his plastic boots four feet below on the hand ledge as he casually traipsed across. 'Hello!' he exclaimed cheerfully as he pulled up beside me, took the rack, and continued up the ice-choked chimney. He hacked steps with his adze in fast, powerful strokes and quickly disappeared out of sight.

> **I remember ... the improbability of pelicans rising in spirals above Jackson Hole ...**

For my benefit we stayed roped up for the entire climb. Snow and ice clogged every crack and cranny, and by the top I was exhilarated with the thrill of the day. The world stretched out below us, and not even a breeze stirred the still beauty. We shook hands, and laughed, and remained on the summit for an hour.

Since then I've climbed the Grand 20 more times by half as many routes, and with each one the mystique draws back a bit more. Down at Dornan's Bar in Moose, as I look out at the mountain through the walls of plate-glass window, its different aspects merge with my emotional and mental recollections to create a tapestry of rich intensity. Slowly I am coming to know the Grand. I remember it in my calves when I think about hiking up the switchbacks on an early summer morning and emerging into the rock-walled amphitheatre of Garnet Canyon. I can feel it in my lungs when I think of the final few hundred feet to the Lower Saddle, in my eyes when I remember the thickening light at sunset on its orange western walls, in my chest when I think of the hours before dawn, as we brew up a mug of something to fill the insides with resolve.

Images go deep, some more than others: once, descending from the Upper Saddle, we discovered footprints in the snow,

these turned into a path, and then we came to the jagged drop down the Dartmouth Couloir and saw the bunched-up blue form five hundred feet below. I remember a man wailing while he worked his way down the cliffs, and my partner and I staring at each other in the moment before realization was complete. I remember, too, the improbability of pelicans rising in spirals above Jackson Hole and the quiet wonder of a belay on the East Face as clouds formed out of thin blue air and the eery whistle of glider planes, silent save for the air around their wings, that circled, white as ghosts, while a partner and I ascended in running belays. I can still see myself cursing with frustration in the Chockstone Chimney as I struggled to ascend, still recall the searing humility as I grabbed the rope and climbed hand over hand past moves I'd tried for 30 minutes to climb free.

When I think of the Grand, I think of one of these moments, then another tumbles on top of it, and then another – as we used to do as children at the local swimming hole back in Maine. I love this mountain, fear it, wonder if, in the end, I will come to rest on its sides. It would be a good place for that. The shimmer of familiarity grows.

But even as I marvel at the complexity of the mountain revealed by each new route, I wonder: will I one day be able to climb it amid recollections as intricate as when I return to the lands of my childhood home? N Scott Momaday, the American writer, notes that at one point in every man's life he must come to know a piece of land intimately, must come to familiar terms with a place he calls home.

Familiarity takes years to come by. I'd be a fool to think that it will come without time. Perhaps some day – if I'm lucky, if the mountain gods are willing, if perseverance joins persistence in the long, slow journey to the summit – I will become familiar with this mountain. It would seem to be a worthy goal.

1858 The earliest recorded sighting of Devil's Tower was made by a white explorer, Lt G L Warren.

1875 'Devil's Tower' was named by Col R Dodge, who was sent into the area to search for gold, in violation of Indian treaty rights.

1893 First ascent of Devil's Tower was made by two local ranchers, W Rogers and W Ripley, using a crude ladder of wooden stakes driven into a 100m (330ft) crack on the South East Side. On the 4th of July, a thousand people gathered at the base of the Tower to watch the pair ascend the ladder and plant a flag on the summit.

1906 Theodore Roosevelt declared Devil's Tower to be America's first National Monument.

1927 The Park Service removed the lower 30m (100ft) of the deteriorating ladder to discourage climbing. (At least 46 ascents were made using the original stake ladder.)

1937 The first technical climbing ascent (without the use of the ladder) of the Tower was made by F Wiessner, W House, and L Coveney. Wiessner led the entire route on the South Face, which, at 5.7, was equal in difficulty to state-of-the-art rock climbs being undertaken in the Alps.

1938 J Durrance and H Butterworth made the second technical ascent, pioneering what is now called the Durrance Route – still the easiest and by far the most popular route.

1941 A parachutist, G Hopkins, landed on the top of Devil's Tower in a publicity

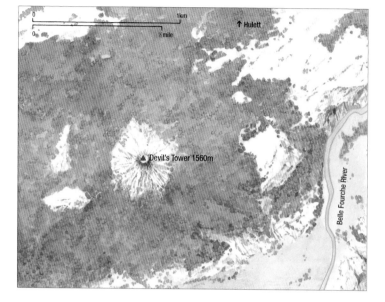

devil's tower

beth wald

In the north-eastern corner of Wyoming, close to the town of Hulett, Devil's Tower erupts out of the horizontal plains, an arrogant monolith, 1560m (5117ft) high, dominating the landscape. The Northern Plains Indian tribes, the original inhabitants of the region, revered the mysterious rock mountain. The Lakota called it Bear Lodge, or Mato Teepee, in honour of its creation legend: long ago, seven girls climbed onto a small rock to escape from a large bear. As they appealed to the spirits for help, the rock grew upwards. The angry bear clawed cracks into the new tower; the girls were pushed into the sky where they became the seven stars in the constellation we call the Pleiades.

Eventually geologists came up with a different explanation of its origins. About 60 million years ago, a vein of magma intruded into sedimentary layers. As the molten rock cooled and then hardened underground, contraction and fracturing formed the 4- to 6-sided columns of extremely hard rock called phonolite porphyry. Over millions of years, the softer sedimentary layers eroded away, exposing the volcanic plug, now rising 400m (1300ft) above the surrounding Belle Fourche River Valley.

Whatever the story of its origin, Devil's Tower, dense with cracks of the purest form, seems to have been created especially for climbers. The elegant dihedrals and columns, sweeping in almost unbroken lines, 260m (850ft) from the base to the summit, have long been a lure for the best climbers in the world.

ridges, faces, and peaks

Devil's Tower is distinguished from many other mountains by its uniformity of shape, the symmetry of its columns, and the consistent high quality of rock. Only near the top, where the ancient magma has been exposed to the elements for much longer than the clean cracks below, does the rock become fractured and loose. The West Face, glowing gold as it catches the last low rays of the setting sun, sits high above a large talus field and is the cleanest and most dramatic of the Tower's many angles, with the highest concentration of difficult routes. Moving around the Tower reveals the gentler aspect of the South and South East Faces, with the easiest, and by far the most popular, routes climbing to the Meadows, a series of high grassy ledges that wind their way to the summit. Facing directly to the east are the intimidating overhangs of The Window, the location of the Tower's most difficult aid routes. The shady North Side extends from the North East Buttress to the North West Shoulder, and sports long, varied lines with excellent rock all the way to the summit. Below the North Face are large columns, which have fallen into the forest, affording good bouldering.

future climbing

Ever since the 1950s, claims that the last climbable crack on the Tower has been done have been disproven again and again. With the explosion of rock climbing, especially sport climbing, in the United States in the 1990s, climbers looking for new routes on the Tower have moved out of the cracks and onto the columns and buttresses, establishing thin, difficult face routes protected by bolts. But fierce and elegant crack climbing has been the Tower's past and is still its future. Dozens of beautiful, unclimbed dihedrals await creative and committed climbers, particularly on the West and South West Faces. Moreover, the ominous roofs of The Window still await a free ascent – a feat that will launch rock climbing at the Tower into the next century.

Right **Charlie Mace (top) crack climbing on Devil's Tower, the famous monolith in Wyoming.**

stunt, and remained stranded there for six days until a climbing team headed by J Durrance was able to reach and rescue him.

1948 Jan Conn became the first woman to reach the summit of the Tower by technical climbing.

1955 The West Face was climbed by J McCarthy and J Rupley; their route went at 5.8, A3.

1964 An extraordinary year of activity, with 10 first ascents. R Robbins put up two significant climbs: 'The Window', a difficult A4 climb through roofs, and 'Danse Macabre', free climbed at 5.10d. Both routes far exceeded contemporary standards at the Tower and worldwide.

1977 H Barber established the first 5.11, 'Mr Clean' (5.11a), and D Horning put up many classic 5.10s, such as 'Belle Fourche Buttress' (5.10b).

1981 The grade 5.12 route was firmly established by S Hong with free ascents of 'Object Cathexis', 5.12b, and 'Brokedown Palace', 5.12a.

1984–5 High standards of free climbing were boosted with the addition of at least 13 new 5.12 routes established by a handful of climbers including S Hong, Karin Budding, T Skinner, P Piana, B Hatcher, and Beth Wald.

1988 The Tower's first 5.13, 'Mystery Express', 5.13a, was established on a steep arête by A Petefish.

1995 A voluntary ban on climbing on the Tower during June was introduced in a gesture of respect to Native Americans.

south face and south east corner

The routes on the South Face are reached by a well trodden path from the Tower nature trail. The established rappel route on this face is the most common way of descent from the summit.

1 Durrance Route 5.6
J Durrance and H Butterworth 1938
The most popular route. Starts at the obvious leaning pillar and winds its way through chimneys and cracks for six pitches to the Meadows, where you can scramble to the summit. 120m (390ft); takes 4–8 hours.

2 Bonne Home Variation 5.8
D Horning and H Hauck 1972
Varied climbing for the grade, with face, off-width, and hand crack moves. Climb to the Meadows, then continue to the summit. 128m (420ft); 2–3 hours.

3 Walt Bailey Memorial 5.9
J Overton and S Woodruff 1974
Very long (50+m/165+ft), 1-pitch hand and finger crack, ending in the Meadows. 100m (330ft); two hours.

east face and east buttress

Routes on the East Face are approached via a ramp running from the South Face, while the East Buttress route is accessed from the north-east.

4 Soler 5.9
L Kor and R Jacquot 1959
A Devil's Tower classic, 2-pitch hand crack to the Meadows. 130m (430ft); allow 2–3 hours.

5 The Window 5.6, A4
R Robbins and P Robinson 1964
A cutting-edge route, and still rarely repeated. It climbs through the obvious tiers of overhangs on fixed and thin gear. Third pitch leads to the summit. 125m (410ft); 4–6 hours.

6 Belle Fourche Buttress 5.10b
D Horning and D Rasmussen 1977
An excellent, 3- or 4-pitch route of hand and finger jams, starting as a straight-in crack splitting the East Buttress. 125m (410ft); three hours.

west face

The West Face has arguably the most aesthetic routes on the Tower and is approached via the talus field above the visitors' centre. Most climbers choose to rappel routes after two or three pitches rather than climb to the summit through the upper, loose band of rock.

7 Carols Crack 5.11a
B Yoho, C Black, C Holtkamp, and J Baird 1978
Three pitches of thin fingerlocks and stemming, finishing in a pitch of chimney climbing. 135m (440ft); allow 3–4 hours.

8 Brokedown Palace 5.12a
S Hong and M Sonnenfeld 1981
Three pitches of thin crack climbing and very technical stemming. Continue for two more pitches of loose rock and chimneys or rappel. 140m (460ft); allow four hours.

9 Mr Clean 5.11a
H Barber and C Lee 1977
The ultimate classic hand and finger crack. 135ft (440ft); about 3–4 hours.

10 Mystery Express 5.13a
A Petefish and K Hjelle 1988
Currently the most difficult route on the Tower, one pitch of thin face and arête climbing. Rappel from the bolts on the ledge at the end of the route. 43m (140ft); allow an hour.

11 El Matador 5.11a/5.10d
B Yoho and C Holtkamp 1978
Five pitches, the second of which is the classic stemming pitch of the Tower, climbing a dihedral box to a good ledge (harder for shorter people). 140m (460ft); four hours.

north face and north east corner

From the Tower trail, take a path north-east, and angle north up easy

The lengths of routes are measured from the beginning of the technical climbing to the summit, but do not consider unroped approach scrambles. Times given are approximations and assume that the climbing party is adept at climbing the given grade of the route.

WEST FACE

EAST AND NORTH FACES

East Face

North Face

ledges to the base of the routes. From here, you can traverse to the North West Shoulder and West Face.

12 Assembly Line 5.9

D Horning and J Jennerjahn 1975

Starting from a large ledge one pitch up, a stemming and finger jams climb leads to a long, classic hand crack. This route is 135m (440ft) and takes two hours.

13 Maid in the Shaid 5.11d

S and A Hong, and K Budding 1983

One of the finest stemming routes at the Tower. 150m (500ft); it takes about three hours.

14 McCarthy North Face 5.11a

D Horning and F Sanders 1978

Mostly a tricky finger crack through a couple of roofs, which widens to hands on pitch three. Then a chimney leads to the summit. 170m (560ft); allow 3–4 hours.

15 Spiney Norman 5.11d

T Skinner and B Wald 1985

A 1-pitch classic, thin finger and stemming problem. 45m (150ft); takes about one hour.

how to get to devil's tower

Devil's Tower is in Wyoming, 64km (40 miles) north-east of the Black Hills of South Dakota. You can reach the Tower via Interstate 90 to the south, via Moorcroft to the south-west, or via Sundance to the south-east.

The nearest airports are in Gillette, Wyoming, and Rapid City, South Dakota, but there is no public transport to Devil's Tower from these cities. A car is the easiest way to get there.

facilities

The closest town, Hulett, Wyoming, is 15km (9 miles) north of the Tower, and has basic services (hotels, café, grocery shops, gas); the two larger towns of Moorcroft and Sundance are 42km (26 miles) and 34km (21 miles) away respectively.

At the entrance to the National Monument is a petrol station, a private campsite with showers, a restaurant, a souvenir shop with limited groceries, and a post office. Guiding services are also available here. There is a campsite

within the Monument for tents and trailers, although it can fill up at weekends. There is a nominal fee for entrance and for camping.

when to climb

Late April–June and September–early November. The Tower is voluntarily closed to climbing in June as a gesture of respect for Native American religious ceremonies. The weather in July and August is often very hot, with frequent, violent, afternoon thunderstorms. However, you can climb in relative comfort during these months by following the shade and finishing early. In very mild years, ascents may be possible even in winter.

gear

Many of the routes are very long, with cracks of uniform size, and often require double or triple sets of stoppers and camming units. The more difficult routes are usually thin, so a set of RPs is recommended. A standard rack consists of two sets of stoppers and two sets of friends size 0.5–3. Two ropes of at least

50m (165ft) are necessary. A comfortable harness is also highly recommended.

maps and guidebooks

Devil's Tower National Monument, A Climber's Guide (second edition), S Gardiner and D Guilmette, and *A Poorperson's Guidebook: Free Climbs of Devil's Tower* are sold at the Visitor centre, where you can also find photos with route descriptions. Maps available locally.

language

English.

rescue and insurance

No rescue team is maintained. Insurance is not required, but is highly recommended.

red tape

No climbing permit is required, but climbers must sign in and out at the Visitor Centre. There may be temporary route closures due to nesting raptors. The Park Service has prohibited the placement of new bolts and pitons, although the replacement of bolts already in place is allowed.

Nationalities: American unless stated.

1936-8 An escalating reputation as 'America's toughest climbing problem' attracted climbers from across the States to this volcanic plug in the New Mexico desert. R Ormes made several strong attempts to reach the summit. In September 1937, after climbing halfway up the lower North Summit, Ormes sustained a 10m (30ft) fall. The fall

bent his piton alarmingly, but held. Demoralized, he retreated.

1939 Sierran mountaineers D Brower, B Robinson, R Bedayn, and J Dyer, utilizing the latest hardware (but sparingly), found the key to the summit via the Rappel Gully and, after four days of climbing, made the first ascent.

1953 Legendary desert climber H T Carter made the fifth ascent of

Shiprock, via the 'Standard Route', with R Craig. This was the first of many climbs for the man who became Shiprock's most prolific pioneer.

1957 The first ascent of Ormes Rib was made by H T Carter.

1958 The first ascent of the Black Bowl Cutoff was made by H T Carter.

1959 The first free ascent of Shiprock (47th ascent overall) was made by

P Rogowski and T McCalla, via Carter's route up Ormes Rib.

1965 F Beckey began climbing the South Buttress with various partners. He spent 18 days with E Bjørnstad, three days with A Bertulis, and two days with H T Carter. After 30 days on the route, and placing 100 bolts in 20 pitches of climbing, Beckey and Carter reached the summit.

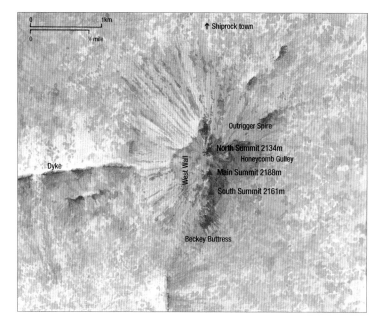

shiprock

cameron m burns

To the casual observer, Shiprock, at 2188m (7178ft), is a solitary monolith standing tall above an ocean of flat, dull scrub and sand in north-west New Mexico. Yet, upon closer inspection, it is more than one peak. It is actually a massif, a complex maze of gullies, towers, and walls, all created out of weirdly shaped and convoluted volcanic breccia. The name, Shiprock, was given to the peak by anglo explorers but, to the Navajo, who inhabit the vast desert regions around Shiprock, the mountain is Tse Beh Tai, or the Rock With Wings.

In pre-World War II North America, the two greatest remaining mountaineering problems on the continent were Mount Waddington, in British Columbia, and Shiprock. In 1936, after Fritz Wiessner and Bill House had conquered Waddington, all American mountaineers turned their eyes towards Shiprock.

The allure of the mountain was heightened by a widespread rumour that $1000 awaited the first mountaineers to climb the fantastic spire. The rumoured prize resulted in dozens of

attempts by the experienced and inexperienced alike. One party even attempted the peak with ladders. In October 1939, a group of Californian climbers drove in from Berkeley, bringing with them 400m (1300ft) of rope, 70 pitons, 18 karabiners, two hammers, and four cameras. They also brought a small supply of expansion bolts, items that had never before been used by American mountaineers. Although they did agree that using expansion bolts was really taboo, they argued that, on this mountain, their safety really depended on them.

Using newly invented aid-climbing techniques and ice pitons for protection, the climbers reached the final summit spire late on the third day. Another bivouac and the last difficult section of rock, the Horn, brought them to the most coveted summit on the continent. On the afternoon of 12 October 1939, David Brower, Raffi Bedayn, Bestor Robinson, and John Dyer became the first men to climb the Rock with Wings. In all, only four bolts had been employed but, according to historical accounts, they were the first bolts used for mountaineering in the Americas.

The man to rack more new routes, first ascents of subsidiary summits, and route variations on Shiprock than anyone else was legendary desert climber, Harvey Carter, active here in the 1950s and 1960s. He was also the first to solo Shiprock.

ridges, faces, and peaks

Shiprock, as its name suggests, is shaped, more or less, like a ship. Rising about 600m (2000ft) above the plains, it is orientated with its bow facing directly north, and its bigger, and steeper, stern to the south. The East and West Faces of the mountain are extremely broad (over 1km/½ mile wide).

It has three major summits, likened to a series of masts. In order of size they are the Main or Central Summit; the South Summit, 2161m (7090ft); and the North Summit, 2134m (7000ft), also known as the Fin. Ormes Rib is a basalt rib that lies on the North West Face of the North Summit.

The West Face, where most of Shiprock's routes lie, is a complex jumble of buttresses, ridges, and gullies. The northern portion of the West Face includes a huge black basalt intrusion called the Black Bowl.

The East Face is much less complex. It is broad and uniform – its most prominent feature is the Honeycomb Gully, a large vertical cleft that splits the face in half.

Right **According to Navajo legend, Shiprock is the petrified remains of a bird that carried their people from 'the netherland' to their present home; the harsh desert of the Four Corners area of the American South West.**

1966 The first ascent of 'Masthead Traverse' by H T Carter (this was also the first solo ascent).

1968 The first ascent of 'West Indies' by H T Carter.

1969 Attention turned to the then-untouched East Face of Shiprock. A Howells, D Doucette, and S Wilman made a bold attempt on the 3000m (10,000ft) buttress left of the Honeycomb Gully, but a storm forced retreat. Shortly afterwards, H T Carter, this time together with Denver climber B Forrest, climbed a line of thin cracks on the same face to produce 'Secret Passage'.

1994 L Laeser and C M Burns made the second ascent of the East Face, completing the route 'Friggin' in the Riggin' attempted by Howells, Doucette, and Wilman. This is of special interest as, although we had done extensive research into the legalities of climbing on the Navajo reservation, and had received permission from a Navajo 'grazing permit' holder, we began our route under the impression that no particular Navajo owned Shiprock. This was straightened out when Brandon Paul rode up to complain that we were trespassing on his family's land. After descending, and a brief meeting with Paul, we were allowed to complete our route. It is believed to be the first time Shiprock has ever been climbed with the permission of the local grazing permit holder.

1996 S Haston (British) and L Goualt (French) free climbed Spinnaker Tower, a subsidiary summit, at 5.11+.

Outrigger Spire

Main Summit

South Summit

South Col

Shiprock has numerous subsidiary summits rising from various points 'on deck'. The biggest and most prominent subsidiary spires lie on the north-western side of the mountain, and include Outrigger Spire and Spinnaker Tower. There are also numerous subsidiary summits on the plain surrounding Shiprock.

future climbing

Unlike most prominent landmarks in the American West, Shiprock's still-uncertain status for climbers has left the monolith virtually untouched. Indeed, on its South East Side, there is a full 1½km (1 mile) stretch of rock where not a single route exists. Tse Beh Tai has potential for hundreds of new routes and thousands of variations.

One of the biggest challenges remaining is an all-free route to the summit, requiring no jumaring or rappelling – in short, a route that does not rely on ropes and hardware.

Harvey Carter, now in his 60s, says he thinks he knows where such a route could exist. 'I've still got my eye on something,' he said recently. 'But I'm not going to tell you!'

west face

The five climbing routes on Shiprock's West Face begin on either the North Side or the South Side of the Main Summit Rib, which extends vertically down the face. Routes (1) and (2) start left of this, while routes (3), (4), and (5) start to its right.

1 Shiprock, the Standard Route IV, 5.9, A1

(A modification of the first ascent by D Brower, B Robinson, R Dedayn, and J Dyer 1939)
The Standard Route follows the line of least resistance up the Black Bowl before crossing the entire mountain at a point called the Sierra Col (just north of the North Summit), and descending onto the East Face via the Rappel Gully. The rock is firm, and the climbing extremely pleasant and safe. Ascent 550m (1800ft). Takes five hours.

2 Masthead Traverse V, 5.11, A2

H T Carter and S Mack 1966
This intricate route takes in the North and Main Summits. It leaves route (1) at the Colorado Col, climbs Ormes Rib, descends to the notch between the Summits, then climbs the North East corner of the Main Summit. The basalt on Ormes Rib is notoriously loose and difficult to protect. Height 550m (1800ft). Takes two days.

3 West Indies VI, 5.10, A3

H T Carter, P Sibley, and T Jennings 1968
This route climbs the rib below the Main Summit on the West Face, then the West Face of the Main Tower. It used to be called 'Wild West Wall'. Ascent 520m (1700ft). Three days.

4 Cowboys and Indians V, 5.9, A4

R Sylvester, K Cooney, and C Kroger 1982
Takes the left side of the West Wall

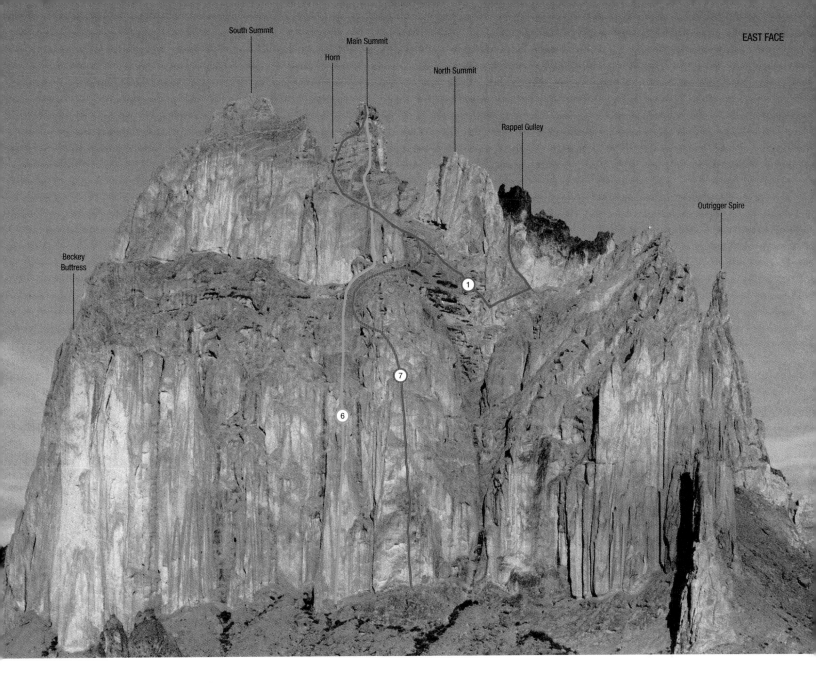

from behind the basalt Roost, a small subsidiary summit, to the notch below the Horn. This route features difficult, big-wall style climbing. Ascent 550m (1800ft). Two days.

5 Beckey Buttress VI, 5.9, A4
F Beckey and H T Carter 1965
This route climbs a crack system on the South West Face to join the massive South Buttress. Cracks and face climbing lead to the South Summit, from which a descent is made to join the 'Standard Route' (1). Probably the longest and most demanding climb on the mountain. Ascent 580m (1900ft). Seven days.

east face
Both routes on this face lie south of the Honeycomb Gully. Route (7) follows a major crack system on the large buttress immediately south of the gully, while route (6) climbs a wall 100m (330ft) south of route (7).

6 Secret Passage VI, 5.9, A3
H T Carter and B Forrest 1969
A bold route up a thin line of cracks in the centre of the East Face, just to the left of the Lower Honeycomb Gully. Above the initial 300m (100ft) wall, this route climbs the North East ridge of the South Summit before crossing Upper Honeycomb Gully to the North Summit. This difficult climb, 490m (1600ft), takes four days.

7 Friggin' in the Riggin' VI, 5.9, A3+
C Burns and L Laeser 1994
An extremely 'natural' route following a prominent crack system between 'Secret Passage' (6) and the Lower Honeycomb Gully. After 13 pitches, it joins the 'Standard Route' (1) in the Upper Honeycomb Gully. Ascent 1600m (490ft) in seven days.

how to get to shiprock
Located in the north-west corner of New Mexico, USA, 16km (10 miles) south of Shiprock town, Shiprock is reached via US Highway 666 from the town.

facilities
There are no facilities at the mountain. Nearest hotels are in Farmington and gear shops are in Durango, Colorado.

when to climb
The climbing season is generally considered to be the spring and autumn months, but it is possible to climb the mountain all year round.

gear
One set of wired stoppers, one set of friends, many slings and karabiners, and jumars. Bring an extra rope to leave fixed in Rappel Gully.

maps and guidebooks
There is no map of Shiprock. The recommended guide is Eric Bjørnstad's book, *Desert Rock* (1988).

language
English.

rescue and insurance
There is no mountain-rescue group and insurance is not usually carried.

red tape
The issue of climbing within the Navajo Nation appears to be still unresolved. Navajo Nation officials recommend that climbers get permission to climb from 'grazing permit' holders.

1545–66 The last recorded eruption of Orizaba volcano.

1796 Ferrer calculated the summit of El Pico de Orizaba to be 5453m (17,879ft).

1804 Baron Alexander von Humboldt, the German naturalist, explored the lower reaches of the volcano and calculated its height to be 5300m (17,375ft).

1848 While occupying the city of Orizaba as a part of General Scott's army in the war with Mexico, American Lt W F Raynolds organized an expedition consisting of eight army officers, two naval officers, and 36 enlisted men. The party ascended from the south-east via a route which is now known as 'El Perfil del Diablo'. On 10 May Raynolds, Maynard, and three soldiers erected a makeshift American flag on the summit in order to mark the first ascent.

1851 Doubting that Raynolds had really made the ascent, a group of 40 Mexican residents attempted to climb the peak. The summit was reached by a lone Frenchman, A Doignon, who found a tattered American flag there with '1848' whittled into its shaft.

1890 Professor A Heilprin, who came from America, organized an expedition from Philadelphia and ascended Orizaba, Popocatepetl, and Iztaccihuatl. He calculated the height of Orizaba to be 5553m (18,205ft) and at that time it was believed to be the highest peak in North America.

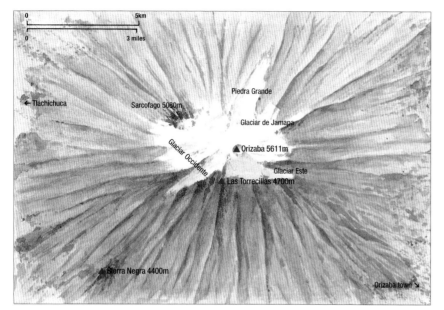

el pico de orizaba

barry blanchard

El Pico de Orizaba, which stands at 5611m (18,410ft), is the third-highest peak in North America. Close to the rural town of Tlachichuca, and anchoring the eastern end of Mexico's Cordillera de Anahuac, El Pico de Orizaba rises with its long hyperbolic skylines above golden fields of corn. A dormant volcano, Orizaba's composite cone is nearly perfect. To the Aztecs it was known as Cetlaltépetl, or Star Mountain – the place where Quetzalcoatl, the plumed serpent god, was consumed by divine fire in the crater. To the east of the mountain lie fertile and flat high plains; to the west, deep ravines and lush tropical forests slope down to the Gulf of Mexico. Orizaba alone soars above it all.

'El Pico' has long been a required ascent for any aspiring Mexican mountaineer and, over the last 25 years, in combination with the range's other two high volcanoes, Popocatepetl and Iztaccihuatl, it has become a popular first taste of altitude – and perhaps foreign culture – for many American and Canadian climbers. The three peaks, often coined 'Los Tres Picos', can be sensibly ascended over a 2-week itinerary and via moderate mountaineering terrain. As a volcano, Orizaba offers little steep ground, which is perhaps a blessing as the rock is hideously loose. Overall, the Mexican volcanoes are a place for mountaineers to attain moderate altitudes with little to no technical difficulty. Although offering good views and Mexican colour, they have very little for the serious climber.

ridges, faces, and peaks

The summit of Orizaba is the high point of a perfectly circular volcanic crater which is over 150m (500ft) deep and contains a lake. One expedition abseiled to the lake and then scuba-dived into it! Permanent snow and glaciers cling to all aspects of the crater rim, except in the south.

The Glaciar de Jamapa forms the North Slope of the mountain, flowing down to 4900m (16,100ft). The Piedra Grande Hut is situated at its base, in the plateau that gives it its name. The dark cliffs of the Sarcofago – eroded remnants of a previous crater at 5080m (16,700ft) – interrupt the volcano's constant slope on the west. The West Side sweeps from there to the Ruta Sur in a series of ice tongues descending from the Glaciar Occidente, which are delineated by weak ridges.

One of the few defined ridges of this relatively young volcano marks the traditional route of ascent and the beginning of the very dry and rocky South Side. This side is basically a sweep of scree and talus slopes, perforated by shattered ridges and small towers. To the east, the glaciation creeps lower towards the two large couloirs, the Glaciar Este and the eastern edge of the Glaciar de Jamapa.

The Aguja de Hielo, the 'Ice Needle', is an anomalous rock pinnacle at the crater rim.

future climbing

There is definitely some potential for more modern ice routes on the West Side of El Pico, between it and its satellite, the Sarcofago.

Right **The near-perfect cone of the Mexican volcano El Pico de Orizaba, viewed from the north-west. From base to summit the climate runs through the range from tropical jungle to arctic snow.**

1922 O McAllister, a Harvard graduate living in Mexico, formed the Club de Exploraciones de Mexico, AC (CEMAC). Throughout the early 1920s, members of CEMAC made ascents of Orizaba. In the early 1930s one of the club's groups, in search of more technical challenges, climbed Las Torrecillas, the Little Towers, on the South Side of the mountain.

c. **1960** Early in this decade road access was established to Piedre Grande and the 'regular' route up the mountain changed from the Ruta Sur (the southern approach) to the Glaciar de Jamapa .

1962 A group from the Socorro Alpino de Mexico opened the 'Ruta Juventud'.

1978 J Israels soloed 'Horror Frost', a steeper new line on the West Side.

1988 Canadians W Barron and B Blanchard discovered some waterfall-type ice climbing on the cliff between the Sarcofago and Orizaba.

Glaciar de Jamapa

north side

This provides the most pleasant way up the peak, offering the most glaciated travel and, therefore, the least amount of crumbly volcanic stumbling. There is also a dependable year-round water source. Routes on the North Side usually start on the Piedra Grande – the plateau just above the tree-line at 4260m (14,000ft).

1 Glaciar de Jamapa F

The normal route up the mountain. Basic 30° glacial travel and possibly the occasional crevasse. A disturbing number of people have slid to their deaths in icy, hard snow conditions. Take a rope and know self-arrest skills. This takes 6–9 hours from Piedra Grande – a 1350m (4400ft) elevation gain from the hut.

2 Ruta Espinoza F

A variation to the Glaciar de Jamapa, offering the option of a traverse of the Sarcofago. Given the prevailing westerly winds it is often scoured down to ice or hard snow. Allow 6–12 hours from Piedra Grande. This route is a 1350m (4400ft) elevation gain.

west side

This side has some of the worthwhile and rare steeper climbing, and is pleasantly free of people. Water can be a problem in the drier periods of the year.

3 Horror Frost PD

J Israels 1978
The crux is 30m (100ft) of 60° ice. A 1000m (3300ft) ascent from the ruins of the Jose Llaca Hut, taking 4–8 hrs.

4 The Serpent's Head AD

W Barron and B Blanchard 1988
Fine grade 3 waterfall ice at 4875m (16,000ft) – the only technical climbing on the mountain. A pre-dawn start from a high camp is recommended as there is a threat from rockfall on a hot day. Named for a window and fangs of ice climbed through on the first ascent; like stepping through the jaws of Quetzalcoatl, the serpent god. It is 1000m (3300ft) from the ruins of the Jose Llaca Hut, and takes 6–10 hours.

5 Ruta Juventud PD-

G Caballero, A Alvarez, C Castillo, R Garcia, D Aguero, and J Rodea 1962
This is a scramble to the western edge of the Glaciar de Jamapa. It is a 1000m (3300ft) elevation gain from the ruins of the Jose Llaca hut, taking 4–8 hours.

6 Ruta Alejandre PD-

This route follows a ridge scrambling to 5000m (16,400ft) then a traversing line to snow and ice and the summit. It is a 900m (3000ft) gain from a high camp and takes 4–8 hours.

7 Ruta Abrego PD- ⊠

This a ridge scramble to a low lobe of glacial ice and follows 30° ice to the summit. A 1000m (3300ft) elevation gain from the ruins of the Jose Llaca Hut; 6–10 hours.

8 La Cara del Muerto PD-

This route is called 'The Face of Death', probably because of the loose scree and sand leading to the ice of the summit slopes. A 1000m (3300ft) elevation gain from the ruins of the Jose Llaca Hut, it takes 6–10 hours.

9 Ruta Vazquez PD-

Ascending the south-west ice tongue of the Glaciar Occidente, this route has possibly the best-quality climbing after 'The Serpent's Head' (4). It is a 1000m (3300ft) elevation gain from the ruins of the Jose Llaca Hut, taking 6–10 hours.

south side ⊠

This side of the mountain suffers from a lack of snow and water. The best time to attempt to climb it is from late September–early December. There are two satellite peaks offering scrambles from the Fausto Gomez Gomar Hut, which is at 4660m (15,300ft) on the Ruta Sur. Las Torrecillas, at 4700m (15,400ft),

Sarcofago

is just south-east of the hut and Sierra Negra, at 4400m (14,400ft), is approximately 6km (4 miles) to the south-west.

10 Ruta Sur F-
This used to be the old regular route and is a rock scramble for all but the last few metres. It is still particularly popular with Mexican climbers. There is a 950m (3100ft) elevation gain from Fausto Gomez Gomar Hut. This route takes 5–7 hours to climb.

11 El Perfil del Diablo F-
Lt W Raynolds, Maynard, and party 1848
This route was the line of the first ascent party. It is a rock scramble similar to the Ruta Sur, but a little longer. There is a 950m (3100ft) elevation gain from the Fausto Gomez Gomar Hut and the route takes 6–8 hours to climb.

east side
Because of the prevailing westerly winds, more snow, giving more

secure footing, is often found here when the Glaciar de Jamapa is icy. Heading east across the Jamapa in dry conditions will often create a safer ascent.

12 Glaciar Este PD+
Two couloir options. The left offering 40° climbing, the right up to 50° with potential rockfall. Reached via a traverse at the 5000m (16,400ft) level from the Glaciar de Jamapa. The 1350m (4400ft) elevation gain from Piedra Grande Hut takes 8–12 hours.

13 El Filo de Chichimeco PD
A moonscape ridge scramble that narrows towards the eastern edge of the Glaciar de Jamapa. Up the glacier to the Aguja de Hielo, the route goes on to the summit. It is a 1300m (4300ft) elevation gain from high camp and takes 6–10 hours.

how to get to el pico de orizaba
International flights are frequent into Mexico City or Vera Cruz. Tlachichuca, Coscomatepec, and Ciudad Serdan can be reached by bus or car. The Reyes family bus service offers airport packages. 4WD needed to get to the right hut or trailhead.

facilities
There are all levels of accommodation and shops in Mexico City, Vera Cruz, and Orizaba. Some equipment is made and sold in Mexico City. Simple lodging and meals, and 4WD transport to roadheads are available in Tlachichuca, Coscomatepec, and Ciudad Serdan.

when to climb
November–March is the dry season, giving the best chance of success. October–early December has more snow.

gear
Standard mountaineering kit plus snow pickets. Clothing to protect from possible

-30°C (-20°F) wind chills. Waterfall ice gear including 10 screws for route (4).

maps and guidebooks
Four 1:50,000 topographical maps are needed: 'Coscomatepec' (E14B46), 'San Salvador El Secon' (E14B45), 'Ciudad Serdan' (E14B55), and 'Orizaba' (E14B56). All are available at the INEGI office, Balderas 71, Mexico City. *Mexico's Volcanoes, A Climbing Guide,* R J Secor (The Mountaineers, 2nd edition, 1993) is essential.

language
Spanish. English is understood in the bigger cities, but not in the rural towns.

rescue and insurance
There is no organized rescue service but the Reyes family often evacuates people from the Piedro Grande Hut.

red tape
None.

Caribbean Sea

North Atlantic
Ocean

Pacific
Ocean

E C U A D O R
● Quito
▲ Chimborazo
*Cordillera
Occidental*

*Cordillera
Blanca*
▲ Huascarán
● Huaraz

P E R U

● Lima

B R A Z I L

● La Paz
▲ Illimani
Cordillera Real

B O L I V I A

Cordillera Andes
▲ Aconcagua
● Santiago

South Atlantic
Ocean

A R G E N T I N A

C H I L E

*Campo de
Hielo Sur*
▲ Cerro Torre

Falkland Islands

south america

Hundreds of years before mountaineers arrived on the continent from Europe, the native Incas, for whom the mountains were sacred, had climbed many of the South American high summits.

The Andes, extending some 9000km (5500 miles) along the western edge of the continent, form the longest mountain system in the world and offer some of the world's finest mountaineering. They comprise a labyrinth of separate chains of peaks, or *cordillera* – 20 or more within Peru alone, where Huascarán dominates the Cordillera Blanca. Easily accessible from Lima, this is perhaps the most popular range of all, with its steep, shapely peaks – many over 6000m (19,700ft) – draped in exotic ice flutings with notoriously unstable cornice ridges. Bolivia's Illimani, with its three main summits, is the highest mountain of the Cordillera Real. In Ecuador, the volcanoes of Cotopaxi and Chimborazo have long presented a most exciting attraction.

The spectacular granite towers that characterize Patagonian peaks are represented here by Cerro Torre, which has been described as a scream in stone. Many believe it to be the world's most difficult mountain. Certainly, it is one of the most savage, with its howling winds and atrocious weather. These characteristics, and its controversial climbing history, lend Cerro Torre an aura that makes it a prize coveted by accomplished climbers of many nations.

Below left: **Cerro Torre at dawn** Below right: **South Face of Aconcagua**

1802 Famous scientists Aimé Bonpland (French) and Alexander von Humbolt (German) claimed to have reached a height of 5900m (19,300ft) on the South Side of the mountain before being stopped by an 'insurmountable cleft'.
1880 The first ascent of Chimborazo was made by J A and L Carrel (Italian) and E Whymper (British) via the South West Ridge and Face.
1911 N Martínez and M Tul followed Whymper's route from the north-west. Tradition credits this as the first Ecuadorian ascent.
1939 P Ghiglione claimed to have made a third new route by climbing to the Main Summit directly from the South East, via the Totorillas Glacier.
1968 A party of Americans and Germans opened the first technically interesting route to the summit when they climbed the North Ridge via the Abraspungo Glacier. This was done in six days.
1971 A Holguin, L Meneses, C Ortiz, S Rivadeneira, R Sáenz, and D Terán (Ecuadorian) made the first ascent of Cima Politécnica by climbing directly to the col between this and the Whymper Summit, via the Boussingault Glacier.
1972 J Dobrzysky, G Grizez, and A Paulo from Poland scored a considerable *coup* by making the first ascent of the technically difficult Cima Nicolás Martínez.
1979 M Jácome (Ecuadorian) and five other members from Quito's Cumbres Andinas Club made the first complete traverse of the Main Summit. Swiss climbers F Kulin and R Menzi claimed

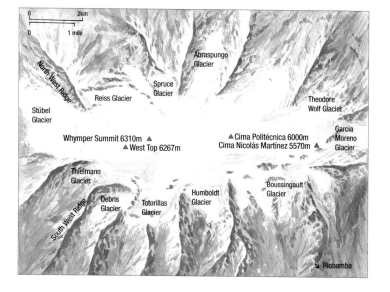

chimborazo

lindsay griffin

Most of Ecuador's mountains are to be found in two parallel chains of volcanic origin running north to south through the country. Between the two lies a main valley system, often referred to as the Avenue of Volcanoes, that holds the major towns and villages of Ecuador. The highest of all the peaks in these two chains, Chimborazo, lies in the western range, or Cordillera Occidental, and to the north-west of the large town of Riobamba.

Because the earth bulges in the region of the equator, Chimborazo's summit is actually the point furthest from the centre of the Earth. Its accepted altitude of 6310m (20,702ft) is taken from the country's most accurate source, the Instituto Geográfico Militar. However, an exhaustive differential Global Positioning Systems satellite survey by the British military in 1993 computed a slightly lower height of 6268m (20,565ft) and this may in future become the standard.

Chimborazo is simply an Indian word meaning 'great snowy mountain'. As one of the world's best-known mountains, it attracts a large international clientele, offering the rare opportunity to ascend to 'high altitude' in the timescale of a short holiday; it is also within the scope of mountaineers of limited technical competence – a Mont Blanc of the Andes. For the unacclimatized the ascent may prove the ultimate in purgatory, but to stand on the summit during one of those rare Ecuadorian days of crystal clarity is to experience that spendid awareness of true isolation only volcanoes can bring.

From the summit dome an almost complete panorama across the Avenue of Volcanoes is visible, from Cayambe, 5789m (18,993ft), and the active jungle cone of Reventador, 3485m (11,434ft), in the north to the highly technical El Altar massif, 5319m (17,452ft), and extremely active Sangay, 5230m (17,160ft), to the south. Not far away to the north-east stands Ecuador's other world-renowned summit, the classic and beautiful volcanic cone of Cotopaxi, at 5897m (19,348ft). And, if you are lucky, you may catch a glimpse of the Pacific Ocean.

ridges, faces, and peaks

The mountain has a complex structure with many different glaciers but no volcanic activity. Where the volcanic rock does make an appearance, it is generally of very poor quality. Chimborazo has a broad, elongated crest more than 8km (5 miles) in length that supports five individual tops. Hidden away on the flanks are subsidiary ridges, spurs, and facets of steeper terrain. These pose interesting and complex technical problems for the mountaineer.

The most easterly and lowest summit, *c.*5570m (*c.*18,275ft), is Cima Nicolás Martínez. It owes its name to the 'father' of Ecuadorian climbing. There is, in addition, a small lower rocky point on the East Ridge known as Cima Nicolás Dueñas. Moving west, the Cima Politécnica, or the Central Summit, 6000m (19,686ft), is next; followed by the Main, or Whymper, Summit, 6310m (20,700ft); Veintemilla, the West Top or foresummit, 6267m (20,562ft); and the North Top, or México Summit, *c.*6200m (*c.*20,340ft). The Main Summit is the highest point of a large plateau rising only 50m (165ft), over a distance of more than 1km (½ mile), from Veintemilla.

Minimal visibility is the norm on Chimborazo, making orientation difficult for mountaineers, though marker flags are often in place during the most popular climbing seasons. The rarely traversed connecting ridge to Politécnica and beyond to Nicolás Martínez is often far from straightforward and, while the extensive glaciated slopes of its sunnier northern slopes remain more or less uniform, the southern flanks are very sheer another new route on the South Face via the tongue and moderately steep slopes of the Boussingault Glacier.

1980 To celebrate the 100th anniversary of the first ascent, a large hut named the Refugio Whymper, was opened below the South West Ridge close to the foot of the Thielmann Glacier.

The first complete traverse of the three distinct summits, Cima Nicolás Martinez, Cima Politécnica, and the Main Summit, was successfully made.

1983 J Anhalzer, R Cárdenas, and R Navarrete (Ecuadorian) made the first ascent of the North East Ridge of Nicolás Martînez, calling it the 'Arista del Sol'. This is probably the hardest route to date on Chimborazo and possibly the best established high-mountain rock route in Ecuador. The

first ascent was made of the prominent South Ridge of Cima Politécnica.

1984 The South East Spur of the Cima Politécnica received its first ascent and is one of the few routes on the mountain to offer significant rock climbing in its lower section. Another new route to the Main Summit, on the South-South-West Face, was climbed by M Woolridge and L Griffin (British).

1993 In one of the worst accidents to occur in the history of Ecuadorian climbing, 13 people were avalanched from the upper slopes of the mountain, resulting in 10 fatalities.

1996 The most recent new route was the result of a fast solo ascent of a series of ephemeral icefalls on the rocky West Face by the American guide, S House.

and impressive. For these reasons, while few climbers choose to tread summits other than the Whymper and Veintemilla, Nicolás Martínez is by far the most interesting for technical alpinists.

future climbing

In the coming years, Chimborazo will undoubtedly attract greater and greater numbers of non-technical mountaineers to its summit as the explosion of organized commercial mountain expeditions continues. This is largely due to the rapid improvement in the infrastructure for climbing throughout Ecuador in recent years. However, having said this, it seems unlikely that a large number of new routes will be established in the near future. While there are a few undiscovered secrets hidden on northern and eastern flanks, together with some hard unclimbed lines on the south faces of the lesser summits, the lengthy access and certain degree of objective danger will mean that only the most adventurous opportunist is likely to try anything new.

Above **Chimborazo from the slopes of Carahuarazo to the north-east. The Arista del Sol is the narrow rocky ridge falling directly towards the camera from the smallest summit, Cima Nicolás Martínez, on the left.**

Labels on image: North Face · West Face · South West Ridge · Thielmann Glacier

north side

The more gentle glacier slopes of the North Side, which were followed by Edward Whymper during the second ascent of the mountain, provided the most popular ascent route in former times. There are now three established approaches to the upper slopes.

1 North Side – Las Murallas Rojas PD

D Beltran, J Campaña, J-A and L Carrel, and E Whymper 1880

The most interesting feature of the ascent is passing a band of red rocks (the Murallas Rojas) via steep snow/ice on its right side at around 5700m (18,700ft). The snow can start to become sloppy after midday and quickly prone to avalanche so it is essential to make a very early start. Climbers sometimes use a high camp, known as the Japanese Camp, on a level area at around 5400m (17,700ft) as a take-off point, but from the Nido de Condores at least 8–9 hours should be allowed for an ascent. Since the introduction of the Whymper Hut below the South West Ridge this route has rarely been followed. *c.*1200m (*c.*3900ft) of ascent.

2 North Side via the Castillo PD/PD+

First ascent unknown

This line became popular after the construction of the Whymper Hut and forms the Standard Route during periods when the original Whymper Route (5) is dry and exposed to rockfall. It reaches the spur of route (1) by using a right-slanting snow ramp below the rocky ridge north-west of the Hut. The eastern end of this ridge has a prominent tower named the Castillo or Peñon. The route is approximately 1200m (3900ft) and normally takes 8–9 hours.

3 North Side via the Thielmann Glacier PD–AD-

First ascent unknown

Climbs the lower Thielmann Glacier direct to the spur mentioned above. The glacier has some interesting ice steps but can be objectively dangerous. The slope can contain large crevasses but is little more than 40°. Eight hours for an acclimatized party. *c.*1300m (*c.*4300ft).

west face

A steep face of rock and ice bounded on the right by the South West Ridge, followed by the original ascent.

4 West Face

S House 1996

This route climbs the thin ice runnels through the rocky area to the right of the Thielmann Glacier. It was given an American water-ice grade of 4 and has sections of 85° with mixed climbing. *c.*1200m (*c.*3900ft). This route probably needs to be climbed fast or not at all, so aim for a 1-day ascent.

5 Original Route PD/PD+

J-A and L Carrel, and E Whymper 1880

This historic route, following the South West Ridge and Face, is characterized by long, moderately angled snow slopes which are reached by a crux ice runnel of *c.*45° above a well-defined ridge. It is inadvisable for climbers to attempt this if the rock barrier is bare of ice or if the upper séracs threaten the routes. *c.*1300m (*c.*4300ft) of ascent that will take approximately 8–9 hours.

6 South-South-West Face AD

L Griffin and M Woolridge 1984

After a steep, loose, but relatively easy rock band close to the base of the route, the climb follows uniform slopes then finds a way through a succession of sérac barriers to reach the plateau. 50°, with short steeper sections, there is some objective danger, and potentially avalanche-prone slopes. *c.*1500m (*c.*5000ft). Allow 1½ days for this route, although a well-acclimatized pary could complete it in a day.

7 Arista del Sol TD

J Anhalzer, R Cardenas, and R Navarrete 1983

The first two-thirds of the North East Ridge's height are more or less entirely on rock (up to V maximum). The upper section is a fine snow arête. The route is 1000m (3300ft); allow two full days to climb it.

Murallas Rojas

West Face

how to get to chimborazo

It is very easy – you can take a flight to Quito, then get public transport to Riobamba, then local taxi to the (gravelled) roadhead 30–45 mins' walk from the Whymper Hut below the South West Ridge. This is the usual starting place, which is at about 4950m (16,250ft).

when to climb

There are supposed to be two seasons when the weather is drier and more predictable: July/August and December/January are the best times to attempt a climb. However, these seasons do not always happen – parties have sometimes experienced very bad periods of weather at all times of the year, although serious storms are uncommon. The biggest problem for climbers tends to be lack of visibility caused by thick mist (though this can disperse at night).

gear

Good boots, an axe, and crampons are essential for anyone attempting to climb the gentler slopes of Chimborazo.

If you plan to embark on one of the harder routes, you will need to take with you the usual assortment of Andean hardware, including snowstakes, deadmen, long ice screws, and very good bivouac equipment. Also make sure you take plenty of warm clothing with you because a night out on the mountain can often be extremely cold.

facilities

Riobamba caters for all grades of accommodation, as well as food shops and markets. Quito, Ecuador's capital, is the point of entry for most climbers. There is an association of guides situated here who offer good accommodation and information, and may be able to help climbers find the necessary equipment. The Whymper Hut has a permanent warden and cooking facilities.

language

Latin-American Spanish and local dialects. English is not widely understood – especially once you get away from the main cities.

rescue and insurance

The local guides offer a rescue service, but do not count on anything more elaborate than a party of climbers organized from Quito. Full expedition insurance is strongly advised.

maps and guidebooks

The Instituto Geográfico Militar (IGM) produces 1:50,000 maps.

The Spanish-language guide *Montañas del Sol*, Landazuri, Rojas, and Serrano (Campo Abierto), and the English guide *Ecuador, a Climbing Guide*, Yossi Brain (The Mountaineers) are the most comprehensive books on the area.

red tape

Permits are not needed.

1904 British explorer R Enock made the first attempt on Huascarán, only reaching 5100m (16,700) on the South West Flank, but accurately guessing the summit to be around 6800m (22,300ft).
1908 Annie Peck (American) reached the summit of Norte, with Swiss guides R Taugwalder and G zum Taugwald.
1932 P Borchers's Austro-German team made the first ascent of Sur.

1958 The first technical route on the mountain was made by six Americans who completed the upper South East Ridge to Sur. The summit party included Irene Ortenburger, making the first female ascent of the highest point.
1966 A French team made the first impression on the North Face of Norte, completing a siege of the prominent spur on the right side of this wall.

1969 A 3-man Canadian team created 'The Shield' on the West Spur.
1970 14 members of A Cernik's Czechoslovakian expedition were killed when a 40-second earth tremor (7.8 on the Richter Scale) triggered a cataclysmic rockfall from the West Face of Norte. The resulting avalanche swept down the Rio Santa Valley, wiping out the town of Yungay and most of

Huaraz. 80,000 people died and a million were left homeless.
1971 Three New Zealanders made the first integral ascent of the South East Ridge. They crossed the Main Summit, then descended the 1961 'Spanish Route' (*see route 10*) on the North East Ridge back down to the Matara Glacier to complete the first traverse of Sur. A few days later four other members of

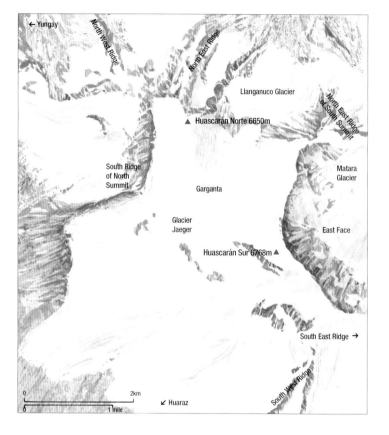

huascarán

lindsay griffin

Standing close to the thriving city of Huaraz in northern Peru, Huascarán is part of the chain of dramatic icy peaks known as the Cordillera Blanca and, at 6768m (22,200ft), is the fourth-highest mountain on the whole of the American continent. Most of the Cordillera Blanca chain lies within the Huascarán National Park, which was officially created in 1975. The area is the most popular climbing and trekking venue in Peru and the reasons for its popularity are clear: access to it is very easy, there are no bureaucratic problems, the climbing is brilliant, and the mountains are as stunning as those found almost anywhere else in the world.

Huascarán attracts considerable international attention because of its altitude, and the fact that it is the highest point in the Peruvian Andes and can be reached by a relatively non-technical route. While most summiteers now follow the 'Standard Route' on Sur, there have been, over the years, a number of ground-breaking ascents on the various ridges and faces – several of which, such as the 'French Route' on Huascarán Norte, have become quasi-classic test-pieces for ambitious visitors.

ridges, faces, and peaks

Huascarán has twin summits. Huascarán Sur is the South, and higher, Summit; approximately 3km (2 miles) to the north-west is the North Summit, or Huascarán Norte, which, at 6650m (21,800ft), is 118m (400ft) lower. Separating the two is a broad, icy, and often windswept col called the Garganta, at 6000m (19,700ft).

The Huascarán massif is defined by four river valleys: the Santa to the west, holding the main centres of habitation and dividing the Cordillera Blanca from the snowless Cordillera Negra; Llanganuco to the north; Huaripampa flowing down towards the jungle to the east; and Ulta to the south.

huascarán norte Probably the most impressive face in the entire massif is the North Face of Norte, overlooking the Llanganuco Lakes. It is an awesome 1600m (5300ft) high wall that in the drier conditions of late season can become almost entirely rocky. The true face is defined on the right by the largely snowy North West Ridge, although the right edge of the rock wall is formed by a prominent spur with a large buttress, christened the Pear, in the lower section. Separating the North Face from the 1350m (4400ft) high, mixed rock-and-ice wall of the North East Face is the elegant, arrow-like line of the North East Ridge, a 4km (2½ mile) icy crest with several rock steps.

A narrow, inset North West Face is largely rock, but to its right the West Face continues as a jumble of sérac-torn ice, towards the more gentle snow slopes of the South Ridge. The latter is the only real line of weakness on the mountain.

huascarán sur The South West Face on Huascarán Sur is a hideous jumble of life-threatening sérac barriers set above a high, gently angled glacier. It is bounded on the left by the knife-edged West Spur. On the opposite side of the mountain, the 6km (3¾ mile) wide East Face, at the head of the Matara Valley,

Right **High on the 1966 'French Route' on the North Face of Huascarán Norte during the second ascent.**

the group made the first ascent of the vast East Face and then completed a second traverse, descending the 'Standard Route'.

1972 J Frehel's 4-man French team climbed the North East Ridge of Norte. K Kochi (Japanese) made probably the first true solo ascent of the Sur.

1973 A powerful French team created an outstanding mixed climb on the North East Face, using 1500m (5000ft) of rope, over a period of 14 days.

1977 R Casarotto (Italian) made the first direct ascent of the North Face of Norte. All attempts to repeat this route have failed and at least three climbers have died trying. The 'Standard Route' on Norte was climbed by N Croucher (British) – a remarkable achievement as he lost both legs below the knee at 19.

1979 N Jaeger (French) spent 70 days alone just below the Main Summit to conduct high-altitude medical tests.

1980 A Spanish team became the first to reach the Garganta from the east.

1985 B Grison (French) made first ascent of the North East Face of Sur in a bold solo effort, but did not continue to the summit after joining the North East Ridge. Two weeks later C Buhler (American) and Sharon Wood (Canadian), unaware of the ascent, climbed a parallel line, joined his route, continued over the summit, and down the 'Standard Route'.

1991 The last certain new route on Sur climbed a 1000m (3000ft) open gully on the South West Face between the West Rib and the huge sérac barrier to the right. Slovenian ace S Sveticic made a fast solo ascent.

is a steep icy wall, raked by stonefall from a capping rock barrier that starts around 6400m (21,000ft). Between the two lies the South East Ridge, a heavily corniced crest that loses height gradually from the summit to the small pyramid referred to as 'Point' 6410m (21,030ft), below which it divides. The east branch has alternate sections of rock and ice, while the south-west branch makes a long descent over snow, then rock, to the Ulta Valley. Between the two lies a relatively steep, triangular, glaciated slope of variable difficulty.

The wide, stone-swept North East Face rises to the complex and corniced North East Ridge. It is bounded on the right side by the broad, crevassed, north-west-facing slopes above the Garganta, leading at a moderate angle to the extensive summit plateau. These snow slopes are now often referred to as the Glacier Jaeger after the well-known French alpinist and medic who died on Lhoste Shar in the Himalaya in 1980.

future climbing

Despite a total of well over 20 different routes currently completed on both summits, the variety of high faces and fine ridges ensures that the scope for additional lines is still vast. The highly dangerous West Face on Norte remains unclimbed. New routes will be subject to variable amounts of objective danger and they will most likely succumb to light and fast ascents by talented performers who are lucky with conditions, weather, and timing.

Nowadays the great lines are being climbed in alpine style and most visiting parties are of the small, informal, and environmentally friendly type which come to climb a selection of routes in the region, treating it as a high-altitude alpine venue.

As other countries increase their climbing restrictions and bureaucracy, it is likely that more parties will be drawn back to the freedom offered by Peru. I hope that the national authorities realize that this is the Cordillera Blanca's greatest attraction.

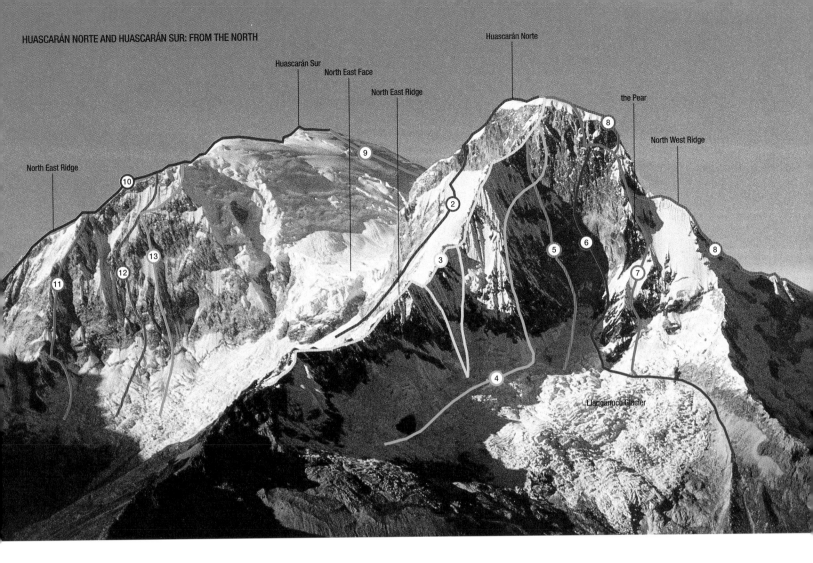

Although alpine grades are quoted, these do not take into account the increased seriousness of climbing on Huascarán due to factors such as the far greater altitude, and should not be taken as a direct comparison with standards in the European Alps.

huascarán norte

The lower of the two summits, but possibly the most important for the ambitious technical alpinist due to the groundbreaking routes on the North Face.

1 South Ridge: Standard Route PD+

A Peck, G zum Taugwald, and R Taugwalder 1908
The easiest route to either summit, this first reaches the Garganta from the west. Normally straightforward 40° snow slopes above. Takes several days from base camp.

2 North East Face TD+

M Barrard, L Desrivieres, G Narbaud, and J Ricouard 1973
An outstanding 1350m (4400ft) route of great quality, following the prominent 50–60° ice slope then breaking through the rock barrier at V+ and A1. Takes at least two days.

3 North East Ridge TD+

R Coene, M Fevrier J Frehel, and J Porret 1972
A splendid and objectively safe line up an icy crest interrupted by four steps of generally poor rock (V maximum). This route is climbed fairly regularly and is probably better later in the season. It is around 1700m (5500ft) and will take at least three days.

north face

This 1600m (5250ft), largely rocky face gives some of the most serious and committing mixed routes in the Cordillera Blanca; only the original line, which is largely sheltered from stonefall, has become a classic climb. Allow at least four days for an ascent of any of the routes on this face.

4 Spanish Route ED2

J Moreno, J Tomas, and C Valles 1983
An extremely steep line that is best climbed in very dry conditions when the face is almost entirely rock. (Earlier in the season the rock will probably be covered in ice.) Short sections of vertical ice with a crux rock pillar at the top, originally graded VI and A3.

5 Swiss Route ED1/2

D Anker and K Saurer 1986
After a big quasi-vertical icefall in the lower section, this climb crosses the 'Spanish Route' (4) to avoid the latter's crux pillar on the left.

6 Italian Directissima ED3

R Casarotto 1977
A direct line to the exit cracks of the 'French Route' (7) that is mainly steep, free and aid climbing VI+ and A2/3 on both good and bad granite, interspersed with difficult mixed terrain. This route took 20 days on the first ascent.

7 French Route ED1

R Jacob, C Jaccoux, D Leprince-Ringuet, and R Paragot 1966
This *tour de force* has become the classic hard route and is ascended relatively frequently. Nowadays, parties avoid the rotten rock of the Pear by 60° ice to the right. The crux lies above on the right side of the crest (V and A1).

8 North West Ridge TD+

E Detomasi, C Piazzo, D Saettone, and T Vidone 1974
A long snowy section with possible cornice difficulty leads to a junction with the 'French Route' (7). The crux lies directly above, with the crest taken on the right side.

huascarán sur

The higher of the two summits, Huascarán Sur is rarely climbed other than by route (9).

9 North West Slopes: Standard Route PD/PD+

H Bernard, P Borchers, E Hein, H Hoerlin, and E Schneider 1932
The standard route via the Garganta is technically straightforward and understandably popular, though certainly not suitable for an inexperienced party. It is a serious glacier expedition that can involve complicated route finding through séracs, crevasses, and icefalls if there is not a well-beaten track. It is often badly exposed to falling ice below the Garganta. This route takes several days from the base camp.

10 North East Ridge (Spanish Route) TD

P Acuna, F Mautino, A Perez, and S Rivas 1961
This route is long, committing, and often badly corniced but the

difficulties do vary. Recent ascents have involved time-consuming climbing over and around precarious mushroom-like ice formations. Allow several days to climb the 1350m (4400ft) route.

north east face

This broad face, stone-swept on the left and exposed to sérac avalanche on the right, has few objectively safe lines. All routes are around 1500m (5000ft) to the summit and will probably take 3–4 days.

11 The Road to Hell ED2
M Kovac, B Lozar, and T Petac 1993
Mostly hard rock climbing (VI+ and A1) up the wide pillar on the left side of the face. Finishes on the ridge at 6100m (20,000ft).

12 American Route TD/TD+
C Buhler and S Wood 1985
Not too steep with 50–75° ice, mixed terrain, and a little V on poor rock. Objectively a very serious route.

13 French Route ED1
B Grison 1985
Very intricate climbing, reaching the ridge at 6400m (21,000ft).

how to get to huascarán
Easy access – many flights are available to Lima and from there is it is a day's bus ride to Huaraz, the most popular and convenient centre. The base camp for the 'Standard Route' is 3-hours' walk above the roadhead at Musho, east of Mancos, and the standard site on the North Side is close to the road in the Llanganuco Valley. A regular tourist bus runs north from Huaraz via Mancos and Yungay to the valley, or you can use cargo trucks and local taxis. Mules for carrying equipment can be hired from the nearest village.

facilities
Huaraz has basic hotels, cafés, and restaurants. It is possible to buy just about every type of food and equipment necessary for base camp, but specialized mountain food should be brought into the country. Standard camping-gas cartridges are normally available in Huaraz, at a price.

when to climb
The main season is the dry austral winter that runs from early May–early

September. The weather tends to be at its most stable in June and begins to break down during August. Snow and ice conditions are generally better before mid-July.

gear
It gets cold at night so a good tent and sleeping/bivouac equipment are essential. The deep powder snow (for which Peru is famous) necessitates big deadmen and long snowstakes. A snow shovel can also prove useful. The usual array of rock gear, pegs, and good ice screws are essential for the harder routes.

maps and guidebooks
There are various 1:100,000 maps to the northern Cordillera Blanca region, and a good German 1:25,000 map to Huascarán specifically.

By far the best guide to the Blanca is *Climbs of the Cordillera Blanca of Peru*, David Sharman, although the inspiring but now outdated *Yuraq Janka*, John Ricker, with its fine black-and-white panoramas, is still a useful source of reference for climbers.

language
Latin-American Spanish. English is not widely spoken, though this does not usually present a problem in the tourist resorts such as Huaraz.

rescue and insurance
Rescues normally have to be carried out by climbers themselves. A helicopter rescue may be possible up to 4500m (14,800ft) but this has to be initiated by an embassy and requires a very substantial deposit. Full expedition insurance is advised.

red tape
None.

1883 P Güssfeldt (German) reached 6560m (21,522ft) on the North West Ridge from the Rio Volcan.

1896-7 E FitzGerald's (British) expedition first climbed the 'Normal Route'. M Zurbriggen, his Swiss guide, summited alone on 14 January 1897. A month later S Vines (British) and Nicola Lanti (Italian) also reached the top. FitzGerald wrote his classic

book *The Highest Andes*, a splendid account of the adventure.

1934 The Polish Glacier was opened by Polish climbers S Daszyinski, K Narkievicz-Jodko, S Osiecki, and W Ostrowski.

1953 In search of terrain more like the Alps, F Marmillod, his wife Dorly (Swiss residents of Argentina), and F Grahales and F Ibanez (Argentine) made a

circuitous line up the South West Ridge, summiting on 23 January.

1947 A guanaco skeleton found on the ridge crest between the North and South Summits fuelled speculation that this wild relative of the llama was taken there by the Incas. The discovery, in 1985, of an Inca mummy at 5200m (17,000ft) on the nearby peak Cerro Piramidal supported the notion that

perhaps the Incas made the first ascent of Aconcagua.

1954 R Ferlet's French expedition climbed the Central Spur of the South Face. Having fixed the lower part of the face, the summit push was made in alpine style by G Poulet, R Paragot, E Denis, P Lasueur, L Bernadini, and A Dagory from a high camp at 6400m (21,000ft) on 24 February.

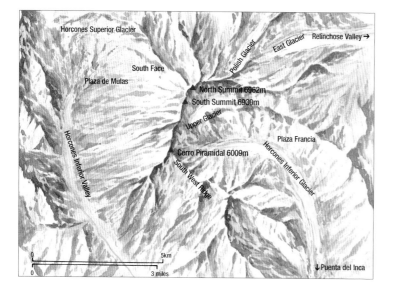

aconcagua

barry blanchard

Named Acconcahuac (the stone sentinel) by the Incas and rising to 6962m (22,840ft), Aconcagua is the highest peak in the southern and western hemispheres, and the world's highest summit outside Asia. An eroding volcano, Aconcagua sits 32–33° South Latitude in western central Argentina, 15km (9 miles) from the Chilean border. The surrounding mountains are steeply sloped and incredibly arid, a wasteland of broken rock and scree. There is little green, and few people visit the area apart from skiers, mountaineers, and the military. A trans-Andean highway links Aconcagua's roadheads to the nearest centres – Santiago in Chile 159km (100 miles) to the east, and Mendoza in Argentina 182km (110 miles) to the west.

Climbers have long been attracted to Aconcagua because of its height. The mountain is also unique because its 'normal route' of ascent involves no glaciation and practically no 'fall-offable' terrain. Novice climbers are regularly guided to the summit without ropes or crampons – a practice virtually impossible anywhere else on the globe!

ridges, faces, and peaks

Aconcagua is a massif from whose flanks fall numerous hanging glaciers, three major valley glaciers, and four river valley approaches: the Vacas to the north-east, the Relinchos to the east, the Horcones Inferior to the south, and the Horcones Superior to the west. Its summit ridge draws a line between the 6962m (22,800ft) North and 6930m (22,700ft) South Summits, and two broad flanks fall away south and west. Both flanks taper, following the ridgeline down in a 3km (2 mile) run to form the South West Ridge, and anchor to Piramidal, a 6009m (19,700ft) satellite peak. A lesser East Flank is contained by the North West and South East Ridges, which fall from the North Summit.

The South Face is a sheer 2400m (8000ft). A truly awesome view of it comes after a day's walk up the Horcones River and Glacier to Plaza Francia (the base-camp site used during the 1954 ascent of the face). From here, the wall rears abruptly as if the earth's crust has been bent into a hard corner. Scythes of séracs front the Middle and Upper Glaciers. Calving over cliffs of charcoal-coloured rock 1.6km (1 mile) high, these séracs negate much of the climbing potential on the eastern side of the face. Above the Upper Glacier is 1000m (3300ft) of what a northern alpinist would call 'North Face terrain'. This face has by far the hardest climbing routes, and much of it is composed of a disintegrating rock that climbers have likened to vertical cat litter.

The West Flank is aproned in fields of rust- and chalk-coloured scree. Stratified cliffs of ochre and black stand from the scree to the south, and wind-eroded pillars march in lines everywhere. It is dry and dusty, and the climbing is mostly novice hiking up established scree trails. Recently, several new lines have been pushed through the steep cliffs that bastion the southern end of the flank, necessitating a lot of hard climbing on vertical, rotten rock.

On the East Flank, the East and Polish Glaciers carve valley lines against vast cliffs and create the look of a boreal alpine environment. Most people find the best climbing experience here on the intermediate-level glacier routes.

future climbing

Other interesting climbs may be found on the icefalls falling from the Pasic Glacier on the South Face. A line on the tumbling glacier left of the 'Slovene Route' may make a quality variation or even an extreme new route.

Right **Climbers on Aconcagua's summit ridge after climbing the 'Polish Glacier Route'.**

1966 R Rocker, O Horak, and D Sause climbed the South East Ridge from the Relinchos Valley.

1974 R Messner's Austro-Italian expedition straightened out the 'French (South Face) Route'.

1978 Argentines J Jasson, G Vieiro, and E Porcellana climbed 'East Glacier Route'.

1982 Slovenians Z Gantar, twins P and P Podgornik, and I Rejc persevered through nine days of storm to open the 'Slovene Route' on the South Face, the hardest route on the mountain.

1988 S Sveticic and M Romih (Slovene) stuck to the crest of the South East Ridge to create the 'Sun Line Route'. Argentines D Alessio and D Rodriguez opened 'La Ruta de la Tapia del Felipe' on the West Face.

1991 T Bubendorfer (Austrian) soloed the 'French Route with Messner Variation' on the South Face in just 15 hours. D Varela and A Mir climbed the 'Esteban Ecaiola Route' on the mountain's West Face.

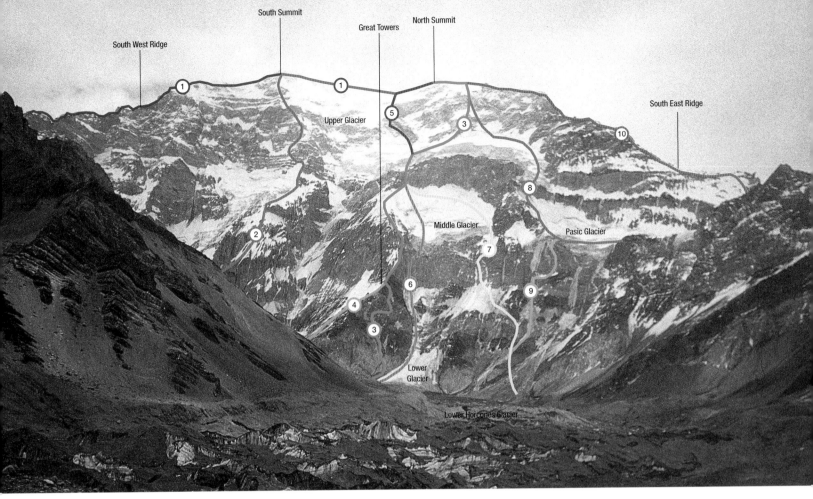

South West Ridge

South Summit

Great Towers

North Summit

South East Ridge

Upper Glacier

Middle Glacier

Pasic Glacier

Lower Glacier

Lower Horcones Glacier

south face

Approach up the Horcones Inferior Glacier from the Lower Horcones Valley to Plaza Francia, 4500m (14,800ft), the most secluded camping below Aconcagua and the starting point for the South Face routes – some of the hardest high-altitude climbing in South America.

1 Sun Line Route EDI

S Seveticic and M Romih 1988

A route that takes on the South West Ridge directly and forces through its difficulties at 5.10+ on rotten rock and vertical ice. Ascent from Plaza Francia 2462m (8100ft); 2–4 days.

2 Slovene Route ED1/2

Z Gantar, Pavel Podgornik, Peter Podgornik, and I Rejc 1982

Extreme modern alpine endeavour with climbing to 5.9, A3 and vertical ice. The first ascent took nine days. Ascent 2462m (8100ft); 4–6 days.

3 French Route EDI

A Dagory, G Poulet, E Denis, R Paragot, P Lasueur, and L Bernardini 1954

The original route up the South Face and now the preferred line when

combined with the 'Slovene Variation' (4) to start and the 'Messner Variation' (5) to finish. Climbing to 5.9, some of which is on the relatively solid rust-coloured rock below the Upper Glacier. Ascent 2462m (8100ft); 2–4 days.

4 French Route: Slovene Variation EDI

M Crnilogar, I Skamperle, S Sveticic, and B Biscak 1982

Avoids the rockfall hazard on the original start joining the 'French Route' (3) at the base of the Great Towers – several 70m (230ft) high towers forming the crux (5.8) on the lower half of the 'French Route'. Ascent 2462m (8100ft); 2–4 days.

5 French Route: Messner Variation EDI

R Messner 1974

Provides a better finish in normal conditions – when there is little snow, avalanche hazard, or, at the other end of the extreme, no rockfall hazard. Ascent 1000m (3300ft) and one day from the Upper Glacier on the 'French Route'.

6 La Ruta de la Ruleta EDI

S Seveticic and M Romih 1988

A dangerous dash to join the French

Route at the Upper Glacier. (The route name is Spanish for roulette.) Ascent 2462m (8100ft); 2–4 days.

7 Central Route D

J Fonrouge and H Schonberger 1966

This is the easiest route up the wall but is exposed to considerable threat from sérac fall. Ascent 2462m (8100ft); 2–4 days.

8 Argentine Route D

O Pellegrini and J Aikes 1966

Takes the most glaciated line on the face to avoid most of the disintegrating rock. Possibly the best-quality climbing on the South Face. Ascent 2462m (8100ft); 2–4 days.

9 The French Direct Route EDI

J Chassagne, P Raveneau, J Dufour, and B Vallet 1985

A moderate technical variation (5.7) to the 'Argentine Route' (8). Ascent 1000m (3300ft) to the junction with the Argentine Route. Four days.

east side

This, the classic mountaineer's side of Aconcagua, can be climbed with one ice axe and crampons.

10 South East Ridge Route AD

R Rocker, O Horak, and D Sause 1966

Follows the crest of the South East Ridge to join the 'East Glacier Route' (11) at about 6000m (19,700ft), above which a 200m (650ft) step forms the crux of both routes – climbing to 5.9 on horribly loose rock. Ascent 2762m (9100ft) from Plaza Argentina; takes 3–5 days.

11 East Glacier Route AD

G Vieiro, E Porcellana, and J Jasson 1978

This route gains the 6000m (19,700ft) junction with the South East Ridge via intermediately difficult ice gulleys and glaciers; it shares the same hard and loose crux as the 'South East Ridge Route' (10). The ascent of 2762m (9100ft) takes 3–5 days.

12 Polish Glacier Route PD

K Narkievitcz-Jodko, S Daszynski, W Ostowski, and S Osiecki 1934

This route is the finest intermediate mountaineering objective on the mountain. It is possible to traverse to, and from, the 'Normal Route' (14) at and above 5900m (19,350ft). The ascent is 2762m (9100ft) and it takes 4–8 days.

13 Polish Glacier Direct PD
O Bravo, T Bellomio, and D Liebich 1961
This route tackles the steeper right-hand side of the Polish Glacier. The ascent is 2762m (9100ft) and takes 4–8 days.

west flank ⊠
The West Flank of Aconcagua is approached via a 2-day, 30km (18½ mile) dry, dry, desert walk. From the roadhead at Laguna

Horcones, 2950m (9700ft), walk up the Horcones Superior Valley to the traditional base camp at the Plaza de Mulas, 4230m (14,000ft), or the new Hotel Refugio, 4370m (14,300ft) – an actual hotel! Access is to the heavily used 'Normal Route' (14) and to all the routes on the West Flank. This is the novice side of Aconcagua. The climbing is mostly on dry scree; any steep rock is inevitably rotten. Dealing with altitude and, possibly, storms, are the real challenges.

14 Normal Route F
M Zurbriggen 1887
An established scree trail. It can be easy to slide on snow traversing into the Canaleta (talus-filled gully). Summit reached over non-glaciated terrain with no technical difficulties. Ascent 2730m (9000ft) from Plaza del Mulas; 5–9 days.

15 La Ruta de la Tapia del Felipe D+
D Alessio and D Rodriguez 1988
Climbing to 5.9 on rotten rock and

some vertical ice. The ascent of 2730m (9000ft) from Plaza del Mulas takes four days.

16 Ibanez-Marmillod Route PD
F and D Marmillod, F Grahales, and F Ibanez 1953
A corkscrew route that bypasses difficulties with a large traverse to weaknesses on the West Flank, then follows the upper reaches of the South Ridge. Ascent 2730m (9000ft) from Plaza del Mulas; 5–7 days.

how to get to aconcagua
Fly to Santiago, Chile or Mendoza, Argentina. From Mendoza, the regular bus service is slow, so tour buses that travel to the border may be better. Bus travel from Chile loses time to border formalities. Taxis and private vehicles are expensive but convenient for reaching the trailheads at Puenta del Inca or Puenta de Vacas.

You can walk the 41km (25½ miles) to the East Side base camp Plaza Argentina.

facilities
A variety of accommodation is available in Mendoza and Santiago. You can buy all provisions in both cities; bring equipment with you. Accommodation and food are available at the roadheads, but little else. Spend a night or two here to aid acclimatization.

From either 'Puenta' you can hire mules to one of the three common base camps. Expensive expedition outfitters can arrange everything you need in Mendoza .

when to climb
The traditional climbing season is December–early March; Febuary is best.

gear
Clothing to protect to -30°C (-22°F). Gales can shred tents. You'll need an ice axe and crampons on the normal route some years. Take technical racks for all hard routes, especially South Face routes.

maps and guidebooks
You'll need: 'Cerro Aconcagua' (3369-7-4), 'Las Cuevas' (3369-13-2), 'Puenta del Inca' (3369-14-1), and 'Cerro Ameghino' (3369-8-3), all 1:50,000, available from Instituto Geográfico Militar, Cabildo 301, Buenos Aires. *Aconcagua, A Climbing Guide*, R J Secor (The Mountaineers, 1994) is highly recommended.

language
Spanish.

rescue and insurance
Helicopter rescue is unusual and expensive, so take out rescue insurance.

red tape
Buy required permits at the Parque office in Mendoza; they're checked at the Parque Provincial Aconcagua trailheads.

1877 French geographer C Wiener, J de Grumkow (Russian), and J M Ocampo (Peruvian) attempted Illimani from the south, reaching a subsidiary South East Summit. Calling this Pico de Paris, they gave it a height of 6131m (20,112ft).

1898 Sir Martin Conway (British) with two Swiss guides, A Maquignaz and L Pellissier, made the first ascent of the mountain, traversing across the South Flank of the Pico de Paris, which Conway later renamed Pico del Indio after discovering a piece of Indian rope close to the top.

1938 An aeroplane, reputedly carrying a huge cargo of gold, crashed into the North Ridge. Any subsequent attempts on this ridge caused great uneasiness to the Bolivian authorities (see 1969).

1940 R Boetcher, F Fritz, and W Kühn (German) made the first ascent of what is now the 'Standard Route'.

1950 H Ertl (German) made the first solo and sixth overall ascent of the Main Summit via the West Ridge and, with G Schröder, made the first ascent of the Central Summit. They then went on to make the first ascent of the North Summit.

1958 W Karl, H Richter, and H Wimmer were the first climbers to make the three peaks traverse.

1964 Anneliese Stobl (German) made the first recorded female ascent.

1968 H Imai and H Ono (Japan) made the first traverse from the South to North Summits.

1969 Three members from J Monfort's Spanish team were first to climb the

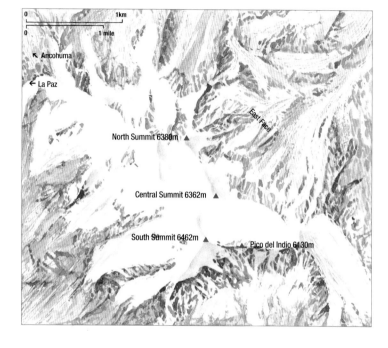

illimani

lindsay griffin

Clearly visible from the thriving Bolivian city of La Paz, Illimani forms the solitary southern outpost of a splendid group of Andean mountains that make up the Cordillera Real. This 160km (100 mile) long chain of snowy peaks has more than 600 summits above 5000m (16,400ft). The two highest peaks of the Cordillera Real, Illimani and Ancohuma, lie at opposite ends of the chain. No really accurate height survey of the Cordillera has taken place and for a long time Illimani has been awarded an altitude of 6462m (21,200ft). The most recent differential GPS (Global Positioning Satellite) survey wants to reduce this slightly to 6439m (21,126ft). Ancohuma seems 'confirmed' at 6427m (21,090).

Illimani's spendid isolation, elegant sweeping ridges, and dream-like summit crest have consistently drawn high-altitude mountaineers. The 'Standard Route' is a non-technical and now well-travelled ascent in a magnificent situation and it is no coincidence that the new breed of commercial expeditions with a strong clientele put it top of their list. Although many of the other routes on the mountain are outstanding climbs, they are also long, serious, and only rarely attempted.

ridges, faces, and peaks

The topography of Illimani is complex: it is more of a massif than a single mountain, having three main tops and several less well-defined subsidiary summits. The highest point is the South Summit. A little below this on the Yungas (or jungle) side a large glacier plateau falls gently towards the south-east and has a subsidiary summit of around 6130m (20,110ft), referred to as the Pico del Indio, and various features such as the Pyramide de los Dioses. Between this and the long South West Ridge lies the steep 1300m (4300ft) high South Face, a broad wall of rock and ice liberally sprinkled with threatening sérac formations. The exquisite crest of the South West Ridge ends in an impressive rock buttress which has still to be climbed. Separating this from the West Ridge is the convoluted West-South-West Face.

The little crescent-shaped Central Summit is 6362m (20,872ft) and the prominent pyramidal North Summit 6380m (20,932ft). A huge ridge, west at first, then running north-west, descends gradually from the North Summit, at one stage rising over a high point of about 6100m (20,000ft), often confusingly called the Pico del Indio. Various other long mixed ridges with bifurcations and ancillary spurs also lead to the North Summit, and most have been climbed. All parts of the mountain have tangled glaciers with chaotic icefalls in their lower sections, separating the objectively safer lines up the ridges and spurs.

The least known and most awesome aspect of Illimani is the 9km (5½ mile) wide East Face that looks out towards the Yungas. The height of this immense wall of rock and ice varies from 1000m (3300ft) to 1400m (4600ft). Access to a lot of this face is difficult, and rock- and icefall is a constant threat.

future climbing

The greatest contribution to climbing on Illimani has come from Alain Mesili, who has climbed the massif by at least eight different routes – many of these first ascents. Only Mesili has put up a route on the East Face, but there is still considerable scope for future pioneers.

Right **Descending the North Ridge of the South Summit. The right-slanting snow crest is the Via Khoya-Khoya; the Cordillera Real lies in the background.**

North Ridge to the North Summit. At one point the party was shot at by an armed patrol (*see 1938*).

1974 Americans R Laba and J Thackray made the first ascent of the South Face in five days. A Mesili (French) made first solo ascent of the 1969 Spanish route.

1976 A large Italian expedition led by C Zappelli climbed both the Spanish route and the western branch of the North Ridge. The latter was repeated two months later by the talented South Africans D Cheesmond and P Dawson.

1978 C Jacquier and A Mesili created a very direct route up a shallow couloir a little to the right of the summit fall-line on the South Face. Mesili teamed up with Bruce Card (American) to climb the very difficult South Face of the Pyramide de los Dioses that leads to the vast hanging glacier situated South East of the Main Summit.

1979 A and R Putz (German) made the first complete south–north traverse of the entire massif in five days.

1982 Over eight days in July, A Mesili and F Pimienta opened the first route on the vast and objectively dangerous East Face, climbing the most prominent snow/ice couloir. L Griffin (British) soloed the upper part of the West-South-West Face more or less directly to the summit.

1988 French guide P Gabarrou soloed a new ice/mixed route on the South Face, which he named 'Hubert Ducroz'. The biggest single climbing accident in the country resulted in the deaths of six Chileans on the 'Standard Route'.

North Summit

North Ridge

North East Ridge

North West Ridge

north side

Routes on this side of the mountain are lengthy expeditions that generally follow the big ridge lines. Although the technical difficulties are never extreme, the routes are major undertakings and are rarely repeated. Routes are generally 1300–1400m (4300–4600ft) vertical intervals and take 2–3 days from the foot of the mountain to the top of the routes.

1 North East Ridge
J Miller and D Young 1977
Possibly unrepeated. A *tour de force* on difficult ground in poor conditions. The first ascensionists spent 10 days on their alpine style ascent, then reversed the route using rappels and downclimbing.

2 North Ridge to North Summit
J Monfort and team 1969
This is a superb mountaineering route with sections of 50°. Overall, it is probably no more difficult than an alpine climb rated D. However, the route is very long and the various descent options from the

summit are all equally lengthy. A well-acclimatized party should allow three days for the ascent.

3 West Branch of North Ridge
G Ferrari and A Gelmi 1976
Undoubtedly one of the finest rock ridges in Bolivia and possibly the best of the more difficult crests on Illimani. Allow five days for an alpine style ascent followed by a descent of the North West Ridge. The route has 5km (3 miles) of climbing on surprisingly good rock, and the lower east-facing rock buttress gives pitches from III to V+.

4 North Face of North Summit
F de Fachinetti, R Gieberna, R Ive, T Klingendrath, and G Chiriaco 1979
This is a long, involved, and fairly committing expedition. The convoluted icefall low down on the route has sections of technical ice climbing and some objective danger. The icy rock spur leading onto the upper section of the North West Ridge gives sustained climbing at a more moderate standard, but can give increasing difficulties on mixed ground as the season progresses.

west side

The west is the most accessible side of the mountain – the long ridges give magnificent expeditions, though generally easier than those on the North Side. The faces give classic medium-grade snow/ice routes, reached via complex glacier approaches. All routes are 1400–1500m (4500–4600ft) from the base of the mountain, and are generally multi-day affairs.

5 North West Ridge
P Barker and team 1966
A superb mountaineering route and the usual start to the greater traverse of the three summits. Generally a 3-day ascent.

6 South West Face to North West Ridge – Via Khoya-Khoya D-/D
A Mesli and E Sanchez 1972
An aesthetic and appealing line up a perfect snow crest of *c.*55° reached after a lengthy glacier approach.

7 North Summit – South Face D- ⊠
W Bauer, L Kerschbaumsteiner, and R Streif 1973
A glacier crossing of variable difficulty that leads to a moderately

steep 300m (1000ft) snow/ice face of *c.*50°.

8 North Summit – Original Route
H Ertl and G Schröder 1950
Variable difficulties on the glacier crossing and ascent to the ridge, followed by a fine narrow snow crest to finish.

9 West Face of Central Summit
M Edlinger, S Friehuber, and R Wurzer 1973
A short and relatively steep snow/ice route. Variable sérac structure can considerably affect the difficulty and objective danger of this route.

10 North West Face
M Abelein and J Eloriaga 1977
Steep snow/ice face that is reached by the upper section of the 'Standard Route' (11).

11 West Ridge – Standard Route PD+/AD-
R Boetcher, F Fritz, and W Kühn 1940
The only route climbed with any frequency. It begins from the old mining road at Puente Roto. A fine snow arête and broader glacier

slopes with an exposed section of *c.*40° lead onto the North Ridge. A superb mountaineering experience with great views. Normally completed with two camps.

12 West-South-West Face AD+

Probably first climbed integrally in 1988. Upper section: L Griffin 1982

A serious, though not technically difficult, route that finds a way through the séracs on this convoluted glacier face. The variable state of the séracs determines the exact line and the amount of objective danger. Should take about two days.

13 South West Ridge to Main Summit

T Dowbenka and H Ziegenhardt 1983

This 4-day outing more or less follows the line descended by Meili and Sánchez in 1972 during the third north–south traverse of the mountain. Grade III rock low down, crevassed slopes left of the crest, and a final 70° wall above the 6250m (20,500ft) foresummit form the major difficulties.

how to get to illimani

Fly direct to La Paz. This tourist area is at an altitude of 3700–3800m (12,150–12,500ft) so allow plenty of time for acclimatization before moving out to the hills. Due to the extensive mining that took place below Illimani, 4WD roads lead past its foot. Landcruiser transport can be hired, but villages close to the mountain are also served by cargo trucks and buses. Departure points for the cargo trucks that ply from La Paz to the Mina Urania can be elusive; daily buses leave from Calle Boqueron, San Petro.

facilities

All grades of hotel accommodation are available in La Paz, as well as all the food you will need, although more 'western' items will take time to locate. There are agencies that hire or might sell certain items of climbing equipment and camping gas, but there is not much gear available.

when to climb

Mid-May–September is the best time to climb. The climate is generally very settled from mid-May–July with clear days, cold nights, and an often continuous chilly breeze coming south off the altiplano. In August, the weather gradually starts to deteriorate, although storms are rarely prolonged and are still relatively infrequent. Deep powder lying at a remarkably steep angle is characteristic of all the south faces in the Cordillera Real during early season, but this usually burns off by August to leave good firm névé and/or hard ice.

gear

Good mountain tents and bivouac equipment are essential – the temperature can easily drop to -20°C (-4°F) at nights when above 5800m (19,000ft). A selection of ice screws, large deadmen and snowstakes should be taken on the harder routes.

maps and guidebooks

The *Cordillera Real Süd – Illimani*, 1:50,000 German (DAV) map is the best.

The most useful guide is the 1996 reprint (in Spanish) of *La Cordillera Real de los Andes*, Alain Mesili (Editorial los Amigos del Libro). Also try *Bolivia, a Climbing Guide*, Yossi Brain (The Mountaineers).

language

Latin-American Spanish and local Indian are spoken. English is not widely understood, although this is changing.

rescue and insurance

Expedition insurance is essential. The rescue service is very poor, so do not count on anything more than a team of climbers organized from La Paz.

red tape

No permits are needed but the Club Andindo Boliviano, Calle México 1648, La Paz would appreciate parties registering their climbing activity before leaving the country.

*c.***1876** Cerro Torre was named by the Argentinian F Moreno on his journeys to establish the Chilean-Argentine border.
1916–44 Padre Alberto María de Agostini (Italian) explored Patagonia and took superb mountain photographs.
1958 Two Italian expeditions attempted the mountain. B Detassis, approaching up the Torre Valley, scrutinized the East Side and declared the mountain impossible. W Bonatti and C Mauri led climbers up the West Side, but, after over a month, they abandoned their climb after reaching the Col of Hope.
1959 C Maestri (Italian), accompanied by expert Austrian ice climber T Egger, made an attempt on the mountain. Six days after they had set out on an alpine style assault of the North Face, Maestri was found half-buried in the snow of the glacier. He declared they had reached the summit, but Egger was killed by an avalanche during the descent – many dispute their ascent.
1968 A British expedition was beaten by the blank rock of the South East Ridge.
1970 An Italian expedition led by C Mauri attempted the West Side again, this time reaching a much higher point but still missing the summit. In an incredible *tour de force*, Maestri stormed the South East Ridge during winter but ran out of food 350m (1150ft) short of the summit. He returned in the summer to finish the task. Controversy arose over his use of a compressed-air drill and his refusal to climb the final ice mushroom.
1974 An Italian team led by C Ferrari reached the summit via the West Face.

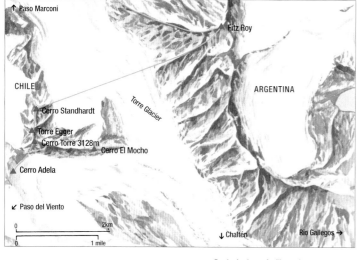

Border is shown for illustrative purposes only.

cerro torre

rodrigo jordan

I dedicate this piece to the memory of my friend Dagoberto Delgado (1956–97) who made the first Chilean ascent of Cerro Torre.

Cerro Torre (El Torre) is the most imposing, threatening, and, undoubtedly, the most coveted peak in Patagonia. Rising on the border between Chile and Argentina at the edge of the Southern Patagonian Icecap, it stands tall against the full fury of the weather, seeming to defy all physical laws.

At 3128m (10,263ft), Cerro Torre is the highest summit of a stupendous 30km (18 mile) long range running north–south at the eastern edge of the Southern Patagonian Icecap between Paso Marconi and Paso del Viento. It towers magnificently over its elegant companion spires, Cerro Standhardt, 2800m (9185ft), and Torre Egger, 2900m (9515ft), to the north, and the broad, glacier-covered Cerro Adela, 2960m (9710ft), to the south. A deep notch, the Col of Conquest, separates Cerro Torre from Torre Egger, and the Col of Hope forms a saddle to Cerro Adela. The peak is separated from Mount Fitz Roy by a deep valley carved by the Torre Glacier and is inside the Parque Nacional Los Glaciares.

ridges, faces, and peaks

The mountain has two main sides of approach, west and east, and the Hope and Conquest Cols are the landmarks of these approaches: the West Side faces the huge freezing plain of the Southern Patagonian Icecap; the East Side faces the Argentinian pampas and the small town of Chaltén.

the east side The North West Ridge rises directly to the summit from the Col of Conquest. It is the unrepeated route climbed by Cesare Maestri and Toni Egger in 1959. From it, clockwise, it is possible to distinguish: the North Face rising from the deep gorge between El Torre and Torre Egger, comprising a notorious 150m (820ft) overhanging dihedral; the East Face forming an impressive granite wall of more than 1300m (4300ft); and the South East Ridge, a prominent buttress that starts on the Col of Patience and finishes on the headwall just below the summit. On the other side of this col is Cerro El Mocho, 1980m (6500ft), and the South Face, a 1300m (4300ft) polished, crackless wall of granite which is, without doubt, the most difficult and challenging face on the mountain. The Col of Hope is at the western edge of the South Face.

the west side The West Side of Cerro Torre is made up of a single, almost featureless, 1200m (3900ft) face. It is an impressive vertical precipice continually hit by very strong winds that accumulate moisture as they cross the Icecap from the Pacific. As these winds lash the face they produce magnificent ice-encrusted features, giving the mountain an air of impossibility and creating very hard climbing conditions as the granite wall is almost always covered by thin layers of ice.

The main feature on this side, and the most elegant route, is a huge dihedral, 250m (820ft) high, in the last third of the face. It ends in the crowning mushroom, an ice-cream-like, 100m (330ft) cone of snow and ice topping the summit – it is the most distinguishable characteristic of Cerro Torre.

future climbing

There is scope for new routes, especially on the West Side, but the difficulty involved is so tremendous they may never be tried. Still, the routes already opened were once deemed impossible: this is a mountain where 'the impossible' is continuously passed.

Right **The South Side of Cerro Torre seen from the Grande Glacier. Typical Patagonian clouds all but obliterate Torre Egger, behind.**

1979 Maestri's 'Compressor Route' was climbed alpine style by Americans J Bridwell and S Brewer in 1½ days.

1981 T Proctor and P Burke (British) made a first ascent of the North Face in seven days. The ice mushroom made it impossible to reach the summit.

1985 The Swiss-Italian climber M Pedrini made an incredible first solo ascent by the 'Compressor Route'.

1986 M Bearzi and E Winkelmann (American) made the first free ascent of Ferrari's 'South West Ridge' route, but could not cross the ice-mushroom. S Karo and J Jeglic (Slovenian) opened 'Devil's Direttissima' (2) on the East Face using fixed ropes for 31 pitches.

1988 S Karo and J Jeglic made the first ascent of the South Face. D Delgado made first Chilean ascent of Cerro Torre.

1994 D Autheman, F Valet, and P Pessi (French) made the first (and only) traverse of Cerro Torre. After climbing Ferrari's 'South West Ridge' route they mistakenly descended the Slovenian 'Devil's Direttissima' (2) on the East Face, although the original plan was to descend by the 'Compressor Route'. J Jeglic, M Lukic, and M Prapontik (Slovenian) completed an impressive

route on the right of the South Face to connect with the 'Compressor Route' just a few pitches above the Col of Patience. M Giarolli, E Orlandi, and O Ravizza (Italian) opened a new route on the West Face.

1995 E Salvaterra, P Vidi, and R Manni (Italian) opened 'Infinito Sud' (6), a third route on the South Face in a continuous 24-day push, using a hanging box-tent.

Cerro Torre

North Face

North West Ridge

East Face

Torre Egger

Col of Conquest

South East Ridge

Col of Patience

Conditions vary, especially on the West Side, from bare rock to rime ice 30–100cm (12–40in) thick.

east side

Three faces and one ridge can be attempted from this side. The present 'normal route' up the South East Ridge (1) is the only one that has been repeated. The North and East Faces have seen only one ascent each. Three absolutely unbelievable routes have been opened on the difficult South Face.

1 South East Ridge: Compressor Route ED

C Maestri, C Claus, and E Alimonta 1970
The standard route, made more accessible by the pitons bolted by Maestri. Difficulties start at the Col of Patience where an ice cave serves as a bivouac. Total ascent 1200m (2300ft) – first 500m (1600ft) to the Col of Patience are mixed IV. The last 700m (3900ft) are up mixed terrain with ice up to 75°, 5.10 and A1. The final two pitches are on the headwall of the East Face, where the compressor still hangs. The last 20m (65ft) of the headwall are A2. Takes one bivouac above Col of Patience, but has been done in 12 hours.

2 East Face: Devil's Direttissima EX

S Karo and J Jeglic 1986
Total height 1100m (3600ft), of which 950m (3100ft) were first climbed by this expedition. The last 150m (500ft) join the 'Compressor Route' (1) at the base of the headwall. The climbers reported highly technical grade VIII and A4, 5.12 climbing. It was climbed using fixed ropes and took several weeks to complete.

3 North Face EX

T Proctor and P Burke 1981
Initially follows the Maestri-Egger line, route (4), (V, VI, A1, A2, mixed, objective dangers), moves left to the 300m (1000ft) overhanging dihedral (VI, A3, A4) in the middle of the face, then goes right on a direct line up a system of smaller dihedrals at 70°. Ascent 1100m (3600ft). First ascensionists had to stop 45m (150ft) from the summit. Seven days.

4 North West Ridge EX

C Maestri and T Egger 1959
First (and only ascensionists) reported pitches of A3 and 5.9/A1 in the lower section. Maestri described the route as 760m (2500ft) of steep ice and snow that took five days.

south face

5 South Face EX+

S Karo and J Jeglic 1988
With 45 pitches, Grade VII climbing, 75° ice, and many objective dangers, it's easy to see why this route was at the time considered the most difficult and adventurous big-wall climb in the world (A4, 5.11). Fixed ropes were used and it took several weeks of hard climbing to complete the 1300m (4300ft) route.

6 Infinito Sud EX+

E Salvaterra, P Vidi, and R Manni 1995
This super route is 1350m (4400ft) high with 36 pitches (VII, 5.11, A4). The route was climbed using a portable hanging box-tent – no fixed ropes were used. It took just over three weeks to complete the ascent.

7 What's Love Got To Do With It? EX+

J Jeglic, M Lukic, and M Prapontik 1994
This impressive route connects with Maestri's 'Compressor Route' (1), just a few pitches above the Col of Patience. The first 600m (2000ft) are the most difficult as they are on the South Face proper. Difficulties reported VII, 5.11, A4. The route was climbed using fixed ropes and took several weeks to complete. Ascent 1300m (4300ft).

west side

Only two routes on this side have been opened due to the lack of features, the awful weather, and the difficulty of access. This is entirely different to the alpine style approach possible on the East Side.

8 South West Ridge ED+

M Conti, C Ferrari, D Chiappa, and P Negri 1974
Considered the easiest route, but still demanding. Rock pitches become ice-covered, making it a serious mixed climb. It is also committing as access is from the Southern Icecap. Siege tactics were used in 1974 but it was climbed alpine style in 1986. Difficulties reported were VI, A2 with ice pitches of 70°–85°. The alpine style ascent required three bivouacs. Ascent 1200m (3900ft).

9 West Face: Cristalli Nel Vento ED+

M Giarolli, E Orlandi, and O Ravizza 1994
One of the most recently opened routes with difficulties starting at the very beginning of the 1300m (4300ft) climb. The first ascensionists retreated 210m (700ft) below the summit.

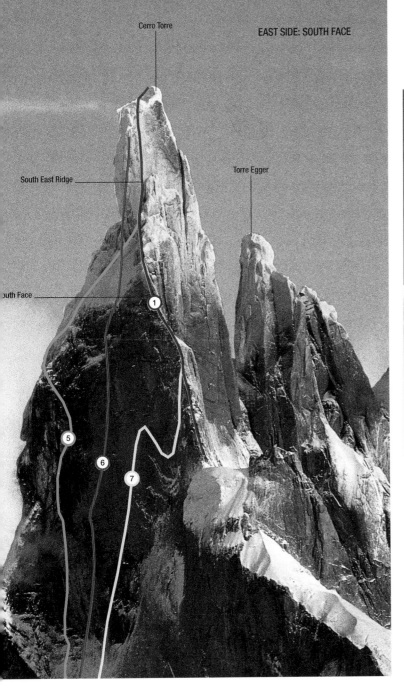

Cerro Torre

EAST SIDE: SOUTH FACE

South East Ridge

Torre Egger

South Face

Above **The remote West Side of the group. Summits left to right: Cerro Standhardt, Punta Herron, Torre Egger, and Cerro Torre.**

how to get to cerro torre

Access to the East Side of Cerro Torre is from the small Argentinian town of Chaltén, reached easily by road from Río Gallegos, the main city of southern Argentina. Inside the Parque Nacional Los Glaciares, good trails take climbers to the base camp for all the routes on this side in a few hours.

The West Side was traditionally reached from Argentina by crossing Paso del Viento, to the south of Cordón Adela. At present, because of a new dirt road opened to Lago del Desierto, it seems better to approach via Paso Marconi, which is to the north of Cordón Marconi. Both alternatives require several days' hard marching.

facilities

The Maestri and Bridwell Base Camps are both under forest-cover so guarantee reasonable protection from the weather. Chaltén is an ill-supplied village where only very basic supplies can be obtained.

when to climb

The main concern is the awful weather. No firm conclusions as to when it is least bad have been reached, but it is generally accepted that late October–January offer the best conditions.

gear

The 'Compressor Route' can be done with a normal climbing rack: two climbers will use something like two 50m (165ft) ropes, four ice screws, some free

karabiners, seven varied friends, a complete set of stoppers, four rappel pitons, one pair of ascenders, two pairs of étriers, and three ice hammers. All other routes are highly technical and require matching gear. Every route will need at least two, if not several, bivouacs.

maps and guidebooks

The best map is the 'Monte Fitz Roy Cerro Torre Trekking-Mountaineering', 1:50,000, (Zagier & Urruty).

The nearest thing to a guidebook is *Patagonia, Terra Magica per Alpinisti e Viaggiatori*, Gino Buscaini and Silvia Metzeltin (dall'Oglio, Italy, 1987). The other excellent source is *Mountaineering in Patagonia*, Alan Kearney (Cloudcap, USA, 1993).

language

Spanish; some Patagonians will speak English.

rescue and insurance

There is a rural medical post but helicopter rescue is generally impossible. Insurance is not compulsory.

red tape

The use of Bridwell Base Camp is restricted and burning wood for fuel is forbidden in the National Park.

triple high jinks on cerro torre

paul moores

"My first visit to Patagonia in 1993, when we failed to climb Fitz Roy, taught me that a different approach might be necessary, and a better alternative to the traditional 'big mountain' siege tactics, with fixed ropes and camps. I remember thinking that, if I returned, I must arrive fully fit to climb right away and be prepared to move fast with some serious load-carrying and uncomfortable bivouacs. Two years later, Adrian (Aid) Burgess and I met up to put theory to practice on Cerro Torre.

Setting out at 2.30am meant getting up just after midnight. Nothing is fast at that time of day. Any attempt to organize yourself the night before is difficult in the confined space of an ice cave. This time, five of us were crammed into a frigid burrow high on the Col of Patience, terrified of breaking through the few centimetres that protected us from the sheer South Face. We struggled out with headtorches and heavy packs.

I partnered Max Berger, a young Austrian guide we had just met. He and his friend Luis had tried Cerro Torre several times already, with only frostnipped toes to show for the effort. Luis decided it was no longer his idea of fun, so Max asked if he could join us. Aid teamed up with Mark Wilford, who had originally planned to solo something.

As Max had been up this part of the climb three times already, the first four ropelengths went by reasonably quickly, though climbing with a new partner in the dark was daunting. It soon got light, but there was no time to enjoy the dawn. We moved as fast as we dared, all the while scanning the horizon for clouds.

Max asked me to take over the lead on the next pitch as he felt I would be quicker. It was an icy, narrow chimney that turned out to be awkward and led to some scary iced-up slabs. This continued for four ropelengths, the sort of climbing that eats up time. The next section climbed thin, overhanging cracks, leading to a hanging, undercut wall – it was like being on a diving board with a 1000m drop. We started to traverse the Maestri Bolt Ladder, which veers horizontally right above the void for 3½ pitches. I found this intimidating at first, and it was certainly no easier for the second. As I belayed Max across the last of these pitches, great blocks of ice came ricochetting down a shallow couloir over my right shoulder. I ducked to avoid being hit, all the time thinking that we couldn't possibly cross the couloir under this constant barrage. It was just too dangerous.

It looked as if we might have to retreat. My first reaction was one of sheer relief that we could go down! Then came the disappointment. And, after that – for some unknown reason – I 'got brave', just as Max arrived at the stance. Realizing the sun had strengthened sufficiently to loosen the snow and ice from the headwall hundreds of metres above – and this all seemed to be funnelling directly towards us – we started counting. By studying the rate at which the blocks came flying down, we could choose the best moment to cross the couloir.

It worked. We escaped being pounded to death, and set up our next stance on a pedestal beneath another overhanging wall. Water was pouring down so, tied to a tiny ledge, we struggled into waterproofs. Water still found its way into every aperture as we climbed, streaming down our necks and sleeves. Yet, as we reached the end of the pitch, the sun dropped behind Cerro Torre and within a few minutes the water had stopped.

It was nearly 4pm. We had been on the go for almost 14 hours. Surely it could not be far now? Ahead, the climbing was mixed – icy corners, hands on rock, feet on ice – but still steep, and all the anchors were hidden under ice. We started to move together, trusting one another not to fall. Soon it opened up onto a steep, exposed, icy slope. We needed to traverse right for three rope-lengths. Armed with only one ice tool each, it felt very precarious. Then, it was straight up vertical ice – much less hazardous than traversing. The final headwall was at last getting closer. Three more difficult ice pitches and we came upon a leaning tower with Maestri's bolts spaced every 2m or so.

This was overhanging, unfortunately, making for strenuous climbing. The light was fading and the temperature dropping fast. The tower led to steep icy grooves and onto a very small

brèche and the base of the headwall. It was 9.30pm. When Max joined me in the dim light, he remarked that his friend had climbed this headwall in the dark, by headtorch – so, knowing that the weather might not hold another day, we set out.

I left my rucksack tied to a piton in the brèche, taking only the headtorch. Max carried clothing and food for both of us. Aid and Mark, who were right behind us, decided to look for a bivouac close to the brèche. There was nothing very appropriate. Mark ended up hacking into the ice mushroom above a rock pinnacle which, after about 45 minutes, provided them with a very small, slippery, icy platform. I was still trying to lead up loose, rotten rock and, after some difficulty, found a stance in the dark. Max followed.

Cerro Torre's headwall is about 300m, about six full ropelengths. We were starting up the second when, after 25m, I reached a very blank section and could not work out how to climb it. Out on a thin limb in the dark and with a very cold wind starting to blow, my imagination began to run riot. We decided to abseil back to the brèche.

> As the descent became … treacherous, our lives hung by the narrow threads of our ropes …

There was no room near Aid and Mark, so Max and I set about excavating a small ledge while hanging onto the ends of our abseil ropes. The slope was about 65° and dropped away for 2000m into dark emptiness. No room for the slightest error. By midnight we had enough room for two backsides. After hot drinks and snacks, we shivered through the long early hours.

At 5.30am we set off again. The weather seemed good and, returning to our high point in the daylight, the climbing did not look too bad either. Five fantastic pitches later we came upon Maestri's Compressor.

The Compressor, the size of a small table, sticks out like a sore thumb. Above it, Maestri had smashed the heads off all his bolts during descent, leaving minute stubs of mild steel punctuating the pitch. This made for some very spooky climbing, as we tried to re-use the remnants for our skyhooks. It was the most difficult pitch by far, but brought us to the top of the headwall.

The mountain top was much larger than I'd imagined. We had to climb three ropelengths back from the edge, traversing behind the huge crowning mushrooms of ice to reach the summit.

What a fantastic view. We could see all of the Patagonian ice-cap, but clouds were on the horizon and racing towards us. We waited 15 minutes for Aid and Mark, but thin, misty clouds started to engulf the summit. It was time to start descending. We had just as many ropelengths to reach the Col of Patience as we did on our ascent. We met the others just starting the last pitch and gave each other momentary congratulations as we passed. They would soon be on the summit.

The route down was just as complex as the ascent, with much traversing, and route finding was very difficult in the worsening conditions. As the descent became more and more treacherous, our lives hung by the narrow threads of our ropes, and their anchors. Our ropes became encased with ice and got stuck as we tried to release them after each abseil, often meaning we had to re-climb in order to free them. Arriving at the ice cave just before dark, we were very tired, but extremely elated: we had climbed Cerro Torre.

Below left **Looking down the Col of Patience from halfway up Cerro Torre.**

Below **Morning after the chilly bivouac on a home-made ledge in the brèche before the headwall.**

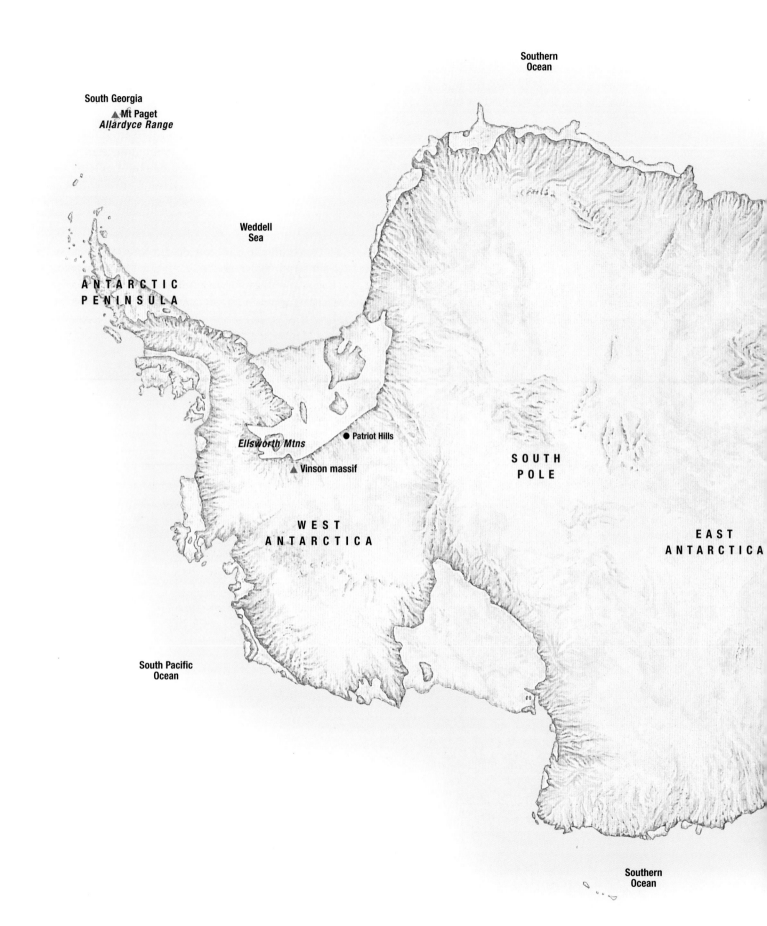

South Georgia
▲ Mt Paget
Allardyce Range

Southern
Ocean

Weddell
Sea

ANTARCTIC
PENINSULA

Ellsworth Mtns
● Patriot Hills
▲ Vinson massif

SOUTH
POLE

WEST
ANTARCTICA

EAST
ANTARCTICA

South Pacific
Ocean

Southern
Ocean

antarctica

The vast continent of Antarctica, although completely covered by an icecap, contains extensive mountain ranges, the highest peaks being found in the Sentinel Range of the Ellsworth Mountains inland from the west coast. Number One choice for mountaineers is inevitably the highest, Mount Vinson, at 4897m (16,067ft); and, while it is very expensive to reach, there is sufficient demand for something of a tourist service.

Despite the great scope for development, general mountaineering on the 'Last Continent' will remain difficult, partly on account of the natural obstacles of the short Antarctic summer, the world's wildest weather, and the sheer remoteness and distances involved; but also because of bureaucratic reluctance to sanction high-risk ventures where support and rescue in an emergency are virtually impossible.

Many of the bleak sub-Antarctic islands offer promise to private parties. South Georgia – famous first as the scene of Ernest Shackleton's 1916 epic of endurance, and subsequently for the unauthorized landing by the Argentine forces in 1982 which launched the Falklands War – has seen several mountaineering forays and ascents of its major peaks; Mount Paget is included here.

Clockwise from left: **On the Vinson-Shinn Col; Mount Paget seen from Mount Carse; on Vinson's summit looking towards Shinn**

Nationalities: American unless stated.
1935 Lincoln Ellsworth on his Trans-Antarctic flight caught sight of a range of mountains, which he romantically named the Sentinel Range.
1959 A US Navy reconnaissance trip discovered a group of high mountains in the Sentinel Range. The exploratory Marie Bird Land Traverse expedition led by Dr C Bentley surveyed it; the highest

summit was named Vinson massif after Carl G Vinson, an American senator.
1966 The first ascent of Vinson massif by all 10 members of the American Antarctic Mountaineering Expedition.
1979 The second ascent was made by Germans, P von Gizycki and W Buggisch, and the Soviet, V Samsonov.
1983 F Wells and D Bass, and invited 'guest' mountaineers, were flown into

Vinson by pilot G Kershaw (British), climbing it as part of their attempt on the 'Seven Summits'.
1985 G Kershaw founded Adventure Network International (ANI), opening Antarctica to private expeditions and enabling P Morrow (Canadian) to climb Vinson on his 'Seven Summits' quest.
1992 Base camp was moved from the Nimitz Glacier to Branscomb Glacier,

eliminating the need to negotiate the icefall encountered by early ascensionists. J Smith and C Anker led a guided party on an ascent via a new route from the south, gaining the Summit Glacier via the Vinson-Craddock Col. They came within 50m (165ft) of the summit.
1993 The broad gully to the right of the hanging glacier, leading directly to the

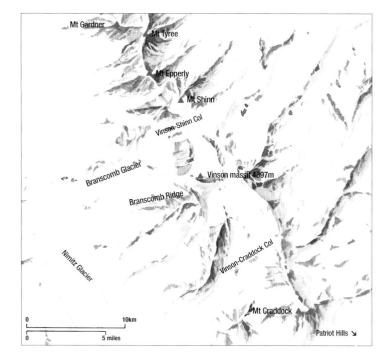

vinson massif

roger mear

Antarctica is the coldest, most windswept continent on Earth. Its mean altitude of 2290m (7500ft) is three times greater than that of any other land mass, and it holds 90 per cent of the world's ice, which at its deepest lies up to 4785m (15,700ft) thick. This ice covers the whole continent – only a few mountain tops project through it. Winds, which normally blow at 10–15 knots, can reach up to 100 knots. Antarctica holds the record for the lowest temperature ever recorded, -89°C (-126°F), yet during the summer the South Pole receives more solar radiation than the equator in any equivalent period.

The Antarctic has attracted mariners, explorers, scientists, and – most recently – climbers. Activity is, of necessity, concentrated during the Antarctic summer when there are 24 hours of daylight. During the other half of the year the continent is in darkness.

Antarctica's highest mountain is Mt Vinson, in the Sentinel Range of the Ellsworth Mountains, at the base of the Antarctic Peninsula. The Sentinel Range stretches for more than 130km (80 miles), drawn up like pieces on a chess board against the edge of the greatest sweep of ice in the world – a vast, barren plain, bigger than North America. The elegant symmetrical pyramids of striated metamorphic rock, laced with icy runnels, grow in stature towards the heart of the range, culminating at the centre in the complex high-glacial massif of Vinson. Its summit is 1190km (700 miles) from the South Pole and, from the top, there are breathtaking views to the neighbouring peaks of Mt Shinn and Mt Gardner. The most recent remeasurement of the range puts Mount Vinson at 4897m (16,067ft), 52m (170ft) higher than nearby Mount Tyree.

ridges, faces, and peaks
Rising from the Nimitz Glacier, the Vinson massif presents black, fluted ridges and huge faces of up to 3000m (9850ft) in height. It has a vast summit plateau of wind-scoured ice and snow, from which Vinson and the massif's lesser summits rise. The standard approach is from the West Side, where the Branscomb Glacier offers the most direct route to the summit. This glacier descends steeply from the Vinson-Shinn Col into a high basin, before swinging in a southerly direction towards base camp, 5km (3 miles) away.

The technical crux of the southern side, climbed in 1992, is another icefall barrier guarding the summit plateau, which is gained on this side by the Vinson-Craddock Col.

Vinson has been climbed by more than 360 people since 1985 and all but two of these ascents have been by the 'Normal Route'. Ascents of new routes in the Sentinel Range, like those by Yvon Chouinard on Mt Tyree, or the remarkable solo first ascent of Mt Epperly by Erhard Loretan, have also been confined to objectives accessible from the West Side of Vinson and are unrepeated.

future climbing
Expense and inaccessibility will continue to limit activity; most of those who come to the massif are commercially guided clients whose main interest is to bag the high summit within a limited time period. But those who do the guiding regularly make variations and put up new lines, for which there is ample scope.

Right **The route to Mount Vinson. Climbers on the col between Shinn and Vinson in the Ellsworth Mountains of Antarctica.**

summit from 2700m (9000ft) on the Branscomb Glacier, was climbed by Jay and Jo Smith in two days.

1994 M Hood and R Mear (British) traversed the Branscomb Ridge in a descent from the summit to Camp 3. A steep snow gully leading to the southern summit on the Branscomb Ridge was soloed by Jay Smith in seven hours.

Labels on image: Mt Shinn · Vinson-Shinn Col · West Face · Vinson massif · Branscomb Ridge · Branscomb Glacier

1 The Normal Route
By way of the Branscomb Glacier and the Vinson-Shinn Col F (Alpine)

Adventure Network International's (ANI) Airstrip and base camp are situated on the Branscomb Glacier at 2100m (6900ft). The route climbs the glacier for 3km (2 miles) where it turns north under the West Face of the mountain. Here a steep hanging glacier provides a direct route to the summit. Just beyond this bend, poorly sheltered among pressure ridges at 2700m (8800ft), is Camp 1. Camp 2, a further 2km (1¼ miles) up the glacier at 3100m (10,200ft), is often placed in a windscoop at the base of the Branscomb Ridge, within sight of the icefall leading to the Vinson-Shinn Col. The route climbs this icefall to Camp 3, which is situated at 3700m (12,100ft). From here the route turns south, ascending the Vinson summit glacier for 5km (3 miles) to 4500m (14,800ft), where a short snow and ice slope leads to a small col and the Summit Ridge.

The entire route from the col on the Summit Ridge has been skied, but most parties deposit their skis below the icefall at Camp 2.

At these high latitudes the effects of altitude must not be underestimated. Objective dangers on the 'Normal Route' are small: crevassing is minor but extensive, and risk of avalanche is generally minimal, though sérac collapse in the icefall is not uncommon. All parts of the route, apart from the area immediately surrounding base camp, are windswept. The most serious concern is to avoid being caught by high winds.

This 13½km (8½ mile) route can take from two days to two weeks, but the average is 10 days.

2 Branscomb Ridge West Face
Solo: Jay Smith 1994

A thin snow ribbon that becomes a pronounced gully on the 2000m (6500ft) West Face, gaining the Branscomb Ridge south of its northern summit. The crux is a short rock band at 4100m (13,400ft). This route takes seven hours.

3 West Face
Rüdiger Lang 1990-91

A direct route to the summit up the hanging glacier on the West Face from 2700m (9000ft) on the Branscomb Glacier.

how to get to vinson massif

Adventure Network International (ANI) provides the only reasonable means for private individuals to reach Vinson, as the area is only accessible by air. It is a 6-hour flight from Chile to ANI's camp at Patriot Hills, and then another 80 minutes' flight to base camp on Vinson when the weather permits. The company can be reached at Canon House, 27 London End, Beaconsfield, Bucks, HP9 2HN, UK.

facilities

You will have to bring everything you require for subsistence, survival, and ascent. At Patriot Hills, the private camp caters for up to 48 people, providing fresh food flown in from Chile. Visitors sleep in insulated tents, which are normally heated up by the sun.

The base camp on Vinson consists of one main tent for dining and living, and smaller tents for sleeping. The latter are normally brought by individual climbers – take a strong one! Radios are situated at every camp on the mountain and each climber is given an individual radio to use while climbing.

when to climb

The climbing season starts in early November, when base camp opens, and finishes at the end of January, when Patriot Hills is evacuated for the winter. The precise dates are unpredictable as all activity in Antarctica depends on the changeable weather. It is significantly colder at Patriot Hills and on the mountain in the early part of the season. Expect temperatures to range from -5°C to -35°C (25°F to -29°F). The weather will be the biggest problem and you should always allow an extra two weeks for hold-ups.

gear

The 'Normal Route' should only require a light rope, a harness, an ice axe, and crampons. Skis are used by many parties and, while they are not essential, they are helpful during descent. Multi-fuel stoves are the norm. A good tent, a snow saw, and a macho snow shovel are advisable, as are marker wands. The ability to navigate is essential. The ANI guide will give you a complete equipment list before you go.

maps and guidebooks

There are no maps and guidebooks to the mountain, but ANI will give you all the information you need.

language

English.

rescue and insurance

Insurance is essential as there is obviously no organized emergency service, although ANI does provide an emergency back-up system. Do remember that it is a wasteland, and all rescues will be difficult.

red tape

The Antarctic Treaty is in place to ensure that Antarctica is kept in pristine condition. Everything, including human waste, must be taken off with you.

Above **Climbers approaching the Vinson-Shinn Col on skis from Camp 3 on Vinson.**

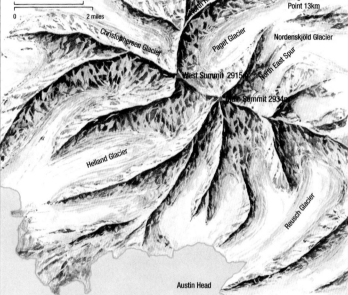

mount paget

lindsay griffin

Mt Paget, 2934m (9625ft), is in South Georgia, the highest and most mountainous island in the seas surrounding Antarctica. Although just outside the Antarctic Circle, it lies wholly within the Convergence, the line where cold water flowing up from the continent meets warmer water moving south from the Atlantic. This means the island has immense glaciation (mostly down to sea level), superb icy peaks, and one of the most inhospitable climates in the world. At these latitudes, a depression track sends almost continuous violent weather across the South Atlantic: South Georgia is the only interruption in its path, so climbing here is a primeval struggle against the elements.

Situated centrally on the crest of the Allardyce Range, Mt Paget is not only the island's highest peak, it is also the highest mountain on British soil. The range runs from the Kohl-Larsen Plateau in the north-west to the Ross Pass in the south-east. To date the

mountain has received no more than four ascents, and only a handful of the major peaks in the range have been climbed.

ridges, faces, and peaks

Mt Paget's two summits, the higher East or Main Summit and the 2915m (9564ft) West Summit are connected by an almost horizontal ridge 2km (1½ miles) long. The northerly aspect is impressive, falling nearly 3000m (10,000ft) to the nearest coastline in less than 7km (4½ miles). Below the Main Summit is the triangular North East Face bounded on the right by the North East Spur. However, the most notable feature on the mountain is the huge, precipitous rock-and-ice wall below the West Summit. The jumbled glacial slopes to the south, dropping to the Helland Glacier, are more reasonably angled, and it was from this side that the first attempts were made. The two main features here are the long West-South-West Ridge and a broad South-South-West Spur. Between the two, the face is heavily seraced and shows few obvious objectively safe lines. The South East Face, bounded on the right by the East-South-East Ridge, is steep and icy, but the North West Face above the Christophersen Glacier is more hospitable and leads directly to the West Summit.

The extreme difficulty of access, combined with the logistical problems of penetrating such a wild environment, has meant that climbing expeditions are very sporadic. However, once there, climbers will find superb climbing conditions, with perfect 'styrofoam' ice and, in general, a surprisingly low risk of avalanche. Indeed, those who succeed in climbing anything, after spending weeks hiding in snow caves from white-out conditions and wind speeds often in excess of 150kph (90mph), will find a magical panorama that makes any ascent a unique and lasting memory.

future climbing

There are immense possibilities for those with the time and resources to stick it out. Paget has never been approached from the south and there is a possible landing at Austin Head by the snout of the Reusch Glacier. This could give access to a number of unclimbed problems such as the South-South-West Spur, the much harder South East Face, and even the East-South-East Ridge, though the latter can be reached from the north. The long, curving North Ridge leading to the West Summit and overlooking the north-west bank of the Paget Glacier has never been attempted, and the futuristic North East Wall below the West Summit would give plenty of hard mixed climbing.

Main Summit

West Summit

Paget
Glacier

Glacier travel begins close to sea level and can involve fairly complex route-finding difficulties; all routes should therefore be considered to be around 2500m (8200ft). Because of constantly changing conditions and the fact that so few ascents have been completed, the routes are generally not graded.

north side

Far more accessible than the West Side, with an approach up the Nordenskjöld Glacier from a sheltered anchorage in Cumberland Bay. However, snow conditions deteriorate more rapidly during periods of good weather, as this side receives maximum sun.

1 North East Face

Anglo-American-Austrian-German Expedition 1994
The six climbers spent three days reaching 1200m (3900ft), then made

a 16-hour round trip to the summit, finding excellent névé and several 60° ice pitches in the upper section. They descended via the upper part of the North East Spur.

2 North East Spur

French Expedition 1980
Probably the most accessible means of ascent; has been repeated.

west side

The most straightforward aspect of the mountain, but remotely sited; presenting serious glacier terrain and moderately angled snow slopes.

3 From the West

British Combined Services Expedition 1964
Although technically very straightforward, this route would be a logistical nightmare for a private party due to the lack of good anchorage available on the south-west coast of the island.

how to get to mount paget

There are several charter ships with very experienced skippers who will take you to South Georgia – at a price. In the past some teams have managed to negotiate a ride on visiting vessels.

facilities

None. Bring all you need with you.

when to climb

Most ascents take place in summer (December–February), but the most stable period of high pressure often occurs in mid-winter. The best plan is to have a snow cave close to your route, then to wait for a break in the weather.

gear

Take snowshoes, skis, snow shovels and saws, waterproofs, resilient tents, and plenty of reading material. For extended

forays into the interior, you will need pulks. You must be very good at navigating in white-out conditions.

maps and guidebooks

The British military and British Antarctic Survey have reasonable maps. The best books are: *The Island of South Georgia*, Robert Headland and *Island at the Edge of the World*, Stephen Venables.

language

English.

rescue and insurance

A privately organized rescue would be required. Insurance is essential.

red tape

Permission to land must be obtained from the local harbourmaster and the military commander at King Edward Point.

Kinabalu
Kota Kinabalu● S A B A H

Crocker Range

B O R N E O

I R I A N
J A Y A ● Jayapura

Carstensz Pyramid

Sudirman
Range

P A P U A
N E W
G U I N E A

● Port Morseby

Coral
Sea

Pacific
Ocean

A U S T R A L I A

Tasman
Sea

indonesia & oceania

Mountaineering among New Zealand's Southern Alps has been popular for more than a century, and 'Kiwi' mountaineers are renowned the world over for their stoicism and endurance. We have chosen to illustrate the highest, Aoraki-Mount Cook, and the lesser Mount Tutoko in the densely vegetated Darran range, as representatives of the rugged and exploratory nature of New Zealand climbing.

By contrast, mountaineering is in its infancy elsewhere on the islands of Oceania and in Indonesia, though there is plenty of potential. Carstensz Pyramid in Irian Jaya, at 4884m (16,021ft), is the highest in the region, surmounting anything in the Southern Alps. Close to the equator, it carries little snow and ice. Set amid dense jungle, its remoteness and delicate internal politics seem set to keep this area off the tourist track. At the other end of the scale, Kinabalu, which is at the north end of the island of Borneo, has a standard route that is well provided with ladders and handrails, and sees thousands of visitors every year.

Clockwise from left: **Aoraki-Mount Cook; the Caroline Face of Aoraki-Mount Cook; view of Kinabalu with Donkey's Ears in the right-hand background**

NEW ZEALAND
Southern Alps
Aoraki-Mt Cook
Christchurch
Mt Tutoko
Queenstown
Darran Mtns

15th century Chinese traders of the Ming Dynasty first identified Kinabalu.

1851 H Low (British), the first person known to have reached the summit area, arrived at Cauldron Gap on 11 March. He travelled from Kampong Kiau via the South Ridge, but did not reach the top itself.

1858 H Low and S St John (British Consul in Brunei) climbed to within 40m (130ft) of the summit of St John's Peak, believing it to be the highest point.

1888 On 3 March J Whitehead, a British natural-history collector, became the first Westerner to climb Low's Peak.

1931 Rev J Clemens (American) and W Gill (British) climbed Victoria Peak.

1957 The first traverse was made between the West and East Plateaux by M Bowen (British).

1961 A British expedition of The Royal Society climbed King George Peak (4063m/13,330ft) via the East Ridge from Poring.

1964 The first ascent of King Edward Peak was made by Sheridon, Heath, and Bosworth (British).

1967 Craig and Wilson (British) made the first ascent of Tunku Abdul Rahman Peak.

1987 On 6 March the first descent into the bottom of Low's Gully was made by S Pinfield (British), and R Alderhalden and R Brandli (Swiss). The first ascent of the 'Marai Parai Route' was made by S Pinfield, R New (British), and A Gunsalam (Malaysian).

1988 The first known ascent of King George Peak by the North Ridge via North Peak was made

kinabalu

robert new

Kinabalu, at 4095m (13,436ft), is the highest mountain in South East Asia, but what makes the mountain impressive is the fact that it is twice the height of almost anything else on the island of Borneo and is, therefore, unique in rising clear above the forest canopy.

To the Westerner the name Borneo conjures up a picture of a great island covered in rainforest, incised by well-fed rivers, and inhabited by primitive jungle tribes. This romantic picture overlooks the reality of kilometre upon kilometre of oil palm plantations, modern towns, and mountains that are, today, more in evidence than the deepest jungle. And it is this almost universal misconception that is partly to blame for the general lack of interest in Kinabalu among mountaineering circles.

Kinabalu is the high point of the Crocker Range that runs almost from the north tip of Borneo to its centre. Consisting mostly of sandstone, this range was pushed up at the point of collision between three tectonic plates and is said to be still rising. A large pluton of hard granite, which formed underground many eons ago, was uplifted with the range and now stands proud as its surroundings have eroded away.

Kinabalu is the emblem of Sabah, one of the two Bornean states of Malaysia. The mountain dominates the lives of all who live on the west coast of Sabah (formerly known as North Borneo) and many who live in the interior. In the days of sailing ships it was a navigation landmark, and it is the feature most remarked on in the accounts of early explorers, so it is hardly surprising that it has had an important spiritual significance to the people of this state and is the subject of both local and Chinese folklore. People living in the immediate vicinity of Kinabalu believe that the spirits of their departed live in the summit area of the mountain. For this reason they did not, until comparatively recently, climb above the tree-line, and actively discouraged European explorers from doing so. Even today, sacrifices and incantations are made from time to time to appease the spirits of the mountain.

Until the late 1800s Kinabalu was completely surrounded by deep rainforest; the only known approach was by a 3-week hike from the west coast to Kampong Kiau, from where the South Ridge was climbed via a spur on its western side. Then the Tenombok Pass, over the Crocker Range at the base of the South Ridge, was found to be a viable, and easier, route and a bridle path was opened up. Today, this route forms the principal connection between the east and west coasts of Sabah. The route encouraged the opening up and development of surrounding lands, threatening the natural habitats around Kinabalu, and this led to the establishment of an area of 754 sq km (470 sq miles) – which includes the mountain – as a protected park.

Three kilometres (2 miles) beyond the Tenombok Pass to the east is the small town of Kundasang, which has a growing number of holiday chalets. Ranau, which is 16km (10 miles) further to the east, is the main town in the area and gives access to Poring, located at the base of Kinabalu's East Ridge where climbers can relax their weary limbs in the hot springs.

The other major change is that, nowadays, far from avoiding Kinabalu, almost every young person in Malaysia hopes to climb the mountain. The normal South Ridge route has been developed with ladders and fixed ropes along its steeper and more difficult sections to make this possible. About 40,000 people do the climb every year, and each September there is an

by Kinabalu Park Warden E Wong (Malaysian) with Kinabalu Park staff.
1994 A British Army expedition down Low's Gully ended with five climbers being rescued from the bottom of the Gully by helicopter after two weeks without food. The rescue was a massive joint Malaysian/British Army effort and was saturated with international media attention.

1997 A survey expedition remeasured the heights of the principal peaks on Kinabalu to confirm Low's Peak as the highest at 4095m (13,436ft).
1998 A joint Malaysian and British expedition successfully descended Low's Gully. They were led by Pat Gunson, and 17 members of the expedition completed the route.

international race up and down this route. (The record time for completing the race has been whittled down to below two hours, 20 minutes.) These statistics, and the fact that a 'stand-alone' mountain is no match for the great mountain ranges, also help to explain the almost total but unjustified lack of interest shown in Kinabalu by serious mountaineers.

ridges, faces, and peaks

Kinabalu is a mostly steep-sided mass of granite. It has three prominent ridges (South, East, and North) and the deep Low's Gully that splits the mountain in two. The mountain top is characterized by sweeping easy slabs, referred to as the West and East Plateaux, and numerous rock peaks and pinnacles of varying severity. Although it often freezes at night, snow and ice are rare so it is a potential playground for rock climbers. The larger summit peaks mostly offer choices between slabby dip-slopes, undercut and often overhanging faces, and faces and ridges that range between these extremes. Many of the peaks have easy ways up for climbers, although everyday visitors are restricted to climbing Low's Peak, which is the easiest of all and happens also to be the highest by a whisker at 4095m (13,436ft).

The other major peaks that can be accessed from the West Plateau include Victoria Peak, which, with its characteristic summit spire at 4094m (13,432ft), is only marginally lower than Low's Peak; and St John's Peak, which is a few metres lower still at 4091m (13,420ft). King Edward Peak, 4081m (13,388ft), is on the less frequented East Side of the mountain and is the only high peak without an easy way up. King George Peak, at 4063m (13,330ft), is an easy scramble and more often climbed. At the head of Low's Gully in the centre of the mountain is Tunku Abdul Rahman Peak (3948m/12,952ft), which is separated by Cauldron Gap from two rock pinnacles known as Donkey's Ears (4054m/13,301ft). Most of these provide routes with 200–300m (650–1000ft) of climbing, although the abundant pinnacles offer shorter climbs.

The peaks of Kinabalu supply good climbing at any grade, on clean and mostly reliable granite, with some fine positions, classic lines, and wonderful panoramas. Nevertheless, it is in Low's Gully that the mountain's magnificence is fully realized. This dramatic cleft features the mountain's highest rock faces, some of which are unrelenting for over 1000m (3300ft). The great depth of the gully means that the

Right A view towards North Peak of Kinabalu from the West Plateau, showing the steep drop into Low's Gully. This separates the West and East Plateaux.

North Buttress

bottom of it can only be viewed from a few locations, and it was not until 1987 that a way into it was found from above. Indeed, it was one almost tragic expedition into Low's Gully in 1994 (*see timeline*) that, through worldwide media exposure, bestowed general recognition on Kinabalu. The complete descent of Low's Gully was only successfully done in 1998. However, as the main drain for the mountain, the risk from rainfall will always be a serious one – early 1998 had the driest months on record, giving the expedition the ideal conditions.

future climbing

While sightseers clamber up the South Ridge, there are difficult alternatives for those prepared for the challenge of fighting uphill through dense, mossy, or bamboo forest for a day or two before reaching rock. Fascinating endemic flora and fauna are found on approach routes up the East Ridge and North Ridge, and from Kampong Kiau on the West Side via either Paka Cave or Marai Parai. With the exception of these routes, the outer sides of the mountain are accessible only after a long jungle trek of several days, or involve somewhat featureless slabs or very broken pinnacled ridges. The lack of classic lines has resulted in climbing normally being concentrated on the upper peak areas.

None of the outer faces of Kinabalu has been climbed, and the difficulties involved in reaching them through the dense vegetation discourages routes. The ridges offer more scenic opportunities but water is scarce.

The South Ridge 'Standard Route' needs no description: just follow the crowds on the path.

1 Mesilau Route – no technical difficulty ⊠
Kotal 1963
This is the most famous route to the East Plateau from the East Side of the mountain. An arduous but scenic 3-day route that crosses the East Ridge and makes its final approach via the Mekado Valley on the North Side.

2 Marai Parai Route – no technical difficulty ⊠
S Pinfield, R New, and A Gunsalam 1987
A 2-day route up the north-west corner of the mountain from Kampong Kiau to the West Plateau via the West Cwm.

routes on the peaks
Most rock routes on the peaks have been put up since the mid-1960s. Although the route options are extensive, very few have ever been recorded. However, many unrecorded climbs appear to have been made, particularly by Japanese climbers, and this is evident from the hardware left in place.

3 St John's Peak: West Ridge D ⊠
First ascent not known
The classic line along the spine of the peak with just two short pitches of climbing. It is one hour from the base of the peak.

4 Victoria Peak: South East Face HVS ⊠
S Pinfield, Alderhalden, and Brandli 1987
This unrelenting route follows one of the few lines of weakness up the centre of the South East Face, but offers fine positions. The ascent is 200m (650ft) long in four pitches.

North East Face

East Ear

West Ear

DONKEY'S EARS

5 Tunku Abdul Rahman Peak: East Flank and South Face VD

Craig and Wilson 1967

A route with delightfully varied climbing and some fine positions. This peak is one of the finest viewpoints on Kinabalu. Ascent 150m (500ft) in four pitches.

6 King Edward Peak: North Buttress VS

First ascent not known

A short, steep climb taking a classic line and offering fine positions. Ascent 50m (165ft).

7 Donkey's Ears: East Ear, North East Face S

Pendleton and Heat 1964

A short, exposed climb via a prominent flake. There are several harder variations. Bolts left in place on the West Ear now enable it to be free climbed at HVS. Ascent of the East Ear route is 50m (165ft) in two pitches.

how to get to kinabalu

There are daily flights to Kota Kinabalu, the capital of Sabah, from Hong Kong, Singapore, and Kuala Lumpur. From here it is a 2-hour drive on good roads to Kinabalu Park Headquarters, and the start of the 'Standard Route'. There is a frequent bus service.

facilities

There is mountain-hut accommodation at 3270m (10,700ft), 3666m (12,000ft) on the 'Standard Route', and at 3838m (12,600ft) in the West Cwm, as well as at the Park Headquarters. There is a restaurant at the 3270m (10,700ft) hut. All accommodation needs to be pre-booked at the Kota Kinabalu office of Sabah Parks, PO Box 10626, 88806 Kota Kinabalu, Sabah, Malaysia.

Only small shops selling local-type food can be found in Ranau and Kundasang so it is best to stop in Kota Kinabalu before departing for the mountain. Gear cannot be purchased locally.

when to climb

Weather has become unpredictable and any time of the year can be dry or wet. December–February and June–August are, however, more likely to be wet than other months.

gear

No special requirements – you will need general gear for rock climbing in spring or autumn at temperate latitudes.

maps and guidebooks

No climbing guidebooks are yet available and the maps are hopelessly inaccurate. Sabah Parks publish leaflets about Kinabalu that are geared towards the 'Standard Route', so you can contact them for general enquiries.

language

English is widely spoken. Malay is the national language spoken by everyone, but the mother tongue for porters and guides comprises Dusun dialects.

rescue and insurance

All climbers are required to take out a modest insurance arranged by the Park authority; this only covers the 'Standard Route'. There is no mountain-rescue service but the Park authority is able to evacuate casualties from the 'Standard Route'. However, do not expect rescue services on the technical routes.

red tape

You will be asked to hire a guide, but they mostly know only the 'Standard Route'. You need special clearance from the Park Warden to climb any of the other routes without a guide. He/she has the right to request evidence of competence, refuse consent, or give approval subject to conditions. Obtaining written agreement from Sabah Parks authority, before arrival, will make the Park Warden's consent a mere formality. You will be charged a climbing fee. Some parts of the mountain are especially hard to access because of rare plants or research projects.

malaysia's playground above the clouds

mike banks

"There are climbers' mountains and there are people's mountains. On the summit of the Dru the mountaineer will meet only kindred spirits. However, if a mountain is the highest in its country, or if it has religious importance, it will attract the crowds and is best avoided by the élitist.

Kinabalu is very much a people's mountain. The highest in Borneo and, indeed, in South East Asia, it is also deeply venerated locally as the resting place of the departed. In a uniformly jungle landscape, Kinabalu thrusts its dramatic ramparts high above the rainforest and is visible from afar. Its flora and fauna are also quite remarkable. Little wonder that it has been designated a National Park by the Malaysian (Sabah) authorities.

Every year some 30,000 people, mostly young office workers from cities such as Kuala Lumpur or Singapore, toil up to the summit. Despite the fact that the *voie normale* is a busy tourist highway, the committed mountaineer can still enjoy the ascent, provided he is flexible enough in mind. Forget your heavy rucksack bulging with climbing gear and food; chuck out your reserved attitude. Instead, tune into the vibrancy and wonder of the groups of young people experiencing their first big mountain and the effects of altitude and cold. They are excited, a little apprehensive, but very friendly and curious.

I climbed Kinabalu with mountain photographer John Cleare. I suspect that our (mandatory) guide was curious to see how far I would totter before I collapsed as I am white-haired and 73. I decided to keep to the alpine maxim of ascending without halt and without haste. Setting a slow and steady pace, I had leisure to enjoy the superb forest.

Every half hour or so we came across a solidly built, gazebo-like shelter where there were seats, drinking water, and a map to show you how far you had progressed. As time passed, the forest became more open and on a fine day there would have been long views. However, by now it was mid-morning and, exactly on cue, the clouds formed and the rain started. Having been moving steadily for more than two hours, we stopped for lunch at Layang Layang, or Carson's Camp, and then trudged on at the same pace.

Our thoughts dwelt increasingly on a hot drink at the hostel of Laban Rata, somewhere up there in the murk. Then a cheerful

It was a rock climber's playground set against the backdrop of limitless rainforest.

man who spoke English called out, 'Keep going, it's only three minutes to the hotel!' Just the sort of message to send a surge of energy into tired legs. Sure enough, a chunky slab of a building materialized out of the mist and we stepped into the cavernous restaurant and lounge. We had ascended 1430m in well under four hours. What Laban Rata lacked in architectural charm, it amply made up for in good, quick, and cheap food.

Because cloud normally forms over the upper mountain by mid-morning, it is the custom for climbers to get up at 2am, have a cup of coffee, and set off from Laban Rata at 3am. This ensures that even the slower ones attain the summit in time to witness the normally spectacular dawn. As we started out next morning it was raining. Five minutes later it became a horizontal shower bath. 'This is nuts!' I shouted against the wind. With one accord we turned and scuttled back to the hostel and bed.

Our decision turned out to be a wise one. We were, in fact, on the edge of a small typhoon. All that day rain lashed against the windows and a rivulet we had noticed earlier was transformed into a demented cataract of terrifying force.

By next morning the storm had blown itself out and we set off into a dark, misty world at 3am. We climbed a few ladders and then came to a thick, fixed, white rope that was to continue without a break for about 2.5km, all the way to the summit. In a few places the rope was necessary to haul yourself up steep rocks, but for the most part it was merely showing the way. The purist mountaineer would regard this rope as a defacement. However, it must be remembered that visibility is usually very poor on this

Above left **The view from 3800m (12,500ft) on Kinabalu, looking south-east to where the Crocker Range summits rise above monsoon cloud.**

Above right **Photographer John Cleare (on right) with the guide at the start of the Kinabalu ascent.**

mountain, with tremendous cliffs falling away from the summit plateau. Most people climbing it are totally inexperienced in mountain navigation. It is, therefore, an extremely effective and absolutely necessary safety measure.

Because of the anticipated cloud, we had allowed three days on the upper mountain for John Cleare to get his Kinabalu pictures. So we were moving our base to a higher hut, Sayat Sayat, which provided cooking facilities. We reached the hut in 1½ hours, dumped our heavy gear, then continued the ascent.

We now debouched onto the huge, smooth granite slabs of the summit plateau. The slope was gentle and our headtorch beams cut through the mist to show the white rope snaking ahead of us. An hour brought us to a sudden steepening, a scramble up a rocky ridge, and then to the outline of the notice marking the summit, Low's Peak.

It was now the grey half-light of pre-dawn. The cloud was still thick – there would be no glorious dawn. We put on all our warm and waterproof clothing to wait for the day to brighten and to snatch what photographs we could. As we sat under the shelter of a summit rock, we watched a succession of inadequately clad, half-frozen figures appear out of the mist and arrive at the summit. Although there was an occasional triumphal whoop, for the most part the visitors only gave a cold shudder, a sigh of relief, and made a quick departure.

The cloud persisted, so we gave up and retreated to Sayat Sayat where a rat hopped hopefully onto the kitchen table to help me prepare supper. That night I hung the food from a roof girder and went smugly to bed. However, my enterprising friend found his way into my toilet bag, ate all my vitamin tablets and, I hope, emerged as Super Rat!

So far we had been blinkered in clouds. On the second day they thinned and we stared in amazement at the array of soaring rock towers that surrounded us. Most unmistakable were the slender twin spires aptly named the Donkey's Ears. It was a rock climber's playground set against the backdrop of limitless rainforest. We scampered back up onto the summit plateau where John Cleare got busy with his camera. The cloud later thickened, but not before we caught a glimpse of the forbidding North Side of Kinabalu. Peeping over the summit ridge, we could see the ground fall abruptly towards the massive rock scoop of Commando Cauldron and Low's Gully that cuts a narrow slit in a vast and precipitous rock face.

On our descent the weather pattern was repeated. Back at Laban Rata we awoke to a brilliant morning to see a skyline filled with jagged peaks. They disported themselves just long enough for us to take in their grandeur before the spirits of the dead, who inhabit these upper reaches, drew thin curtains of mist across this elusive and beguiling mountain landscape.

1623 The Dutch navigator J Carstensz was the first to bring to Europe news of tropical ice in West New Guinea. His observations were met with ridicule.
1913 British naturalist A F R Wollaston reached the snout of a glacier on the South Side of Carstensz after horrendous jungle-bashing from the southern coast. It took him 92 days to cover the last 50km (30 miles).

1936 A Dutch party, led by Dr A H Colijn, with the assistance of aerial reconnaissance and parachute drops, came into the mountains and climbed neighbouring Ngga Pulu, 4860m (15,590ft). He failed to climb Carstensz East and also Carstensz Pyramid, which he attempted via the East Ridge and the North Face, but produced a useful map and published equally

useful aerial photographs of the range. (It was the geologist in the group, J V Dozy, who first discovered the rich copper-ore deposits on the 'copper mountain' of the Ertsberg.)
1961 P Temple led a 6-man New Zealand team into the Carstensz Massif via Wamena airstrip. The pre-arranged air drop of supplies never came, so they were unable to climb the Pyramid.

1962 Carstensz Pyramid was first climbed by an expedition organized by Austrian climber H Harrer with guide P Temple (New Zealander). The other two members of this team were a Dutch District Officer, A Huzenga, and R Kippax (Australian). Some of their supplies were dropped by aeroplane. Their approach was from Illaga to the north, which had been opened up

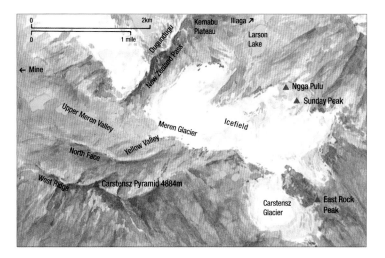

carstensz pyramid

doug scott

Carstensz Pyramid lies in Irian Jaya – what used to be known as West New Guinea – and, at 4884m (16,021ft), is the highest peak in Indonesia. It is also the highest peak in Australasia, making it a target for those mountaineers collecting the so-called Seven Summits. It is one of at least 10 peaks over 4500m (14,800ft) that rise up out of the series of cordillera running medially west to east through Irian Jaya into Papua New Guinea. Previously known as the Central Highlands, the section in Irian Jaya is now known as the Maoke Mountains. The principal ranges within the Maoke are the Sudirman (formerly Nassau), of which Carstensz is the highest; the Jayawiyaya (Oranje), at 4702m (15,427ft); and the Trikora (Wilhelmina Top), at 4750m (15,500ft).

Rising from dense jungle and frequently wreathed in mist, Carstensz is a remote and mysterious mountain. An expedition to it is not just a climbing venture, but a journey into the Stone Age and an incredibly rich experience.

Unfortunately, this experience is set to change as the Indonesian government continues its trans-migration policy and as mining interests massively expand their operations. The tribespeople of these highlands, such as the Dani, fear that their way of life is under threat. Every day of the year a major mining company dumps 120,000 tons of highly toxic tailings into the Ajkwe River. The locals are displaced from their ancestral homelands, often with force, as miners gobble up whole mountains. Tragically, these mountains have religious significance to tribes such as the Amungme; as one leader put it, the mining company 'is digging out our mothers' brains.'

However, much of Irian Jaya is still covered in prime forest and there are said to be tribes living in the north-east that have never been visited by people from outside the island. A trek to Carstensz takes you through the aboriginal lands of the Dani, where the men still prefer to wear traditional penis gourds and birds of paradise feathers in their hair and the women have raffia skirts. These people are welcoming to climbers, displaying honesty, spontaneous humour, and warmth, and will provide the porters needed for the approach march. This is a rugged 4- or 5-day trek from the village of Illaga, taking in jungle, several steep passes, and ridge crossings, and it can be very humid, to say the least. The base camp is located by a glacial melt lake in the midst of the high mountain limestone. Other summits in the area include the East Rock Peak, two miles east of Carstensz Pyramid: Ngga Pulu and Sunday Peak are high points on the rim above the icefield.

The remoteness and, more particularly, political volatility of the area, and an unbelievable amount of red tape, have combined to limit the number of independent climbers who visit the area. There are several commercial climbing tour operators that include Carstensz Pyramid in their annual programmes at considerable cost. However, since the 1996 hostage-taking, the area has been closed to foreign climbers for the foreseeable future.

ridges, faces, and peaks

The peak is named after the Dutch navigator, Jan Carstensz, whose reports of tropical ice after his voyage of 1623 were widely disbelieved. It was only in the early years of the 20th century that explorers were able to reach the snowline. An annual rainfall of as much as 710cm (280in) has been recorded, and yet the crests of all the porous, limestone mountains remain relatively dry.

by missionaries and their light aircraft since World War II. This has become the standard approach to the area, and the North Face route is the regular way up the mountain.

1971 R Messner (Italian) made the second ascent of Carstensz Pyramid with an Italian client, S Bigarella. They climbed the knife-edged East Ridge of the mountain and had an epic

and hungry return to Illaga, going without food for five days.

1972 The British expedition of D Isherwood, L Murray, and J Baines climbed the North Face of Carstensz Pyramid via a line directly up to the East Summit. This was the first hard direct route on the face. Isherwood went on to solo, for the first time, the North Face of nearby Sunday Peak from Larson Lake.

1973 The mountain was soloed for the first time by a new route. The ascensionist was the brilliant young American climber, B Carson. His party ascended Carstensz three times in all, on one occasion with the first Indonesian to reach the summit, E Wurjantoro.

1978 P Boardman and Hilary Collins (British) were the first to climb the South

Face of Carstensz. They descended the North Face via the first ascent route (1962), thus also making the first crossing of the mountain. They were the first to approach the massif from the north-west (*see pages 182–3*).

With one-and-a-half days of walking through dense jungle, stumbling across tussock grass, karst country, and usually in drenching rain with mud underfoot for two more days, it is a wonderful moment when the clouds crossing the Kemabu Plateau part to reveal the mountain. The final approach is over the New Zealand Pass, through an area of great natural beauty, with forests and lakes that nestle in secluded cwms. After crossing the pass, Carstensz's North Face can be seen – head-on with all its lines showing if the sun is slanting across the face.

north side 'The Original Route' (12), which slopes from left to right through a scree basin and up onto the West Ridge, is clearly visible. To its right is the huge blank White Slab; to its left is another snow or scree basin and, further left, huge walls seamed with cracks. Two-thirds of the way up the face is the Great Terrace, which is more a sloping ridge. This water-worn high mountain limestone is quite often prickly wherever indentations coalesce. Much of it is fluted or seamed with deep cracks. It is immediately obvious that this is good rock for climbing.

At its highest point the North Face is at least 610m (2000ft). As it has been scoured by glacier and is washed by the almost daily deluge of rain, the rock is mainly solid. Areas of loose rock are obvious – in the gullies or below basins holding scree. In general, the climbing on the North Face is delectable. As far as is known, no one has found it necessary to drill holes for bolt belays and it should continue to be considered a bolt-free zone.

The East Ridge is long, crenellated, and gendarmed – the East Summit is the most prominent crenellation before the summit.

south side The mountain's South Side is constantly enveloped in mist, and is full of ledges and loose broken ground.

future climbing

The 0.5km (1 mile) wide North Face may give the best climbing in the whole of Irian Jaya, but there are also good routes to repeat and establish in the immediate environs of Carstensz; such opportunities will be immediately apparent on visiting the area. It is a lot more than a rock climber's paradise; it is good for anyone interested in wild mountain country. The glaciers are shrinking, revealing smooth, striated limestone rock. In fact, since 1936, the Carstensz and Meren Glaciers have receded by 0.5km (1 mile). Sadly, within 50 years they may all have melted away completely.

Right **Mark Bowen climbing the 'Anglo-American Route' on the North Face.**

East Ridge

East Summit

Main Summit

West Ridge

Great Terrace

White Slab

north face

The usual base camp is in the Upper Meren Valley on the flat gravel shoreline on the south side of the lake. To save an hour in the morning you can camp in the Yellow Valley, right under the North Face.

One unfortunate aspect of the Meren Valley is that it is only about 2–3 hours away from the mine – at weekends mineworkers and their guards come up here, leaving their litter and graffiti and firing off their AK-47s. However, this is a small price to pay for being in an otherwise pristine area of great natural beauty.

New routes have been put up on the North Face in ever-increasing numbers, and now there are 11 new routes achieved mostly by Europeans and North Americans. The face itself is 610m (2000ft) and most of the following routes are that length. Unless otherwise stated, they require a day to complete.

1 Messner Line
R Messner and S Bigarella 1971
Takes the East Ridge and is a fine outing in good weather apart from loose rock and several steps to cross.

2 Carson-Emmett Route
B Carson and D Emmett 1973
This climbs up the far-left side of the face to the East Ridge and then traverses along ledges on the South Side to reach the summit. 3½ hours.

3 The Anglo-American Route
M Bowen, T Callaghan, and D Scott 1995
This is on the left of the face, on the solid bulging rock to the right of two parallel cracks joining together below the East Ridge. The first five pitches are the most difficult: 5.8/5.9. The route then goes up the steeper wall and into a gully out of sight from below, and leads up to the East Ridge just beneath the East Summit of Carstensz (V+/IV). The route provides extremely good, solid climbing except for the final scramble to the ridge.

4 The Munich Route
H Huber and party 1974
Hermann Huber and Herbert Karasek climbed up gullies and grooves to the left of 'The Isherwood Line' (5). At half-height they then joined the Isherwood route. For the Germans, the route was particularly icy.

5 The Isherwood Line
D Isherwood, L Murray, and J Baines 1973
This route takes fairly easy ground to start with, up broken gullies (III and IV) to the Great Terrace where it steepens into open face and chimney climbing until the East Summit of Carstensz is reached. All in all it is a fairly direct line from the start to the top of the East Summit (V+).

Routes 6–10 all claim to have gone direct to the summit. Whether they were independent, crossed existing routes, or involved climbing pitches of existing routes is not known for sure. Only the line of route (8) can be ascertained precisely.

6 The French Route V/V+, A1 ⊠
B Domenech and J Fabre 1979
As far as is known, this is the most direct way up the face, reaching the West Ridge just short of the summit.

7 The Carson Line ⊠
Solo: B Carson 1973
There were 12 pitches of up to 5.8 in grade on this almost direct route to the summit – all done in 3½ hours. Carson then downclimbed

the 'Carson-Emmett Route' (2) – a remarkable *tour de force*.

8 The American Direct V, 5.8
G Tabin, R Shapiro, and S Moses 1980
Another very direct route on the North Face, this required a bivouac halfway up. The rock again was found to be excellent, giving 5.6 and 5.7 pitches continuously with two cruxes of 5.8 on the headwall.

9 Indonesian Route ⊠
Adiseno and members of the Mapala University Climbing Club and Indonesian Army 1992
They reported ascending more or less directly to the summit. The main difficulties (5.9) were in negotiating the overlaps at the start of the headwall.

10 The Italian Route ⊠
A de Felice, E de Luca, and P Sabbatini
They reported the route as being grade VI.

11 Ferrière Route
L de la Ferrière and G Vionnet 1994
A new route to the west of the summit, finishing up the obvious tower. The Main Summit was reached via the East Ridge.

12 The Original Route
H Harrer, P Temple, A Huzenga, and R Kipax 1962
The route takes a line of weakness slanting left to right into a scree basin and then a gully system above, onto the West Ridge; from here a long traverse leads to the summit. Variations have since been made, particularly up the last 60m (200ft) to the West Ridge, by leaving the scree terrace and climbing direct up the highly featured face. 800m (2600ft). AD, mainly IV with one pitch of V 5.8 (5.9 in the wet).

13 Spanish-German Climb (Aquarius) IV
R Portilla and W Treibel 1993
This pioneered a route up the obvious gully and crack system on the left side of the big White Slab. Rain prevented the original climbers going directly to the West Ridge, so they traversed left and joined 'The Original Route' (12) in the big scree basin. They did not make it to the summit due to the pouring rain.

south side
Much more mist-prone and has very broken, loose rock between ledges.

14 German Traverse
B Schrechenback and G Kirner 1974
A long, meandering route starting to the right of the White Slab, traversing over its top, then joining with 'The Original Route' (12).

15 The Boardman Line V ⊠
P Boardman and H Collins 1978
Crosses the East Ridge to gain the South Face. After traversing loose ledges and a lead up 50m (160ft) of ice, it continues up chimneys and over rotten ledges. The first climbers descended 'The Original Route' (12) to make the first crossing from south to north.

16 South Side Variation ⊠
N Banks, C Monteath, and party 1995
A commercial group reached the summit via this route.

Left **A neighbouring summit, Sunday Peak, which is one of the high points on the rim above the icefield.**

---

how to get to carstensz pyramid
Most people fly to Jakarta and make a connection to Wamena via Jayapura, Irian Jaya's capital city. Wamena is the main town in the mountains and from there it is possible to take another flight to Illaga, the nearest village north of Carstensz. Alternatively, you may be able to get a local flight from Biak to Nabire, then arrange a charter flight from Nabire to Illaga, which will shorten the approach to a few days' trek. You can take a helicopter onto Nasidome but, if you have the time, it is best to trek and meet the Dani tribespeople.

Flights can be expensive, and you are recommended to check with your local travel agent to see if Indonesian Airlines offers a special–rate air pass for multiple domestic stopovers.

The easiest way to reach the Carstensz Massif is via the Ertsberg Mountain mine, which is 2½ hours' walk from base camp. However, it is very unusual for access via the mine to be allowed. In 1986 Canadian Pat Morrow's party took 17 months of high-level negotiation between the Canadian and Indonesian politicians and the Indonesian Army to gain access via Timika and the mine.

Note: in 1987 the Swiss Markus Itten and Diego Wellig were shot at by military patrols on the perimeter of the mine.

facilities
Every basic commodity can be bought at Nabire and excellent vegetables are available at Illaga.

when to climb
There is no best season to climb on Carstensz because it can rain at any time of the year. It is always advisable to complete climbing by midday as heavy rainfall can be expected most afternoons. An alpine start (3–4am) is invaluable.

gear
Besides rain, climbers should be prepared for quite heavy dumps of snow. On occasions, the North Face has been considerably iced-up. Depending on what route you contemplate, you should take a range of equipment including a set of friends, wires, sling, and a selection of pegs, and mainly knife blades, but no bolts! It is always necessary to take plenty of tape for the fingers and backs of hands; in fact, a light pair of leather industrial gloves could be useful against wear and tear on the hands.

maps and guidebooks
There are no guidebooks or maps to assist in climbing the Carstensz Range although the *Lonely Planet Guide to Indonesia and Irian Jaya* has useful general information. *The Periplus Travel Guide to New Guinea – Irian Jaya* can also be useful. It will be necessary to comb through the various Alpine Journals (especially 1977) for the most accurate information, and it is also worth reading *Nawok!*, Philip Temple (1962); *I Come From the Stone Age*, Heinrich Harrer (1964); and *Sacred Summits*, Peter Boardman (1982) – the latter currently in print as part of the *Boardman Tasker Omnibus*. All have useful sketch maps.

Note: bear in mind that the ice keeps on retreating, alternative heights are given, and the names are forever changing. So far, Carstensz massif has largely escaped this last annoying occurrence except that, on some maps, Carstensz Pyramid will be named Puncak Jayakesuma or, more simply, Puncak Jaya.

language
Indonesian or one of 600 local dialects. English is sometimes understood.

rescue and insurance
There are no rescue facilities laid on by the government but in a real emergency it may be possible to activate a helicopter rescue from the mine. They may then allow you to pass through their property and provide you with transport to the airport at Timika, from where it is possible to fly to Biak and from there onto regular services back home.

Insurance is not necessary, but always highly recommended.

red tape
You will need to make contact with an experienced local trekking agency. The whole procedure can take six months so you should send out biographical data and 12 passport photographs well in advance to aid the agents when they are chasing the relevant government officials for the necessary permits. If this is not done ahead of your visit you may have several frustrating weeks – and perhaps several journeys back and forth across Indonesia.

Once the relevant permits have been acquired, your journey should proceed without any major hitches, at least as far as Illaga. Always allow for the weather and for a backlog of passengers wanting to join the local flights to Illaga.

Local guides and porters can be hired at Illaga. It will facilitate the hiring process to have your Indonesian agent there with you – they will be able to help translate and make your onward journey more interesting.

carstensz's initiation test

hilary boardman

Carstensz Pyramid is a prize for mountaineers who wish to climb the highest peaks on all the continents. In 1978 my fiancé Peter Boardman had already climbed Everest, McKinley, and Kilimanjaro, so Carstensz, 'an easy climb for a lady', was his next objective. However, it took 18 months to get travel permits for the primitive interior of West Irian. Mountaineering, along with a list of other activities, such as surveying, was on the 'forbidden list'.

Two weeks of frustrating travel around the coast had brought us into contact with many altruistic people, particularly the Catholic Fathers who were working so hard to bring an adapted Christianity to West Irian. They were always willing to help us – the selfish mountaineering parasites. 'Someone has to climb mountains', Father Verheijen declared, laughing at our apologies when we begged for his help, 'I know the Head of Intelligence, maybe I can persuade him to let you travel to the interior.'

The next day we followed him past guards and secretaries to wait outside the office of the Head of Intelligence. He entered alone. My heart was in my mouth as I tried to overhear the rapid exchange of incomprehensible words in the next room. The tone of their conversation oscillated from friendly, to suspicious, to indifferent. We were, therefore, astonished when a secretary emerged with two new Surat Jalans (permits) to fill in. He told us that we could visit Bilorai and Beoga and the Moni tribe, but that we must not embark on a mountaineering expedition. I could not help the size of the grin that spread across my face – at least we were going to see the people of the interior.

As we skimmed ridge after ridge in a tiny, snub-nosed Cessna the following day, I was thrilled to watch the undulating jungle sea. However, everything seemed to speed up uncomfortably when our bags were dumped onto the earth-beaten runway and the plane took off into the blue. Children and tribesmen with penis gourds instantly whisked our precious belongings away and we stumbled after them in a state of shock.

Father Jan van der Horst looked bemused when we joined the pile of gear in front of his house. He had had no idea that he was about to have visitors. The expedition seemed to have taken on a tempo of its own, with complete disregard for normal manners.

Now that we were so near to the mountain, the dilemma that faced us was that we had no permission to go any further. We knew we would be breaking a promise to continue, but the thought of having to repeat the same expenditure and effort made us determined.

Without involving the mission directly, we managed to employ 11 porters from a neighbouring village, although I was annoyed to hear that they were not at all keen on going to Carstensz with a woman! However, as we ran behind our diminutive porters, it was Pete who suffered all the indignity. Tallness was no advantage in Irian Jaya. The low jungle forced him to stoop uncomfortably to avoid branches and to enable him to place his feet in the safe footsteps of our guides. Not to do so was to encounter holes that swallowed your legs up to your knees.

The forest sucked at my shoes, scratched at every surface of skin, tripped me up, and filled my nostrils with the foetid stench of rotting vegetation. It offered only steep uphill or slithery downhill to my aching legs. Relief came at last with a 200m root-ladder up a nearly vertical escarpment. A vista opened across a flat plateau with incredible tree ferns. What a fantastic present – to witness this scene on Christmas Day, and to feel a cooling mountain air after the humidity of the forest.

Boxing Day was unusually clear and by 10am magnificent limestone walls appeared in the distance. From the top of the Bakopa Valley we only had five minutes to view the elusive Snow Mountains of New Guinea and the shark's fin of Carstensz itself, before the mist re-enveloped them.

> **How delicious it was to let gravity take my body downhill.**

From a col, we could see the copper-mine site where some of our porters had gone to buy food. The resulting visit from the 'Commandant' could have been the end of our expedition, so I rushed about trying to hide obvious climbing gear. However, he had only come to be paid for the food the porters had bought. With relief we walked through the Meren Valley to be greeted by a shocking sight – the base camp was littered with rubbish from a previous expedition. But this could not dampen the excitement of being there at last, with Carstensz in front of us and seven days to explore. Nine excited porters called and hooted as they left for the mine to spend their pay. Just two, Ans and Fones, stayed to guard the camp, wistfully watching the others descend.

The North Face of Carstensz, with its solid-looking slabs, reassured me – at least I could see where our descent route should be. Why is it that mountaineers always need to find a new route? Carson's statement that 'the best climb yet to be done is the South Face' had fired Pete's enthusiasm. He visualized superb ice pitches on hanging glaciers, with buttresses of solid limestone in-between. However, we had not bargained with the speed of retreat of the glaciers since the last aerial photographs, seven years before. They certainly seemed very much shorter than we had imagined when we saw them momentarily the next day.

Morning drizzle and the weight of my rucksack seemed to guarantee that we would have to bivouac that night as we front-pointed up the toe of the Carstensz Glacier. I knew we were unlikely to see much of the route if the mists did not clear with the dawn. Predictably, from the notch between Wollaston Peak and Carstensz's East Ridge, the grey scree merged with the clouds about 200m away. We knew we had to go down and turn right at some point to gain access to the South Face, but how far down and when to turn right was an unknown gamble. The thrill of covering previously untrodden ground was with us as we sped downwards – remarkably, without encountering any major cliffs. Relying on intuition, we turned right and Pete shot ahead to a small outcrop. Through a momentary window in the cloud he saw the South Face, a forbidding amphitheatre with the glacier split into two. I was cheated of this view as the cloud closed in again, spitting chilling rain.

We started up a series of very loose ledges, donning helmets but not daring to rope up as that would only have catapulted snagged boulders down onto me. Two hours of uninspiring climbing brought us to 50m of ice, the only technical climbing on the face. This quickly over, we dropped behind the bergschrund. The upper overhang to a ledge traversing directly under the summit ridge was so crumbly, I marvelled that Pete was daring to climb it. 'What happens if he falls off?' stirred something

Top **Hilary Boardman and a Dani guide, in the jungle of Irian Jaya on the way to Carstensz.**

Above **Dani tribesmen at 3800m.**

close to anger in my heart. The wind was whistling across the ridge 7m above us, but here we could find no obvious way up. Eventually, a chimney gave an apparent key to the ridge. As I stepped onto the arête, the wind pierced to my core, whistling through my sodden clothes. However, it also cleared the clouds and we were able to spot the summit beyond a row of towers. It still looked a long way off, and it was already midday.

A deep gash in the ridge refused to let us pass. This was just unbearable; we had to retrace our route to the chimney. As Pete towed me behind him, shouting against the wind, 'We'll have to get a move on if we don't want to spend the night up here', I wondered if I'd ever have a 'normal' holiday if I married him.

Back on the ledge below the ridge we were sheltered from the wind and at last knew which direction to take. Ledges of rotten rock led us to just below the summit, marked by a wooden pole. We saw tins with notes from Carson's and Huber's expeditions of 1973 and 1974, New Zealand and Indonesian flags, and some locks of hair in a film case. I didn't even have the strength to

speculate who they might belong to, nor to smile for a summit shot as Pete reminded me that I was the first 'bird' to climb Carstensz. Too tired to be angry with him, I just wished I had wings, instead of the dead-weight rucksack to lug around with me. I felt ashamed of my slowness, and everything conspired against me: the rock on the ridge was the sharpest that I had ever encountered, there were holes in my gloves, my camera was always in the way inside my anorak, my pocket split, and my sunglasses made the descent of the North Face without me. We stayed, shivering, just long enough to replace the summit treasures and add our names to one of the tins. It was already 3pm and 2$\frac{1}{2}$ hours of daylight seemed a dauntingly short time to descend an unknown mountain face of alpine structure. Finally, after a deceptive abseil into nothingness, we came across a cairn that marked ledges diagonally traversing the North Face.

How delicious it was to let gravity take my body downhill. Suddenly I was aware of Pete yelling at me to stop. I had gone into the lead and was now soloing down steep water runnels. I had gone beyond tiredness and was in that state of euphoria that has killed so many climbers. After three sensible abseils, our feet touched horizontal ground at 5.30pm with dusk rapidly fading. There was no question of bivouacking. It was slow going for two hours, in relentless rain, but eventually we walked over the boulder field to the col and down to our tent haven. My heart went out to Ans and Fones whose massive grins glinted in the torchlight, clearly showing their delight at having us back with them. Carstensz had allowed us to pass the gruelling initiation test intact.

postscript Hilary married Peter Boardman in August 1980. Sadly, he was killed alongside Joe Tasker while attempting the unclimbed Pinnacles on Everest in 1982. He will always be remembered for his outstanding climbs on the Changabang West Wall and the North Ridge of Kangchenjunga, among many others. He and Joe are commemorated by the Boardman Tasker Award for Mountain Literature, which is presented annually.

Nationalities: New Zealand unless stated.

1895 J Clarke made an attempt but his party was thwarted by the seriousness of the undertaking.

1897 W Grave, the Don brothers, and A C Gifford also gave up on their attempt.

1919 British eccentric, S Turner, resident in New Zealand, made his first serious attempt on Tutoko from the south.

1920 Turner returned with A Cowling and J Cowan and made the first ascent of nearby Mt Madeline. Bad weather forced them to abandon the Tutoko attempt.

1921 Turner tried again, this time with F Milne, but bad weather and a disagreement turned them back only 200m (660ft) from the summit.

1924 Spurred on by the near success of W Grave, E Williams, and B Johns,

Turner finally reached the peak by the North West Ridge with P Graham.

1951 R Rodda, J Ede, G Ellis, and G Longbottom succeeded via a spur on the south of the West Face.

1952 L Stewart, C Lea, and R Ryan climbed the easiest route up the Age Glacier on the South Face.

1956 The South East Ridge was successfully climbed by M Jones and

L Warburton, with P Robinson and D Irwin (American).

1959 The North East Ridge was descended by M Gill and P Houghton after ascending the South East Ridge.

1968 M Jones and H Jacobs climbed the north of the West Face to Ngapunatoru Plateau, then up the North West Ridge.

1973 R Price and C Powell completed the South West Ridge.

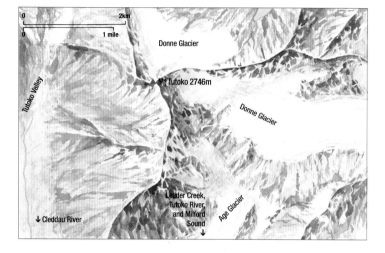

mount tutoko

guy cotter

In the hidden south-west corner of New Zealand's South Island lies the Darran mountain range, protected from invasions of the climbing masses by extreme rainfall, distance from any population base, and the obnoxious, irritating sandfly. Its highest point, Mount Tutoko, 2746m (9009ft), though no more than an arduous day's struggle from the road through sub-alpine scrub and snowgrass, remains an explorer's mountain. Only a stolid, determined few know the Darrans for the alpinist's utopia they are.

The Darrans are encompassed within the Fjordland National Park, a World Heritage Site. Their deep, vegetated valley walls make the approach scarier than the climbs themselves. Virtually inpenetrable forest and outsized jumbled blocks on the valley floor make it an expedition just to reach the base of a close peak. However, once you are free of the valleys and sandflies, and into the crisp air of the alpine heights, there are few places on earth that can offer the same sense of wilderness and beauty.

Huge sweeping walls and peaks of granite/diorite soar prominently over deep U-shaped valleys of 1000m (3300ft), testifying to the once-heavy glaciation in the region. Remnant glaciers still cling to the shady slopes of some of the higher

peaks. The valley bottoms are lush with beech rainforest and spongy mosses where abundant birdlife thrives. Deep-cut gorges allow the frequent rains passage to the nearby sea. The phenomenon most responsible for shaping this region is the precipitation – on average 7.5m (25ft) of rain and snow every year! Strong westerly winds lash the area; roaring almost uninterruptedly around the globe, they collect moisture to unleash primarily on this range of mountains before washing over the rest of the country. The main drainage is the Cleddau River, flowing into picturesque Milford Sound, a 3km (2 mile) fjord with frequent waterfalls cascading down its sheer walls. The Sound is best known as the finishing point for the famous Milford Track, one of the great walks of the world.

In the 1950s, as a boost to the region's tourism, a road was carved through the range to Milford Sound from Te Anau in the east, opening up one of the most spectacular climbing areas in New Zealand. Driving along this road with its looming walls, you are apt to bash heads on the windscreen, trying to peer at the craggy peaks 1000m (3300ft) above. But even with the road, climbing is still mainly restricted to mountains within a day's walk of it, and few peaks have more than one or two routes.

The implications of getting caught in a storm that can drop 100cm (40in) of rain and snow within 12 hours, the ferocity of the driving rain that physically hurts, and the potential misery of descent in such conditions are obvious deterrents. Yet in many ways Tutoko exemplifies the essence of mountaineering. Perseverance can lead to a fruitful and rewarding experience that would lose its appeal if it were too easy.

ridges, faces, and peaks

Less than 25km (16 miles) from the ocean, and dominant by virtue of both height and bulk is Mount Tutoko. At the south-west tip of its base, it is only 270m (900ft) above sea level. Capped by heavy glaciation that tumbles in chaotic forms down its 2000m (6600ft) South Face to the Age Glacier, and with huge sweeping walls on the west culminating sharply at the head of the Tutoko Valley, Mt Tutoko gives the impression that it is somewhat out of place here – a mountain of this stature belongs in the great ranges.

The rocky western aspect of Tutoko falls away 2500m (8200ft) into the head of the Tutoko Valley in a vast wall complicated by gully systems, while the North West Side bears a 500m (1650ft) rock triangle rearing out from the top of the Donne Glacier. The rocky North and North West Ridges define both edges of this face.

Above **Mount Tutoko, in the Darran Mountains of New Zealand. This photograph shows its first ski descent.** The West Face extends 4km (2½ miles) and is 2000m (6500ft) high. It is a huge rock face convoluted by gullies and two hanging glaciers on the upper third. The South West Ridge extends into the bushline to the right as you look at the West Face. The North West Ridge, route of the first ascent, drops to the upper Donne Glacier from the summit.

The North and East Faces extend from the gently sloping Donne Glacier to the summit and, at the southern end of this aspect, the dramatic serrated South East Ridge defines the demarcation line between the more rocky North and Eastern side and the glacier-laden Southern Face.

Due to difficult access, the East Side of Tutoko is almost never visited, although there has been one route put up. Glacial recession has reduced the access points to the eastern side.

The awesome South Face holds the Age Glacier, a steeply inclined feature that cascades ice blocks from its lower ice cliffs into Leader Creek, a tributary to the Tutoko River. Outlining the opposite edge of the South Face is the long South Ridge, rearing out from the rainforest to the elongated and glaciated summit.

future climbing

Tutoko offers some astoundingly good climbing, despite the often problematic weather conditions. Probably the most classic route is the South East Ridge, which ascends three rock buttresses connected by steep snow arêtes, finishing on the squat summit. There are now nine routes on Tutoko and room for more. The North (Donne) Face promises the climber long, clean rock routes direct to the summit that have yet to be exploited, and the South Side has awe-inspiring lines to the South Ridge for the winter ice climber, although icefall potential from the Age Glacier could threaten the better lines. The left side of the face would offer good leads through complicated gully systems when iced-up for 1200–1500m (3900–5000ft). Major routes are yet to be established on the West Face, which would probably yield some formidable and spectacular ice lines in winter. However, so far, extreme avalanche activity in the Darrans during the winter months has deterred climbers from all but those routes accessible by road.

Tutoko surely offers great potential for future generations, but it is only for those prepared to put in an appreciable amount of effort to crest a fine summit on an exceptional peak.

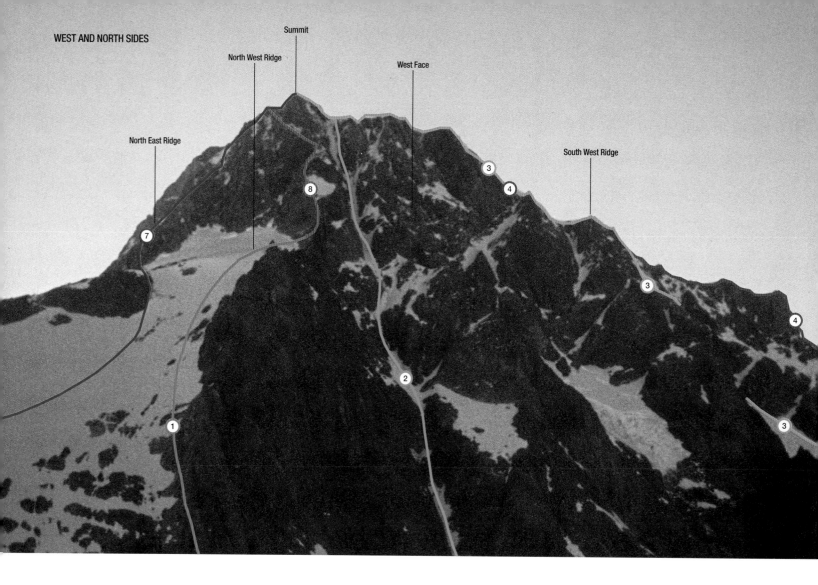

Most of these routes take a minimum of three days to complete; the walk into the base of the routes on the South Side of the mountain takes a minimum of eight hours, but to gain the North Side can be a lengthy process of two days via the Grave Couloir. This is a 100m (3300ft) couloir leading to the Ngapunatoru Glacier, which is ascended. You must then climb a snowfield at the head of the Donne Glacier to meet the North Face. In 1971, however, the West Face to the North West Ridge was climbed in 18 hours – this type of ascent is only possible by those who know the route well and are familiar with the surrounding area.

Note: in order to protect the 'wilderness' aspect of the area, no grades are published for climbs on Mount Tutoko, a policy to be respected.

west side

The western aspect of Tutoko has seen little traffic, yet is a vast 2100m (7000ft) face which leads directly up to the summit of the mountain. It is lined with several gullies along the way that would give good possibilities to ascensionists in winter conditions. However, there is some loose rock on the face, which has been a problem for those attempting to climb via these routes during the summer months.

1 West Face

H Jacobs and M Jones 1968
A route following ledges to gain the North West Ridge.

2 West Face Direct

P Moore, D Bouchier, and B Hill 1974
A rock gully leads to the summit snowfields. The route did not reach the summit.

3 Rodda Route

R Rodda, J Ede, G Ellis, and G Longbottom 1951
This route begins at 460m (1500ft), up bush and tussock bluffs past a snowfield and couloir to the South West Ridge and then onto the summit of the mountain.

4 South West Ridge

R Price and C Powell 1973
This 2289m (7510ft) long route starts in rainforest and follows the South West Ridge to the summit.

south side

There are, to date, only two routes mapped out on the awesome southern aspect of Tutoko. They are both ascents of 1500m (5000ft) from Turner's Bivouac, a popular rock bivvy used prior to climbs on this side – access is gained via Leader Creek.

5 Age Glacier Route

L Stewart, C Lea, and R Ryan 1952
The route ascends the steep Age Glacier along a similar line to the South East Ridge but avoids the rock steps. A good route to attempt during the early season, and a potential descent route.

6 South East Ridge

L Warburton, G Hall-Jones, P Robinson, and D Irwin 1956
Possibly the most classic alpine route in New Zealand due to good-quality rock and its situation. Never desperately hard but does involve continuous climbing, demanding good route-finding skills on the approach. It ascends three rock steps with steep snow arêtes between.

north side

A short rock pyramid at the head of the Donne Glacier leads to an arête and final headwall to the summit. The North and East Side routes are between 600–1500m (2000–5000ft). They get shorter on the northern side and are longer on the eastern aspects.

7 North East Ridge

M Gill and P Houghton 1959 (descended)
A broken rock scramble leading to the original 'North West Ridge' route and spectacular finish.

8 North West Ridge

S Turner and P Graham 1924
The line of the first ascent. A rock ridge of dubious quality, but only moderate difficulty, leads to the headwall beneath the summit; here a chimney with good holds gives access to easy ground and the top.

South West Ridge

South East Ridge

East Face

Summit

North East Ridge

Age Glacier

Donne Glacier

how to get to mount tutoko

Mount Tutoko is best approached via Queenstown. A car is almost essential so that you can escape if the weather turns sour, but buses or scenic flights leave Queenstown daily for Milford Sound, which is 2km (1¼ miles) from the Tutoko River where the access track starts.

facilities

The New Zealand Alpine Club has a climbers' hut (car access) near Homer Tunnel in the heart of the Darran mountain range, 20 minutes' drive from the walking track to Tutoko. Otherwise, the nearest accommodation and a few shops are at Milford Sound. Shop for groceries in Te Anau, 95km (60 miles) away.

when to climb

The best time to plan your ascent of Tutoko is in summer, especially January–February. Any later and access to the South East Ridge is more difficult, but rock routes in the region are fine throughout March. For winter routes the spring months of September–November can produce the best conditions, but watch out for climax avalanches on upper slopes as the spring thaw sets in. Proximity to the sea means that any westerly airstream brings precipitation on Tutoko, so check weather maps on arrival in New Zealand and only go there when the weather is forecast to clear – unless you want to see how hard rain can fall.

gear

Light alpine equipment is sufficient in the summer months, but be prepared for rogue storms that can deposit snow or heavy rain at any time of year. Tents are not usually carried even though there are no huts in the Tutoko region. Bivvy rocks are the normal form of shelter in inclement weather here in Fjordland. Remember to take insect repellent with you!

language

English.

maps and guidebooks

Maps are available from the Department of Conservation (DoC). The best is the NZMS 1 series #S113 'Tutoko'. *The Darrans Guide,* Murray Judge and Hugh Widdowson, obtainable from the New Zealand Alpine Club, PO Box 3040, Wellington, NZ, is the best book.

rescue and insurance

The closest DoC office is in Te Anau, so it is best to register intentions in the hut book at nearby Homer Hut and ask someone to look out for your return, in case your plans get upset. This is still a very remote region with little or no visits to most routes each year, so you must be self-reliant. However, the DoC in Te Anau does co-ordinate the rescue services in the region.

It is advisable to carry insurance but at present rescues are free if the police initiate them. If you need help contact the Department of Conservation or Police.

red tape

You are not required to carry a permit, but you must sign the book at the DoC office in Te Anau, regardless of whether you register at the Homer Hut.

Nationalities: New Zealand unless stated.

1882 First climbing attempt by Rev W Green (Irish), E Boss (Swiss), and U Kaufman (Swiss guide) via the Linda Glacier route. They came within 50m (160ft) of the summit before being turned back by wind and nightfall.

1894 First ascent of Mt Cook made by a young New Zealand group on hearing of the imminent arrival of Irishman E Fitzgerald and his Swiss/Italian guide M Zurbriggen. J Clarke, G Graham, and T Fyfe made the ascent on Christmas Day via Fyfe's Gut (a gully below the Sheila Face) and the North Ridge, a serious route even by today's standards.

1895 Zurbriggen's Ridge was climbed by M Zurbriggen, who guided J Adamson to Linda Shelf. Zurbriggen then continued on to the top to complete the second ascent.

1910 The first female ascent of the mountain was made by visiting Australian Freda du Faur with guides P and A Graham via 'Earle's Route'. This young Australian woman was to go on to achieve numerous climbs within the Mt Cook region, all escorted by guides as was the fashion at the time.

1913 Grand Traverse completed. Ascent of the 1.6km (1 mile) long ridge line encompassing the Low, Middle, and High Peaks, again by Freda du Faur with guides P Graham and D Thompson.

1938 The East Ridge was ascended by D Bryant and L Mahan.

1947 The South Ridge was climbed by H Ayres and M Sullivan, guiding R Adams and E Hillary.

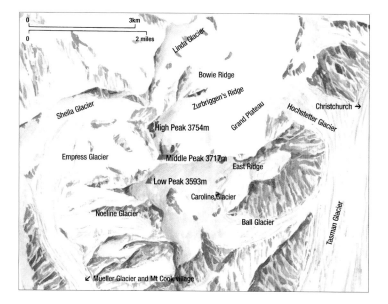

aoraki-mount cook

guy cotter

The Southern Alps are a relatively young mountain range aligned north to south in South Island, New Zealand. Mount Cook is their highest point, at 3754m (12,316ft), and is easily distinguishable from its neighbours. Rearing above the numerous heavily glaciated and weather-patterned peaks, just to the east of the Main Divide that separates the west coast from the east coast, it is visible from both shores of central South Island. The mountain lies across the path of the prevailing westerlies, so its summit is often graced by brightly tinted lenticular clouds, rolling in from the Tasman Sea, 30km (18½ miles) to the west. The rock – principally schists and greywacke – is generally poor throughout the range.

Named by European settlers after the 18th-century British navigator, Captain James Cook, the mountain already had a very apt name: to the Maori, it was known as Aoraki, meaning Cloud Piercer. It is situated in the Mt Cook National Park, which contains the peaks and glaciers on the eastern aspect and borders onto the Westland National Park on the western side of the Main Divide. Mt Cook village is situated near the junction of the Hooker, Tasman, and Mueller Glaciers. This is the base for climbing, with accommodation, a hotel, and the Department of Conservation headquarters, where information on the climbing options within the region, conditions, and weather forecasts can be obtained and registration details completed.

Climbers base themselves in huts that are placed around the mountain and provide excellent protection from the weather. The eastern climbs are serviced by Plateau Hut, which has ski-plane access, while the Hooker Valley to the west has the Gardiner Hut and the Empress Hut, both only accessible by foot.

Though low by international standards, because its line of perpetual snow is also lower, Mt Cook equates in stature and form with all but the biggest Himalayan giants. Abundant moisture, collected from the Tasman Sea by the prevailing winds, is forced over the Alps, drenching the thirsty rainforests of the West Coast and falling as heavy rain and snow at higher elevations to contribute to large permanent snowfields, starting at 2500m (8200ft), and feeding turbulent glaciers with ice cliffs.

The oxygen-rich environment of Mt Cook makes for alpinism at its best. The routes are generally long, requiring a lightweight approach. The ability to travel over moderate ground unroped is paramount to gain the summits, as is the necessity to travel fast to avoid the horrendous winds and storms that can miraculously appear and stay for weeks. Overly security-conscious climbers will find themselves benighted while still on the lower reaches of a climb. Exploiting the smallest of weather windows is a skill fostered by Kiwi climbers.

ridges, faces, and peaks

Cook is a very complex mountain with five sides, six faces altogether, and seven main ridges. It is a soaring peak with three main summits, High 3754m (12,316ft), Middle 3717m (12,195ft), and Low 3593m (11,789ft), linked by the impressive ice-bound Summit Ridge. Such elongation has created long flanks to the west and east, and short triangular northern and southern faces. Rising sharply above the Hooker and Tasman Glacier Valleys, the mountain has a vertical rise from valley to summit of over 2500m (8200ft).

The Linda and East Face Glaciers feed into the Grand Plateau, which exits through the constriction of the Hochstetter Icefall, which in turn feeds into the Tasman Glacier flowing from the large catchment area 10km (6 miles) further up valley. To the

Above **Near the middle peak of Aoraki-Mount Cook, approaching the summit peak. Mount Tasman is on the right.**

south, the Caroline Face feeds into the Ball Glacier entering the Tasman 2km (1¼ miles) below the Hochstetter Dome, which is 15km (9 miles) from Mt Cook at the head of the Tasman Glacier.

On the opposite (western) side of the mountain, where the angle of the massif eases, the Upper and Lower Empress shelves fall off into the Hooker Glacier which heads south, as does the Tasman. The Sheila Glacier also contributes to the Hooker from the north-western end of Mt Cook, and the Noeline Glacier deposits its bulk from below the South Face close to the Gardiner Hut.

Further west of the Mt Cook massif, the Fox and Franz Josef Glaciers tumble to below the 1500m (4900ft) tree-line in the more temperate zones near the Tasman Sea. East of the Main Divide the two glaciers flow for up to 20km (12 miles) before they stop short of the alluvial plains, and the rainshadow effect of the westerly winds creates a drier climate.

east side The eastern side of Mt Cook extends for over 3.5km (2 miles). The two distinct faces on this side, the Caroline and East Faces, are separated by the classical arête of the East Ridge, which culminates on the Middle Peak. Heavily glaciated, this side accumulates large ice cliffs built by the incessant westerly winds, which transport snow onto that lee side, and is bordered to the north by Zurbriggen's Ridge. Today, climbing this ridge is still considered a serious undertaking, and it is worth noting that the first two ascents on Mt Cook were by technical routes many years before the term 'modern alpinism' had been flaunted. Joining Zurbriggen's Ridge below the summit ridge is a rock arête known as Bowie Ridge, which begins low in the Linda Glacier.

The huge Caroline Face drops 2500m (8200ft) and is threatened by a serious band of ice cliffs at half-height. This is the largest face in New Zealand, and was the last great face to be climbed on Mt Cook.

The East Face dominates the scenery above the Grand Plateau where most of the climbing activity occurs. In 1991 six

million cubic tonnes of rock thundered down the East Face, robbing the mountain of 10m (30ft) of height and leaving the summit highly unstable. The top of the mountain is now a precipice hanging above the East Face, and is constantly changing.

north side The North Side is the lowest-angled of all the flanks, and without it Mt Cook would repel more climbers and provide no easy descent routes.

west side The Hooker and Sheila Glaciers give access to the western Sheila and Hooker Faces. The Hooker Face is short and is gained from the Upper Empress Shelf. The Sheila is a large face tucked away at the head of the Sheila Glacier.

the south side The South Face of Mt Cook dominates the Hooker Valley and is very prominent when viewed from Mt Cook village. Adorned in huge ice cliffs and presenting smooth ridgelines, this is the most commonly viewed aspect. It impresses on the observer that Mt Cook is indeed a serious mountain.

Left **Near the summit, looking down to the Grand Plateau.**

Below **Looking over the Tasman Glacier towards Aoraki-Mount Cook in the north-west.**

climbing on mount cook

Within 20 years of Cook's first ascent all the major peaks in New Zealand had been climbed, some 26 of them over 3000m (10,000ft). With the exception of the South and East Ridges, Mt Cook's other ridges quickly fell to keen alpinists, mostly accompanied by a charter of local guides. The first female ascent was made as early as 1910 by Freda du Faur in the company of guides Peter and Alec Graham. Being so far away from the rest of the world has kept Mt Cook out of the international climbing limelight. However, the area is popular with New Zealand and Australian alpinists who are used to whiling away the many storms in a system of mountain huts, conveniently positioned to take advantage of the hours between weather fronts.

New Zealand climbing found its identity in men like Bill Denz, who made daring solo first ascents of the Caroline Face and South Face, and Jon Fantini, whose same-day *enchainement* of Mt Cook and neighbouring Mt Tasman – New Zealand's second-highest mountain at 3498m (11,500ft) – was followed by two ascents of Mt Cook in one day from both the east and west. Essentially the 'last great problems' had been achieved. Paul Aubrey's ascent of 'David and Goliath' (*see route 25 on page 195*) on the South Side of the mountain, a smooth ice smear below an 100m (330ft) ice cliff, brought European standards to Mt Cook, with routes finishing not at the summit but at the end of the difficult pitches.

future climbing

For the next generation there may be a few lines between existing routes that can yet tempt alpinists, or the future may lie in the *enchainement* of routes and ski descents of all the major faces. When the world gets fed up with first, fastest, hardest, highest, and longest ascents, the mountain will still be there (and hopefully still neglected by the masses) to remind us that classic alpinism on New Zealand's highest peak just cannot be surpassed.

South Ridge · Low Peak · Caroline Face · East Ridge · Middle Peak · Summit Rocks · High Peak · East Face · Zurbriggen's Ridge · Bowie Ridge · Bowie Couloir · Grand Plateau · Hochstetter Icefall · Linda Glacier

All of the routes on Mount Cook are climbable in a day if conditions are good and the climbers are versed in efficient movement on this type of terrain. However, times can vary from 5–55 hours depending on variable weather – it is not uncommon for climbers to be caught out with a forced bivvy.

caroline face

By today's standards these routes are long snow and ice climbs, often with significant objective hazard from the numerous ice cliffs on the face. The lower part of the face is a steep and broken glacier, creating significant hazards in the approach.

1 Denz Route 5 (TD)
W Denz 1973
A rarely climbed route ascending directly to the Low Peak from a small hanging glacier left of the normal route. Involves 1000m (3300ft) of technical ground but, if accessed from the left side, avoids the threatening ice cliffs.

2 The Clit Route 5 (TD)
J Glasgow and P Gough 1970
This direct route, done in the era of straight ice picks, involves 2100m (7000ft) of moderate climbing on ice with a technical ice cliff at half-height. Sees few repeats due to its serious and committing nature.

3 The East Ridge 4 (D)
L V Bryant and L Mahan 1938
An arête climb of the highest class. While not technically too demanding, the route is long and finishes on the upper region of the Caroline Face to Middle Peak. Descent can be made over the High Peak or down the West Side of the mountain.

east face

The East Face rears above the Grand Plateau and is where most climbing activity on the mountain takes place. Routes to either side of the 1991 avalanche site are still climbable, but a constantly flowing rockfall from the summit region has rendered the central routes impossible to ascend. Other routes also suffer from rockfall and are best climbed in cold weather. Most ascensionists have completed one variation or another from the several routes on this large face, but each of the major lines is defined below.

4 Jones Route 4+ (D+)
M Jones 1974
A predominantly snow and ice route directly to the summit ridge left of the summit.

5 High Peak Route 5- (TD-)
D Cowie, L Crawford, P Farrell, and V Walsh 1961
This is the original route on the face. It has become a spectacular bowling alley due to rockfall, and as a result is best avoided.

6 Zurbriggen's Ridge 3+ (AD+)
M Zurbriggen 1895
This is one of the most coveted routes on the mountain and probably the most direct route leading to the summit. Climbers will marvel at the prowess of Zurbriggen to climb this line over 100 years ago. 750m (2400ft) of 50-55° snow and ice leads to what are now known as the Summit Rocks, followed by 150m (500ft) of climbing, then 300m (1000ft) of exposed arête to the top. This is a fantastic climb.

north side

Access to these easier-angled routes is via the Linda Glacier, which is severely threatened by ice cliffs and complicated by often difficult crevasse travel.

7 Bowie Couloir 4- (D-)
J Barry and D Nicholls 1967
Prominent gully route, often cut off at the bottom in late season due to the large bergschrund.

8 Bowie Ridge 4- (D-)
R K Irvin, H MacInnes, and P Robinson 1956
A classic ridge route on fairly good rock, climbed originally from near the head of the Linda Glacier. A longer route can be made by also climbing the lower buttress.

9 Linda Glacier Route 3 (AD)
J M Clarke, J P Murphy, H Chambers, and H F Wright 1912
Glacier travel to the head of the Linda leads to increasingly steeper ground. This route is the most commonly climbed and is a classic mountaineering adventure, requiring good technical skills and stamina. Most common descent route.

Summit Rocks

Bowie Ridge

Middle Peak

East Face

Zurbriggen's Ridge

North Ridge

Bowie Couloir

East Ridge

Linda Shelf

Linda Glacier

west side

After the 2-day walk up the Hooker Glacier, the Gardiner and Empress Huts provide shelter and are the starting points for these climbs.

10 North Ridge 4- (D-)
J M Clarke, T Fyfe, and G Graham 1894
Originally climbed from this western quarter at the head of the Sheila Glacier, the North Ridge is prone to rockfall in its lower sections. Now the North Ridge is more commonly accessed from the Linda Glacier.

sheila face

This face has long routes of varying difficulty and provides stunning mixed routes in winter, yet it is rarely visited due to the long approach.

11 Left Buttress 5 (TD)
W Denz and P Gough 1973
A rock corner leads to an obvious traverse left, then up slabs and ice to meet the North Ridge.

12 Central Buttress 5- (TD-)
A Brookes, A Dickie, and R Miller 1967
An obvious buttress on relatively easy but sometimes loose rock leads to the summit icecap.

13 Right Buttress 5 (TD)
H Logan and D Pluth 1974
The crest of the buttress is followed on the left to a final pitch involving some difficulty to join 'Earle's Route'.

14 Earle's Route 4- (D-)
J M Clarke, A and P Graham, and L M Earle 1909
True to form during that era, the route was named after the client who paid the guides' wages. A fine mixed route leading directly to the summit. Often iced-up due to its windward orientation.

hooker face

This is a fairly short face, once access is gained to the Upper Empress Shelf via the Sheila Glacier. Most of these climbs have short technical sections.

15 Hooker Face Route
H P Barcham, D Herron, G McCallum, and R Tornquist 1956
Three variations exist across this face, involving short cruxes to gain the summit icefield.

16 Porter Col Route 3 (AD)
T Fyfe and G Graham 1894
A short gully from the Upper Empress Shelf leads to the Summit Ridge near Middle Peak. Often used as a descent route.

17 North West Couloir Grade 3- (AD-)
F Du Faur, P Graham, and D Thompson 1913
A striking couloir leads to the West Ridge, which flattens below Low Peak. Gained from the Lower Empress Shelf, it can also provide access to the Upper Empress Shelf and the other Hooker Face routes.

18 West Ridge 3+ (AD+)
P Graham and H Sillem 1906
A long and meandering rock ridge with little difficulty leads to Low Peak by several variations.

south face

These climbs are accessed from the Hooker Valley and Gardiner Hut.

19 Sweet Dreams 5 (TD)
A Harris, M Roberts, and P Sinclair 1983
An ice climb following gullies and a smear on the left side of the face to join the West Ridge higher up.

20 Wet Dream 5 (TD)
K Logan 1983
Ice climbing through steep ice smears over rock to the left of 'White Dream' (21).

21 White Dream 5 (TD)
C Brodie and N Perry 1980
A popular ice climb on this face due to its not being exposed to the ice-cliff hazard further right. Chimney systems lead to the upper icefields and Low Peak.

22 Original Route 4 (D)
J R McKinnon, J S Milne, R J Steward, and P J Strang 1962
A sojourn up the obvious flank leading into the centre of the face, the route then traverses below the towering ice cliffs to the South Ridge.

23 Direct Route 5- (TD-)
W Denz 1972
Denz did this alone and was way ahead of his time. A steep and icy gully/smear below an active ice cliff leads to the 'Original Route'.

24 The Gates Of Steel 5 (TD)
N Perry and W Denz 1981
A prominent rock arête splits the

Low Peak

Middle Peak

East Ridge

Caroline Face

South Ridge

28

23

22

27

20

21

19

26

25

24

22

22

right-hand ice cliffs, so this route is safe compared to others on this part of the face. 609m (2000ft).

25 David And Goliath 5 (TD)

P Aubrey and P Axford 1991

A fierce line from the Upper Noeline Glacier. This ice streak extends for 11 pitches of up to 80° ice. Goliath is the huge ice cliff that is poised right above the whole route. Recommended at the coldest time of year only! 609m (2000ft).

26 Nerve Runner 5+ (TD+)

N Cradock and B Dyson 1992

Begins as for 'David and Goliath' (25) then veers right along breaks to a gully system that leads to an exit point through ice cliffs. 609m (2000ft).

27 South Ridge 4- (D-)

H Ayres, E Hillary, R Adams, and M Sullivan 1947

A classic ridge line that is an ideal start for the Grand Traverse.

28 The Grand Traverse

F du Faur, P Graham, and D Thompson 1913

Possibly the most classical mountaineering adventure in the country, the Grand Traverse links the three peaks of Mt Cook.

how to get to mount cook

You can drive south from Christchurch to Mount Cook in four hours. Alternatively, there is a 40-minute flight from Christchurch that lands at the Mt Cook airport, and the airport is within walking distance of the New Zealand Alpine Club Hut. An airport courtesy coach serves Hermitage Hotel, in Mt Cook village.

Access to the mountain is usually via ski plane, which lands at the Grand Plateau, 2300m (7500 ft). In order to reach the western and southern routes, climbers approach via the Hooker Glacier on foot from Mt Cook village. Nowadays they must endure considerable moraine travel to get to the ice of the glacier, but it is worth it in the case of the Hooker Valley.

facilities

Besides the Hermitage Hotel, there is a youth hostel and some other budget accommodation in Mt Cook village. Department of Conservation (DoC) huts throughout Mt Cook National Park are basic but provide you with a mattress, fuel, stoves, and water as well as a well-run radio system that gives daily weather forecasts. The huts are fairly cheap and you pay by the night.

when to climb

At 45° South with no landmass between it and South America to disturb the weather flows, New Zealand's weather is classically maritime. Unsettled weather can happen any time of the year (as can settled weather), but the summer months of January and February are traditionally better overall. Good freezes tend to disappear over the late December–early January period but return from mid- to late January. Good weather often extends into March, but access on the glaciers is more difficult and the days are noticeably shorter.

gear

There are few mountain ranges in the world that require so much versatility of gear due to the weather fluctuations. While it rarely gets very cold in the summer, most storms start warm (wet) and end cold, creating classic hypothermia conditions; storms can also last for long periods. Tents are rarely used because of the rain and very strong winds, so most climbers base themselves at the established huts.

maps and guidebooks

The best map is # H36, 1:50,000. The *Mount Cook Guidebook* can be purchased from the DoC headquarters in Mt Cook village, or from the New Zealand Alpine Club, PO Box 3040, Wellington, New Zealand.

language

English.

rescue and insurance

As well as providing hut facilities, the Department of Conservation (DoC) co-ordinates the mountain-rescue service. It is best to carry insurance but at present rescues are free if initiated by the Police, so if you need help contact the DoC or Police.

red tape

No permits required but climbers must sign their intentions into a book at the DoC headquarters at Mt Cook village.

Arctic
Ocean

RUSSIA

MONGOLIA

Mt Huithen ▲
Altai Mtns

Tien Shan

Almaty ● ▲ Khan Tengri

Tashkent ●   ▲ Pik Kommunizma

Pamirs

MIDDLE
EAST

CHINA

Hindu Kush
Tirich Mir massif ▲
Chitral ●
Nanga Parbat ▲   ▲ K2
Gasherbrum IV

Karakoram

ARABIA

PAKISTAN

Shivling ▲ ▲ Nanda Devi

TIBET

Himalaya

● Islamabad

NEPAL

Red
Sea

Delhi ●

Kathmandu ● ▲ Mt Everest

AFRICA

Kangchenjunga
● Darjeeling

INDIA

Arabian
Sea

Bay of
Bengal

high asia, korea, & japan

Kamchatka
Peninsula

▲ Kamchatka Volcanoes

● Petro-Pavlovsk

Sea of
Japan

J A P A N

▲ Yari-ga Take

● Sorak San

K O R E A

Kita Alps

South China
Sea

The Himalaya chain is the greatest physical feature on Earth, encompassing the Hindu Kush and Karakoram mountains as well as the various ranges that make up the Himalaya proper. In a sweeping curve of some 2700km (1700 miles), it separates the wedge of India from the high plateau of Tibet and, at its widest, the chain is 240km (150 miles) across. Here are the youngest mountains on earth, formed over 40 million years ago when a piece of Antarctica (now India) crashed into the Asia and began sliding underneath it. The force of the impact ruched up the mountains, and continues to do so: the Himalaya are still rising.

Every mountaineer dreams of climbing in the Himalaya and Karakoram, as all the world's highest mountains are to be found here: 14 of them over 8000m (26,000ft), and more than 80 towering over anything anywhere else. The Asian mountains of Kamchatka, Mongolia, Japan, and Korea are less often visited by climbers from outside, so little has been written about them in the West.

Clockwise from left: **Khan Tengri Icefall; prayer stone below Everest; Everest and its neighbouring peaks; Chun-bul-dong Valley of Sorak San**

Nationalities: Kazakh unless stated.

7th century The first recorded existence of Khan Tengri is contained in the writings of a Chinese monk.

1866 P Semeynov (Russian) searched unsuccessfully for a route to the foot of Khan Tengri, but discovered the legends of Khan Tengri from local nomads.

1927 A team of Soviet climbers reached Khan Tengri's foot, but did not climb it.

1931 The first ascent of Khan Tengri by a Soviet team led by M Pogrebetsky (Ukrainian) via the West Ridge.

1936 The second ascent (first by a Kazakh) was led by E Kolokolnikov.

1964 Two important new routes were put up: one climbing the Marble Rib from the south, by B Romanov and party; and the other following the North East Ridge, by K Kuzmin and party.

1973 The first ascent of the South East Ridge by V Voronin and party.

1974 The first ascent of the very difficult North Wall of Khan Tengri. The 14-day alpine style ascent was completed by five Kazakh climbers led by B Studenin. A second route was completed on the North Wall by E Myslovsky and a party from Moscow. B Solomatov and team put up a new route up the North Side of

Chapaev to the West Ridge. The now standard route from the north starts up this then traverses Pik Chapaev, as climbed by V Khrischaty in 1988.

1982 V Sviredenko and party climbed the South Wall to the Marble Rib, which was the first foray onto this very difficult face.

1988 Two new routes were established on the East Face and North Wall by

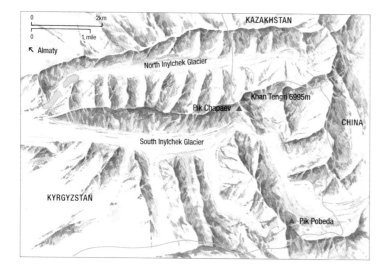

khan tengri

steve bell

The Tien Shan is the most northerly of Asia's great mountain ranges. Otherwise known as the 'celestial mountains', it comprises an isolated forest of peaks 2400km (1500 miles) from the nearest ocean. The striking pyramid of Khan Tengri stands proud among these peaks, the undisputed jewel of the Tien Shan. Although Pobeda, 20km (12 miles) to the south, is the highest mountain in the range at 7434m (24,405ft), it is Khan Tengri, 6995m (22,949ft), that catches the eye. Its elegant ridges and sweeping faces are extremely smooth, and the top of the mountain is capped by yellow marble that almost glows when touched by the rays of the setting sun.

Khan Tengri is on the border between Kazakhstan to the north and Kyrgyzstan to the south. It is the highest of a long ridge of mountains running east to west and separating the North Inylchek Glacier, to the north of Pobeda, from the South Inylchek Glacier. These glaciers converge at the termination of the ridge, 25km (15 miles) to the west.

The isolated location of Khan Tengri has left it largely neglected by climbers outside the countries of the former Soviet Union. Yet, in those countries, it has forced up the standards of high-altitude mountaineering, giving the former Soviet Union's top Himalayan climbers experience of weather conditions equal to those in the Himalaya. However, it is misleading to describe Khan Tengri merely as a training peak for the Himalaya. Some of its routes contain extremely technical climbs and offer a challenge to Westerners, for none of the harder routes has yet been done by climbers from overseas. All of the routes have been pioneered by local or Russian climbers. Since the mountain's first British ascent in 1990 it has been climbed by other British and European teams, but all have taken the 'West Ridge' normal route. American climbers have been a little more adventurous, with at least one team climbing the Marble Rib (South Ridge).

ridges, faces, and peaks

The awesome 2600m (8500ft) North Wall has an average angle of 60°, steepening further at the summit rocks. It is bounded on the north-east by the heavily glaciated North East Ridge, beyond which is the extensive East Face, 2500m (8200ft). The centre of this face is joined at mid-height by the continuing ridge of peaks extending east to China.

The snow- and ice-covered East Face is raked by avalanches from a hanging glacier near the summit. Its left side is bounded by the long, superb-looking South East Ridge, which forms the right edge of the impressive 3000m (9800ft) South Face. This face is still unclimbed; its smooth marble rocks offer little security, and would-be first ascensionists have so far been forced left onto the beautiful Marble Rib, or South Ridge. Left of the Marble Rib is the West Ridge, which rises from the col between Khan Tengri and Pik Chapaev (6371m/20,903ft), and the ridge of mountains leading west. This is the usual route of ascent, the 6000m (20,000ft) col being gained from either the south or north.

future climbing

The next few years should see a significant increase in the number of climbers going to Khan Tengri. Improved access and lack of red tape will draw people from many countries. It is already a popular objective for commercial expeditions, and an annual race to the summit survives as a testimony to the competitions of the Soviet era. It is only a matter of time before Western mountaineers fully recognize the potential of this exceptional mountain.

Right **Khan Tengri, or Celestial Mountains, is the jewel of the Tien Shan, and can be one of the coldest and harshest mountains on the planet.**

teams led by A Savin and N Zakharov (Russian). J Moiseev's team climbed a similar route to Zakharov's in a record six days. Two routes were also established on the East Face.

1990 A 5-man team led by V Khrischaty, Kazakhstan's most celebrated climber, completed the first traverse of the central Tien Shan, from Pobeda to Khan Tengri, in 15 days.

1992 In February V Khrischaty led the first (and only) winter ascent by the standard, 'West Ridge', route. It took eight days. Extreme temperatures and strong winds make the mountain a formidable winter undertaking.

1993 Two British climbers and two Kazakhs, including V Khrischaty, were killed when the icefall on the West Ridge avalanched.

Pik Chapaev

West Col

West Ridge

South Wall

Marble Rib

South East Ridge

There are no grades available at the moment for the routes on this mountain. However, they are all serious undertakings.

south side

Up until 1974, the usual route of ascent was (2), despite the southerly approach to the West Col being badly threatened by an icefall. It is now more common – and considerably safer – to gain the West Col from the north via Pik Chapaev (1).

1 West Ridge

B Solomatov 1974; V Khrischaty 1988

This is the northern approach to the West Ridge via Pik Chapaev. From the North Inylchek Glacier the route climbs the North Ridge of Pik Chapaev. This is a straightforward snow climb with one or two rock steps (usually fixed with ropes); the high altitude makes it hard work. Two camps are usually placed. The summit of Chapaev is traversed, followed by a 300m (1000ft) descent to the West Col where there are snow caves. It is usual to climb to the summit of Khan Tengri in a day

from here, following snowy ramps through rocks and a final couloir to gain the summit slopes.

2 West Ridge

M T Pogrebetsky and team 1931

The first climbers gained the West Col from the south through the dangerous Peter Semeynov Glacier.

3 Marble Rib

B Romanov and party 1964

This is the striking South Ridge of Khan Tengri, which was gained from the west.

4 South Wall to Marble Rib

V Sviridenko 1982

First foray onto the very difficult South Face, the main challenge of which remains unclimbed. The climbing to gain the base of the Marble Rib was very hard.

5 South East Ridge

V Voronin 1973

The longest and purest climb on the whole mountain. The ridge was gained by Voronin after he climbed a buttress on the East Face.

north side

The North Side of the mountain has an immense, very steep face that currently has five very hard, direct routes, all climbed during Soviet competitions. The face is still far from being 'worked out', and there is probably scope for improving on the style of some of the existing ascents, which – as speed is a more measurable and visible component to competition organizers – were originally climbed with speed, rather than ethics, in mind.

6 North East Ridge

K Kuzmin 1964

Kuzmin's group climbed along a series of marble chimneys on the North East Ridge.

7 Eastern Buttress of North Wall

O Hudiyakov 1970

The expedition led by O Hudiyakov reached the summit via the Eastern Spur of the North Wall from the North Inylchek Glacier. The route is difficult and interesting, and took a long time – 25 days. Middle steepness of 70°.

8 North Wall

M Gorbenko 1987

This route climbs the left-hand buttress of the North Wall.

9 North Wall

B Studenin 1974

This was a 14-day alpine style ascent following a very hard, direct route up the 2800m (9200ft) face.

10 North Wall

E Myslovsky 1974

The overall acent was 2800m (9200ft). The most difficult part is at 450m (1500ft) with 60° steepness. The first ascensionists took nine days.

11 North Wall

M Zakharov 1988

Direct route up the centre of the face. A similar route was also climbed by J Moiseev. Both are very hard climbs on often vertical terrain.

North Wall

North East Ridge

Eastern Buttress

West Ridge

Pik Chapaev

how to get to khan tengri

The quickest way to reach the Tien Shan is to fly to Almaty, the former capital of Kazakhstan. From Almaty, it is a 5-hour drive to Karkara, on the north-east edge of the Tien Shan. During summer, weather permitting, helicopters fly daily from here to base camps on the North Inylchek and South Inylchek Glaciers, depending on the route to be climbed. It is not really practical to walk into Khan Tengri as, apart from being a very long hike, Kazakhstan does not have the sort of porterage that is found in Himalayan countries.

facilities

Karkara and the South and North Inylchek Base Camps are large tented camps, set up at the start of each summer climbing season. For a modest price, these camps provide accommodation, messing facilities, and even a sauna! Radio communications link all the camps for scheduling helicopter flights and so on. The base camps are staffed by Kazakh and Kyrgyz mountaineers. No good

climbing gear is available to purchase (except ice screws and snowstakes) so bring your own. Cooking fuel is unreliable and local food is generally unsuitable for high-altitude use, so it is best to pay for base-camp facilities.

when to climb

The best time to climb is during July and August, but even then the weather is notoriously capricious. September is a 'dry' season, giving comparatively stable, but cold weather. Winter climbing in the Tien Shan is growing in popularity among local climbers, but this hardy option has yet to attract climbers from overseas. To date, Khan Tengri has only received one winter ascent.

gear

Clothing and tents need to be able to cope with very bad weather conditions, such as temperatures as low as -25°C (-45°F) and winds of 130kph (80mph). The type of climbing equipment required obviously depends on the route to be undertaken and the style in which it is

to be climbed. The normal 'West Ridge' route (2) is largely fixed with ropes, making ascenders useful. For harder routes a good selection of both rock and ice climbing gear will be needed.

maps and guidebooks

There are no guidebooks to Khan Tengri and maps are of poor quality and detail. Russian military maps are excellent, but difficult to obtain. Your national mountaineering club or association may be able to help. One useful book is *Forbidden Mountains*, Paoloa Pozzolini Sicouri and Vladimir Kopylov (Indutech spa, 1994).

language

The official languages are either Kazakh or Kyrgyz depending on the country you are in, with most people speaking Russian. Those people involved in tourism often speak English, but efforts to speak the local language are greatly appreciated.

rescue and insurance

The local mountaineers provide a very

capable rescue service, for which insurance is advised.

red tape

You will need a Kazakhstan visa which is currently available only if you have an official invitation, obtainable from any of the companies that set up the base camps and arrange the helicopter flights. The main operator in the region is Khan Tengri Mountain Service, headed by the Kazakh climber, Kazbek Valiev.

For climbs on the South Side of Khan Tengri, you also need a visa for Kyrgyzstan and a special permit for the region that is on the frontier with China. All these can be obtained through the Mountain Service.

The lack of commercial infrastructure in Kazakhstan creates considerable logistical problems for overseas expeditions. For instance, the chance of air-freighted equipment being lost or stolen is considerable.

The Tien Shan is a free climbing zone, although you will be required to pay a nominal peak fee.

khan tengri revisited

simon yates

It is July 1995 and I have returned to Khan Tengri after a four year absence, in the company of five friends – Peta Watts, Kenny Forster, Pat Holborn, Joe Lyons, Yvonne Holland, and Paul Briggs. A lot has changed. Soviet communism has collapsed. Kazakhstan is now a separate sovereign state, its people no longer cushioned from the harsh realities of the free market. Our host, the Central Sports Club of the Army, is, like many others, venturing into business and selling their services. The aim of our trip is to climb Khan Tengri from the north.

We acclimatize by climbing along the long, sweeping ridge on the 6400m peak Mramornaya Stena (Marble Wall), which involves a couple of days of absorbing climbing and a difficult night camping in a snowstorm. But the views are superb, from the foothills in the north to peaks stretching off eastwards into the Chinese Tien Shan, with Khan Tengri dominating the horizon, its enormous North Face rearing straight out of the Northern Inylchek Glacier. Having climbed it from the south on my previous visit, it is good to see this aspect.

The descent from Mramornaya is sensational. Dropping off the plateau into an icefall, we head along a knife-edged snow ridge that ends abruptly in a sweeping slope down to the glacier far below. Abseil follows abseil, until at last we are in a small valley at the side of the lower part of the icefall. All that remains is a little easy downclimbing to take us out of harm's way. The climb is over and, as we walk down the Inylchek Glacier, my eyes are drawn to Khan Tengri, our next, and main, objective.

Rest days at the base camp are most welcome. Supply by helicopter allows these camps to be elaborate affairs with huge mess tents, kitchens, and generators providing power for lighting. Fresh food arrives almost daily and the larger camp lower down the glacier even has a sauna. It is also good to spend some time chatting with our hosts, all of whom are exceptional mountaineers. Valodia shows me lines on Khan Tengri's 3000m North Face, which is a focus for pushing the standards of Soviet mountaineering. I am amazed at how many there are, all looking incredibly hard. 'We climbed one new route,' he says, indicating two young friends. 'Very, very, difficult. It took nine days.' He breaks into a smile. 'Near the top, very bad weather. We have no place to sleep. Misha thinks we are going to die.' He adds, 'I also do first winter ascent of Khan Tengri in 1992.' 'What was that like?' I ask and Valodia simply puts his arms round himself and starts shaking. I can do little but admire their fortitude.

We are going to climb the standard route on the north side of the mountain. This follows a spur to the right of Khan Tengri's

North Face proper to a subsidiary summit of Pik Chapaev, before dropping down to a col below Khan Tengri's South West Ridge, the final section to the summit.

After an easy first day, the next is much more demanding. The ridge becomes steeper with short buttresses – fortunately fixed with rope. But the biggest problem is the weather, as the entire day is spent in swirling cloud and falling snow. Wading through the ever-deepening snow becomes increasingly tiring. By the time we reach a camp at 5500m, everyone has had enough; we've come up nearly 1000m in a day.

That night it snows even more and in the morning, although the weather has cleared, the snow is knee-deep. We are happy to pack up the camp slowly while another group breaks trail up a steepening snow ridge above. Others have the same idea, resulting in a jam of people below a vertical wall higher up, further confused by more climbers coming down.

Despite the delay, by early afternoon all the climbing is completed and I sit at the top of Pik Chapaev's subsidiary contemplating an easy walk down to the camp at the col below. From here, it is possible to see both branches of the Inylchek Glacier merging to the east. Merzbacher shimmers at the junction of the two mighty glaciers. This strange glacial lake fills through the summer every year and then suddenly empties virtually overnight. To the south is the huge bulk of Pobeda (7434m), the highest mountain in the Tien Shan and the world's most northerly peak over 7000m. Nevertheless, it has none of the beauty of Khan Tengri, which captures my attention as I walk down the slopes towards the camp.

On the col there is much activity, with people enlarging a labyrinth of enormous snow caves. Our Kazakh friends secure us one of the largest snow holes – to call it a snow hole seems

> **With height gained comes wind and cold – Khan Tengri really is a cold mountain.**

inadequate as the chamber is large enough to sleep maybe 30 people. 'I think it best to go to the top from here,' says Anatoli. I nod in agreement. I know that it is still 1000m to the summit and that it is possible to camp higher up the ridge, but the thought of spending a night perched on a tiny platform, buffeted by the wind, holds no appeal when compared to a night in this ready-made palace.

We leave the cave in darkness into the bitter cold of early morning. Already the wind is blowing hard. With light sacks, our progress is steady, but the group soon splits into two. Peta and Kenny, along with our Kazakh hosts, are faster and go in front. I stay back and climb with Yvonne. The climbing becomes more technical with short, steep steps on the ridge. As we slow to a crawl, the others get further and further ahead. All too quickly people are coming down again. The day is slipping by, but I feel sure we can make it.

I find my movement and perception taking on a dream-like state. With height gained comes wind and cold – Khan Tengri really is a cold mountain. Eventually we reach the summit snow slopes and meet Peta. I start to feel cold just stopping to talk, and am amazed to discover that Anatoli and Valodia have waited an hour and a half on top for her.

The final slopes take an eternity and Yvonne insists that we go on above the summit tripod, where I had been happy to stop in 1991. A few minutes later it is over. Yvonne is elated, and for me the experience has been just as good from the north as it was from the south.

The descent passes uneventfully and a few days later we are saying our goodbyes. There are celebrations at base camp, an incredible helicopter flight out past Khan Tengri's North Face and Marble Wall, a sea of alpine flowers in Bayankol, sightseeing and saunas in Almaty, and a party laid on by our Kazakh friends. It was an exceptional month in a unique range of mountains – Khan Tengri remains on my list of the world's most beautiful peaks, from whatever angle it is viewed, or climbed.

Far left above **Climbing above Camp 2 on Khan Tengri's North Ridge, with Pik Chapaev's subsidiary summit above. From here the route drops to a col before the final steep pull to the summit.**

Centre above **Climbing on the summit of Khan Tengri.**

Above **The view from the top of the basin on the South West Ridge before exiting onto the summit slopes.**

Nationalities: former USSR unless stated.

1871 A P Fedchenko (Russian) reached the northern foothills of the Pamirs.

1877–8 N A Severtsov (Russian) mapped the range's basic structure.

1878 V F Oshanin (Russian) discovered the 72km (45 mile) Fedchenko Glacier.

1928 Soviet Academy of Sciences expedition explored Fedchenko Glacier region to give first accurate maps.

1933 Russian-Tadjikistan expedition, led by E M Abalakov, climbed (the then) Pik Stalin by the East (Pioneer) Ridge.

1955 South Ridge was climbed from the Belyaev Glacier by a Georgian party that was led by O Gigineishvily and A Ivanishvily.

1957 K Kuzmin's party from the Moscow Burevestnik Sports Society climbed the West Ridge from Belyaev Glacier.

1959 K Kuzmin and team made a difficult route from the Belyaev Glacier, skirting the left edge of the South (South West) Face to the West Ridge.

1962 A British-Soviet expedition led by Sir John Hunt and A Ovchinnikov climbed Kommunizma's South Face.

1965 A party led by V Nekrassov (Russian) climbed from the Belyaev Glacier up the rib between Piks Pravady

and Rossija, then via the South Ridge (1955 Georgian Route) to the summit.

1967 A Ukrainian Spartak Sports Society team climbed the South East Ridge.

1968 South (South West) Face was first climbed by E Mislovsky, V Gluckhov, V Ivanov, and A Ovchinnikov. South East Ridge was climbed via Central (Budanov) Buttress by a Leningrad team under P Budanov. J Borodkin

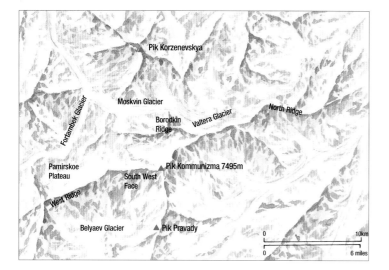

pik kommunizma

mike smith

Pik Kommunizma, formerly known as Pik Stalin, is the highest summit in the former Soviet Union. At 7495m (24,590ft) high, it dominates the complicated geography of the Pamirs. Lying across the now independent republics of Central Asia, the Pamirs form the western end of the Himalaya, to the north of the Hindu Kush. Kommunizma is part of a knot of inaccessible mountains in the Republic of Tadjikistan – a final flourish of the Himalaya before they peter out into the vast steppes of Central Asia.

The mountain is Himalayan in stature and Alpine in nature, featuring numerous walls, faces, ridges, long glaciers, towering séracs, and a summit high in the realms of hypoxia.

Before 1990 not many non-Soviet-bloc climbers had visited the region, and nearly all the routes had been established by Russian and East European climbers. Now the mountain has received a great many Western ascents, mostly by commercial groups on the standard route, 'The Borodkin', from the north. Kommunizma is seen by many as a good testing ground for larger 8000m (26,000ft) peaks – a technically straightforward ascent of a big mountain that can be undertaken in a shorter time than is usual for the Himalaya. The mountain also provides numerous alpine style routes. There are at least 25 established lines, including a full traverse, yet they are infrequently climbed. The reasons for this are the limiting factors of time, access, and acclimatization.

ridges, faces, and peaks

At 4200m (13,800ft), the base camp Alp Navruz, to the northwest of the mountain, is so high that it is necessary to acclimatize there for a couple of days. From it, looking south across the Valtera Glacier, the imposing North Wall seems to bar access to the Main Peak of Kommunizma, rearing up from the moraine and topped by an impressive sérac barrier that provides regular demonstrations of the power and spectacle of avalanches. To the north is Pik Korzenevskaya, 7105m (23,200ft).

A distinctive feature of Pik Kommunizma is the enormous Pamirskoe Plateau. This almost flat glacier lies on the North Side of the peak and is 11km (7 miles) long by 2–3 km (1¼–2 miles) wide. It rises gradually from the south-west to the north-east from 4700m (15,400ft) to 6300m (20,700ft). At the north-east end a mass of rock rises sharply to join the long North Ridge running to the summit. The northern edge of the plateau drops over cliffs 1000m (3300ft) down the North Wall to the Valtera Glacier, and is punctuated by small tops and long icefalls. At the north-east end of the plateau is a face that forms the western flank of the North Ridge. It has a number of routes on it. The southern rim of the plateau is the West Ridge, a long spine of five tops.

Where the snow-covered North and West Ridges meet, the summit of Kommunizma rises as a steep equilateral triangle of rock and ice, shorn of snow by the wind, and with a South, or South West, Face dropping away for over 2000m (6560ft). To the west is a separate top, Pik Dunshanbe (6956m/22,823ft).

The views from the summit are staggering: a vast sweep of the western Himalaya with numerous peaks; away to the east the triangle of K2 marks the horizon; and to the south are the southern Pamirs, an area of outstanding mountaineering interest that has hardly been touched.

future climbing

Access to the southern and eastern faces would require helicopters, which, even if available, would be very expensive. It is on these faces that the main possibilities for new variation routes are.

Right **The steep and forbidding North Wall of Pik Kommunizma, with the North Ridge and summit behind.**

opened 'The Borodkin' on the North Side, from the Valtera Glacier.

The North West (Burevestnik) Buttress was climbed from Fortambek Glacier by Moscow Burevestnik Sports Society.

1970 A new North East Rib route ('Uzbek Route') was climbed to the East Ridge. The South (South West) Wall was climbed via the left-hand buttress by W Onishtchenko (Russian) and Trud Sports Society. V Voronin (Russian) led a team up the South East Buttress.

1972 O Borisenok and party climbed the North East Face's left-hand edge from the Ordzhonikidze Glacier. The South (South West) Face was climbed by a party led by A Kustovsky.

1977 Americans D Dietz and C Pizzo climbed the 'Nekrassov Route' from the Belyaev Glacier. A Nepomnjaschiy climbed the South (South West) Face by the 'Paunch Route'.

1980 The South (South West) Face was climbed via the right-hand buttress on the South West Flank by nine Soviet Army climbers led by K Valiev.

1981 The West Face was climbed by a party led by V Solonnikov.

1982 Czechoslovakian P Ratjar and a companion climbed the North West Buttress and skied across the Pamirskoe Plateau. Ratjar then soloed the summit and skied down.

1986 A winter ascent of the Borodkin Buttress was completed by a combined team of Russian and Uzbek climbers.

1988 A party led by P Chotchia (Yugoslavian) climbed the left-hand side of the North Ridge's North West Face.

North Ridge
Pamirskoe Plateau
Pik Dushanbe
Valtera Glacier

north side

There are numerous lines up this north-facing wall, all alpine in nature. All are equally threatened by enormous séracs above as the snow from the plateau slowly shuffles over the edge in huge chunks and crashes down to the valley floor, leaving fresh white debris fanned out over the ancient black ice of the glacier.

1 The Borodkin 5a
J Borodkin 1968

This is the standard route, providing the easiest access to the Pamirskoe Plateau from the north. If you are fit and, more importantly, acclimatized, the whole route can be comfortably done in six days, up and down, weather permitting.

The Borodkin Ridge rises from the Valtera Glacier to the south-east of the base camp at 4600m (15,100ft). The base of the ridge is a rocky triangle that is prone to rockfall, and access is easiest by traversing onto it from the left, via a sérac ramp that is

regularly swept by avalanche and stonefall. This is best done early in the morning, and speedily. Once safely on the crest of the ridge a camp is usually established just above the snowline, at about 5300m (17,400ft). Camps can be put higher, at 5800m (19,000ft); if climbers are doing the route in one push, this is a good option, but would perhaps add a day to the ascent. In the clear weather of July and August these camps, and the track running up the Borodkin Ridge on the rib above, can be seen clearly from base camp, as can the other lines breaching these ramparts.

A separate rib of snow and rock running directly from the glacier up Pik Dunshanbe provides the most straightforward route to a high camp. There are some crevasses in this area and care must be taken; fixed rope crosses them, but later in the season these need checking. Some groups put a camp on this rib, but it is invariably windy, and it is best to push on. Between the insignificant

top of Dunshanbe (rarely visited) and the final summit triangle there is a col at 6900m (22,600ft); this is often used as the site of the top camp. Again it is a windy spot and it is more comfortable to shelter the tent in the bergschrunds that are just above the traverse into the col.

From the high camp it is a long slog up to a notch in the skyline to the left of the final summit ridge. These slopes are steep and often quite icy, having been hardened by the wind, and up here you are very aware of being on a Himalayan peak. The air is thin and progress slow, and it is not a place to be caught out or benighted. At the notch, turning to the right, is an exposed final arête up to the rocks sticking through wind-blasted snow, which marks the summit. At the top a metal cross seems to lean against the elements, and a plaque commemorating the 50th anniversary of the Revolution lies among the rocks and ice. The total height of the ascent is about 2900m (9515ft).

2 The Bezzubkin 5b
V Bezzubkin 1971

This route tackles the thin rib that rises to the edge of the plateau (ascent 1500m/4920ft), and then continues up the flank of the North Ridge to the top. Depending on snow conditions, climbers then either traverse out left and over the lip of the sérac band, or climb higher to the top of 'The Borodkin' (1) and then drop down 150m (500ft), on a long slanting traverse to the plateau and Camp 2. Takes 2–3 days to ascend and about a day to descend.

3 The Yugoslav Route 5b
P Chochia 1989

Looking over to the left from 'The Borodkin' (1), this route rises from the bergschrund in a line finishing through the cracks of the sérac on the edge of the plateau (ascent 1500m/4920ft). 'The Borodkin' or 'The Bezzubkin' (2) can then be joined to reach the summit. A long day, with two more days to the summit from a pre-stocked camp on the plateau.

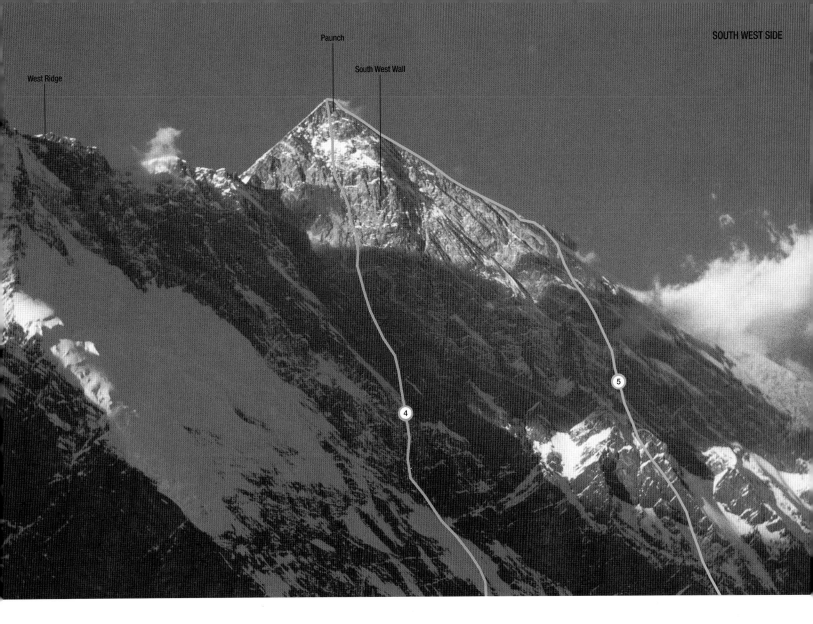

West Ridge

Paunch

South West Wall

4

5

south west side

With rockfall an ever-present threat, the 2000m (6560ft) South (or South West) Wall is a serious undertaking. It is uncompromisingly steep and, in places, overhanging. A recognizable feature near the top is a 600–900m (1970–2950ft) section pitched at 80-85°, known as *Pusa* (Paunch).

4 South (South West) Wall Direct: The Terrible 6b

K Valiev and party 1980

Intensive rockfalls up to 6800m (22,300ft). With few useful cracks, the Paunch was climbed direct on poor protection with some very bold leads. Ascent 3000m (10,000ft). Took the first ascensionists 11 days, with nine nights spent in a sitting position.

5 South (South West) Wall: Onischenko Route 6a

W Onischenko and party 1970

Takes the left spur of the face and a curving line to avoid the Paunch.

how to get to pik kommunizma

Fly to Tashkent via Frankfurt, or to Dunshanbe from Moscow. From either place the only feasible way into the area is by helicopter, which takes two hours from Tashkent to the Alp Navruz base camp, in the junction of the Moskvin Glacier and Valtera Glacier at about 4200m (14,000ft), just to the north of the Kommunizma massif. A former Soviet mountaineering camp, it is now run on commercial lines by the government of Tadjikistan.

Access problems are not confined to the terrain – political instability in the region as a whole means that it can be difficult even to reach the mountain. It is often impossible to fly direct from Tashkent or Dunshanbe, and sometimes incredibly circuitous journeys are necessary to get within helicopter range of the base camp. It is best to use an agent or tour operator to sort out travel to the camp, permits, and in-country supplies before arrival. Arranging relevant visas can also be difficult.

facilities

Alp Navruz has a basic hospital and a radio; other amenities include a restaurant, bar, and sauna. You can rent tents for base-camp use, and buy staples such as rice, potatoes, powdered milk, and sugar. It is also possible to camp without using the facilities. The camp is in operation from late June–late August.

when to climb

Early July–mid–late August. The mixed circulation air systems of western (cyclonic) and southern (monsoonal) make the weather unstable for most of the year, and it is intensely cold in the winter. Winter starts on 21 August, and the base camp starts to empty then.

gear

Alpine clothing with a Himalayan supplement, good high-altitude gloves, and lots of sun cream. A good layering system is essential for temperature extremes. An ascender is useful for fixed rope sections. Most movement is unroped, but there are heavily crevassed sections higher up. You will need a helmet for lower down on 'The Borodkin'.

maps and guidebooks

US air charts have a large-scale map of the area. There is also a 1:70,000 map produced by the Profsport Alpine Department in Moscow. *Forbidden Mountains*, (English and Italian), Paola Pozzolini Sicouri and Vladimir Kopylov (Indutech spa, 1994) is the only guide.

language

Russian, English, French, and German.

rescue and insurance

Alp Navruz has a mountain-rescue crew, but it charges. Insurance recommended.

red tape

Climbers are charged a peak fee and fees for the use of fixed rope and radios. US dollars is the most useful currency.

1697 This was the year of the discovery and annexation of Kamchatka by the Cossack Atlasov.

1788 Daniil Gauss (Russian), who was a mining engineer and member of the Billings and Sarychev Expedition, made the first ascent of Kliuchevskaya with two companions. His personal account of the ascent was lost right up until the 1940s.

1931 After two previous attempts, A Bylinkina and N Ogorodov, two members of a 6-strong Russian expedition led by G Semionova and V Dinges, made the first 20th-century ascent of Kliuchevskaya. Bylinkina, a female volcanologist, was killed by rockfall descending from the summit, leaving the 16-year-old Ogorodov to return alone.

1958 The first ascent of Kamen, from the north-west, was made by a party led by F Chelnikov (Russian).

1965 First ascents of Ostry Tolbachik: from the east by A Berezin, and from the north by V Sergeyev. In the same year Ovalnaya Zimina was climbed from the north and west by N Sergeyev.

1968 Khrestovsky was first climbed by the East Rib by a Russian party led by

O Alekseyeva. In the same year L Maksimov (Russian) climbed the steep North Rib of Kamen, the first serious mixed route in the area (at 4A).

1983 Kamen's most impressive side, the horrifying South East Face, was climbed by its right-hand edge by Kaluzhny (Russian) and his team.

1991 Kamchatka was opened to foreign climbers and Kliuchevskaya became a

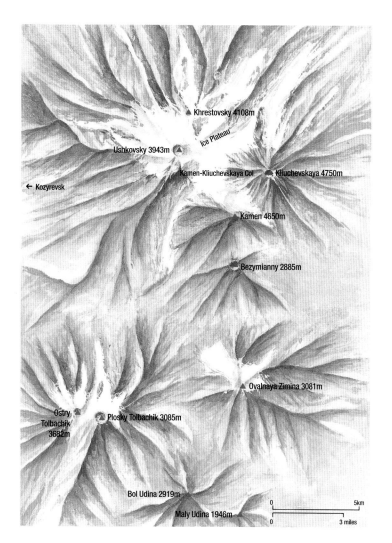

Khrestovsky 4108m
Ice Plateau
Ushkovsky 3943m
Kamen-Kliuchevskaya Col · Kliuchevskaya 4750m
← Kozyrevsk
Kamen 4650m
Bezymianny 2885m
Ovalnaya Zimina 3081m
Ostry Tolbachik 3682m · Plosky Tolbachik 3085m
Bol Udina 2919m
Maly Udina 1946m
0 _____ 5km
0 _____ 3 miles

kamchatka

john town

The Kamchatka peninsula extends 1300km (800 miles) down from the easternmost part of Siberia. A chain of hundreds of volcanoes runs its length, and the highest and most impressive group, Kliuchevskaya, lies 350km (220 miles) north of its only city, Petro-Pavlovsk, about 80km (50 miles) inland from the Pacific coast.

Kamchatka's volcanoes are set in one of the world's most pristine natural environments – rich in wildlife and mainly free of roads, tracks, and people (Petro-Pavlovsk is accessible only by sea or air). Conditions are harsh, and temperatures can drop to -50°C (-58°F) in winter. Many of the volcanoes are highly active and the proximity of the sea produces unpredictable weather.

The indigenous people thought the volcanoes were the home of evil spirits, and they, and the incoming Russians (with the exception of Daniil Gauss), kept well away until the 20th century. Even when climbing began elsewhere in the former USSR, Kamchatka's inaccessibility and its hazards meant that activity here remained very limited. Despite an average of less than one ascent a year since 1931, over 40 people have reportedly been killed on Kliuchevskaya.

The area was opened to foreign climbers in 1991 and there have been just a handful of foreign ascents; the routes climbed so far have all been pioneered by Russians.

ridges, faces, and peaks

The Kliuchevskaya group consists of 12 volcanoes spread over an uplifted area 50km (30 miles) across and 65km (40 miles) wide. It is bounded to the east by the Bolshaya Khapitsa River and to the north and west by the valley of the Kamchatka River, along which runs the area's only major highway. The large village of Kliuchy, home to both a military missile-testing range and a monitoring station for the local volcanoes, is sited on the Kamchatka River to the north-west of the group.

Massive explosions have shaped much of the landscape, resulting in little sound rock. Climbers can confront still-warm lava flows in intimate contact with recently surged glaciers. Summit vents often pour out high concentrations of sulphur dioxide and hydrogen sulphide, making gas masks a wise precaution. There is also the possibility of multiple 'first ascents' up the same mountain, as peaks can change shape completely.

kliuchevskaya At 4750m (15,585ft), the 'Kliuchy volcano' is the highest peak in the group. One of the most active volcanoes in the world, it is less than 7000 years old. Kliuchevskaya can be climbed from most directions, although it is wise to avoid routes in the vicinity of the Khrestovsky (NW) and Apakhonchich (SE) trenches. The escape routes for summit lava flows, these remain warm for months after an eruption and seriously disrupt local ice features. There have been 12 flank eruptions in the last 65 years and four summit eruptions in the last 10 years, with each of the latter

closing the mountain for six months or more. The region's hardest
and most beautiful peak is immediately south of Kliuchevskaya,
and joined to it by a 3280m (10,700ft) col. This is Kamen (The
Rock), 4650m (15,256ft), a rock tooth swathed in ice on its West
Side and falling in a steep, broken 2500m (8200ft) East Face.

Across the Ice Plateau are two further peaks: Khrestovsky,
4108m (13,500ft), and Ushkovsky 3943m (13,000ft). Khrestovsky,
or Ploskaya Blizhnaya, has a tightly defined summit and
subsidiary ridge. Ushkovsky, or Plosky Dalny, is a large, mildly
active strato-volcano. A huge, smoothly glaciated, upturned
saucer, it has two shallow, ice-filled craters on the summit, and is
a superb viewpoint for the two giants to the east.

Bezymianny (No-name) at 2885m (9465ft) is a much lower but
highly active volcano lying just to the south of Kamen. In 1956
a Mount St Helens-type eruption blew out its final 200m (700ft),
creating new opportunities for climbers.

ostry tolbachik, 3682m (12,080ft), and Plosky Tolbachik, 3085m
(10,121ft), lie about 30km (18½ miles) south-west. They rise
impressively to the south-east of the village of Kozyrevsk, and are
the first peaks that greet travellers after the long journey from the
south. They are good climbing alternatives to Kliuchevskaya if it is
erupting or for those seeking a safer ascent. Ostry Tolbachik is the
higher, and more shapely, extinct snow cone attached to the flatter
lump of the worryingly active Plosky. To those who ascend it,
Plosky reveals a huge cauldron crater 1200m (3937ft) across,
whose depth has varied between 100m (330ft) and 400m (1300ft)
over the last 50 years. At different times, home to lakes of both
scalding water and molten lava, it has been dry for about 20 years.

ovalnaya zimina This smaller, 3081m (10,108ft), extinct peak lies
17km (10½ miles) south of Kamen. It offers a variety of moderate
routes and there are two attractive summits crowning its upper
slopes. It is probably the safest peak in the region.

future climbing

There is still much climbing to be done here. Kamen's South
East Face offers the greatest potential for putting up hard new
routes, while the North West
Side of Khrestovsky and the
remote, eastern approaches to
Ovalnaya Zimina offer the
possibility of fine lines that are
almost certainly unexplored.

Right **The impressive tooth of Kamen
from the slopes of Kliuchevskaya.
Eruptions, poisonous fumes,
and wild bears are among the hazards
of climbing Kamchatka's volcanoes.**

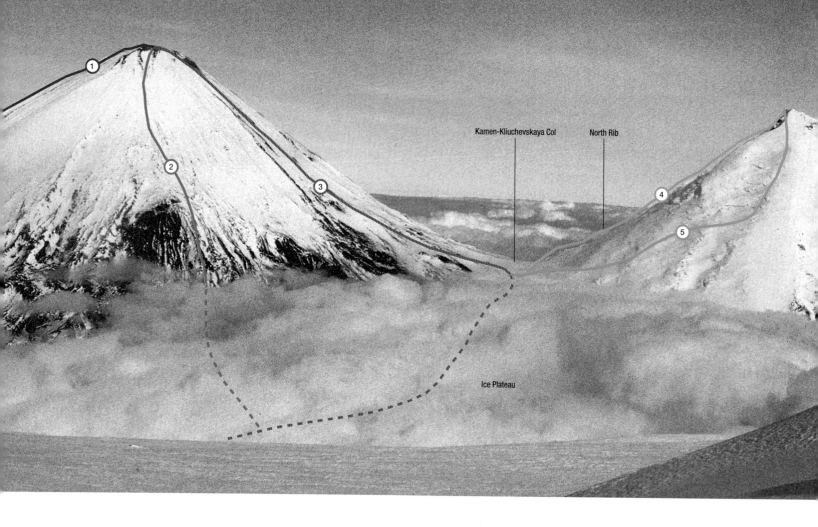

Kamen-Kliuchevskaya Col   North Rib

Ice Plateau

Due to the extensive area this volcanic group covers, and the few visits made by foreign climbers, it is impossible to illustrate all of the routes that are described in the following section.

kliuchevskaya

1 North West Slope 2A

V Sergeyev 1966

A direct route up the unremitting and exposed northern slopes. 2–3 days, 22km (13½ miles), and 3800m (12,500ft) of climbing.

2 West Slope 2A

V Nikonovich 1971

A direct route from the Ice Plateau, this takes 3 days, covers 25km (15½ miles), and involves 3800m (12,500ft) of climbing.

3 South Slope via Ice Plateau and Kamen-Kliuchevskaya Col 2A

First ascent unknown

The route ascends directly from Padkova Hut, at 980m (3200ft), to the Tsirkovaya Hut (*c.*2 hours). It then follows a long rising rightward traverse of the lower slopes, crossing the lava flow and small glacier

to the Ice Plateau (2700m/8900ft; 6–7 hours) whose edge is then followed to a small bivouac hut. From there it climbs east to the Kamen-Kliuchevskaya Col (3280m/ 10,800ft; 1–2 hours). From a camp on the col, the south-western slope is climbed direct to the summit area (4700m/15,400ft; 5–7 hours). There is serious stonefall danger. It takes three days to cover the 28km (17½ miles) from Padkova and there is 3800m (12,500ft) of climbing.

kamen

4 North Rib from Kamen-Kliuchevskaya Col 4A

L Maksimov and party 1968

The harder North Rib route rises 1300m (4200ft) direct from the Kamen-Kliuchevskaya Col.

5 North West Route from Kamen-Kliuchevskaya Col 3 B

F Chelnikov and party 1958

This is the easiest route up the peak, by a rising rightward traverse from the Kamen-Kliuchevskaya Col onto the West Face. The route involves 50° ice and a final exposed and

sometimes awkward rock section. There is 1300m (4300ft) of climbing from the col.

6 East Ridge 4B ⊠

N Katiuzhny and party 1983

This is the hardest route on the mountain and climbs the formidable South East Face. The base could be reached from Kamen-Kliuchevskaya Col but this would involve a very extended line of communication; it may be easier to reach it from a base camp east of Kamen. Almost certainly unrepeated.

ushkovsky

7 East Face 2A

A straightforward climb from the Ice Plateau up steep glacier ice, merging gradually into long snow slopes. Climbing the 1250m (4100ft) route takes 5–7 hours from the plateau.

khrestovsky

8 East Rib 2B

O Alekseyeva and party 1968

An interesting route directly from the Ice Plateau up snow and ice.

The route involves 1400m (4600ft) of climbing and takes 6–8 hours from the plateau.

bezymianny ⊠

9 North West Ridge 2B

V Maligin and party 1965

A highly unstable area: gas masks are essential and check the volcanic activity forecast. The partially destroyed cone is 1300m (4300ft) above and 4km (2½ miles) north of the Plotina Bivouac. The bivouac is approximately 50km (30 miles) from Kozyrevsk.

ostry tolbachik ⊠

10 From Plosky Tolbachik 2B

A Berezin and party 1965

About 2000m (6500ft) in total.

Routes (11) and (12) are closest to the Studenaya Valley, with the base of the climbs about 35km (22 miles) from Kozyrevsk.

11 From the North 2B

V Sergeyev and party 1965

This route is approximately 2000m (6500ft) long.

East Face

East Rib

7

8

Ice Plateau

12 North West Ridge 3A
V Skvortsov and party 1971
About 2000m (6500ft).

13 West Ridge 3A
V Kosov and party 1971
About 2000m (6500ft).

14 Plosky Tolbachik
Vloadavets 1936
No information available.

ovalnaya zimina ☒
The base of this mountain is approximately 50km (30 miles) from Kozyrevsk. All of these routes are about 1500m (5000ft).

15 North Ridge 2A
N Sergeyev and party 1965

16 West Ridge 2A
N Sergeyev and party 1965

17 South West Ridge 2B
V Kosov and party 1971

18 South Ridge 3A
L Skvortsova and party 1971

how to get to kamchatka
Petro-Pavlovsk can be reached daily by a 9-hour flight, direct from Moscow Domodedova. Flights can be subject to extensive delays and seats for both inward and return flights should be reserved well in advance. Alaska Airlines fly direct once a week from Anchorage to Petro-Pavlovsk.

There is a public bus service between Petro-Pavlovsk and Kliuchy as well as Kozyrevsk, but it is best to hire a 4WD vehicle. Approaches on foot from the main road are lengthy, but primitive tracks run onto and around the lower slopes of some of the volcanoes. You can hire helicopters in Petro-Pavlovsk to fly to Kliuchy and also to the mountains, but this is expensive.

facilities
The nearest hotels and reliable food supplies are 350km (220 miles) away in Petro-Pavlovsk.

when to climb
The peaks can be climbed at any time but winter conditions are extremely severe.

gear
Rope, crampons, and an axe will suffice on all peaks apart from Kamen, where ice screws and some rock gear may be needed. Much of the climbing on the easier volcanoes can be achieved unroped but a sound helmet is advisable. Industrial filter masks are recommended for the summits of Kliuchevskaya, Tolbachik, and Bezymianny. Mosquito-proof head nets are essential in summer.

maps and guidebooks
The US Defense Mapping Agency Tactical Pilotage Chart 'TPC E-10B', 1:500,000 is the best map of the whole peninsula (try your local map stockists – it is available in Stanfords, London).

The *Lonely Planet Guide to Russia* and *Trekking in Russia and Central Asia*, Frith Maier are essential reading; the latter includes maps. Both books provide details of agencies in Kamchatka, the USA, and the UK that can arrange access to the area. *Kamchatka: Land of Fire and Ice*, Vadim Gippenreiter has excellent aerial photos of all the peaks described.

language
Russian. If you cannot speak Russian, you will definitely need a guide once you get beyond Petro-Pavlovsk.

rescue and insurance
There is no full-time rescue organization. Although local authorities will probably do their best to respond to emergencies, it is best not to rely on them as their resources are limited. Full insurance is advisable, given the high cost of hiring helicopters in Kamchatka. Warning: bears are a considerable problem in Kamchatka and regularly attack and kill people.

red tape
Access to the area, by helicopter or road, is subject to local weather conditions, military sensitivities, and volcanic hazard. Avoid advertising your presence to the military authorities in Kliuchy village since this is, in theory, a closed area. There does not appear to be any explicit permit system for the peaks themselves, but unaccompanied foreigners could find themselves turned back by local police.

1938 A British reconnaissance expedition attempted the mountain from the south, with G Finch reaching about 6100m (20,000ft).

1949 Norway's A Naess and A Randers Heen reconnoitred an approach up the South Barum Glacier to the South Ridge.

1950 On 22 July P Kvernberg from Naess's Norwegian expedition reached the summit. Incredibly, he managed to drag a 14kg (31lb) rock from the North West Flank to the highest point of the snowy summit plateau to mark his ascent. The following day H Berg, A Naess, and T Streather (British) also reached the summit.

1964 R Høibakk and A Opdal (Norwegian) made the first ascent of Tirich Mir East; a lightweight dash from 6500m (21,000ft) on the South Face.

1965 K Diemberger (Austrian) climbed Tirich North.

1967 A 13-man Czechoslovakian team led by I Galfy climbed the North West Ridge from the Upper Tirich Glacier to make the second ascent of the mountain. J Cervinka, I Galfy, M Jaskovsky, V Smida, and I Urbanovic reached the summit, and on the following day (without Jaskovsky) made the first ascent of Tirich West I via the tricky South East Ridge. K Diemberger made the first ascent of Tirich West IV with D Proske (German).

1971 S Masue's Japanese expedition climbed the South Ridge via a traverse of South Glacier Peak and the 6450m (21,160ft) South Col.

1974 A French expedition, with J Kelle, J-F Lemoine, G Lucazeau, M Pompei,

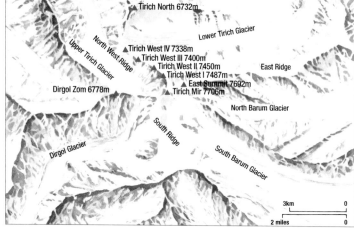

tirich mir massif

lindsay griffin

The Asian mountains of the Hindu Kush run almost 500km (300 miles) south-west from the head of the Wakhan Corridor, along the Pakistani–Afghan frontier, to the foothills surrounding Mir Samir in Nuristan. The eastern section between the Baroghil and Dorah Passes contains the main collection of high peaks – over 20 of more than 7000m (23,000ft) – and is sometimes referred to as the High Hindu Kush. Towards the south-western end of this section, and south of the frontier, is the complex Tirich Massif. Its highest summit, Tirich Mir (King Tirich) at 7706m (25,283ft), is also the highest throughout the Hindu Kush. Its South Side can be easily approached from the well-travelled Chitral Valley.

ridges, peaks, and faces

The Main Summit, Tirich Mir, is surrounded by four glaciers and has four main ridges descending from the highest point. All are long and carry several subsidiary summits.

The South Ridge, which divides the Dirgol and South Barum Glaciers, is sharp and snowy where it crosses the South Glacier Peak, 6700m (21,983ft), but becomes broader and more inviting to climbers higher up.

The West Ridge rises from a high col between the Main Summit and Dirgol Zom (6778m/22,239ft). The ridge has a steep rocky section above 7000m (23,000ft).

The North West Ridge, separating the broad and generally easy-angled Upper and Lower Tirich Glaciers, is undoubtedly the finest, containing five major summits: Tirich West I 7487m (24,565ft), Tirich West II 7450m (24,443ft), Tirich West III 7400m (24,279ft), Tirich West IV 7338m (24,076ft) and, slightly off the line of the ridge, Tirich North 6732m (22,088ft). These superb rock and ice peaks have all been climbed, often by high-quality lines, but subsequent ascents have been few in number.

The East Ridge is an imposing crest of rock and ice rising above the North Barum Glacier to the East Summit of Tirich Mir. It then falls to a col at 7550m (24,800ft) before rising again to the main top. Although this ridge has been climbed to Tirich Mir East, no one has as yet made the 1½ km (1 mile) continuation traverse to the highest summit. From a point on the East Ridge, just below the East Summit, 7692m (25,257ft), a well-defined and objectively safe rocky spur descends south-east to the Barum Glacier.

Between the ridges on the mountain lie convoluted faces of rock and ice. Apart from the Norwegian lines on the South Face, they remain unclimbed. Rockfall and avalanches pose the most threat on all but the relatively short North West Face. The latter, sporting several clearly defined granite pillars, resembles the Brouillard Face of Mont Blanc (see pages 40–47), and gives the opportunity for high-standard rock climbing at 7300m (24,000ft).

future climbing

A number of technical routes have now been climbed in the massif, but few have yet seen alpine style ascents. As long ago as 1975 the Iranian, Mischa Saleki, envisaged, but never managed, a continuous traverse of all four Tirich West Peaks, starting at IV and ending on the Main Summit, Tirich Mir. It would undoubtedly be one of the great high-altitude traverses of Asia. So, too, would be the traverse over the East and West Summits, seriously attempted by the Norwegians in 1991. Perhaps less logical would be a bold north–south traverse of the Main Summit, but an on-sight descent of the 1950 Norwegian 'South Face' route will pose serious route-finding problems. The East Side, above the Lower Tirich Glacier, is unexplored. There are some awesome lines, on West II particularly, but much of the initial ground is threatened by sérac avalanches.

Right **Tirich West I seen from the 'Standard Route' on Tirich Mir, with Camp 4 on the col.**

and S Sartou, reached the summit of Tirich West III via the West Face from the Upper Tirich Glacier. The team survived an earthquake. G Machetto and B Re (Italian) made first ascent of Tirich West II via Tirich West III.

1975 G Machetto and G Calcagno (Italian) attacked the unclimbed West Ridge. Fixing ropes, they reached the summit from a 7300m (24,000ft) bivouac.

1978 S Rudzinski led nine Poles and five Yugoslavs to the unclimbed East Ridge of Tirich Mir East. J Kukuczka, T Piotrowski, and W Wroczynski were the first to reach the summit.

1979 G Calcagno, with S Casaleggio, A Enzio, and T Vidoni (Italian), made an unsupported alpine style traverse over the summit of Tirich West I to West IV.

1985 G Van Sprang's 4-man Dutch team put up a new, technically difficult, mixed route up the c.2000m (c.6560ft) North-West-West Face of Tirich North. Their line went up to the right of K Diemberger's original 1965 line. They survived a severe earthquake close to the summit.

1991 J Gangdal's Norwegian team made the first ascent of the South East Ridge of Tirich Mir East to a 7620m (25,000ft) forepeak where it joins the East Ridge.

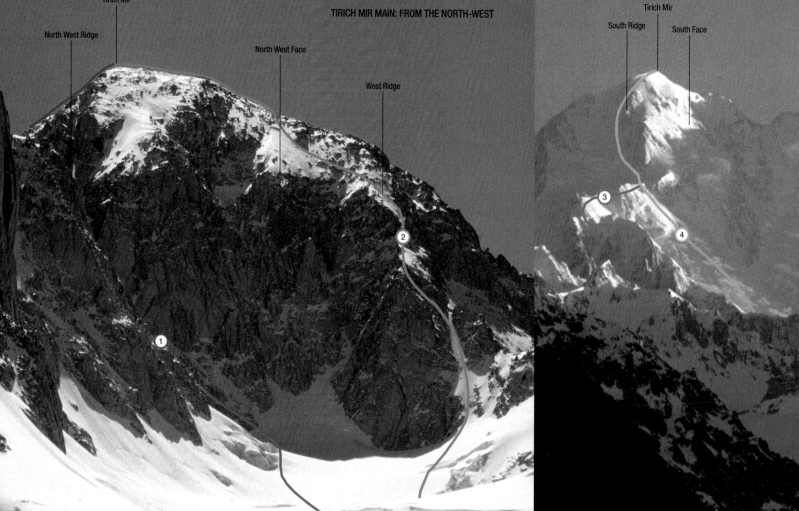

Route grades are not given, but grades of certain sections, or the maximum technical difficulty, are provided where possible. Heights quoted are the vertical intervals of the summit above base camp. How long a climb takes is difficult to indicate as climbers will spend weeks or months on the mountain acclimatizing. Due to the complex nature of the massif, some of the routes are not shown.

tirich mir main

Apart from the 'Standard Route' (1), other routes to the Main Summit have been rarely or never repeated.

1 North West Ridge: Standard Route
Czechoslovakian Expedition 1967
Assessment of the technical difficulty of the crux couloir on this route varies from one expedition to the next. 2800m (9200ft).

2 West Ridge
Italian Expedition 1975
After a steep rocky section above 7000m (23,000ft) of maximum V difficulty, easier climbing leads across the upper North West Face. Unrepeated. 2800m (9200ft).

3 South Ridge
Japanese Expedition 1971; Polish variation 1983
A lengthy approach over the sharp crest of South Glacier Peak (6700m/22,000ft) with technical difficulties easing as the ridge broadens and the 'South Face' route (4) is joined. 4000m (13,000ft).

4 South Face
Norwegian Expedition 1950
The upper part of the spur leading to the South Ridge can be quite prone to avalanches. This route has seen several ascents. 4000m (13,000ft).

tirich mir east ☒

A snowy dome that appears to have been reached on only two occasions.

5 South Face
Norwegian Expedition 1964
A succession of steep icefields separated by mixed ground and rock (V). Not without a certain amount of objective danger. As yet, unrepeated. 4000m (13,000ft).

6 South East Ridge
Norwegian Expedition 1991
The scene of many previous failures and in the end only climbed to the junction with the East Ridge. A technically difficult climb at altitude with a steep rock band between 6000m and 6700m (19,700–22,000ft). Five camps were placed on the first ascent. Unrepeated.

tirich west I ☒

The most southerly and highest of the Tirich West peaks.

7 South East Ridge
Czechoslovakian Expedition 1967
A steep, exposed, and fairly sharp snow crest leads to more gentle ground and a fine, pointed summit. Several ascents. 2600m (8530ft). (*The ridge can be seen on page 213.*)

tirich west II ☒

Not a particularly distinct summit – more a high point on the ridge.

8 North West Ridge from West III
Italian Expedition 1974
A reasonably short but interesting and exposed snow crest. Unrepeated, but crossed in reverse direction on the 1979 traverse. 2550m (8400ft).

tirich west III ☒

Like Tirich West II, this is more of a high point on the ridge than a distinct summit. The West Face has a very fine route, put up by the French. It climbs a rock buttress (V), then crosses easier mixed ground and snow slopes. At least three ascents. 2500m (8200ft).

tirich west IV

The most northerly and rocky of the four Tirich West Peaks, this has several different routes to its summit.

9 North Ridge/North Face
K Diemberger and D Proske 1967
A superb mixed climb much more easily approached than most of the other routes on the Tirich Massif. 2400m (7900ft).

10 South West Face ☒
Spanish Expedition 1976
A mixed route on 45–70° snow and ice slopes interspersed with rock barriers of grade V. Relatively safe from objective dangers but probably still unrepeated. It is 2400m (7900ft) in length.

TIRICH MIR MAIN: FROM THE SOUTH

TIRICH WEST AND TIRICH NORTH

Tirich East

Tirich West II

Tirich Mir

Tirich West I

Tirich West III

Tirich West IV

Dirgo Zom

Tirich North

North Face

North Spur

9

12

13

3

3

Upper Tirich Glacier

11 South West Face Direct ⊠
Italian Expedition 1977
Technically difficult rock and ice climbing leading to easier mixed ground directly below the summit. Probably unrepeated. The route is 2400m (7900ft).

tirich north
The North Side of this attractive snow dome lies up the Lower Tirich Glacier and needs a different base camp from that used to access the other Tirich peaks. Both routes are about 2000m (6500ft) of climbing, but the base camp is further away from the face.

12 North Spur
Austrian Expedition 1965
This is a superb line of reasonable difficulty. The route is mainly snow/ice with some short sections of mixed ground.

13 North Face
Dutch Expedition 1985
An unrepeated, 2-day alpine style ascent up a direct line, right of the central sérac. Difficult ice runnels in the lower section.

how to get to tirich mir massif
You can fly to Islamabad and hire transport (transit or bus) to take food, equipment, and personnel to Chitral. From here it is a short jeep ride and walk up the lower reaches of the South Barum Glacier to a base camp on the South Side. However, most teams will head towards the northern side. This involves a much longer approach – a jeep ride from Chitral to Shagrom is a particularly hair-raising, 7-hour experience (and in 1986 an Italian expedition failed to reach the roadhead when their jeep plunged off the track killing two members). Porters are available in Shagrom for the three (or four) long days needed to walk to the 4900m (16,000ft) base camp on the Upper Tirich Glacier.

facilities
Some staple food can be obtained in Chitral, but is is best to bring it from Rawalpindi/Islamabad. There are basic hotels in Chitral and jeeps can be hired for your journey to the mountain. There are no facilities beyond Chitral, except for small roadside stalls that can provide you with tea and basic meals.

when to climb
June and July are the prime months for climbing. Later in the year, the weather gets more unsettled and, as the temperatures drop, fresh snowfall fails to consolidate, making the avalanche risk higher and glacier travel hard work. This area has a well known history of earth tremors and a surprising number of expeditions have been affected, so far without loss of life.

gear
Full Himalayan clothing, tentage, and equipment. Skis or snowshoes can be invaluable on the Upper Tirich Glacier.

maps and guidebooks
Jerzy Wala's Polish maps and the Japanese Atlas *Mountaineering Maps of the World* (Karakoram volume) cover this region in full. There are numerous expedition reports in the standard national alpine club journals, some with good sketch maps and photographs.
   A useful book for the history up to 1975 is *Sette Anni Contre il Tirich*, Guido Machetto and Riccardo Varvelli.

language
The local language is Urdu but many people, especially in Chitral, understand some English.

rescue and insurance
Helicopter rescues below a certain altitude are possible. A helicopter bond must be deposited with the Ministry of Tourism to guarantee this service. On the mountain it will be the responsibility of the other climbers in your expedition to bring down an injured person.

red tape
Any expedition attempting peaks over 6000m (19,686ft) in Pakistan must apply to the Ministry of Tourism for permission, and a royalty has to be paid well in advance. A Liaison Officer will be assigned to your expedition and an environmental bond must be deposited before you leave for the mountain. This will be refunded if the Liaison Officer is happy with the expedition's environmental strategy. Porter insurance is also obligatory.

1856 K2 received its name in the course of mapping the Karakoram, when T G Montgomerie of the Survey of India logged the Karakoram peaks as K1, K2, K3 etc from distant observations on Mt Haramukh in Kashmir.

1890 Mystery still surrounds a reconnaissance expedition undertaken by R Lerco (Italian). He may have been the first to set foot on K2.

1892 W Martin Conway (British) led a scientific and mountaineering expedition to the Baltoro Glacier, reaching the enormous glacier junction at the base of K2, which he named 'Concordia'.

1902 An international expedition led by O Eckenstein climbed K2's North East Ridge to a height of 6525m (21,400ft).

1909 Luigi Amedeo di Savoia, Duke of Abruzzi (Italian), explored the area and attempted K2's South East Ridge, attaining a height of 6250m (20,500ft). The Abruzzi Spur, now known in his honour, has become the 'standard' route. V Sella, photographer to the expedition, took pictures from all round the mountain – these rank among the best ever.

1938 A 6-man American team, led by Dr C S Houston, made a concerted attempt on the Abruzzi Spur, erected seven high camps, and reached 7925m (26,000ft).

1939 Another American attempt, led by ex-patriate German climber F Wiessner, pushed to 8382m (27,500ft), but Dudley Wolfe (the team's sponser) and three Sherpas died.

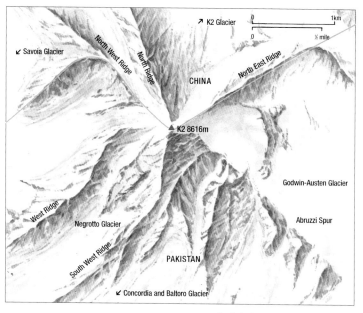

Border is shown for illustrative purposes only.

k2

julie-ann clyma

K2, at 8616m (28,267ft), is the second-highest mountain in the world. While it may rate less in stature and popularity than Everest, to the mountaineer it is the 'mountain of mountains'. With only just over 100 successful ascents and a mortality total of 30, K2 is a serious but compelling objective. Its allure arises from the combination of its isolation, extremes of weather, great altitude, and difficulty of climbing. Its challenge is as profound today as ever.

Unlike many of the other giants of the Himalaya, K2 lies in such isolation that it is not visible from any inhabited place. When travelling by road from the town of Skardu (the capital of Baltistan) you reach the last village of Askole, from where it is seven long days of walking to reach the mountain. K2 has no known native name (Chogori, which the Balti sometimes call it, means merely 'Big Mountain').

K2 lies within the Karakoram range, strategically situated at its westerly margin near the junction of three great nations –

China, India, and Pakistan. Significant sections of the borders between these countries are in dispute and, with a strong military presence in the area, the problems of geographical isolation of the mountain have been compounded by politics.

The Karakoram is a great range of mountains, over 180km (100 miles) wide and running for over 400km (250 miles) to the north-west of the main Himalayan chain. It holds four of the 8000m (26,000ft) giants – K2, Broad Peak, 8047m (26,402ft); Gasherbrum II, 8035m (26,363ft); and Gasherbrum I/Hidden Peak, 8068m (26,471ft) – and has four of the world's longest glaciers outside the polar regions. K2 lies at the head of one of these – the Baltoro Glacier. Positioned so far inland, 1500km (900 miles) from the sea, K2 is not subject to the effects of the monsoon, but, nevertheless, its weather can range from clear and sunny to the most protracted and ferocious storms.

ridges, faces, and peaks

K2 rises in six great ridges to form a classical summit pyramid of rock and ice. Between these ridges are four major faces. The most frequently visited of these is the great South Face, which rises above the traditional base-camp site on the Godwin-Austen Glacier. The face is defined on its left side by the South West Pillar, which is gained from the Negrotto Col and has a distinct snow patch called 'the Mushroom' at about two-thirds of the height of the mountain. The right side of the South Face is defined by the classic line of the first ascent – the South East Ridge or Abruzzi Spur. A notorious feature of this route is the Shoulder, a large snow shelf at around 8000m (26,000ft), which has been the site of many fatalities. Between the South West Pillar and the Abruzzi Spur the face is broken by two spurs. The Hockey Stick Gully is a distinctive feature on the left of these, marking the line of the Polish Route of 1986.

Around to the west and rising above the Savoia Glacier, the West Face is typified by its steep, horizontal, striated rock bands. The classic line of the West Ridge rises from the left side, gained from the subsidiary Negrotto Glacier. A distinctive feature of this area is a band of rocky slabs between two snowfields at c.7300m (c.23,950ft) called The Slide. The right edge of the West Face abuts the South Face at the line of the South West Pillar.

To the east, and rising up above the head of the Godwin-Austen Glacier as it curves around to its end, lies

Right **Balti porters struggle up the Baltoro Glacier** *en route* **for K2. So remote, the mountain has no known local name, nor is it visible from any inhabited place.**

1953 Dr C S Houston returned to the Abruzzi Spur, where his team reached 7900m (26,000ft), but an ailing A Gilkey was lost in an avalanche during a brave bid to bring him off the mountain. P Schoening, with great presence of mind and a remarkable feat of strength, held six men in a fall of tangled ropes.
1954 First ascent made by L Lacedelli and A Compagnoni of a strong Italian expedition, led by Professor Desio. They took additional oxygen, but it ran out shortly below the summit. Team member M Puchoz died of pneumonia at Camp 2.
1975 J Whittaker led an American expedition in an attempt on the North West Ridge from the Savoia Saddle. The highest point reached was 6700m (22,000ft).

1976 A strong Polish team surmounted the difficult North East Ridge only to be thwarted by lack of oxygen on the summit pyramid – 8400m (27,500ft).
1978 First attempt on the West Ridge by a British team under C Bonington was abandoned at 6700m (22,000ft) when N Estcourt perished in an avalanche. Americans, again led by J Whittaker, repeated the Polish North East Ridge, then traversed to the normal 'South East Ridge' route to successfully complete the mountain's third ascent.
1979 French climbers attempted the South-South-West Ridge, made five summit bids but were unable to get above 8400m (27,500ft). R Messner (Italian) and M Dacher reached the top via 'South East (Abruzzi Spur) Route' without using bottled oxygen.

the East Face. A huge snow shelf crosses the face at half-height linking the North East Ridge, and bounding the face on its right side, with the Abruzzi Spur, which defines the left edge.

Finally, to the north, and rising from the K2 Glacier, is the North Face. Its most striking feature is the North Ridge, which bisects the face in a clean sweep from glacier to summit. The face is bounded on its left side by the North East Ridge, and on its right by the North West Ridge.

climbing on K2

Nowhere on the mountain is there a line that could be fairly described as a trade route. The Abruzzi Spur, now the most often ascended line, was an outstanding mountaineering feat for its time, and still remains a formidable climb. Other routes on the mountain present even greater technical challenges, often combined with serious objective risk. The human endeavour on K2 has been great, and the struggle between man and this mountain has resulted in some of the most gripping and poignant mountaineering dramas ever recorded.

High on the mountain and far from assistance, many climbers, often successful summiteers, have succumbed to exhaustion, illness, and the weather. These problems have sometimes been compounded by misunderstandings between teams and overcrowding at critical campsites. The media attention arising from events

Above **Negotiating a way through crevasses on the long Baltoro Glacier approach to K2.**

Right **Julie-Ann Clyma at the start of House's Chimney on the Abruzzi Spur.**

1980 Four British climbers (leader P Boardman) climbed the West Ridge to 7000m (23,000ft).

1981 E Ohtani (Japanese) and N Sabir (Pakistani), from a Japanese group led by T Matsuura, reached the summit via the West Ridge/South West Side.

1982 Large Polish expedition with a strong Mexican contingent attempted a new route, avoiding the Savoia Saddle: 8200m (27,000ft) was gained on the Chinese side before they were observed and ordered back! Japanese mountaineers made the first ascent from China via the North Ridge.

1983 An Italian expedition led by F Santon made the second ascent of the North Ridge.

1986 R Casarotto died in a crevasse after climbing high on the South-South-West Ridge. Two Americans perished while attempting the same ridge. Two Poles climbed the South Face, but T Piotrowski fell to his death during their descent. Two more Poles and a Czech completed the South West Pillar – this time W Wroz was lost during the descent. Altogether, 13 died during the worst season on K2, five after being trapped in an 8000m (26,000ft) camp by prolonged bad weather. Slovenian climber T Cesen soloed a new route to the left of the Abruzzi Spur to 7800m (25,500ft).

1987 Based on (mistaken) satellite readings, rumours circulated that K2 was higher than Everest. The veteran Professor Desio quickly organized resurveys of K2 and Everest, which reaffirmed Everest's superiority.

However, in the process, by the latest measuring techniques, K2 was found to be 8616m (28,267ft), rather than the (remarkably accurate) 8611m (28,250ft) established by traditional methods 150 years before by the Great Trigonometric Survey. The older measurement is still widely used today.

1988 French climbers reached 8000m (26,000ft) on the North Spur.

1989 An Austrian attempt on the unclimbed East Face reached a height of 7200m (24,000ft).

1990 Three members of a 4-person expedition (S Svenson, G Child, G Mortimer – American/Australian) reached the summit by the North Spur. Two Japanese climbers completed a new route on the North West Face and the North Spur.

1992 A 2-man alpine style attempt was made on the West Face by E Loretan and V Kurtyka. Unfortunately it had to be abandoned because of great avalanche danger.

1993 A Canadian expedition under B Blanchard climbed to above the Negrotto Col on the 'South-South-West Ridge' route, switching first to the South Face and then to the Abruzzi

Spur where they reached the shoulder before joining in the rescue of a stricken climber.

1995 Alison Hargreaves (British) soloed K2 alongside other climbers, but they were all blown to their deaths in a stormy descent.

Left **To climb on the North Side of K2 requires a long approach through the Shaksgam region (when the river is low enough). Camels are used to cross the wild Shaksgam River.**

Above **Crossing the river on an approach.**

such as these has made K2 a familiar name, but has also popularized its nickname 'the Savage Mountain'.

The style of climbing adopted on K2 prior to the first ascent was characterized by relatively small teams – achievable because bottled oxygen was not used. This diminished the scale of the associated logistical pyramid. Despite their small size, two of these early expeditions reached over 8000m (26,000ft). It is significant, then, that the successful first-ascent team in 1954 did use oxygen to increase its chances, and employed 500 porters to get the climbers to base camp. The second ascent team in 1977 had 52 climbers and employed 1500 porters. Fortunately, this was seen as a retrograde step, and the third and fourth ascents were again by smaller teams using little or no bottled oxygen. Today, it is rare to find an expedition that employs high-altitude porters or uses supplementary oxygen. The use of fixed rope is also lessening because of the logistical move toward smaller teams favouring alpine style climbing. The

ethic is generally towards a lighter 'footprint' with a minimum number of smaller camps.

Because of its inaccessibility and technical difficulties, K2 has not attracted commercial expeditions on the same scale as some of the other 8000m (26,000ft) peaks. It may be partly for this reason that the lighter-weight approach has been sustained on this mountain.

future climbing

Despite its long history, K2 still presents a number of significant mountaineering challenges. Many of the routes already climbed up the main ridges take significant deviations in line, so direct ascents are awaited. The 'West Ridge', 'Japanese North West Face', and 'North East Ridge' lines all cross the upper section of their adjoining faces, but none of the West, North, or East Faces have had a direct ascent. There has not yet been a true traverse of the mountain, nor a winter ascent of any route. There is no doubt that K2 is a mountain with a history that commands respect, and yet it still has the capacity to excite and inspire. For all these reasons K2 remains a powerful magnet to mountaineers.

West Ridge

the Mushroom

Hockey Stick Gully

Bottleneck

Shoulder

Black Pyramid

House's Chimney

Abuzzi Spur

pakistani side

There are nine separate routes. Seven of these – moving clockwise around the mountain from the 'North West Ridge' to the 'South Face' route, to the 'North East Ridge' – fall under the jurisdiction of Pakistan. Only the 'North Ridge' and the 'North West Face' routes are climbed entirely from the Chinese side.

The vertical height gain from base camp to the summit of K2 by any route is over 3500m (11,500ft). Most expeditions allow 10–12 weeks to undertake an ascent. About 3–4 weeks can be spent on logistical preparations and on the walk-in and out from base camp. Of the remaining time, perhaps three or four weeks will be taken up with acclimatization and establishing a chain of camps. It will then be entirely dependent on the weather and conditions underfoot as to how long a summit attempt will take. Under ideal conditions, and without taking any rest days, it would be possible to climb from base camp to the summit via the Abruzzi Spur in five days, with another 2–3 days required for the descent. Realistically, however, with the probability of bad weather, a round trip is more likely to take 8–10 days, and may be considerably longer on the more difficult routes.

pakistani side

To approach the mountain on its Pakistani side you must hike the full length of the Baltoro Glacier to Concordia, the meeting place of its tributary glaciers, the Godwin-Austen, the upper Baltoro, and the Vigne Glaciers. There you are granted your first view of the peak, as you look due north up to K2's impressive South Face.

1 North West Ridge
(see Chinese side picture)
P Béghin and C Profit 1991
This route covered very little new ground but was notable because the difficult climbing was done in alpine style in very fast time. Rising from the Savoia Glacier it only briefly follows the North West Ridge before taking a traverse line similar to the Japanese 'North West Face' route, to finish up the North Ridge.

west face
The West Face is easily identifiable by its striking, striated rock bands. The fact that there is only one route on it gives a measure of the difficulty of the climbing it presents. In addition to its technical difficulty, there is a high objective danger with the face being very prone to avalanches.

2 West Ridge
E Ohtani and N Sabir 1981
Starting from the Negrotto Glacier the main crest is gained at 5800m (19,000ft). Difficult climbing adjacent to the ridge pushes through rock bands broken by snowfields, before a traverse across the top of the West Face. The route finishes up the line of the South West Pillar.

south face
The South Face is a complex mass, punctuated by rocky spurs and avalanche-prone ice cliffs. The characteristics of objective danger and difficult climbing are present here, as with all the faces on the mountain, but the South Face is notable as being the only one to have received a direct ascent.

3 South West Pillar: 'Magic Line'
W Wroz, P Piasecki, and P Bozik 1986
This route possibly gives the most technical climbing so far undertaken on K2, with hard, steep sections of icy rock at high altitude.

4 South Face: Polish Route
J Kukuczka and T Piotrowski 1986
Exposed to sérac danger in the lower section, with extremely difficult climbing in the upper section, composed of a curved gully (the Hockey Stick), this route culminates in a rock barrier below the summit.

5 South-South-East Spur (Basque variation to the Abruzzi)

J Oiarzabal, J Tomas, A and F Inuirrategi, and E de Pablo 1994

This route is possibly the best and safest way up the mountain. The spur is climbed to a junction with the Shoulder on the Abruzzi Spur, then continues up to the summit on this line.

6 Abruzzi Spur (South East Ridge)

A Compagnoni and L Lacedelli 1954

The most commonly attempted and ascended line. Although described as a spur, the ground is very open and the line indistinct. The climbing varies from steep snow slopes to loose and difficult rock steps. Its named features include House's Chimney, Black Pyramid, the Shoulder and, above that, the Bottleneck. The Spur is very exposed and suffers badly from the strong winds funnelling between Broad Peak and K2.

east face ⊠

The East Face is characterized by a large snow shelf located at about three-quarters-height, providing the upper part of the only route on this facet of the mountain.

7 North East Ridge

J Wickwire, L Reichardt, J Roskelly, and R Ridgeway 1978

From the head of the Godwin-Austen Glacier a snowy rib leads to the crest of the difficult, corniced North East Ridge. This is followed to around 7900m (26,000 ft), then the route traverses the East Face to finish up the Abruzzi Spur.

North Ridge

North West Ridge

North Side

chinese side

Approaching K2 from the Chinese side presents a major logistical problem. The journey is long and arduous, and final access to the mountain is dependent on the volume of meltwater in the Shaksham River. On reaching the oasis of Suget Jangal you may be rewarded with the sight of the North Ridge rising from the K2 Glacier, but it is still another 16km (10 miles) to reach base camp on the glacier itself. Because there are no porters available locally, and because no load-carrying animals can continue to the foot of the mountain due to the difficult glacial terain, it is necessary for climbers to ferry every load up this final section.

8 North Ridge

N Sakashita, Y Yanagisawa, H Yoshino, K Takami, H Kawamura, T Shigeno, and H Kamuro 1982

Perhaps the most compelling route on the mountain – an almost direct line from the K2 Glacier to the summit. Sustained climbing, but without great difficulty and at a moderate angle.

9 North West Face

H Nazuka and H Imamura, 1990

A huge, rising, leftward traverse. Starting from the K2 Glacier, the route climbs to the North West Ridge, then crosses the North West Face in a diagonal line to a junction with the North Ridge to reach the summit.

how to get to k2

International flights connect to Islamabad, then you can travel to Skardu by air with PIA, or by vehicle along the Karakoram Highway. From Skardu, you can now take local jeeps as far as Askole, where the walk-in begins. The main base campsite is situated on the Godwin-Austen Glacier beneath the South Face and can be reached in about seven days.

For approaches from China, international flights connect with Beijing. To the north of the range, the land which lies in the Sinkiang Province of China is extremely barren. This means a long journey with camels through harsh gorges, and crossing the Aghil Pass, at 4780m (15,700ft), then the Shaksgam River (only possible in the driest months) to the Sarpo Laggo Valley and the green oasis of grass and willow called Suget Jangal, which serves as a first base camp. Then the K2 Glacier leads up to the peak.

facilities

There are large military camps close to the mountain, but these cannot be relied on as sources for provisions or equipment. Base camp (in Pakistan) lies 10 days from a major town, so you must be self-sufficient.

when to climb

It is possible to climb throughout the summer months, with most expeditions visiting the mountain from June–August.

gear

It is best to take some fixed rope, although there is a great deal left on the mountain. The amount of technical gear that is required will depend on the route and style of climbing. A basic rack for the Abruzzi Spur might include 3–4 ice screws, a set of chocks, 2–3 hexes, 6–10 pitons, a few friends, and a good selection of different-length tapes. If using *in-situ* ropes, take a jumar. You will need tents, food, and fuel for four camps.

maps and guidebooks

Maps are available from travel book shops worldwide. There are no guidebooks, but route information can be found in books, journals, and magazines.

language

Your Liaison Officer will generally speak English, Urdu, and other dialects, and will act as an interpreter (*see red tape*). Local employees speak Urdu and Balti.

rescue and insurance

Take out comprehensive travel insurance, to include rescue costs. Rescue operations are conducted by the military.

red tape

To climb K2 it is necessary to apply for permission to the Ministry of Tourism in Islamabad and you will have to pay a peak fee. Expeditions are expected to attend a briefing meeting at the Ministry before climbing, and to attend a debriefing before leaving the country. Financial bonds for environment and rescue cover are required. As K2 lies in a restricted military area, a Liaison Officer will be assigned to your expedition and will accompany you throughout to assist with police and military checkpoints and all other matters. This will be at your expense.

the unforgiving peak
barry
blanchard

"In 1984 I stood on top of Rakaposhi and gazed over to the mutinous, black pyramid of K2. I knew then that I wanted to climb it, and that I was afraid of it. Like all Himalayan climbers, I posted a picture of K2 on the wall, I read about it, and I talked to friends who had been there. In 1992 I applied for permission, and in the spring of 1993 The Banff/Dead Man's Flats K2 Expedition left Canada for its attempt on the South-South-West Ridge, the 'Magic Line'. Peter Arbic and Troy Kirwan made up the Banff contingent, while I represented the hamlet of Dead Man's Flats. We were going for alpine style because we believed in entrusting ourselves to the mountain, totally.

In Rawalpindi we hide from the midday heat. Temperatures climb to over 45°C. We stay close to the air conditioning and sip on ice-cooled Murree beer. Our Liaison Officer will be arriving in five days and, as our organizational chores get ticked off, the torment of doubt and fear starts prying into me. Is what we're trying ridiculous? Three men, 3650m of technical climbing on the second-highest peak of the planet, the earth's boldest thrust into thin air? I know how precarious the margins are up there – how a storm can smash us like china figurines hurled at a brick wall. How truly impotent we are against the atmosphere when it unloads on a high mountain. Over the restaurant table Peter nails me with eyes, deep brown, engaging – and unwavering. 'Don't get psyched out, Bubba. We're some of the best climbers in Canada. We will get our chance.'

june 14 Sitting cross-legged beside the Dumordu River, I watch 300 porters queue up and push into the man-basket to cable across the river. The basket holds two men and each of the crossings takes four long minutes. I've been sitting here for 3½ hours. Our 90 porters are at the end of the line and I'm beginning to doubt there will be enough time in the day to get us across.

june 20 We finally arrive at K2 Base Camp – the 'strip' – and plop down between Swedes and some Canadian/American friends. We are the fifth expedition to arrive and the only team attempting a route other than the Abruzzi Spur. Our friends Jim Haberl and Dan Culver visit from the 'CanAm' team and describe how a Slovenian climber had died trying to escape from Camp 4 high on the Abruzzi during a storm five days earlier. Over tea, I tell Troy and Peter that in half-a-dozen expeditions over here I have never been on a peak where people were dying.

june 30 'This slope is the endless pig of misery,' says Troy. He leans heavily on both his tools, picketed into the softening 50° steep melt/freeze rubbish that leads to the Negrotto Col. We have come to hate the relentless insecurity of balled-up cramponing, points shearing through its structurelessness. Too long to rappel (900m); tortuous to downclimb. We make our second reconnaissance during the first of the two 4-day high-pressure windows we see during our 68-day stay below K2.

july 4 Crunching out of base camp at 10pm, we are determined to climb the 'endless pig' at night, when it is frozen.

july 6 We leave our camp at the col where Peter has excavated a Slovenian Bible and a vintage 1970s ice axe from crushed tent remains of previous sieges. We enjoy the day: fine climbing on incut edges, which we discover after throwing aside the caving ladders from the sieges and getting at the rock. At 400m above the col, we turn around and are back in base camp the next morning. We feel ready to go for the 'Magic Line' with the next good weather.

In the afternoon we hear our 'CanAm' friend Phil Powers summit on the radio. 'What in the wide world of sports is a hick from Wyoming doing on top of K2!' I shout into the radio. 'Enjoying the view, friend, enjoying the view.' An hour afterwards Jim and Dan become the first from our country to summit the mountain.

> ... I have never been on a peak where people were dying.

Above **Peter Arbic climbing the 'Magic Line' on K2.**
Chogolisa can be seen in the background.

the next morning we confront the sérac barrier. It is ugly and terrifying. We opt for the traverse to the South Spur used by Afanassieff and Seigneur. High-tailing it, we're out from under the chopping séracs and onto the South Spur in half an hour. We shout hellos to two Catalonians, fixing rope not 50m above where we've gatecrashed their route, and continue on our merry alpine way, ignoring the fixed lines. That night we bivvy in a cold but comfortable crevasse at 6900m.

july 29 Morning sees Troy unable to continue because of a crushing headache that won't go away. We radio the Catalonians who, without hesitation, agree to allow Troy to descend their lines. (They seemed surprised we even asked.) It is hard to part. Harder for Troy, who badly wants to keep going.

Peter and I slog on. At about 7500m it hurts to continue, and to keep outguessing the slope, to go where the footing is good, yet stay out of the windslabs – precarious margins. And the weather is far from perfect: late in the day a fog envelops us just short of the Shoulder. Instantly it is frostbitingly cold. Peter and I armour ourselves in layers. At 7900m the day is done and we dig in against some exposed rock, exhausted. Finally, we climb into the tent. Frost grows inside it. My crampon straps are frozen and for the first time in my climbing career I cannot get them off. Peter helps me.

july 30 Next morning we stagger onto the Shoulder. My balance is off; I am very tired. Six climbers in front of us are heading into the Bottleneck. Peter and I decide to descend. It just isn't in control enough; there are clouds to the east.

'God, those guys must be doing better than us,' I say, looking to the Bottleneck. 'No, Bubba. I don't think so. We've been gaining on them,' Pete replies. 'How come they keep going if they feel like I do?' I say. 'They're taking their chance, I guess.' Pete turns as he says it and heads towards the Abruzzi.

Late that afternoon we stumble into base camp, completely wasted. Troy is joyful to see us. All six of the climbers ahead of us make the summit. We know them all. You get acquainted with almost everyone on the 'strip'. But Peter and Reamer from Germany and Daniel from Sweden all die descending from the top and into a storm. Gone forever.

Pete, Troy, and I, along with many others, help to rescue Raphael who is frostbitten. The storm continues, lasting for most of August. Twelve hours of good weather on August 14 had the three of us dashing up to Camp 2 on the Abruzzi, still trying to climb K2. But climbing is now a chore to commit to, interrupting the social life on the 'strip': cappuccino with Dutch internationals at 9am, tea with the Brits, reading in the tent, a stroll down the glacier in the afternoon, late tea with the Catalonians. We got stormed off anyway.

august 26 Our porters come, and we walk out through the second high-pressure window of the summer of 1993. Dawn light splashes golden fire across the Baltoro peaks, making me quiver. The earth's ultimate expression of Mountain.

People still ask me if I intend to climb K2. I say that I will return in my 40s, when I can deal with the boredom and suffering better. To climbers I now give this advice: 'If you see a storm coming, drop everything and run for your life. Do not hesitate ... RUN!'

Peter, Troy, and I are proud of the lads. But later that night we hear that Dan has fallen on the descent. He is dead.

july 8 We walk out of base, along the 'strip', and past the last camp. We continue up the Godwin-Austen Glacier and meet our friends. I hug Stacey, their leader, the first American woman to climb Everest. She pushes down tears: 'I don't want to cry any more. I can't cry any more.'

Later, a plaque for Dan Culver is added to the Gilkey Memorial at the southernmost foot of K2.

july 15 Two days of climbable weather lure us back up and into a storm. Descending, we agree that none of us can face that endless 'pig of misery' again and that we are never going to see the six days of good weather we need to get up the 'Magic Line' and down the Abruzzi safely. We decide to switch our efforts to the Kukuczka/Piotrowski route on the South Face. We cache our gear there, and are able to move it higher on the 22nd.

In base camp I catalogue the different sounds that the various forms of snow drum out against the taut nylon of my tent ... one month and three days in base camp waiting to climb K2.

july 27, climbable: Peter, Troy, and I leave before dawn and climb to the cache, which is buried in a windslab and takes some digging to retrieve. We continue on to 6000m and camp. Early

gasherbrum IV

stephen venables

Gasherbrum IV, 7925m (26,000ft) is not the highest of the six Gasherbrum peaks but its gigantic pyramid outline is the showpiece of the group, at the heart of the Karakoram. It straddles the frontier between Chinese Sinkiang to the north, and the Pakistan province of Baltistan to the south. The name means Shining Wall in Balti and is most apt at sunset when the West Face glows orange above Concordia, the confluence of the Baltoro and Godwin-Austen Glaciers.

Gasherbrum IV is a real mountaineer's mountain: not quite attaining the magic 8000m (26,000ft) status, it appeals through beauty of form and obvious difficulty. To date, only three parties have reached the Main Summit, and a fourth turned back from the North Summit. The peak remains a symbol of the commitment and challenge of high-altitude mountaineering.

ridges, faces, and peaks

Gasherbrum IV has two summits, separated by an almost horizontal ridge. The Main Summit, 7925m (26,000ft), is the apex of the South-South-West Ridge and the less prominent South East Ridge. From the slightly lower North Summit, 6950m (22,803ft), drop the North East Ridge and North West Ridge.

south side From the South Gasherbrum Glacier, Gasherbrum IV appears as a magnificent pyramid. The left skyline is formed by the long South Ridge. To its right is a triangular face of snow topped by steep rock banks. The right-hand edge of this triangle is a rocky buttress rising from a chaotic icefall, Serracata degli Italiani. Above the icefall, a glacier cwm leads beneath the East Face to the distant, high North East Col between Gasherbrum IV and III. Slanting left from the col, forming the right-hand skyline of Gasherbrum IV, is the rocky North East Ridge.

west side Dominating the Baltoro Glacier, the West Face is an immense trapezoid of pale marble, with a great streak of black diorite sweeping up its left-hand side. The upper bowl of the face is a huge snowfield, topped by the rock turrets of the ridge linking the North and Main Summits. The face is framed by the South Ridge on the right and the North West Ridge on the left. Running down the face from the North Summit, just left of centre, is a shattered rib of rocky towers – the South-South-West Spur.

north side The North Face, rising above the extremely remote North Gasherbrum Glacier in Sinkiang, has never been seen in detail. Distant views from Broad Peak, the 8000m (26,000ft) peak between Gasherbrum and K2, show huge snow-laden hanging glaciers.

future climbing

No one has ever set foot on the North Face, which might offer a comparatively easy approach to the North East Col. On the Pakistani side there are challenges: the South-South-West Ridge and the East Face have still not been conquered; nor has the South-South-West Spur on the West Face.

Right **Camp beneath the ice 'ships' on the Gasherbrum Glacier, the route to the northern side of the mountain.**

R Schauer for one of the boldest Himalayan ascents of all time up the West Face (*see pages 230–1*).

1986 An American-Australian team made the first ascent of the North West Ridge. Travelling light up the final section, without sleeping bags, G Child and T Macartney-Snape (Australian) and T Hargis (American) bivouacked in a snow hole at the North Summit, continuing the following morning, 22 June, to reach the Main Summit.

1992 An American team attempted the South-South-West Ridge, approaching it by the South Face, from the South Gasherbrum Glacier.

1993 Y Yamanoi (Japanese) made a solo attempt on the East Face. During his first outing he was avalanched in the icefall area of the Serracata degli Italiani.

Two days later, he reached 7000m (23,000ft) on the face, before being driven into a retreat by bad weather.

1995 One of Slovenia's top alpinists, S Sveticic, made an audacious solo attempt on the still unclimbed Central Spur of the West Face, passing rockfall to reach 7100m (23,300ft) on the fourth day before bad weather forced him to retreat. A Korean team also attempting the face spotted him descending on the fifth day, but he never returned.

1997 Korean climbers, including Cho Sung-Dae, Yoo Hak-Jae, Bang Jung-Ho, and Kim Tong-Kwan, returned to the West Face. Using thousands of metres of rope, they finally managed to climb the Central Spur. They found Sveticic's body on their descent.

Main Summit

North Summit

South Face

East Face

North East Ridge

North East Col

①

On all routes, any heavy new snow makes rock climbing very awkward and snow slopes avalanche-prone. This, plus the long, complex nature of all the routes, will always mean that success can be elusive. Even very strong teams should expect to take at least five days on their final push from base camp to summit.

south side

The South Side is hidden from the Baltoro and has to be approached from round the back, by the South Gasherbrum Glacier (as do the approaches to Gasherbrums I, II, and III). Base camp is usually sited at the junction of the Abruzzi and South Gasherbrum Glaciers.

1 North East Ridge

W Bonatti and C Mauri 1958
A classic expedition, with a long glacier approach to the North East Col and including a difficult 500m (1600ft) icefall – the Serracata degli

Italiani. There is hard mixed and rock climbing (pitches of V) on the ridge itself, with more difficulties on the final ridge from North to Main Summit. In purely technical terms, it might equate to a D+ alpine climb, but such comparisons are almost meaningless on a multi-day route at extreme altitude. It is about 10km (6 miles) to the North East Col, from base camp. Ascent 2800m (9200ft).

west side

From Concordia, the West Face looks very close, but it is actually a long approach from base camp, which is at the junction of the Baltoro and West Gasherbrum Glaciers. The final corridor curving around to the North West Ridge only becomes visible after reaching the upper part of the West Gasherbrum Glacier.

2 North West Ridge

G Child, T Hargis, and T Macartney-Snape 1986
This is a more reasonable alternative

to the 'West Face' (4). Like the 'North East Ridge' route (1), it has a long glacier approach and involves mainly snow and ice climbing on the ridge, until the crux marble band, with pitches of V, starting at 7350m (24,100ft). From the North Summit, unlike the Bonatti group, the 1986 team stayed mainly on the West Face, traversing beneath the crest. This is a sustained and committing climb, as hard or harder than the 'North East Ridge' (1). It is 7km (4 miles) from base camp to the North West Col. Ascent 2500m (8200ft) from gully at head of glacier; 3300m (10,800ft) from base camp.

3 Central Spur

Yoo Hak-Jae, Bang Jung-Hoe, and Kim Tong-Kwan 1997
A dangerous line, as hard or harder than route (2). 70–80° snow and ice on the left side of the lower spur, threatened by serious rock and sérac fall. Grade IV and V+ rock climbing on the Black Towers and a vertical

rock step of V+ above 7000m (23,000ft). The team followed a rising rightward traverse from the top of the spur to the Main Summit with sections of 70° mixed ground. A very difficult and serious route.

4 West Face

V Kurtyka and R Schauer 1985
One of the outstanding alpine style achievements of the 1980s and a huge committing route with sustained difficulties. The line slants from the right to left, first up a prominent ice runnel, then up tenuous mixed ground to emerge in the huge snow basin beneath the North Summit. The marble is both loose and compact, making belays sketchy and retreat by this route virtually impossible. Probably one of the hardest big-mountain routes in the world – ED+ alpine climbing transposed to nearly 8000m (26,000ft). It is about 5km (3 miles) to the start of the face, which is 2500m (8200ft) high. Ascent 3300m (10,800ft) from base camp.

North Summit

Main Summit

West Face

2

North West Ridge

3

4

Black
Towers

2

how to get to gasherbrum IV

Travel by air or road to Skardu. From there a jeep track leads most of the way to the village of Askole in the Braldu Valley. The walk-in from the roadhead to a base camp on the West Side takes about seven days. The South Side base camp is two days further. Both journeys can be shortened by taking the alternative approach from Hushe, over the Gondoro La, which is the high pass now used frequently to approach the upper Boltoro Glacier.

facilities

There is nothing in the way of stores or accommodation beyond Skardu and Askole, so all provisions and equipment must be carried.

when to climb

The normal Karakoram climbing season is June–September. The best chance of getting reasonable snow conditions

and fine weather is probably during July and August. Because all of the routes on Gasherbrum IV are long, difficult, and complex, your success will always depend on a clear spell, which will need to last for several days.

gear

Gasherbrum IV is one of the world's highest mountains, requiring the very best in high-altitude clothing and tents. On the lower reaches, most attempts on the mountain have used varying amounts of fixed rope. However, unless a large team is providing sustained back-up, as happened on the first ascent, the summit push will probably have to be made fast and light, with minimal gear. A shovel for digging an emergency snow cave could well be a life-saver. All routes require both ice and rock gear, although on the West Face it can be hard to find any good anchors.

maps and guidebooks

Among the available maps are 'K2, Baltoro, Gasherbrum, Masherbrum, Saltoro Groups', 1:200,000 ('No 3' from Leomann Maps, Germany, 1990) and 'Eight Thousand Metre Peaks of the Karakoram', 1:50,000 (Jerzy Wala/Climbing Company Buxton, 1994).

There are no guidebooks, but it is worth reading: *Karakoram, The Ascent of Gasherbrum IV*, Fosco Maraini (Hutchinson, 1961), *Himalaya Alpine Style*, Andy Fanshawe & Stephen Venables (Hodder, 1995), and *Thin Air*, Greg Child (Patrick Stephens, 1988).

language

English is understood in the major towns and by the Liaison Officer (*see red tape*). Locals speak Urdu and Balti.

rescue and insurance

There are military camps in the mountains and these can be contacted for rescue

and emergencies. It is strongly advisable to take out comprehensive travel insurance to include possible rescue costs.

red tape

You will need to apply for permission to climb, and pay a peak fee to the Ministry of Tourism in Islamabad. This will involve attending a briefing meeting at the Ministry before going to the mountains, and a debriefing on your return. Financial bonds for environment and rescue cover are required. A Liaison Officer will be assigned to the expedition to accompany it throughout.

death zone, pleasure zone
robert schauer

"There is a fascination in pushing limits: finding out who you are and what you are capable of at the extreme edge of existence. Many mountaineers have their consciousness widened in the so-called 'Death Zone'. During some moments of mountaineering, only the narrowest of lines separates death and that heightened state of awareness that approaches meditation. Surviving such an experience is almost a form of pleasure. This natural 'high' can be compelling. You feel irresistibly urged to climb again – but probably under more stringent conditions.

I took one such reversible step into the realm of death in 1985 during an expedition to the Karakoram with Vojtek Kurtyka. Our object was the West Face of Gasherbrum IV, almost 3000m high. Known as the Shining Wall, its serious technical difficulties, coupled with altitude and the frequent bad conditions, had defied all previous attempts to climb it.

It soon became clear that, without the help of porters, our only real chance was to go for it in a single push, rather than repeatedly climbing up and down, banging in pitons and fixing ropes, as you would normally do on a mountain of its scale.

Surviving on that face took every last ounce of our will and skill. The difficult first half took far longer than we expected, with the result that we ran out of food and fuel. Yet the summit looked within our grasp – until our plans were completely destroyed by the onset of a fierce storm. Already exhausted, we dug ourselves into a snow hole at 7700m – and remained pinned there for the next two days. We had scarcely eaten or drunk in 72 hours and, after such long deprivation, had become inured to the constant cold.

In our apathy, it took conscious effort to separate the real problems from images conjured up by our imaginations. I was convinced there were three of us on this expedition, and I blamed my imaginary third for our slow progress. I believed he was preventing us from sleeping by shaking and pulling at our bivvy tent, and was opposing all our arrangements.

The snowstorm brought avalanches thundering down at fairly regular intervals. Ensconced in our deep hole, they passed harmlessly over our feet, but I fancied the 'unseen other' was trying to squeeze me out. In reality I was being pushed by Vojtek on one side and by the pressure of mounting snow on the other. The feeling of being crushed made me desperate to escape.

Soon I was hovering like a raven. In a most intense fashion I felt every sensation of flying – the wind in my face, the biting cold, the weightlessness. I could look down and see myself in my sleeping bag, hanging like a tiny dot against the gigantic wall. How foolish to be weighted down like that, when up here I could steer myself in any direction, at any height I wished.

It was exhilarating and I had no desire to go back to my frigid sleeping bag in that cramped hole. At the same time I was aware of the need to get off the mountain safely. We'd been arguing about it, coming close to a solution at one stage as we racked our brains for it. If the blizzard lasted many days, any movement of ours would set off a deadly avalanche. And how long could we hold out without food or drink, up here where a body needs 5–6 litres of fluid daily to counter dehydration and keep the organs functioning?

I was so weak already that making the smallest movement took all my willpower. Vojtek proposed climbing straight down, a recipe for disaster with only six pitons and a couple of ropes. We'd never have reached the bottom – quite apart from the

Far left **Vojtek Kurtyka on the previously unclimbed West Face of Gasherbrum IV – the Shining Wall.**

Left **Though accomplished back in 1985, the ascent of the Shining Wall by Vojtek Kurtyka and Robert Schauer is still regarded as one of the boldest alpine style achievements ever.**

avalanche danger. I felt he was losing touch with reality, when till then he'd been so prudent and practical. Despite being in as bad a way as I was, he'd always talked of reaching the top, a target which for me had long receded into the distance. We both knew that if we continued our ascent we'd need to find a different way down, and that meant a host of unknowns.

In the event we were condemned to wait, by our own physical weakness and by the storm. No amount of rest at high altitude can help you to recuperate. Above 6000m the body weakens all the time, feeding off its stored fat, digesting itself. Scientists tell us that this triggers mechanisms that provide our subjective perception with very pleasurable sensations. Certainly, as we waited, our sense of security made our thinking more focused. After my stint as a raven, I suddenly found myself among a heaving mass of people, all radiating a comfortable feeling of warmth and safety. I saw road signs and traffic lights, as if I were being pointed in the right direction. Then I was in a supermarket, tucking into the most delicious sausages and other goodies, like in a speeded-up film. A short interlude of reality interrupted this bizarre collage when squalls of snow whipped my face. But soon I was back, this time in an elegant restaurant in Graz, gobbling like one possessed. All these images enhanced my eerie sense of wellbeing. I felt I had nothing to fear. Yet why, in that one moment of lucidity, had I not panicked? Was my inner excitement releasing energy, supporting the notion that I was doing the right thing, generating movement and activity? I wouldn't have believed it possible before then, but I am convinced of it now. Where was this energy coming from, given that there was so little strength left in the body? Other mountaineers, I knew, had experienced similar sensations. Hermann Buhl soloed Nanga Parbat in a partial trance. At 8000m he felt he was walking through

> **If the blizzard lasted … any movement of ours would set off a deadly avalanche.**

an orchard of flowers and was convinced a second climber accompanied him. You can find many such examples.

Our nightmare continued for two days. The cold was almost unbearable. When the sun finally reached the Wall, it took hours to penetrate our stiff bodies while we struggled to escape the clutches of our dream world. It was hard to make decisions and take action as vision and reality blurred together.

I stuffed snow into my mouth. For days I'd had an excruciatingly swollen throat and my voice was long gone. I definitely should have drunk more. Trying to make up for it now was only a drop on a hot stone. Slowly our bodies began to move in the warming sun, almost like a reflex. It was clear to both of us that our only chance of salvation lay in continuing the climb. We would have to wade through thigh-deep snow towards the summit. Although less steep, we moved at snail speed. At last, late in the afternoon, we reached the top of the face. A little nick in the ridge indicated a way to go down. We said nothing. Neither of us wanted to climb the few extra metres to the summit.

Intuitively, I nosed out the only way down across high rock steps and ice barriers. As if by magic, on a face so vertical and depressingly smooth, safe places appeared for us to stand on, and when it grew dark we found a 'comfortable' spot to bivouac at 6500m. This was our the 10th night on Gasherbrum IV. As our abseil descent became increasingly dangerous, still I believed nothing could harm us. After a whole day and night we reached the level surface of the glacier. I felt I was floating half a metre above the ground. The first stream did not make us crave water as might have been expected. Reality had become unreal. It took days before we could think and feel clearly again, and in a strange way I enjoyed this state of 'absence'.

The climb had released a tide of emotions and insights. I'd already discovered that, once you've survived intense situations like this, you immediately find yourself becoming determined not to repeat them. I had thought of abandoning this level of climbing after the Shining Wall. But the horrors fade. Soon there is something new. You never finish.

1956 The Russian climber Pieskariow and 12 Mongolians made the first ascent of Huithen. Their route took them up the North East Spur to the North Summit. It is presumed that they also went to the Main Summit, as the linking ridge is not a difficult proposition.
1967 A Polish/Mongolian expedition, led by R Palczewski, made an array of satellite first ascents on neighbouring

peaks such as Malczyn Chajrchan (4020m/13,200ft); Selenge (3840m/12,600ft), which is named after the Mongolian river; Birkut or Eagle Peak (4068m/13,350ft); Snow Church (4073m/13,360ft); and others.
1967–70 Two expeditions visited in 1967 and 1970 but little is known about them except that their principal objective was to make ascents by the 'Original Route'.

1991 British climber J Town climbed Monch Chajrchan at 4362m (14,300ft), 320km (200 miles) to the south of Huithen, and was probably the first Westerner allowed to climb post-independence. The Dutchman R Naar also made a ski descent of the 'Original Route' on Huithen.
1992 J Freeman-Attwood and L Griffin (British), and E Webster (American)

climbed a new route on Huithen's South Ridge, which they unofficially named 'The Back of Beyond Ridge'. Another British expedition, led by S Berry with D Hillebrandt and other colleagues, climbed to just marginally below the top of Mount Huithen by the East Ridge, and then made a successful ascent of the North East Ridge.

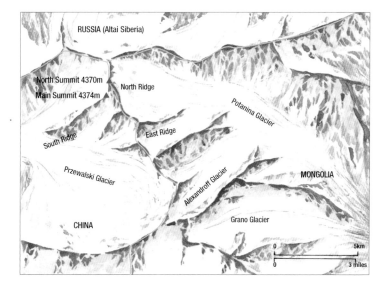

mount huithen

julian freeman-attwood

Mount Huithen, at 4374m (14,350ft) the highest mountain in Outer Mongolia, straddles the far north-western triple border between Mongolia, China's Dzungarian Basin, and Altai Siberia. This one point could rightly be judged as the meeting place of the great cultures of Central Asia. A more remote part of the great continent would be hard to find: the nearest town, Olgy, is 240km (150 miles) away. This remoteness is still a reality and Mongolia is surely one of the emptiest places on earth. Just 2.3 million inhabitants occupy an area three-quarters of the size of the Indian subcontinent. At least one million are nomadic, living in Gers, or Yorts (tents).

The Altai Range, in which lie Mt Huithen and the whole Tabun Bogdo group, rises at Mount Belukha in Siberia, within Kazakh and Pazyruk country. From Belukha, the range runs south-east into Mongolia and peters out on the western fringes of the Gobi Desert. But it is in the Tabun Bogdo group (the Mountains of the Five Gods), on the triple border of Mongolia, China, and Siberia, that the range becomes intriguing. The group is roughly the size

of the French Alps and contains nine 4000m (13,100ft) peaks, and numerous smaller satellites. Many of these are unclimbed, so the area is of interest to exploratory climbers.

The earliest explorers were mostly Russian, but little climbing seems to have been done until after the break-up of the Soviet Union in 1990; even since then there have been very few visits by Westerners. In 1992, the Mongolian authorities gave me and colleagues Lindsay Griffin and Ed Webster permission to climb Huithen and surrounding peaks. We decided on a new route from the previously unexplored Chinese Przewalski Glacier, which included an unpermitted crossing of a high pass. The successful ascent ended in near tragedy when Griffin badly damaged his leg. An extraordinary, unofficial rescue took place involving a Mongolian helicopter flying over 3200km (2000 miles) each way, and into Chinese airspace.

ridges, faces, and peaks

The glaciation on Huithen is more extensive than might be expected on a mountain of this height. The longest glaciers are the Potanina and Przewalski, each some 13km (8 miles) long, which run off Huithen's East and South West Faces respectively. There is little glaciation flowing north into Siberia. The major Mongolian glaciers such as the Alexandroff and Grano, both of which join the Potanina, flow south-east into the arid steppe of the Olgy Aimag (region); and the major Chinese glaciers (mostly unnamed) flow into the Przewalski and run into the arid desert of the Dzungarian Basin, an area long since out of bounds and containing many of the Tabun Bogdo mountains.

Huithen is mostly composed of granite, both sound and rotten. It has two summits: the Main Summit, 4374m (14,350ft), and the slightly lower North Summit, 4370m (14,300ft), with a ridge linking the two. The North Ridge drops with hanging séracs to a col linking it with the triple-border peak. A branch of this North Ridge runs down north-east onto the Potanina Glacier, the route of the first ascent. There is also an East Ridge that again drops onto the Potanina. The South Ridge falls by a series of ice ridges and rock towers to the Chinese Przewalski Glacier.

Most of the East Face and the whole of the West Face of Huithen drains into China.

future climbing

The Chinese section of the East Face looks devoid of obviously good lines and is threatened by séracs over much of its length, but the West Face may hold some good unclimbed routes.

South Ridge · **South Summit** · **North Summit** · **East Ridge**

1 South Ridge Route D-

J Freeman-Attwood, L Griffin, and E Webster 1992
Starts from Przewalski Glacier at 3000m (10,000ft), through 460m (1500ft) of steep boulder-strewn moraine to the snow ridge proper. This broadens for 90m (300ft) into a wider face before constricting again into a harder section where an ice traverse is necessary. A broadened plateau is reached 75m (250ft) below the top, and after this the snow climb becomes easier. It took the group 10 hours from its advance base camp. 1125m (3700ft) from Przewalski Glacier.

2 North East Ridge: Original Route PD

Pieskariow and party 1956
A straightforward snow climb that takes about 10 hours. It is 1000m (3300ft) from the advance base camp at the edge of Potanina. Many parties bivouac once on the ascent.

3 East Ridge AD

First ascent by Mongolians, date unknown
A little more difficult than the original route. 1000m (3300ft) from Potanina Base Camp.

how to get to mount huithen

Fly to Peking and then travel to Ulan Bator by air or rail (rail is best). The same railway line links up with the trans-Siberian Express so you can also reach Ulan Bator through Russia.

To get to Huithen, take an internal Mongolian flight to Olgy from Ulan Bator. From there, you can hire a truck to travel for a couple of days towards the mountain. The last 1–3 days of the journey will have to be done on camel or pony. You must haggle for these with the local Kazakh nomads, but don't be in any rush!

facilities

There are none. You will need to bring specialized food with you, or be prepared to live only on yak milk, fatty lamb, and strong bitter tea. You can buy rice, sugar, and some tinned produce in Olgy.

when to climb

The best time to visit is May and June, but July and August are also possible though wetter. Outside of these months the cold can be terrific with winter lows of -30°C (-22°F); even -45°C (-49°F) is not unknown.

gear

Fibre pile and waterproofs, and normal alpine gear. (Goose or duck down is only needed in the winter and as yet no climbing has been done then.) Take ice screws, snowstakes, slings, a few nuts, and karabiners, but you will not need too much hardware for any of the routes described. The ability to navigate in poor visibility is essential.

maps and guidebooks

The best maps for the area are the Air Navigation series (try your local map stockists or Stanfords, London). Mongolian maps are useless apart from a restricted army map, 'Tabun Bogdo'No: M-45-104, 1:100,000, probably only obtainable through the Mongolian forces.

The *Lonely Planet Guide to Mongolia* would be a useful reference for anyone travelling to the area, but there are no specific books on Huithen.

language

Mongolian – you will need an interpreter to obtain camels or ponies.

rescue and insurance

It is best to have insurance, but do not expect to be rescued.

red tape

Despite the relative ease of obtaining official permission to climb Mount Huithen from the Ulan Bator authorities, the Olgy Aimag, in which the mountains lie, is principally Kazakh and semi-autonomous. Recently a Westerner was thrown in gaol despite obtaining the correct paperwork. It is vital to employ an interpreter, who will also act as a Liaison Officer for you.

To obtain information about permits, write to the Ministry of Environment (Chairman of Protected Areas and Ecotourism Department) in Ulan Bator. The correct postal address and a booklet giving further information can be obtained through the Mongolian Embassy at 7 Kensington Court, London, W8 5DL, UK.

1856 The first known reports of Nanga Parbat were sent to Europe after the German explorer and suspected spy A Schlagintweit reached its foot.
1895 A F Mummery (British) made the very first attempt on an 8000m (26,000ft) peak when he climbed alpine style past 6000m (20,000ft) on the Diamir Flank with Raghobir Thapa, his Gurkha porter. His presumed route is now called the Mummery Rib. He and two porters disappeared attempting to cross a pass to the Rakhiot Glacier.
1932 W Merkl led the first German expedition. They climbed the Rakhiot Peak but failed on the Main Summit.
1934 P Aschenbrenner and cartographer E Schneider (Austrian) achieved a high point of 7850m (25,800ft) above Silver Saddle on the northerly Rakhiot Side in a disastrous expedition – 10 people died. Schneider and others collected data for a map that is still used by the majority of climbers today.
1937 16 climbers and porters, including leader K Wien (German), died during another German expedition. An avalanche at Camp 4 just below Rakhiot Peak killed them.
1953 In an extraordinary effort without oxygen, Austrian climber H Buhl made the first ascent, reaching the summit on all fours on 4 July after climbing the last 1300m (4000ft) on his own.
1962 Germans T Kinshofer, S Low, and A Mannhardt reached the summit via the 'Kinshofer Route' on the left-hand side of the westerly Diamir Flank. Low died after a storm on the descent.

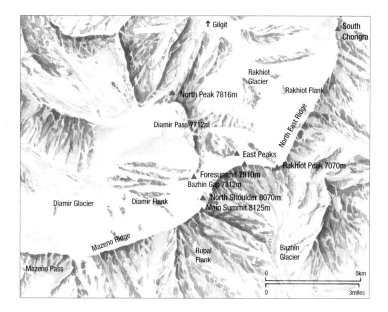

nanga parbat

richard cowper

The ninth-highest peak in the world, Nanga Parbat (naked mountain), 8125m (26,700ft), stands in splendid isolation in north-eastern Pakistan: the dazzling culmination of the westernmost end of the Himalayan chain. Not far from disputed Kashmir, it is bounded to the north and west by the mighty River Indus, while, to the south, its Rupal Face rises almost sheer for upwards of 4500m (14,800ft), the greatest single face on any mountain in the world.

The mountain has a reputation for committing climbs and considerable objective dangers. None of its seven major routes offers an 'easy' way to the top. Given its size and stunning beauty, Nanga Parbat is remarkably little visited by climbers or trekkers: it is rare for it to receive more than three or four expeditions in a year. Remarkably, it has yet to receive a winter ascent.

Sadly, even the few visitors have left their mark. At the start of the traditional route, Fairy Meadow is no longer the idyllic field idealized in the memoirs of pre-war climbers; it is scattered with rubbish and many of its trees have been felled for firewood.

ridges, faces, and peaks

Nanga Parbat is one of the most formidable of the 8000m (26,000ft) giants. A highly complex massif, it is usually considered as one giant ridge, running over 25km (15½ miles), from the Mazeno Pass in the south-west to the Chongra Peaks in the north-east. It has a number of lengthy subsidiary ridges, an array of steep-sided spurs and buttresses, and three great flanks, which have almost a dozen other peaks of over 6000m (19,700ft) on them. Its highest part is a trapezoid of snow, ice, and rock, with its Main Summit at 8125m (26,700ft) and its second-highest summit to the north, the North Shoulder, 8070m (26,500ft).

mazeno ridge From the Mazeno Pass, 5377m (17,600ft), in the south-west, the ridge climbs east for 13km (8 miles), over seven Mazeno Peaks (several over 7000m/23,000ft), to the Mazeno Gap, 6700m (22,000ft). It then rises steeply to the Main Summit.

north east ridge and rakhiot flank From the Main Summit, the North East Ridge continues across the summit plateau, northwards to the North Shoulder and the Bazhin Gap, 7812m (25,600ft), before shifting north-east to take in the Foresummit 7910m (25,952ft) and some famous pre-war expedition landmarks. These include the Silver Saddle, between the North West Peak, 7597m (25,000ft), and the South East Peak, 7530m (24,700ft); the Rakhiot Peak, 7070m (23,200ft); the Moor's Head; and the Chongra Peaks (South Chongra 6488m/21,300ft and Central Chongra 6455m/21,200ft). From the Foresummit another ridge to the north-west crosses the Diamir Pass to the North Peak 7816m (25,645ft).

diamir and rupal flanks The complex 3500m (11,500ft) West Face, or Diamir Flank, is the scene of the first attempt on the mountain by Mummery in 1895. Its lower half consists of a series of hanging glaciers above an array of steep rocky ribs. This face is subject to regular avalanches, some of gigantic proportions.

The magnificent South Face of Nanga Parbat, the Rupal Face, boasts the biggest vertical drop in the world.

future climbing

A winter ascent is perhaps the biggest challenge. Then there is the Mummery Rib on the Diamir Flank. The Mazeno Ridge, with its seven summits, is regarded by many as the greatest ridge challenge left on an 8000m (26,000ft) peak.

Right **The massive Rupal Face of Nanga Parbat, first climbed in 1970 by the Messner brothers.**

1970 Italian brothers R and G Messner made the first traverse of the mountain. They ascended via the Rupal Face ('Rupal Direct'), then descended on the Diamir Side via the Mummery Rib. Günther died in an avalanche and Reinhold lost six toes to frostbite.

1976 H Schell led R Schauer, H Sturm, and S Gimpel (Austrian) to the top via a route on the left of the Rupal Flank.

1978 R Messner made the first completely solo ascent of an 8000m (26,000ft) peak, climbing an audacious new route on the Diamir Flank. He returned by a different and new route.

1984 Liliane Barrard (French) became the first woman to climb Nanga Parbat – this was via the 'Kinshofer Route'.

1985 Wanda Rutkiewicz and two companions, Anna Czerwinska and Krystyna Palmowska (Polish) became the first all-woman team on the summit.

1985 J Kukuczka and P Kalmas (Polish) put up a new route on the South East Pillar. Kalmas died in an avalanche.

1992–5 Britain's D Scott mounted three unsuccessful expeditions in 1992, 1993, and 1995 to climb the seemingly endless Mazeno Ridge. Dogged by avalanches and despite the presence of great climbers like Poland's V Kurtyka and Russia's S Efimov, Scott managed to complete only the first three of the seven Mazeno Peaks.

1995 The last new route was put up by Japanese climbers led by H Sakai. It is a direct ascent, via the North West Spur, onto the Silver Saddle, at 7400m (24,300ft). It then follows the original 1953 'Buhl Route' to the top.

RAKHIOT (NORTH EAST) FLANK

Rakhiot Peak

Moor's Head

North East Ridge

Silver Saddle

North Peak

North East Face

North West Ridge

Rakhiot Glacier

As for all expeditionary climbing, times taken and grades are subject to conditions on the day, and to climber fitness and acclimatization. Most climbing on Nanga Parbat is still a lengthy business, undertaken with the preliminary build-up of camps, though there have been notable alpine ascents.

rakhiot (north east) flank
1 Rakhiot Route

H Buhl 1953

Famous first ascent route. It is long and arduous, requiring at least five camps. Starting from Fairy Meadow, it passes beneath Rakhiot Peak and onto the enormous North East Ridge, past the Moor's Head rock outcrop, beneath the two Silver Peaks, and over the North Peak. Below the Moor's Head there are steep avalanche-prone slopes. The length of the route and its high objective dangers mean it has received only one other ascent in 43 years – it is not ideal for modern climbing techniques.

2 North West Spur

H Sakai and Tchibe Institute Expedition 1995

To avoid some of the dangers on the

Rakhiot, this route follows a quicker and more direct way onto the North West Ridge, via a spur rising to the North West Peak of the Silver Saddle. The route required four camps and comprised a 600m (2000ft) rock face up to Grade IV, a 300m (1000ft) ice tower (4 pitches of 65°), and a crack of Grade V before joining the 'Rakhiot Route' at Camp IV, 7350m (24,000ft).

diamir (west) flank
3 Kinshofer Route

T Kinshofer, A Mannhardt, and S Low 1962

Accepted as today's normal route, but not an easy climb. A tough start up a steep snow couloir (often fixed), a 60m (200ft) rock step at 5900m (19,400ft) to the Kinshofer Icefield, and then the Bhazin basin to join route (1). Most expeditions follow the final variation first done in 1978, which cuts below the summit ridge. 4025m (13,200ft) of vertical ascent.

4 Messner Solo Route

R Messner 1978

Unrepeated and highly dangerous climb to the right of the Mummery Rib; constantly swept by avalanches.

An earthquake forced Messner to descend via a different route. This remarkable solo took five days.

rupal (south) flank
5 Schell Route

H Schell, R Schauer, H Sturm, and S Gimpel 1976

To the left of the main Rupal Face, this is one of the most direct routes to the summit. Most attempts have been beset by rockfall and injuries.

6 Messner Direct

R and G Messner 1970

Severe route directly up the centre of the Rupal Face. The most difficult climbing is above 7300m (24,000ft) in the Merkl Gully (70°), and is subject to sustained avalanches and rockfall. Vertical height gain 4500m (14,800ft).

7 Polish Spur

J Kukuczka, Z Heinrich, C Carsolio, and S Lobodzinski 1985

On the right-hand side of the Rupal Buttress, another awesome route by Kukuczka. An endless stream of avalanches bedevil the steep runnels and couloirs that make up much of the unrepeated climb.

how to get to nanga parbat

Fly to Islamabad. Base camps for most routes lie up to three days' march and a 12-hour jeep ride away from the regional capital of Gilgit, so it is best to hire a minibus and drive down the Chinese-built Karakoram highway to Gilgit (two days) or fly there from the capital. The latter option gives splendid views of the Nanga Parbat massif but is subject to weather delays.

At Gilgit, hire a jeep and obtain any remaining supplies. It is then a 12-hour drive to Astor and onto Tarshing, where you can hire porters for climbing on the Rupal Side; or three hours by jeep to Rakhiot bridge over the River Indus for Fairy Meadow and the Rakhiot Flank; and four hours by jeep to Bunar, where you can hire porters on the Indus for the Diamir Side.

Note: take care when hiring porters; hire a representative sample, not all from one village or headman. This avoids strikes and grievances in an area where the waving of Kalashnikovs is not uncommon. Porter standards are not in the Sherpa league – be self-sufficient.

North Peak

Kinshofer Icefield

North Shoulder   Main Summit

Bazhin Gap

Mummery Rib

DIAMIR (WEST) FLANK

Bazhin Basin

Mazeno Gap

Main Summit   **RUPAL (SOUTH) FLANK**

Merkl Gully

Silver Saddle

facilities

You will have to buy most of your supplies in Islamabad. Vegetables and eggs can be bought in areas local to the mountain, but shops have very little.

when to climb

June–August are the main summer climbing months. Nanga Parbat is much less effected by the monsoon than the Himalayan peaks in Nepal.

gear

Full high-Himalayan gear.

maps and guidebooks

The 1936 German map of the Nanga Parbat massif, 1:50,000, printed by Alpenvereinskarte (DAV), is essential. There is also a good map in *Mountaineering Maps of the World, vol II; Karakoram and Hindu Kush*. *The Pakistan Trekking Guide*, Isobel Shaw (Odyssey Guides, Hong Kong, 1993) is useful. I recommend anyone going to Nanga Parbat to read the following texts: *Alpine Journal* vol 18, 1896, no 131, pages 17–32: Collie's account of

A F Mummery's 1895 attempt on the mountain; *Nanga Parbat Pilgrimage, the autobiography of Hermann Buhl* (1954, and Hodder & Stoughton, 1981); and *Solo Nanga Parbat*, Reinhold Messner, translated by Audrey Salkeld (Kaye & Ward, 1980).

language

Urdu and local dialects. Your Liaison Officer will speak good English, and so too might some of your porters.

rescue and insurance

There are no organized rescue services, and insurance is recommended.

red tape

Formalities are completed at the Ministry of Tourism, including the appointment of a military Liaison Officer who will accompany your expedition to base camp and possibly remain with you until you have completed your climb. An agency, such as Nazir Sabir Expeditions, can secure climbing permits and porter insurance as well as overseeing the import of vital gas cylinders.

breaking surface
roger mear

"By 4am we were ready to emerge from our tent. Periodic glances through the flap had revealed a continuous deterioration in the weather. Now it was snowing. We stepped out as the dawn turned the blackness to grey and then to an eerie white fog that hid, but in some way intensified, the power of the void that slid from beneath us.

We stood at either end of our inadequate home-made platform, the tent between us. Snow fell in minute flakes, each adding its weight to the scale that was tipping against us. I felt a surge of frustration, drawn from the energy I was holding for this day. It raged in silence against the acceptance of this soft futility. Better to be stopped by forces that blast the need for reasonable decisions to hell. The dream was lost. We both knew it.

But, if we were to return now it would be because we had prejudged the outcome, not because we could no longer raise our bodies higher, nor because the margin of survival was too small. I needed to do battle before giving in, to bang my head against the wall until I, and not reason, cried 'enough'! So we agreed not to decide, agreed to make the mountain force the issue.

Leaving our shelter and carrying no more then we might for a winter walk in Scotland, we made our way upwards into the cloud through knee-deep snow with a weight of pessimism adding to the gloom. A band of sombre cliffs loomed up before us, vertical and streaked with black, higher and wider than we could discern. We traversed right beneath them until there was only white above, and then back left on steepening ground below the threat of icy slabs. Occasional isolated outcroppings of rock protruded through the snow. These features were less parts of a mountain than events that floated vaguely within the fixed whiteness of some abstract space. Gradually the conditions worsened. The further we went, the greater became the force that called us back. Visibility was down to a few metres, snowfall was increasing and, worse, a wind threatened the makings of a blizzard. Our way, if not lost, was not found, and the deep snow that brought such drudgery to each upward step grew deeper.

Our 9am deadline came without improvement and passed without a word. At 10am we stopped to gulp a drink. The altimeter confirmed our slow progress. We resolved to continue, but only so long as we felt strong and in control. Somehow it then became easier. Though I knew Dave felt it all to be a waste of energy, I no longer sensed his unvoiced call to be gone. There was no

... the impossibility of maintaining a rhythm of steps and breath was debilitating.

Top left **Dave Walsh on the Diamir Glacier approaching the Diamir Face.**

Above **Dave Walsh passing an abandoned Spanish tent at Camp 3.**

Right **Climbing towards the summit couloir.**

arbitrary time by which all the answers had to be in place, only a continual assessment of the rightness of what we were doing. We were keeping open the option of continuing; nothing more. We were living our dream – climbing upwards into a storm somewhere near the top of Nanga Parbat.

Then, at noon, we emerged from the whiteness, breaking surface above an ocean of cloud to a new world of hard sunlight and deep blue sky, golden rock and glittering snows. A cold wind blew flags of spindrift from the summit ridge 400m above us. There was a feeling of joy, of justice, of thankfulness at being given a chance. We deserved our chance and understood that success now rested solely with us.

The 500m we had climbed from the tent had taken us more than seven hours. That rate had to be bettered, or the sun would set before we reached the summit. An unprotected bivouac was not to be contemplated. Both of us, I think, were confident of surviving a night in the open, but not with the inevitable price of frozen hands and feet. With such injuries, how would we get

break and we would plunge through to our knees. Trying to read the nuances of the snow proved an absorbing game, with each step bringing reward or disappointment. Yet the impossibility of maintaining a rhythm of steps and breath was debilitating. Climbing at altitude is extremely humbling. The horizon of possibility closes in. Only simple intellectual tasks and gentler physical goals are achievable. Only well practised routines and techniques so ingrained as to be automatic keep you from making an error.

Armed with ice axe and ski stick, we took turns to break a zigzag trail between the confines of the gully. 100m in the hour. It is a slow race but exciting none the less. At around 8000m we were lured out of the gully by the promise of swifter progress on the warm-coloured rock to our right. We had been joined by the rope all day. Though it did little more than hang between us, it offered the comforting reassurance that it was ready to hand; it guarded against loneliness. The idea of adding its weight to the pack was discouraging but, as we began to follow more independent and less predictable paths among the broken rocks, the thin cord snagged at every turn. Either its tautness was hurrying me into breathlessness or, if Dave paused, it gathered under my feet, threatening to tangle my crampons.

'Take the rope off?' I asked, hoping to rid ourselves of its encumbrance. But if we left it, would we ever find it? I was too knackered to take it. 'I'll coil it if you carry it,' I offered, praying that would seem fair deal enough.

8000m was higher than I'd climbed before. This arbitrary barrier was a personal frontier. I was apprehensive of the unknown, worried my body might not perform. Dave had been there before, had climbed Cho Oyu alone. He had been strong enough, his brain had survived. Was he stronger than me?

Ahead on the ridge a shattered mound of stones stood proud, a white crown against a blue sky. It deserved to be the summit but I knew it was not. Attracted, I worked my path of little decisions towards it. This foot here, that foot there. There is pleasure when a choice leads to an unbroken pattern of steps. Each breath a step … each step a breath.

We reached the top at 4.15pm. Dave stood above me with his feet firmly astride, braced against the wind, and the straps of his near-empty pack flaying. It was an emotional meeting and one of unexpected strength, for I did not at first share his euphoria. Summits have never held great importance for me, other than playing a vital part in the form of a climb: without a summit a climb is aesthetically faulted, its end too arbitrary. The summit provides a reason for turning back and climbing down, but rarely, in my experience, a climax. For me the emotional peak had been when we rose from the ocean of cloud when, emerging from the storm, we were presented with the gift of a chance.

We hugged, a single, long, strong hug – a deep and honest hug of thanks and friendship – that charged the moment of the summit with a significance I shall always treasure. It would have been good to linger on the top. To soak up that beautiful, enchanted place in the golden light and watch the sun sink into the sea of boiling cloud that flowed, in a slow, interminable current, out of Asia and washed upon the mountain island, the westernmost bastion of the Himalaya.

ourselves down the mountain? We agreed to keep going until 5pm when, summit or not, we would return.

The clouds had parted to reveal the mouth of a narrow, snow-filled gully cutting the final rocks. I had worried that in the storm we might miss this key to the summit, but instinctively we had groped our way to it. As we climbed out of the storm, we also climbed out of the deepening snow onto an older surface of wind-carved sastrugi. Sometimes we walked with delightful ease upon plates of soft meringue, into which the points of our crampons sank without complaint; more often the crust would

1898 The geography of the mountain and potential approaches for climbing were established during Douglas Freshfield's celebrated circuit of the massif, with geologist Edmund Garwood and the Italian photographer Vittorio Sella.
1905 The first attempt on the South West or Yalung Face, organized by the Swiss Dr Jacot-Guillarmod and

A Crowley (British), did not get above 6100m (20,000ft). It led to the deaths of Lt A Pache (Swiss) and three porters in an avalanche.
1930 An international expedition, led by Swiss Professor G O Dyhrenfurth, withdrew from the North West Face after its most experienced Sherpa, Chettan, was crushed in a torrent of ice blocks.

1929 and 1931 Two Bavarian expeditions led by P Bauer concentrated on the North East Spur. Two years after their first attempt, they reached a point at 7730m (25,360ft) where the Spur abuts the North Ridge, but were defeated by dangerous windslab conditions.
1955 The first ascent by a British party led by C Evans followed the general line on the South West Face investigated

the year before. Two pairs reached the summit: J Brown and G Band on 25 May, and N Hardie and T Streather on 26 May. In deference to the religious feelings of the Sikkimese, the final cone of snow was left untrodden.
1973 The West (Yalung Kang) Summit was climbed by a Japanese party.
1977 The second ascent was made by an Indian Army team, led by

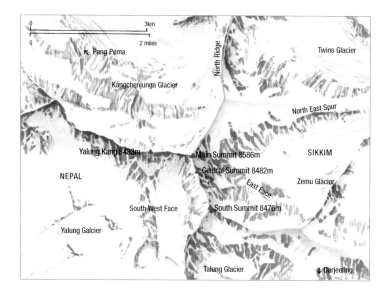

kangchenjunga

george band

Kangchenjunga, at 8586m (28,170ft), is the world's third-highest mountain, after Everest and K2. Visible from the Indian hill station of Darjeeling, 70km (over 40 miles) away, it dominates the north-western horizon. Forming the frontier ridge between Nepal and Sikkim, Kangchenjunga is only 18km (11 miles) from the Tibetan border. It lies slightly south of the main Himalayan chain and so bears the brunt of the summer monsoon, which provides it with a heavy snow cover; it is renowned for its avalanches.

The people of Sikkim regard Kangchenjunga as a holy mountain, and worship it at the Festival of Snows. Its many summits give it its name, meaning the Five Sacred Treasuries of the Snows.

faces, ridges, and peaks

There are four separate summits on the mountain: the Main 8586m (28,170ft); Central, 8482m (27,829ft); South, 8476m (27,810ft); and West, 8433m (27,668ft), also known as Yalung Kang.

The Main Summit is bounded by three faces: the East Face, from which the Zemu Glacier flows; the North West Face, where

the Kangchenjunga Glacier starts; and the South West Face, from where the Yalung Glacier runs.

A prominent feature of the very steep East Face is the North East Spur, which has provided the only route on this side and is a succession of icy towers and cornices abutting the North Ridge. The North West Face is enormously impressive seen from the base camp at Pang Pema. It consists of several horizontal rock bands, alternating with hanging glaciers. Both of these faces have had very few ascents. They are especially exposed to the jetstream winds that batter the upper slopes.

The majority of ascents, and particularly those of the satellite peaks, are by the South West Face. A major feature of this face is the glaciated Great Shelf at 7000m (23,000ft), which is reached by climbing a rock buttress and steep icefall. Summit routes are launched from a camp on this shelf. This 'Original Route' has been climbed solo and is often accomplished without the aid of supplementary oxygen. However, the unexplained disappearance of renowned climbers like Wanda Rutkiewitz in 1992 and Benoit Chamoux and Pierre Royer in 1995 have emphasized the need to treat the mountain with respect – do not underestimate the debilitating effect of overexertion at extreme altitudes.

The South Face, on which no one has yet set foot because of its sheer difficulty, falls from the South Summit to the Talung Glacier. It can be seen magnificently from the Guicha La, 4940m (16,200ft), which is a popular Sikkimese trekking objective.

Kangchenjunga is reckoned to be one of the hardest 8000m (26,000ft) peaks. It has a reputation for having harder technical climbing problems and objective dangers. Because of this reputation, and its relative isolation in the north-east corner of Nepal, it has had far fewer ascents than Everest: less than 50 separate ascents of the Main Peak by the end of 1996. The mountain was not successfully climbed by a woman until 1998.

future climbing

The East and South Faces in Sikkim present ample scope for modern mixed routes, spiced with objective danger. The left-bounding ridge of the South Face was partly followed from the South West (Nepalese) Side by Andrej Stremfelj and Marko Prezelj in 1991, but the very long, right-bounding ridge, rising from the Zemu Gap at 5861m (19,230ft), is still untouched, leaving plenty of scope for future generations.

Right **Peter Boardman (foreground) and Joe Tasker resting at the Pinnacles on the West Ridge, just below the Main Summit of Kangchenjunga.**

Col N Kumar. They completed the Bavarians' route via the North East Spur.

1978 The Central and South Peaks were climbed by a Polish expedition.

1979 The third ascent of the Main Peak, the first from the North West, without supplementary oxygen, was achieved by a lightweight British/French party – D Scott, P Boardman, J Tasker, and G Bettembourg.

1980 Ascents became more frequent, and were normally via the South West Face. The Japanese were the first to risk the North West Face direct.

1986 First winter ascent of the South West Face by a Polish/Mexican group.

1989 A massive Russian expedition made the first traverse of all four peaks in both directions. 28 climbers reached one or more of these summits.

1991 Slovenians A Stremfelj and M Prezelj put up a remarkable route to the South Peak.

1998 Ginette Harrison (British) became the first woman to successfully summit the mountain.

Yalung
Kang

Main Summit

Central Summit

South Summit

Great Shelf

Because of their long and difficult nature, Himalayan climbs are not often given grades.

south west face

Most of the climbing is done via this face – Yalung Kang and the Central and South Summits are normally climbed from the Great Shelf.

1 Original Route – Main Summit
British Team led by C Evans 1955
This has now become the standard route being relatively free from objective danger. The original team spent a month setting up the route using siege tactics. Nowadays, if well-acclimatized, a party could do this route in about a week.

central and south summits
Polish teams made the first ascents of the Central and South Summits in 1978. These were later repeated by Russians (*see below*).

2 Russian Route
Russian Expedition 1989
The Russians climbed and traversed all four peaks – an outstanding and unrepeated achievement.

3 Slovene Route
A Stremfelj and M Prezelj 1991
This route climbs the South Peak by way of the South Ridge, a most remarkable ascent that is still unrepeated. The whole expedition was later awarded the prestigious Piolet d'Or for its achievement.

north west face

The North West Face is protected by formidable bands of ice cliffs that either have to be tackled direct, which is a very risky and dangerous undertaking, or circumvented via the North Col.

4 North Col Route
D Scott, P Boardman, J Tasker, and G Bettembourg 1979
When putting up this route, the original team avoided the ice cliffs by climbing steeply to the North Col and then, after experiencing very severe winds and storms, climbing slightly below the line of the North Ridge to join the West Ridge and the 1955 original line of ascent.

5 Messner Route
R Messner 1982
Messner climbed the lower ice cliff direct, and went on to join the 'North Col Route' (4).

6 Japanese Route
Japanese Expedition 1980
The Japanese were the first successful team to tackle the ice cliffs directly. Their route is still unrepeated.

east face

The approach by the Zemu Glacier and the North East Spur used by the Bavarians and Indians has only had a handful of ascents, and is the only route on this side.

Main Summit

North Col

④

⑥

⑤

④

④

how to get to kangchenjunga

Travel from Kathmandu by road via Dharan Baza to Basantpur roadhead, then trek for two weeks to get to Pang Pema, the base camp for the North Side. Alternatively, fly to Biratnagar in south-east Nepal or take a light aircraft to Suketar, 2300m (7550ft). It is then a 10-day trek either to the north-west or south-west base camps. Approach the East Side through Sikkim via Darjeeling and Gangtok. Green Lake Base Camp, beside the Zemu Glacier, is a 3-day trek from the Lachen roadhead.

facilities

The nearest settlement in Nepal is Ghunsa, which is slowly developing into a trekking village. It has a police post, a shop, and a small 'hotel' and is a 3-day trek from the base camps.

when to climb

The two main seasons are April–May or September–October, either before or after the summer monsoon. Trekking parties usually favour the more stable autumn, but, if you wish to climb at extreme altitude, the wind and cold may be more favourable in May than October.

gear

The average climber benefits from supplementary oxygen, although an increasing number climb without it.

On the 'North Col Route' (4), fixed ropes assist a quick descent in bad weather. On the 'Original Route' (1), light sectional ladders keep the supply lines open at bergschrunds and in the lower icefall.

maps and guidebooks

There is a rare Marcel Kurz map of Kangchenjunga, 1:100,000 (1931), and a Swiss Foundation for Alpine Research map of the Sikkim Himalaya, 1:150,000 (1981). Various trekking guidebooks of Nepal Himalaya (eg Lonely Planet) describe the approach routes.

language

Your sirdar will understand English.

rescue and insurance

In a real emergency, helicopters can reach the base camps, but there are no organized services. It is best to carry full climbing insurance.

red tape

In the 1950s climbers had free access to the Nepalese side of Kangchenjunga from Darjeeling by crossing the Singalila Ridge that forms the frontier with Sikkim. Now only Indians and Nepalese are given access. In both Nepal and Sikikim, permits are expensive. Sikkim is most expensive: an entry permit is required and fees have to be paid to the Indian Mountaineering Federation and the Sikkim authorities.

9th century Legendary ascent of Everest on a ray of sunlight by the Buddhist Saint Padma Sambhava, also known as Guru Rinpoche, when he introduced Buddhism to the inhabitants of Tibet.
1808 The India Survey was undertaken by the British military to provide reliable maps for maintaining dominion over India. This effort led to the incredibly accurate Great Trigonometrical Survey

of India and the Himalaya, and the discovery of Everest as the world's highest peak.
1854 Surveyor General A Waugh (British) calibrated figures from the previous decade and ascertained that the Survey's 'Peak XV' at 8840m (29,002ft) stood higher than K2, in Pakistan, and Kangchenjunga, further to the east in the Nepal Himalaya.

1865 The Royal Geographical Society in London officially adopted 'Everest' as the name for the peak, despite the reservations of Sir George Everest, the Surveyor General of India whom this was meant to honour.
1903-4 During the Younghusband Mission to Lhasa (a chapter in 'the Great Game' conflict between Russia and Britain), Everest was photographed

from Khamba Dzong, 150km (90 miles) away. Two officers from Younghusband's party came within 96km (60 miles) of the mountain on a reconnaissance.
1913 British photographer and entrepreneur Captain J Noel, travelling illicitly from India, also reached a point within 96km (60 miles) of Everest. After World War I he lectured at the Royal

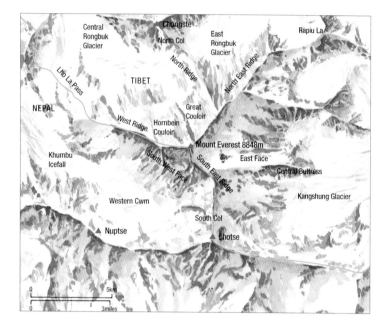

mount everest

peter athans

Situated on the frontier of north-east Nepal and south-east Tibet, Everest dominates the furthest eastern grouping of 8000m (26,000ft) peaks, of which there are six. Lhotse, Makalu, and Kangchenjunga may be found to the south-east, while Cho Oyo and Shisha Pangma are due west.

When George Mallory saw Everest for the first time in 1921, it was as a dream-like, fragmented vision, through cloud. Being unable to perceive its entire form only heightened the mystery for him. Piercing the veil to understand what Everest represented to Mallory and, more expansively, what it represents today and what motivates mountaineers to climb it, is no less daunting a task than scaling the mountain itself.

George Mallory took part in all the expeditions of the 1920s and became entranced with the dream of Everest's summit. In his last attempt to climb it, with novice Andrew Irvine, in 1924, he disappeared, and one of mountaineering's greatest mysteries was born. His name is enshrined in climbing history along with

his cryptic utterance that he climbed Everest 'because it's there'. Rendered to hackneyed cliché by constant repetition, the phrase echoes emptily through nearly 75 years of climbing. The first unqualified ascent of Everest, by Edmund Hillary and Sherpa Tenzing Norgay, was made in 1953 but, even without this triumph, Everest is a more timely media topic than ever today – and, usually, not in the most flattering terms.

Though routinely denounced as a 'mountain of garbage' and popularly believed to be overrun by wealthy, unqualified, and luckless clients, shepherded by avaricious and unprofessional guides, the truth is less damning. While the environmental ethics of the past have allowed desecrations, current practices in Nepal have improved the aesthetics of Everest's Base Camp and Camp 2, concentrating the need for further action above the Western Cwm. To forbid guided expeditions would not, in itself, exclude unqualified climbers from the mountain: it is often the case that private expeditions have equally or less qualified teams. Having said that, any guides willing to take on this most difficult of objectives need to understand the qualifications of the climbers they guide and, further, to approach the ascent of Everest conservatively and with the utmost humility.

ridges, faces, and peaks
The name 'Everest' was chosen in 1865 to honour the Surveyor General Sir George Everest who undetook the tremendous effort of the Great Trigonometrical Survey, although he himself found the choice embarrassing. Previously it had been known merely as 'Peak XV'. The name Everest supplanted the fine local Tibetan name, Chomolungma (Mother Goddess of the Earth); the mountain's Nepalese name is Sagamartha (Head of the Ocean).

Everest can be described as a monolithic, massive, and somewhat distorted pyramid with three dramatic ridges and an equal number of precipitous faces. Its Nepalese side is approached via the Khumbu Glacier – a steep and serious icefall that leads into the Western Cwm, the high basin circumscribed by Everest, Lhotse, and Nuptse. In Tibet the Rongbuk Valley gives access to the North Side of the mountain.

The first expeditions to Everest were incredulous at its rocky character since, from a distance, it looked like a massive, supernal white spire. Its varied strata are wonderfully visible, on the

Right **Looking down the awe-inspiring Khumbu Icefall where the glacier squeezes between the West Shoulder of Everest and the flanks of Nuptse, falling steeply for 600m (2000ft). The broken ice, scarred by huge crevasses, is constantly on the move.**

Geographical Society, aiming to inspire the early climbing efforts.

1921 Led by Lieutenant Howard-Bury, the first British expedition reconnoitred the possibility of climbing Everest. Among members of the team was the charismatic G Mallory, who would play a part in all three of the British expeditions of the 1920s. The party reached the North Col.

1922 The second pre-World War II British expedition reached 8320m (27,300ft) on Everest.

1924 Mallory and young A Irvine disappeared during a climb on Everest; no one knows how high they climbed but their story has slipped into legend (*see pages 252–3*). H Somervell and Major E Norton reached 8578m (28,126ft) without oxygen equipment.

1933–6 A series of five – four official and one illicit – British expeditions gained dramatic heights on Everest but each one failed to reach the summit. M Wilson, the 'Mad Yorkshireman', piloted his Gypsy Moth aeroplane *Ever Wrest* to India, travelled overland to Everest, and then sadly perished during a solo attempt on the peak.

1951 The Everest Reconnaissance expedition, led by E Shipton (British) went to the south of Everest after Nepal opened its borders to foreign explorers. The team, including E Hillary (New Zealander), reached the entrance of the Western Cwm above the icefall.

1952 A Swiss expedition (with Sherpa Tenzing Norgay) led by R Lambert almost climbed the South Summit.

1953 Hillary and Tenzing became the first to gain Everest's summit during the British expedition led by J Hunt.

1960 Wang Fu-chou and Chu Yin-hua (Chinese) with Gonbu (Tibetan) summited via the North and North East Ridges.

1963 Americans T Hornbein and W Unsoeld succeeded in climbing the West Ridge and then descended via the South East Ridge, completing both a

new route and making the first traverse of the mountain.

1975 Climbers on a British expedition – D Haston, D Scott, P Boardman, Sherpa Pertemba, and (probably) M Burke – summited Everest via the 'South West Face' route (9). Film-maker Burke disappeared on summit day. Junko Tabei (Japanese) became the first woman to climb Everest. She

climbed the mountain via the 'South Col' route (10).

1978 R Messner (Italian) and P Habeler (Austrian) were the first to climb Everest without supplementary oxygen,

1979 A Stremflez and N Zaplotnik (Slovenian) ascended the difficult and continuous 'West Ridge Direct' (7).

1980 R Messner became the first to solo Everest, climbing the North Face. He

used no supplementary oxygen, and no other expeditions were present. In the same year, also on the North Face, T Shigehiro and T Ozaki (Japanese) established an elegant superdirect route by climbing the lower extension of the Hornbein Couloir (see route 5).

1982 Soviet mountaineers completed a bold, hard new line (see route 8) on the sheer buttress to the east of the

Above **Picking a safe route through the Khumbu Icefall is always complex. These days, for a fee, one of the expeditions on the mountain usually equips and monitors the safest passage on behalf of all the others.**

north east ridge From the summit down into Tibet, the sinuous North East Ridge runs for 5km (3 miles), terminating at a high pass known as the Rapiu La and separating the East Rongbuk Glacier from the Kangshung Glacier like a great blade. More than 1km (¾ mile) from Everest's summit along this ridge, at a height of approximately 8300m (27,230ft), there is a distinctive

South West and North West Faces particularly, the most prominent feature being the golden limestone layer, known as the Yellow Band, that extends around the peak.

shoulder from which another ridge descends to the north towards a glaciated pass, Chang La, or North Col, with the dramatic peak Changste, also known as Everest's North Peak, positioned behind it.

The North East Ridge was the objective of remarkable early British expeditions, and ascends two obvious uplifts or steps, where harder limestone surmounts the Yellow Band. It was somewhere in the vicinity of these First and Second Steps that Mallory and Irvine disappeared in 1924.

west ridge The West Ridge is of similar length to the North East Ridge but drops irregularly: first quite steeply to around 7500m (24,600ft), where it is then nearly horizontal, with a slight uplift towards the West Shoulder at 7300m (23,950ft). From there, it descends to the Lho La (a pass to the south, not to be confused with the South Col) and the top of the Central Rongbuk Glacier. With its great length and steep nature, especially above 7500m (24,600ft), the West Ridge offers some of the most technically difficult climbing on the peak.

south east ridge The last major ridge is the South East Ridge, which runs down to the South Col at 7990m (26,200ft) in about 1.5 km (1 mile). This provided the line of ascent for Hillary and Sherpa Tenzing in 1953. Its most prominent feature is the South Summit at 8600m (28,200ft). Approximately 100m (325ft) summitwards from the South Summit is the Hillary Step, a 12m (40ft) ramp and chimney.

south west face The expansive face between the South East and West Ridges is the overpowering and technical South West Face. For all practical purposes a rock wall, the upper 700m (2300ft) is composed of friable schistose shale and so precipitous that it offers an extreme challenge to modern mountaineers.

north west face The massive North West Face extends in a concave plane (averaging approximately 45°) between the West Ridge and the North Col. Its most distinctive features are its couloirs, which provide the most frequent lines of ascent for modern parties. To the right (west) is the Hornbein Couloir, below which an expansive snow band, aptly named the White Limbo by an Australian group, extends across the face. Below that, positioned elegantly in line with the Hornbein, is the Japanese Couloir. When these two are linked, they provide an impressively direct line above the Central Rongbuk Glacier.

Closer to the North Col, and above the amorphous White Limbo, rises the Great (or Norton) Couloir. This is recognizable as a huge gouge, almost in the centre of the face, beginning at around 7400m (24,280ft).

Access to the entire North West Face may be achieved from the North Col or the Central Rongbuk Glacier. The strata of the face is such that traverses are possible on discontinuous, rock-strewn ledges.

A variety of couloirs lower down, the most notable being the Japanese, gains the upper ramparts of the face. It should be noted, however,

that the angle of the lower face is critical to loading snow and, consequently, there is high avalanche danger. The upper, steeper regions of the face are less prone to this risk.

east face Everest's last major facet is the East Face, enormous and broad, and flanking not only the North East Ridge but also the summit and the South East Ridge to the South Col. Dropping from a height of 7884m (25,870ft) from the North East Ridge, is the East Rib (or 'Fantasy Ridge'), which descends abruptly to the Kangshung Glacier. Further south-west are the Trinity Gullies, which plunge from a broad, hanging glacier at about 7500m (24,610ft). At the very head of the Kangshung Glacier, the face above separates into two buttresses: the first, northern, one, the Central Buttress, has as its apex the South Summit; the second,

Right **A cluster of box tents on the South West Face. Finding a way up this steep face was the major problem of the early 1970s, solved by a team led by Chris Bonington.**

to its left, the South East Spur, rises to the South Col. Both have been climbed and include in their lower sections some of the most technical mixed rock

Above The prominent easternmost rib of the East Face has become known as 'Fantasy Ridge' – one of the great challenges awaiting future climbers.

and ice on Mount Everest. The regions above 7000m (23,000ft) are less devious, but present prolonged snow and ice climbing.

future climbing

In considering the future of climbing on Everest, the question of motivation and what the peak might represent arises again: one person may climb to escape our over-mechanized and complicated society; another may choose Everest because it is the absolute limit to which we can climb; yet another may be inspired by the camaraderie that exists between Western and Sherpa climbers and by the desire to be a part of the great common objective – the climb. Everest's current routes offer objectives and answers to all these motives, with room for new ones as well.

In the 1950s the ascent of Everest by its 'South Col Route' was the *sine qua non* of mountaineering challenge. As the 21st century looms, will mountaineers take on such extreme projects as the traverse of Everest-Lhotse-Nuptse, the complete ascent of the East Face's 'Fantasy Ridge', or attempt the ultimate direct line on Everest's South West Face? If the answer is 'yes' (which it must be), to these or any number of new firsts, Everest will remain in the forefront of high-altitude mountaineering endeavour.

north side

Base camp is at the snout of the Rongbuk (or Rongphu) Glacier, a short distance below the junction with the East Rongbuk Valley.

1 North Ridge/North East Ridge
F Wang, Gonbu, and Y Chu 1960
The most popular route from the Tibetan side, this begins by ascending the East Rongbuk Glacier and climbing to the North Col via avalanche-prone snow slopes. After establishing a series of camps above the col and negotiating the obstacles of the First and Second Steps, the summit is reached via a moderately angled ridge.

2 The North East Ridge or Integral Route
Pinnacles section: H Taylor and R Brice 1982
Takes a line from the Rapiu La, over the North East Shoulder and on towards the summit dome, a total length of about 5.5km (3½ miles). It includes difficult mixed alpine climbing, especially below the North East Shoulder and the Main Summit. Three prominent gendarmes, the Pinnacles, must be surmounted before the junction with the North Ridge. From here to the summit dome is along the moderately angled arête described under route (1). Once the Pinnacles had been negotiated for the first time, all sections of this route had been climbed. However, to date no one has completed it as a single enterprise.

3 Messner Variant
R Messner 1980
While not an independent line for its entire length (joins route 4), the Messner variation is important for its futuristic concept of climbing alpine style and even solo, without supplementary oxygen in the high Himalaya. After reaching the North Col, it continues to approximately 7500m (24,600ft) and, over broken rising terrain, traverses into the Great Couloir, ascending this to the summit dome and final ridge.

4 The Great (Norton) Couloir Direct
T Macartney-Snape and G Mortimer 1984
From the 'White Limbo' area in the centre of the North West Face, the Great Couloir (first approached by Norton in 1924) rises to the North Ridge just below the Main Summit. Access to this route is via a shallow couloir leading into the White Limbo directly below the conspicuously massive Great Couloir.

5 The Japanese Couloir
T Shigehiro and T Ozaki 1980
Ascends from the Central Rongbuk Glacier into the White Limbo snow slopes directly below the Hornbein Couloir, then moderates to steep alpine and mixed climbing through the couloir itself, from where the route finishes with a rising traverse south towards the West Ridge. Camps may be found above the glacier at 6870m (22,540ft), 7650m (25,100ft), and 8200m (26,900ft).

west side

This side offers the most direct line on the peak and the longest climb (7). The West Ridge is accessible from either Nepal or (much more easily) Tibet.

6 West Ridge
W Unsoeld and T Hornbein 1963
(exiting via the Hornbein Couloir)
In 1963 the Americans came from the Western Cwm at 6470m (21,200ft) to gain the West Shoulder in a rising traverse. The same spot can also be attained from the Central Rongbuk Glacier in Tibet. The route then follows the ridge proper, usually on the northern flank, to where it steepens and abuts the summit pyramid at 7620m (25,000ft). Camps may be located at: 6100m (20,000ft), 6550m (21,500ft), 7170m (23,525ft), 7520m (24,700ft), and 8290m (27,200ft).

7 West Ridge Direct
J Zaplotnik, A Stremfelj, and S Belak 1979
Climbers attempting this 'integrale' must gain the Lho La, either via the Central Rongbuk Glacier in Tibet or directly up the Lho La South Face from Nepal's Everest Base Camp. The latter requires difficult aid and free climbing with some interesting route finding. From the Lho La, the route ascends on the northern flank of the ridge proper through mixed terrain and a series of discontinuous gullies to just north-east of the West Shoulder. It then follows the ridgeline towards the summit pyramid, traverses north into a broad concave face, and ascends to the last camp at 8395m (27,520ft) via a series of ridges and a short chimney. It finishes with mixed climbing through the Yellow Band in steep gullies and onward through the rock and snow of the final ridge. Camps may be located at: 6770m (22,200ft), 7170m (23,525ft), 7520m (24,700ft), and 8120m (26,600ft).

Labels on image: Main Summit · Great Couloir · Hornbein Couloir · Second Step · White Limbo · First Step · North East Ridge · West Ridge · North Ridge · North East Shoulder · Pinnacles · Japanese Couloir · Changste

how to get to mount everest

For all routes on the Nepalese (southern) side of the mountain, you start from Kathmandu (connections with Europe or Thailand). After protocol formalities are completed (*see red tape*), it is possible to fly to the village of Lukla, which is quite literally the gateway to the Everest region, the Khumbu. You can also reach Lukla by taking a bus to the eastern city of Jiri (eight hours from Kathmandu) and then walking for approximately one week. After Lukla, proceed to the commercial centre of Khumbu, Namche Bazaar, then follow the Dudh Kosi watershed to the Great Khumbu Glacier and Everest Base Camp at 5335m (17,500ft). If unacclimatized, plan on at least a week to get from Namche Bazaar to base camp.

All the Tibetan routes may be approached from Kathmandu as well by chartering ground vehicles to the border at Kodari/Zhangmu. If the road is intact, this is about five hours' drive. Allow (at least) another two hours for

crossing the border. From Zhangmu, Chinese or Tibetan hired vehicles take you to the northern-side base camps in approximately one full day of driving. Road damage is extremely common in the post-monsoon season and vehicle woes equally common.

The northern routes may also be approached via Lhasa (reached by air from Kathmandu or Hong Kong; by air and rail from Beijing via Chengdu). From Lhasa, it is customary for trucks to take two days to reach Everest Base Camp. Either way, it should be noted that you will arrive at the 5000m (16,400ft) base camp by vehicle, having had little opportunity to build up any acclimatization, so it would be wise to spend one or two days in Lhasa and Xegar Dzong before completing the journey.

While travel to the East Face (Kharta Valley) base camp does require several days' walking with porters and yaks, the drive time is essentially the same and an altitude break is appropriate.

facilities

There is vehicle access to the northern base camp at Rongbuk and, within a few hours' drive, the chance to purchase (in Xegar Dzong) limited fresh produce with some sundry items. Constructions there in recent years may, at some time in the future, serve as an expedition lodge.

The Nepalese base camp does not have access to motorized transport; however, once you are acclimatized, the Saturday market at Namche Bazaar is only a 2-day walk and provisions there have reached almost legendary proportions. Nearly everything – from titanium ice screws to cinnamon rolls – is available, though often in only limited supply! Every Saturday fresh produce is on sale, as well as kerosene and, occasionally, propane cylinders. However, larger teams should arrive completely self-sufficient, other than for fresh food.

There is a medical clinic in Pheriche operated by the Himalayan Rescue Association, and another more extensive

clinic in Khumjung village operated by the Himalayan Trust.

when to climb

Spring and autumn (pre- and post-monsoon) are the most favourable times to climb Everest. The spring (officially 1 March–1 June) boasts more than twice as many ascents as the autumn (1 September–1 December), being warmer, less windy, and having longer periods of daylight during the traditional summit weather 'window' in late May. Everest has been climbed in winter, but not often due to low temperatures, short daylight hours, and high wind.

It has been rumoured that the Nepalese government will grant monsoon permits, but climbing routes on the South Side of the peak might be extremely problematic due to increased rain and warmth. Monsoonal storms characteristically shed more snow on the Nepalese flanks; consequently, the (continued on page 251)

North Col   North Ridge   West Shoulder   North East Ridge   South West Face   Main Summit   Hillary Step   South Summit   South Col   Lhotse Face

Western Cwm

south side

The South Side Base Camp remains the most favoured for a successful climb of Everest.

8 Soviet Central Buttress

W Balyberdin and E Myslovsky 1982
Starts west of the buttress defining the Central Couloir's western edge. Following difficult, discontinuous ice couloirs, it becomes rock and mixed to 8300m (27,230ft), where the Central Buttress joins the West Ridge Route (6). Camps above the Western Cwm: 7250m (23,800ft), 7800m (25,600ft), 8250m (27,100ft), and 8500m (27,900ft).

9 South West Face

D Haston and D Scott 1975
The couloir up the centre of this face appears to end in a band of dark rock; in reality, it by-passes this to the west, via a steeper and concealed deep cleft that gains the highest western edge of the face. The line continues upwards into the snowfield to the east, rising until it tops the gully just north-west of the South Summit. The South East Ridge is then followed over the Hillary Step and, difficulties concluded, continues to the Summit. Camps above the Western Cwm: 6900m (22,600ft), 7200m (23,600ft), 7750m (25,400ft), and 8250m (27,100ft).

10 The South Col/South East Ridge

E P Hillary and Sherpa Tenzing Norgay 1953
This, the standard route, follows a circuitous path through the Khumbu Icefall, into the Western Cwm, and onto Lhotse. After a line of séracs, it traverses north over the Yellow Band and a rib – the 'Geneva Spur' – to the South Col. After a 70m (230ft) ice step and a climb up gullies and short rock bands, it traverses east and up to the South East Ridge, over the South Summit and Hillary Step, and, shortly thereafter, the Summit. Camps: 6100m (20,000ft), 6550m (21,500ft), 7250m (23,800ft), and 7990m (26,200ft) on the South Col. Technically moderate but not trivial.

11 The South Pillar

Polish: A Czok and J Kukuczka 1980; Czech: Z Demjan, J Psotka, and Sherpa Ang Rita 1984
Climbs to the Lhotse Face then, from the bergschrund, climbs into the Lhotse Couloir. At 7400m (24,280ft), the Polish Line climbs icefields, then the pillar's right-hand side to 8000m (26,245ft); it then ascends rock, 200m (655ft), to reach snowfields and the South East Ridge at the South Summit. Camps above the Western Cwm: 6900m (22,600ft), 8050m (26,400ft), and 8300m (27,200ft). The Czech route takes the right-hand edge of the pillar itself to 8500m (27,900ft), then traverses to join route (10). Camps above the Western Cwm: 7400m (24,300ft), 8050m (26,400ft), and 8300m (27,200ft). Yet another variation goes directly to a camp on the South Col.

east side

All climbing here is extremely serious and threatened by snow slides and falling séracs from the North East Ridge cornice above.

12 The South East Spur

S Venables 1988
After the Kangshung Glacier the chief difficulties are quickly reached in the first half of the route to the South Col, where the route follows the prominent buttress just south of route (13). Here is difficult ice, rock, and mixed ground. Beyond the last South Col camp, it joins route (10). Camps: 5450m (17,900ft), 6300m (20,700ft), 7450m (24,450ft), and 7990m (26,200ft).

13 Central Rib

L Reichardt, K Momb, and C Buhler 1983
From the Kangshung Glacier, this ascends the prominent left pillar to join the South East Ridge near the South Summit at 8500m (27,900ft). There is a big-wall rock climb before the pillar's crest. Six camps: 5800m (19,000ft), 6100m (20,000ft), 6600m (21,650ft), 7160m (23,500ft), 7590m (25,000ft), and 7865m (25,800ft).

Lhotse

Main Summit

South Summit

South East
Spur

South Col

10

13

Central
Buttress

Trinity Gullies

12

Kangshung Glacier

Northern routes can enjoy excellent conditions in late August or early September. Even with a post-monsoon permit it is best to be climbing by early August. Winter comes quickly and, after the first week of October, conditions are usually far more challenging.

gear
To withstand cold and wind above 8000m (26,250ft), climbers usually wear 1-piece full down climbing suits, boots, and overboots, along with gloves/mittens and other protective gear. They may also choose to use oxygen equipment. However, the Western Cwm can be extremely hot and it is advisable to have sun protection and long white underwear.

An entire volume could be written on the technical equipment needed for the hardest routes on Everest. Essentially, if one were contemplating the West Ridge via Lho La or the South West Face, it is necessary to amass technical hardware and thousands of metres of rope if an

expedition or capsule-style approach is chosen. Less technical routes on snow and ice require less equipment.

It is customary to cross the notorious Khumbu Icefall with up to 60 2.5–3m (8–10ft) aluminium ladders, obviating the need for rope crossings or bridges made from other materials.

maps and guidebooks
Both 'Mount Everest', Brad Washburn, 1:50,000 (Boston Museum of Science) and 'Chomolongma-Mount Everest', Erwin Schneider, 1:25,000 (Alpenvereinskarte) are excellent. Another recently released map from the Chinese Academy is wonderfully detailed.

Mount Everest Massif, Jan Kielkowski (Explo Publishers, 1993) is a useful guidebook. *Everest*, Walt Unsworth (Grafton, 1989), and *Everest, the Best Writing and Pictures from Seventy Years of Human Endeavour*, Peter Gillman (Little Brown, 1993) are also recommended as background reading.

language
In Nepal the two principal languages of commerce are Nepali and English. Colloquial Nepali is not impossible to learn and a smattering goes a long way towards friendly communication.

In Tibet, a Tibetan or Chinese Liaison Officer will be able to communicate with local people as well as with any Sherpa-speaking staff in your group. A Tibetan phrasebook can be helpful – and entertaining with the wrong pronunciations you are sure to make!

rescue and insurance
There are excellent clinics in Kathmandu, but invasive surgery is best obtained outside Nepal. It is advisable to carry comprehensive travel insurance including rescue costs, if only to cover repatriation or transfer to medical facilities outside Nepal or Tibet. For helicopter-rescue flights to Everest Base Camp, it is necessary to leave a deposit with the expedition agent in Kathmandu.

(Despite the widely publicized rescue of two climbers from 5980m/19,600ft in 1996, air support is extremely unlikely above Everest Base Camp.)

Air support is not a possiblility at the Tibetan base camp. Vehicle transport to Kathmandu and Med-evac outside Nepal is probably the most efficient option.

red tape
In Nepal, permits are obligatory. Your group will be assigned a Liaison Officer. If a film permit is secured, you will also have to have an Environmental Officer. Contact the Ministry of Tourism in Kathmandu direct for salary/equipment disbursement figures.

On the Chinese side a peak registration fee is charged. A service charge for transport, yak transport, a Liaison Officer, and vehicle expedition duration is also imposed. This quickly mounts up, and can mean that Chinese-side expeditions are just as expensive as those in Nepal.

finishing family business
george mallory II

> "I first became aware of my legendary grandfather when I was very young. I didn't fully grasp what he had done and could not understand why he had done it. I wished that I could know for certain if he was the first to climb Everest – and how and why he had died up there in 1924.

As the years went by – and my own passion for rock climbing matured – I read all the books about my grandfather and understood that nobody knew exactly what had happened after he and his partner disappeared into mist, high on the roof of the world. Some felt the pair could have reached the summit. Others thought Odell (who was last to see them) had actually spotted Mallory and Irvine climbing the First Step at 12.50pm and not, as he had reported at the time, the more abrupt Second Step. If that were so, they could not have reached the top. My curiosity grew, and the more I read, the more I wanted to see Everest's North Ridge.

When Paul Pfau invited me to join him and his friends on Everest's Mallory Route, I could not refuse.

Everest has not shrunk in the 71 years since Mallory and Irvine died in their attempt to make the first ascent, but the difficulties involved in climbing it have. In 1995 our 4-day drive to the Rongbuk Glacier was almost luxurious and, on the mountain, our Sherpas led the way, preparing the mountain for our dash to the summit. Down suits, lightweight oxygen cylinders, and, most significantly, prior knowledge of the route, have removed some of the adventure from the climb, though the challenge and the necessity for team harmony are still there. The significance of an ascent has also changed. Mallory and Irvine were heroes – an inspiration for future climbers. These days, risking death on a mountain attracts public criticism, besides annoying other mountaineers who have to share the same route.

By May 1995, members of our expedition were poised ready for a summit bid, hoping that we would have the speed on 'summit day' to reach the top before prudence dictated we turn around. Although I was as keen as anyone to reach the highest point, I had no desire to become the second Mallory to die on Everest. Freezing or falling to my death held no appeal. Neither did I want to lose fingers or toes on what was more a personal journey than a climb. My closest friend on the expedition and summit partner Jeff Hall was like-minded – we decided to turn back no later than 2pm. If my grandfather's death were not reason enough for caution, then the death of fellow-Australian

Mike Rheinberger certainly was. In 1994 Mike had doggedly persevered over a long day and reached the summit at sunset, only to die tragically on the descent.

So when Jeff, Chhiring Sherpa, and I set out at 1am from our high camp at 8300m, I was obsessed with climbing as fast as my lungs would permit. I felt confident of being able to sustain this effort because my pre-expedition training, which had culminated in a 340km bicycle ride, including 11,000m of ascent in 23 hours, had provided me with the stamina I expected to need on 'summit day', a task that generally takes at least 16 hours. But there is only one place in the world where a mountaineer can prove beyond all doubt that he or she has what it takes to climb to 8848m and, on 14 May 1995, I made my one and only bid for success.

Despite perfect conditions, -20°C, brilliant moonlight, and not a hint of wind, we were forced to pause after every 10 steps and repeatedly ventilate every cubic millimetre of lung capacity. You may imagine that up there, finally covering the ground on which my grandfather had disappeared, I might have been distracted by thoughts of his mysterious end. But the demands of the terrain, my sense of urgency, and, above all, the awesome view of Everest's vast North Face, crystal clear in pale white moonlight, dominated my diminished mental capacity.

We soon warmed to our task – clambering up the rocks which have been dubbed the 'Yellow Band' – then, surprisingly easily,

Above **The precarious Chinese ladder at the top of Everest's Second Step.**

Far right **Kaji Sherpa and George Mallory II on top of the world.**

Right **George Leigh Mallory, pictured here with his wife Ruth. He has been an inspiration and hero to generations of climbers.**

we surmounted the First Step. Some easier ground led to a knife-edge, from where we could look out to the east for the first time. The exposure was tremendous. The Kangshung Face gaped below us and, across the void, the image of Makalu's carved ridges etched itself into my brain. From here, the difficulties increased. The route traversed steep rocky ground where exacting footwork was essential. Then, suddenly, ahead of us in the gloom loomed the Second Step, the technical crux.

If my grandfather had ... looked up from here, would he, could he have turned around?

The moon had virtually set by now and we started up the 20m cliff using head-torches. I had rock climbed in the dark before, but never wearing gloves, crampons, and a bulky down suit, and carrying a 10kg pack. Nor had I ever rock climbed at such an altitude. The situation might have been daunting, but in these special circumstances – with a major prize almost within grasp – mountaineers often draw on inner inspiration and perform far above their norm.

Naturally, I made use of the rope placed by others to belay myself and was relieved to see an aluminium ladder anchored against the uppermost 4m of the cliff. Chinese mountaineers hauled the ladder up to this unlikely spot in 1975 and, until it became dislodged in 1996, everyone used it to surmount the most difficult part of the Second Step. The slab acquired its reputation for difficulty because Chu Yin-hua, the Chinese climber who led this section during its (accepted) first ascent in 1960, had to remove his boots to get a better footing. To pragmatists, this was taken as proof that the pitch would have thwarted my grandfather. I scanned the feasible 'lines' up the rock and wondered, fleetingly, whether I might try the easiest-looking one, then, with a twinge of guilt, I grabbed the ladder.

At 4am we paused at the top of the Second Step to change oxygen bottles. We were above all difficulties now, and ahead of schedule. Urgency was replaced with optimism. I gazed towards the summit. It looked close – but that was because the ridge is foreshortened and the true summit was hidden. If my grandfather had, indeed, looked up from here, would he, could he have turned around?

The knoll called the Third Step posed little problem, and we started up the final pyramid. The technical difficulty was nominal, but at times I could only manage three steps between breathers. Halfway up the slope, sunlight on the snow announced dawn. Minutes later we were able to look out to the south-west and see Everest's gigantic shadow extending to the horizon past innumerable lesser Himalayan peaks. I paused to capture some of this magic on film, then pressed on up the slope.

From its crest, we could see, just 100m away, a tripod festooned in prayer flags. Realizing I was within minutes of reaching mountaineering's most celebrated summit – something that until that moment had always seemed so improbable – opened the flood gates of emotion. It took us another five minutes to reach the tripod, minutes of desperate panting mingled with tears of relief. I stepped up onto the small, level patch of snow and immediately took a set of photographs. To the west, the familiar shapes of Pumori or Daughter-Peak (named by my grandfather for my Aunt Clare) and Cho Oyu were clearly lower than us; and the view of Makalu, emerging from a sea of low cloud, was utterly spectacular. It was 5.30am; we were on top of the world and could afford to indulge for a while.

For nearly 50 minutes we reeled off photos and admired that most magnificent, most moving of views. I wondered, had my grandfather seen it in 1924? I certainly hoped so. We were about to start our descent when I remembered my mission. From my pack, I retrieved a photograph of my grandparents, George and Ruth, and knelt down to plant it in the snow. This act symbolized the unarguable completion of a family project begun seven decades earlier. Again, I was moved to tears by what will remain with me as a moment of profound meaning. Jeff, empathizing, said, 'George, your grandfather would be proud of you.'

Emotion was quickly replaced with grim reality. We were a very long way from home, with what we knew to be the most dangerous part of the climb yet to survive. Any success so far would be rendered meaningless if we could not complete the round trip. Turning my thoughts to my grandmother and her three children, I became even more determined to finish my climb of Everest safely. Because, to each of them, George Mallory was not just a hero of his generation – he was also the husband and father who did not come back.

1883 First explorations by W W Graham (British). His claim to have ascended several peaks on the Sanctuary Wall was disbelieved.

1905–1907 Dr T Longstaff (British) explored approaches to the Inner Sanctuary. He climbed Trisul on the Outer Sanctuary Wall. With guides, A and H Brocherel, Longstaff reached Longstaff Col on Nanda Devi East.

1927–32 H Ruttledge (British) explored various approaches from the south and discovered the Sunderdhunga Khal (col) on the South Sanctuary Wall.

1934 E Shipton and H W Tilman (British) first attempted the Rishi Ganga Gorge in spring, and finally forced their way through to the Inner Sanctuary post-monsoon. They left via the

Sunderdhunga Khal. (It has only been crossed this once, and in this direction.)

1936 An Anglo-American expedition made the first ascent of the Main Summit. H W Tilman and N Odell reached it via the South Ridge during August. Two members made an exit by the Longstaff Col to the Lawan Gad.

1939 J Klaner and J Bujak (Polish) made the first ascent of Nanda Devi East.

1951 A French expedition attempted to traverse from the Main to the East Peak by the 2km (1¼ mile) wide connecting high ridge. R Duplat and G Vignes disappeared after being last seen below the Main Summit. T Norgay and L Dubost climbed Nanda Devi East.

1964 An Indian expedition under Colonel N Kumar climbed the Main Summit via the 'Original (1936) Route'.

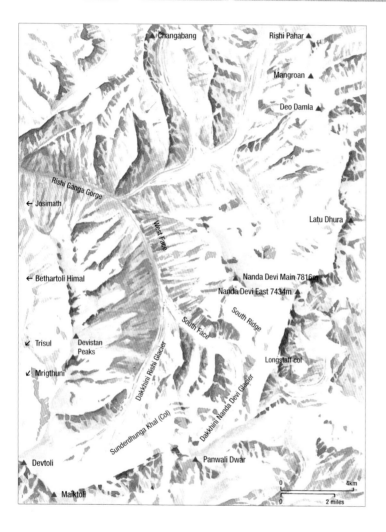

nanda devi

harish kapadia

Viewed from any angle, the twin peaks of Nanda Devi – Main Summit 7816m (25,600ft) and Nanda Devi East 7434m (24,400ft) – rise majestically from the centre of a ring of peaks that makes up the Nanda Devi Sanctuary.

Nanda Devi is the highest mountain in the Indian Garhwal Himalaya. Encircled by a 110km (70 mile) 'barrier ring' of 12 peaks of over 6400m (21,000ft), it is also one of the most difficult mountains in the world to reach. The circle of peaks effectively thwarted all early approaches to the mountain. There are no access depressions lower than 5180m (17,000ft), except in the west where the Rishi Ganga, rising at the foot of Nanda Devi, creates a terrific gorge.

The high peaks of the Sanctuary are the major barriers between the cold Tibetan winds and the Gangetic plains of India. Without them to absorb the main thrust of these icy blasts, the 'granary of India' would be stripped bare. No wonder Nanda Devi, meaning the bliss-giving Goddess, is worshipped locally; the peak is steeped in legend and romance.

Permission to climb in the Inner Sanctuary has never been easy to obtain, especially during the mid-1960s when 'hush-hush' attempts were made to install a listening device on the summit for monitoring Chinese nuclear activity on the Tibetan plateau. The plan misfired, leading to a diplomatic incident some years later.

There was a short period after 1974 when the Sanctuary was opened to Western mountaineers and trekkers, and several impressive new routes were put up on the Nanda Devi peaks and on the Sanctuary Wall. Local shepherds also forged an alternative route into the Inner Sanctuary, enabling their herds to graze inside its walls for the first time. However, all this put pressure on the fragile ecology of the area and, as a result, the government decided to close it to mountaineers and locals; it remains closed today.

ridges, faces, and peaks

The Rishi Ganga Gorge, approached from the roadheads of Josimath or Lata, offers the only access to the peaks of the Inner Sanctuary. The Rishi Gorge is an adventure in itself: a gripping climb, culminating in what is aptly named the Vaikunth Seedi, or Staircase to Heaven. And Heaven it is, inside the Sanctuary: green meadows with a vast view of the West Face of Nanda Devi rising almost 2500m (8200ft) from the Rishi Ganga. From the top of the Rishi Gorge, going southwards around Nanda Devi, is the Dakkhini Nanda Devi Glacier, the site of the original base camp. This gives easy access to the South Face with its rocky 'coxcomb' South Ridge which, though very exposed on both sides, and composed of poor rock, provides the mountain's *voie normale*.

Right **Guarded by a near-impregnable ring of peaks, no one was able to approach the foot of the majestic Nanda Devi until 1934.**

1965–68 Secret attempts were made to monitor nuclear activity in Tibet from the Main Summit. Loss of the nuclear listening device in an avalanche led to the closure of the Sanctuary and fears that the Rishi Ganga had been polluted.

1974 The Sanctuary was opened to Western mountaineers. Changabang and Devtoli, the northern- and southernmost peaks of the Inner Sanctuary, were climbed within days of each other during June.

1975 A Japanese expedition climbed several peaks on the North Sanctuary Wall. French climbers led by Y Pollet-Villard scaled both Nanda peaks but did not complete the traverse in-between.

1976 Y Hasegawa and K Takami from an Indo-Japanese expedition traversed the ridge from the East to the Main Summit in three days. An American expedition climbed the Main Summit by a new North Ridge Route. It ended in the tragic death of Nanda Devi Unsoeld.

1977 Environmentalists reported serious eco-imbalances in the Sanctuary.

1981 A new route on the Main Summit (North Ridge to North East Buttress) was climbed by a Czech (M Martins) expedition. An Indian expedition led by Col Balwant Sandhu climbed the Main Summit. Another expedition of Indian Army paratroopers led by Major Kiran Kumar climbed both peaks, but five climbers died during the expedition.

1983 The Sanctuary was closed for environmental reasons.

1993 An Indian Army expedition studied the condition of the Sanctuary, and they recommended its continued closure.

Main Summit · South (Coxcomb) Ridge · Nanda Devi East · South Ridge · Longstaff Col

the peaks of the nanda devi sanctuary The Nanda Devi Sanctuary has a rim or ridge known as the Sanctuary Wall, which also encloses the Inner Sanctuary Ridge. Several famous peaks stand on these walls. From Nanda Devi East, the North Sanctuary Wall has peaks like Latu Dhura, 6392m (21,000ft); Deo Damla, 6620m (21,700ft); Mangroan, 6568m (21,500ft); and Rishi Pahar, 6992m (22,900ft). The Sanctuary Wall turns west at this point and leads to Kalanka, 6991m (22,900ft) and Changabang, 6864m (22,500ft). It ends at Dunagiri, 7066m (23,000ft).

Towards the south stand the small but challenging twin tops of Bethartoli Himal, 6352m (20,800ft) and Bethartoli South, 6318m (20,700ft). Further south still stands Trisul, 7120m (23,400ft). The Wall now turns east and leads to Mrigthuni, 6855m (22,500ft); Devtoli, 6788m (22,300ft); and Maiktoli, 6803m (22,300ft). Next, across the depression of Sunderdhunga Khal (col), stand Panwali Dwar, 6663m (22,000ft) and Nanda Khat 6611m, (21,700ft) to complete the circle. Finally, on the Inner Sanctuary Ridge, west of the Main Summit and east of Trisul, stand the Devistan peaks.

future climbing

The Nanda Devi Sanctuary will always be a highly prized mountain wilderness; some people even regard it as one of the wonders of the world. There is a lot to look forward to if and when it is re-opened. Nanda Devi's West Face is perhaps the most stupendous rock face that awaits mountaineers, but there are many other peaks and routes that are yet to be climbed.

Times for the routes have not been given; so much depends on conditions and the style of climbing adopted. Allow 2–3 weeks from base camp, and a further five days to return to civilization.

south side

Base camp is established at 4600m (15,000ft) on the Dakkhini Nanda Devi Glacier, approached from the grazing area of Sarso Patal.

1 Main Summit: Original Route (Coxcomb or South Ridge)
H W Tilman and N E Odell 1936
From base camp, four camps should be established on the South Ridge.

2 Nanda Devi East: Polish Route
J Bujak, D Tsering Sherpa, and J Klaner 1939
Alpine style: R Payne and Julie-Ann Clyma 1994
This route climbs the South Ridge from the Longstaff Col.

3 Nanda Devi East: South West Face ⊠
Three parties: P Lal and P Dorje; U K Palat, C Tashi, T Tashi, and P Tsering; A K Srivastava, H D Chand, U Singh, P Wangyal, and Sanjay Sherpa 1982
The route follows the length of the South West Ridge.

4 Indo-Japanese Traverse
Y Hasegawa and K Takami 1976
Both summits were climbed by the expedition, and two camps (East Four and West Five) were established on the ridge by climbing down from Nanda Devi East, and traversing the avalanche-prone snow of the South Face of the Main Summit. There are several overhanging sections on the 200m (650ft) 'hump' and a knife-edged ridge on the descent, which took five hours. Not repeated.

north side

The north side is reached from the open grazing ground of Patal Khan by crossing the North Rishi Ganga River. The base camp for routes on this side is generally established near a lake called Haj Tal at around 4600m (15,000ft).

5 Main Summit: North West Face and North Ridge: American Route ⊠
J States, L Reichardt, and J Roskelley 1976
After a complicated approach, the North West Face was climbed with two intermediate camps. In its upper sections, the North Buttress is steep

Nanda Devi East

Main Summit

North Ridge

with holdless slabs and awkward, shallow chimneys before the final snow slope.

6 Main Summit: North East Face: Czech Route

Two parties: O Svronal, B Kadlcík, L Horka, L Palecek, and K Karafa; J Rakoncaj and L Sulovsky 1981

This route follows the prominent ridge on the North East Face. Four camps were placed.

7 Main Summit: North Ridge Direct

L Horka, L Palecek, K Karafa, O Strounal, and B Kaplcik 1981 (J Rakoncaj and L Sulovshy summited three days later)

This route had been attempted in 1978 by a Czech team that reached a foresummit at 7055m (23,000ft) before the monsoon broke, blocking further progress.

how to get to nanda devi

From Delhi, travel to Haridwar-Rishikesh. From there, a road leads to Josimath and Lata, the usual starting points. There follows a tiring 5-day trek into the Sanctuary, via Dhranshi Pass and the Rishi Gorge, to base camp.

facilities

Josimath, where there is a rest house, is the nearest town. Local porters can be hired and basic food purchased here. There are no supplies available in the village of Lata.

During an expedition weather bulletins can be obtained from the Indian Mountaineering Foundation.

when to climb

Generally either the pre-monsoon period (mid-May–end June) or the post-monsoon period (early September–end October) are suitable times to attempt the peaks. The monsoon is heavy and the winter severe.

gear

Full expedition gear is needed in order to climb Nanda Devi.

maps and guidebooks

Recommended maps are the 'Garhwal-Himalaya East', 1:150,000 (Swiss Foundation for Alpine Research Map), and the 'Garhwal Region – Nanda Devi and Ganges Source' (2 sheets), 1:250,000, available via Cordee and specialist distributors. The Survey of India has excellent maps, but they are restricted: 1:250,000 No 53N; 1:50,000 Nos 53N/13, N/14, and N/15. There are no guidebooks to the area.

language

Locals speak Hindi or the Garhwali dialect. Josimath officials understand English.

rescue and insurance

Rescue helicopters are arranged by the Indian Air Force. Prior arrangements for such an eventuality must be made with the Indian Mountaineering Foundation or your Embassy. Foreign climbers also have to get a bond and guarantee from their Embassy. In case of emergency, you must inform the the Sub-Divisional Magistrate at Josimath or the nearest police post, but you will be charged.

red tape

At present no teams are allowed to penetrate the Sanctuary, but peaks on the Sanctuary Walls can be climbed from 'outside' the Sanctuary. This allows for attempts of Nanda Devi East (from the Lawan Gad to the east), Changabang, Kalanka (from the north, Dunagiri Gad), Trisul (from the west, the Nandakini Valley), and Maiktoli (from the south, the Sunderdhunga Valley). Many other peaks can be climbed but the Main Summit is, unfortunately, currently out of bounds.

To climb any peaks in the Sanctuary you must get permission from the Indian Mountaineering Foundation, which can be contacted at Benito Juarez Road, New Delhi. Peak fees are payable (in accordance with height) and a Liaison Officer must accompany the team. Certain other charges for environmental protection are also levied.

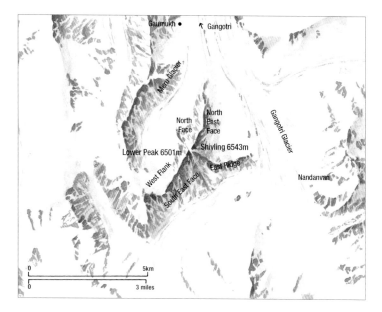

shivling

ed douglas

Shivling, 6543m (21,468ft), is a stunning, huge granite tooth, topped with ice and snow. It is in the Western Garhwal, not far from the western border of Nepal (in fact this area was once part of the Nepalese kingdom). The nearest village is Gangotri, 15km (9¼ miles) away, which has several lodges and a beautiful temple, and is half a day's drive from Uttarkashi, the nearest town.

Shivling, meaning Shiva's lingam (a reference to the phallic shape of the mountain), towers over the Gangotri Glacier. The glacier's snout is Gaumukh (the cow's mouth), the source of the Bhagirathi, the holiest tributary of the Ganges. Each year thousands of Hindu pilgrims make the trek up here to bathe in the freezing river at its base. Some continue to the beautiful alpine meadow, Tapovan, at 4400m (14,100ft), which is where the base camp is normally situated. Shivling is a site of pilgrimage for mountaineers, too, drawn by what the first explorers called 'Matterhorn Peak'. In truth, Shivling is even more beautiful than its famous alpine counterpart and considerably harder to climb.

ridges, faces, and peaks

Shivling has an elegantly simple form but its sheer sides make it a forbidding prospect of ice-draped granite, too steep except on its West Flank for any substantial build-up of snow. From high up on the Meru Glacier, to the west, or from across the Gangotri Glacier at Nandanvan (base camp for neighbouring Bhagirathi Peaks), Shivling's fish-tail shape becomes obvious: it has two summits, almost symmetrical and almost the same height at 6543m (21,468ft) and 6501m (21,330ft), with the Lower Peak to the south-west separated by a sweeping col.

Viewed from the meadow at Tapovan, Shivling presents its most forbidding aspect: the North East and North Faces, separated by the slender North Ridge, which has an improbable overhang at its apex, just below the summit. The North East Face is bounded on its left by the long and intricate East Ridge, which offers an airy route to the summit but demands so much time and effort that it has only been climbed twice in 15 years.

The southern aspects are more rocky. The huge South East Face holds much less snow than the shadowy North Faces, but Shivling's remarkable symmetry is sustained in other ways. The East Ridge is balanced at the other end of the mountain's southern aspect by the elegant South East Ridge, with the South East Spur in the middle of the face corresponding to the West Ridge on the other side.

Shivling's South West Ridge is the shortest, but is reached by a long approach up the Meru Glacier and requires substantial effort in load-carrying before an attempt can be made. Its upper reaches are steep and technical, and few have attempted to follow the example of the Australian first ascensionists (1986).

The West Face is set at a more amenable angle but is overhung by a huge sérac band that periodically collapses. The route up the West Ridge has seen the bulk of climbing activity, despite the objective danger, because of its short technical difficulties. Nevertheless, only 50 per cent of expeditions are successful.

future climbing

All the major lines have been climbed. Nevertheless, all routes, bar the West Ridge, have only had either one or two ascents and will continue to offer difficult challenges to mountaineers for generations to come. The rock gendarmes on the South Side of the mountain will provide good long rock climbs.

Right **The sacred summit of Shivling in the Himalaya, considered by many to be the most beautiful mountain in the world. The evening sun lights up the West Face after a storm.**

then finished up on the East Ridge of Shivling.

1987 Czech climbers made the first ascent of the North Face up steep ice and mixed ground.

1993 Tyroleans H Kammerlander and C Hainz straightened the Japanese line (1980) up the North Ridge, climbing the last 850m (2800ft), including vertical and overhanging rock, in 12 hours.

1995 British mountaineer S Haston and his French wife Laurence Gouault climbed the 'Indo-Tibetan Border Police Route' (1974) in nine hours from the base camp to the Main Summit.

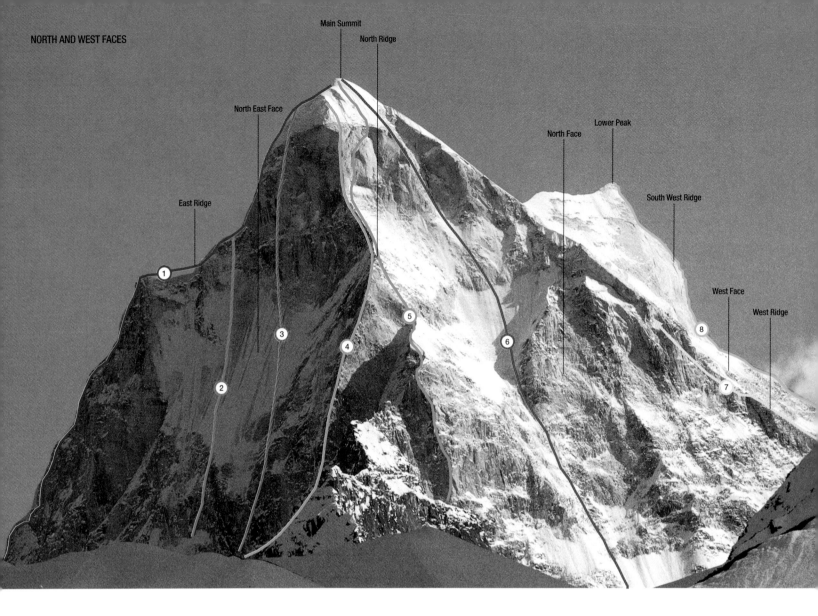

north face

Giving grades is difficult in the Himalaya, and on unrepeated routes they would be meaningless as there has to be a consensus on these things. The time taken to complete a route depends on many factors, including weather conditions and climbing style. Expeditions spend up to four weeks in preparation at base camp; the climbs take up only part of this time.

north face

The North Face is bounded by the West Ridge and the North Ridge, and is one of the most dramatic aspects found in the Himalaya. Steep, technically difficult, and intimidating – all the routes on it are hard and around 1500m (4900ft).

1 East Ridge

G Bettembourg, G Child, R White, and D Scott 1981
A vast and audacious undertaking. Some 60 pitches over a range of ground, including A3 wall climbing and difficult mixed and alpine terrain. Originally done in 12 days.

2 North East Face

A Popelnik, D Vidmar, and D Tic 1987
The team took six days to climb this line on the left of the Face. Most of the difficulties are in the lower part.

3 North East Face

P Bernascone, F Manoni, and E Rosso 1986
After climbing a rock band at 5000m (16,400ft) at VI and A1, the first ascensionists were faced with a mixed section of VI and 85˚ ice before they reached an icefield with an easier angle. An 8-day climb.

4 North Ridge

H Kammerlander and C Hainz 1993
A brilliant effort; these two climbers took the challenge of the summit prow head on. Takes about 12 hours.

5 North Ridge

M Fujita, M Yamamoto, and I Kubo 1980
This takes the right-hand spur at the bottom of the ridge, moving right onto the North Face to avoid the steep, and at times overhanging, granite prow just below the summit.

6 North Face

B Adamec, P Rajif, and J Svedja 1987
After an initial avalanche-threatened ice couloir, a mixed section of 70˚ ice and IV+ rock leads to an 80˚ ice couloir and then a second icefield. More steep ice leads to a rotten chimney before the final steep section to the summit.

west face

This is the most amenable face, but a sérac barrier at 6000m (19,700ft) threatens much of it.

7 West Ridge

H Singh, A and P Tharkey, L Singh, Dorje, and P Sherpa 1974
The route of the first ascent is the easiest on the mountain, with the main difficulties starting at around 5400m (17,700ft). A mixed spur with two sections of UIAA V lead to the sérac. The line through the sérac alters almost year to year: in 1995 a straightforward line directly above the ridge led to the col between the two peaks, and then up a steep snowfield to the Main Summit. This route takes between one and three days; ascent of 1000m (3300ft) from the main difficulties.

south side

There has been much less activity on the southern aspects of Shivling despite the reported excellence and safety of the Japanese route (11). A number of the gendarmes on this side of the mountain, offering excellent rock climbing, have recently been explored.

8 South West Route: Australian

B and J Muir, and G Hill 1986
The South West Ridge was reached from the Meru Glacier up steep mixed ground. The original team spent three days fixing rope along the difficult rocky ridge. They then moved their camp up and spent another four days solving the summit headwall, with the crux pitch going at VI/A4.

Labels on image: Lower Peak, East Face, Main Summit, South East Ridge, South West Ridge, East Ridge, 9, 8, 10, 1, 11

9 South West Route: British

C Bonington and J Fotheringham 1983

This route avoids the rotten lower section of the South East Ridge and climbs a dangerous ice couloir below a sérac before breaking right towards the ridge. The upper section of the ridge is superb granite, giving a crux pitch of V before it relents and becomes more shattered. The original team made five bivouacs.

10 South West Route: American

C Warner, D Jenkins, and A Weiss 1989

After initially starting up the South East Ridge, the American first ascensionists were forced onto the East Face by bad weather when they were 400m (1300ft) below the top. However, they eventually reached the Lower Peak after six days.

11 South East Face: Japanese

M Nakao, K Ohama, and M Yamagata 1983

This route was climbed in 51 pitches over eight days; the final pitch onto the col is said to be the most dramatic of all.

how to get to shivling

It is possible to take public transport from Delhi to Rishikesh, then on to Uttarkashi and Gangotri, but it is a fraught and crowded affair. There are plenty of agents in Delhi who will take care of all travel arrangements and hiring of porters; however, it can be more beneficial to ask someone who has already climbed in India for recommendations. Tapovan, Shivling's base camp, is a 2-day walk from the roadhead at Gangotri and all the routes can be accessed from this point.

facilities

There are lodges in Uttarkashi and Gangotri. Vegetables and supplies are available at Gangotri; Uttarkashi has more shops, but you should bring all your climbing equipment with you. A stream supplies water at Tapovan.

when to climb

The monsoon in the Garhwal begins in early June and ends, more or less, in early September, and during this time conditions are too snowy. The optimum seasons are late March–late May and late August–late October. The spring season is slightly warmer, while the weather in the autumn is more settled. By October the days are clear and warm, but at night temperatures drop well below freezing.

gear

First-time visitors to the Himalaya should read and consult widely on appropriate gear. During the day, up to around 5500m (18,000ft), normal alpine clothing is fine; above that, temperatures are more like those during an alpine winter. A good sleeping bag is obligatory. Hardware requirements for these routes are the same as for a demanding alpine route.

maps and guidebooks

The Swiss 'Garhwal-Himalaya-West', 1:150,000 (Schweizerischen Stiftung fur alpine Forschungen – update of Survey of India data) is the best map.

Peaks and Passes of the Garhwal Himalaya (Alpinistyczny Klub Eksploracyjny, Hungary, 1990) is a useful guidebook.

language

The local language is Hindi but English is spoken by many people. Your obligatory Liaison Officer will act as interpreter.

rescue and insurance

There is a limited rescue service. Climbers should carry insurance.

red tape

Expeditions must apply for permission from the Indian Mountaineering Foundation in Delhi at least six months before departure and then attend a briefing there before they leave for the mountains. If at all possible, talk to someone who has climbed in India before to avoid the many pitfalls this process can involve.

1955 In July, M S Jung and S K Lee of Seoul National University Alpine Club, explored the Misi Pass and Outer Sorak, investigating climbing Sorak. In October, H R Ryu and 13 members of SNUAC stayed at Sin Heung Temple with Korean Army Guards. They made first ascents of the First, Second, and Third peaks of Ul San Am.

1957 In July S J Park and Laterne members climbed Tae Chung via Death Valley. They descended to Sin Heung Temple by way of Soo Ryum Dong and Ma-deung Pass, naming the ridge Dinosaur Ridge. After climbing all the ridges on Ul San Am, they climbed Tal Ma Peak, 635m (2100ft).

1958 E J Lee and members of SNUAC introduced winter climbing to Outer Sorak on the gentler icefalls of Death Valley. D Chun and Schuteinman Club members made the first ascent of a frozen waterfall in Chun-bul-dong Valley.

1959–60 H Y Lee and J H Cho explored the North West Ridge. From Nam Gyo Ri, they climbed the Twelve Angels Valley to Tae-seung Pass.

1966–7 The first winter climbs on the North West Ridge of Sorak were made by K S Sohn and 23 members of SNUAC.

1967 Yodel Alpine Club climbed a 50m (165ft) icefall in Jajeun Bawi Valley.

1968 Kyung Buk Alpine Federation completed the Dinosaur Ridge in winter.

1970 Sorak North Main Ridge received its first ascent by SNUAC. The jagged Yong-Ah Ridge was first climbed by J H Song and members of Yodel AC.

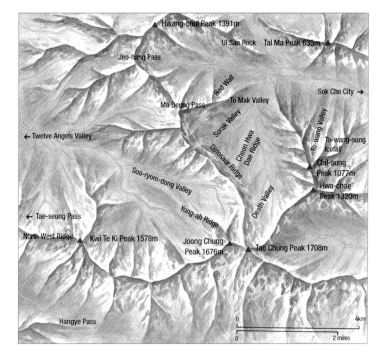

sorak san

sun woo nam

Sorak San is a cluster of peaks situated mid-way along the Korean peninsula, near the east coast, not far from the city of Kangnung. The Demilitarized Zone (DMZ) between North and South Korea lies only 20km (12 miles) to the north. Sorak's highest peak, Tae Chung, 1708m (5604ft), the third-highest mountain in South Korea, is the central feature of the Baek Du Range, which extends from Mount Baek Du, 2744m (9000ft), to Mount Ji Ri, 1915m (6300ft), some 1400km (850 miles) in a north–south direction.

After the Korean War (1950–3), Sorak San took over from Mount Diamond, 1638m (5400ft), now north of the DMZ and out of bounds to South Koreans, as the most popular peak with mountaineers and hikers. In March 1970, it was designated as Korea's third National Park, and in 1982 appointed by UNESCO as the only Wildlife Conservation Area in Korea.

ridges, faces, and peaks

Sorak San and its neighbours are bristling with granite walls and ridges riven by abundant watercourses in deep, narrow valleys. The mountain and ridge tops tend to be bare and smooth, while lower and gentler slopes are thickly wooded, as are the valleys. Rock climbing is good on the canyon walls. Popular trails have been fixed with metal ropes, ramps, and ladders.

Sorak San is divided into two parts, Inner Sorak (to the west) and Outer Sorak (to the east), the boundary line extending from the Ma Deung Pass, 1327m (4400ft), to Dinosaur Ridge. The area to the south of the North West Ridge and Hangye Pass, 1000m (3300ft), is classified as Southern Sorak.

Six main ridges converge on the summit slopes of Tae Chung and the lesser summits, too, are endowed with ridges of their own. It makes for an intricate network, as follows.

chung-bul-dong valley The largest valley in Outer Sorak, this connects to the smaller valleys, such as Jajeun Bawi and Death Valley, through which Tae Chung Peak is reached. It is the normal approach route.

twelve angels valley and north west ridge In Inner Sorak, this 10km (6 mile) granite valley, starting from Nam-gyo-ri, is steep and dangerous. There is a trail through it to Tae-seung Pass, 1210m (3970ft), on the North West Ridge. Stretching from the Tae-seung Pass to Tae Chung Peak, this ridge is 20km (12½ miles) long and in winter is characterized by deep snow and strong winds. From its middle rises Kwi Te Ki Peak, 1578m (5177ft).

death valley Only 2km (1¼ mile) long, Death Valley, in Outer Sorak, boasts a 100m (330ft) waterfall and precipitious gorge.

to-wang valley and to-wang-sung icefall This striking, three-stepped, 320m (1050ft) fall, located in the upper part of the 2km (1¼ mile) To-wang Valley, drains both Hwa-chae Peak, 1320m (4331ft), and Chil-sung Peak, 1077m (3534ft). In winter the fall turns into a huge wall of ice. It is the longest icefall in Korea – and vertical in its upper and lower parts.

dinosaur ridge This runs in a north-west direction starting from the Moo-neo-mi Pass, 1050m (3445ft), through to the Ma Deung Pass, 1327m (4354ft), and on to Tae Chung. A north-east branch is the Cheon Hwa Dae, running

Right **Just before the highest area of the Yong-ah Ridge.**

1971 S M Kim and 15 members of SNUAC succeeded in the first winter ascent of Sorak North Main Ridge. It took 20 days to complete.

1972 C G Yu and seven members of Yodel AC made the first winter climb of Yong-ah Ridge. The last ridge of Sorak, the Cheon Hwa Dae, was climbed by SNUAC members. (This may possibly have been done in 1973.)

1973 Dong Kug University Alpine Club (leader J H Park) completed the first winter climb of Southern Main Ridge.

1974 The first winter ascent of Cheon Hwa Dae Ridge was made by D S Chun and members of Ascent Alpine Club.

1976 First free winter ascent of 1275m (4183ft) peak was made by Ascent AC.

1977 The Crony Alpine Club of Seoul, led by Y B Park, made the first ascent of the upper and lower To-wang-sung Icefalls. Seven Brothers Peak climbed.

1978 Red Wall of Jang Kun Peak climbed by B Park and Crony AC members.

1981 Pusan Chung Bong Alpine Club completed the first ascent of To-wang-sung Icefall and its two walls.

1984 B S Lee of Hong Ik University Alpine Club made the first 'on sight' climb of To-wang-sung Icefall suceeding in seven hours. The South East Wall of Ul San Am was climbed.

1985 Dae Seung Icefall near Dae Sung Pass, South Sorak San, was climbed by J B Lee, D P Yun, H J Chung, and Y K Kim in six hours, 10 minutes.

1989 Little To-wang-sung Icefall climbed by Chung Hwa Alpine Club members. Big-wall climbers of Rock Party Alpine Club blitzed some of the long ridges.

Heuk Bum Ridge   Suk Joo Ridge   Bum-bong   Dinosaur Ridge   Sorak Valley

for 2km (1¼ miles) from the unnamed 1275m (4183ft) Peak to the Chung-bul-dong Valley and including Bum-bong (Tiger Peak). On either side of the ridge are the Sorak Valley (north) and the Jajeun Bawi Valley (south; also known for its ice climbing).

north main ridge From the Missi Pass, 826m (2700ft), this ridge, the longest and roughest on Sorak San, runs south to the Ma Deung Pass by way of Hwang-chul Peak, 1391m (4600ft), and Jeo-hang Pass, 1110m (3600ft).

yong-ah ridge The jagged Yong-ah Ridge has many sharp, steep pinnacles, like dragon's teeth, and runs north-west from Tae Chung. On both sides of the ridge are beautiful valleys: the Soo-ryom-dong Valley and the Ka-ya-dong Valley. In the upper part of the Soo-ryom-dong Valley are the Ssang-pok (Twin Waterfalls).

ul san am This is a huge granite wall in Outer Sorak, near Sok Cho city, offering a whole line of cliffs. It is about one-fifth the size of El Cap in Yosemite (*see pages 114–17*).

future climbing

No Juk Peak, the North Wall of Ul San Am, and several walls of To Mak Valley offer future climbing potential – most are unexplored.

north east side

The North East Side is where most of the climbing is done. The mountain is steeper on this side and has more rock walls and waterfalls.

1 Cheon Hwa Dae Ridge 5.7–5.9

Members of SNUAC 1972 or 1973

This ridge branches off the Dinosaur Ridge and was the last of Sorak's ridges to be climbed. In summer it takes about seven or eight hours to climb to the summit, or four hours to climb one of the subsidiary ridges, such as Heuk Bum (Black Leopard), Yum Ra, and Suk Joo (5.7–5.9). Ascent is 500m (1600ft).

2 To-wang-sung Icefall IV

Y B Park and members of Crony AC 1976–7

Both the upper and lower falls were climbed by club members, who adapted ice techniques learned in Chamonix. The lower falls needed three days with 18 pitons, and the upper ones eight days and 32 pitons. This amazing winter-climbing feat

was agreed to be of a grade IV level. Ascent 200m (660ft) upper and 80m (260ft) lower.

3 To-wang-sung Two Walls 5.9

Pusan Chung Bong Alpine Club 1981

This route follows the two walls of the fall, left and right. The total climbing height is about 700m (2300ft). It is great wall climbing and can be done in both summer and winter. It takes about 13 hours to climb both walls.

4 Dinosaur Ridge 5.6–5.8 ⊠

First ascent not recorded

Climbing pinnacle by pinnacle along the Dinosaur Ridge will take two days, but the detour route takes only six hours. The ascent is 700m (2300ft). The ridge also has many other classic climbing routes, grade 5.8–5.10, which can be done from either the Sorak or the Jajeun Bawi Valleys. The latter, flowing into Chun-bul-dong Valley, is also particularly known for its ice climbing.

5 Red Wall of Jang Kun Peak
5.11–5.12 ☒

Y B Park and members of Crony AC 1978

The Red Wall is only an hour
from Sok Cho City, at Bi-sun-dae.
Park's climbing of it was memorable
because of the successive overhangs
and poor belay positions. Ascent
150m (500ft), takes 4–5 hours;
or 70m (230ft), takes 3 hours.

6 Dol Jan Chi Route ☒

Rock Party Alpine Club 1989

This route, on Ul San Am, was the
club's most noteworthy – 4km
(2½ miles) long, it covered 30
intermediate peaks, starting from
Hell's Gate (a large cave on the right
side of Ul San Am) and ending at the
30th, the Twin Peak. This route takes
about three days, the hardest peaks
being P3 and P20. P3's grade is 5.11b
and composed of three pitches.
The first pitch is a 40m (130ft) crack,
the second is 50m (165ft), and the
third 20m (65ft). P20's grade is 5.10c
and also composed of three pitches
of crack and slab.

how to get to sorak san

From Seoul, it takes approximately
six hours to reach Sorak San by express
bus line. However, by air it is only one
hour from Seoul Kim Po airport to Sok
Cho City, from where Sorak San is less
than 20 minutes' drive.

facilities

There are six refuges and shelters in the
park: Baek Dam shelter, Sorak shelter
(contact Sorak National Park Branch
Office), So Chung shelter, Yang Pok
refuge, Soo-ryum-dong refuge,
and Hee Woon Kag refuge.

The rescue parties can help foreign
climbers to find guides who can speak
a bit of English and Japanese.

when to climb

December–February are the best
months for the icefalls. July–August
is the rainy season, so avoid climbing
on Sorak during these months.

gear

In order to climb the various routes
and ridges of Sorak San, a helmet
is essential because of the frequent
stonefall. For climbing the To-wang-sung
Icefall, a 100m (330ft) rope (11mm/½in)
and at least 20 screws should be taken.

maps and guidebooks

The following map is useful: 'Mount Sorak
National Park', 1:50,000 (1995).

Very little has been written in English
on climbing in Korea. *Korea – A Lonely
Planet Guide Travel Survival Kit*, Robert
Storey and Geoff Crowther has a brief
introduction to the area.

language

Korean. English is not widely understood,
even in the areas frequented by tourists.

rescue and insurance

Five rescue parties operate around Sorak.
They are co-ordinated by the Korean

Alpine Club and the Korean Red Cross
Party. Insurance is not compulsory.

red tape

For environmental reasons, there
are some areas at Sorak San that
are periodically put out of bounds.
Camping is permitted only within
specified sites around shelters and
refuges, and only with the permission
of the National Park Office.

There are two periods during which
the forest is closed to protect it
from fire: 1 March–31 May and
15 November–15 December. But even
during these exclusion periods, there
are some routes that remain open.

1828 The 'Yarisawa Route', identified the previous year, was followed to the summit by a monk, Bannryu, carrying three Buddhist effigies. He was supported by local people. He spent six years preparing the attempt, and made four ascents altogether to supply the climbing route with safety chains.

1878 Professor W Gowland, a British metallurgist, became the first foreigner

to reach the summit. He wrote up his field investigations in his *Handbook for Travellers in Central and North Japan* (1881), describing the mountains as the 'Japanese Northern Alps' and Yari-ga Take as the 'Japanese Matterhorn'.

1892 Yari-ga Take was climbed by its 'Original Route'.

1893 Having failed the previous year on another line the Rev W Weston, British

missionary, became the first foreigner to repeat the 1892 route. He went on to have a great influence on mopuntaineering in Japan, and is known as the father of Japanese mountaineering. He wrote two books on the Japanese Alps: *Mountaineering and Exploration in the Japanese Alps* (1896) and *The Playground of the Far East* (1918).

1902 Japanese alpinists U Kojima and K Okano climbed Yari-ga Take. They provided the inspiration for the Japanese Alpine Club (formed in 1905).

1909 The traverse route to Yari-ga Take from the neighbouring peak of Hotaka Dake was first done by M Udono (Japanese) in August.

1912 The first ascent of the upper part of the North Ridge was completed

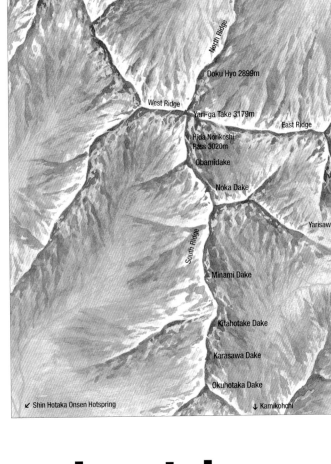

0 | 2km
0 | 1 mile

↗ Nakabusa Onsen Hotspring

North Ridge

Doku Hyo 2899m

West Ridge

Yari-ga Take 3179m

East Ridge

Hida Norikoshi Pass 3020m

Obamidake

Noka Dake

Yarisawa Valley

South Ridge

Minami Dake

Kitahotake Dake

Karasawa Dake

Okuhotaka Dake

↙ Shin Hotaka Onsen Hotspring   ↓ Kamikohchi

yari-ga take

sumiyo tsuzuki

Yari-ga Take, 3179m (10,430ft), lies in the Kita or Northern Japanese Alps, almost exactly in the middle of Honshu Island, the main island of Japan. The fourth-highest peak in Japan, it is named after a spear (Yari), because of the distinctive shape of its rocky summit. The Japanese Alps are composed mostly of metamorphic rock.

The Kita Alps consist of a magnificent series of 3000m (10,000ft) peaks, which include Okuhotaka Dake, 3190m (10,500ft), the third-highest mountain in Japan. A long, rugged ridge connects Okuhotaka Dake and Yari-ga Take and other high summits, offering a popular high traverse that takes two days.

In Japan, mountains have traditionally been respected as religious symbols and power places. Yari-ga Take was first climbed by a Buddhist monk and a Buddhist shrine still exists on its summit, maintaining the holy atmosphere. Climbing mountains for religious or ascetic reasons has always been important among devout Japanese. Alpinism, as such, began late in the 19th century and Yari-ga Take played a role of unparalleled importance in its development, providing climbing of all grades in the different seasons. Its popular routes are generally grade 3–4; however, the unstable conditions can make the climbing difficult.

ridges, faces, and peaks

Yari-ga Take is made up of four long, sharp-crested ridges with one main peak. The three least difficult ridges – the South, East, and West – meet below the Summit Peak at the South Shoulder, where there is a big lodge with a medical centre and facilities. From here, a single trail leads to the final sharp 'spear'.

Below the Main Summit are Doku Hyo, 2899m (9500ft), on the North Shoulder, and Ko-yari (Little Yari Pinnacle), a sharp tower, with good rock climbing, on the north of the West Ridge.

south and east sides Between the South and East Ridges, the vast Yarisawa Valley has traces of former glaciation, but Japan no longer has any glaciers. At the head of the valley, Yari-ga Take rises before you as a conspicuous symmetrical pyramid – recognizable from a long way off. The valley offers access to the 'Original Route' (1892), which was repeated by Walter Weston the following year and popularized by him.

The South Ridge of Yari-ga Take stands like a wall at the end of the valley, and links the mountain with the other 3000m (10,000ft) peaks.

Higashi Kama-one (East Ridge) is the site of the route called 'Kisaku Shindo' (new path), which was opened by Kisaku Kobayashi in 1921. It is a long, beautiful ridge, rising gently from the lower peaks, and takes a day to climb. This new approach made the

Right **Aerial shot of the North East Face. The ridge on the right is the North Ridge; Higashi Kama-one (the East Ridge) can be seen on the left.**

by Rev W Weston and S Nemoto (Japanese) with two porters.

1921 East Ridge climbed by K Kobayashi who was a hunter and mountain guide.

1922 The first complete climb of the North Ridge was done by Waseda University Alpine Club. There was something of a race to reach the summit by the same route, on the same day, by teams from two universities;

this has gone down in the mountain's history as a famous and dramatic story.

1927 A solo ascent of Ko-yari was made by Mr Itoh.

Ko-yari Pinnacle

South Face

East Ridge

ascent of Yari-ga Take from the north-east a much more feasible proposition. The South East Ridge gives access to the South Side of the peak from the East Ridge.

north and west sides Compared to the other side, the ridges on these sides see fewer trekkers, and contain some serious sections. From the Shin Hotaka Onsen Hotspring, it is a day's trek, through forest and romantic alpine meadows and up to the Hida Norikoshi Pass, 3020m (1000ft), to the South Shoulder.

Nishi Kama-one, the West Ridge, reaches directly up to the South Shoulder. The needle-sharp Ko-yari (Little Yari Pinnacle) is on its North Side.

The North Ridge, Kitakama-one, was the last to be climbed, even though more difficult ascents had been done elsewhere in the range. Above the point of Doku Hyo, the ridge becomes rockier and steeper as it nears the summit.

future climbing

There are probably no unclimbed routes on Yari-ga Take, but winter climbing on the North Ridge is challenging and difficult, and good training for the Himalaya.

All routes described on South, East, and West Ridges pass the South Shoulder.

south and east sides

Both sides start with a basic walk to the South Shoulder.

1 Yarisawa Route (South Face) Grade 3

Bannryu Matajyuro 1828

Traditional route for climbing Yari, completely equipped with ladders and chains. There is some difference in the lines of ascent and descent. Rocks are very loose and there is stonefall danger. Takes 1½ hours.

2 Higashi Kama-one (East Ridge or Kisaku Shindo)

K Kobayashi 1921

Opened by a hunter to provide a new approach as the new road made access easier from this side. The route follows a long, beautiful ridge, rising gently from lesser peaks and taking a day to climb.

3 South East Ridge ⊠

First ascent unknown

This branches off from route (2), and joins the South Shoulder. 1½ days.

4 East Rib ⊠

First ascent unknown

Also branching off from route (2), this reaches the summit via a traverse to the North Ridge. Complicated access and rockfall danger; one of the hardest routes in winter. Sees few ascents. It takes approximately five hours after separating from route (2).

north and west sides

Less frequented, with a quieter atmosphere. Beautiful forest lower down with alpine meadows above.

5 Nishi Kama-one (West Ridge) ⊠

First ascent unknown; opened by a hunter

Leads to South Shoulder, then completes the South Face to the summit. Takes 1–1½ days.

North Ridge

6

6 Kitakama-one (North Ridge) Grade 4
Waseda University team 1922

Line of the first complete ascent of the North Ridge. A serious route, but sees a lot of climbers in the high season. In winter, unstable weather conditions and vicious cold winds make it dangerous. Taking in Doku Hyo (on the North Shoulder), the ridge reaches directly to the summit. The long approach and height gain make it a much harder proposition than any other route. Two days.

7 Ko-yari: Little Yari Pinnacle Route ⊠
S Tsuchihashi and team 1922

Ko-yari has a number of routes and variations, from 1–6 hours long. To climb the longest of these requires a descent into one of the steep gullies. The most fantastic rock climbing on Yari-ga Take is found on Little Yari Pinnacle. This route climbs down from the South Shoulder or the North Ridge to the foot of the pinnacle; completing the climb over the pinnacle and onto the Main Peak is considered the ultimate challenge. The last steep section directly up to the summit is the most exciting.

how to get to yari-ga take

The famous resort of Kamikohchi is the most popular and simplest starting point. It is 5–6 hours by train and bus from Tokyo. Alternatively, you can go from the hotsprings of Shin Hotaka Onsen or Nakabusa Onsen. Private cars are not allowed into Kamikohchi: park 13km (8 miles) away at Sawando and take a bus or taxi in. There is no public transport in winter.

The most popular routes on the mountain are reached by walking up the Yarisawa Valley, by traversing from Tsubakuro Take to Higashi Kama, or from Hotaka Dake along the South Ridge.

facilities

From April–September finding accommodation and places to eat out is easy, but the lodges are closed in winter. Drinking water is always very scarce and, therefore, expensive.

You should bring all climbing equipment with you as there are no shops to buy it in the area.

when to climb

High season is late April–mid-November. July and August are especially enjoyable when there is plenty of colour and lots of flowers. Winter climbing requires careful planning, knowledge, technique, and weather information. Rock climbing is clearly best in summer, but the greatest fun and excitement is derived from trying some routes on the mixed ice and rock terrain of winter. However, be warned that, as for so many peaks around the world, conditions are completely different in winter. The area is then very remote and route finding in the strong wind is very difficult. Avalanches, severe cold, and blizzards from the north-west are particular hazards to alpinists.

gear

For winter, it's necessary to have full alpine equipment. In summer, good comfortable trekking shoes will be sufficient for most routes; however, as there is snow until early June, crampons will make walking easier and safer. Always carry warm clothing, waterproofs, and a pack cover, as heavy rain is frequent. Additionally, on normal routes at holiday times, a fund of patience is important in coping with the long queues!

maps and guidebooks

The best map is the 'North Alps', 1:130,000 (Geo Co Ltd).

There are no guidebooks in English but guidebooks in Japanese can be purchased locally.

language

Japanese. Most notices and signs are not in English, but Yari-ga Take is so well known that the way to go is clear once you are in the area.

rescue and insurance

There are books at the starting points in which to register your name, the date, your intended route, and so on, in case of emergency, but there is no system in place to check this. Be prepared to be self-sufficient. Rescue is undertaken by the police.

Insurance is not obligatory, but it is advisable as the rescue helicopters can be expensive.

red tape

Since this is a national park, you must not collect or disturb plants, creatures, or rocks and stones. Camping places are strictly limited.

North Atlantic
Ocean

Mediterranean
Sea

● Marrakech

Atlas Mtns

Jebel Toubkal

Red
Sea

M O R O C C O

S U D A N

U G A N D A

K E N Y A

*Ruwenzori
Mtns*

Margherita

C O N G O

Kampala ●

▲ Mt Keny

Nairobi ●

Kilimanjaro ▲

T A N Z A N I A

South Atlantic
Ocean

africa

Travellers to the Dark Continent were told of mountains covered in silver, or in salt, for the concept of snow was baffling to people from the plains. Even Europeans were sceptical for a long time that snow-capped mountains could exist in the vicinity of the equator. Now that we all do believe it, the sad thing is that the ice and snow of Africa's tallest peaks are diminishing year by year, due to global warming.

The peaks of Kilimanjaro and Mount Kenya were 'bagged' towards the end of the 19th century; those of the mysterious Ruwenzori had to wait until 1906, when the Duke of Abruzzi led an expedition that conquered most of its major summits. More extensive climbing development was undertaken during colonial rule, although the greatest advances of all were made during the late 1960s and the 1970s.

Africa's most northerly mountains are the Atlas, which rise behind the Atlantic and Mediterranean coasts of Morocco, Algeria, and Tunisia. Most of the climbing takes place on the higher summits south of Marrakech, where the High Atlas culminates in Jebel Toubkal.

Clockwise from left: **Kilimanjaro at sunrise; giant heather forest in the Ruwenzori; trekker on Pt Lenana of Mount Kenya**

1861–2 G Rohlfs (German) crossed the Atlas Mountains in disguise (the country was anti-European).

1871 A British scientific/botanical expedition of Alpine Club members, J D Hooker, J Ball, and G Maw, had the Sultan's approval to explore the area, but Berber hill tribes obstructed them at every opportunity. They climbed Jebel Gourza, 3280m (10,800ft), and reached the Tizi n' Tagharat, 3465m (11,400ft), above the Mizane Valley near Toubkal.

1901–14 French penetration of Morocco and the start of mountain explorations by geologists and others.

1923 Marquis de Segonzac (French) and party made the first European ascent (it may have had local ascents) of Toubkal. Surveying the next year gave the height as 4165m (13,700ft).

1924 The first explorations of the South Face were made by French parties: J Balay, M de Prandières, and L Neltner.

1927 South East Ridge was climbed by J de Lépiney and A Stofer (French).

1930 British B Beetham and Dr Brogden climbed the West-South-West Ridge.

1932 A major Italian expedition to the area, led by M A de Pollitzer-Pollenghi, traversed all the Mizane Valley peaks.

1934 A major Polish expedition climbed on Tichki and Afekoï.

1936 The West-North-West Ridge was descended by a party that included J de Lépiney.

1956 Morocco gained independence. Few climbs in a modern idiom have been made on Jebel Toubkal, as exploration has been shifted to other Atlas areas.

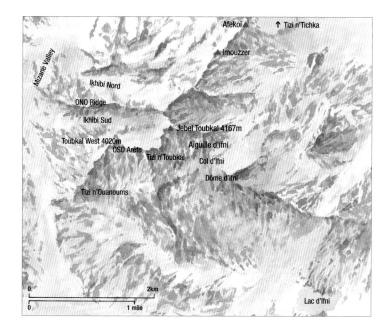

jebel toubkal

hamish brown

Jebel Toubkal, 4167m (13,700ft), the highest peak in North Africa, is the most popular mountain objective in the Atlas Mountains, which have their culmination in this Moroccan massif, 80km (50 miles) south of magical Marrakech. It lies in a compact group around the high Mizane Valley, which drains to Imlil, Asni, and the Haouz Plain of Marrakech. The sight of Toubkal's snowy horizon rimming the view southwards from the medieval walls and palm groves of Marrakech gives it an air of romantic unreality.

The first foreign ascent of Toubkal was made only in 1923. Morocco was a land of mystery well into the 20th century, its mountains the secretive abode of warrior Berbers. While now suffering the 'honeypot' effect of any highest summit, the romance remains. Jebel Toubkal is popular with trekkers and ski mountaineers; it is surprisingly neglected by climbers, given its easy access, sunny climate, and pleasant people, which should make it a tempting, and different, exotic mountain world.

ridges, faces, and peaks

Most of the Atlas Mountains are sedimentary rock, giving long, sweeping crests and bergs with deeply eroded canyons. But the Toubkal massif, contained by the Atlas road-passes of the Tizi n' Tichka, 2260m (7400ft), and the Tizi n' Test, 2092m (6900ft), is an area of volcanic activity, weathered into alpine crests and deep, narrow valleys: a satisfying 'architecture' with defined ridges and faces, while valleys between offer easy access.

south side The South Side of Toubkal plunges down about 1800m (6000ft) to the oddity of a small lake, the Lac d'Ifni, bounded on the south-east by a stepped ridge, falling to a col and the striated Ouimlilene or Dôme d'Ifni, 3876m (12,700ft), a complex world of crags, arêtes, gullies, and scree. The west edge is demarcated by the Tizi n' Ouanoums, 3664m (12,000ft), the first pass over the watershed west of Toubkal and giving access to the lake. From the Tizi rises the classic OSO Arête (West-South-West Ridge), which ends on a shoulder, Toubkal West, 4020m (13,200ft), before linking with the tourist route beyond.

west and north west side This side is drained by the Mizane Valley with the Tizi n'Ouanoums and Tizi n'Ouagane at its head, the former leading to Lac d'Ifni, the latter to the Agoundis Valley. Two hanging valleys, the Ikhibi Nord and the Ikhibi Sud, overlook the Mizane and offer easy routes of ascent. The former was the original *voie normale* (and is still the pleasanter route) before a Club Alpin Français (CAF) refuge was built below the Ikhibi Sud at 3207m (10,500ft). Between the Tizi and the Ikhibi Sud is a nameless face with gullies and rock bands offering winter routes; between the two Ikhibis is a long, jagged rock crest of alpine character.

Working north-east down the Mizane, there is an area of rocks and gullies before a big corrie dominates. It is marked by rock bands (ice walls in winter) and leads up to shapely Afekoï, one of several peaks along the watershed ridge running north-east from Toubkal to the Tizi n' Tagharat, 3442m (11,300ft). The remaining east slopes are broken and scree-covered, offering no climbing.

future climbing

There are some long winter routes on the South Face, opportunities in the Mizane Valley, and some gap-filling, but new lines are limited.

Right **The south-western aspect of Toubkal from Ouanoukrim, the second-highest peak in the Atlas Mountains. The classic West-South-West Ridge slants up left from the Tizi n'Ouanoums in the centre of the picture.**

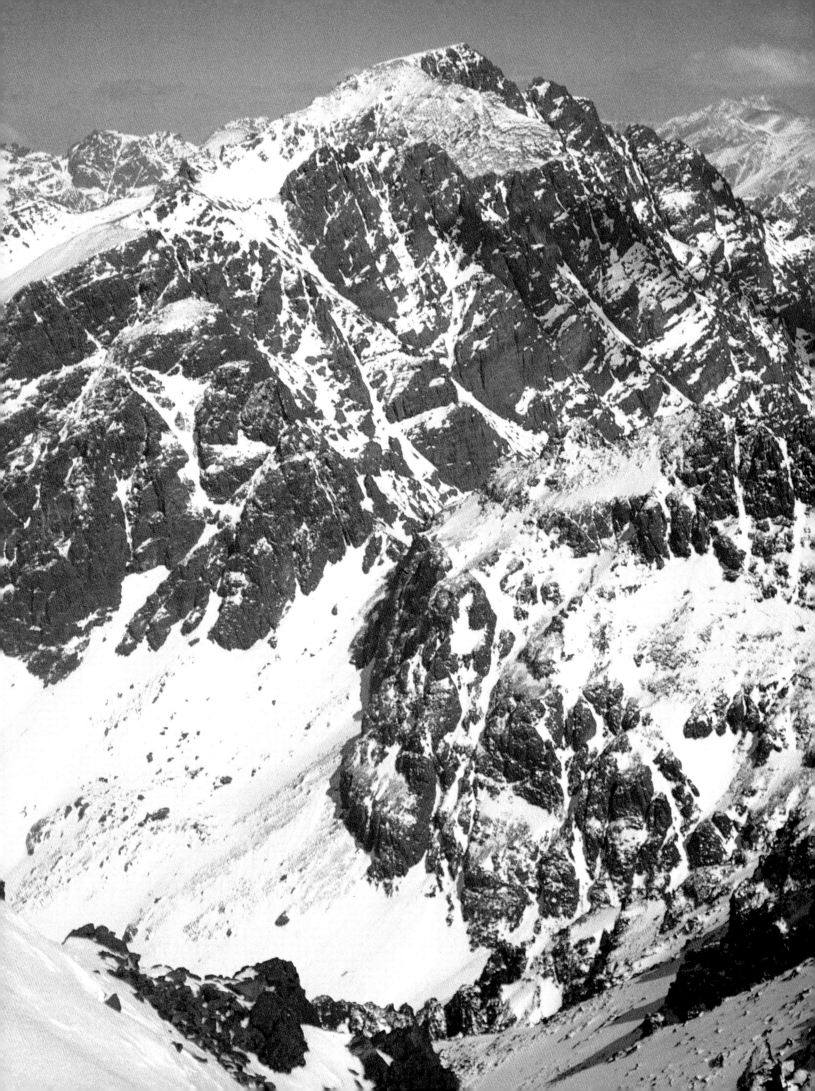

Ikhibi Nord

West-North-West Ridge

Ikhibi Sud

West-South-West Ridge

Warning! Because many tourist guidebooks describe Toubkal as an easy ascent there is a tendency to attempt it ill-equipped, in the wrong conditions, and without proper acclimatization. Heat, dryness, and altitude can overtake even the fit. Toubkal should be treated with all the respect that would be due to a comparable Alpine peak.

Also note that names and heights are often given differently on the various maps and guidebooks and can mislead the careless.

1 Afekoï Valley Approaches

The Afekoï is guarded by a rock band (a curtain of ice in winter), which tends to stop exploration. There is a route up the left (north) side of the band, or a scrambling route can be picked to the south. There is plane wreckage high in the valley and some fine towers on the Toubkal side, where some interesting climbs must be waiting. Afekoï itself, 3755m (12,300ft), gives a good scramble, then a satisfying ridge or gullies lead on over Imouzzer or Tibherine for Toubkal. The full traverse over the crest peaks of Afekoï, Agoujdad

n'Tichki, 3607m (11,840ft), and Tichki, 3753m (12,300ft), is enjoyable and is classic in winter.

west side

This offers both non-technical routes and good winter, alpine style climbs.

2 Ikhibi Nord

First ascensionists unknown, probably 1923
This route starts slightly down-valley from the CAF refuge so it escapes most tourists, although there is now a track up the hanging valley. Plane wreckage (from a 1970 crash) may call for a diversion on Tibherine, 3887m (12,750ft), and Imouzzer, 4010m (13,150ft), offers a short climb. For the non-technical, this is the best ascent route. 1000m (3300ft); 3–4 hours.

3 West-North-West Ridge (ONO Arête) III/IV

J de Lépiney and party 1936
Seldom done but an enjoyable, long traverse with many towers and gaps. Some difficulties can be turned or abseiled. Allow seven hours.

4 The Ikhibi Sud 'Tourist Route'

In winter this will merit crampons and respect. The route climbs steeply from the CAF refuge to a hanging valley, then breaks right towards a col, Tizi n' Toubkal, to take easy slopes up to a final narrow crest and the small summit plateau topped by an iron trigonometrical marker. In summer, an eroded scree horror of a route! Ascent 960m (3150ft); 2½–3 hours.

5 Face between OSO Arête and Ikhibi Sud III/IV

This is a large and obvious face (500m/1640ft), seamed with gullies offering mixed climbs in winter.

6 West-South-West Ridge (OSO Arête) III/IV

B Beetham and Dr Brogden 1930
Something of a classic alpine style climb with marked steps and a fine situation. Leads to a shoulder, Toubkal West, and the col, beyond which the normal route (4) is joined. A splendid winter route taking six hours with an ascent of 360m (1180ft) from Toubkal West to the col.

south face

This high face has plenty of scope but is disappointingly loose and scrappy. It offers many steep lines of III/IV.

7 Ouimlilene or Dôme d'Ifni

This is the notable feature on the South Side, occasionally reached from the Col d'Ifni, 3750m (12,300ft). The col can be gained by a 3-hour, but easy, traverse from the Tizi n'Ouanoums.

8 Over the Aiguille d'Ifni III/IV

J de Lépiney and A Stofer 1927
From the Col d'Ifni 'an impressive staircase' of ridge leads to the summit of Toubkal over the Aiguille d'Ifni, with pitches of III/IV if keeping to the crest. Four hours from the col; 470m (1540ft) of ascent.

Aiguille d'Ifni

Dôme d'Ifni

Col d'Ifni

how to reach toubkal

You can fly to Marrakech or reach it by train from Tangier. From Marrakech you can hire a minibus or Land Rover and drive to Imlil, or take a bus or taxi from the city's Bab er Rob terminus to Asni (Saturday souk or market), then to Imlil. Toubkal (Neltner) Hut, 3200m (10,500ft), is a 5-hour walk up the Mizane Valley via Around and the pilgrim shrine of Sidi Chamarouch. It is the base for most Toubkal climbs but it can be overcrowded at peak periods.

facilities

Imlil, 1740m (5700ft), the nearest village base, has a CAF refuge, small hotels, restaurants, shops, gear-hire, a guides bureau, and mules for carrying equipment to the Toubkal Hut. Around has village accommodation. Camping is possible at the Toubkal Hut area.

when to climb

Toubkal is climbed year-round but November–January is least practical. February–April can give excellent clear spells with mixed winter routes in condition, while June–September can be hot with the snow disappearing in spring.

gear

Standard requirements should be brought. In winter it is pleasant to ski to reach rock climbs. Toubkal is a fine ski ascent by either Ikhibi Nord or Ikhibi Sud and, in good conditions, one can descend as far as Sidi Chamarouch.

maps and guidebooks

Maps are something of a problem as the issuing authority in Rabat takes days to supply maps (or doesn't!), and will not sell them abroad. Some local guides and Marrakech hotels (Hotel Ali) may be able to provide the 'Oukaïmeden-Toubkal', 1:100,000 or the 'Toubkal', 1:50,000 sheets. Try a major map stockist or try AMIS (Atlas Mountains Information Service), 26 Kirkcaldy Road, Burntisland, Fife, KY3 9HQ, Scotland. (SAE please.)

Le Massif du Toubkal, J Dresch and J de Lépiney (1942, re-issued) is the only climbing guide. Atlas Mountains, Morocco, R G Collomb (West Col,1987), while dated, is the best general work in English. Ski Dans le Haut Atlas de Marrakech, C Cominelli (1984) is useful for its maps and diagrams, and describes some climbs. For background reading try the updated Rough Guide to Morocco.

language

French is the generally understood language but some guides speak English and other major European languages such as German, Spanish, and Italian.

rescue and insurance

There are minimal rescue services and parties should be self-sufficient and take out adequate insurance cover.

red tape

For practical, diplomatic, and social reasons employing a certificated local guide is a good idea as a first visit can be something of a culture shock. There are no particular restrictions on climbing in the Toubkal massif.

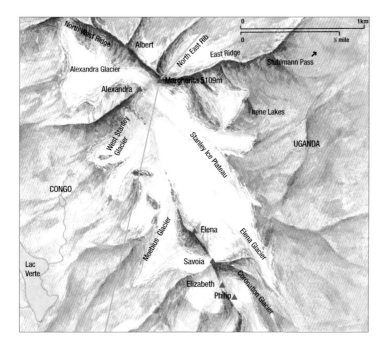

margherita

john cleare

Margherita, 5109m (16,763ft), is the highest of 10 summits over 4800m (15,700ft) in the remote Ruwenzori Range, which stands on the Uganda/Congo (lately Zaire) frontier in Central Africa, just 50km (30 miles) north of the equator. This 'block mountain' of ancient Pre-Cambrian rock extends some 80km by 30km (1000 square miles) above 2000m (6500ft). The six highest massifs of the range each rise to several individual summits and hold permanent ice. Mt Stanley is the highest of these massifs, and Margherita is its highest summit. Also known as the Mountains of the Moon and translated as Hills of Rain, the Ruwenzori Range produces copious waters, which feed the River Nile.

Access to the Ruwenzori has never been easy, always logistically and often also for political reasons. Of the comparatively few parties that do visit, very few include serious high-standard mountaineers. This means that its importance lies not in the technical mountaineering it presents, but in its remoteness and its aura of mystery, besides its incongruity as a glacier-bearing range at such a latitude, and the characteristic and exotic vegetation and ice formations that clothe it.

ridges, faces, and peaks

Margherita is one of the three northern summits on Mt Stanley. The Stanley massif forms an elevated crest, some 7km (4½ miles) long and about 3km (2 miles) wide, between the high Bujuku Valley below its eastern (Ugandan) slopes and the tangled cwms and hills beneath its western (Congolese) flank. The Stanley Ice Plateau drapes over the middle third of the Stanley crest, and glacier tongues hang from it on all sides.

The South Stanley Peaks are clustered beyond the end of the Ice Plateau. Elena, 4968m (16,300ft); Savoia, 4977m (16,330ft); Elizabeth, 4929m (16,170ft); Philip, 4919m (16,140ft); and their satellites are monolithic, ice-hung peaks, linked by a narrow ridge (the latter two cradle the beautiful, hanging Coronation Glacier). Steep, savage icefalls characterize their western flanks while, eastward, vertiginous rock walls and buttresses rise from the Elena Glacier, the gentle south-eastern tongue of the Ice Plateau.

At its northern end, the icy whaleback of the Ice Plateau rears up to form the three North Stanley summits; first the narrow, wave-like, transverse crests of Alexandra, 5091m (16,703ft), and Margherita – separated by a steep ice saddle – and then via some 300m (1000ft) of narrow ice ridge to the rocky pyramid of Albert, 5087m (16,690ft), where the Mt Stanley crest ends with a large triangular North Face.

The summits of both Alexandra and Margherita rise at the western extremities of their respective crests, which are hung with large cornices and encrusted with bizarre ice formations. On the Congolese side, Margherita's summit drops abruptly to the steep, hanging ice of the comparatively extensive Alexandra Glacier, crossed by several sérac bands before its wide tongue terminates at around 4500m (14,800ft). In the opposite direction, Margherita's crest falls as a well-defined East Ridge initially of ice, then of steep mixed ground before dropping as craggy cliffs into the boggy moorland of Stuhlmann Pass, some 950m (3100ft) below.

Margherita also throws down a West Face (the Alexandra Glacier) and an East Ridge of its own, while a short North East Rib springs from the wide glacier-fringed hollow between the East Ridge and the North East Ridge of Albert.

It is difficult to divorce climbing on Margherita from climbing on its close neighbours, Alexandra and Albert. Indeed, an ascent

Above **Two climbers on the Stanley Ice Plateau looking north towards Alexandra and Margherita, in the Ruwenzori Range. Margherita is the right-hand peak.**

of one will usually involve a traverse of another, either on the way up or down. In all, 16 different climbing routes have been described on the three North Stanley summits, 11 of them reaching the summit of Margherita itself.

future climbing

The few powerful parties that have visited Mt Stanley over the years have ascended all major features and the more obvious variations. While there is scope for new climbs, they are likely to be unaesthetic routes, searching out difficulties for their own sake. Logistical problems, poor weather, and typically vegetated rock mean that even strong parties will need serious research, determination, and luck to achieve anything ambitious.

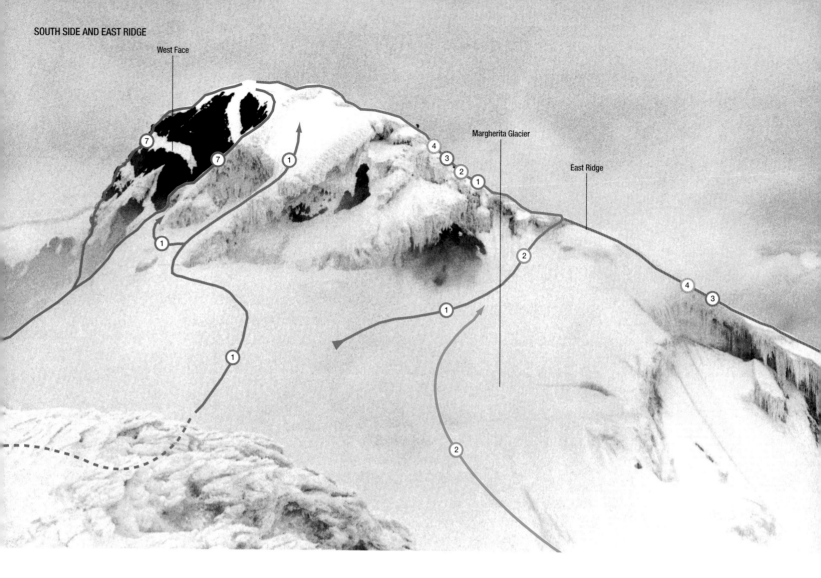

West Face

Margherita Glacier

East Ridge

south side

Routes must first traverse Alexandra having gained its upper ridge (1), or work around the foot of Alexandra to gain Margherita's East Ridge (2).

1 From Stanley Ice Plateau via Alexandra AD

Duke of the Abruzzi, guides J Petigax and C Ollier, and porter J Brocherel 1906

Route of first ascent, now a classic and frequently climbed. Dangerous cornices may make the route harder while best line may be elusive in typical thick mist. Ascent 350m (1150ft); 3–4 hours.

2 From Stanley Ice Plateau via Margherita Glacier and Upper East Ridge AD-

G N Humphreys, E H Armitage, R T Wickham, and G Oliver 1926

Regular route contours below the end of Alexandra's East Ridge, crosses Margherita Glacier, and climbs up onto the final section of the snow/ice East Ridge. Similar problems to (1); also crevasses to negotiate on glacier section. Ascent 300m (1000ft); 3–4 hours.

east ridge

In its entirety well over 1km (¾ mile) in length, the difficult and confusing lower section of this great ridge is rarely attempted (3).

3 East Ridge Integrale from Stuhlmann Pass D/V

T Bernardzikiewicz and T Pawlowski 1939

Ascends the ridge's blunt end on steep, mossy, and difficult rock for 300m (1000ft) to gain its crest. Mixed ground follows, broken by a rock step (III) leading to the final snow/ ice ridge. Main problems are route finding on lower sections and greasy, lichenous rock. Ascent 600m (2000ft); technical climbing; 6–10 hours.

4 East Ridge from Irene Lakes AD/III

R Bere, R Ladkin, and P Hicks 1945; R F Davies and R L Forsyth 1953

Two variations lead from the bivouac hut in the south-east cwm of Margherita onto the East Ridge above the first and second steep sections respectively. The latter, easy to find in mist, is the simplest on Margherita. 450m (1480ft); technical climbing; 4–7 hours.

north side

More accurately Margherita's North West Ridge, this easiest of final approaches can only be gained by first climbing Albert. Albert's North West and North East Ridges are fine mixed routes, the former a superb classic; the North Face is a steep and serious Scottish style ice couloir.

5 North Ridge from Albert F

Count X de Grunne and party, guide J Georges 1932

An easy and heavily corniced snow ridge. Vertical interval about 60m (200ft); 15 minutes.

west side

Margherita's lone buttress rises from the upper Alexandra Glacier (7). Although almost any line up the glacier is possible, the easiest (6) gains the ridge linking Margherita to Albert (5) just above its lowest point, also making a good descent route.

6 West Face via Alexandra Glacier PD

Count X de Grunne and party, guide J Georges 1932

Glacier route long considered *the* ice route of the Ruwenzori. Dangers include sérac and snow avalanche. Ascent of 600m (2000ft); 2–3 hours from Moraine Hut site.

7 West Face Integral AD

P Ghiglione, Carlo Mauri, and B Ferrario 1960

The Alexandra Glacier is gained direct via the rock wall forming the foot of Alexandra's West Ridge, while the summit is reached directly from below, up a steep rock/ice buttress. Ascent 600m (2000ft); 4–6 hours from Moraine Hut site.

north east flank

Large and complex, the flank's upper part is divided by a prominent rib into twin cwms, the left one holding a small glacier.

8 North East Face/North East Rib via Margherita North East Glacier AD/IV

E Eisenmann and T Schnackig 1938

This small, hanging glacier is reached by climbing the broken cliffs beneath via ledges, slabs, and an awkward chimney (IV). About 550m (1800ft); technical climbing; 6–8 hours from Bujuku Hut.

The image is labelled (from left to right): North East Face, North Ridge, Margherita, Alexandra, West Face, Alexandra Glacier, with route markers numbered 8, 5, 3, 2, 4, 1, 7, 6.

how to reach margherita

Travel in eastern Congo is extremely difficult, so access from Uganda is recommended. Private overland travel from Nairobi is convenient, but Kampala is served by scheduled flights (to Entebbe) where you can catch a bus for the 12-hour ride to Kasese, the nearest village. You will then need to walk or catch a lift to the mountain.

Now in ruins (as are all seven Ruwenzori huts), Bujuku Hut, 3980m (13,000ft), near Lake Bujuku is the best centre for Mt Stanley climbs. It is best to bring your own tents but there are rock shelters and caves that the porters will use. Bujuku is reached from the Ibanda roadhead, which is 14km (9 miles) from Kasese. The hard 3-day trek from the roadhead is over 2350m (7700ft) of strenuous and boggy ascent.

facilities

There are no facilities in the area, and only very basic food is available in Uganda. Climbing rations and camping stoves/utensils must be imported. You can hire porters to carry your gear and food (see red tape).

when to climb

The weather is characteristically awful. A good day starts clear and frosty, by midday clouds wreath the tops, and snow is falling by mid-afternoon, yet at dusk the sky clears again. The best weather is likely in January–February and June–August, and pre-dawn starts are recommended. Other times of the year should be avoided.

gear

Ruwenzori climbing is expeditionary, acclimatization to altitude is essential, and all movement is slow and laborious. Without reasonable logistical support climbers cannot remain in the field long enough to achieve anything ambitious. Clothing should reflect a climate that is never excessively cold but always damp, and frequently wet. If your clothes get wet, they are likely to remain so for the duration, so warm and weatherproof clothing suitable for a Scottish winter is more appropriate than high-altitude Himalayan gear. Rock is typically lichenous and slippery except at the highest altitudes, while most ice is encrusted rime and only rarely hard and blue. Both climbing boots and expendable approach-march boots are suggested while usual alpine climbing gear – crampons, axes, ropes, rock and ice pitons, etc – is essential.

maps and guidebooks

'Margherita', 1:50,000, Uganda Sheet 65/11 (Directorate of Overseas Surveys/ DOS, 1957) is the definitive map but is difficult to obtain.

Ruwenzori Map & Guide, Andrew Wielochowski (West Col Productions, 1989), is a useful map-cum-miniguide. It includes both a 1:50,000 survey map of central Ruwenzori and a 1:20,000 survey map of Mts Stanley, Speke, and Baker, based on DOS publications. *Guide to the Ruwenzori*, H A Osmaston and D Pasteur (West Col Productions, 1972) is the definitive climbing and trekking guide. *Africa's Mountains of the Moon*, Guy Yeoman (Elm Tree Books, 1989) is an interesting general book on the Ruwenzori.

language

Swahili – some English is spoken.

rescue and insurance

There are no organized rescue services. Insurance is recommended, not obligatory.

red tape

The co-operative Ruwenzori Mountain Services will arrange permits and organize the guide and porter crews that are obligatory.

Civil war seems endemic in this part of Africa and, although Uganda now appears comparatively tranquil, recent trouble in Rwanda and Congo/Zaire hardly encourages travellers to this area. The West Flank rises within the Parc National Albert and has its own entry restrictions, but its future is uncertain.

Warning: although Margherita stands on the frontier, the border is a hypothetical line and does not follow the ridge crest of Mt Stanley. Thus it is frequently impossible to tell if you are in Uganda or Congo. Certainly routes (4) and (5) lie totally within Congolese territory and should be approached cautiously, as it is not unknown for unsuspecting climbers to be arrested for illegal entry by border patrols.

picnic on the equator

stephen venables

"It was all thanks to Willoughby that I climbed Margherita. He and his wife Victoria had met in Lhasa, bicycled through Tibet, and honeymooned in the New Guinea jungle. Deciding that they wanted to climb mountains, they had organized a group of friends to attempt the three highest peaks in Africa in early 1986. I was enrolled as guide, cook, and general dogsbody, in an attempt to add some clout to what was probably the most inexperienced group of people ever to set off on an expedition."

We warmed up painfully on Kilimanjaro, ascending in just a week from sea level to nearly 6000m, spending Boxing Day night camped on the summit plateau. Never have I felt so ill on a mountain. But from there things improved all the way. Acclimatized, we celebrated New Year's Eve joyously, with copious champagne, at an idyllic camp on Mt Kenya, and two days later four of the group did their first ever rock climb to the summit of Nelion. But for me, the real excitement of our 4-week safari was its third stage – the journey west, across Uganda to the elusive Ruwenzori, the Mountains of the Moon.

Years of civil war had demolished Uganda. Buildings were scarred by shellfire and tanks rusted at street corners. Our bus stopped at endless checkpoints (on one occasion the driver had to ask a uniformed youth to unload his rocket-launcher before coming aboard to check passports), and in between we lurched through giant potholes, splattered with the red mud of Africa.

In Kasese, at the foot of the mountains, we stocked up with supplies for our porters. Then a short steep drive took us up to the roadhead at Ibanda, where we were hustled into the office of the Mountain Club of Uganda to sign up our porters. Back in England, Henry Osmaston, co-author of the Ruwenzori guide-book, had asked me to say 'wobukiri' to his old friend John Matte, father of 45 children and undisputed head of the local portering closed shop. Matte smiled at the greeting and introduced us to a son, Aloysius, who was to be our head porter and who proved an able leader, presiding over a cheerful, hardworking team of local Bakonjo tribesmen.

The first day in the usually tough Ruwenzori mountains was quite gentle. The sun shone, birds flitted amid semi-tropical vegetation, butterflies shimmered in the balmy air, and we had only a fairly short climb to the first hut on the ridge of Nyabitaba.

In the morning, the sun still shone as we slithered down through bamboo jungle to the crossing of the Bujuku River and contoured up the far side, through a zone of giant brambles. But then it started to rain, real Ruwenzori rain – thick, luxuriant

sheets of it, seeping inexorably through clothing and turning the narrow trail into a quagmire. By lunchtime we had climbed out of the semi-tropical belt into a higher zone of giant heathers.

We emerged from this tangled confusion to negotiate Bigo Bog. Hopping from tussock to tussock, we missed repeatedly and lurched into the intervening channels of black slime. Bigo Bog fills a great hanging plain, encircled on three sides by mountains smothered in dense vegetation. In the soft blue light of a misty evening it was incredibly beautiful, and it was with a mood of deep contentment that we settled into our camp on the far side of the Bog, washing out sodden garments and changing into dry overnight clothes. Rotten stumps of giant *Lobelia wollastonii* were coaxed into flame and wood smoke soon mingled with the glorious aroma of cinnamon, cloves, and wine as we prepared a cauldron-full of heart-warming glüwein.

... trying to match ... ill-assorted crampons to 11 pairs of bog-sodden boots ...

Day three was our toughest. From Bigo Bog, the trail climbed up a long steep ridge, weaving through giant spikes of lobelia. It rained all morning and, when we finally emerged onto the next hanging valley level to skirt round Bujuku Lake, I couldn't help agreeing with Bill Tilman's dismissal of this 'mournful, shallow mere which, with its foetid, mud-lined shores, was in harmony with the desolate landscape ...'

Our porters also seemed disenchanted and threatened to strike but somehow, with my own cajoling and Willoughby's diplomacy, we persuaded them to continue up the vertiginous,

Far left **A rare clearing on the Elena Glacier allows the group to check its position.**

Left **Looking down on Bigo Bog with its weird and luxuriant vegetation.**

rotting trench of Groundsel Gully and over the final ridge of snow-sprinkled rocks, where we slithered in our boots while they, despite their loads, balanced nimbly on frozen bare feet.

Depositing their loads, they left immediately, to return to the comparative comfort of a cave at Bujuku Lake, leaving us to settle into the Elena Huts – two semi-dilapidated wooden cabins, perched on the rocks at about 4540m, close to the tongue of the Stanley Glacier, which lurked just above us, invisible in the mist. My task was to find the route up this glacier to the summit of Margherita. Tied to my rope would be Georgina, James, Louisa, and Peter from London; Anthony, Victoria, and Doune from Tokyo; and Isabelle and Didier from Lyon, with their 70-year-old father, Maurice. Didier had some climbing experience; the rest had never set foot on a glacier.

I prevaricated for a whole day, using the mist and drizzle as an excuse for inaction. Cut off from the world on our bleak rocky perch, I was moved by the extraordinary camaraderie that our group had developed during its month on the equatorial snows. No one grumbled about the cold and the damp. Instead, they got on cheerfully with the job of trying to match 11 pairs of ill-assorted crampons to 11 pairs of bog-sodden boots in readiness for the climb. However, the skies remained resolutely dank and the next morning – our last available day for the climb – we had to set off regardless, into the white-out.

The pre-dawn departure was chaotic, but we got away soon after first light, a long line of roped figures, black against grey, recalling, as someone pointed out, images of herded convicts. Compass bearings guided us up the featureless snowy hump of the Stanley Glacier until we glimpsed a hint of a ridge on our left. I hoped that this was the South East Ridge of Alexandra, in

which case we had to skirt beneath it, heading north. So we set a new course and found ourselves descending slightly into a bowl. Was this right? Were those crevasses supposed to be there? I began to dither, suggesting that we might consider a judicious retreat, pointing out that Eric Shipton and Bill Tilman, arguably the finest mountain explorers of all time, had got lost up here. My charges were having none of it and insisted on continuing, so we had another look at the Osmaston/Pasteur sketch map, took another bearing, and groped our way forward again, shuffling towards what I hoped would be the East Ridge of Margherita.

Soon we were climbing again, weaving our way through a labyrinth of icicle-fringed caverns and weird rime gargoyles that seemed to mirror the surreal vegetation of the lower slopes. Suddenly, much sooner than I expected, we emerged onto the ridge crest. The recommended route hits the ridge some way from the summit, but we seemed to have climbed some new, direct variation and almost immediately we found ourselves on top of a mountain. As we posed in the mist for a triumphal photo I made no promises that this was actually the summit of Margherita and it was only later, after checking the details with Aloysius, that our success was confirmed.

We never actually saw Margherita but, descending the Stanley Glacier that afternoon, we did get a glimpse of the magnificent ice-draped rock turrets of the outlying Stanley peaks. There was clearly good work to be done there, but the glorious greenery of the valley beckoned. Margherita was a wonderfully unique summit, but what made it really special was the whole experience of getting there – and getting back. We completed the popular circuit over the Freshfield Pass to the Mubuku Valley to get back to Ibanda. It was all magical, from the dream-like Kitandara Lakes to the vertical quagmire over the Freshfield Pass (where Isabelle hurled herself in reckless muddy somersaults), to the great rock shelter of Bujongolo, to the cave of Kabamba, where we made our last camp, watching a full moon rise above the ghostly outlines of the giant heathers. I found the heather forest, on our last morning, a place of total enchantment. The dew-beaded pearls of the 'everlasting' helichrysum flowers burst suddenly into orange flower with the first rays of sunshine, and the hanging mosses glowed yellow, green, and crimson. Soon we were down in the semi-tropical bamboo, enjoying a quick swim and sunbathe in the Mubuku River, then rushing back up to Nyabitaba, then down again, through a farewell drenching of afternoon Ruwenzori rain to Ibanda, where our minibus was waiting with the last reserves of expedition wine.

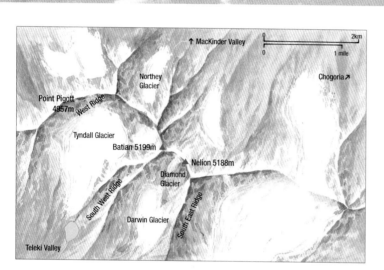

mount kenya

iain allan

Mount Kenya, 5199m (17,058ft), is Africa's second-highest mountain. It rises from the plains of central Kenya, some 95km (60 miles) east of the Great Rift Valley, and 180km (120 miles) north of Nairobi. From the plains, its twin peaks, Batian and Nelion, seem to float like a distant fortress in the sky, or – in the words of the Wakamba people, living some 200km (120 miles) away – like a 'Cock Ostrich'. To them, the white glaciers and contrasting dark rock of Mount Kenya have the appearance of black-and-white plumage.

For the mountaineer, this beautiful peak will always be the most important mountain on the African continent. It was immortalized by the brilliant climbing achievements of Eric Shipton, Percy Wyn Harris, and Bill Tilman in the 1920s and early 1930s. Modern climbing techniques were introduced by Barry Cliff in 1963, and ice climbing came of age in the 1970s with resident Park Warden Phil Snyder. To such illustrious names should be added Ian Howell, who arrived in Kenya from England in 1967. More than any other person, he has set standards that have brought Mt Kenya into a position where it can rate alongside the great mountains of the world. Howell has climbed nearly all of the

33 routes on Batian and Nelion, and has pioneered 11 of them. He also single-handedly built a comfortable bivouac hut on the summit of Nelion in 1970 – something that checked the fatality rate caused by climbers descending Nelion's South East Face in the dark, which until then had been a huge problem.

In the 1970s, he formed a strong partnership with me, and we searched out every major unclimbed line we could find on the mountain. In 1980, our first ascent of the very serious (and unrepeated) 'North Gate' (21), which ascends the great Super-couloir between Batian and Nelion, brought an end to our highly productive decade.

ridges, faces, and peaks

As well as Nelion and Batian, the two main peaks, the Mount Kenya massif has many subsidiary summits, such as Point Pigott, 4957m (16,265ft), and Point John, 4883m (16,020ft), on one of the southern spurs of the mountain. The rock is near-perfect, composed mainly of basalt and trachyte, and the fact that the mountain straddles the equator enhances the climbing potential: for nearly half the year one side of the peak is free of snow and ice, while the other side is plastered. When the sun passes its zenith the situation reverses. However, like many mountains around the world that lie in the proximity of the equator, the glaciers and icefalls of Mount Kenya are receding at a dramatic rate.

south face When viewed from the south-west in the Teleki Valley, the great buttresses of Batian (to the west) and Nelion (to the south) are split by the Diamond Glacier, which is perhaps the most spectacular and obvious feature on the mountain. From the base of this glacier falls the Diamond Couloir, one of the world's great ice climbs, although now barely joined together for half of the year due to glacial recession. Between these icefalls and the South West Ridge to the left stands the impressive Diamond Buttress, location of some of the hardest rock climbing on Mount Kenya. Left of the South West Ridge, and rising in a grand sweep from the Tyndall Glacier, is the West Face, with the elegant West Ridge forming the dominant left skyline of the South Face. To the right of the Diamond Couloir is the steep Darwin Glacier and its bordering South East Ridge.

north face There are few hanging ice forms on this face; it is composed of a series of large grey-brown rock buttresses, interspersed with occasional rubble-strewn amphitheatres. This

1980 I F Howell and I Allan forged 'North Gate' (21) up the Supercouloir between Batian and Nelion.

Above **A circular rainbow reflects onto the impressive rocky flanks of Nelion, Mount Kenya.**

side has an altogether darker, more brooding presence, lacking the subtle play of light that so characterizes the South Face. When viewed from the MacKinder Valley, Batian and Nelion are split by the shadowed deep gash of the Supercouloir. Left of this is the spectacular North East Face of Nelion, where many superb-quality rock routes exist. Bordering the right side of the North Face is the hanging, but rapidly dwindling, Northey Glacier.

future climbing

The big lines on Mount Kenya may have already fallen, but a world of fine new climbing awaits a fresh generation of climbers. The sheer walls and buttresses found on the East and North East Sides of Nelion present numerous challenges for the free rock climber, and prominent gaps also still exist on Batian's Diamond Buttress.

Free climbers should also look to the occasional aid sections on existing routes. Many of these have only been ascended once or twice, and would go free with some effort.

Batian
West Ridge
South West Ridge
Nelion
Diamond Couloir
Gate of the Mists
Diamond Glacier
Darwin Glacier

spidery couloir right of the Diamond Couloir with all the exposure of its more famous counterpart. From the end of the couloir, the first party of the season often has to cut a window through the icicle curtain that forms the snout of the Diamond Glacier. Only worth doing May–October.

7 South Face Route 4
A H Firmin and J S Bagenal 1950
Nowadays this is climbed as a pure ice route during the June to October season.

8 MacKinder's Route 4 ⊠
H J MacKinder, C Ollier, and J Brocherel 1899
Not often done. The 'Normal Route' (9) is easier, and ice recession has made the Diamond Glacier increasingly difficult.

9 Normal Route 4
E E Shipton and P Wyn Harris 1929
A great classic. Long with complex route finding. Much of the climbing is Grade 3, but the crux pitch is 4. Owing to ice recession the Gate of the Mists has become more difficult.

10 Heim Direct 6 ⊠
L Gouault and A Parkin 1990
A very bold mixed route that takes the right side of the West Face.

west face
11 West Face 5 ⊠
R A Caukwell and G W Rose 1955
Predominantly an ice climb, this has suffered owing to glacier recession. Climbers should be prepared for sections of hard verglas climbing.

12 The Untravelled World 6 ⊠
R Barton and D Morris 1978
An ice route that has altered considerably since the first ascent owing to glacier recession. Probably a harder undertaking today.

13 West Ridge Route 5
E E Shipton and H W Tilman 1930
The grand route of Mount Kenya.

north and east sides
14 Grand Traverse 5 ⊠
R W Baillie and T Phillips 1974
A great traverse of Point Pigott, Batian (West Ridge), Nelion, and Point John.

15 East Face Route 6, A3
H Klier, S Aeberli, and G B Cliff 1963
A fine direct line up an exceptionally steep face. It will probably go free.

Unless you are exceptionally well acclimatized, all the routes should be regarded as 2-day climbs. Ian Howell's hut on Nelion's summit can be used for climbs on that peak; on Batian plan for a bivouac.

south face
1 South West Ridge Route 4
A H Firmin and J W Howard 1946
A frequently climbed classic and, although more sustained, no harder than Batian's 'Standard Route' (25).

2 Diamond Buttress Direct 6, A3
I F Howell and I J Allan 1978
More meandering than direct, but excellent nevertheless.

3 Diamond Buttress: Equator 6+, AI
I F Howell and I J Allan 1979
A major direct line on the Diamond Buttress. Sustained and technical on brilliant rock.

4 Diamond Buttress: Original Route 7
I F Howell and J Temple 1976
A long, technical classic.

5 Diamond Couloir 6
P Snyder and T Mathenge 1973
The definitive ice climb. An extraordinary line that has come to symbolize Mount Kenya. The main difficulties lie in the first pitch and the headwall. Only worth doing in May–October as the ice is barely formed at any other time.

6 Ice Window Route 5
P Snyder, Y Laulan, and B LeDain 1973
Perhaps the outstanding ice climb of Africa, this takes an unobvious

East Face · Nelion · North East Face · Gate of the Mists · Supercouloir · North East Buttress · Batian · West Ridge · North Face

16 North East Face of Nelion 6

I F Howell and R Higgins 1969

Climbed infrequently. Surpassed by other routes in its vicinity.

17 Eastern Groove of Nelion 7

I F Howell and I J Allan 1978

A very sustained direct climb that is regarded as the finest on Nelion's eastern walls.

18 Scott-Braithwaite Route 7

D K Scott and P Braithwaite 1976

Another excellent hard route on superb rock.

19 North East Pillar of Nelion 6+

G B Cliff and D Rutowitz 1963

A spectacular route, often climbed. Aid has slowly been whittled away through the years.

20 East Gate 5+

I F Howell and P Brettle 1980

An interesting climb up a daunting wall at a surprisingly mild grade.

21 North Gate 6

I J Allan and I F Howell 1980

One of the boldest routes on Mount Kenya, this climb ascends the Supercouloir directly below the Gate of the Mists. A rock route of great quality, with considerable stonefall danger in the lower half.

22 Northern Slabs Route 6-, A2

I F Howell and D J Temple 1973

Meandering but distinguished, with excellent and exposed climbing. Rockfall danger in lower part.

23 North East Buttress of Batian 5+, AI

I F Howell, P Snyder, and I J Allan 1976

This is a direct climb that joins 'The French Route' (24) just below the West Ridge.

24 The French Route 5, AI

M Martin and R Rangaux 1952

Exposed to rockfall in the lower section; sustained in the upper parts.

25 North Face: Standard Route 4+

A H Firmin and P Hicks 1944

This is the normal route of Batian during the July–October season. It is long, and most parties will bivouac. The hardest climbing is in the upper sections.

how to get to mount kenya

Nairobi is 180km (120 miles) to the south and connected by good roads to Mt Kenya's nearest towns, Naro Moru (2½ hours away) and Chogoria (4 hours away). Hike to the roadheads or arrange transport from the nearby lodges.

facilities

The Naro Moru River Lodge is a good hotel at the south-western base of the mountain. The town of Nanyuki on the West Side has a food store, but get provisions in Nairobi. Climbing equipment cannot be bought in Kenya.

when to climb

Between Christmas–mid-March the 'Normal Route' is in condition, as well as the South West Ridge and the Diamond Buttress. From June–mid-October it is the turn of the 'North Face Standard Route', the West Ridge, and the North East Faces. The 'Diamond Couloir' and the 'Ice Window Route' are best in June–mid-October. Avoid the 'long rains' in April and May.

gear

A normal comprehensive rack, including a full set of wires and camming devices, will suffice on most rock routes. On the ice routes take a small selection of thin-blade pitons, as well as normal ice gear.

maps and guidebooks

Map and Guide of Mount Kenya, Wielochowski and Savage, 1:50,000 (West Col). *Guide to Mount Kenya and Kilimanjaro* (ed Iain Allan, Mountain Club of Kenya), *East Africa International Mountain Guide* (ed Andre Wielochowski, West Col), *Kilimanjaro and Mount Kenya: A climbing and trekking guide*, Cameron Burns.

language

English and Swahili.

rescue and insurance

The National Park has a rescue team.

red tape

Daily park entrance fee charged – you will be expected to adhere to the park rules.

from a dream to a memory
jim Curran

"Nelion, Batian, MacKinder, Shipton, Wyn Harris, Tilman: these names had rolled around my brain for over 30 years, periodically surfacing in a succession of foiled plans to climb Mt Kenya, perhaps the most charismatic of Africa's mountains. Each of my attempts to travel to the 'Dark Continent' had been abandoned in favour of Himalayan projects. Consequently, it was not until I was well into my 50s, in mid-December 1994, that I found myself driving north from Nairobi in the company of Ian McNaught-Davis (Mac) *en route* for the Naro Moru roadhead.

We had just climbed Kilimanjaro by the Arrow Glacier in torrential rain – I have never been so wet for so long in my life. Now, as we approached our destination, the forested hillside disappeared into lowering clouds. Not very promising.

We were pleasantly surprised when we awoke the next morning to a cloudless sky and saw the characteristic spiky silhouette of the Mt Kenya massif jutting above the eastern horizon. I couldn't believe that the weather would last for the four days we would need to walk in and do the climb but, if nothing else, we'd got one spectacular long-distance view of the mountain.

Perhaps because we were well acclimatized and reasonably fit, the approach, via the infamous Vertical Bog, the MacKinder Hut, and the semi-derelict Austrian Hut, seemed fairly painless. I had imagined the Vertical Bog to be a battlefield of sorts, tilted through 90°, and was relieved to find a gently inclined swamp. We had clear views of the Diamond Couloir. Global warming has reduced it to an evil runnel of dirty ice with an ominous gap at its base. I was glad we had no intention of climbing it.

In Nairobi we had contacted Ian Howell, an old climbing partner of Mac's. He had strongly recommended that we bivouacked in the Howell Hut on the summit of Nelion. He explained that, from there, we would get better views from the top first thing in the morning and could take our time to do the route in comfort. This, I think, was his tactful way of saying we were unlikely to get up and down in a day, which was certainly correct.

So it was that dawn, on yet another fine day, saw us slithering cramponless across the hard, frozen snow of the Lewis Glacier to the foot of the climb. Up close, the elegant architecture of the mountain seemed surprisingly broken but, once we'd started, we found that the rock was generally sound and enjoyable to climb, though route finding on the bottom half was quite difficult.

Quite early on we came across an incredibly ancient piece of bleached rope, reputed to be a relic of the first ascent in 1899. Could it really have survived for nearly a hundred years? Our meanderings had taken in various time-honoured features such as the Keyhole, the Rabbit Hole, and One O'clock Gully. None were particularly difficult, apart from when I climbed an arête to avoid an awkward-looking chimney crack and failed to spot an easy traverse at the top, which meant I climbed an unnecessary little overhang and earned Mac's justified disapproval. I was wearing rock shoes, gambling on the whole climb being on rock; Mac sensibly wore boots and carried a short hammer axe. From the Austrian Hut, Nelion had appeared to be snow-free but, as we gained height, old snow patches started to appear and streaks of old ice filled some of the cracks.

The weather was still settled, with wisps of innocuous cloud drifting up the valleys. We were level with Point Lenana, shamelessly hyped as the 'third summit' of Mt Kenya by trekking companies anxious to make a mountain out of a molehill.

After crossing a snow-filled gully, we arrived at the foot of De Graaf's Variation, a long corner crack that in good condition

Right **Jim Curran relaxing in the luxury of the '5-star' Howell bivouac hut on the summit of Nelion.**

Far right **Jim Curran in action on the enjoyable rock of Nelion's South East Face.**

provides the crux of the climb. It looked steep but straightforward and I could see several protection pegs in place. After about 10m I decided to climb without my sack, which I hung on a peg. Delightfully unencumbered, I carried on, revelling in a really enjoyable pitch. At the top I belayed happily, knowing that the rest of the route would be easier.

Twenty minutes later I brought up Mac in a fury, cursing my stupidity as, while hauling them up, I'd managed to get the sacks stuck under overhangs and tangled in rope. Suddenly I felt tired.

> **I plodded shakily across almost flat ground in a tangle of ropes and slings …**

Mac led up to a broken arête around which we climbed to make a descending traverse across a gully.

The atmosphere changed abruptly, and it became cold and gloomy, and the bed of the gully was seamed with ice. Climbing at 5000m didn't help even though we'd been about 1000m higher on Kilimanjaro. Mac led everything as I was too tired to lead through by the time I had followed a pitch. One pitch in particular still sticks in my memory – Mac climbed a steep wall to avoid cracks bulging with water ice. It felt much harder to me than anything else on the route. I was impressed.

Above, the granite walls stretched away, catching the late afternoon sun playing on what I hoped would be the summit.

Mac climbed on, almost scrambling. He shouted down that there were only two or three more pitches. Wearily I followed. As I joined him, I found with great relief that he had been kidding – the summit was only a few metres away. I plodded shakily across almost flat ground in a tangle of ropes and slings to the glinting aluminium biscuit tin that is the Howell Hut. Inside it were rotting pieces of foam, frozen snow, and some dubious remnants of ancient dried food. It felt like a 5-star hotel, even though there was only just room for the two of us to stretch out.

We wriggled in and within minutes were in our sleeping bags, melting snow for the first of many brews, then preparing a meal of sorts. Soon we had made the cramped interior our home and crashed into dreamless sleep.

We awoke early to a freezing, stunning dawn. Below us was a fabulous panorama across Kenya, though a cloud ceiling blocked the 'ultimate' view to Kilimanjaro, over 300km away to the south. While I brewed up our remaining tea bag and tried to swallow a piece of stale bread, Mac found the hut book in which we made the first entries since August. He wrote a fantasy description of our breakfast: bacon, liver, sausages, quails' eggs, salmon kedgeree, fried bread, black pudding, coffee, toast, and marmalade. Months later it provoked a bewildered climber who had spent a miserable night in the hut to ask me how we'd managed to carry up all that food!

We scrambled the few metres to the highest point of Nelion and looked across at Batian, now so close we could almost touch it. But to gain those final 11m would mean crossing the Gate of the Mists, which seemed out of the question – bits of old fixed rope disappeared into hard, frozen snow, its rocks were rimed with hoar frost, verglas gleamed evilly: it would have taken hours. We settled for retracing our steps. It took several hours of abseiling and downclimbing to reach the Lewis Glacier. Apart from getting the ropes well and truly jammed and having to reclimb a pitch to free them, it passed uneventfully. But, in the late afternoon sunshine, recrossing the glacier was a desperate affair and we floundered through slushy waist-deep snow. At last it was done and we walked unsteadily down the path to the MacKinder Hut. Behind us the last rays of the sun turned the mountain gold. Already it was becoming a memory. Deep down though, I felt a sense of fulfillment.

Hugely satisfied, we slept late and next morning watched in amazement as an awesome wall of cloud and snow billowed over the mountain like a breaking wave in a surfer's nightmare. We fled down the Vertical Bog in mist and drizzle to regain the road-head. Behind us the vast expanse of damp forested hillside once again disappeared into a lowering cloud base that looked as though it had been there forever.

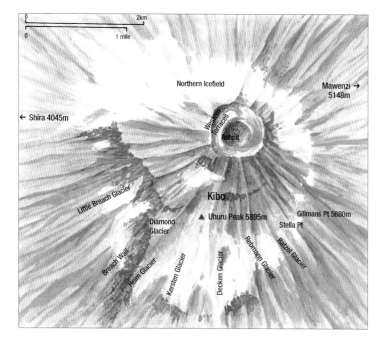

kilimanjaro

ed february

Straddling the border between Kenya and Tanzania, Kilimanjaro's snow-capped summit rises majestically above the surrounding savannah. Just over 80km (50 miles) east of the eastern branch of the Rift Valley (the Gregory Rift), 'Kili' – as the mountain is affectionately known – has a base about 80km (50 miles) long by 40km (25 miles) wide. This almost perfectly formed volcano is the highest mountain in Africa and one of the highest volcanoes in the world. All three of its peaks – Shira, 4045m (13,300ft); Mawenzi, 5148m (17,000ft); and Kibo, 5895m (19,340ft) – are within Kilimanjaro National Park, which is in Tanzanian territory. The nearest town is Moshi, 40km (25 miles) away from the big tourist route, the 'Marangu Route'.

Since the beginning of the 20th century the glaciers on Kilimanjaro have been in constant retreat, so no guidebook can be relied on for accurate descriptions and grades. For example, the lower third of the Heim Glacier has now gone. This recession, combined with poor-quality rock and high peak fees, has meant that Kilimanjaro has attracted few foreign climbers. The mountain's importance is undoubtedly in its altitude and the relative ease with which the average tourist can reach the summit. Each year many hundreds of people climb Kilimanjaro. The vast majority do so via the 'Marangu Route', which is not much more than a stiff walk. However, very few are black Africans: Tanzania is one of the poorest countries in the world and the average citizen has neither the leisure nor the means to climb mountains.

ridges, faces, and peaks

From the south, Shira, the westernmost peak, is hardly discernible from the general contours of the ridgeline flowing up to Uhuru Peak, 5895m (19,340ft), the highest point on Kibo. Shira is very rarely climbed because, being no more than a rounded dome, it does not pose any physical challenge. Uhuru Peak is also the highest point in Africa, which means the climbing on Kilimanjaro does tend to focus around Kibo. It is the middle peak and is very different in appearance to Mawenzi in the east. Where Kibo is symmetrical and perfect, Mawenzi is rugged and gnarled.

A closer look at Kibo reveals that the crater itself has collapsed, forming a number of concentric craters within. Uhuru Peak lies on the southern rim of the outermost crater. Moving in from this are the Western Terraces, the inner crater, and the central vent called the Ashpit. The summit of Kibo is partially covered by three large icefields from which hang 15 glaciers, offering the most interesting and variable climbing on 'Kili'.

Access to Uhuru Peak from the northern part of the mountain is barred by the Northern Icefield, through which there is only one recorded route. This side of the mountain is little frequented, as its glacier climbs are too steep for walking but not steep enough for climbing.

The majority of the routes on Kibo are on the southern and western sides of the mountain. Separating these two aspects is the massive, 1400m (4600ft) Breach Wall. This is seen as one of the greatest alpine challenges in Africa because of its remoteness and the friable nature of the rock. Global warming has meant that the glaciers on the South Side of the mountain no longer offer the interesting and varied climbing they gave 20 years ago. On top of the Breach Wall is the Diamond Glacier, from which hangs the 80m (250ft) icicle first climbed by Messner in 1978. This icicle touches the the upper snowfields at

1977 The Kilimanjaro National Park was officially opened by President Julius Nyerere of Tanzania.

1978 R Messner (Italian) and K Renzler (Austrian) climbed 'Breach Wall Direct'.

Right **Burchell's zebra in the national park with Kilimanjaro, Africa's highest mountain, in the background.**

the top of the Heim Glacier. To the east of this are the remains of the Kersten, Decken, Rebmann, and Ratzel Glaciers. The 'Maweka Route' approaches the summit via Stella Point, the highest point between the Rebmann and Ratzel Glaciers. Gillmans Point slightly north-east of Stella Point marks the crater rim on the 'Marangu Route'. West of the Breach Wall is the Little Breach Glacier and the Great Western Notch, the point where the 'Western Breach Route' reaches the crater.

East of Kibo, and separated from that peak by a magnificent moonscape almost 7km (4 miles) wide, known as the Saddle, lies the rugged and spectacular Mawenzi. Its 1200m (3900ft) East Face is a veritable jumble of crags, pinnacles, and rock ridges, split by two enormous clefts, the Greater and Lesser Barrancos. Poor rock quality combined with no hiking access to its summit, Hans Meyer Peak, makes Mawenzi a serious undertaking with real danger of rockfall, especially if descended after midday.

future climbing

While the most notable recent achievements on Kilimanjaro were in the 1970s with three new routes on the Breach Wall, future development is possible on the impressive East Face of Mawenzi, despite its incessant stonefall and access difficulties.

Breach Wall

Diamond Glacier

Kersten
Glacier

Heim Glacier

south side of kibo

There are more than 20 routes
on Kibo; most are on the south or
south-western sides of the mountain
where it is steepest. The main
attraction is the glacier routes.

1 Heim Glacier: Original Route D
A Nelson, H J Cooke, and D N Goodall 1957
One of the classic routes in East
Africa and one of the more popular
glacier climbs on Kibo. Not
technically very difficult, it takes
1–2 days. The approach has changed
considerably recently, becoming
horrible loose scree and polished
slabs. The easiest approach is via
the 'Umbwe Route' (*see route 11*).

2 Heim Glacier: Direct Route
R Barton and D Morris 1977
No longer the technical ice climb
it once was, due to the glacier's
retreat. Start left of the rock buttress
separating the Heim and Kersten
Glaciers and climb diagonally right
to meet the 'Original Route' (1).

3 Kersten Glacier: Original Route ED1
W Welsch and L Herncarek 1962
Also approached via the 'Umbwe
Route' (*see route 11*). The technical
part of this climb has to be done
in one push because of the lack
of suitable bivouac sites on the lower
sections, where there is also a high
risk of stonefall. Allow 1–2 days.

4 Kersten Glacier: Direct Route ED1
I F Howell, W O'Connor, and J Cleare 1975
The major difficulties are in the first
600m (2000ft), where the ice is steep
and broken. On the original ascent,
direct aid was occasionally used
here. Technical difficulty combined
with stonefall danger makes this
a serious route that takes two days.

5 Kersten Glacier: Right Side TD
I J Allan and M Savage 1976
Lower sections prone to stonefall.
Many of the more than 50 pitches
are on reasonably angled (40–50˚)
ice with a 4-pitch vertical sting in the
tail to summit 300m (1000ft) from
Uhuru Peak. A serious 2-day route.

6 Decken Glacier AD
E Eisenmann and T Schnackig 1938
The lower sections of the Decken
Glacier are very steep with many
sections of more than 65˚.
The guidebook grade of AD may
however no longer apply as, due to
glacier retreat, the bottom sections
have changed quite considerably
in recent times. Allow two days.

7 Marangu Route (Tourist Route)
M Lange and Weigele 1909
Besides the easy routes on Table
Mountain and Lion's Head in Cape
Town, this must be the most climbed
route on any mountain in Africa
with more than 10,000 people a year
attempting to get to the summit.
It is not much more than a stiff
walk, with the final section to the
crater rim at Gillmans Point up
an interminable scree slope – the
summit is more likely to be reached
with relief than euphoria. The well-
used path has formed an erosion
gully that is often hip-deep. Allow
five days from Marangu village.

breach wall on kibo

This impressive 1400m (4600ft) wall
is considered one of the most
significant mountaineering
challenges on the African continent.
Objective dangers on this huge and
remote wall include friable rock and
a high incidence of rockfall, making
any attempt to climb here a very
serious undertaking.

8 Breach Wall: East End TD+
D J Temple and A Charlton 1974
In good condition this route offers
a very viable alternative to the
degraded lower sections of the Heim
Glacier, via the Balletto Icefield
to the upper Heim Glacier.
It takes 1–2 days.

9 Breach Wall: Direct Route ED2
R Messner and K Renzler 1978
Considered one of the most serious
and dangerous routes on
Kilimanjaro, the Direct has probably
only had one repeat ascent.
Messner's ascent of the 80m (250ft)

icicle to the Diamond Glacier is said to be the hardest ice climb in Africa. Allow 1–2 days.

10 Breach Wall: Balletto Icefield ED1
D Cheesmond and D J Temple 1975
Where the 'Direct Route' (9) has some of the most technical and serious ice climbing on the African continent, this route is equally dangerous, but this time because of the poor quality of the rock. It takes 2–3 days.

11 Western Breach ⊠
E Oehler and F Klute (descent) 1912
Access to the Western Breach is via the 'Umbwe', 'Shira', or 'Machame' Routes through the lower slopes of the mountain. This is not a technical route, with just some scrambling on rock and scree. There are now some tourists on this route but it definitely sees less traffic than the 'Marangu Route'. The 'Umbwe Route' starts at Umbwe Gate 15km (9 miles) east of Moshi. The 'Machame Route' starts at Machame Gate 30km (18 miles) south of Moshi. Allow five days from Umbwe village for this route.

how to get to kilimanjaro
Most climbers fly to Nairobi in Kenya then catch a bus or Matatu (a pick-up truck that is usually overloaded and ill-serviced but cheap). You can also fly directly to Kilimanjaro International Airport, 35km (22 miles) west of Moshi, from Europe or Dar Es Salaam in Tanzania. It is possible to get to Moshi (at the base of Kilimanjaro) using local transport on good tarred roads.

There are a number of routes through the lower rainforest section of the mountain, all of which eventually meet with the north and south circuit paths that circle Kibo at about 4000m (13,000ft). From these paths you can then gain access to the climbing routes on both Kibo and Mawenzi.

Remember that when climbing Kilimanjaro acute mountain sickness is a very real possibility. You should spend at least two days acclimatizing between 3700m–4000m (12,000–13,000ft) before attempting an ascent of the mountain.

facilities
Moshi itself has everything you need when catering for climbing, with a wide variety of shops, hotels, boarding houses, and even campsites. Most of the hotels will arrange for climbing, the hiring of guides and porters, and generally give you any information you may need. Except on the 'Marangu Route', there are no huts or refuges on the mountain. On any other route you will need to bring a tent.

when to climb
The majority of people only want to walk up the Marangu route, for which the time of year is not important. The driest months are August–October, with the wet periods between November and December and March and May. The best time to do any of the glacier routes is between January and April.

gear
An ascent of the normal routes requires little more than a strong pair of hiking boots. The easier glacier routes need a rope, harness, axe, and crampons. For the harder mixed routes you should take a full rack of nuts and friends along with a couple of ice screws.

maps and guidebooks
The best maps are the Kilimanjaro map published by Mark Savage and 'Kilimanjaro' (Ordnance Survey (UK) world series).

The best guidebooks for Kilimanjaro include the *Lonely Planet walking guide, Trekking in East Africa*, which also has some good information on maps, and, for more technical climbing, *The Guide to Mount Kenya and Kilimanjaro* (Mountain Club of Kenya).

A recent publication detailing routes and treks in the area is *Kilimanjaro and Mount Kenya: A Climbing and Trekking Guide*, Cameron Burns.

language
English.

rescue and insurance
Rescue by the Kilimanjaro National Park authorities cannot be expected on any other route than the 'Marangu Route' as there is no formal rescue service on the mountain. Insurance is recommended.

red tape
The National Park authorities insist that you hire both a guide and porter through a licensed tour operator. Special permission has to be obtained from the park authorities to climb any of the routes other than the 'Marangu Route'. A letter of competence from your national climbing authority will help to cut the red tape if you wish to deviate from the tourist routes.

the authors

iain allan

Iain Allan is one of Kenya's foremost mountaineers and mountain guides. The strong partnership he formed with Ian Howell has dominated East African climbing since the 1970s, with many pioneering ascents on Mt Kenya and Kilimanjaro, as well as on Kenya's countless outlying crags.

pete athans

Pete Athans has been active on Everest: since 1985 he has led 12 expeditions, attempted five routes from both the Nepalese and Tibetan sides, and has stood on the summit five times. He guides independently and for such organizations as Alpine Ascents International and The Exum Guide Service in Wyoming's Teton range.

george band

George Band was the youngest member of the first successful Everest expedition in 1953. Two years later he was the first to climb Kangchenjunga. He still enjoys modest climbing, recently visiting Nepal, Sikkim, and Bhutan. A former President of the Alpine Club, he is currently President of the British Mountaineering Council.

mike banks

Among many other expeditions, Mike Banks crossed the Greenland icecap in 1952–4 and made the first ascent of Rakaposhi in 1958. At 71 he attained the age record for climbing the Old Man of Hoy. An ex-Royal Marine Commando, he is author of six books and has been awarded the Polar Medal and the MBE.

christian beckwith

American-born Christian Beckwith began climbing in Llanberis, Wales in 1990 before returning to the USA where he 'putzed around on a bit of rock'. He admits it wasn't until moving to Jackson, Wyoming in 1993 that he 'applied any diligence to the pursuit'. He now edits the *American Alpine Journal*.

steve bell

Steve Bell is a qualified mountain guide, and is the principal of Himalayan Kingdoms Expeditions, based in Sheffield, UK. His achievements include ascents of the Eiger's North Face and Mt Huntington's East Face. Recently he became the 38th person to complete the Seven Summits.

josé luis bermúdez

Colombian-born José Luis Bermúdez, now a lecturer in philosophy at the University of Stirling, Scotland, has climbed in Britain, the Alps, the Caucasus, and the Himalaya. In 1993 he co-authored (with Audrey Salkeld) *On the Edge of Europe*. He is currently Area Notes Editor for the British *Alpine Journal*.

barry blanchard

Born in Calgary, Canada in 1959, Barry Blanchard is a UIAGM (IFMGA) Mountain Guide and one of Canada's leading Alpinists and Himalayan climbers. Among his successes are a 6-day ascent of the North Ridge of Rakaposhi and the first ascent of the North Pillar of North Twin in the Canadian Rockies.

hilary boardman

Hilary Boardman's love of the mountains was kindled by school trips to the Lake District. After training as a teacher, she climbed in the Alps, Africa, Iceland, New Guinea, and the Himalaya. Now working in a Swiss international school, her love affair with mountains and rock climbing still continues.

hamish brown

Hamish Brown is an author, travel writer, mountaineer, and poet. He is based in Scotland, but wanders worldwide, making extended visits particularly to Morocco. Two of his popular books, *Hamish's Mountain Walk* (on the Munros) and *Climbing the Corbetts*, have recently been reissued in an omnibus edition.

cameron m burns

Australian-born Cameron Burns, aged 32, has lived and climbed throughout the American West for the past 15 years. A freelance writer, he is author of guides to climbing in California, Colorado, and East Africa. He lives in a small town in the Rocky Mountains, Colorado, with his wife Ann, a dog, and two cats.

greg child

Greg Child is well known for his Himalayan expeditions and first ascents on rock walls in Australia and the United States. His first book, *Thin Air, Encounters in the Himalayas*, described three seasons of climbing, and his two collections of writings, *Mixed Emotions* and *Postcards from the Ledge*, are hard-hitting and direct.

john cleare

A climber for over 40 years, John Cleare has visited mountains all over the world. He is a freelance photographer, writer, and lecturer. His many books include *Rock Climbers in Action in Snowdonia* (with Tony Smythe), *Collins Guide to Mountains and Mountaineering,* and *Trekking - Great Walks of the World.*

julie-ann clyma

Julie-Ann Clyma started climbing in the New Zealand Alps and has done extensive rock, winter, and alpine climbing. Her highlights include K2, Changabang, the first alpine style ascent of Nanda Devi East, and being the first non-Soviet woman to climb both Khan Tengri and Pobeda in Kazakhstan.

guy cotter

Guy Cotter has ascended many of the highest peaks in New Zealand and made the first solo ascent of the South Face of Mt Hicks. He has also climbed Everest, Gasherbrum II, and Cho Oyo. He now specializes in high-altitude guiding – his company Adventure Consultants Ltd is based on South Island, New Zealand.

richard cowper

Mountaineer and Asia specialist, Richard Cowper works on the foreign desk of *The Financial Times*. He has been on many expeditions, including to Latok I in the Karakoram, Nanga Parbat, and the Caucasus – all with Doug Scott. He has also attempted Everest with Alan Hinkes.

jim curran

Jim Curran is a freelance writer and film maker. He has taken part in more than a dozen expeditions to the Himalaya and South America. His books include *Trango, the Nameless Tower; K2, Triumph and Tragedy; Suspended Sentences*; and the award-winning *K2, the Story of the Savage Mountain.*

kurt diemberger

The only person alive to have made first ascents of two 8000m (26,000ft) mountains (without oxygen), Broad Peak (1957) and Dhaulagirii (1960), Kurt has since climbed Makalu, Everest, K2, and Gasherbrum II. He has written three autobiographical volumes – *Summits and Secrets, The Endless Knot, Spirits of the Air* – and made a number of films.

ed douglas

In his 17 years as a climber, Ed Douglas has travelled from Alaska to the fringes of the Sahara, including an ascent of Shivling via the West Ridge in 1995. Ed is a climbing journalist, and his book on Everest's environment, *Chomolungma Sings the Blues*, was published in 1997. He is married with two children and lives in London.

ed february

Edmund February was not welcomed into the South African climbing fold during the dark days of apartheid. Despite this, he has made a major contribution to rock climbing in South Africa, including first ascents of more than 200 routes. He has climbed extensively in America, Europe, and the rest of southern Africa.

julian freeman-attwood

Julian Freeman-Attwood has participated in over 17 expeditions to the Karakoram, India, Nepal, Sikkim, Bhutan, Tibet, Africa, Mongolia, Tierra del Fuego, and Antarctica, and specializes in exploratory climbs, new routes, and first ascents. As well as lecturing and writing, he has been involved in four mountaineering films.

lindsay griffin

Lindsay Griffin began climbing regularly in the 1970s in the Alps. He has climbed in the Arctic, the Andes, Antarctica, and Africa, as well as the Himalaya, Karakoram, and Central Asia. Author of four alpine guidebooks, he now works on *High* Magazine and is Vice President of the British Mountaineering Council and Alpine Club.

anderl heckmair

Anderl Heckmair was born in 1906. He became a mountain guide in 1933 and made many impressive climbs in the Alps. In 1938 he led three companions on the first ascent of the North Face of the Eiger. He has been on numerous expeditions to Africa, South and North America, and the Himalaya.

rodrigo jordan

Rodrigo Jordan has made numerous high-altitude climbs in South America and been involved in Chilean expeditions to Mt McKinley, Mt Everest, and K2. He was named Best Mountaineering Sportsman in 1985, and is Vice-President of both the International Union of Alpine Associations (UIAA) and Chilean Olympic Committee.

harish kapadia

A cloth merchant by profession, Harish Kapadia has climbed and trekked in the Himalaya since 1960. He is Honorary Editor of the *Himalayan Journal* and compiler of the *Himalayan Club Newsletter*. In 1993 he was awarded the Gold Medal of the Indian Mountaineering Federation.

piotr konopka

Piotr Konopka has been on expeditions to Lhotse, Aconcagua, Nanga Parbat, Cho Oyu, and Nilgiri North. He has put up several new climbs and made first winter ascents and some extreme ski descents in the Tatra. He is President of the Polish Mountain Guides Association and a member of the Rescue Service in the Tatra Mountains.

anders lundahl

Anders Lundahl started climbing in 1973; he has made the first hammerless ascent of the Philipp-Flamm and the first free ascent of Messner's 'Friends Route' on the North Face of the Civetta. In Norway, he has made several first ascents of virgin big-walls, always emphasizing free climbing with no bolts.

george mallory II

George Mallory II started rock climbing aged 16. During the 1980s he established many new routes throughout South Africa, particularly multi-pitch routes at Blouberg in the northern Transvaal. He has also climbed Mt Everest, Mt Cook, and Gangotri in the Garhwal Himalaya. He now lives in Victoria, Australia.

roger mear

Roger Mear climbed the Eiger in winter and made the first winter ascent of McKinley's Cassin Ridge. He walked to the South Pole and attempted a solo crossing of Antarctica. He made the first British ascent of Nanga Parbat. His book *In the Footsteps of Scott* (with Robert Swan) won the 1987 Boardman Tasker Award for Mountain Literature.

paul moores

Paul Moores has climbed in the Alps, Himalaya, Andes, Alaska, and Africa. For many years a civilian climbing instructor for the British Forces and Special Forces, he is now a UIAGM Mountain Guide, owns a climbing shop and guiding business in Glencoe, Scotland, and is a member of the famous Glencoe Mountain Rescue Team.

sun woo nam

Sun Woo Nam joined the Korean Makalu expedition in 1982 and climbed the North Face of the Eiger. During the 1980s he climbed Pumo Ri in winter, Ama Dablam in a solo winter ascent, and Everest, and in 1992 he succeeded in successive ascents of Cho Oyu and Xixabangma. He is editor of *The Man and Mountain*.

robert new

Robert New has lived in Kota Kinabalu for almost 20 years, making over 50 expeditions to Mt Kinabalu. As a student, he climbed in the Alps, Romsdal in Norway, and in East Africa. In the early 1970s he was President of the Mountain Club of Uganda.

bernard newman

Bernard Newman has been an active climber in Britain, Europe, and North America since 1966. A graduate in geology from Leeds University, he edited *Mountain* magazine from 1984–92 and co-produced 'Extreme Rock' with Ken Wilson in 1987. He works in electronic publishing and is the editor of *Climber* magazine.

marko prezelj

Marko Prezelj, born in 1965, works as a climbing instructor. His new routes include the North Face of Cho Oyu in 1988, Kangchenjunga South, alpine style, in 1991, and the East Face of the North Tower of Paine, Chile in 1995. In 1992 he made the first ascent of Menlungtse Main Summit, alpine style, by the East Face.

al read

Al Read was part of the American Dhaulagiri expedition in 1969 and the American expedition to Everest's North Ridge. He led the first ascent to Gaurishankar and co-led the first ascent of McKinley's East Buttress. He is President of Exum Mountain Guides in Grand Teton National Park and Vice-Chairman of Geographic Expeditions.

steve roper

During the 1960s Steve Roper ascended about 500 routes in Yosemite Valley. He has also climbed in Canada, Mexico, Turkey, the Dolomites, and Wales. He wrote *Fifty Classic Climbs of North America* with Allen Steck, and his *Camp 4: Recollections of a Yosemite Rockclimber* won first prize for non-fiction at the 1994 Banff Book Festival.

victor saunders

Victor Saunders has climbed extensively in Scotland, the Alps, and the Himalaya. An architect and UIAGM Mountain Guide, he is the author of two books: *Elusive Summits* and *No Place to Fall*. The former won him the Boardman Tasker prize for mountain literature in 1990. He is now based again in his native Scotland.

robert schauer

Robert Schauer has reached the summits of five different 8000m (26,000ft) peaks, including Everest. He has produced many natural history films, including 'Focus on Karakoram', and was cinematographer for David Breashears' IMAX film 'Everest'. He orchestrates the annual International Mountain Film Festival in Graz, Austria.

chic scott

Chic Scott has climbed in Europe, Alaska, Yosemite, Nepal, and Canada. During the 1960s and 1970s he worked as a guide at the International School of Mountaineering in Switzerland. Now a mountain writer, he has worked on several ski-mountaineering guidebooks to the Canadian Alps and is writing a history of Canadian climbing.

doug scott

Doug Scott CBE has made 32 expeditions to Asia. Apart from his first ascent of the South West Face, Everest, he has made all his climbs alpine style, without the use of bottled oxygen, and has completed the 'Seven Summits'. His books include *Big Wall Climbing*, *The Shishapangma Expedition*, and *Himalayan Climber*.

araceli segarra roca

Araceli Segarra Roca began climbing in 1988 in Spain, going on to classic routes in the Alps and Dolomites. She has climbed in Yosemite Valley; on Devil's Tower; in Morocco; and on Mt Kenya. She reached 7300m (23,950ft) on Broad Peak and, in 1996, became the first Catalán and Spanish woman to summit Everest.

nigel shepherd

Beginning climbing at 11 years old, Nigel Shepherd has gone on to climb in the Alps, South Africa, North America, New Zealand, and Australia. A member of the UIAGM, he has guided and instructed in many parts of the world. He is author of three books and a regular contributor to outdoor and climbing magazines.

mike smith

Born in Kidderminster, England in 1961, and now based in Chamonix, France, Mike Smith has climbed and guided extensively in Scotland, Alaska, the Himalaya, and Central Asia, including to the summit of Pik Kommunizma, Tajikistan, in 1994 and 1995.

john town

John Town's preference for climbing in little-explored mountain areas has taken him to the Caucasus, Eastern Turkey, the Siberian and Mongolian Altai, Kamchatka, central and north-eastern Tibet, Yunnan, and the Andes. He is Academic Secretary at the University of Bradford, England.

sumiyo tsuzuki

Sumiyo Tsuzuki's first attempt at climbing Everest was in 1996 with the IMAX Everest team; the second was in spring 1997 when she reached 8400m (27,560ft). She is a magazine journalist and also works in television; her latest project was as NHK TV interviewer for the Winter Olympics held in Nagano, Japan in 1998.

stephen venables

Stephen Venables has climbed particularly in the Himalaya, where his first ascents have included a route on the Kangshung Face, Everest in 1988, solo (without oxygen). Of his books, *Painted Mountains* won the Boardman Tasker Prize (1986) and *Himalaya Alpine Style* (with Andy Fanshawe) won the Banff Festival Grand Prize (1995).

beth wald

Beth Wald is a professional photographer – she began photographing her rock-climbing adventures for *Climbing* magazine in 1983. Among her many achievements are a 1996 Banff Book Festival Award for photographs of Tibetan people of the Humla and, in 1995, an award from *Summit* magazine for photography of remote mountain culture.

ed webster

Back climbing again with his usual vigour after sustaining severe frostbite in the late 1980s, Ed Webster is known for his diverse ascents and travels. Along with pioneering routes in Norway, Mongolia, and Utah, he was part of a 4-man, 'no oxygen', first ascent up the Kangshung Face of Everest.

rob wood

Rob Wood made the first British ascent of the Nose on El Capitan with Mick Burke. He emigrated to Canada in 1970 where he pioneered waterfall climbing in the Rockies and, in 1978, climbed Mt Waddington in winter. His book *Towards the Unknown Mountains* explores some of the inner workings of mountaineering.

simon yates

Simon Yates has climbed extensively, including making a first ascent of Siula Grande in the Andes, with Joe Simpson, and the first British ascents of Khan Tengri and Marble Wall in Kazakhstan. He wrote *Against The Wall* (1997) about his experiences putting up a new route on the Central Tower of Paine, Chile.

international route grades

The technical grading of climbs is constantly evolving and, being subjective, is something of an inexact science, and frequently controversial. The intention is to describe both the physical nature of the climb, and the level of expertise and commitment it demands of the climber. Difficult moves, length, objective factors, the possible existence of escape lines, remoteness – all these are taken into account.

Different systems are adopted in (and for) different areas, which are a nightmare to correlate, although attempts have been made at universal systems. The UIAA rock-grading system is recognized as a standard, yet usually supplanted in the field by local gradings.

In this book our policy has been to quote the form of grading most frequently used in the area under description, or in the most readily obtainable guidebooks to that area. Among the anomalies this throws up are the use of the American 'Yosemite decimal system' for big-wall grades in the Norwegian area of the Romsdal; and the use of Alpine grading systems in the Himalaya and Great Ranges, where much of the development has been done by visiting climbers.

We have two comparison tables below: one a selection of international rock grades, the other of international ice-climbing grades. They should be considered as approximate only.

rock grades

BRITAIN		FRANCE	USA (YDC)	UIAA
		I	5.2	I
D		2	5.3	II
VD		3	5.4	III
S	4a	4	5.5	IV
			5.6	V-
HS	4b			
VS	4c	5	5.7	V
HVS			5.8	V+
	5a	5+		VI-
E1			5.9	VI
	5b		5.10a	VI+
		6a–6a+	5.10b	
E2			5.10c	VII-
E3	5c	6b–6b+	5.10d	VII
			5.11a	
		6c–6c+	5.11b	VII+
	6a		5.11c	VIII-
E4		7a–7a+	5.11d	VIII
			5.12a	
	6b	7b–7b+	5.12b	VIII+
E5			5.12c	IX-
			5.12d	
	6c	7c–7c+	5.13a	IX
E6				IX+
		8a–8a+	5.13b	X-
			5.13c	
E7	7a	8b–8b+	5.13d	X
	7b	8c	5.14a	X+
				XI-
E8				

Artificial climbs have their own grades of severity. In British climbing, where there are pitches requiring aid, a rising numerical system is employed: ie A1, A2.

ice-climbing grades

FRANCE	USA	SCOTLAND	RUSSIA	N ZEALAND
F	AI 1	I	3A	I
PD		II	3B	
AD		III		3
D	AI 2, AI 3	IV	4A, 4B	4
TD	AI 4, AI 5	V	5A	5
ED1	WI 5	VI	6A, 6B	
ED2	WI 6, WI 7			

The table above correlates the ice-climbing grades that appear in the book. Rating snow and ice, or mixed climbs, is a far more difficult proposition than categorizing rock alone. One of the most widely used systems, which has stood the test of time, is the French Alpine Adjectival System. This gives seven grades that can be further defined by the application of a plus or minus; or Sup (Supérior) and Inf (Inférior).

In his book *Ice World* (the 'Bible' of modern ice climbing), Jeff Lowe analyses different snow and ice types and offers for them a classification grade 1–8, comparing this roughly with technical rock classification. Additionally, the prefix 'AI' indicates Alpine ice and 'WI' water ice, whereas a predominantly mixed climb would be preface by 'M'.

Alaska has its own grading system, based upon ideas by Boyd N Everett, and taking special account of storms, cold, altitude, and extensive cornicing. Grade 1 would be an easy glacier route, Grade 5 requiring sustained technical climbing and intense commitment, and Grade 6 combines all these with great objective danger and few opportunities for bivouacs.

Russian grading, a hangover from Soviet days, is – rather like the Soviet political system itself – a doomed attempt to impose a single structure on wildly disparate raw materials. The system was conceived to apply equally to the long rock routes in the Crimea, to the alpine and super-alpine routes in the Caucasus, the Altai and the Pamir Alai, and to the almost Himalayan 7000m (23,000ft) peaks of the Pamir and the Tien Shan. Routes of Russian grade 6B and higher tend to involve a lot of aid climbing.

We have not attempted to grade the highest Himalayan peaks, nor Mount Paget in Antarctica, beyond describing certain individual pitches; this is because conditions can vary wildly and so much depends on the fitness and acclimatization of the party.

glossary

abseil Method of descending steep terrain by sliding down a rope. Colloquially 'abbing off'. The same as rappelling.

acclimatization Process of physiological adaptation to living and climbing at high altitude where the air is at lower pressure and delivers less oxygen to the body. Above 8000m (26,000ft) only one-third as much oxygen is available as at sea level.

aid climbing Direct use of inserted devices (pitons, ice screws, bolts, etc) to assist progress up a climb, rather than simply for protection. Also referred to (archaically) as 'artificial climbing'.

aider See 'étrier'.

aiguille (French for needle.) A sharply pointed mountain, or pinnacle.

alpine style Practice of climbing large mountains in a single push, without previously setting up and stocking camps. This effectively means forgoing supplementary oxygen and Sherpa support. There are recognized degrees at which climbers can dispense with equipment, assistance, and companions for ultra-lightweight alpine style ascents.

altiplano A high plateau.

anchor The point to which a fixed belay rope is attached – either a natural rock feature, a piton in a rock crack or ice, or a deadman in snow.

angle A folded steel piton.

arête A sharp ridge of rock or snow.

artificial climbing See 'aid climbing'.

ascender (Also 'ascendeur'.) Mechanical clamp for climbing a rope, manually operated. Special cams allow the ascender to slide up the rope, but lock and hold when weight is applied, as in a fall. Two are employed: one attached to the waist harness, the other to a foot loop; by taking the weight alternately on foot or waist, the freed ascender can

be moved up the rope. See also 'jumar clamp' and 'prusiking'.

bandolier A shoulder sling for carrying equipment.

BASE jump A spectacular and hazardous form of parachuting (from buildings, antennae, spans, earth), occasionally employed in conjunction with climbing. Some big-walls and towers are also meccas to BASE jumpers.

belaying The taking in or letting out of rope (often through a 'belay device') to safeguard the other climber(s) in a roped group. This will often entail being tied to a firm anchor on a 'stance'. Solo climbers have developed self-belaying tactics to safeguard dangerous moves.

belay device A small device clipped to the belayer's harness, through which the climber's rope is passed, enabling a fall to be easily held. A range of devices is used for different climbing situations; these work either by friction or camming. (Sticht Plate, ATC, Gri Gri, Tuber.)

bergschrund The crevasse or gap where a glacier pulls away from the mountain proper; often a serious obstacle at the start of an alpine climb.

big-wall climbing Attempting sheer faces of great height, often requiring several days to climb. A vast range of techniques has been developed for the special conditions encountered and the activity has a glossary all its own.

bivouac (bivvy) Temporary overnight stop without a standard tent. Bivvy bags are a sensible item when a bivouac is anticipated – and more so when it's not! Some of the smaller alpine huts, often little more than metal boxes, are also known as bivouac huts.

bolts/bolting Metal expansion bolts placed in pre-drilled holes in rock as anchors. Their use is highly controversial, not only for the damage they cause to the rock, but since they allow a climber to go any-where, regardless of natural features.

brèche A deep notch in the skyline; a gap in a ridge.

bridging A method of climbing a wide chimney, one hand and a foot on either side.

bouldering Exercising on boulders and small cliffs that offer climbing to a high level of expertise but with reduced risk.

camming unit A popular tool used for protection in rock climbing to supply a secure fixture in a crack or hollow. See 'friends'.

chock/chockstone Originally, a stone found wedged or placed in a crack and employed as an anchor or to restrain a running belay. Various wedges and nuts are now manufactured for the same purpose.

cirque A deep, rounded hollow with steep sides, formed by ice erosion, and characteristic of areas that are or have been glaciated. Corrie and cwm are (Scottish and Welsh) synonyms.

col A pass or dip in a ridge, generally between two peaks and usually offering the easiest passage from one side to the other. Also known as a saddle.

copperhead A cylindrical copper swage or cable used for incipient grooves.

cornice An overhanging mass of wind-sculpted snow projecting beyond the crest of a ridge. A potentially dangerous feature.

corrie (Also 'coire'.) See 'cirque'.

couloir An open gully.

crampon A frame of metal spikes that straps to the soles of a climbing boot for snow and ice work. Usually 10 or 12 point, the latter incorporating a forward-pointing pair for steep ice.

crevasse A rift in a glacier's surface, made as ice moves over irregularities in the glacier bed, or when the flow is constricted or released. Some can be very deep, and all are most dangerous when concealed by new snow.

cwm See 'cirque'.

deadman An alloy fluke or plate that is dug into the snow to provide an anchor. The harder it is pulled, the deeper it bites.

descender (Also 'descendeur'.) Friction device for abseiling. The 'figure of eight' is a popular form.

dihedral/dièdre The term for a wide-angled or 'open book' crack or corner.

direttissima The most direct line up a face and, by the same token, the most highly prized.

EBS A type of tight-fitting rock boot.

enchainement The stringing together of two or more hard routes as a single enterprise. Often facilitated by speeding up the descents in between by skiing, or parapenting.

étrier Portable step or footsling used in aid climbing, usually of a light alloy or nylon webbing. Also known as an 'aider'.

exposure In a non-medical sense, the word is used to describe vertigo-inducing steepness or precariousness.

finger lock Act of inserting fingers into a vertical crack of finger-width and twisting them to create a cam.

fixed rope On the steep ground of prolonged climbs, the lead climber – having run out the full length of rope – attaches it to anchors, so that all who follow can clip into it as a safety line. It remains in place throughout the expedition.

free climbing To climb using your body only – the rope is solely an insurance against falling, not a climbing aid. 'Freeing' a route is to dispense with the aid used in earlier ascents.

friend Revolutionary camming device invented in the 1970s for protecting rock climbs.

front-pointing Climbing straight up steep snow and ice by digging in the forward points of crampons and supporting a balance with hand-held tools.

goulotte A water channel.

GPS A satellite navigation system. A small hand-held receiver picks up two dozen satellite signals, calculates, and displays coordinates on its screen. Accurate to within 100m (330ft) anywhere on the earth's surface.

gendarme A sharp pinnacle or tower impeding progress along a ridge.

grading Systems for describing the difficulty of a climb. Degrees and terminology vary from one area to another (*see page 298*).

HACE, HAPE Life-threatening, altitude-induced medical conditions: high-altitude cerebral œdema and high-altitude pulmonary œdema. In both cases the most effective treatment is to lose height quickly.

hanging glacier A (tributary) glacier entering the main glacier or valley from a considerable height above the bed of the latter, and thus often presenting ice cliffs or an icefall.

headwall A cliff at the head of a valley.

hex/hexentric A type of alloy, with irregular hexagonal cross-section to fit in cracks and pockets for protection or belay.

hooks, hooking In big-wall climbing, the process of setting steel hook-shaped devices on edges and knobs.

icefall Steep and broken section of a glacier where it flows over a sizeable step in its bed. Unstable, its features continually change.

jamming Means of ascending cracks by wedging fingers, hands, or feet.

jumar clamp A type of ascender. 'Jumaring' has become a generic term for climbing ropes using ascenders.

karabiner Oval or D-shaped metal snap-link, offering a universal

means of attachment: climber to rope, ropes to belay, as a runner, for abseiling, etc. Can be shortened to 'krab' or even 'biner'. In North America, it is usually spelt 'carabiner'.

klettergarten A training ground for rock climbing.

massif A mountainous mass with several summits, but recognizably of a piece.

moraine Rock debris piled up by the movement of glaciers, or accumulated in hollows under ice.

névé Permanent snow above the level of the bergschrund. Feeds glaciers. Often granular.

nut Same as 'chock': a wedge or mechanical device for providing a secure anchor in cracks.

œdema (edema) An accumulation of fluid in the tissues. *See also 'HACE' and 'HAPE'.*

off-width Cracks too wide for a fist jam and too narrow for more than an arm or leg. Awkward and strenuous to climb, to descend, and also to protect.

pitch The section of a rock climb between two stances or belay positions.

piton Metal peg hammered into cracks to support a belay. A wide variety is manufactured for different contingencies, such as: angles, leepers, bongs, bugaboos, rurps. Sometimes called 'nails' or 'pegs' or 'pins', and the act of using them 'nailing' etc.

portaledge Now a generic term for a hanging platform, on which to sleep during multi-day big-wall climbs.

protection The number and quality of running belays used to make a pitch safer and psychologically easier to lead. Not an aid to climbing, but a safeguard against falling.

prusiking Originally a method of directly ascending a rope with the aid of sliding 'prusik knots', or friction hitches, with foot loops.

These days various mechanical devices have replaced the rope knot, but the original term 'prusiking' survives.

pulk Small sledge designed for 1-person hauling.

puja Ceremony of purification and propitiation, held at the start of most expeditions where Sherpas are employed.

quick-draw Manufactured tape 'extender' that has replaced the tied short slings of pioneers; with a karabiner at each end it is mainly for connecting wired nut runners to the rope.

rack The selection of equipment (nuts, friends etc) carried on a climb.

rappel *See 'abseil'.*

rivet Steel screw for hammering into shallow drilled hole.

RP The original brass nut; now a universal term for small nuts.

rurp (Realized ultimate reality piton.) Razor-thin peg for the slimmest cracks.

sastrugi Wave-like sculpting of the snow by wind.

scree Rock debris at the foot of a crag.

sérac A tower, or pinnacle of ice, found especially in icefalls or calving off ice cliffs. Usually unstable.

Sherpas Properly an ethnic group, living below Everest in the Sola Khumbu region (female: Sherpani). Because of their pre-eminence as high-altitude porters, the name has been applied to all who work in that profession, whether Sherpa by birth or from other ethnic Nepalese groups, such as the Tamangs.

siege style The traditional method by which high Himalayan peaks were climbed, involving the establishment of a chain of well-stocked camps, frequently connected by fixed ropes, and slow progress up the mountain.

Usually requiring the aid of relays of porters and, for the highest mountains, the use also of supplementary oxygen.

sirdar The head Sherpa on an expedition, who works directly with the leader.

skyhook One of many specialized hooks available, offering precarious support on tiny flakes.

spindrift Loose powder snow carried by wind or avalanche.

sport climbing Where the element of risk is eliminated by the use of bolt runners, and the emphasis is on technical and gymnastic skill.

stance The place where a climber makes his or her belay – preferably a comfortable ledge.

talus *See 'scree'.*

TriCam A passive camming unit, designed by Jeff Lowe.

UIAA (Union Internationale des Associations d'Alpinisme.) International governing body of alpinism.

via ferratta A prepared route up or across a mountain, protected by steel cables and sometimes other features such as ladders in the more awkward sections. Climbers can clip into the cable for protection. The word is Italian – in Germany it is known as Klettersteige.

verglas A thin layer of ice coating the surface of rock.

Warthog A solid-steel ice piton with an angular thread along its tapered length.

windslab A type of avalanche that can occur when a layer of wind-compacted snow settles insecurely on old snow. It falls as enormous blocks or slabs.

index

acknowledgements

The publishers, contributors, and Audrey Salkeld would like to thank the following people who gave invaluable help collecting/checking information: the Alpine Club Library, the ANI, Aldo Boitano, Anatoli Boukreev, the British Mountaineering Council, Brot Coburn, Xavier Eguskitza, Simon Harriss, Ian Howell, Suz Kelly, Marjeta Keršič-Svetel, Stanko Klinav, Vladimir Kopylov, Göran Kropp, Andreas Kubin, Danielle Lawrence, Nick Lewis, Roger Metcalfe, Charles Oliver, Kev Reynolds, Dawn Rowley, the Royal Geographical Society, Don Serl, Malcolm Slesser, Kazbek Valiev, Alex White, and Linda Wylie.

Photographic credits

Front endpapers Pat & Baiba Morrow; back endpapers Roger Mear; 1 Doug Scott; 2–3 Kurt Diemberger; 4–5 Pat & Baiba Morrow; 8–9 Roger Mear; 11 Cameron M Burns; 12 Roger Mear; 13 left Audrey Salkeld/Swiss National Tourist Office and Swiss Federal Railways; 13 right Hulton Getty Picture Collection; 14 Audrey Salkeld; 15 Steve Bell; 16 Doug Scott; 17 Beth Wald; 18 Roger Mear; 19 Roger Payne and Julie-Ann Clyma; 23 left Victor Saunders; 23 right Roger Payne and Julie-Ann Clyma; 24–5 Mountain Camera/Bill O'Connor; 25 Doug Scott; 26 Anders Lundahl; 27 John Amatt Collection; 28–29 Mountain Camera/Bill O'Connor; 29 Phil Coates; 30 Mountain Camera/John Cleare; 31 Mick Fowler; 32–3 Mountain Camera/Bill O'Connor; 33 Al Phizaclea; 34 Bernard Newman/Andy Rowell; 35 top Bernard Newman/Andy Rowell; 35 bottom Judy Todd; 36–7 Mountain Camera/Bill O'Connor; 37 Lindsay Griffin; 38 Piotr Konopka; 39 Piotr Konopka; 40–41 Mountain Camera/Bill O'Connor; 41 Roger Payne and Julie-Ann Clyma; 42 Marko Prezelj; 42–3 Mountain Camera/Bill O'Connor; 43 Bill O'Connor; 44 ©Bradford Washburn, Courtesy of Panopticon Gallery, Boston; 45 Roger Payne and Julie-Ann Clyma; 46 ©Bradford Washburn, Courtesy of Panopticon Gallery, Boston; 47 Gino Buscaini; 49 top left Kurt Diemberger; 49 bottom left Kurt Diemberger; 49 right Kurt Diemberger; 50–1 Mountain Camera/Bill O'Connor; 51 Leo Dickinson; 52 ©Bradford Washburn, Courtesy of Panopticon Gallery, Boston; 53 left ©Bradford Washburn, Courtesy of Panopticon Gallery, Boston; 53 right Stock Shot/Jess Stock; 54–5 Mountain Camera/Bill O'Connor; 55 Roger Mear; 56 Bill O'Connor; 57 Mountain Camera/John Cleare; 59 top left Audrey Salkeld; 59 bottom left Audrey Salkeld; 59 right Audrey Salkeld; 60–1 Mountain Camera/Bill O'Connor; 61 bottom Marko Prezelj; 62 Marko Prezelj; 63 Marko Prezelj; 64–5 Mountain Camera/Bill O'Connor; 65 Neil McAdie; 66 Igor Koller; 67 Igor Koller; 68 Mountain Camera/Bill O'Connor; 69 José Luis Bermúdez; 70 George C Band; 71 José Luis Bermúdez; 72 José Luis Bermúdez, 73 José Luis Bermúdez; 74–5 Mountain Camera/Bill O'Connor; 75 Miguel Angulo; 76 Araceli Segarra Roca; 77 Kev Reynolds; 78 Mountain Camera/Bill O'Connor; 79 Lorenzo Arribas; 81 left Paul Pritchard; 81 top right Tyler Stableford; 81 bottom right James Balog; 82 Mountain Camera/Bill O'Connor; 83 Nigel Shepherd; 84 Nigel Shepherd; 85 Doug Scott; 86–7 Mountain Camera/Bill O'Connor; 87 Doug Scott; 88 left Paul Pritchard; 88 right Doug Scott; 89 Doug Scott; 90–1 Mountain Camera/Bill O'Connor; 91 James Balog; 92 Pat & Baiba Morrow; 92–3 Mountain Camera/Bill O'Connor; 93 Roger Mear; 94 ©Bradford Washburn, Courtesy of Panopticon Gallery, Boston; 95 ©Bradford Washburn, Courtesy of Panopticon Gallery, Boston; 96 ©Bradford Washburn, Courtesy of Panopticon Gallery, Boston; 97 ©Bradford Washburn, Courtesy of Panopticon Gallery, Boston; 98 Barry Blanchard/Kevin Doyle; 99 Barry Blanchard/Kevin Doyle; 100–1 Mountain Camera/Bill O'Connor; 101 Pat & Baiba Morrow; 102 Chic Scott; 102–3 ©Bradford Washburn, Courtesy of Panopticon Gallery, Boston; 103 ©Bradford Washburn, Courtesy of Panopticon Gallery, Boston; 104–5 Mountain Camera/Bill O'Connor; 105 Ed Cooper; 106 Ed Cooper; 107 Ed Cooper; 108 top Ed Webster/Mountain Imagery; 108 bottom Ed Webster/Mountain Imagery/Bryan Becker; 110 Mountain Camera/Bill O'Connor; 111 Doug Scott; 112 left Doug Scott; 112 right Rob Wood; 113 Rob Wood; 114–15 Mountain Camera/Bill O'Connor; 115 Beth Wald; 116 Mountain Camera/John Cleare; 117 Ed Webster/Mountain Imagery; 118 Greg Child; 119 Greg Child; 120–1 Mountain Camera/Bill O'Connor; 121 Ed Cooper; 122 Ed Cooper; 123 Carolyn Ortenberger (Courtesy, the Family and Estate of Leigh Ortenberger); 125 left Christian Beckwith; 125 centre Christian Beckwith/Stephen Koch; 125 right Christian Beckwith/Stephen Koch; 126–7 Mountain Camera/Bill O'Connor; 127 Beth Wald; 128 left Beth Wald; 128–9 Beth Wald; 129 Beth Wald; 130–1 Mountain Camera/Bill O'Connor; 131 Ed Webster/Mountain Imagery; 132 Cameron M Burns; 133 Cameron M Burns; 134–5 Mountain Camera/Bill O'Connor; 135 Barry Blanchard; 136 Barry Blanchard; 137 Barry Blanchard; 139 left Beth Wald; 139 right Barry Blanchard; 140–1 Mountain Camera/Bill O'Connor; 141 Royal Geographical Society Picture Library/Eric Lawrie; 142 Royal Geographical Society Picture Library/Eric Lawrie; 143 Lindsay Griffin; 144–5 Mountain Camera/Bill O'Connor; 145 Brian Hall; 146 Phil Coates; 147 Mountain Camera/John Cleare; 148–9 Mountain Camera/Bill O'Connor; 149 Pat & Baiba Morrow; 150 Phil Coates; 151 Doug Scott; 152–3 Mountain Camera/Bill O'Connor; 153 Yossi Brain; 154 Michael R Kelsey; 155 Lindsay Griffin; 156–7 Mountain Camera/Bill O'Connor; 157 Beth Wald; 158 Mountain Camera/John Cleare; 159 left Beth Wald; 159 right Beth Wald; 160 Paul Moores; 161 Paul Moores; 163 top left Hedgehog House/Colin Monteath; 163 bottom left Hedgehog House/Colin Monteath; 163 right Stephen Venables; 164–5 Mountain Camera/Bill O'Connor; 165 Hedgehog House/Colin Monteath; 166 US Geological Survey; 167 Roger Mear; 168 Mountain Camera/Bill O'Connor; 169 Stephen Venables; 171 left Hedgehog House/Tom Hopkins; 171 top right

Hedgehog House/Nick Groves; 171 bottom right Ed February; 172–3 Mountain Camera/Bill O'Connor; 173 right Robert New; 174 left Robert New; 174 right Robert New; 175 Robert New; 176–7 Mountain Camera/John Cleare; 177 Mike Banks; 178–9 Mountain Camera/Bill O'Connor; 179 Doug Scott; 180 Hedgehog House/Colin Monteath; 181 Doug Scott; 183 top Peter Boardman; 183 bottom Doug Scott; 184 Mountain Camera/Bill O'Connor; 185 Hedgehog House/Geoff Wayatt; 186 Guy Cotter/R Price; 187 Hedgehog House/Ian Whitehouse; 188 Mountain Camera/Bill O'Connor; 189 Hedgehog House/Jo Haines; 190 Hedgehog House/Grant Dixon; 191 top Mountain Camera/Bill O'Connor; 191 bottom Hedgehog House/Colin Monteath; 192 Hedgehog House/Colin Monteath; 193 Hedgehog House/Ian Brown; 194 Hedgehog House/Rob Brown; 195 Guy Cotter/Geoff Mason; 197 top left Ace Kvale; 197 bottom left Sun Woo Nam; 197 top right Roger Mear; 197 bottom right Ed Webster/Mountain Imagery; 198–9 Mountain Camera/Bill O'Connor; 199 Roger Payne and Julie-Ann Clyma; 200 Roger Payne and Julie-Ann Clyma; 201 Steve Bell/Kazbek Valiev; 202 Simon Yates; 203 left Simon Yates; 203 right Simon Yates; 204–5 Mountain Camera/Bill O'Connor; 205 Mark Twight; 206 Mountain Camera/Tadashi Kajiyama; 207 Vladimir Kopylov; 208–9 Mountain Camera/Bill O'Connor; 209 John Town; 210 John Town; 211 John Town; 212–13 Mountain Camera/Bill O'Connor; 213 Neil Goldsmith; 214 David Hamilton, High Adventure; 214–15 Henry Day; 215 David Hamilton, High Adventure; 216 Mountain Camera/Bill O'Connor; 217 Bill O'Connor; 218 Bill O'Connor; 218–19 Mountain Camera/Bill O'Connor; 219 Roger Payne and Julie-Ann Clyma; 220 top Mountain Camera/Bill O'Connor; 220 bottom Hedgehog House/Colin Monteath; 221 Roger Payne and Julie-Ann Clyma; 222 Barry Blanchard; 223 Paul Moores; 224–5 Barry Blanchard; 226–7 Mountain Camera/Bill O'Connor; 227 Kurt Diemberger; 228 Paul Nunn; 229 Hedgehog House/Nick Groves;

230 Robert Schauer; 231 Robert Schauer; 232 Mountain Camera/Bill O'Connor; 233 Julian Freeman-Attwood; 234–5 Mountain Camera/Bill O'Connor; 235 Doug Scott; 236 Doug Scott; 237 top Roger Mear; 237 bottom Doug Scott; 238 top inset Roger Mear; 238–9 Roger Mear; 239 Roger Mear; 240–1 Mountain Camera/Bill O'Connor; 241 Doug Scott; 242 Mountain Camera/John Cleare; 243 Doug Scott; 244–5 Mountain Camera/Bill O'Connor; 245 Ed Webster/Mountain Imagery; 246 Kurt Diemberger; 246–7 Mountain Camera/Bill O'Connor; 247 Doug Scott; 248 Chris Bonington Picture Library/Chris Bonington; 249 Chris Bonington Picture Library/Chris Bonington; 250 Chris Bonington Picture Library/Chris Bonington; 251 Stephen Venables; 252 top George Mallory; 252 bottom Audrey Salkeld; 253 George Mallory II; 254–5 Mountain Camera/Bill O'Connor; 255 Harish Kapadia; 256 Harish Kapadia; 257 Doug Scott; 258–9 Mountain Camera/Bill O'Connor; 259 Mountain Camera/John Cleare; 260 Hedgehog House/Colin Monteath; 261 Mountain Camera/ John Cleare; 262 Mountain Camera/Bill O'Connor; 263 Sun Woo Nam; 264 Sun Woo Nam; 265 left Sun Woo Nam; 265 right Sun Woo Nam; 266–7 Mountain Camera/Bill O'Connor; 267 Sumiyo Tsuzuki; 268 Sumiyo Tsuzuki/Hiroshi Seo; 269 Sumiyo Tsuzuki/K Olmori; 271 top left Ed Webster/Mountain Imagery; 271 bottom left Hedgehog House/Colin Monteath; 271 right Stephen Venables; 272 Mountain Camera/Bill O'Connor; 273 Hamish Brown; 274 Lindsay Griffin; 275 Hamish Brown; 276 Mountain Camera/Bill O'Connor; 277 Mountain Camera/John Cleare; 278 Mountain Camera/John Cleare; 279 Mountain Camera/John Cleare; 280 Stephen Venables; 281 Stephen Venables; 282–3 Mountain Camera/Bill O'Connor; 283 Ed Webster/Mountain Imagery; 284 Iain Allan; 285 Mountain Camera/John Cleare; 286–7 Jim Curran/Ian McNaught Davis; 287 Jim Curran/Ian McNaught Davis; 288–9 Mountain Camera/Bill O'Connor;

289 Bruce Coleman Ltd/Christer Fredriksson; 290 Steve Bell; 291 Doug Scott; 292 top left Iain Allan/Clive Ward; 292 top centre Pete Athans; 292 top right George C Band; 292 centre left Mike Banks; 292 centre Christian Beckwith/Lindsay Griffin; 292 centre right Steve Bell; 292 bottom left José Luis Bermúdez; 292 bottom centre Barry Blanchard/Pat Morrow; 292 bottom right Chris Bonington Picture Library/Chris Bonington; 293 top left Hamish Brown; 293 top centre Cameron M Burns; 293 top right Leo Dickinson; 293 centre left Mountain Camera/Colin Monteath; 293 centre Roger Payne and Julie-Ann Clyma; 293 centre right Guy Cotter; 293 bottom left Richard Cowper; 293 bottom centre Jim Curran; 293 bottom right Leo Dickinson; 294 top left Ed Douglas; 294 top centre Ed February; 294 top right Julian Freeman-Attwood; 294 centre left Lindsay Griffin; 294 centre Leo Dickinson; 294 centre right Rodrigo Jordan; 294 bottom left Harish Kapadia/Rajesh Gadgil; 294 bottom centre Piotr Konopka/Andrzej Lejczak; 294 bottom right Anders Lundahl; 295 top left George Mallory II; 295 top centre Roger Mear; 295 top right Paul Moores; 295 centre left Sun Woo Nam; 295 centre Robert New; 295 centre right Bernard Newman/Jim Perrin; 295 bottom left Marko Prezelj/Andrej Stremfelj; 295 bottom centre Al Read; 295 bottom right Steve Roper; 296 top left Victor Saunder/Chris Saunders; 296 top centre Robert Schauer; 296 top right Chic Scott; 296 centre left Cameron M Burns; 296 centre Araceli Segarra Roca; 296 centre right Nigel Shepherd; 296 bottom left Mike Smith; 296 bottom centre John Town; 296 bottom right Sumiyo Tsuzuki; 297 top left Stephen Venables/Bruno Schrecker; 297 top centre Beth Wald/William Hatcher; 297 top right Ed Webster/Mountain Imagery/John Climago; 297 centre left Rob Wood/Philip Stone; 297 centre Simon Yates.